# Fish Population Dynamics in Tropical Waters: A Manual for Use with Programmable Calculators

*To Sandra, Ilya and Angela*

Fish Population Dynamics in Tropical Waters: A Manual
for Use with Programmable Calculators

D. Pauly

1984

INTERNATIONAL CENTER FOR LIVING AQUATIC RESOURCES MANAGEMENT
MANILA, PHILIPPINES

Fish Population Dynamics in Tropical
Waters: A Manual for Use with
Programmable Calculators

D. Pauly

1984

Published by the International Center for Living
Aquatic Resources Management, MCC P.O. Box
1501, Makati, Metro Manila, Philippines

Copyright 1984 by Daniel Pauly and the
International Center for Living Aquatic
Resources Management

Printed in Manila, Philippines

Pauly, D. 1984. Fish population dynamics in tropical waters:
a manual for use with programmable calculators. ICLARM
Studies and Reviews 8, 325 p. International Center for
Living Aquatic Resources Management, Manila,
Philippines.

ISSN 0115-4389
ISBN 971-1022-03-6 cloth
ISBN 971-1022-04-4 paper

ICLARM Contribution No. 143

## Table of Contents

| | |
|---|---|
| List of Figures | vi |
| List of Tables | ix |
| List of Examples | xi |
| Foreword | xiii |
| Acknowledgements | xiv |
| Abstract | xv |
| 1. How to Use this Manual | 1 |
| 2. Length-Weight Relationships | 5 |
|     Introduction | 5 |
|     Parameter Estimation | 5 |
| 3. Mesh Selection | 10 |
|     Introduction | 10 |
|     Trawl Mesh Selection | 10 |
|     Gillnet Selection | 12 |
|     Using a Selection Curve to Adjust Catch Samples | 17 |
| 4. Fish Growth | 23 |
|     Introduction | 23 |
|     Data Needed for Parameter Estimation | 26 |
|     Methods for Parameter Estimation | 28 |
|         The von Bertalanffy plot | 29 |
|         The Ford-Walford plot | 31 |
|         The Gulland and Holt plot | 33 |
|         The Munro plot | 35 |
|         Fitting seasonally oscillating length-growth data | 37 |
|         Extended Gulland and Holt plot | 39 |
|     Growth: A Concluding Program | 41 |
| 5. Total, Natural and Fishing Mortalities | 52 |
|     Introduction | 52 |
|     Estimating Total Mortality | 53 |
|         Total mortality from the oldest animal in the catch | 53 |
|         Total mortality from the mean size in the catch | 55 |
|         Estimation of Z from cumulative plots | 56 |
|         Catch curves and length-converted catch curves | 58 |
|         Further inferences from length-converted catch curves | 64 |
|         Estimating Z from a pseudo-catch curve | 66 |
|     Simultaneous Estimation of Z and K | 67 |

|   | Estimation of Z/K...................................................... | 70 |
|---|---|---|
|   | 1st case: the Beverton and Holt formula of 1956 ................ | 70 |
|   | 2nd case: using the variance of the mean length ................ | 70 |
|   | 3rd case: using a nomogram and the mean weight of fish in the catch ........................................................ | 70 |
|   | 4th case: estimating Z/K from the shape of the length-frequency distribution........................ | 70 |
|   | Methods for Splitting Z into M and F .......................... | 71 |
|   | Plot of Z on effort........................................... | 72 |
|   | Analysis of tagging data...................................... | 73 |
|   | Method for Obtaining Independent Estimates of M ................ | 74 |
|   | Exploitation Rates and Potential Yields ......................... | 76 |
| 6. | **Estimation of Population Size** ..................................... | 91 |
|   | Introduction............................................... | 91 |
|   | Population Size Through Tagging (Petersen Estimates)............... | 91 |
|   | Standing Stock Estimation with the Swept-Area Method ............ | 92 |
|   | Population Size from Catch and Fishing Mortality ................. | 93 |
|   | Population Size as Estimated by Leslie's Method ................. | 94 |
| 7. | **Estimation of Past Population Sizes Using Virtual Population Analysis and Cohort Analysis** ....................................... | 100 |
|   | Introduction............................................... | 100 |
|   | Derivation of a Length-Structured VPA Model..................... | 101 |
|   | Discussion of the Length-Structured VPA Model .................. | 103 |
|   | Applications of Age-Structured VPA and Cohort Analysis ........... | 105 |
|   | Application of Length Cohort Analysis and Length-Structured VPA ... | 105 |
| 8. | **Yield-Per-Recruit Assessment** ....................................... | 114 |
|   | Introduction............................................... | 114 |
|   | Estimation of Yield Per Recruit ............................... | 115 |
|   | Comparison of Various Equations for Yield-Per-Recruit Estimation.... | 119 |
|   | The Use of the Yield-Per-Recruit Model: A Warning................ | 120 |
|   | An Alternative Use of Beverton and Holt's Yield Equation........... | 121 |
| 9. | **Stock-Recruitment Relationships** .................................... | 129 |
|   | Introduction............................................... | 129 |
|   | The Stock-Recruitment Relationship of Beverton and Holt .......... | 129 |
|   | Ricker's Stock-Recruitment Relationships ....................... | 132 |
|   | First form of Ricker's curve ................................. | 132 |
|   | Second form of Ricker's curve ............................... | 134 |
| 10. | **Surplus-Yield Models**............................................. | 138 |
|   | Introduction............................................... | 138 |
|   | The "Equilibrium" Problem ................................... | 141 |
|   | Some Modifications of the Parabolic Model ...................... | 143 |
|   | Applying Surplus-Yield Models to Multispecies Stocks .............. | 146 |
| 11. | **The Intrinsic Rate of Population Increase**............................. | 152 |
|   | Introduction............................................... | 152 |
|   | Maximum Sustainable Yields and $r_m$........................... | 152 |
|   | Stock-Recruitment Relationships and $r_m$ ....................... | 155 |

| | |
|---|---|
| 12. Multispecies Fisheries | 161 |
|     Introduction | 161 |
|     Modelling Multispecies Systems | 163 |
|         Two-species systems | 163 |
|         N-species systems | 167 |
|     Method for Constructing Quantitative "Box Models" | 168 |
|     Managing Multispecies Fisheries | 171 |
| **Appendix I. Testing Models and Their Results: An Introduction to Sensitivity Analysis and the Jackknife** | 177 |
| **Appendix II. List of Programs and Program Listings** | 180 |
| **Appendix III. Use of Calculators Other Than HP 67/97** | 305 |
| **List of Symbols and Their Definitions** | 309 |
| **References** | 314 |
| **Author Index** | 323 |

**Program Card Holder**

## List of Figures

| | | |
|---|---|---|
| 1.1 | Factors responsible for stock size increase and decrease | 2 |
| 1.2 | Geographic distribution of examples used in this book | 4 |
| 2.1 | Length-weight relationship for the threadfin bream *(Nemipterus marginatus)* from the South China Sea. | 7 |
| 3.1 | Selection curve of slipmouth *(Leiognathus equulus)* caught with 7.8-cm mesh nets | 11 |
| 3.2 | Nomogram for estimation of selection factors of fishes from their body proportion | 11 |
| 3.3 | Logarithm of catch ratios plotted on length for *Tilapia esculenta* caught with gillnets of two different mesh sizes. | 15 |
| 3.4 | Selection curves for *Tilapia esculenta* caught with gillnets of two different mesh sizes. | 15 |
| 3.5 | Plot of natural logarithms of catch ratios against length and ln length to show effect of logarithmic transformation of length. | 16 |
| 3.6 | Selection curve of *Tilapia galilaea* caught with gillnets of two mesh sizes | 16 |
| 3.7 | Difference between a gillnet sample and the same sample, adjusted for mesh selection | 17 |
| 4.1 | Relationship between the maximum body weight reached in different groups of fish and the power linking their weight to their metabolic rate or gill surface area | 25 |
| 4.2 | Growth curve of millet-seed butterflyfish *(Chaetodon miliaris)* off Oahu, Hawaii | 27 |
| 4.3 | Relationship between the goodness of fit of a von Bertalanffy plot and the selected value of $L_{(\infty)}$ | 30 |
| 4.4 | Two Ford-Walford plots for Atlantic yellowfin *(Thunnus albacares)* based on the special and generalized VBGF | 32 |
| 4.5 | Differences between the special and generalized VBGF as applied to growth data for Atlantic yellowfin *(Thunnus albacares)* | 32 |
| 4.6 | Estimation of growth parameters for the ocean surgeon fish *(Acanthurus bahianus)* off the Virgin Islands by means of a Gulland and Holt plot | 34 |
| 4.7 | Scattergram of growth increment for ocean surgeon fish *(Acanthurus bahianus)*, as obtained from tagging data | 35 |
| 4.8 | Gulland and Holt plot and "forced" Gulland and Holt plot for the Queen parrot fish *(Scarus vetula)* off the Virgin Islands. | 36 |
| 4.9 | Graph showing how the coefficient of variation of the K-values obtained from a Munro plot depends on the selected value of $L_{(\infty)}$. | 36 |
| 4.10 | Seasonally oscillating growth of the halfbeak *(Hemirhamphus brasiliensis)* off Florida. | 37 |
| 4.11 | Graph showing how an optimal value of $L_{(\infty)}$ can be selected when fitting seasonally oscillating length-growth data. | 38 |
| 4.12 | Relationship between the amplitude of seasonal growth oscillations of fish and shrimps and the difference between highest and lowest mean monthly temperature of their habitats. | 40 |
| 5.1 | Decrease of a cohort of 100 fish subjected to different levels of mortality | 52 |
| 5.2 | Jones' cumulative plot for the estimation of Z/K (or Z) | 57 |
| 5.3 | Sparre's cumulative plot for the estimation of Z (or Z/K) | 58 |
| 5.4 | Catch curve for red porgy *(Pagrus pagrus)* caught off North and South Carolina, U.S.A. | 59 |

| | | |
|---|---|---|
| 5.5 | A length-converted catch curve | 61 |
| 5.6 | Length-converted catch curve for yellow striped goatfish *(Upeneus vittatus)* from Manila Bay, Philippines. | 63 |
| 5.7 | Length-converted catch curve | 63 |
| 5.8 | Relationship between mean length and water depth in slipmouths *(Leiognathus splendens)* caught off Southeast Kalimantan, Indonesia | 66 |
| 5.9 | Relationship between average catch per effort of *Leiognathus splendens* and water depth in western Indonesian waters. | 67 |
| 5.10 | Pseudo-catch curve for *Leiognathus splendens* in western Indonesian waters | 67 |
| 5.11 | Growth curve of the white goby *(Glossogobius giurus)* in Laguna de Bay, Philippines as estimated using Ebert's method. | 69 |
| 5.12 | Powell's nomogram for the estimation of Z/K from the relationship between the mean weight in the catch, the asymptotic length and the lowest size at full retention. | 71 |
| 5.13 | Overall shapes of length-frequency plots, given different values of Z/K | 71 |
| 5.14 | Length-frequency data from Table 5.4, fitted with an exponential curve to demonstrate that Z/K for *Epinephelus sexfasciatus* is 2 or greater. | 72 |
| 5.15 | Plot of total mortality (Z) on effort for the yellow striped trevally *(Selaroides leptolepis)* in the Gulf of Thailand trawl fishery. | 73 |
| 5.16 | Analysis of tag return data for chub mackerel *(Rastrelliger neglectus)* from the Gulf of Thailand. | 75 |
| 6.1 | Leslie plots for reef eels *(Kaupichthys hyoproroides)* and bluehead wrasses *(Thalassoma bifasciatum)* from an isolated Bahamian reef patch. | 95 |
| 7.1 | Relationship between the length class interval in which catch data are grouped and the percentage difference between the results obtained using Jones' length cohort analysis and length-structured VPA. | 104 |
| 7.2 | Population sizes of a cohort of Moroccan sardines *(Sardina pilchardus)* as estimated by (age-structured) virtual population analysis | 106 |
| 8.1 | Yield per recruit as a function of fishing mortality for the slipmouth *(Leiognathus splendens)* | 115 |
| 8.2 | Yield isopleth diagram for the snapper *(Lutjanus sanguineus)* of the South China Sea | 116 |
| 8.3 | Stock assessment of the swordfish *(Xiphias gladius)* off Florida, based on the relative yield-per-recruit concept. | 117 |
| 8.4 | Comparison of yield curves based on different methods to compensate for allometry when performing a yield-per-recruit analysis. | 118 |
| 8.5 | Yield-per-recruit curve of the threadfin bream *(Nemipterus marginatus)* from the South China Sea | 121 |
| 9.1 | Types of stock-recruitment relationships used in fishery research | 130 |
| 9.2 | Beverton and Holt type stock-recruitment relationship for the sea bream *(Taius tumifrons)* (East China Sea) | 131 |
| 9.3 | Stock-recruitment data of false trevally *(Lactarius lactarius)* in the Gulf of Thailand, fitted with Ricker curves. | 131 |
| 10.1 | The simple Schaefer model. A) the logistic curve and its first derivative. B) the yield-biomass and the yield-effort relationships | 138 |
| 10.2 | Yield curve of Peruvian anchoveta *(Engraulis ringens)* off Peru. | 141 |
| 10.3 | Yield curves for the red snapper *(Lutjanus campecheanus)* fishery on the Bank of Campeche, Mexico | 142 |
| 10.4 | Yield curve for the north Java coast trawl fishery | 144 |
| 10.5 | Yield curve of shorthead anchovy *(Stolephorus heterolobus)* at Ysabel Passage, Papua New Guinea. | 145 |
| 11.1 | Logistic growth curve fitted to catch-per-effort data on a newly established Mediterranean population of lizardfish *(Saurida undosquamis)*. | 153 |
| 11.2 | Relationship between intrinsic rate of population increase and adult body weight for various organisms | 154 |
| 12.1 | Combined yield of two similar species, one preying to a small extent on the other | 165 |

| | | |
|---|---|---|
| 12.2 | Combined yield from a predator-prey system | 165 |
| 12.3 | Combined yield from a system in which each species strongly benefits from the presence of the other | 166 |
| 12.4 | Combined yield from a system in which each species, to a small extent, benefits from the presence of the other | 166 |
| 12.5 | Graph showing how the choice of a given constant ratio of fishing mortalities affects the shape and height of a yield curve | 167 |
| 12.6 | Simplified trophic model of Bukit Merah Reservoir, Malaysia. | 168 |
| 12.7 | A simple economic model of a fishery with fishing costs linearly proportional to effort. | 169 |
| 12.8 | Comparison of two yield models fitted to catch-and-effort data from a tropical multispecies fishery. | 172 |

## Appendix Figures

| | | |
|---|---|---|
| III.1 | Program for implementing RPN on TI-58/59 calculators | 307 |
| III.2 | Basic structure of several programs in Appendix II. | 308 |

## List of Tables

2.1 Data for establishing a length-weight relationship for the threadfin bream *(Nemipterus marginatus)* from the southern tip of the South China Sea. . . . . . . . . . . 6

2.2 Data for establishing the length-weight relationship of *Leiognathus splendens* from the Eastern Java Sea. . . . . . . . . . . . . . . . . . . . . . . . . . . 7

3.1 Trawl selection data for *Leiognathus equulus* obtained with 7.8-cm meshed nets in Mombasa Harbour, Kenya . . . . . . . . . . . . . . . . . . . . . . 10

3.2 Morphometric data for *Leiognathus equulus* for rapid estimation of mean length at first capture. . . . . . . . . . . . . . . . . . . . . . . . . . . . . . . 13

3.3 Catch by length of two gillnets to estimate their selection for *Tilapia esculenta* in Lake Victoria. . . . . . . . . . . . . . . . . . . . . . . . . . . . . . . . 14

3.4 Catch by length of two gillnets for estimation of their selection for *Tilapia galilaea* in Volta Lake, Ghana. . . . . . . . . . . . . . . . . . . . . . . . . . . . 17

4.1 Data for and results of the comparison of growth parameters obtained from length- and from weight-at-age data. . . . . . . . . . . . . . . . . . . . . . . . 26

4.2 A set of length-at-(absolute) age data, pertaining to millet-seed butterflyfish *(Chaetodon miliaris)* from Oahu, Hawaii. . . . . . . . . . . . . . . . . . . 27

4.3 A set of length-at-(relative) age data, pertaining to male Nile carps *(Labeo niloticus)* from a freshwater body near Alexandria (Egypt) . . . . . . . . . . . . 28

4.4 Length-at-age data for the Atlantic yellowfin *(Thunnus albacares)* off Senegal for use with a Ford-Walford plot. . . . . . . . . . . . . . . . . . . . . . . 31

4.5 Length at tagging, length at recapture and time at large for tagged ocean surgeon fish *(Acanthurus bahianus)* from the Virgin Islands. . . . . . . . . . . . 33

4.6 Length at tagging, length at recapture and days at large of tagged Queen parrot fish *(Scarus vetula)* from the Virgin Islands . . . . . . . . . . . . . . . . . 34

4.7 Seasonal growth of halfbeak *(Hemirhamphus brasiliensis)* off Western Florida. . . . . . 39

4.8 Constants to be stored for each of the solutions of the generalized von Bertalanffy Growth Formula. . . . . . . . . . . . . . . . . . . . . . . . . . . . . . 41

5.1 Maximum observed size, maximum observed age and estimated mortality for 12 coral reef fish of New Caledonia . . . . . . . . . . . . . . . . . . . . . . . 54

5.2 Table of coefficients for estimating Z and its standard error. . . . . . . . . . . . . . . 54

5.3 Maximum reported age and estimated total mortality of selected Brazilian freshwater and marine fish . . . . . . . . . . . . . . . . . . . . . . . . . . . . . . 55

5.4 Data for the estimation of Z/K and Z for the banded grouper *(Epinephelus sexfasciatus)* of the Visayan Sea, Philippines. . . . . . . . . . . . . . . . . . . . . . 60

5.5 Criteria for assessing the suitability of length-frequency samples for estimating Z. . . . . . . . . . . . . . . . . . . . . . . . . . . . . . . . . . . . . . . 60

5.6 Derivation of a selection curve from the left side of a length-converted catch curve. . . . . . . . . . . . . . . . . . . . . . . . . . . . . . . . . . . . . . . 65

5.7 Values of $t_1$ and $t_2$ for use with $L_1$ and $L_2$ values, given the month of recruitment . . . . . . . . . . . . . . . . . . . . . . . . . . . . . . . . . . . . . . 68

5.8 Length-frequency data for the goby *(Glossogobius giurus)* from Cardona, Laguna de Bay, Philippines . . . . . . . . . . . . . . . . . . . . . . . . . . . . . . 69

5.9 Data for estimating M and q for *Selaroides leptolepis* from the Gulf of Thailand . . . . . . . . . . . . . . . . . . . . . . . . . . . . . . . . . . . . . . . . 72

5.10 Number of tagged and recovered chub mackerels *(Rastrelliger neglectus)* grouped according to time spent at large after releasing. . . . . . . . . . . . . . . 74

6.1 Variants of equations for Petersen estimates of population, as suggested by various authors. . . . . . . . . . . . . . . . . . . . . . . . . . . . . . . . . . . 92

| | | |
|---|---|---|
| 6.2 | Successive sample sizes of reef eels *(Kaupichthys hyoproroides)* from an isolated Bahamian patch reef. | 94 |
| 6.3 | Successive sample sizes of blueheard wrasses *(Thalassoma bifasciatum)* from an isolated Bahamian patch reef | 94 |
| 7.1 | Review of work on the sensitivity of virtual population analysis and cohort analysis | 101 |
| 7.2 | Comparison of results obtained using Jones' length cohort analysis and VPA using catch-at-length data on *Merluccius merluccius* off Senegal (6-cm classes) | 103 |
| 7.3 | Comparison of results using Jones' length cohort analysis and length-structured VPA (24-cm classes) | 104 |
| 7.4 | Some properties of four methods for the analysis of sequential catch data | 105 |
| 7.5 | Estimation by means of Gulland's virtual population analysis of the population (in numbers) and the fishing mortality of a cohort of sardines *(Sardina pilchardus)* caught off Morocco | 106 |
| 7.6 | Estimation of the population size and fishing mortality of a cohort of Peruvian anchovy *(Engraulis ringens)* by means of Pope's cohort analysis | 107 |
| 7.7 | Estimation of population size and exploitation rate for a West African stock of hake *(Merluccius merluccius)* based on Jones' length cohort analysis | 108 |
| 8.1 | Growth data of a hypothetical tuna | 117 |
| 8.2 | Parameter values of different growth equations for use in yield-per-recruit analysis | 118 |
| 8.3 | Data for the estimation of $F_{0.1}$ for *Nemipterus marginatus* from the South China Sea | 121 |
| 9.1 | Data for the derivation a Beverton and Holt type relationship for sea bream *(Taius tumifrons)* from the East China Sea | 132 |
| 9.2 | Data for the derivation of Ricker type stock-recruitment relationships for the false trevally *(Lactarius lactarius)* from the Gulf of Thailand | 133 |
| 10.1 | Catch-and-effort data for anchoveta *(Engraulis ringens)* off Peru. | 141 |
| 10.2 | Catch-and-effort data for the red snapper fishery on Campeche Bank, Gulf of Mexico | 143 |
| 10.3 | Catch-and-effort data from the north Java demersal trawl fishery | 145 |
| 10.4 | Catch and total mortality estimates of shorthead anchovy *(Stolephorus heterolobus)* in Ysabel Passage, Papua New Guinea | 147 |
| 11.1 | Data on the growth of a newly established Mediterranean population of *Saurida undosquamis* | 153 |
| 12.1 | A typical trawler catch from the Java Sea made on 5 September 1976 by R/V *Mutiara IV* | 161 |
| 12.2 | Constants used for drawing Figs. 12.1 to 12.4. | 165 |
| 12.3 | Data for the construction of a quantitative box-model of Bukit Merah Reservoir, Malaysia | 169 |
| 12.4 | Nominal catch-and-effort data from the Gulf of Thailand Trawl Fishery | 173 |

## Appendix Tables

| | | |
|---|---|---|
| I.1 | Values of the D-measure (formula 1) for various perturbations in the input parameters | 178 |
| I.2 | Application of the jackknife method to the surplus model. | 179 |
| III.1 | Guide for the conversion of the HP 97 keystrokes to HP 41C/41CV functions | 306 |

## List of Examples

| | | |
|---|---|---|
| 2.1 | Computation of a length-weight relationship in *Nemipterus marginatus* | 8 |
| 2.2 | Computation of a length-weight relationship in *Leiognathus splendens* | 9 |
| 2.3 | Calculating the condition factor in a stock of fish when only one length-weight data pair is available | 9 |
| 3.1 | Estimation of the mean length at first capture and selection factor of *Leiognathus equulus* by means of a trawl selection experiment. | 19 |
| 3.2 | Fitting the logistic curve to trawl selection data. | 20 |
| 3.3 | Estimation of the selection factor of *Leiognathus equulus* by means of morphometric data and a nomogram. | 21 |
| 3.4 | Estimation of the selection curves for *Tilapia esculenta* caught with gillnets of two different mesh sizes | 21 |
| 3.5 | Estimation of asymmetrical selection curves for *Tilapia galilaea* caught with gillnets of two different sizes | 22 |
| 4.1 | Calculating values of $L_\infty$, K and $t_o$ in the millet-seed butterflyfish *(Chaetodon miliaris)* by means of a von Bertalanffy plot. | 42 |
| 4.2 | Calculating a value of K, and improving a first trial value of $L_{(\infty)}$ for Nile carps *(Labeo niloticus)* by means of the von Bertalanffy plot. | 43 |
| 4.3 | Estimation of $L_\infty$ and K for *Thunnus albacares* off Senegal by means of a Ford-Walford plot, special and generalized VBGF | 44 |
| 4.4 | Using a Gulland and Holt plot to estimate $L_\infty$ and K for ocean surgeon fish *(Acanthurus bahianus)* from the Virgin Islands. | 45 |
| 4.5 | Using a "forced" Gulland and Holt plot to estimate K when a value of $L_{max}$ and growth increment data are available. | 46 |
| 4.6 | Calculating values of K, and using these to improve a first trial value of $L_{(\infty)}$ for ocean surgeon fish *(Acanthurus bahianus)* by means of a Munro plot. | 47 |
| 4.7 | Determination of growth parameters from seasonally oscillating length-at-age data for the halfbeak *(Hemirhamphus brasiliensis)*. | 48 |
| 4.8 | Estimating the growth parameters and the seasonal growth oscillations of *Acanthurus bahianus* from the Virgin Islands | 49 |
| 4.9 | Solutions of the generalized VBGF. | 50 |
| 4.10 | Estimation of the parameters d and D in Atlantic yellowfin by means of Program FB 9 | 51 |
| 5.1 | Estimation of Z and its standard error from the maximum age of a fish sample. | 78 |
| 5.2 | Estimation of Z from the mean weight of the catch (iterative solution) | 78 |
| 5.3 | Estimation of Z from the mean length of the catch | 79 |
| 5.4 | Estimation of Z using Jones' method. | 80 |
| 5.5 | Estimation of Z using Sparre's method | 81 |
| 5.6 | Estimating Z from length-frequency data using a length-converted catch curve in which the "piling-up" effect is corrected for using growth rates. | 82 |
| 5.7 | Showing that not correcting for the "piling-up" effect leads to biased estimates of Z | 83 |
| 5.8 | Estimation of Z from a length-converted catch curve (using $N/\Delta t$) with subsequent improvement using Sparre's method. | 83 |
| 5.9 | Construction of a pseudo-catch curve for *Leiognathus splendens* caught off Kalimantan, Indonesia | 85 |
| 5.10 | Estimation of K and Z in a stock of the white goby *(Glossogobius giurus)* using Ebert's method. | 86 |

| | | |
|---|---|---|
| 5.11 | Estimating Z/K from length-frequency data | 87 |
| 5.12 | Estimating M and q from a plot of Z values against their corresponding values of effort | 88 |
| 5.13 | Estimating F and M for chub mackerel *(Rastrelliger neglectus)* from tagging data | 88 |
| 5.14 | Obtaining an independent estimate of M for a fish whose growth parameters are known | 89 |
| 5.15 | Estimation of the exploitation rate from mean lengths | 90 |
| 6.1 | Petersen population estimate of tigerfish *(Hydrocynus vittatus)* in the Sanyati Gorge, Lake Kariba, Zimbabwe | 96 |
| 6.2 | Use of the swept-area method to estimate demersal standing stock size and fishing mortality in San Miguel Bay, Philippines | 97 |
| 6.3 | Applications of the relationships linking catch, fishing mortality and mean standing stock size | 98 |
| 6.4 | Estimation of unfished population size by means of Leslie's equation | 99 |
| 7.1 | Population sizes and fishing mortality of Moroccan sardines *(Sardina pilchardus)* as determined by Gulland's virtual population analysis | 109 |
| 7.2 | Population sizes and fishing mortality of Peruvian anchoveta *(Engraulis ringens)* as determined by Pope's cohort analysis | 110 |
| 7.3 | Conversion of length-frequency data to catch-at-length data, given data on bulk catch and a length-weight relationship | 111 |
| 7.4 | Population sizes and exploitation rate of West African hake *(Merluccius merluccius)* as determined by Jones' length cohort analysis | 112 |
| 7.5 | Population sizes and fishing mortality of West African hake as determined by length-structured VPA | 113 |
| 8.1 | Estimating the yield per recruit obtainable from the slipmouth *(Leiognathus splendens)* in western Indonesian waters | 123 |
| 8.2 | Estimating the yield per recruit obtainable from the snapper *(Lutjanus sanguineus)* in the South China Sea | 124 |
| 8.3 | Yield-per-recruit assessment of Atlantic swordfish *(Xiphias gladius)* | 125 |
| 8.4 | Computation of yield per recruit in cases where weight growth is allometric (Jones' method) | 126 |
| 8.5 | Computation of yield per recruit using the generalized VBGF | 126 |
| 8.6 | Estimating $F_{0.1}$ for *Nemipterus marginatus* from the South China Sea | 127 |
| 8.7 | Estimating the proportion of adult slipmouth *(Leiognathus splendens)* in the total stock | 128 |
| 9.1 | Estimating the parameters of a Beverton and Holt type stock-recruitment relationship *(Taius tumifrons,* East China Sea) | 135 |
| 9.2 | Estimating the parameters of Ricker type recruitment curves | 136 |
| 10.1 | Estimating the MSY and optimum effort for a single-species pelagic fishery by means of the Schaefer model | 148 |
| 10.2 | Application of Schnute's model to the red snapper fishery on Campeche Bank, Mexico | 149 |
| 10.3 | Estimating MSY and optimum effort for a multispecies demersal trawl fishery by means of Fox's model | 150 |
| 10.4 | Estimation of MSY and $Z_{opt}$ using Csirke and Caddy's model | 151 |
| 11.1 | Estimating the intrinsic rate of increase for an "exploding" population of lizardfish *(Saurida undosquamis)* | 158 |
| 11.2 | Estimating $r_m$ from the mean weight of the adults in a given stock | 159 |
| 11.3 | Estimating potential yields when catch-and effort data are not available | 160 |
| 12.1 | Yield from a two-species (predator-prey) system | 175 |
| 12.2 | Fitting an asymptotic yield model to bulk catch-and-effort data from a multispecies fishery | 176 |

# Foreword

Fifteen years ago, in Jamaica, I purchased my first electronic calculator, a typewriter-sized affair which had four functions and no memory, and it revolutionized my life. The cheapest of the modern hand-held calculators do more, for less than one hundredth of the price that I paid in 1979. Around the same period, I was using a mainframe computer manned by an army of staff to perform yield-per-recruit computations. The reader will find that their hand-held programmable calculators will execute such computations in a few seconds, by the touch of a button.

It is a feature of our times that new hardware becomes outmoded with remarkable speed. The reader who purchases this book will find that models of the calculators for which the programs were originally written are already difficult to acquire, as they have been replaced by faster and more sophisticated models (which will still run the programs presented here). Likewise, programmable calculators are already being replaced by microcomputers and many readers will wish to translate the programs contained in this book into computer languages.

The scientist working in a sophisticated fisheries laboratory will be aware that many of the routines incorporated in this book are already available in the memories of the mini- or mainframe computers to which they have access and for such individuals, the programs given here will be useful for on-the-spot calculations without moving to a terminal. Convenient yes, but not a remarkable benefit. However, fisheries scientists, particularly in the developing countries, who are working in small, modestly-equipped laboratories, remote from the advanced electronic gadgetry of this decade, will find that their lives and working abilities are radically changed by this book because it will now be possible to do complex analyses of data in the remotest field station or even at sea, and in places without regular power supplies, programmers and systems analysts.

Doubtless, many disastrously erroneous analyses will emerge when inappropriate or poor sample data are used to generate estimates, and the dictum of "garbage in → garbage out" will more frequently be seen in operation—but this will be a small price to pay for the real advances, improved scientific output and scientifically-based fisheries management decisions which will emerge as a result of the publication of this book.

Additionally, ecologists in fields other than fisheries will find that many of the routines given here are easily adapted to non-fisheries applications—which will hopefully help to overcome the needless dichotomy which has tended to separate fisheries science from the rest of ecology.

This book is doubly welcome because, while there are numerous texts which give clear instructions on how to collect data, there are remarkably few which give any instructions on how to analyze what has been collected. W.E. Ricker's *Handbook of Computations and Interpretation of Biological Statistics of Fish Populations* and John Gulland's *Manual of Fish Stock Assessment* have been the mainstays of fish population dynamics for many years and both are sufficiently intimidating—in terms of their mathematics—to have cured many biologists of any inclination to pursue a career in the quantitative aspects of fisheries science. In contrast, readers will not fail to be impresssed by the lucidity and incisiveness which characterizes this manual and which will rightfully earn Dr. Pauly a permanent niche in the annals of fisheries science.

J.L. Munro<br>
Manila<br>
March 1984

## Acknowledgements

I wish to express my gratitude to John Munro, Saul Saila and Erik Ursin for reading the entire draft of this book, and for suggesting various improvements, and to John Gulland and Jorge Csirke, who read and proposed changes for several draft chapters.

Thanks are also due to Lourdes "Deng" Palomares for tracing the program listings by hand, and to Aye Pyo for checking the computational examples.

I would like also to express my most sincere appreciation of the efforts of Per Sparre and John Hoenig. Per not only read the entire draft but also checked the derivation of each equation, spotting in the process a frighteningly large number of errors and ill-defined notions, and developing *en passant* two new models that he was kind enough to let me incorporate into Chapter 5 of this book. John, on the other hand, accepted the dreary task of checking the galley proofs; his efforts led similarly to the identification of a number of errors of the most insidious kind, all of which would have been most deleterious; I would have hated to see them in the printed version.

It must be stressed here that neither he, nor Per, nor the other reviewers agreed entirely with the selection of items presented here, or with my interpretation of them. Here, I bear full responsibility, as I do with regard to any remaining errors, typographical or other, which readers may spot.

Daniel Pauly
Manila
March 1984

## Abstract

This manual is a selection, from the entire field of fish population dynamics, of methods which are applicable to tropical fish and fisheries and can be implemented with the help of programmable calculators.

The methods selected cover the following areas: length-weight relationships, mesh selection, growth, mortality, population size estimation by various methods (e.g., tagging, virtual population analysis), yield-per-recruit assessments, stock-recruitment relationships, surplus-yield models, the rate of increase of populations and aspects of multispecies stocks and fisheries.

The program listing and user instructions of thirty programs for use with HP 67/97 programmable calculators are included; the translation of these programs for use with other types of calculators especially HP 41 and TI 59 is discussed. Sixty computational examples including complete keystroke sequences are provided to illustrate the methods presented in the text. These examples are drawn exclusively from subtropical and tropical stocks and fisheries.

# 1. How to Use this Manual

Students of fishery biology in tropical developing countries generally find their textbooks replete with cod and haddock, salmon and trout. There is not even one little example pertaining say, to the chub mackerels, the scads or the various demersal percoids, although these fish often support significant and well-documented fisheries throughout the tropics (Marr 1978).

A manual, such as the one presented here, cannot alone compensate for this sad state of affairs. What this manual will do, however, is demonstrate that:

  i. there are at present enough original publications on tropical fish and fisheries to exemplify most aspects of fish population dynamics and stock assessment,
  ii. there is no further need, when investigating tropical stocks, to compare one's results with those obtained in temperate areas of the world—"lateral" comparisons, involving several similar tropical stocks being generally far more illuminating.

At this point, the question might arise as to what fish population dynamics are all about. A now classic axiom, formulated by Russel (1931) may be used to answer this question. This axiom states that

$$B_2 = B_1 + (R^* + G^*) - (M^* + Y) \qquad \ldots 1.1)$$

where $B_1$ and $B_2$ are the total weights of the exploited phase of a fish stock (or population) at the beginning and end, respectively, of a given time period, while R denotes the recruitment (in weight) to the exploited phase, $G^*$ the growth of individuals in the exploited phase, $M^*$ the biomass of fish that died due to natural causes in the exploited phase, and Y the yield or catch (in weight) during the aforementioned time period. In other words, the axiom states that in a "closed" population (no emigration, no immigration), the primary factors responsible for weight increments to the stock are recruitment and growth, while the factors responsible for weight loss are natural mortality and capture by the fishery (see also Fig. 1.1).

Population dynamics now can be simply defined as the quantitative study of the four primary factors listed in Russel's axiom. *Tropical* fish population dynamics, then, can be more specifically defined as the set of methods which can be used quantitatively to interpret data on: 1) stock sizes, 2) recruitment, 3) growth and 4) natural mortality of tropical fish, such that potential catches can be predicted or such that existing fisheries can be knowledgeably managed.

As will be seen, the dynamics of tropical fish are not very different from those of their temperate counterparts, the major differences being: 1) the ranges of sizes are generally smaller, 2) the time periods are shorter, 3) the intensity of seasonal phenomena is reduced.

Accounting for the differences between tropical and temperate systems is therefore basically a question of adjusting one's scales, the "trick" with tropical fish being to turn what appears to be a liability (i.e., that they operate on scales different from those of temperate fish) into an asset.

For example, the fact that many demersal stocks in tropical waters consist of short-lived fish sometimes prevents aging by means of annuli, but allows one to follow the growth and decay of a cohort within a period of 12 months. When there are well-defined spawning seasons (as is often the case), one can then:

— determine growth from length-frequency data without encountering many of the problems of applying this method to long-lived temperate fishes,
— estimate the age, in days, of individual fish,
— estimate absolute recruit numbers from the relationship of yield per recruit with the catch, and
— neglect time-lag effects when fitting surplus-production models to catch-and-effort data.

Also, the extremely large number of species often encountered in the tropics (especially in demersal fisheries), which many authors have generally considered a major problem, may be viewed as a beautiful set of replicates from which not only one, but several sets of parameter estimates can

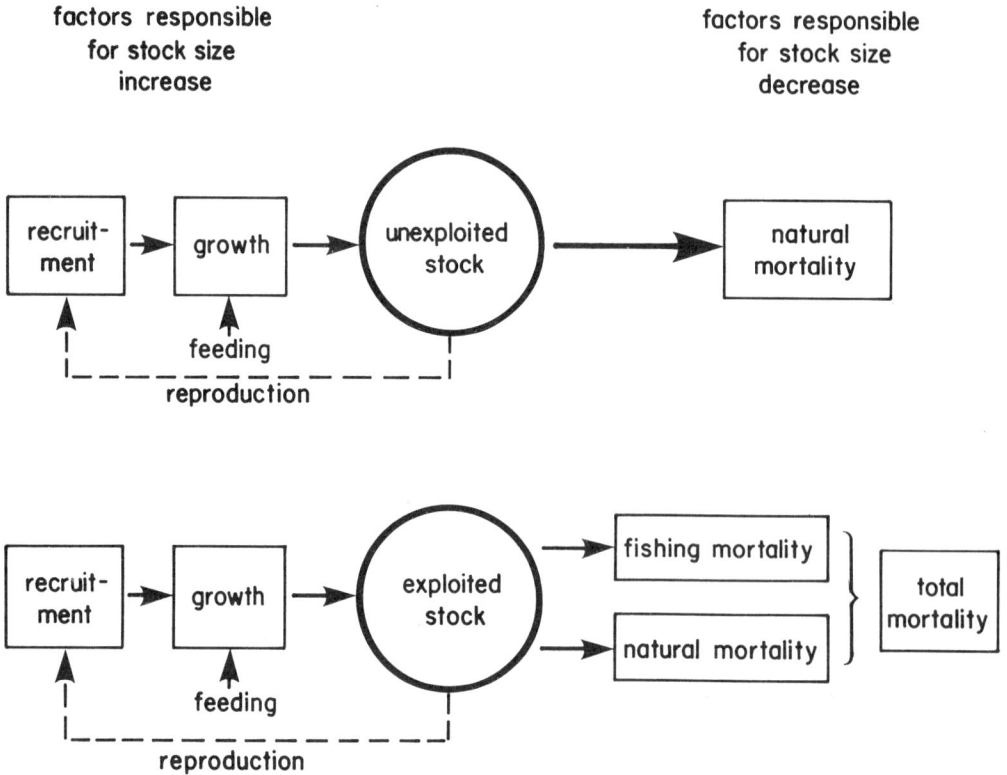

Fig. 1.1. Factors responsible for size increase and decrease in exploited and unexploited stocks (modified after Ricker 1975).

be obtained, for example, to assess the impact of fishing on a multispecies stock (see Chapter 12).

The next 10 chapters of this manual deal with single-species stocks, and only the last chapter deals explicitly with multispecies problems. This 10 to 1 ratio should not conceal the fact that most tropical stocks are part of a multispecies community, and that the other species inevitably affect the dynamics of the stocks under investigation. Chapter 12 is, therefore, very important.

The thirty programs presented here are all original, although a few of them are built around, or incorporate routines written by other authors; the latter are acknowledged in the program descriptions (Appendix II).

The astute reader will note that many, if not all of the programs presented here could be written more elegantly, shortened or otherwise improved. It is only after writing these programs that the author came across such excellent books on calculator programming as Smith (1977), Ball (1978) and Green and Lewis (1979).

Statistical problems *per se* are given little emphasis in this book, for two reasons. First, fish population dynamics, despite recent improvements, are still mainly based on deterministic models (i.e., on models which assume the input data are known perfectly, and which thus ignore the stochastic nature of the inputs). Second, statistics are best learnt from texts explicitly devoted to that subject. Such texts as Draper and Smith (1966), Snedecor and Cochran (1967), Gomez and Gomez (1976), Weber (1980) or Sokal and Rohlf (1981), include both the theoretical background to some of the approaches used for the programs presented here and methods by which these sometimes crude approaches could be refined.

Some possible improvements and refinements are as follows:
- the use of model II instead of model I regressions (or "GM" instead of "AM" regressions) in a number of cases where the former might be more appropriate (Ricker 1973; Laws and Archie 1981),
- the correction of bias in cases where certain parameters are estimated via linear regression by taking the inverse of the variables,
- the correction of bias where a parameter is derived by taking the antilog of a regression intercept (Sprugel 1983),
- the computation of the standard error of parameter estimates where such routines are missing.

Chatterjee and Price (1977) should be consulted for simple methods to deal with these biases, as well as for a detailed account of residual analysis, a method that is extremely useful whenever regression analysis is applied.

Several programs included in this manual provide approximate estimates of standard error (s.e.) for a number of statistics. These were obtained from the square root of the variance in those cases where an equation was readily available which gave the variance of a given statistic, on the assumption that the statistic in question has a normal distribution.

When equations for the estimation of the variance of a given statistic are missing, approximate values of the standard errors can be obtained using the "jackknife" method of Tukey (1977), which is presented in Appendix I.

Confidence intervals are computed by multiplying the "t-statistic" by the standard error. When a large number of degrees of freedom are available, the confidence intervals of a given statistic, A, are thus computed from:

$$A \pm 1.96 \cdot s.e._{(A)} = 95\% \text{ confidence interval of A} \quad \ldots 1.2)$$

or

$$A \pm 2.58 \cdot s.e._{(A)} = 99\% \text{ confidence interval of A} \quad \ldots 1.3)$$

For low numbers of degrees of freedom (d.f. $\leq$ 50), table values of the t-statistic must be used.

It is recalled here, finally, that the term "standard error" is used for the square root of the variance *of a given statistic*, while the term "standard deviation" is used for the square root of the variance of *a set of values* of a given variable (see Sokal and Rohlf 1981).

Two types of readers will make use of this manual: those who "believe" in fish population dynamics, and in whatever comes out of a computer (or calculator), and those who don't.

For the latter, little instruction is needed since they already will know how to deal with the contents of this book. The "believer" readers are likely to be students or unfortunate colleagues who might think that given the equations in this book, and the programs to solve them, all they have to do is press the appropriate buttons of their calculator. Clearly, this would be a recipe for disaster. Fish population dynamics are at present in a state of flux and virtually all of the assumptions, approaches and methods presented here have been challenged at least once by highly competent scientists. Furthermore, the application of many of these methods to tropical stocks is rather new, and their overall applicability to all stocks in many cases still needs to be confirmed, especially the new methods presented in this manual.

To give a "feel" of this, several equally legitimate methods and/or equations are usually presented to solve a given problem; these methods generally give somewhat different results, for reasons that are not obvious in the majority of cases. This will help the "believers" appreciate that nothing can replace one's own thorough knowledge of the various aspects of a given problem. Also, it is imperative when using any of the methods and approaches presented herein to read the *original literature*; references are given throughout the text and in a special "recommended reading" section in each of the following chapters.

The methods presented in this book are illustrated by at least one example, based in all cases on data obtained in the tropics or subtropics (Fig. 1.2). Altogether, 60 examples are provided. All include a full keystroke sequence for HP 67/97 calculators and results, to which a brief comment has generally been added. These examples can also be used for testing the programs numbered FB 1 to FB 30 after they have been entered from the listings in Appendix II, into a calculator. The examples can be easily located in the colored pages at the end of Chapters 2-12. Holders for 30 HP 67/97 (and HP 41C) program cards are provided at the end of this book.

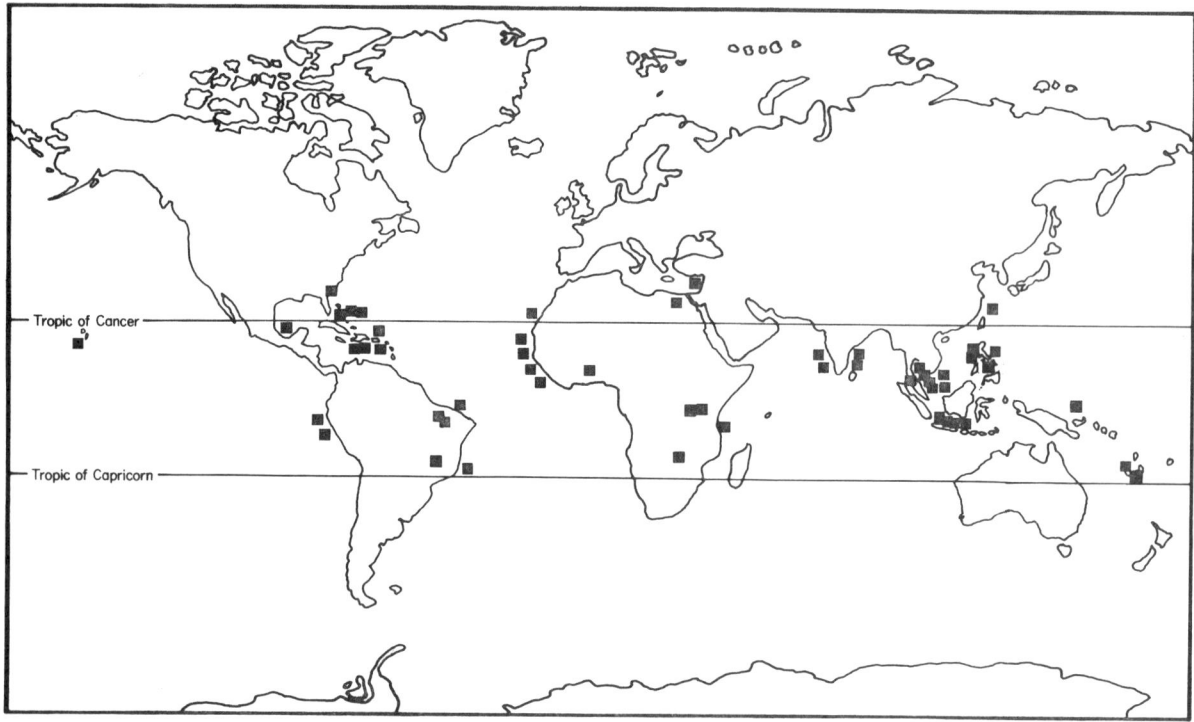

Fig. 1.2. Geographic distribution of examples used in this book, showing that most examples are drawn from the intertropical belt.

The user should follow the procedures below when using this manual and the programs it contains:
1) always read the original literature on the models and approaches presented here,
2) use (whenever possible) several methods to estimate the value of a given parameter and try to identify the sources of the differences in the estimates when such differences occur,
3) estimate standard errors, using the jackknife where appropriate, and perform sensitivity analyses (see Appendix I),
4) always check whether the results obtained make biological sense,
5) try to identify possible sources of biases in the model used here and attempt to improve Programs FB 1 to FB 30,
6) consider that more rigorous methods for estimating certain parameters are possible, and
7) do not blame the author for the nonsensical results that may result from thoughtless applications of the methods and programs given here.

## 2. Length-Weight Relationships

### INTRODUCTION

The relationship between the length (L) and the weight (W) of fish can generally be expressed by the equation:

$$W = a \cdot L^b \qquad \ldots 2.1)$$

where *a* is a factor discussed below and the exponent b lies between 2.5 and 3.5, usually close to 3. Carlander (1969, 1977) has demonstrated from an extraordinarily large number of length-weight data, stemming from a wide variety of fishes, that values of $b < 2.5$ or $b > 3.5$ are generally based on a very small range of sizes and/or that such values of b are most likely to be erroneous. When b = 3, weight growth is called *isometric*, meaning that it proceeds in the "same" dimension as the cube of length. When $b \neq 3$, weight growth is *allometric*, meaning that it proceeds in a "different" dimension (differing from $L^3$). Allometric growth can be either positive ($b > 3$) or negative ($b < 3$). Another way of relating length and weight is to define a condition factor (c.f.) such that

$$c.f. = W \cdot 100/L^3 \qquad \ldots 2.2)$$

When weight growth is isometric (b = 3), we also have

$$c.f./100 = a \qquad \ldots 2.3)$$

where a is the multiplicative factor in equation (2.1). The reason for the multiplication by 100 in equation (2.2), it may be mentioned, is to bring the value of the condition factor of fishes with a "normal" shape close to unity when grams are used to express the weight, and centimeters to express the length. It must be emphasized, however, that the c.f. in a given fish species or stock can be compared to that of another species or stock only if the same units and definitions have been used (e.g., total length in cm and live or ungutted weight in g). The units and definitions must always be stated.

In addition many factors, such as sex, time of year, stage of maturity, stomach contents and others influence the numerical magnitude of the condition factor. Comparisons should only be made when these factors are roughly equivalent among samples to be compared.

The values of a in equation (2.1), on the other hand, cannot be used for interspecies or interstock comparisons, even when the same units and definitions are used, unless the values of b are exactly the same. The values of b, finally, are not affected by the units or definitions used.

### PARAMETER ESTIMATION

The values of a and b in equation (2.1) are estimated in Program FB 1 by means of a "linearized" form of that equation, namely

$$\log W = \log a + b \cdot \log L \qquad \ldots 2.4)$$

that is by taking (base 10) logarithms on both sides and by estimating the values of log a and of b by means of a linear regression.

This procedure of using ordinary least-square regression to estimate a and b only approximate these parameters, and results in estimates of the standard errors that are not very reliable; alternative procedures, e.g., the use of non-linear least-squares estimations should be considered where possible.

Program FB 1 also calculates single values of c.f. when L/W data are entered, computes an individual or mean c.f. value after one or several pairs of L/W values have been entered and estimates L from W and/or W from L when values of a and b, or an estimate of the condition factor are available.

When expression (2.4) is fitted to data, the coefficient of determination ($r^2$) is also estimated by program FB1. This coefficient has the value of the correlation coefficient squared, and is used in all those programs that are presented here in which an estimator of the goodness of fit is given. It has the advantage over the correlation coefficient that it expresses directly the proportion of the variance that is "explained" by the regression (e.g., of log W on log L). For example, $r^2 = 0.92$ means that 92% of the variance in a set of values is accounted for, or explained, by a regression, while $100 - 92 = 8\%$ remains "unexplained", that is, must be attributed to other cause(s), e.g., to random variability.

As will be seen in the following chapters, a number of models (= equations) used in fish population dynamics assume that the exponent of the length-weight relationship is equal to 3. Also some models can be considerably simplified when this exponent is actually equal to 3. For these reasons, Program FB 1 incorporates a routine which calculates the value of $\hat{t}$ that can be used to test whether a value of b calculated by this program is significantly different from 3. The equation used to compute the t-statistic is

$$\hat{t} = \frac{s.d._{(x)}}{s.d._{(y)}} \cdot \frac{|b-3|}{\sqrt{1-r^2}} \cdot \sqrt{n-2} \qquad \ldots 2.5)$$

where $s.d._{(x)}$ is the standard deviation of the log L values, and $s.d._{(y)}$ the standard deviation of the log W values, n being the number of fish used in the computation. The value of b is different from 3 if $\hat{t}$ is greater than the tabled value of t for $n - 2$ d.f. (see Example 2.1).

Table 2.1 presents data which can be used for establishing a length-weight relationship (see also Example 2.1).

Table 2.1. Data for establishing a length-weight relationship for the threadfin bream *(Nemipterus marginatus)* from the southern tip of the South China Sea (live weight in g).

| #  | TL (cm) | W (g) | #  | TL (cm) | W (g) |
|----|---------|-------|----|---------|-------|
| 1  | 8.1     | 6.3   | 9  | 16.6    | 65.5  |
| 2  | 9.1     | 9.6   | 10 | 17.7    | 69.4  |
| 3  | 10.2    | 11.6  | 11 | 18.7    | 76.4  |
| 4  | 11.9    | 18.5  | 12 | 19.0    | 82.5  |
| 5  | 12.2    | 26.2  | 13 | 20.6    | 106.6 |
| 6  | 13.8    | 36.1  | 14 | 21.9    | 119.8 |
| 7  | 14.8    | 40.1  | 15 | 22.9    | 169.8 |
| 8  | 15.7    | 47.3  | 16 | 23.5    | 173.3 |

When large numbers of fish have been measured, entering the L/W data pairs can become quite tedious. In such cases, a common practice is to arrange the data by length groups, and to calculate the mean weight for each length class. The data should then look as in Table 2.2.

Using Program FB 1, the length-weight relationship and/or the mean condition factor may be calculated with the L/W data pairs having been "weighted" by the sample size. Example 2.2 shows how the data of Table 2.2 may be used in this context. Example 2.3, finally, shows how a single data pair (one value each of L and W) can be used to obtain a preliminary estimate of c.f.

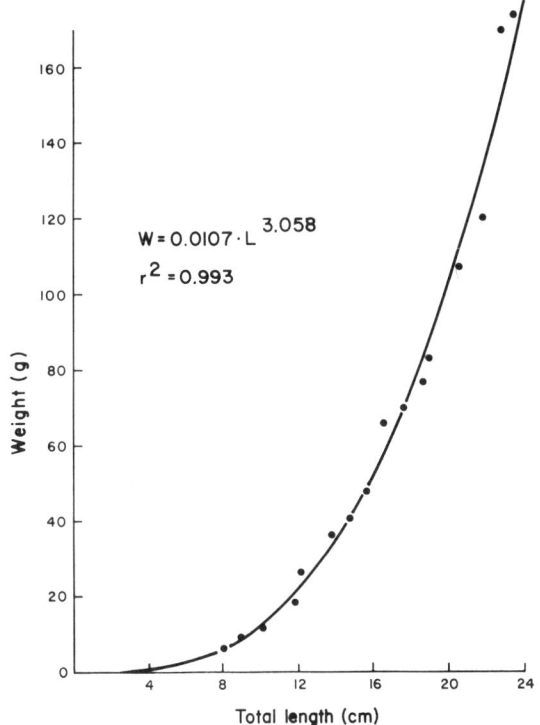

Fig. 2.1. Length-weight relationship for the threadfin bream *(Nemipterus marginatus)* from the South China Sea (based on data in Table 2.1 and Example 2.1).

Table 2.2. Data for establishing the length-weight relationship of *Leiognathus splendens* from the Eastern Java Sea (total length in cm, live weight in g).

| # | Class limits low high | Class midlength | Mean weight | n |
|---|---|---|---|---|
| 1 | 6.00-6.49 | 6.25 | 5.28 | 1 |
| 2 | 6.50-6.99 | 6.75 | 4.07 | 1 |
| 3 | 7.00-7.49 | 7.25 | 6.91 | 11 |
| 4 | 7.50-7.99 | 7.75 | 8.46 | 26 |
| 5 | 8.00-8.49 | 8.25 | 10.15 | 26 |
| 6 | 8.50-8.99 | 8.75 | 11.88 | 23 |
| 7 | 9.00-9.49 | 9.25 | 13.77 | 16 |
| 8 | 9.50-9.99 | 9.75 | 17.13 | 2 |
| 9 | 10.00-10.49 | 10.25 | 19.29 | 7 |
| 10 | 10.50-10.99 | 10.75 | 22.57 | 9 |
| 11 | 11.00-11.49 | 11.25 | 25.54 | 7 |
| 12 | 11.50-11.99 | 11.75 | 28.66 | 3 |
| 13 | 12.00-12.49 | 12.25 | 34.02 | 7 |
| — | 12.50-12.99 | 12.75 | — | 0 |
| 14 | 13.00-13.49 | 13.25 | 46.73 | 1 |
| — | 13.50-13.99 | 13.75 | — | 0 |
| 15 | 14.00-14.49 | 14.25 | 55.91 | 1 |
| 16 | 14.50-14.99 | 14.75 | 65.63 | 1 |
| 17 | 15.00-15.49 | 15.25 | 61.72 | 1 |

Recommended reading: The following papers and books contain useful reviews of aspects of the length-weight relationships of fish: Kesteven (1947), Le Cren (1951), Carlander (1969, 1977), Weatherley (1972), Ricker (1973, 1975), Balon (1974).

Suggested research topics: Estimating a and b in various commercially exploited fish stocks, plotting c.f. values of adults of similar sizes against month of the year to detect changes due to spawning, and comparing the c.f. values of fishes of similar sizes, both parasitized and unparasitized.

**EXAMPLE 2.1**

**Computation of a length-weight relationship in *Nemipterus marginatus*.**

Data from Table 2.1

Computations

1) Read sides 1 and 2 of Program FB 1. The display should show: 0.000.

2) Keystrokes

   f a 8.1 ↑ 6.3 A 9.1 ↑ 9.6 A 10.2 ↑ 11.6 A 11.9 ↑ 18.5 A 12.2 ↑ 26.2 A 13.8 ↑ 36.1 A
   14.8 ↑ 40.1 A 15.7 ↑ 47.3 A 16.6 ↑ 65.5 A 17.7 ↑ 69.4 A 18.7 ↑ 76.4 A 19.0 ↑ 82.5 A
   20.6 ↑ 106.6 A 21.9 ↑ 119.8 A 22.9 ↑ 169.8 A 23.5 ↑ 173.3 A

3) Calculate $r^2$, a and b

   | Keystrokes | Results | |
   |---|---|---|
   | E | 0.993 | ($r^2$) |
   | | 0.010674... | (a) |
   | | 3.058 | (b) |
   | | 0.821 | ($\hat{t}$) |

   Tables of the t-distribution (e.g., Table Q in Rohlf and Sokal 1969) give for 14 degrees of freedom (n − 2) a critical value of t (for P = 0.01) equal to 2.977. Hence the value of b calculated here (3.058) does not significantly differ from 3.

4) Thus, one can recalculate the length-weight relationship using 3 as the exponent, and c.f./100 as the new value of a, or

   | Keystrokes | Results | |
   |---|---|---|
   | C | 1.251 | (c.f.) |
   | 100 ÷ | 0.013 | |
   | DSP 4 | 0.0125 | (new a) |

   and the new length-weight relationship is $W = 0.0125 L^3$.

## EXAMPLE 2.2

**Computation of a length-weight relationship in *Leiognathus splendens* (data weighted by sample size).**

Data from Table 2.2

Computations

1) Read sides 1 and 2 of Program FB 1.

2) Keystrokes

   f a 6.25 ↑ 5.28 ↑ 1 B 6.75 ↑ 4.07 ↑ 1 B 7.25 ↑ 6.91 ↑ 11 B 7.75 ↑ 8.46 ↑ 26 B 8.25 ↑ 10.15 ↑ 26 B 8.75 ↑ 11.88 ↑ 23 B 9.25 ↑ 13.77 ↑ 16 B 9.75 ↑ 17.13 ↑ 2 B 10.25 ↑ 19.29 ↑ 7 B 10.75 ↑ 22.57 ↑ 9 B 11.25 ↑ 25.54 ↑ 7 B 11.75 ↑ 28.66 ↑ 3 B 12.25 ↑ 34.02 ↑ 7 B 13.25 ↑ 46.73 ↑ 1 B 14.25 ↑ 55.91 ↑ 1 B 14.75 ↑ 65.63 ↑ 1 B 15.25 ↑ 61.72 ↑ 1 B

3) Calculate $r^2$, a and b

   | Keystrokes | Results | |
   |---|---|---|
   | E | 0.995 | ($r^2$) |
   | | 0.01680... | (a) |
   | | 3.031 | (b) |
   | | 1.683 | ($\hat{t}$) |

4) Calculate the mean condition factor     C    1.799    ($\overline{c}$.f.)

5) To estimate weight for length, enter the length, and press D (or fc).

6) To estimate length for weight, enter the weight, and press fd (or fe).

## EXAMPLE 2.3

**Calculating the condition factor in a stock of fish when only one length-weight data pair is available.**

Prabhu (1952) gives for the Indian Wolf-herring *(Chirocentrus dorab)* a weight of 800 g for a length of 56 cm (LF). What is the condition factor?

Computation

1) Read sides 1 and 2 of Program FB 1.

2) Keystrokes

   f a 56 ↑ 800 A

   | | Keystrokes | Results | |
   |---|---|---|---|
   | 3) Calculate the condition factor (c.f.) | C | 0.456 | (c.f.) |
   | 4) Calculate the weight corresponding to 20 cm (FL): | 20 fc | 36.443 | (W) |
   | 5) Calculate the length (FL) corresponding to 500 g: | 500 fe | 47.879 | (L) |

Obviously, a c.f. value obtained from only one fish is not too reliable; the method, thus should be used only when comprehensive data are not available. Incidentally: is *C. dorab* a slender fish?

## 3. Mesh Selection

### INTRODUCTION

Generally, fishing gears, whether used by fishermen or by a fishery biologist are "selective" i.e., they catch fish only within a certain range of sizes. Thus, if one wishes to know the true size structure of a fish population (e.g., to assess whether there has been a reduction of mean size over a period of time) it is necessary to account for the effect of selection.

This can be achieved by assessing, for each size class of fish sampled, the probability of capture by the gear in question, then dividing, for each length class, the numbers actually caught by the probability of capture.

Two methods are presented below to estimate the probability of capture (= fraction retained) of different size groups of fish caught by fishing gears. The first of these methods pertains to trawl selection, the second is a simple method applied to gillnets (but also applicable to fishing hooks and some other gears).

### TRAWL MESH SELECTION

The selectivity of trawl meshes is generally determined through trawl selection experiments. Such experiments consist of covering the cod end whose selectivity is to be assessed with a fine-mesh cover. After fishing, in each length group, a certain fraction of the total number of fish caught will be retained in the cod end, and this fraction (the probability of capture) will tend to increase with increasing fish length (Table 3.1).

From such data, the probability of capture can be obtained from a plot of the fractions retained against the corresponding length. A smooth curve can then be drawn (e.g., by eye) from which the probability of capture can be read for each length class (Fig. 3.1).

Table 3.1. Trawl selection data for *Leiognathus equulus* obtained with 7.8-cm meshed nets in Mombasa Harbour, Kenya.[a]

| Lower class limit (cm) | Fishes in cover (No.) | Fishes in cod end (No.) | Total fish caught | P = fishes in cod end as fraction of total (= fraction retained) |
|---|---|---|---|---|
| 8 = $L_{min}$ | 4 | 0 | 4 | 0.000 |
| 9 | 35 | 2 | 37 | 0.054 |
| 10 | 198 | 22 | 220 | 0.100 |
| 11 | 170 | 56 | 226 | 0.248 |
| 12 | 76 | 42 | 118 | 0.356 |
| 13 | 45 | 34 | 79 | 0.430 |
| 14 | 25 | 19 | 44 | 0.432 |
| 15 | 7 | 21 | 28 | 0.750 |
| 16 | 0 | 12 | 12 | 1.000 |
| 17 | 1 | 3 | 4 | 0.750 |
| 18 | 0 | 5 | 5 | 1.000 |
| 19 | 0 | 5 | 5 | 1.000 |
| 20 | 0 | 3 | 3 | 1.000 |
| 21 | 0 | 1 | 1 | 1.000 |
| 22 | 0 | 1 | 1 | 1.000 |
| 23 = $L_n$ | 0 | 1 | 1 | 1.000 |
| 24 = $L_{n+1}$ | — | — | — | $\Sigma P_i$ = 10.120 |

[a]Based on selection experiments conducted during the FAO/DANIDA Training Course on the Methodology of Fisheries Sciences (Biology), held in Mombasa, Kenya, 19 May–14 June 1980.

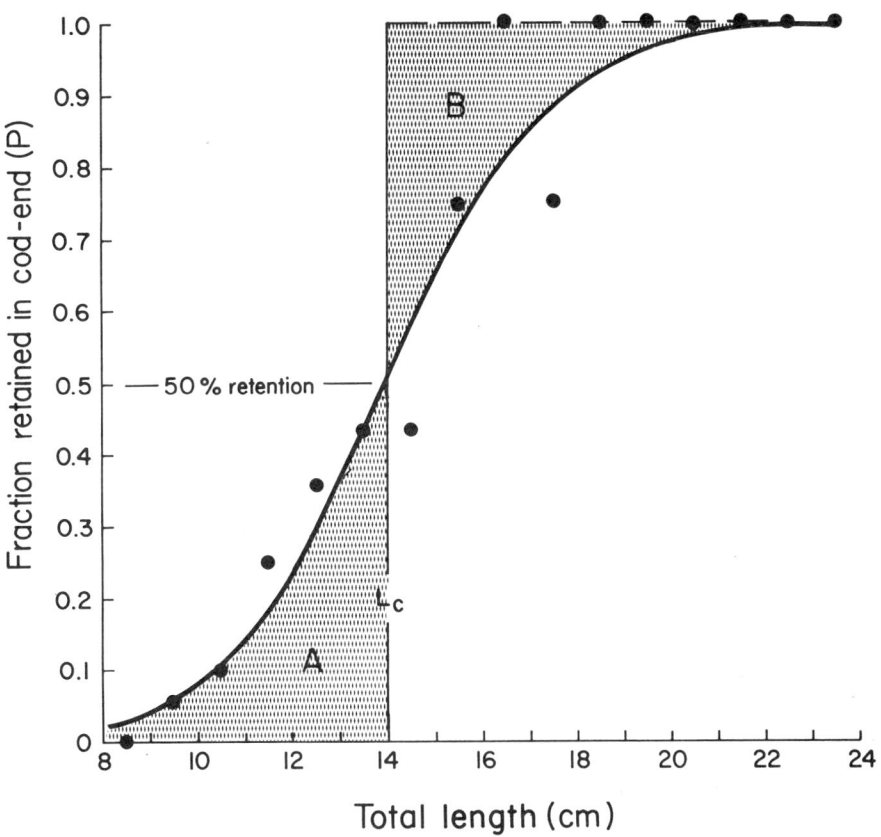

Fig. 3.1. Selection curve of slipmouth *(Leiognathus equulus)* caught with 7.8-cm mesh nets (based on data in Table 3.1 and Example 3.1). Note that area A, representing fish caught below $L_c$ approximately equals area B, representing fish above $L_c$ *not* caught.

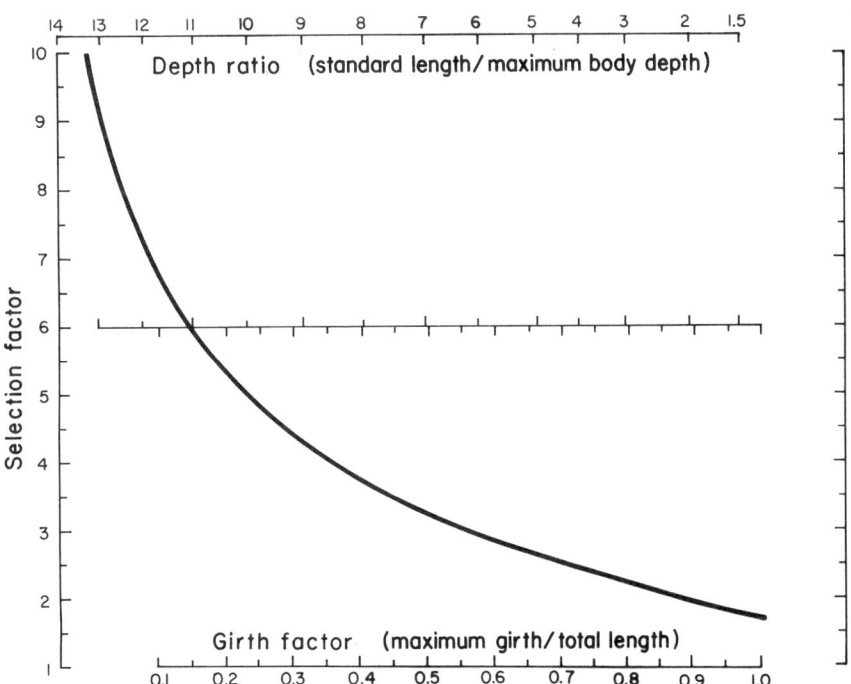

Fig. 3.2. Nomogram for the estimation of selection factors of fishes from their body proportion (from Pauly 1980a).

Several of the models discussed in the following chapters of this manual require estimates of the mean size at first capture, that is the length at which 50% of the fish entering a trawl net are retained by the gear ($L_c$).

The parameter $L_c$ is particularly interesting in that it is the length at which the numbers of smaller fish caught retained by the cod end compensate for the number of larger fish not yet retained by the cod end (see shaded areas in Fig. 3.1).

While $L_c$ can be estimated graphically, a more precise method is to order the catch data as in Table 3.1 and to estimate $L_c$ from

$$L_c = L_{n+1} - \Sigma P_i \qquad \ldots 3.1)$$

where $L_n$ is the lower limit of the highest length class considered (when this equation is used the fish must be grouped in classes of width equal to unity, e.g., 1 cm), while $\Sigma P_i$ is the sum of the fractions retained, as shown in Table 3.1 (see also Example 3.1).

Another method to estimate $L_c$ is to fit the retention data with a logistic curve of the form

$$P = 1/(1 + e^{-r_m (L - L_c)}) \qquad \ldots 3.2)$$

where P is the probability of capture, L the midpoint of a length class and $r_m$ is a constant whose value increases with the steepness of the selection curve; both equations (3.1) and (3.2) assume the selection curve to be symmetrical or nearly so.

A program is provided here (FB 29) which can be used to fit a logistic curve to data obtained by a trawl selection experiment (Example 3.2). However, this approach gives best results when the selection curve is symmetrical about the $L_c$ value, and it is thus necessary to first plot the data to check if the requirement for symmetry is at least reasonably met (see Example 3.2 and Fig. 3.1).

In general, $L_c$ can be considered proportional to the mesh size of the cod-end meshes; the proportionality constant is called the selection factor (S.F.). When known, it can be used to estimate $L_c$ from the relationship

$$L_c = S.F. \times \text{mesh size} \qquad \ldots 3.3)$$

It has been demonstrated by several authors that the selection factor of fishes is generally related to their overall shape, i.e., slender fishes have high selection factors while bulky fishes have low selection factors. This property has been used by the author to derive a nomogram (Fig. 3.2), based on a large number of published results of selection experiments, and which can be used to estimate approximate values of selection factors of fishes, given their "girth factor" (maximum girth/total length) or their "depth ratio" (standard length/maximum body depth). (See Table 3.2 and Example 3.3).

GILLNET SELECTION

Whereas trawl selection is essentially a one-sided affair (with only smaller fish having a reduced probability of capture), gillnets tend to select negatively both small and large fish. The former simply go through the mesh without getting caught, while the latter are too big to insert themselves into a mesh. Thus, when the fish are actually "gilled" (that is caught with their head in the mesh, with the net's twine retaining the fish by their operculum), the resulting selection curve has the shape of a normal distribution, and the length at optimum efficiency (optimum length) will be proportional to mesh size. The selection curve of gillnets can be estimated, when the fish are "gilled" as described above, by using two gillnets of different mesh sizes, if the following applies:

— both selection curves are normally distributed,

Table 3.2. Morphometric data for *Leiognathus equulus* for rapid estimation of mean length at first capture ($L_c$).[a]

|   | Total length (cm) | Standard length (cm) | Maximum girth (cm) | Maximum body depth (cm) |
|---|---|---|---|---|
|   | 10.2 | 8.2 | 9.9 | 4.5 |
|   | 10.5 | 8.6 | 10.6 | 5.0 |
|   | 11.3 | 9.0 | 11.1 | 4.8 |
|   | 14.0 | 11.5 | 14.2 | 6.3 |
|   | 14.3 | 11.8 | 14.0 | 6.1 |
|   | 14.4 | 11.8 | 13.7 | 6.0 |
|   | 16.4 | 13.2 | 16.3 | 7.6 |
|   | 16.7 | 13.2 | 16.5 | 7.4 |
|   | 18.4 | 14.9 | 18.3 | 8.4 |
|   | 22.1 | 17.8 | 22.8 | 10.5 |
| $\Sigma$ | 148.3 | 120.0 | 147.4 | 66.6 |
| $\overline{x}$ | 14.83 | 12.00 | 14.74 | 6.66 |

[a]Based on samples from Mombasa Harbour, obtained during the FAO/DANIDA Training Course on the Methodology of Fisheries Sciences (Biology), held in Mombasa, Kenya, 19 May-14 June 1980.

— the two selection curves have the same standard deviation,
— optimum length is proportional to mesh size,
— the two nets have overlapping selection ranges.

In such cases, given catches obtained by the smaller mesh of size A and the larger mesh of size B, the optimum length corresponding to A ($L_A$) and the optimum length corresponding to B ($L_B$) can be estimated from the catch by length class of each mesh ($C_A$, $C_B$) through a linear regression of the form y = a + bx, where

$$y = \ln \frac{C_B}{C_A} \qquad \ldots 3.4)$$

$$x = L \text{ (class midpoint)} \qquad \ldots 3.5)$$

The ratio $C_A/C_B$ is called the catch ratio.

The intercept and slope of this regression can then be used to estimate the optimum lengths from

$$L_A = \frac{-2a \cdot A}{b(A+B)} \qquad \ldots 3.6)$$

and

$$L_B = \frac{-2a \cdot B}{b(A+B)} \qquad \ldots 3.7)$$

while the standard deviation of both selection curves is estimated from

$$s.d. = \sqrt{\frac{2a(A-B)}{b^2(A+B)}} \qquad \ldots 3.8)$$

Once $L_A$, $L_B$ and s.d. have been estimated, the probability of capture (P) at a given length (L) is given for mesh A by

$$P_A = \exp\left(-\frac{(L-L_A)^2}{2\,\text{s.d.}^2}\right) \quad \ldots 3.9)$$

and for mesh B by

$$P_B = \exp\left(-\frac{(L-L_B)^2}{2\,\text{s.d.}^2}\right) \quad \ldots 3.10)$$

The derivation of these equations may be found in Gulland (1969, p. 90-92); this method was proposed by Holt (1963) on the basis of pioneering work by Baranov (1914).

Although the method gives reasonable results in the case of the example provided here (Example 3.4, Table 3.3, Figs. 3.3 and 3.4), various authors have shown that gillnet selection curves frequently have shapes other than normal (= bell-shaped). This applies especially to large, spiny fishes, which, in addition to being gilled often entangle themselves, which results in asymmetrical selection curves. In such cases, it may be necessary to use more elaborate methods to estimate the selectivity of the net(s) under investigation, e.g., those of Gulland and Harding (1961), or Hamley (1975).

When the selection curves for a given fish species are only slightly asymmetrical and drawn to the right, it is still possible to apply the Baranov/Holt method outlined above using the logarithm

Table 3.3. Catch by length of two gillnets to estimate their selection for *Tilapia esculenta* in Lake Victoria. Simplified from Table 1 in Garrod (1961).

| Midpoint of length group (in cm) | Mesh sizes (cm) | |  |
|---|---|---|---|
| | 8.1 | 9.1[a] | |
| 18.5 | 7 | — | not used, no catch with 9.1-cm meshes |
| 19.5 | 90 | 1 | |
| 20.5 | 199 | 9 | |
| 21.5 | 182 | 53 | used, n = 5 |
| 22.5 | 119 | 290 | |
| 23.5 | 29 | 357 | |
| 24.5 | 17 | 225 | |
| 25.5 | 3 | 82 | not used, see Fig. 3.3 |
| 26.5 | — | 19 | |
| 27.5 | — | 10 | not used, no catch with 8.1-cm meshes |

[a]Note that, when comparing two nets, only those lengths can be used for which there are non-zero catch data on both sides.

of the lengths (and of the mesh sizes) instead of the lengths (and mesh sizes) in all computations. This approach is illustrated in Example 3.5, which is based on the data pertaining to *Tilapia galilaea* caught in Volta Lake, Ghana (Table 3.4). As might be seen in Fig. 3.5A, the plot of the natural logarithm of catch ratio against length is not linear (thus suggesting that the simple Baranov/Holt model is inappropriate). The plot of the natural logarithm of catch ratio against that of length (Fig. 3.5B) is linear however, and provides parameters from which asymmetrical selection curves can be drawn (Fig. 3.6).

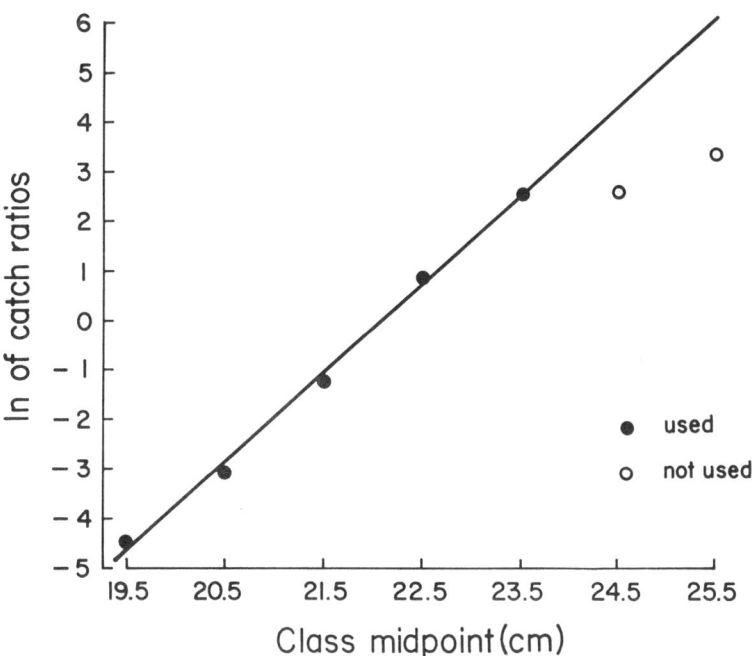

Fig. 3.3. Logarithm of catch ratios plotted for length in *Tilapia esculenta* caught with gillnets of two different mesh sizes (based on data in Table 3.3 and Example 3.4). (Note that one could also argue that the logarithmic model in Fig. 3.5 would fit the data better than the simpler model used here.)

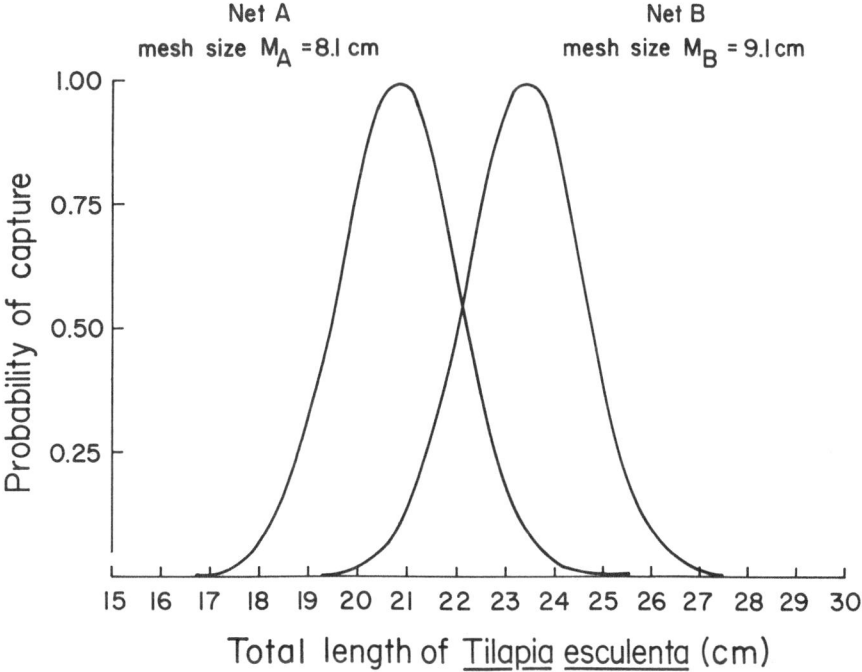

Fig. 3.4. Selection curves for *Tilapia esculenta* caught with gillnets of two different mesh sizes (based on Example 3.4).

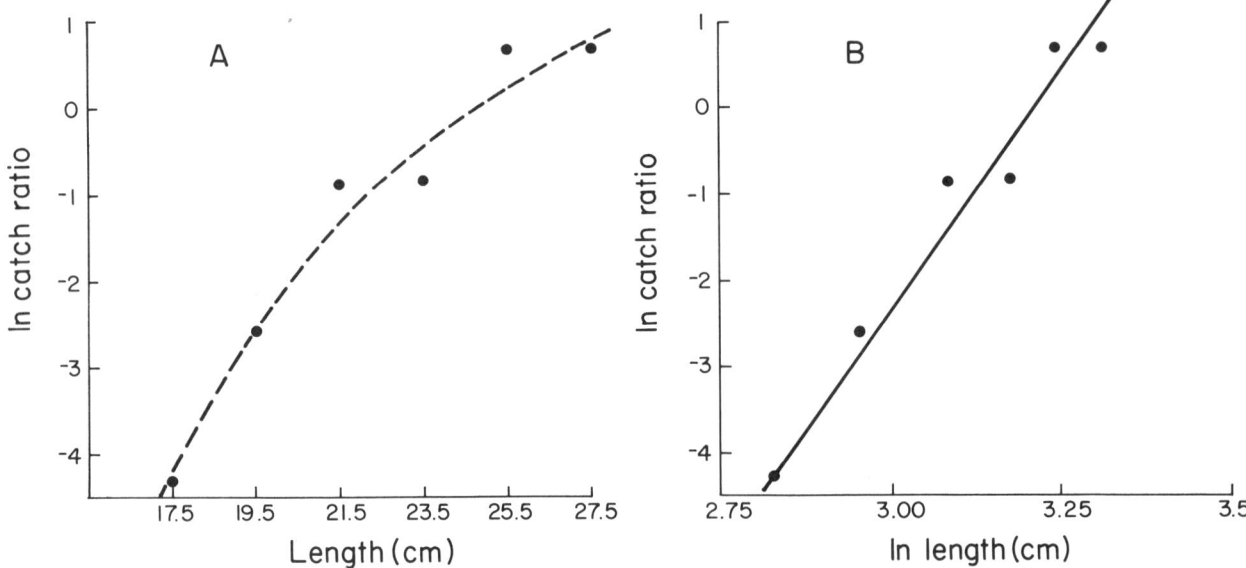

Fig. 3.5. Plot of natural logarithms of catch ratios against length (A) and ln length (B) to show effect of logarithmic transformation of length. Based on data of Table 3.4. Note non-linearity of relationship A (dotted line drawn by eye); see also Example 3.5 and text.

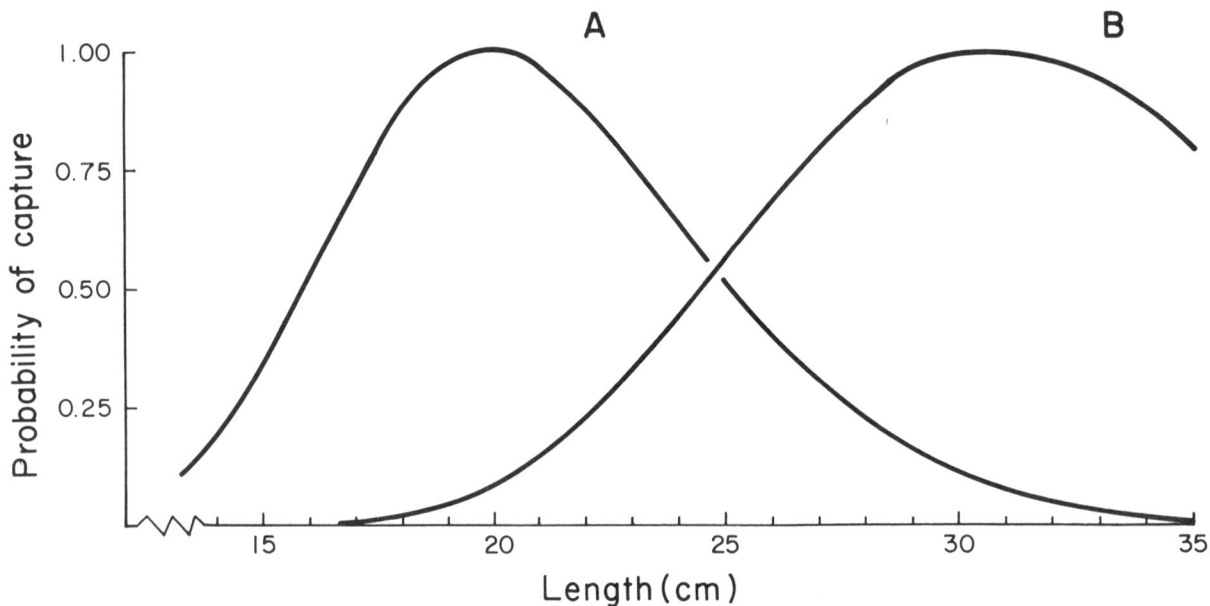

Fig. 3.6. Selection curve of *Tilapia galilaea* caught with gillnets of two mesh sizes (A = 7.6 cm, B = 10.2 cm). Based on data in Table 3.4 and Example 3.5.

Table 3.4. Catch by length of two gillnets for estimation of their selection for *Tilapia galilaea* in Volta Lake, Ghana.[a]

| Midpoint of length class (cm)[b] | Mesh sizes (cm) 7.6 | 10.2 | Probability of capture at mesh sizes 7.6 cm | 10.2 cm |
|---|---|---|---|---|
| | No. of fish caught | | | |
| 17.5 | 75 | 1 | 0.803 | 0.016 |
| 19.5 | 95 | 7 | 0.994 | 0.068 |
| 21.5 | 36 | 15 | 0.929 | 0.190 |
| 23.5 | 14 | 6 | 0.705 | 0.391 |
| 25.5 | 5 | 10 | 0.457 | 0.633 |
| 27.5 | 2 | 4 | 0.262 | 0.849 |

[a]Data read off Fig. 1 in Lelek and Wuddah (1969), including only those lengths for which both mesh sizes had non-zero catches.
[b]Data regrouped in 2-cm classes to reduce number of classes with zero catches.

## USING A SELECTION CURVE TO ADJUST CATCH SAMPLES

Conducting and interpreting selection experiments, e.g., with the models proposed above, represent only half of the work that must be done to obtain catch samples that are representative of a given fish population. The other half of the work, obviously, is to use the selection curves obtained to adjust the available samples. Such adjustment is done by simply dividing the number of fish caught, for each length class, by the probability of capture of that length class, i.e., using the relationship

$$\frac{\text{true relative abundance}}{\text{in the population}} = \frac{\text{relative abundance in sample}}{\text{probability of capture}} \quad \ldots 3.11)$$

Fig. 3.7 shows, as an example, the catch sample of *Tilapia galilaea* in Table 3.4 (7.6-cm meshes) and the computed true (relative) abundances in the population.

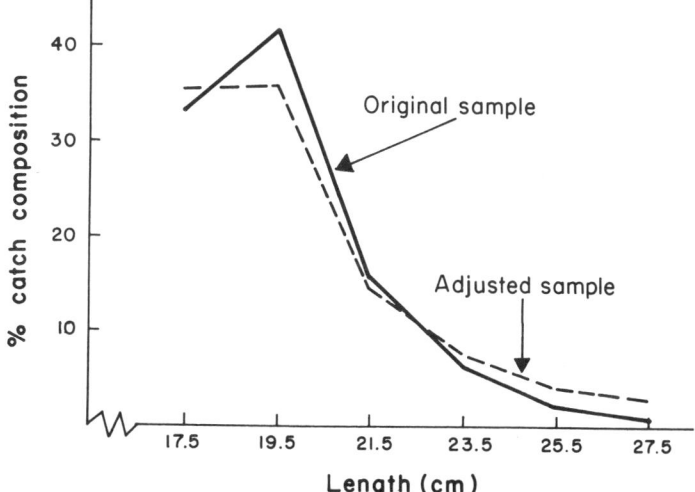

Fig. 3.7. Difference between a gillnet sample and the same sample, adjusted for mesh selection (based on data of Table 3.4, 7.6-cm meshes and Example 3.5). The difference between the two samples is relatively small in this example, but can be quite dramatic when large ranges of sizes are represented in the catch.

Recommended reading: Mesh selection for both trawl and gillnets is discussed in Gulland (1969, p. 84-95) who derives the various equations presented in this chapter. For trawl selection, further details may be found in Beverton and Holt (1957, p. 221-233) and Pope et al. (1975), while McCombie and Fry (1960), Gulland and Harding (1961) and Hamley (1975) describe methods for assessing the selectivity of gillnets when the assumptions of the models presented above are not met, e.g., when the selection curves are strongly asymmetrical.

It is extremely important for fishery biologists to have a good knowledge of the gears used in a given fishery, and of the properties of such gears. Brandt (1972) and Baranov (1976) may be consulted for gear descriptions and the study of gear properties, respectively.

Passive gears, such as traps, longlines, gillnets, etc. tend to interfere with each other and to become saturated. These and related problems are reviewed in Munro (1974) and Eggers et al. (1982).

Suggested research topics: Estimate selection ogives, $L_c$, and selection factors of important commercial species. In multispecies fisheries, use the knowledge gained in the fashion of Sinoda et al. (1979).

**EXAMPLE 3.1**

Estimation of the mean length at first capture ($L_c$) and selection factor of *Leiognathus equulus* by means of a trawl selection experiment.

Data from Table 3.1

Computation

1) Read sides 1 and 2 of Program FB 2

2) Keystrokes

    8 f a 4 ↑ 0A 35 ↑ 2A 198 ↑ 22A 170 ↑ 56A 76 ↑ 42A 45 ↑ 34A 25 ↑ 19A 7 ↑ 21A 0 ↑ 12A 1 ↑ 3A 0 ↑ 5A 0 ↑ 5A 0 ↑ 3A 0 ↑ 1A 0 ↑ 1A 0 ↑ 1A

|  | Keystrokes | Results |  |
|---|---|---|---|
| 3) Calculate $L_c$ | fb | 13.88 | ($L_c$) |
| 4) Calculate the selection factor (S.F.) (i.e., divide by the mesh size used): | 7.88 ÷ | 1.76 | (S.F.) |

See Example 3.2 for another method to estimate S.F., also applied to *Leiognathus equulus*.

**EXAMPLE 3.2**

**Fitting the logistic curve to trawl selection data.**

Data from Table 3.1 (but note that midpoints are used instead of the lower class limits)

Computations

1) Read side 1 of Program FB 29

2) Keystrokes

   1 f a .054 ↑ 9.5 A .1 ↑ 10.5 A .248 ↑ 11.5 A .356 ↑ 12.5 A .43 ↑ 13.5 A .432 ↑ 14.5 A .75 ↑ 15.5 A
   (note that midlengths above 15.5 were skipped; see below)

3) Estimate goodness of fit and $L_c$.

   | Keystroke | Results |
   |---|---|
   | E | 0.938 ($r^2$) |
   | | 0.591 ($r_m$) |
   | | 14.002 ($L_c$) |

4) To draw curve as in Fig. 3.2 enter class midpoint, and obtain fraction retained, as follows

   | | Keystrokes | Results |
   |---|---|---|
   | | 7.5 C | 0.021 (frac. retained) |
   | | 8.5 C | 0.037 (frac. retained) |
   | | ... etc. | |
   | and | 14.002 C | 0.500 (as expected) |

5) Divide $L_c$ by the mesh size used (here 7.88 cm) to estimate the selection factor.

   | Keystrokes | Results |
   |---|---|
   | 14.002 ↑ | — |
   | 7.88 ÷ | 1.777 (S.F.) |

The value of $L_c$ obtained here (14 cm) is very close to the value obtained earlier (13.9 cm). However, this was achieved by omitting all values associated with lengths higher than 15.5 cm. This step was necessary because the program used here does not allow for the entry of 1.00 as a fraction retained. The selective removal of all such values, on the other hand, would cause a bias in the curve estimation. Thus, the best solution here was to omit all lengths from the first which couldn't be entered. As Fig. 3.1 shows, the resulting curve gives a good fit to the data.

**EXAMPLE 3.3**

Estimation of the selection factor of *Leiognathus equulus* by means of morphometric data and a nomogram (Fig. 3.2).

Data from Table 3.2

1) Calculate the "girth factor" (maximum girth/total length)
    Keystrokes: 14.74 ↑ 14.83 ÷
    girth factor = 0.99

2) Calculate the "depth ratio" (standard length/maximum body depth)
    Keystrokes: 12 ↑ 6.66 ÷
    depth ratio = 1.80

3) Use the calculated "girth factor" and "depth ratio" to estimate two values of S.F. via the nomogram in Fig. 3.2. This results in a mean estimate of S.F. of ≈ 1.8 which compares well with the values of 1.76 and 1.78 estimated in Examples 3.1 and 3.2, respectively.

**EXAMPLE 3.4**

Estimation of the selection curves for *Tilapia esculenta* caught with gillnets of two different mesh sizes.

Data from Table 3.3

Computation

1) Read sides 1 and 2 of Program FB 2

2) Keystrokes

    8.1 ↑ 9.1 fe 90 ↑ 1 ↑ 19.5 C 199 ↑ 9 ↑ 20.5 C 182 ↑ 53 ↑ 21.5 C 119 ↑ 290 ↑ 22.5 C 29 ↑ 357 ↑ 23.5 C

3) Calculate parameters of selection curves

| Keystrokes | Results | |
|---|---|---|
| E | 0.996 | ($r^2$) |
| | −39.801 | (a) |
| | 1.801 | (b) |
| | 20.818 | ($L_A$) |
| | 23.388 | ($L_B$) |
| | 1.195 | (s.d.) |

4) Obtain P-values to draw selection curves

| Keystrokes | Results | |
|---|---|---|
| 17 D | 0.006 | (P) |
| 18 D | 0.062 | (P) |
| etc. | | |

Step 4 allows the quick estimation of values of P (= probability of capture) for any length, using mesh A; to obtain values pertaining to mesh B, enter the length value and press fd (see Users' Instruction for Program FB 2 and Fig. 3.4 for selecting the curves pertaining to this example).

**EXAMPLE 3.5** — **Estimation of asymmetrical selection curves for *Tilapia galilaea* caught with gillnets of two different sizes.**

Data from Table 3.4

Computation

1) Read sides 1 and 2 of Program FB 2

2) Keystrokes

fSTF1 7.6 ↑ 10.2 fe 75 ↑ 1 ↑ 17.5 C 95 ↑ 7 ↑ 19.5 C 36 ↑ 15 ↑ 21.5 C 14 ↑ 6 ↑ 23.5 C 5 ↑ 10 ↑ 25.5 C 2 ↑ 4 ↑ 27.5 C

3) Calculate parameters of selection curves

| Keystrokes | Results | |
|---|---|---|
| E | 0.941 | ($r^2$) |
|  | −36.024 | (a) |
|  | 11.224 | (b) |
|  | 19.936 | ($L_A$) |
|  | 30.774 | ($L_B$) |
|  | 0.197 | (s.d.) |

(but note that s.d. is expressed in $\log_e$ units)

4) Obtain P-values to draw selection curve for mesh A

| Keystrokes | Results | |
|---|---|---|
| 17.5 D | 0.803 | (P) |
| 19.5 D | 0.994 | (P) |

etc. (see Table 3.4 and Fig. 3.6)

For mesh B, enter midpoints and press fd instead of D; remember that all computations in this example must be performed *with flag 1 set*, and that it should be cleared to get back to linear plots of ln catch ratio on length and to symmetrical selection curves.

# 4. Fish Growth

## INTRODUCTION

Growth may be defined as the change over time of the body mass ($\cong$ body weight) of a fish, being the net result of two processes with opposite tendencies, one building-up body substances (anabolism) and the other breaking these substances down (catabolism) or

$$dw/dt = HW^d - kW \qquad \ldots 4.1)$$

where dw/dt is the change in body weight per unit time, H is the coefficient of anabolism and k is the coefficient of catabolism. The process of anabolism is here viewed as being proportional to a certain power (d) of the fish weight (W), while catabolism is proportional to weight itself (von Bertalanffy 1938; Pauly 1981).

Equation (4.1) is a differential equation which may be integrated in two ways:
a) by setting the value of d at 2/3. This leads to what is widely known as the *Von Bertalanffy Growth Formula* (VBGF), which is here called *special* VBGF.
b) by allowing d to take a certain range of values, including 2/3. This leads to what will be called the *generalized* VBGF (Pauly 1981).

Most growth-related programs in this manual allow the use of both forms of the VBGF, and there is no need to fear that the use of a "new" growth equation will complicate things. The reason why the generalized VBGF is introduced here is that this form of the growth equation allows smaller deviations when fitting growth data and a biological interpretation of the equation parameters, as intended by von Bertalanffy (1951) (see Pauly 1981).

Details on the integration of expression (4.1) to a growth curve have been presented in Taylor (1962) and Pauly (1979a). It suffices to mention here that, in the course of this integration, the weights in expression (4.1) are replaced by length such that

$$HW^d = pL^a \qquad \ldots 4.2a)$$

and

$$W = qL^b \qquad \ldots 4.2b)$$

Also a "surface factor D" is defined such that

$$D = b - a = b(1 - d) \qquad \ldots 4.3)$$

The integration for length growth yields the equation

$$L_t^D = L_\infty^D (1 - e^{-KD(t - t_o)}) \qquad \ldots 4.4)$$

or

$$L_t = L_\infty (1 - e^{-KD(t - t_o)})^{1/D} \qquad \ldots 4.5)$$

where

$L_\infty$ is the asymptotic length, that is the mean length the fish of a given stock would reach if they were to grow indefinitely.

K is a growth constant which may be conceived as a "stress factor", with $K = k/3$

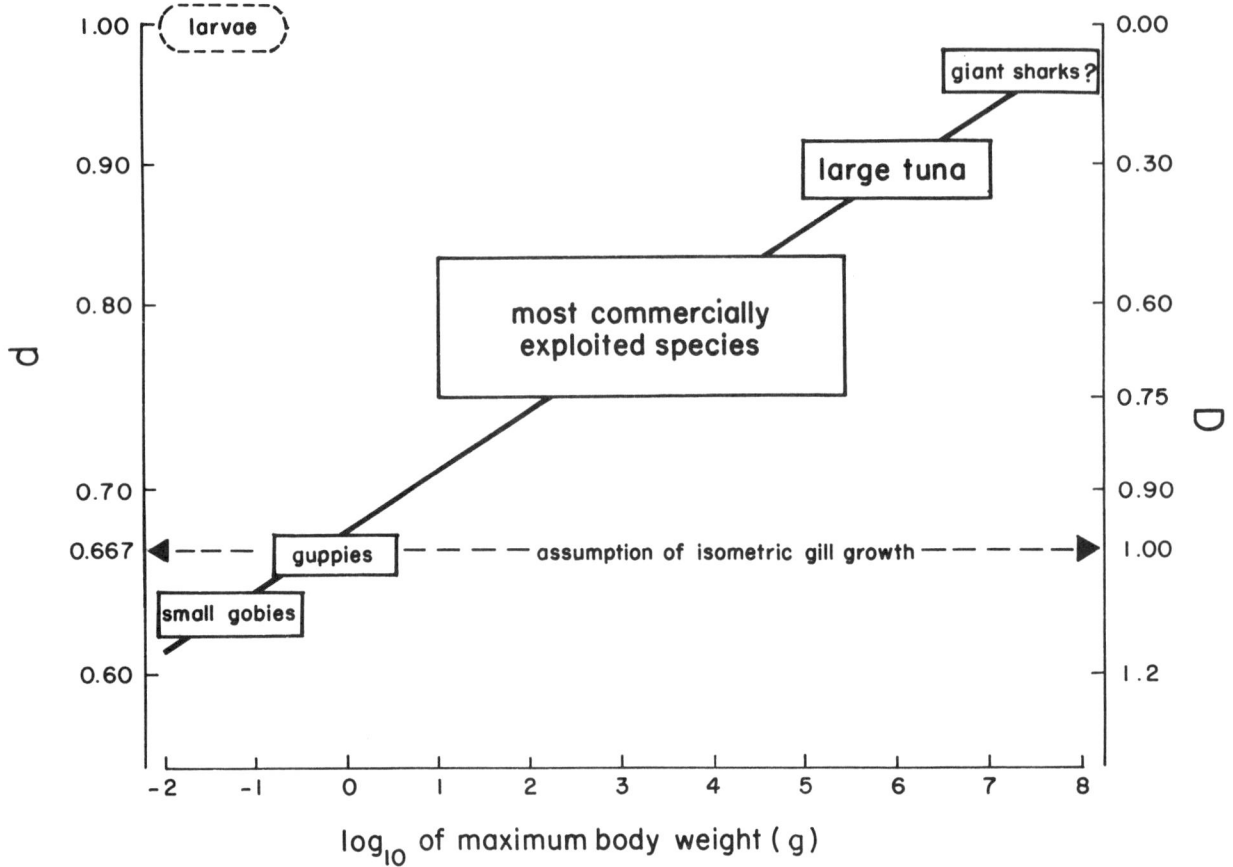

Fig. 4.1. Relationship between the maximum body weight reached in different groups of fish and the power linking their weight to their metabolic rate or gill surface area (d); see text for definition of D (based on Pauly 1981, 1982a, 1982c).

$t_o$ is the "age of the fish at zero length" *if* they had always grown in the manner described by the equation (note that $t_o$ is generally negative) and

D is a "surface factor" (Pauly 1981).

Expression (4.5) is the "generalized" version of the VBGF. It can easily be reduced to its "special" form by setting d = 2/3 in equation (4.1). When weight growth is isometric this would correspond to a = 2 in equation (4.2a) and b = 3 in equation (4.2b); from equation (4.3) this gives

$$D = 1 \qquad \ldots 4.6)$$

and

$$L_t = L_\infty (1 - e^{-K(t - t_o)}) \qquad \ldots 4.7)$$

which is the original or "special" VBGF. (It is here called "special" because it is based on the special case: D = 1).

There are at present few straightforward methods to determine directly the value of d as used in equation (4.1). However, since the anabolic processes of fish generally must be linked with energy-supplying oxidative reactions, the assumption can be made that the power of weight in proportion of which metabolism (= oxygen consumption) increases should be equal to d.

Similarly, the power in proportion of which the surface area of the gills of fish grow should also provide an estimate of d, if the assumption is made that the gill surface area of fish is the surface which limits their growth (Pauly 1981).

Small fish such as the Cyprinodontidae have "metabolic" values of d of about 2/3 (von Bertalanffy 1934, 1938) or lower, down to d = 0.5 (Winberg 1960, 1961), while the study of gill surface areas of tuna revealed that these generally large fish have values of d as high as 0.90 (Muir 1969). In fact, it can be demonstrated that an approximate value of d in a given fish species can be estimated on the basis of a plot of d values in different fish species (as compiled from the literature) against logarithms of their maximum weight (Fig. 4.1).

The relationship between d and $W_{max}$ (in g) can be expressed by the relationship (Pauly 1981):

$$d = 0.674 + 0.0357 \log W_{max} \qquad \ldots 4.8)$$

The definition of a in equation (4.2a), of b in (4.2b) and of D in (4.3) implies, when weight growth is isometric, that

$$D = 3(1-d) \qquad \ldots 4.9)$$

Substituting (4.8) into (4.9) gives for the direct estimation of D the empirical relationship:

$$D \approx 3 \cdot \{1 - (0.674 + 0.0357 \cdot \log W_{max})\} \qquad \ldots 4.10)$$

when $W_{max}$, the maximum weight reached by the fish of a given stock, is expressed in grams. (See Fig. 4.1 and Program FB 9).

Expression (4.8) and Fig. 4.1 show that $d \approx 2/3$ only in very small fish (weighing about 1 g) while $d > 2/3$ in larger fish. This implies that the special VBGF, which assumes that D = 1 (and consequently d = 2/3) is biologically justifiable only in the case of these very small fish, while values of $D < 1$ (hence, $d > 2/3$) should be used for all other fish, especially for large fish such as sharks and tuna.

Since the programs in this manual allow in most cases the use of both special and generalized VBGF, it is suggested that growth parameters be generally computed twice, once with the special VBGF to compare new growth parameter estimates with those already available in the literature, and again with the generalized VBGF and an appropriate value of D, for consistency with the biology of fish growth.

The special VBGF for weight is

$$W_t = W_\infty (1 - e^{-K(t-t_0)})^3 \qquad \ldots 4.11)$$

where $W_\infty$ is the asymptotic weight and all other parameters are as in equations (4.5) and (4.7). It will be noted that the equation, as written here, implies isometric weight growth.

The generalized version of the VBGF for weight growth is

$$W_t = W_\infty (1 - e^{-KD\frac{3}{b}(t-t_0)})^{b/D} \qquad \ldots 4.12)$$

which reduces, when growth is isometric (b = 3) to

$$W_t = W_\infty (1 - e^{-KD(t-t_0)})^{3/D} \qquad \ldots 4.13)$$

It will be noted that equation (4.13) reduces to (4.11) when D = 1.

When weight growth is isometric, as in (4.11) and (4.13), fitting the equation to weight growth data is the same as fitting length-growth data except that the cubic root of all weight values is taken prior to all calculations, these cubic root values being then treated exactly as if they were length values. This is justified because, when weight growth is isometric:

$$L \propto \sqrt[3]{W} \qquad \ldots 4.14)$$

More generally, weights can be rendered proportional to length by raising them to the inverse of the power of the length-weight relationship (b), or

$$L \propto W^{1/b} \quad \ldots 4.15)$$

which can be used when weight growth is either isometric or allometric to obtain growth parameters ($K$, $t_o$) generally equivalent to those that would be obtained by fitting the corresponding length data.*

This is illustrated here by the set of constructed data in Table 4.1 in which values of $L_\infty$, $W_\infty$, K and $t_o$ were obtained for data with the length-weight relationships $W = aL^{2.5}$, $W = aL^{3.0}$ and $W = aL^{3.5}$. This property is used in most growth programs described here to fit weight data with the same programs that fit length data, the sole difference being that a value of b has to be entered when weight growth data are used.

Table 4.1. Data (A) for and results (B) of the comparison of growth parameters obtained from length- and from weight-at-age data. (All computations with D = 1).[a]

| | | | Weight (in arbitrary units) | |
|---|---|---|---|---|
| | Age | Length (cm) | b = 2.5 | b = 3.0 | b = 3.5 |
| A | 1 | 15 | 871.4 | 3,375 | 13,071 |
| | 2 | 18 | 1,375 | 5,832 | 24,743 |
| | 3 | 20 | 1,789 | 8,000 | 35,777 |
| | 4 | 21 | 2,021 | 9,261 | 42,439 |
| B | $W_\infty$ → | | 2,450 | 11,669 | 55,572 |
| | $L_\infty$ | 22.68 | 22.68 ($W_\infty^{1/2.5}$) | 22.68 ($W_\infty^{1/3.0}$) | 22.68 ($W_\infty^{1/3.5}$) |
| | K | 0.511 | 0.511 | 0.511 | 0.511 |
| | $t_o$ | −1.116 | −1.116 | −1.116 | −1.116 |
| | $R^2$ | 0.999 | 0.999 | 0.999 | 0.999 |

[a]The fitting of the data in (A) was performed by means of the computer program described in Gaschütz et al. (1980). The length-weight relationship used was of the form $W = a \cdot L^b$, with "a" set equal to unity.

## DATA NEEDED FOR PARAMETER ESTIMATION

Growth, as defined above relates *weight* and *time*. "Growth data" are therefore such data which connect, directly or indirectly, weight and time such as the growth process expressed by equation (4.1) or by the various forms of the VBGF for weight which can be reconstructed from them. Growth being defined as a process involving mainly body weight (or mass), only those data should be considered "growth data" which pertain to weight. On the other hand, wherever a linear dimension (such as body length) remains in a reasonably constant relationship with body mass, changes in length with time obviously also express growth as defined above—if only indirectly.

In the present manual, the word "size" is used wherever weight or length may be used interchangeably to express the basic growth process.

There are two basic types of growth data—size-at-age data and data on size increase in time.

Table 4.2 gives an example of size-at-age data; from such data, given a value of D, the parameters $L_\infty$ or $W_\infty$, K and $t_o$ of the VBGF can be easily estimated, given one of the methods outlined below. Such data may be called "size-at-(absolute) age". (See also Fig. 4.2.)

There is however, a closely related type of data, the character of which prevents the estimation of one of the VBGF's parameters. These data pertain to sizes at *successive* "ages" or "size-at-

---

*When empirical data are used, slight differences might still occur between values of K and $t_o$ computed from weight and length data, depending on sample size and method of fitting.

Table 4.2. A set of length-at-(absolute) age data, pertaining to millet-seed butterflyfish *(Chaetodon miliaris)* from Oahu, Hawaii.[a]

| Specimen | Standard length (mm) | No. of daily rings |
|---|---|---|
| 1  | 27 | 35  |
| 2  | 29 | 71  |
| 3  | 32 | 51  |
| 4  | 35 | 108 |
| 5  | 42 | 133 |
| 6  | 44 | 118 |
| 7  | 50 | 115 |
| 8  | 52 | 138 |
| 9  | 56 | 147 |
| 10 | 66 | 169 |
| 11 | 70 | 227 |
| 12 | 71 | 228 |
| 13 | 71 | 221 |
| 14 | 86 | 322 |
| 15 | 87 | 375 |

[a] From Table 1 in Ralston (1976).

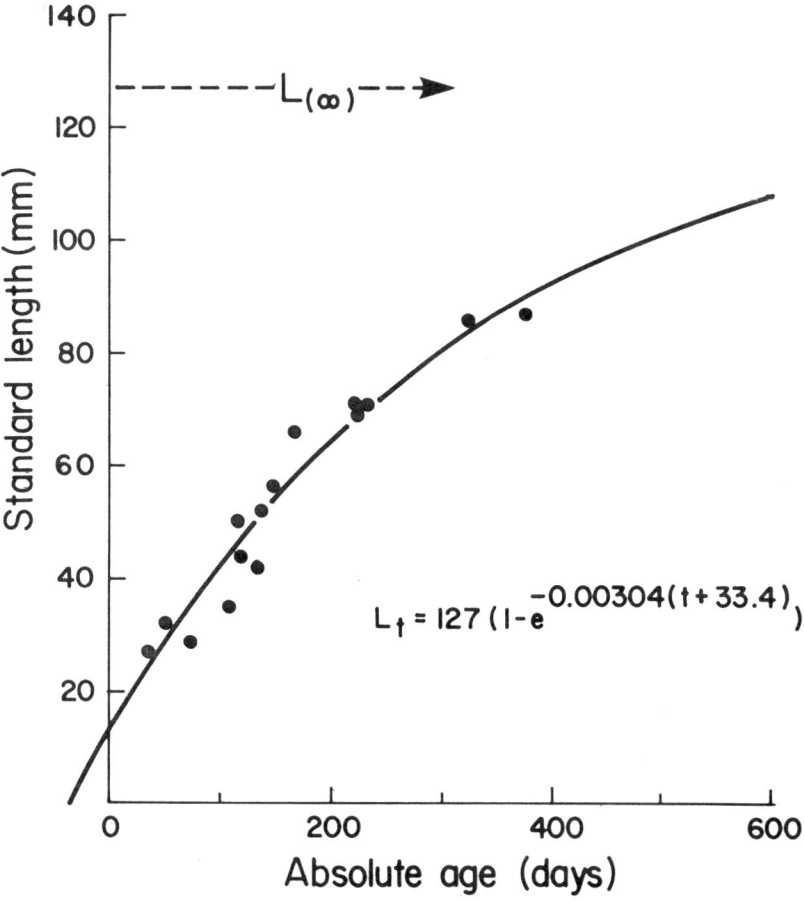

Fig. 4.2. Growth curve of millet-seed butterflyfish *(Chaetodon miliaris)* off Oahu, Hawaii (based on data in Table 4.2 and Example 4.1).

(relative) age". Table 4.3 gives an example of such data. From such data, $L_\infty$, (or $W_\infty$) and K may be estimated, but not $t_o$, which is due to the fact that what is really known are age *differences*, not actual ages. To obtain estimates of $t_o$, a knowledge of the absolute age of fish of given size is necessary, as might be obtained, e.g., from aging by means of daily otolith rings (Pannella 1971) or from a detailed knowledge of the life-history of a fish, inclusive of the exact spawning season.

Table 4.3. A set of length-at-(relative) age data, pertaining to male Nile carps *(Labeo niloticus)* from a freshwater body near Alexandria (Egypt).[a]

| Age group (relative age, in years) | Length (cm) | N |
|---|---|---|
| I | 19.6 | 184 |
| II | 37.4 | 73 |
| III | 45.7 | 11 |
| IV | 51.0 | 3 |

[a] From Hashem (1972).

Throughout most of this manual, I have used the term size-at-age both for data on size at *absolute* and at *relative* age, and distinguished between the two only when the distinction was essential to the point being made.

Size-at-age data (in the wider sense) are required in this manual for Programs FB 3 (von Bertalanffy Plot), FB 4 (Ford-Walford Plot) and FB 7 (seasonal length growth).

Data on size increase in time may be typically represented by the tagging-recapture data of Table 4.4. With this type of data, we do not know the age of any fish, nor do we even have a series of sizes at relative ages. Still, it is possible to derive from data of this type an estimate of asymptotic size and K, given values of D, by means of Program FB 5 (Gulland and Holt Plot) or Program FB 6 (Munro Plot).

This manual, it must be stressed here, shows how to interpret growth data, not how to obtain them. Introductions into the literature on fish aging, including validation techniques applicable to tropical fish, are given by Mohr (1927, 1930 and 1934), Graham (1929), Suvorov (1959), Menon (1950), Bagenal (1974), Pauly (1978), by Brothers (1980), who also reviews techniques for aging tropical fish by means of daily otolith rings, and most recently by Beamish and McFarlane (1983).

METHODS FOR PARAMETER ESTIMATION

A method for obtaining first estimates of asymptotic size

Various authors, notably Beverton (1963) and Taylor (1958), have noted that there is generally a good agreement in various fish stocks, between $L_{max}$, the largest length recorded from a given stock and $L_\infty$, the asymptotic length estimated for that stock.

Taylor (1958) in fact suggested the rule of thumb

$$L_{max}/0.95 \approx L_{(\infty)} \qquad \ldots 4.16)$$

which for weight becomes

$$W_{max}/0.86 \approx W_{(\infty)} \qquad \ldots 4.17)$$

and where $L_{(\infty)}$ and $W_{(\infty)}$ are used (instead of $L_\infty$ and $W_\infty$) to distinguish such preliminary estimates from values of asymptotic size obtained from growth data, e.g., by means of a Ford-Walford plot (see below).

Two problems are associated with this method to obtain preliminary estimates of asymptotic size. The first problem is that of properly defining $L_{max}$ (or $W_{max}$); S. Garcia, FAO (pers. comm.) suggests $L_{max}$ and $W_{max}$ should be derived by averaging the sizes of several large specimens from a well-sampled stock, whenever possible, rather than using only one single value. In either case, it is important to distinguish $L_{max}$ (and $W_{max}$) from $L_{max.\ ever}$ (and $W_{max.\ ever}$), i.e., to distinguish the maximum size on record from a *given stock* from the maximum size recorded from a given *species* of fish (see e.g., Intern. Game Fish Assn. 1978). Obviously, values of $L_{max.\ ever}$ or $W_{max.\ ever}$ will not do for use with equation (4.16) or (4.17), because the "record" fish will most probably have grown under environmental conditions different from those applying to the stock under investigation.

The second problem associated with the use of expression (4.16) or (4.17) to obtain preliminary estimates of asymptotic size lies in the fact that in fish capable of reaching very large sizes, the use of the special VBGF implies that $L_\infty \gg L_{max}$ (and $W_\infty \gg W_{max}$), as shown in Pauly (1981) (see also Example 4.9 and Fig. 4.5). The reason for this is that the assumption embedded in the special VBGF that $D = 1$, which is more or less erroneous in most fish, is most erroneous in those fish that are capable of reaching large sizes (see Fig. 4.1). Using $D = 1$, instead of the appropriate value of D has in these fish the effect of generating values of asymptotic sizes much larger than the maximum known from the stocks in question (Pauly 1981). Thus, in fish capable of reaching large sizes (> 50 cm) it is imperative, when using expression (4.16) or (4.17) to compute and use the appropriate value of D.

The von Bertalanffy plot

Historically, the first method for estimating the parameters of the VBGF was that proposed by von Bertalanffy (1934). The method requires the use of a set value for the asymptotic size ($L_{(\infty)}$, or $W_{(\infty)}$).

The generalized VBGF

$$L_t^D = L_{(\infty)}^D \cdot (1 - e^{-KD\,(t - t_o)}) \qquad \ldots 4.18)$$

can also be written

$$(L_t/L_{(\infty)})^D = 1 - e^{-KD\,(t - t_o)} \qquad \ldots 4.19)$$

and

$$1 - (L_t/L_{(\infty)})^D = e^{-KD\,(t - t_o)} \qquad \ldots 4.20)$$

or

$$-\ln[1 - (L_t/L_{(\infty)})^D] = -KDt_o + KDt \qquad \ldots 4.21)$$

Expression (4.21) has the form of a linear regression, $y = a + bx$,

where

$$y = -\ln[1 - (L_t/L_{(\infty)})^D] \qquad \ldots 4.22)$$

and

$$x = t \qquad \ldots 4.23)$$

which, given a set of length-at-age data, a value of D and an estimate of $L_{(\infty)}$, provides values of intercept (a) and slope (b) which can be used to obtain K and $t_o$ through

$$K = b/D \qquad \ldots 4.24)$$

and

$$t_o = -a/b \qquad \ldots 4.25)$$

Also, a value of $r^2$ is generated which estimates the goodness of fit and which can be used to test whether the use of a different value of $L_{(\infty)}$ improves the linearity of the regression. The latter

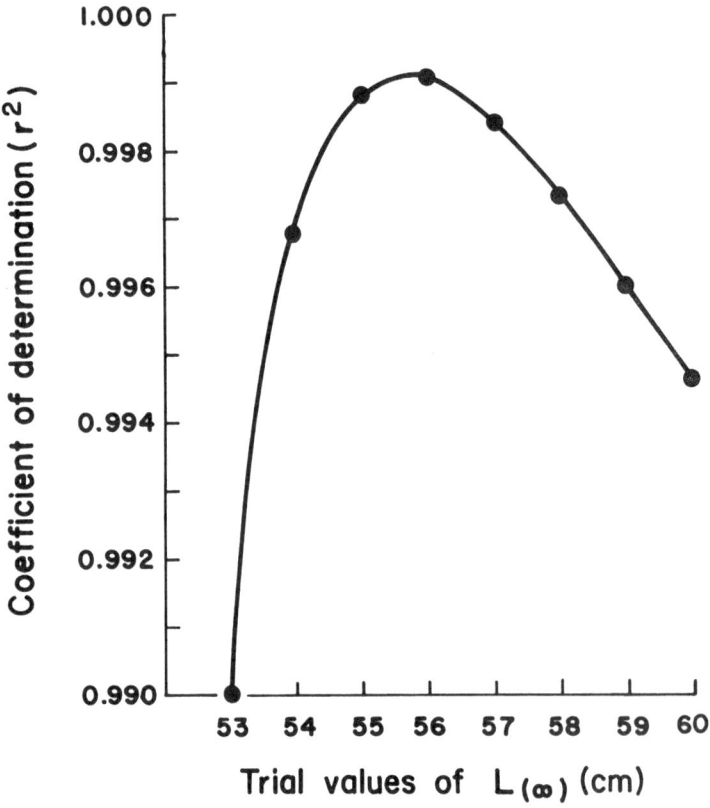

Fig. 4.3. Relationship between the goodness of fit of a von Bertalanffy plot (expressed by the coefficient of determination) and the selected value of $L_{(\infty)}$ (based on data in Table 4.3 and Example 4.2).

feature, therefore, can be used to obtain by trial and error the value of $L_{(\infty)}$ which brings $r^2$ to its maximum. See Example 4.2 and Fig. 4.3.

The use of a von Bertalanffy plot has the following advantages:
a) the values of t (ages) do not need to be equidistant (see Example 4.1)
b) the mean length values used in the regression can be weighed by sample size (as in Example 4.2)
c) the value of $t_o$ is estimated directly when absolute ages are provided (as in Example 4.1)
d) the use of a forcing value of $L_{(\infty)}$ helps in obtaining (rough) estimates of K even when the growth data are not asymptotic.

The Ford-Walford plot

Of all methods used for estimating the parameters of the VBGF, the Ford-Walford plot (Ford 1933; Walford 1946) is the most commonly used. The method is based on a rewritten version of the VBGF:

$$L_{t+1}^D = a + bL_t^D \qquad \ldots 4.26)$$

from which is derived

$$L_\infty = \left(\frac{a}{1-b}\right)^{1/D} \qquad \ldots 4.27)$$

and

$$K = -\frac{\ln b}{D} \qquad \ldots 4.28)$$

Here, $L_t^D$ and $L_{t+1}^D$ pertain to length separated by a constant time interval (1 = year, month or week, etc.). Table 4.4 shows how size-at-age data need to be rearranged for use in a Ford-Walford plot.

A point must be mentioned which pertains to the regression model used in conjunction with the Ford-Walford plot. The linear regression models normally used in this manual (as well as in the HP 67/97 Standard PAC) are arithmetic mean (AM) regressions, also called type I, or predictive regressions. In this regression type, it is implied that the ordinate (y) values are measured with error, or have natural variability, while the abscissa value (x) are measured without error or not to have natural variability. This assumption applies in the case of the von Bertalanffy plot. In the case of the Ford-Walford plot, however, the use of an AM regression introduces a bias, due to the fact that both the y values ($= L_{t+1}^D$) and the x values ($= L_t^D$) are measured with the same error (they are indeed the same data, used twice!). In such a case, a geometric mean (GM) regression (also called type II, or functional regression) has to be used (Ricker 1973; Laws and Archie 1981).

In practice this consists in calculating the a, b and $r^2$ values of an AM regression, then calculating the GM slope (b') from

$$b' = b/r \qquad \ldots 4.29)$$

and the GM intercept (a') from

$$a' = \overline{y} - (b'\,\overline{x}) \qquad \ldots 4.30)$$

where $\overline{x}$ is the mean of the $L_t^D$ values and $\overline{y}$ the mean of the $L_{t+1}^D$ values. The values of a' and b' are then inserted into equation (4.27) and equation (4.28) instead of the values of a and b.

Table 4.4. Length-at-age data for the Atlantic yellowfin *(Thunnus albacares)*[a] off Senegal for use with a Ford-Walford plot.

| Age (years) | FL (cm) | Rearrangement for Ford-Walford plot | |
|---|---|---|---|
| | | $L_t$ ( = x) | $L_{t+1}$ (= y) |
| 1 | 35 | | |
| 2 | 55 | 35 | 55 |
| 3 | 75 | 55 | 75 |
| 4 | 90 | 75 | 90 |
| 5 | 105 | 90 | 105 |
| 6 | 115 | 105 | 115 |

[a] From Postel (1955), who also gives $L_{max}$ = 146.5, corresponding to a value of $W_{max} \approx 60$ kg.

The computations outlined here are all performed by Program FB 4 and data are provided in Table 4.4 for calculating Example 4.3 (see also Figs. 4.4 and 4.5). The Ford-Walford plot has a few advantages over the von Bertalanffy plot—an estimate of $L_\infty$ is obtained immediately, and it is relatively easy to compute.

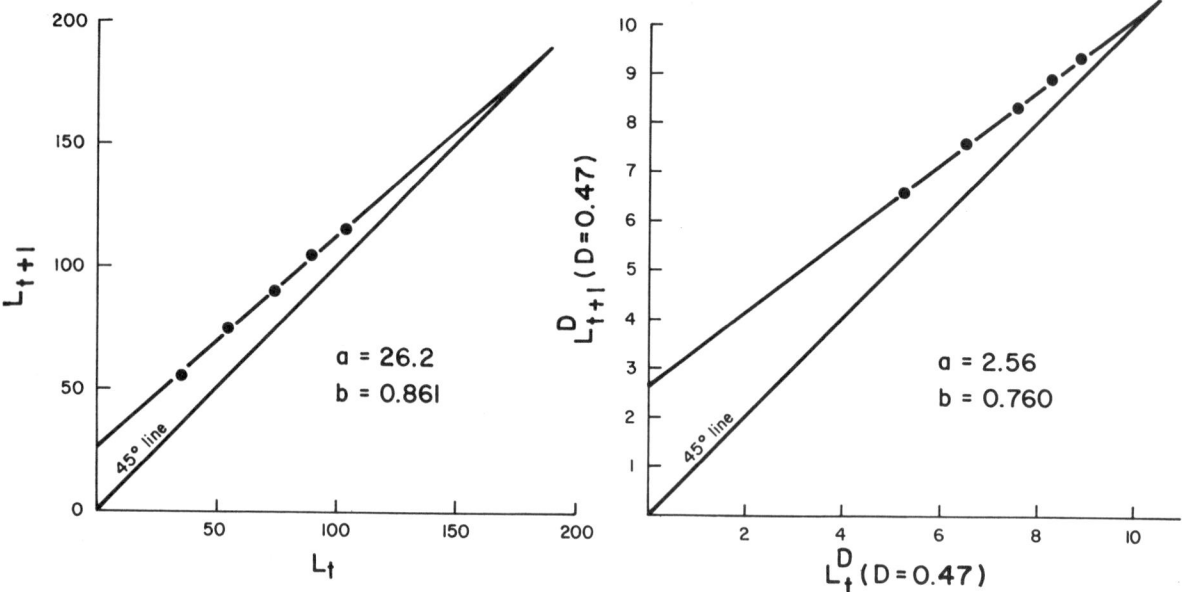

Fig. 4.4. Two Ford-Walford plots for Atlantic yellowfin *(Thunnus albacares)*, based on the special and generalized VBGF (based on Table 4.4 and Example 4.3).

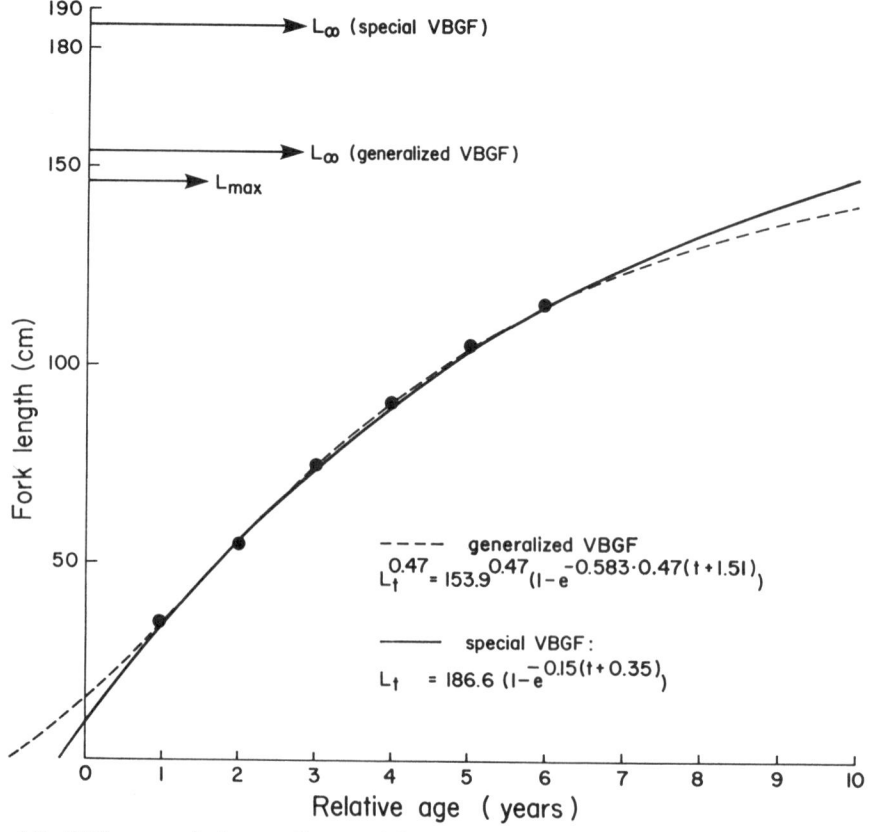

Fig. 4.5. Differences between the special and generalized VBGF as applied to growth data for Atlantic yellowfin *(Thunnus albacares)* (based on Example 4.3).

These advantages, as it seems, are outweighed by the disadvantages of this method, namely:
- The plot requires that the data are equidistant in time (the time between size values being years, months, weeks, etc.).
- The points are unevenly spaced along the plot (see Fig. 4.4) which introduces a slight bias when calculating the regression parameters.
- The points, being combined from *two* values of size-at-age cannot be readily weighed by sample size.
- One value of size-at-age is always lost (because it has no corresponding value of $L_{t+1}$).
- The value of $t_o$ must be estimated separately.

Variants of the basic Ford-Walford plot have been published (e.g., Gulland 1969; Hohendorf 1966), but the negative features of this plot can hardly be compensated for; it would appear that the Ford-Walford plot is in fact inferior to the original von Bertalanffy plot.

The Gulland and Holt plot

Another method for estimating $L_\infty$ and K from growth data is provided by the feature that a plot of size increments per unit time against mean size (for the increment in question) gives a straight line, whose slope—with sign changed—closely corresponds to the value of K, or including the parameter D:

$$\frac{L_2^D - L_1^D}{t_2 - t_1} \approx a - KD\bar{L}^D \qquad \ldots 4.31)$$

where $\bar{L}^D = (L_1^D + L_2^D)/2$, and where $L_1$ and $L_2$ are successive lengths, pertaining to times $t_1$ and $t_2$, respectively (Gulland and Holt 1959).

Table 4.5 gives an example of data of this kind, which are typically obtained from tagging studies or from length-frequency data. The method uses normal size-at-age data, at equal or unequal

Table 4.5. Length at tagging ($L_1$), length at recapture ($L_2$) and time at large for tagged ocean surgeon fish *(Acanthurus bahianus)* from the Virgin Islands.[a]

| No. | $L_1$ (cm) | $L_2$ | Days out | Annual K[b] | Mean temp.[c] (in °C) |
|---|---|---|---|---|---|
| 1 | 9.7 | 10.2 | 53 | 0.370 | 27.48 |
| 2 | 10.5 | 10.9 | 33 | 0.518 | 28.61 |
| 3 | 10.9 | 11.8 | 108 | 0.385 | 27.79 |
| 4 | 11.1 | 12.0 | 102 | 0.419 | 29.29 |
| 5 | 12.4 | 15.5 | 272 | 0.808 | 28.37 |
| 6 | 12.8 | 13.6 | 48 | 1.007 | 28.89 |
| 7 | 14.0 | 14.3 | 53 | 0.405 | 27.55 |
| 8 | 16.1 | 16.4 | 73 | 0.500 | 27.99 |
| 9 | 16.3 | 16.5 | 63 | 0.407 | 27.54 |
| 10 | 17.0 | 17.2 | 106 | 0.321 | 28.00 |
| 11 | 17.7 | 18.0 | 111 | 0.707 | 28.30 |

$\bar{K}$ = 0.532
C.V. = 0.408

[a] Adapted from Table 3 of Randall (1962). Data included pertain to fishes which grew at least 2 mm while at large, which accounts for small measurement errors and cases of no-growth due to tagging wounds.

[b] As calculated from a Munro plot (see Example 4.6) with $L_{(\infty)}$ = 19.25 cm and D = 1 (Fig. 4.9).

[c] As computed from the mean monthly temperatures and the dates at tagging and recapture in Randall (1962), who also gives 29.4°C as highest mean monthly temperature ($T_s$), 27.2°C as lowest mean monthly temperature ($T_w$) and 28.5°C as annual mean ($\bar{T}$).

intervals, granted that the values of $(t_2 - t_1)$ stay small in relation to the longevity of the fish (Gulland and Holt 1959).

Equation (4.31), it will be noted, has the form of a linear regression $y = a + bx$ with

$$x = \overline{L}^D \qquad \ldots 4.32)$$

and

$$y = \frac{L_2^D - L_1^D}{t_2 - t_1} \qquad \ldots 4.33)$$

the intercept (a) and slope (b) of which provide values of K and $L_\infty$ through the relationships

$$K = -b/D \qquad \ldots 4.34)$$

and

$$L_\infty = \left(\frac{a}{KD}\right)^{1/D} \qquad \ldots 4.35)$$

Sometimes, the method does not provide reasonable parameter estimates, when the $\overline{L}^D$ data are too close to each other (Table 4.6, Fig. 4.6). In such a case, a set value of $L_{(\infty)}$ may be used in connec-

Table 4.6. Length at tagging ($L_1$), length at recapture ($L_2$) and days at large of tagged Queen parrot fish *(Scarus vetula)* from the Virgin Islands.[a]

| No. | $L_1$ (cm) | $L_2$ | Days out | $\overline{L}$ | cm/day |
|---|---|---|---|---|---|
| 1 | 14.0 | 16.9 | 48 | 15.45 | 0.0604 |
| 2 | 20.8 | 27.6 | 189 | 24.2 | 0.0360 |
| 3 | 24.8 | 26.5 | 48 | 25.65 | 0.0354 |
| | | | | $\overline{x}$ = 21.77 ; | $\overline{y}$ = 0.0439 |

[a] Adapted from Table 17 in Randall (1962). Randall (1968) gives for this stock a value of $L_{max}$ = "20 inches", hence $L_{(\infty)}$ = 20·2.54/0.95 = 53.5 cm.

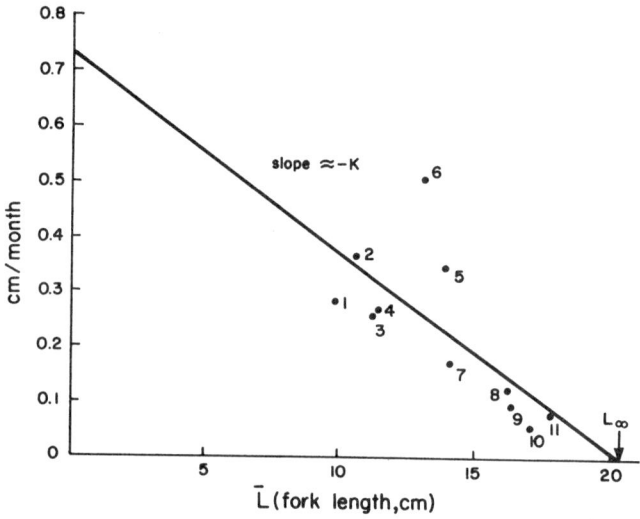

Fig. 4.6. Estimation of growth parameters for the ocean surgeon fish *(Acanthurus bahianus)* off the Virgin Islands by means of a Gulland and Holt plot (based on data in Table 4.5 and Example 4.4).

tion with the means of all $\overline{L}^D$ values ($\overline{x}$) and of all $\dfrac{L_2^D - L_1^D}{t_2 - t_1}$ values ($\overline{y}$) to obtain an estimate of K through

$$K \approx \dfrac{\overline{y}}{(L_\infty^D - \overline{x}) \cdot D} \quad \ldots 4.36)$$

This method, called a "forced" Gulland and Holt plot, allows the estimation of K even when only *one* pair of x and y values is available.

Program FB 5 provides estimation of $L_\infty$ and K, or $W_\infty$ and K given appropriate data (as exemplified in Tables 4.5 and 4.6 and Fig. 4.8). When values of $L_{(\infty)}$, or of $W_{(\infty)}$ are supplied, only K is estimated (Examples 4.4 and 4.5).

Care should be taken, when using tagging data in conjunction with a Gulland and Holt plot, to identify and reject those data pertaining to fish whose growth was severely reduced or halted, e.g., as a result of tagging wounds. It is generally necessary to draw a scattergram prior to all calculations to identify such values of x and y (see Fig. 4.7 for an example). For this purpose, Program FB 5 has been given a routine which provides for the output of the x and y values.

The Munro plot

Munro (1982) suggested that

$$\log_e (L_\infty - L_a) - \log_e (L_\infty - L_b) = K (b - a) \quad \ldots 4.37)$$

which becomes, in the notation used here, and in terms of the generalized VBGF

$$\ln (L_{(\infty)}^D - L_1^D) - \ln (L_{(\infty)}^D - L_2^D) = KD (t_2 - t_1) \quad \ldots 4.38)$$

Given a value of D and trial values of $L_{(\infty)}$, this equation can be used to calculate single values of K (one for each triplet of $L_1$, $L_2$ and time values). The calculated values of K are close to each other when an optimal value of $L_{(\infty)}$ has been selected, and differ widely from each other when the selected value of $L_{(\infty)}$ is too high or too low.

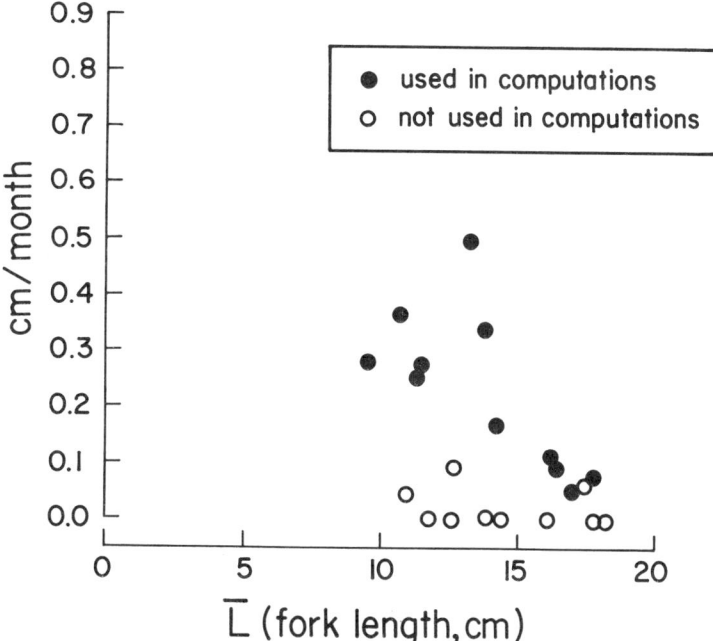

Fig. 4.7. Scattergram of growth increment for ocean surgeon fish (*Acanthurus bahianus*), as obtained from tagging data (the selection of points used was done using a rigorous criterion, see Table 4.5).

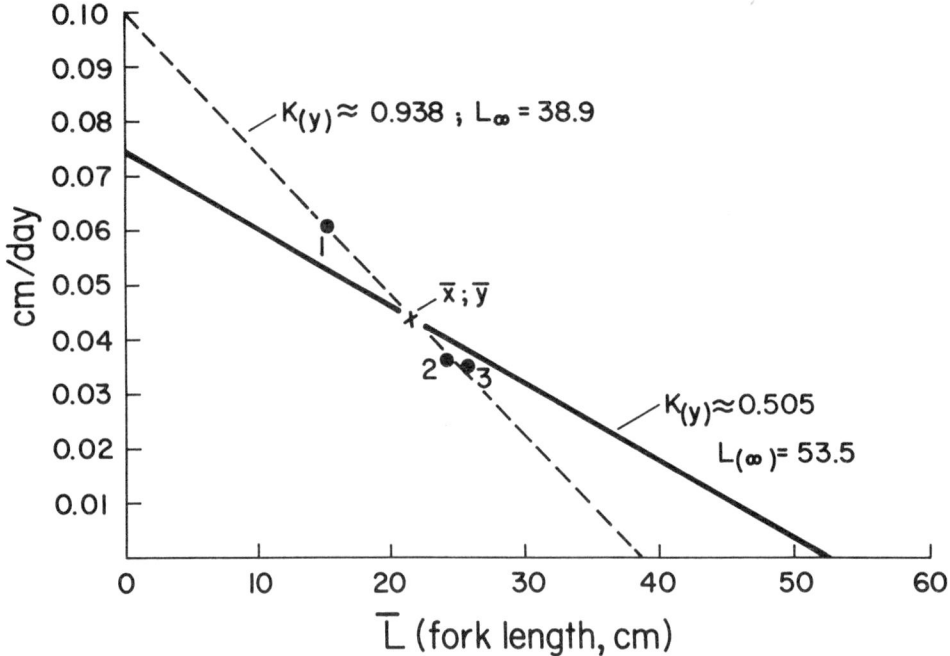

Fig. 4.8. Gulland and Holt plot (dotted line) and "forced" Gulland and Holt plot (solid line) for the Queen parrot fish *(Scarus vetula)* off the Virgin Islands (based on data in Table 4.6 and Example 4.5).

Thus, by calculating, for a given value of $L_{(\infty)}$, the coefficient of variation of the K-values (C.V. of K = $\frac{\text{standard deviation of the K-values}}{\text{mean value of K}}$), one may select by trial and error the value of $L_{(\infty)}$ which produces the lowest coefficient of variation for a given set of data. Program FB 6 (Munro plot) can be used for this purpose (see Table 4.5, Example 4.6, Fig. 4.9).

This method resembles the (forced) Gulland and Holt plot in that data for unequal time intervals can be used, e.g., tagging data. It has, however, the distinct advantage over the Gulland and Holt plot of providing accurate solutions (K values) irrespective of the length of the time interval(s) ($t_2 - t_1$ values).

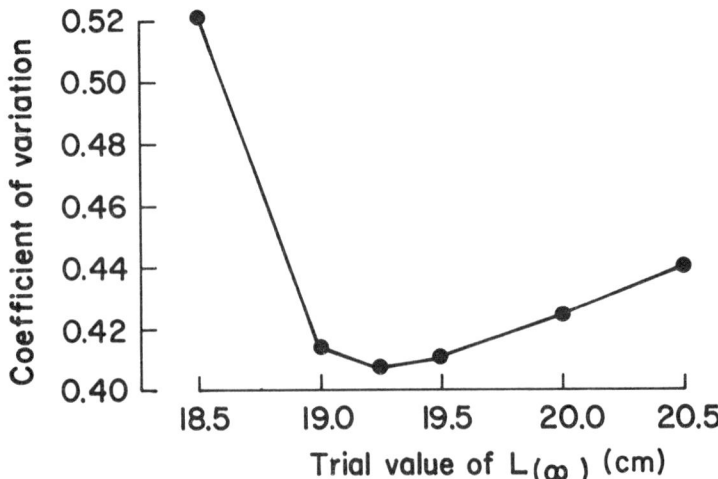

Fig. 4.9. Graph showing how the coefficient of variation (C.V.) of the K-values obtained from a Munro plot depends on the selected value of $L_{(\infty)}$ (based on data in Table 4.5 and Example 4.6).

Alternatively, when a value of $L_\infty$ is reliably known (e.g., as obtained by the procedure outlined above), single values of K can be output (see Table 4.5) which can be compared and/or plotted against any variable likely to affect the growth of individual fish (e.g., mean water temperature during time at large).

Fitting seasonally oscillating length-growth data

In sub-tropical waters, and even more so in temperate waters, the growth of fish is fastest in summer time when temperatures are highest, and slowest in winter time when temperatures are lowest, the growth oscillation roughly following a sine wave curve of period one year (Fig. 4.10).

The inclusion of a sinusoid element of period one year into the VBGF has, therefore, the effect of considerably improving the fit of a growth curve and the accuracy of estimated values of the growth parameters in cases of growth seasonality (Pauly and Gaschütz 1979; Gaschütz et al. 1980).

The "seasonalized" version of the generalized VBGF has the form

$$L_t^D = L_\infty^D (1 - e^{-[KD(t - t_o) + C\frac{KD}{2\pi} \sin 2\pi (t - t_s)]}) \qquad \ldots 4.39)$$

Where $L_\infty$, D, K and $t_o$ are parameters of the "unseasonalized" VBGF while C expresses the amplitude of the growth oscillations and $t_s$ the start of the sinusoid growth oscillations with respect to $t = 0$.

The value of C is defined such that, if C = 1, the growth rate (dl/dt) is zero exactly once a year.[a] Values of $0 < C < 1$ indicate a slowing down of the growth rate in winter time without dl/dt ever reaching zero, while C = 0, finally corresponds to the unseasonalized VBGF. The para-

---

[a]Values of $C > 1$ do not imply that the length of fish is reduced in winter, but rather that the period of no-growth lasts over several weeks or months. This case should not occur in the tropics, however.

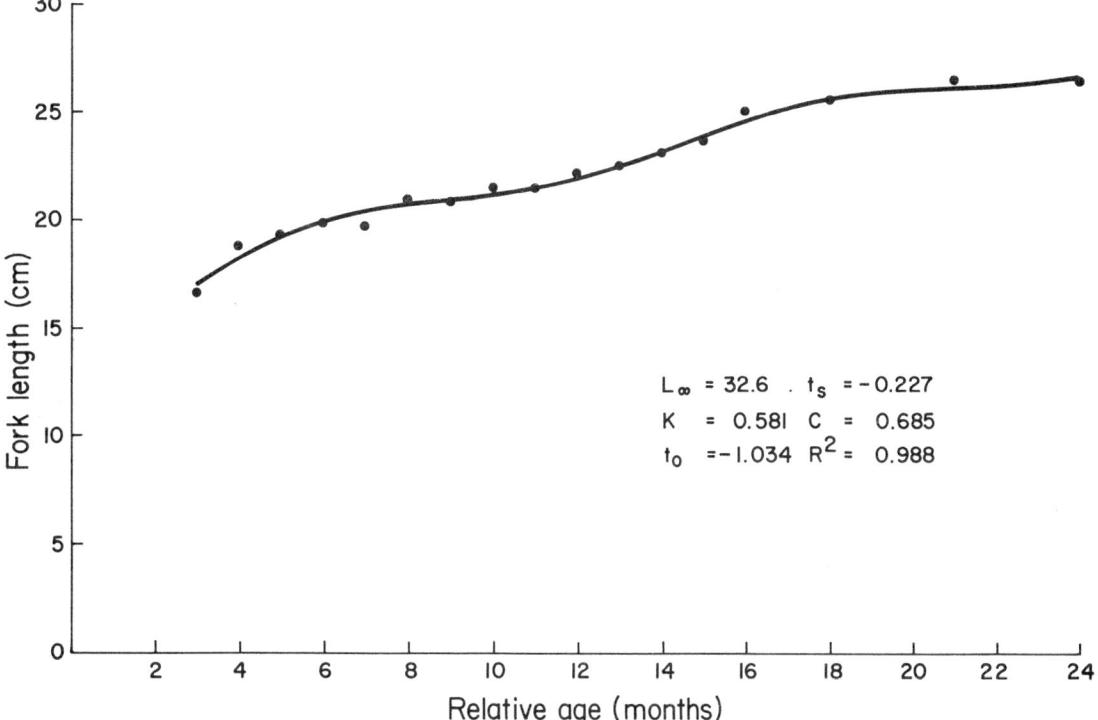

Fig. 4.10. Seasonally oscillating growth of the halfbeak *(Hemirhamphus brasiliensis)* off Florida (based on data in Table 4.7 and Example 4.7).

meter $t_s$ is defined such that $t_s + 0.5$ = "winter point", i.e., the time of the year when growth is slowest.

Given values of $L_{(\infty)}$, D and a set of seasonally oscillating length-at-age data, the parameters K, C, $t_o$ and $t_s$ of equation (4.39) can be easily estimated from a multiple linear regression of the form

$$y = a + b_1 x_1 + b_2 x_2 + b_3 x_3 \qquad \ldots 4.40)$$

where $\quad y = \ln(1 - L_t^D / L_\infty^D)$  $\qquad \ldots 4.41)$

$\quad x_1 = t$ (age must be always expressed in years) $\qquad \ldots 4.42)$

$\quad x_2 = \sin 2\pi t$ $\qquad \ldots 4.43)$

and $\quad x_3 = \cos 2\pi t$ $\qquad \ldots 4.44)$

and where the parameters K, $t_o$, C and $t_s$ are estimated from the relationships

$$a = KDt_o \qquad \ldots 4.45)$$

$$b_1 = -KD \qquad \ldots 4.46)$$

$$b_2 = -KD \frac{C}{2\pi} \cos 2\pi t_s \qquad \ldots 4.47)$$

$$b_3 = KD \frac{C}{2\pi} \sin 2\pi t_s \qquad \ldots 4.48)$$

and $\quad t_s = \{ \arctan(-b_3/b_2) \}/2\pi \qquad \ldots 4.49)$

The only parameters which cannot be estimated directly from the seasonally oscillating growth data are $L_{(\infty)}$ and D. The input value of $L_{(\infty)}$, however, can be improved by means of the same trial and error techniques suggested for the von Bertalanffy and the Munro plots, because Program FB 7 has a routine for computing $R^2$ (multiple coefficient of determination, analogous to $r^2$) the value of which may be maximized by means of a few plots with different estimates of $L_{(\infty)}$ (see Table 4.7, Example 4.7 and Fig. 4.11). Hoenig and Choudary (1983) give a method to derive standard errors of the parameters of equation (4.39).

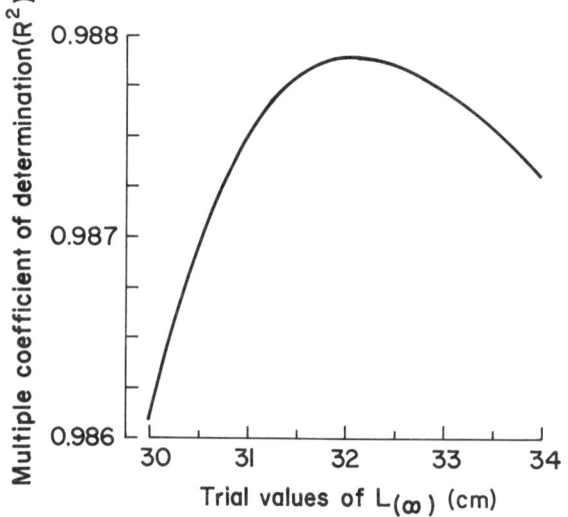

Fig. 4.11. Graph showing how an optimal value of $L_{(\infty)}$ can be selected when fitting seasonally oscillating length-growth data (based on data in Table 4.7 and Example 4.7).

Table 4.7. Seasonal growth of halfbeak *(Hemirhamphus brasiliensis)* off Western Florida, U.S.A.[a]

| Relative age in months | FL (cm) | Relative age in months | FL (cm) |
|---|---|---|---|
| 3 | 16.8 | 12 | 22.2 |
| 4 | 18.9 | 13 | 22.5 |
| 5 | 19.4 | 14 | 23.2 |
| 6 | 20.0 | 15 | 23.6 |
| 7 | 19.8 | 16 | 25.0 |
| 8 | 21.0 | 18 | 25.5 |
| 9 | 20.8 | 21 | 26.4 |
| 10 | 21.5 | 24 | 26.4 |
| 11 | 21.5 | — | — |

[a] As read off Fig. 5 in Berkeley and Houde (1978), who also give 31 cm for $FL_{max}$.

Program FB 7, as opposed to the other programs for estimating the parameters of the VBGF, cannot be used to fit weight growth data, even after conversion of W to $W^{1/b}$, because weight oscillations have in fish a structure different from that of length oscillations (see Shul'man 1974).

Extended Gulland and Holt plot

The seasonally oscillating growth model presented above (equation 4.39) is very sensitive, even to small seasonal oscillations. Using this model, growth oscillations have been demonstrated using data previously thought to depict growth patterns unaffected by the relatively small oscillations of environmental factors that occur in the tropics (Pauly and Ingles 1981). For this reason, it becomes necessary to consider growth oscillations not only with regard to size-at-age data, but also with regard to size increment data (i.e., tagging data), which have been frequently used to estimate the growth parameters of tropical fish.

The method proposed here is a modification of the Gulland and Holt plot, discussed earlier in this chapter. The new method may be called "extended Gulland and Holt plot"; it consists of extending the earlier method

$$\frac{L_2^D - L_1^D}{t_2 - t_1} = a + bX \quad \ldots 4.50)$$

where $b = -KD$ and $x = (L_1^D + L_2^D)/2$ into a multiple regression of the form

$$y = a + b_1 x_1 + b_2 x_2 \quad \ldots 4.51)$$

where $y = (L_2^D - L_1^D)/(t_2 - t_1)$, and $x_1 = (L_1^D + L_2^D)/2$, as in the Gulland and Holt plot, and where $x_2$ is the value, during the time $t_1 - t_2$, of the environmental factor most likely to affect the growth of the fish while at large. (Obviously, the expression may be extended to any number of additional terms, up to $b_n X_n$, but this will not be investigated here.)

As shown in Fig. 4.12, the amplitude of seasonal growth oscillations in different fishes is extremely well correlated with the difference between annual minimum and maximum temperature of the water masses they inhabit, for which reason the most meaningful factor to insert for $X_2$ in expression (4.51) is the average temperature encountered by the fishes while at large (between times $t_1$ and $t_2$).

Thus, the model becomes

$$\frac{L_2^D - L_1^D}{t_2 - t_1} = a + b_1 \left(\frac{L_1^D + L_2^D}{2}\right) + b_2 T \quad \ldots 4.52)$$

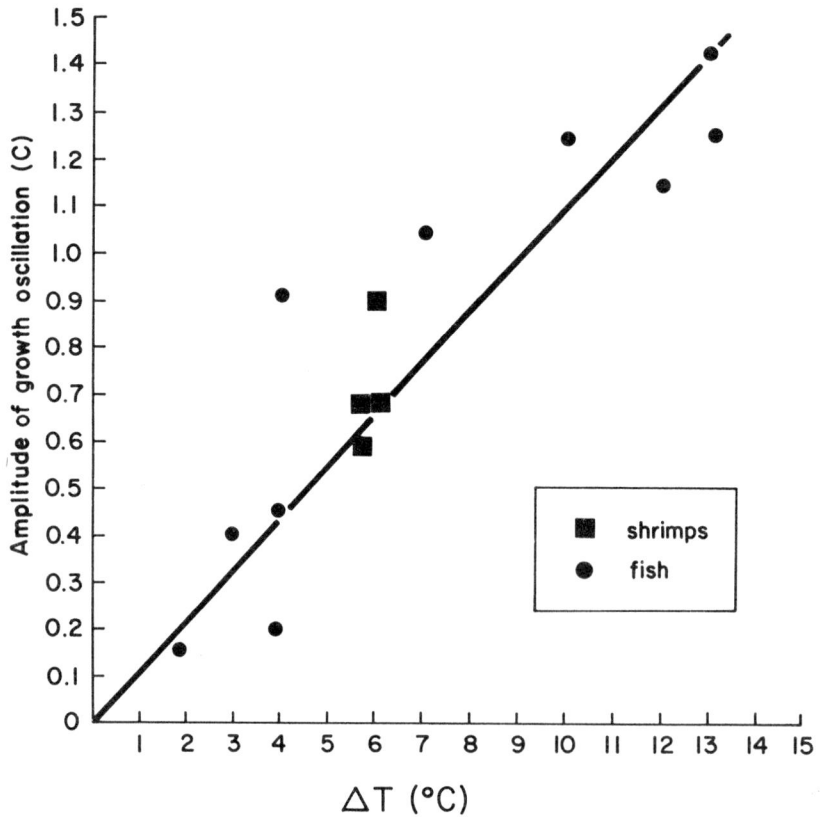

Fig. 4.12. Relationship between the amplitude of seasonal growth oscillations (C) of fish and shrimps and the difference between highest and lowest mean monthly temperature of their habitats ($\Delta T$). Adapted from Pauly et al. (in press).

where T is the mean environmental temperature in °C during an interval $t_1$ to $t_2$. From this, the value of $L_\infty$ corresponding to the mean annual temperature ($\overline{T}$) (hence, to a value of $L_\infty$ unaffected by temperature fluctuations) can be estimated as:

$$L_\infty = \left( \frac{a + (b_2 T_m)}{-b_1} \right)^{1/D} \qquad \ldots 4.53)$$

while K and C can be estimated from

$$K = -b_1/D \qquad \ldots 4.54)$$

and

$$C = \frac{b_2 (T_s - T_w)}{2 [a + (b_2 \overline{T})]} \qquad \ldots 4.55)$$

respectively, $T_s$ ("summer") being the highest and $T_w$ ("winter") the lowest mean monthly temperature of the water body in question.

The method, as might be seen from Example 4.8, is extremely sensitive and can detect and quantify temperature effects that are extremely slight.

In analogy to the "forced Gulland and Holt plot", the method can also be used to estimate K (while accounting for seasonal growth oscillations) with a forcing value of $L_{(\infty)}$, using

$$K \approx [a + (b_2 T_m)]/L_{(\infty)}^D \qquad \ldots 4.56)$$

(See Example 4.8.).

# GROWTH: A CONCLUDING PROGRAM

More methods suitable to estimate growth parameters by means of HP 67/97 calculators are available, especially from the HP "Users Library". The six methods proposed here are quite sufficient, however, for most problems and this chapter concludes with a straightforward, but hopefully helpful program.

Program FB 9 simply gives solutions for the generalized versions of the VBGF and their derivatives and also estimates the parameters d and D from equations (4.8) and (4.9). Table 4.8 gives an overview of the various output values that are calculated, given an appropriate set of values for the parameters needed for the calculation (see Examples 4.9 and 4.10).

Table 4.8. Constants to be stored for each of the solutions of the generalized von Bertalanffy Growth Formula (see Program FB 9).

| Label | Values estimated | Constants required in stores | | | | | | Input | Output |
|---|---|---|---|---|---|---|---|---|---|
| | | $L_\infty$ | $W_\infty$ | K | D | $t_o$ | b | | |
| A | length at a given age | X | — | X | X | X | — | t | $L_t$ |
| B | weight at a given age | — | X | X | X | X | X | t | $W_t$ |
| C | age at a given length | X | — | X | X | X | — | $L_t$ | t |
| c | age at a given weight | — | X | X | X | X | X | $W_t$ | t |
| E | $t_o$ for given length and age[a] | X | — | X | X | — | — | $L_t, t$ | $t_o$ |
| e | $t_o$ for given weight and age[a] | — | X | X | X | — | X | $W_t, t$ | $t_o$ |
| a | length at inflexion point of curve[b] | X | — | X | X | — | — | — | $L_i$ |
| b | weight at inflexion point of curve | — | X | X | X | — | X | — | $W_i$ |
| D | growth rate at a given length | X | — | X | X | — | X | $L_t$ | dl/dt |
| d | growth rate at a given weight | — | X | X | X | — | X | $W_t$ | dw/dt |
| 7 | values of d and D | — | — | — | — | — | — | $W_{max}$[c] | d, D |
| Stores: | | A | B | 1 | D | 0 | E | | |

[a]The values of $t_o$ may be summed up ($\Sigma+$), then averaged ($\bar{x}$).
[b]Applicable only when $D < 1$.
[c]$W_{max}$ must be expressed in grams.

This program, although consisting of very simple steps, can help save a considerable amount of time to whomever has to draw various growth and related curves.

Recommended reading: The literature on fish growth is immense, and a list of recommended reading on this subject is necessarily highly subjective. Nevertheless, here are some useful references: von Bertalanffy (1938), Beverton and Holt (1959), Cushing (1981), Taylor (1962), Pannella (1971), Fryer and Iles (1972), Weatherley (1972), Bagenal (1974), Shul'man (1974), Ricker (1975, Chapter 9), Lowe-McConnell (1975, Chapter 9), Jones (1976a), Ricker (1979), Brothers (1980) and even Pauly (1981).

Suggested research topics: Estimate growth parameters of commercially exploited fishes, and of little-investigated groups (e.g., coral reef fish). Compare growth curves obtained with the special VBGF with growth curves obtained using the generalized VBGF, especially in tuna. Estimate the age of fish by means of daily rings in their otoliths (see Brothers 1980). Assess the intensity of seasonal growth oscillations in tropical fish, and establish the cause for these oscillations.

Reanalyze previously published length-frequency data (or data on file somewhere) by new methods (see, e.g., Pauly and David 1981) and use the resulting growth prameters to derive growth-related parameters (e.g., mortality rates; see next chapter).

**Calculating values of $L_\infty$, K and $t_o$ in the millet-seed butterflyfish *(Chaetodon miliaris)* by means of a von Bertalanffy plot.** EXAMPLE 4.1

---

Data from Table 4.2

Computation

1) Read sides 1 and 2 of Program FB 3.

2) Tinker (1978, p. 50) gives "about 5 inches" for the maximum length reached by *Chaetodon miliaris* in Hawaii, thus $L_{(\infty)}$ = 127 mm. We set D = 1.

3) Keystrokes

   127 ↑ 1 f a 27 ↑ 35 A 29 ↑ 71 A 32 ↑ 51 A 35 ↑ 108 A 42 ↑ 133 A 44 ↑ 118 A 50 ↑ 115 A 52 ↑ 138 A 56 ↑ 147 A 66 ↑ 169 A ↑ 70 ↑ 227 A 71 ↑ 228 A 71 ↑ 221 A 86 ↑ 322 A 87 ↑ 375 A

4) Calculate $r^2$, K and $t_o$

|  | Keystrokes | Results |  |
|---|---|---|---|
|  | E | 0.953 | ($r^2$) |
|  |  | 0.003 | (K) |
|  |  | −33.403 | ($t_o$) |
| 5) Repeat (step 4) with 6 digits | DSP 6 E | 0.952513 | ($r^2$) |
|  |  | 0.003043 | (K) |
|  |  | −33.402913 | ($t_o$) |
| 6) Put K and $t_o$ on an annual basis: | 365 ÷ | −0.091515 |  |
|  | DSP 3 | −0.092 | ($t_o$) |
|  | 0.003043 ↑ | 0.003 |  |
|  | 365 x | 1.111 | (K) |

Using the relationship $3/K \approx t_{max}$ (see p. 75) we may thus infer, among other things, that *Chaetodon miliaris* has a longevity ($t_{max}$) of about 3 years.

**EXAMPLE 4.2**  Calculating a value of K, and improving a first trial value of $L_{(\infty)}$ for Nile carps *(Labeo niloticus)* by means of the von Bertalanffy plot.

Data from Table 4.3

Computation

1) Read sides 1 and 2 of Program FB 3, and perform: DSP 4.

2) Select first value of $L_{(\infty)}$ through $\frac{L_{max}}{0.95} = \frac{51}{0.95} \approx 54$, with D = 1.

3) Keystrokes

   54 ↑ 1 f a 19.6 ↑ 1 ↑ 184 C 37.4 ↑ 2 ↑ 73 C 45.7 ↑ 3 ↑ 11 C 51 ↑ 4 ↑ 3 C

|   | Keystrokes | Results |   |
|---|---|---|---|
| 4) Calculate $r^2$ and K (remember, with *relative* age, the third output is *not* a value of $t_o$!) | E | 0.9967 | ($r^2$) |
|   |   | 0.7417 | (K) |
|   |   | 0.3970 | (not $t_o$) |

5) Repeat steps 2 and 3 with $L_{(\infty)}$ = 53, 55, 56, 57, 58, 59 and 60 cm and note the values of $r^2$. Then plot these values of $r^2$ on the trial values of $L_{(\infty)}$ (as in Fig. 4.3). You will note that the value of 56 cm produces the highest value of $r^2$ (= 0.9990), hence the best fit to the growth curve. At this stage, our preliminary value of $L_{(\infty)}$ turns into a full-fledged value of $L_\infty$, matched by a value of K = 0.655.

**EXAMPLE 4.3**

Estimation of $L_\infty$ and K for *Thunnus albacares* off Senegal by means of a Ford-Walford plot, special and generalized VBGF.

---

Data from Table 4.4

Computations

Case I, with D = 1

1) Read sides 1 and 2 of Program FB 4

2) Keystrokes

   35 ↑ 1 f a 55 A 75 A 90 A 105 A 115 A

|  | Keystrokes | Results |  |
|---|---|---|---|
| 3) Compute $r^2$, K and $L_\infty$ | E | 0.996 | ($r^2$) |
|  |  | 0.150 | (K) |
|  |  | 186.6 | ($L_\infty$) |

Case II, with D = 0.47*

4) Keystrokes

   35 ↑ .47 f a 55 A 75 A 90 A 105 A 115 A

| 5) Compute $r^2$, K and $L_\infty$ | E | 0.998 | ($r^2$) |
|---|---|---|---|
|  |  | 0.583 | (K) |
|  |  | 153.9 | ($L_\infty$) |

Note the slight improvement of the goodness of fit (0.998 > 0.996), the higher value of K and the lower value of $L_\infty$ ($\approx L_{max}$ = 146.5 in Postel 1955) resulting from the use of the generalized VBGF. See Fig. 4.5 for a view of the differences between the special and generalized VBGF.

---

*Obtained from $W_{max}$ = 60 kg and equation 4.10 (see Fig. 4.1 and Program FB 9).

**EXAMPLE 4.4**  Using a Gulland and Holt plot to estimate $L_\infty$ and K for ocean surgeon fish *(Acanthurus bahianus)* from the Virgin Islands.

Data from Table 4.5

Computation

1) Read sides 1 and 2 of Program FB 5.

2) Keystrokes

   1 f a 9.7 ↑ 10.2 ↑ 53 A 10.5 ↑ 10.9 ↑ 33 A 10.9 ↑ 11.8 ↑ 108 A 11.1 ↑ 12 ↑ 102 A 12.4 ↑ 15.5 ↑ 272 A 12.8 ↑ 13.6 ↑ 48 A 14 ↑ 14.3 ↑ 53 A 16.1 ↑ 16.4 ↑ 73 A 16.3 ↑ 16.5 ↑ 63 A 17 ↑ 17.2 ↑ 106 A 17.7 ↑ 18 ↑ 111 A

3) Calculate $r^2$, K and $L_\infty$

|  | Keystrokes | Results |  |
|---|---|---|---|
|  | E | 0.496 | ($r^2$) |
|  |  | 0.001 | (K) |
|  |  | 20.336 | ($L_\infty$) |
| 4) Putting K on an annual basis | X⇌Y | 0.001 |  |
|  | 365 x | 0.432 | (K) |

Hence, the growth parameters are $L_\infty$ = 20.4 and K = 0.432 (see Fig. 4.6). For plotting the data and results on a graph (such as Figs. 4.6, 4.7) press C; the procedure is then as follows (data of Table 4.6):

| Keystrokes: | Output: | $\bar{L}$ | $\Delta L/\Delta t$ | i |
|---|---|---|---|---|
| 14 ↑ 16.9 ↑ 48 A |  | 15.45 | 0.060 | 1 |
| 20.8 ↑ 27.6 ↑ 189 A |  | 24.20 | 0.036 | 2 |
| 24.8 ↑ 26.5 ↑ 48 A |  | 25.65 | 0.035 | 3 |
| etc....... |  | ... | ... | ... |

The intercept and slope of the regression line are in STO A and STO B, respectively, and may be recalled to trace the line.

**EXAMPLE 4.5**

**Using a "forced" Gulland and Holt plot to estimate K when a value of $L_{max}$ and growth increment data are available.**

Tagging data from Table 4.6. Also, Randall (1968) gives for the fish in question a value of $L_{max}$ = "20 inches".

Computations

1) Read sides 1 and 2 of Program FB 5.

2) Estimation of $L_{(\infty)}$, in cm

| Keystrokes | Results | |
|---|---|---|
| 20 ↑ | | |
| 0.95 ÷ | 21.053 | |
| 2.54 x | 53.474 | ($L_{(\infty)}$) |

3) Estimation of K

| Keystrokes: | Results | |
|---|---|---|
| 1 f a 14 ↑ 16.9 ↑ 48 A 20.8 ↑ 27.6 ↑ | 0.001 | (K) |
| 189 A 24.8 ↑ 26.5 ↑ 48 A 53.5 f c | (rounded up) | |

4) Putting K on an annual basis: 365 x         0.505       (K)

Hence, the growth parameters are $L_{(\infty)} \approx 53.5$ cm and $K \approx 0.505$. See Example 4.6 on how to draw the graph.

**EXAMPLE 4.6** — Calculating values of K, and using these to improve a first trial value of $L_{(\infty)}$ for ocean surgeon fish *(Acanthurus bahianus)* by means of a Munro plot.

Data from Table 4.5

Computations

1) Read side 1 of Program FB 6.

2) Select trial value of $L_{(\infty)}$, e.g., as obtained from a Gulland and Holt plot; try $L_{(\infty)}$ = 20 cm.

3) Keystrokes

   20 ↑ 1 f a 9.7 ↑ 10.2 ↑ 53 A 10.5 ↑ 10.9 ↑ 33 A 10.9 ↑ 11.8 ↑ 108 A 11.1 ↑ 12 ↑ 102 A 12.4 ↑ 15.5 ↑ 272 A ↑ 12.8 ↑ 13.6 ↑ 48 A 14 ↑ 14.3 ↑ 53 A 16.1 ↑ 16.4 ↑ 73 A 16.3 ↑ 16.5 ↑ 63 A 17 ↑ 17.2 ↑ 106 A 17.7 ↑ 18 ↑ 111 A

4) Calculate mean value of K and C.V.

| | Keystrokes | Results | |
|---|---|---|---|
| | E | 0.448 | ($\overline{K}$) |
| | | 0.425 | (C.V.) |

5) Compute $\overline{K}$ and C.V. for $L_{(\infty)}$ = 18.5, 19.0, 19.5, 20.5 and plot C.V. values. The results should look as in Fig. 4.9, which allows for an estimate of best $L_{(\infty)}$ (hence, $L_\infty$) = 19.25, corresponding to $\overline{K}$ = 0.532 and C.V. 0.408.

6) To obtain single values of K, select a good value of $L_{(\infty)}$ and perform:

| Keystrokes | Results | |
|---|---|---|
| 19.25 ↑ 1 f a fSTFO ↑ 9.7 ↑ 10.2 ↑ 53A | 0.370 | ($K_1$) |
| 10.5 ↑ 10.9 ↑ 33 A | 0.518 | ($K_2$) |
| 10.9 ↑ 11.8 ↑ 108 A | 0.385 | ($K_3$) |
| etc. (see Table 4.5, right column) | | |

The estimates of K may then be plotted against variables likely to influence growth rate (e.g., water temperature while at large).

**Determination of growth parameters from seasonally oscillating length-at-age data for the halfbeak** *(Hemirhamphus brasiliensis)*.

EXAMPLE 4.7

Data from Table 4.7 (and using D = 1)

Computations

1) Read sides 1 and 2 of Program FB 7 (a).

2) Compute preliminary value of $L_{(\infty)}$ from $L_{max}$ = 31 cm.

|  | Keystrokes | Results |  |
|---|---|---|---|
|  | 31 ↑ |  |  |
|  | .95 ÷ | 32.6 | ($L_{(\infty)}$) |

3) Initialize and enter length-at-age data

   Keystrokes

   10 ↑ 5y$^x$ f a 3 ↑ 12 ÷ 16.8 ↑ 32.6 A 4 ↑ 12 ÷ 18.9 ↑ 32.6 A 5 ↑ 12 ÷ 19.4 ↑ 32.6 A 6 ↑ 12 ÷ 20 ↑ 32.6 A 7 ↑ 12 ÷ 19.8 ↑ 32.6 A 8 ↑ 12 ÷ 21 ↑ 32.6 A 9 ↑ 12 ÷ 20.8 ↑ 32.6 A 10 ↑ 12 ÷ 21.5 ↑ 32.6 A 11 ↑ 12 ÷ 21.5 ↑ 32.6 A 12 ↑ 12 ÷ 22.2 ↑ 32.6 A 13 ↑ 12 ÷ 22.5 ↑ 32.6 A 14 ↑ 12 ÷ 23.2 ↑ 32.6 A 15 ↑ 12 ÷ 23.6 ↑ 32.6 A 16 ↑ 12 ÷ 25 ↑ 32.6 A 18 ↑ 12 ÷ 25.5 ↑ 32.6 A 21 ↑ 12 ÷ 26.4 ↑ 32.6 A 24 ↑ 12 ÷ 26.4 ↑ 32.6 A

4) Read sides 1 and 2 of Program FB 7 (b).

5) Perform:

| Keystrokes | Results |  |
|---|---|---|
| A | 0.98783 | ($R^2$) |
| E | 0.58094 | (K · D) |
|  | −1.03386 | ($t_o$) |
|  | −0.27326 | (old $t_s$) |
|  | −0.68498 | (−C) |

6) Adjust $t_s$ and C values (see User's Instruction FB 7 (b)).

| Keystrokes | Results |  |
|---|---|---|
| CHS | 0.68498 | (C) |
| 0.273 CHS | −0.273 | (old $t_s$) |
| 0.5 + | 0.227 | (new $t_s$) |

7) Repeat steps 3-6 with different values of $L_{(\infty)}$ and plot resulting $R^2$ values against the $L_{(\infty)}$. A figure similar to Fig. 4.11 should emerge from which the best value of $L_\infty$ can be selected. (The best value of $L_{(\infty)}$ happens to 32.6 cm.)

8) To trace the growth curve follow User's Instruction FB 7 (b).

**EXAMPLE 4.8**   **Estimating the growth parameters and the seasonal growth oscillations of** *Acanthurus bahianus* **from the Virgin Islands.**

Data from Table 4.5

1) Read sides 1 and 2 of Program FB 8.

2) D is set equal to unity.

3) Keystrokes

1 f a 9.7 ↑ 10.2 ↑ 53 ↑ 27.48 A 10.5 ↑ 10.9 ↑ 33 ↑ 28.61 A 10.9 ↑ 11.8 ↑ 108 ↑ 27.79 A 11.1 ↑ 12 ↑ 102 ↑ 29.29 A 12.4 ↑ 15.5 ↑ 272 ↑ 28.37 A 12.8 ↑ 13.6 ↑ 48 ↑ 28.89 A 14 ↑ 14.3 ↑ 53 ↑ 27.55 A 16.1 ↑ 16.4 ↑ 73 ↑ 27.99 A 16.3 ↑ 16.5 ↑ 63 ↑ 27.54 A 17 ↑ 17.2 ↑ 106 ↑ 28 A 17.7 ↑ 18 ↑ 111 ↑ 28.3 A

4) Estimate $R^2$, intercept and slopes

| | Keystrokes | Results | |
|---|---|---|---|
| | E | 0.648 | ($R^2$) |
| | | −0.065 | (a) |
| | | 0.001 | ($b_1$) |
| | | 0.003 | ($b_2$) |

5) Calculate value of $L_\infty$ corresponding to the mean annual temperature ($\overline{T}$) and K

| | Keystrokes | Results | |
|---|---|---|---|
| | 28.5 C ($\overline{T}$) | 22.079 | ($L_\infty$) |
| | | 0.001 | ($K_d$) |
| to put value of K on annual basis do: | 365 x | 0.387 | ($K_y$) |

6) To estimate value of C, enter $T_s$, $T_w$ and $\overline{T}$

| | Keystrokes | Results | |
|---|---|---|---|
| | 29.4 ↑ | | |
| | 27.2 ↑ | | |
| | 28.5 f c | 0.146 | (C) |

7) To estimate value of K based on a forcing value of asymptotic length do

| | Keystrokes | Results | |
|---|---|---|---|
| (value of $L_{(\infty)}$ in Example 4.4 = ) | 20.4 ↑ | | |
| ($T_m$ = ) | 28.5 f e | 0.001 | ($K_d$) |
| to put value of K on an annual basis do: | 365 x | 0.419 | ($K_y$) |

This last result (K = 0.419) corresponds well with that obtained with the same data used in conjunction with a simple Gulland and Holt plot (see Example 4.4, where a value of K = 0.432 was estimated for $L_\infty$ = 20.4.)

**EXAMPLE 4.9**

## Solutions of the generalized VBGF.

Case I

Calculate the length ($L_t$) corresponding to a given age t.

1) Read sides 1 and 2 of Program FB 9.

2) Enter constants as required (here: $L_\infty$, K, $t_o$ and D, see Table 4.8)

3) Calculate length-for-age

| Keystrokes | Results |
|---|---|
| Age, A | Length |

Case II

Calculate the growth rate corresponding to a given weight.

1) Enter constants as required (here: $W_\infty$, K, D and b, see Table 4.8)

2) Calculate growth rate at weight

| Keystrokes | Results |
|---|---|
| Weight, fd | dw/dt |

Case III

Calculate $t_o$ corresponding to a given length-at-age.

1) Enter constants as required (here: $L_\infty$, K and D, see Table 4.8)

2) Calculate $t_o$

| Keystrokes | Results |
|---|---|
| $L_t$ ↑ | |
| t E | $t_o$ |

For other cases, see Table 4.8 and User's Instruction to Program FB 9.

**EXAMPLE 4.10**

> **Estimation of the parameters d and D in Atlantic yellowfin by means of Program FB 9.**
>
> The Atlantic yellowfin *(Thunnus albacares)* reaches about 60 kg (see Table 4.4). What are the corresponding values of d and D?
>
> Computations
>
> 1) Read sides 1 and 2 of Program FB 9.
>
> 2) Perform:
>
> | Keystrokes | Results | |
> |---|---|---|
> | 60000 | | |
> | GTO 7 | 0.84 | (d) |
> | R/S | 0.47 | (D) |
>
> The value of D, although approximate, can be used in conjunction with the generalized VBGF, for the stock in question and will generate growth parameters more realistic than obtained with D = 1, as implied in the special VBGF.

# 5. Total, Natural and Fishing Mortalities

## INTRODUCTION

In fishery biology, the most useful manner of expressing the decay (= decrease) through time of a group of fish born at the same time (a cohort) is by means of "instantaneous" rates. These rates, of which there are three (Z, M, F), are defined by the following two expressions:

$$N_t = N_o \cdot e^{-Zt} \qquad \ldots 5.1)$$

where $N_o$ is the (initial) number of fish at time zero, and $N_t$ is the number of remaining fish at the end of time t; Z is the instantaneous rate of total mortality. An advantage of such decay rates is that they can be added or subtracted. Thus we have

$$Z = M + F \qquad \ldots 5.2)$$

where M is the instantaneous rate of natural mortality and F the instantaneous rate of fishing mortality. Obviously, when F = 0, Z = M, which means that natural and total mortality have the same value when there is no fishing, i.e., in an unexploited stock (Fig. 5.1).

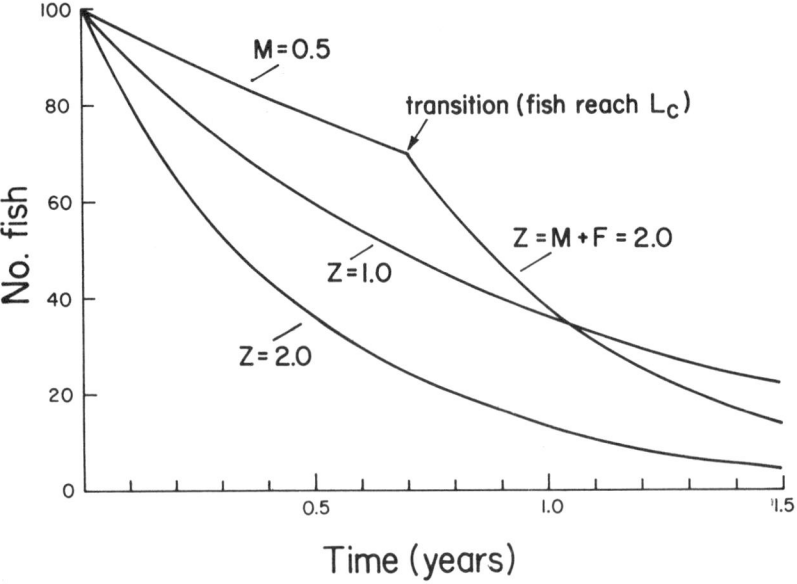

Fig. 5.1. Decrease of a cohort of 100 fish (initially), subjected to different levels of mortality; $L_c$ = mean length at first capture.

Instantaneous rates (i.e., "exponential" rates) of mortality can be converted to the fraction surviving through equations such as

$$S = \frac{N_t}{N_o} \qquad \ldots 5.3)$$

where S is the fraction surviving after time t, while

$$A = 1 - S \qquad \ldots 5.4)$$

is the fraction of the stock dead after time t. Although used by a number of authors, percentage mortalities are not further discussed in this book, because they are too cumbersome to handle in comparison with instantaneous rates (see Beverton and Holt 1956, p. 68 for reasons).

Mortalities, whether expressed as instantaneous rates or as fractions, always refer to a certain period of time. Throughout this book, the *year* is used as the conventional unit, unless mentioned otherwise.

Fishery biologists have two main jobs as far as mortalities are concerned:
a) to estimate total mortality;
b) to split their estimates of total mortality where appropriate into separate estimates of natural and fishing mortalities.

A number of methods are proposed here by which these aims can be achieved, given suitable inputs.

Ecologists, on the other hand, will be pleased to know that Z, as defined here, is equivalent to the inverse of the mean age of the animals in a population (computed from the age when Z is more or less constant) and, hence, as shown by Allen (1971) equal to their "turnover rate", i.e., to the production/biomass ratio (P/B ratio) that is so difficult to estimate reliably using the various methods described in the ecological literature (e.g., Chapman 1968; Winberg 1971).

## ESTIMATING TOTAL MORTALITY

Total mortality from the oldest animal in the catch

Following a number of earlier authors who had demonstrated the existence of a strong relationship between the longevity of fish (in the wild) and their mortality, Hoenig (1984) assembled data on a large number of aquatic animals (molluscs, fish and cetaceans) from which he derived the relationship

$$\ln Z = 1.44 - 0.984 \ln t_{max} \qquad \ldots 5.5)$$

where $t_{max}$ is the maximum age (in years) observed in a given stock, and Z is defined as above.

Although the "fit" of equation (5.5) is rather good ($r^2 = 0.82$ for 130 data pairs), it should be realized, when using this equation, that the estimates of Z thus obtained are very approximate, possibly biased downward (J.M. Hoenig, pers. comm.) and should therefore be revised as additional information becomes available. Table 5.1 gives examples of the application of equation (5.5) which, given its simplicity, needs not be illustrated by a computational example.

When, in addition to $t_{max}$ and $t_c$ the size of the sample (n) from which $t_{max}$ was determined is also known, it becomes possible to estimate Z and its standard error ($s.e._{(Z)}$) from the relationships derived by Hoenig and Lawing (1982),

$$Z = \frac{1}{c_1 \cdot (t_{max} \cdot t_c)} \qquad \ldots 5.6)$$

and

$$s.e._{(Z)} = \sqrt{c_2 \cdot Z^2} \qquad \ldots 5.7)$$

where $c_1$ and $c_2$ are coefficients whose values depend on n (see Table 5.2).

Hoenig and Lawing (1982), whose paper should be consulted for the derivation of equations (5.6), (5.7) and of Table 5.2, stress that "fast growing, short-lived species with minimal variability in length about age are best suited for this method". This is so because in such cases, n, the sample size, is *not* the number of fish actually aged, but the number of fish from which a subsample, consisting of the largest fish was taken. Thus, if say, 200 fish have been inspected, from which the 20 largest were selected for aging, then the value of n will be 200, not 20 (this assumes, obviously that the oldest fish of the sample of 200 will be among the 20 largest). This feature appears particularly valuable in all those cases where fish must be aged by the tedious procedure of counting daily rings (Hoenig and Lawing 1982).

Table 5.1. Maximum observed size ($L_{max}$, $W_{max}$), maximum observed age ($t_{max}$) and estimated mortality (Z) for 12 coral reef fish of New Caledonia.[a]

| Family | Species | $L_{max}$ (standard length, in cm) | $W_{max}$ (live weight, in g) | $t_{max}$ (in years) | $Z$[b] |
|---|---|---|---|---|---|
| Holocentridae | | | | | |
| | *Adioryx spinifer* | 25.8 | 572 | 13 | 0.34 |
| Serranidae | | | | | |
| | *Epinephelus summana* | 20.8 | 263 | 16 | 0.28 |
| Carangidae | | | | | |
| | *Caranx ignobilis* | 76.4 | 10,765 | 9 | 0.49 |
| Lutjanidae | | | | | |
| | *Lutjanus argentimaculatus* | 60.7 | 5,870 | 18 | 0.25 |
| | *Lutjanus gibbus* | 37.0 | 1,735 | 18 | 0.25 |
| | *Lutjanus sebae* | 69.5 | 13,810 | 35 | 0.13 |
| Pomadasyidae | | | | | |
| | *Plectorhynchus chaetodonoides* | 43.1 | 2,715 | 21 | 0.21 |
| | *Plectorhynchus pictus* | 39.2 | 1,970 | 11 | 0.40 |
| | *Pomadasys hasta* | 31.8 | 87.3 | 12 | 0.37 |
| Lethrinidae | | | | | |
| | *Lethrinus harak* | 24.3 | 450 | 15 | 0.29 |
| | *Lethrinus obsoletus* | 25.0 | 501 | 14 | 0.31 |
| | *Monotaris grandoculis* | 39.2 | 2,730 | 11 | 0.40 |

[a]Size and age data adapted from Loubens (1980, Table VI); the values of $t_{max}$ are based on limited samples (sample sizes not given) which, however contained large-sized adults.
[b]Estimated from Equation (5.5).

Table 5.2. Table of coefficients for estimating Z and its standard error using equations (5.6) and (5.7) (from Hoenig and Lawing 1982).

| $n$[a] | $c_1$ | $c_2$ | $n$[a] | $c_1$ | $c_2$ |
|---|---|---|---|---|---|
| 5 | 0.583 | 0.416 | 110 | 0.200 | 0.050 |
| 10 | 0.405 | 0.196 | 120 | 0.196 | 0.048 |
| 15 | 0.344 | 0.142 | 140 | 0.190 | 0.045 |
| 20 | 0.311 | 0.117 | 160 | 0.185 | 0.043 |
| 25 | 0.290 | 0.102 | 180 | 0.181 | 0.041 |
| 30 | 0.274 | 0.091 | 200 | 0.178 | 0.040 |
| 35 | 0.263 | 0.084 | 250 | 0.171 | 0.037 |
| 40 | 0.253 | 0.078 | 300 | 0.165 | 0.035 |
| 45 | 0.245 | 0.074 | 350 | 0.161 | 0.033 |
| 50 | 0.239 | 0.070 | 400 | 0.157 | 0.032 |
| 55 | 0.233 | 0.067 | 450 | 0.155 | 0.031 |
| 60 | 0.228 | 0.064 | 500 | 0.152 | 0.030 |
| 65 | 0.224 | 0.062 | 600 | 0.148 | 0.028 |
| 70 | 0.220 | 0.060 | 700 | 0.144 | 0.027 |
| 75 | 0.217 | 0.058 | 800 | 0.142 | 0.026 |
| 80 | 0.214 | 0.057 | 900 | 0.139 | 0.025 |
| 90 | 0.208 | 0.054 | 1,000 | 0.137 | 0.025 |
| 100 | 0.204 | 0.052 | | | |

[a]Interpolate for intermediate values of n.

Table 5.3 gives values of Z and its standard error as obtained by application of equations (5.6) and (5.7); the method is also illustrated in Example 5.1.

Table 5.3. Maximum reported age and estimated total mortality of selected Brazilian freshwater (F) and marine fish (M).[a]

| Family | Species | $t_{max}$ (yr) | n | Location, sampling date(s) | Author(s) | Estimated Z | s.e.(Z) |
|---|---|---|---|---|---|---|---|
| Auchenipteridae | | | | | | | |
| | Trachychorystes galeatus ♀ | 3.5 | 83 | Banabuiú Reservoir | Nomura | 1.35 | 0.32 |
| | Trachychorystes galeatus ♂ | 3.5 | 99 | Caera State, 1971 (F) | et al. (1976) | 1.40 | 0.32 |
| Characidae | | | | | | | |
| | Prochilodus scrofa ♀ | 13 | 451 | Mossi Guassu River, | Godoy | 0.50 | 0.09 |
| | Prochilodus scrofa ♂ | 9 | 485 | São Paulo State, 1947 (F) | (1959) | 0.73 | 0.13 |
| Sciaenidae | | | | | | | |
| | Plagioscion squamosissimus ♀ | 6 | 103 | Amanari Reservoir, | Nomura and | 0.82 | 0.19 |
| | Plagioscion squamosissimus ♂ | 7 | 134 | Caera State, 1960-2 (F) | Oliviera (1976) | 0.74 | 0.16 |
| | Micropogon furnieri ♀ | 6 | 229 | Off Iguape, Caera | Rodrigues | 0.96 | 0.19 |
| | Micropogon furnieri ♂ | 7 | 115 | State, 1966-7 (M) | (1968) | 0.72 | 0.16 |
| | Macrodon ancylodon ♀ & ♂ | 11 | 9,947 | Off São Paulo, 1975-6 (M) | Lara (1951) | 0.66 | 0.11 |

[a]Total mortality and its standard error estimated from equations (5.6) and (5.7), with $t_c$ set at zero because very small fish were included in the catch samples.

Total mortality from the mean size in the catch

The following expression (Beverton and Holt 1957; Gulland 1969) can be used to estimate Z from the mean weight ($\overline{W}$) of fish in the catch from a given population:

$$\overline{W} = W_\infty \left\{ 1 - \frac{3Z \exp(-a)}{Z + K} + \frac{3Z \exp(-2a)}{Z + 2K} - \frac{Z \exp(-3a)}{Z + 3K} \right\} \quad \ldots 5.8)$$

where $a = K \cdot (t_c - t_o)$, with K and $W_\infty$ pertaining to the special VBGF (i.e., when D = 1) and where $t_c$ is the mean age at first capture (corresponding to $L_c$ as defined in Chapter 2) obtained by a given gear. Equation (5.8) it will be noted, can be solved for Z only iteratively (Program FB 10, Example 5.2). Also, the equation requires an estimate of $t_o$, which may sometimes be difficult to obtain.

Another equation, proposed by Beverton and Holt (1956), is more generally used to estimate Z from the mean size in the catch. When used in conjunction with the generalized VBGF, it has the form

$$Z = \frac{KD (L_\infty^D - \overline{L}^D)}{\overline{L}^D - L'^D} \quad \ldots 5.9)$$

where $\overline{L}$ is the mean length of all fish $\geq L'$, the latter being (a length not smaller than) the smallest length of fish fully represented in the length-frequency data at hand. $L'$ is always $> L_c$, as defined in Chapter 2, except in true cases of "knife-edge selection", where $L' = L_c$. [A method is given further below in connection with a discussion of length-converted catch curves to obtain reasonable estimates of $L'$ from a set of length-frequency data.]

A sensitivity analysis of this widely-used equation is given in Appendix I; on the average, equation (5.9) gives results (values of Z) which are equal to those obtained with length-converted catch curves (see below).

Occasionally, data are available in the literature where the mean length has been computed from the whole range of length in the catch rather than from $L'$ upward. In such cases, minimum estimates of Z can still be obtained, using

$$Z_{min} = \frac{KD(L_\infty^D - \overline{\overline{L}}^D)}{\overline{\overline{L}}^D - L_c^D} \qquad \ldots 5.10)$$

where $\overline{\overline{L}}$ is the overall mean length and $L_c$ is the 50% retention length. See Chapter 2 for various methods to compute $L_c$.

Another type of widely available data is mean weights of fish, as obtained by simply weighing a haul, counting the fish caught and dividing the weight by the number caught. Such values of $\overline{\overline{W}}$, however, do not represent the weight corresponding to a given value of $\overline{\overline{L}}$; rather, they are biased upward. This effect should partly offset the negative bias in equation (5.10) such that

$$Z \approx \frac{KD(W_\infty^{D/3} - \overline{\overline{W}}^{D/3})}{\overline{\overline{W}}^{D/3} - W_c^{D/3}} \qquad \ldots 5.11)$$

where $W_\infty$ and $W_c$ are the weights corresponding to $L_\infty$ and $L_c$, respectively. It will be realized that this equation gives quite approximate results, and that, as in the case of equation (5.5), every effort should be made to revise the estimates of Z based on it as soon as additional information become available.

Example 5.3 presents applications of equations (5.9), (5.10) and (5.11).

Although computationally convenient, simple equations such as (5.9 to 5.11) have two disadvantages, one of them major. Equations (5.9 to 5.11) require estimates of $L_c$ or $L'$; the first of these parameters involves either conducting selection experiments, or using shape measurements and the nomogram presented in Chapter 2. The second of these parameters, on the other hand, can be estimated from length-frequency data; this, however, involves plotting the data in a form akin to a length-converted catch curve, at which point it will be more appropriate to estimate Z from the catch curve itself (see below).

The major objection to the use of mean size data for estimating Z is, however, that one quite literally doesn't *see* what one is doing. While computation of one single value of Z from the mean of a wide range of sizes implies that mortality is constant, the assumption itself cannot be verified. The semi-graphical methods presented further below, particularly the length-converted catch curves, do allow verification of this assumption. Also, they allow the selection of data points to use in the estimation of Z, and hence the estimation of values of Z applying only to certain ranges of size something which cannot be done using summary statistics, such as mean lengths or mean weights. [Mean sizes can be used directly to draw inferences on the status of a stock or fishery without being expressed in terms of Z. Henderson (1972) provides a theoretical background for this approach which was applied to tropical fish by Ita (1980), but won't be discussed here.]

Estimation of Z from cumulative plots

When length-frequency data or catch-at-length data are available which were obtained over a period during which conditions can be considered constant, several methods can be used to estimate Z which are less crude than the ones presented above. The first of these was proposed by Jones (1981) to estimate Z/K; it is presented here, however, among methods for the estimation of Z because it led to another method, developed by Sparre (MS) which is closely related to Jones' method, but allows direct estimation of Z.

The basic equation in Jones' method, expressed in terms of the generalized VBGF, has the form of a linear regression,

$$\ln C(L_i, \infty) = a + \frac{Z}{KD} \cdot \ln(L_\infty^D - L_i^D) \qquad \ldots 5.12)$$

where $C(L_i, \infty)$ is the cumulative catch (computed from the highest length class with non-zero catch) corresponding to a given length class, and $L_i$ is the lower limit of that length class, the $\infty$ symbol expressing that the catch considers a range from $L_i$ to all larger sizes.

However, as shown in Fig. 5.2, the plot of the $\ln C(L_i, \infty)$ values on the $\ln (L_\infty^D - L_i^D)$ values is linear only over the central part of its range and deviates markedly from linearity when very large and very small fish are considered.

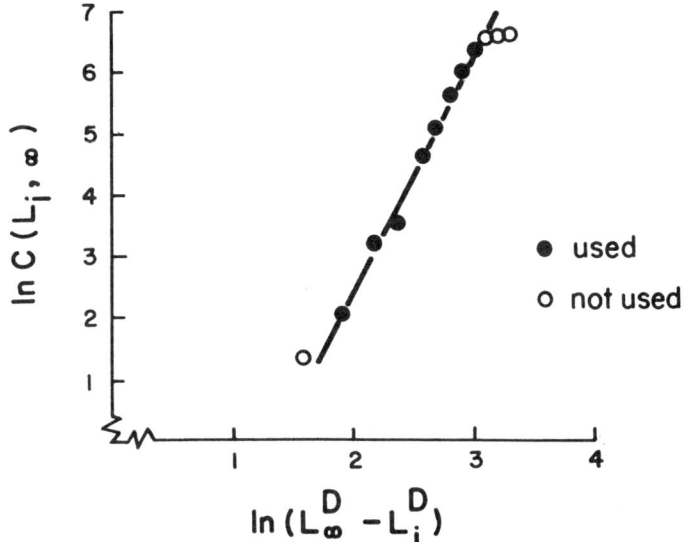

Fig. 5.2. Jones' cumulative plot for the estimation of Z/K (or Z), as applied to the data of Table 5.4. The points to be included in the regression are selected after transformation and plotting of the data (see Example 5.4).

Thus, when applying this method, it is necessary to draw a scattergram of the computed values and to select visually the points belonging to the straight segment of the plot (see Example 5.4). Sparre's modification of equation (5.12) resembles a catch curve (see below for definition) in that the ages (or relative ages) are used for the x-axis and that Z (or Z/K) is estimated from the slope of a descending series of points. The equation used has the form

$$\ln C(L_i, \infty) = a + bt' \qquad \ldots 5.13)$$

where $\ln C(L_i, \infty)$ is defined as above and $t'$ is the (relative) age corresponding to $L_i$, while b, with sign changed, provides an estimate of Z (the relative ages are estimated through conversion from length to age) based on the straight part of the plot. A routine has been incorporated in Program FB 11 which produces values of $C(L_i, \infty)$ and $t'$ such that a scattergram can be drawn, from which the values usable in the estimation of Z can be selected (see Fig. 5.3 and Example 5.5).

When K is not known, Sparre's method can still be used; in this case, a value of one (unity) has to be used instead of K, which results in the relative ages being defined as

$$t' = (t - t_o) \cdot K \qquad \ldots 5.14)$$

The slope (b in equation 5.13) will then be equal to Z/K.

Both Jones' and Sparre's methods are extremely ingenious methods which lead to exact values of Z or Z/K, given suitable data and appropriate selection of data points to be included in the regression. However, both methods give results which, because of the cumulation of the catches, are extremely sensitive to the values of the catches in the largest size groups, even when they are not included in the linear regression. Thus, these methods should not be used when the catch composition data used were obtained from gears that markedly select for or against very large fish.

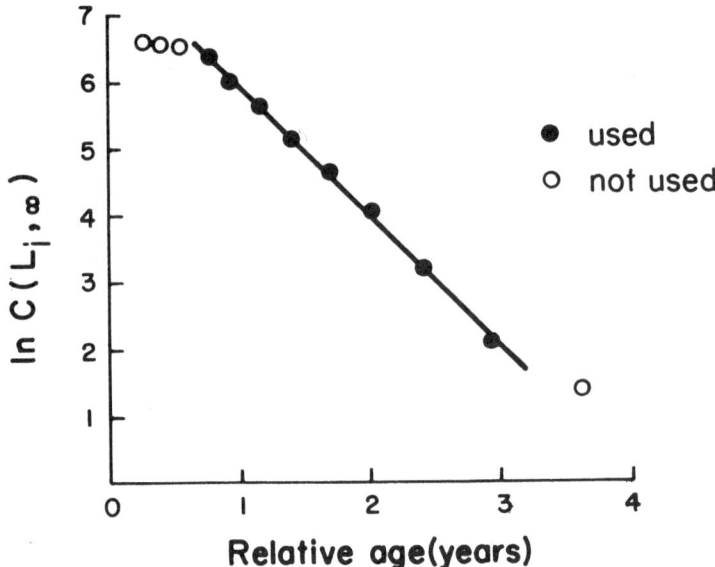

Fig. 5.3. Sparre's cumulative plot for the estimation of Z (or Z/K), as applied to the data of Table 5.4 (see Example 5.5).

Catch curves and length-converted catch curves

One of the methods most commonly applied in temperate waters to estimate the total mortality of fish is the "catch curve" method, which has been reviewed in Beverton and Holt (1956), Chapman and Robson (1960), Robson and Chapman (1961) and Ricker (1975, Chapter 2).

Essentially, the method consists of a plot of the natural logarithm of the number of fish in various age groups ($N_t$) against their corresponding age (t), or

$$\ln N_t = a + bt \qquad \ldots 5.15)$$

Z being estimated from the slope b, with sign changed, or the descending, right arm of the plot (Fig. 5.4).

The following assumptions are involved here:
1) Z is the same in all age groups used in the plot,
2) all age groups used in the plot were recruited with the same abundance (or the recruitment fluctuations have been small and of random character),
3) all age groups used in the plot are equally vulnerable to the gear used for sampling,
4) the sample used is large enough and covers enough age groups to effectively represent the average population structure over the period of time considered.

The authors of this method should be consulted for more detailed treatment of the assumptions involved in catch curves.

Often, in order to broaden the data base from which inferences are drawn (i.e., in order to meet assumption 4 above), the samples used for catch-curve analysis are constructed in three steps, as follows:
i) record the lengths of very large samples of fish,
ii) age a subsample of fish, and construct an "age-length key", and
iii) separate the large length-frequency sample into an **age-frequency sample** by means of the age-length key obtained in (ii).

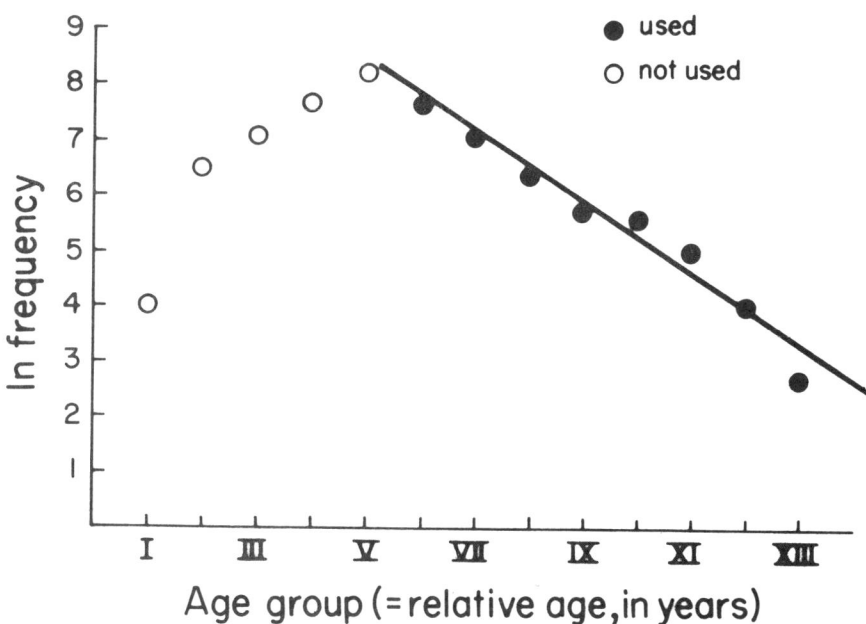

Fig. 5.4. Catch curve for red porgy *(Pagrus pagrus)* caught off North and South Carolina, U.S.A. The curve is based on 13,120 measured specimens, of which 222 were actually aged. Note slight non-linearity of curve which, on the average, suggests a value of Z = 0.65 (adapted, with modifications, from Manooch and Huntsman 1977, Fig. 3).

This indirect procedure was introduced by Fridrikson (1934) and is discussed in detail in Gulland (1966) and Allen (1966), and was applied by Manooch and Huntsman (1977) in their study of red porgy mortality (see Fig. 5.4). However, it has hardly ever been used in tropical waters, where the very few authors who have used catch curves have tended to construct them directly, based on relatively small samples of aged fish. As shown by Kimura (1977), there are several cases where this procedure is indeed more appropriate.

A major disadvantage of the age-structured catch curves represented by equation (5.15) is that they cannot be used in conjunction with animals that presently cannot be aged individually, such as shrimps, lobsters and some molluscs.

"Length-converted catch curves", as will be shown below, allow the use of catch curves with animals that cannot be aged; moreover, the method, being based solely on length-frequency samples, allows the use of large samples without construction of age-length keys.

The estimation of Z from a length-converted catch curve involves the following steps:
i) pooling of length-frequency samples to obtain a single, large length-frequency sample representative of the population for the period under consideration;
ii) construction of the catch curve proper, using the large sample in (i) and a set of growth parameters (see below);
iii) estimation of Z from the descending right arm of the catch curve.

Pooling of length-frequency samples (e.g., of monthly samples) over a longer period of time (at least one year) is particularly needed in short-lived fish and shrimps, because their whole population structure is affected by seasonal "pulses" of recruitment, generally one or two per year (Pauly and Navaluna 1983). Also, to prevent a single, larger (monthly) sample from unduly affecting the total (annual) sample, the various samples may be given the same weight, by conversion to percentages prior to adding to obtain a single overall sample.

There are many alternatives to a scheme where each sample is given the same weight. For example, it might be more appropriate to weigh the samples by the square root of their size when the fishery catch is not known, or by the catch when it is known. However, empirical studies concerning appropriate sample sizes and weighing factors for length-converted catch curves are still lacking. Table 5.5 is given here to suggest sample sizes which at present seem appropriate.

Table 5.4. Data for the estimation of Z/K and Z for the banded grouper *(Epinephelus sexfasciatus)* of the Visayan Sea, Philippines (from Pauly and Ingles 1981).[a]

| Lower class limit (cm) | Midpoint of class (cm) | N[b] |
|---|---|---|
| 4 | 5 | 5 |
| 6 | 7 | 29 |
| 8 | 9 | 114 |
| 10 | 11 | 161 |
| 12 | 13 | 143 |
| 14 | 15 | 118 |
| 16 | 17 | 61 |
| 18 | 19 | 50 |
| 20 | 21 | 32 |
| 22 | 23 | 17 |
| 24 | 25 | 4 |
| 26 | 27 | 4 |

[a]To be used in conjunction with $L_\infty$ = 30.9, K = 0.51 and D = 1.
[b]As obtained by pooling a number of samples representing a whole year.

Table 5.5. Criteria for assessing the suitability of length-frequency samples for estimating Z (modified from Munro and Thompson 1973).

| Total sample size (no. fish) | Time (in months) over which data for total sample were accumulated[a] | | | | |
|---|---|---|---|---|---|
| | 1 | 2 | 4 | 6 | 12 |
| 1 — 99 | 0 | 0 | 0 | 0 | 0 |
| 100 — 499 | 0 | 0 | 1 | 2 | 2 |
| 500 — 999 | 1 | 1 | 2 | 3 | 4 |
| 1,000 — 1,499 | 1 | 2 | 3 | 4 | 5 |
| 1,500 — ∞ | 2 | 3 | 4 | 5 | 5+ |

0 = not usable    2 = fair    4 = very good
1 = poor          3 = good    5 = excellent

[a]It is here assumed (1) that the samples cover a wide range of lengths, (2) that gear selection is accounted for and (3) that the sizes of the monthly samples are more or less equal if the total sample is accumulated over more than one month.

There are also several methods by which a length-converted catch curve may be constructed. However, they all must account for the fact that fish growth in length is not linear, but slows down as length and age increase. This slowing down has the effect that older *size groups* contain more age groups than do younger *size groups*. In other words, it takes larger fishes longer to "leave" a certain size group, they "pile-up" (Baranov 1918), or "stack-up" (van Sickle 1977) in the size classes pertaining to old, large, slow-growing fish. Correcting for this effect is rather straightforward, and three methods by which this can be achieved here will be discussed here.

The first approach, analogous to but improved upon those discussed in Ricker (1975, p. 33 and p. 60-64) and van Sickle (1977), consists of multiplying the number in each length class by the growth rate of the fish in that class. This results in a catch curve equation of the form

$$\log N_i \cdot (dl_i/dt) = a + bt_i' \qquad \ldots 5.16)$$

where $dl_i/dt$ is the growth rate and $t_i'$ the relative age corresponding to length class (i), respectively. In practice ($dl_i/dt$) can be estimated from the VBGF as the growth rate pertaining to the median length, or "midlength" of length class (i), while $t'$ can be estimated as the relative age corresponding to the median of class (i) as estimated, using the appropriate growth parameters, through conversion using the VBGF. "Relative" ages are used here because using $t_o$ (which leads to *absolute* ages) is not necessary in conjunction with catch curves, where Z is estimated from a *slope*.

Fig. 5.5 gives an example of such catch curve, constructed from the data in Table 5.4 and using Program FB 9 with which values of $dl_i/dt$ and $t'$ can be computed (see Example 5.6).

Equation (5.16) allows ready estimation of the bias caused by *not* accounting for the "pile-up" effect mentioned above. This is done by first rewriting equation (5.16) as

$$\ln N - \ln (dl/dt) = a + bt' \qquad \ldots 5.17)$$

or

$$\ln N = a + bt' - \ln (dl/dt) \qquad \ldots 5.18)$$

Now, in terms of the generalized VBGF, the growth rate can be expressed as

$$dl/dt = \ln (K \cdot D \cdot L_\infty^D) + KD (t' - t_o) \qquad \ldots 5.19)$$

where K, D, $L_\infty$ and $t_o$ are parameters of the generalized VBGF, and relative $t'$ is the age corresponding to a given midlength. Inserting (5.19) in (5.13) gives

$$\ln N = a + bt' - \ln (KDL_\infty^D) - KD (t' - t_o) \qquad \ldots 5.20)$$

or

$$\ln N = a + bt' - \ln (KDL_\infty^D) - KDt' + KDt_o \qquad \ldots 5.21)$$

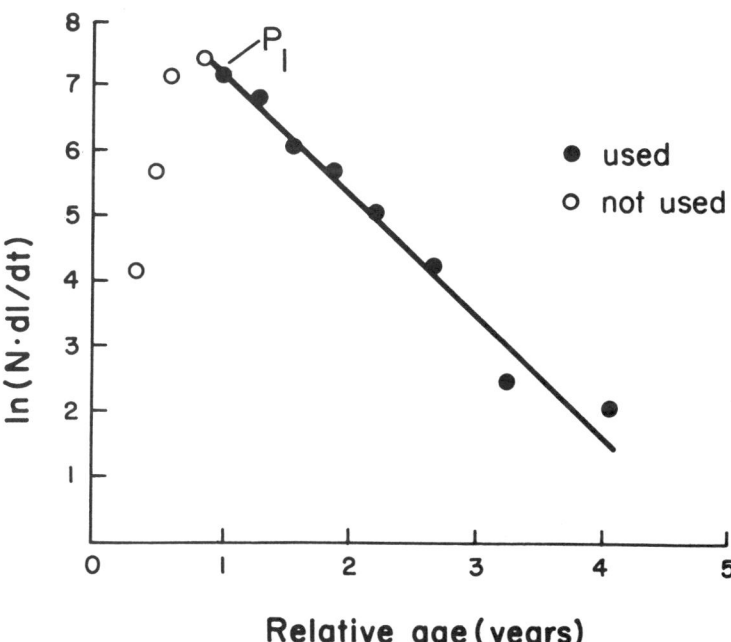

Fig. 5.5. A length-converted catch curve, based on the data of Table 5.4. The first point to be included in the estimation of Z ($P_1$) is clearly defined (see text). Note that each point is independent of all others and thus could be deleted singly from the computation of Z.

Equation (5.21), it will be noted, has 3 constant terms with regard to the variable N and $t'$, namely a, ln ($KDL_\infty^D$) and $KDt_o$. Since Z in equation (5.16) is estimated as a slope, these 3 constant terms can be grouped into one single new term ($a'$) which becomes the intercept of a new equation of the form

$$\ln N = a' + bt' - KDt' \qquad \ldots 5.22)$$

which gives, rearranged

$$\ln N = a' + (b - KD) t' \qquad \ldots 5.23)$$

as a new equation for a length-converted catch curve. Therefore,

$$-b + KD = Z \qquad \ldots 5.24)$$

It follows from this that the bias resulting from the non-consideration of the "pile-up" effect (i.e., resulting from using ln N instead of ln (N · dl/dt) as ordinate of a length-converted catch curve) is equal to KD, or to K when the special VBGF is used (i.e., when D = 1). (See Example 5.7.)

Two practical applications of this finding come to mind:
  (i) It becomes possible to correct biased values of Z obtained by various authors who didn't account for the "pile-up" effect (by simply adding K times D to their (biased) estimate of Z) (see e.g., Berry 1970; Nzioka 1983).
  (ii) The estimation of Z from a length-converted catch curve becomes simpler, since one can first ignore the "pile-up" effect then compensate for it by addking K · D to the absolute value of the curve's slope (see Example 5.7).

When K is not known, equations such as (5.16) and (5.24) can still be used; in such cases, a value of unity (one) should be used instead of K when computing the relative ages, which are then defined by equation (5.14). The slope of the catch curve, with sign changed, will then be equal to (Z/K)–1.

Another type of length-converted catch curve is defined by the equation

$$\ln N_i/\Delta t_i = a + bt'_i \qquad \ldots 5.25)$$

where $N_i$ and $t'_i$ are defined as in equation (5.16), and where $\Delta t_i$ is the time needed, on the average by the fish to grow through length class i. This equation accounts for the "piling-up" effect through division of the $N_i$-values by $\Delta t_i$, the inverse of the growth rates by which the $N_i$ values are multiplied in equation (5.16). Hence, equation (5.25) is a slightly modified version of (5.16), and its properties, e.g., with regard to not accounting for the "piling-up" effect are the same.

Since equations (5.16) and (5.25) are equivalent, only one Program (FB 12) is given here for the computation of length-converted catch curves. This program implements equation (5.25) rather than (5.16) because the former has already been presented and discussed elsewhere (Pauly 1980a, 1982a, 1983; Pauly and Ingles 1981; Gulland 1983).

Example 5.8 shows the application of equation (5.25) and Program FB 12 to the data of Table 5.4. It will be noted that as in the earlier models, the points of a length-converted catch curve must be drawn for selection of the values to include in the regression equation. This selection must account for two features of a length-converted catch curve:
  — as in age-structured catch curves, the points belonging to the ascending, left arm of the curve must not be included because they represent incompletely selected and/or incompletely recruited animals, and
  — the conversion of length to (relative) ages by means of the VBGF, when involving fish whose length is very close to $L_\infty$, generates unrealistically high "ages" which cannot be included either.

Suggested criteria for the selection of points to be included in the computation of Z are:
1) the first point to be included ($P_1$ on Figs. 5.5, 5.6 and 5.7) should be the point immediately to the right of the highest point. The latter may still be affected by incomplete selection and/or recruitment and is considered to be part of the ascending, left part of the curve;
2) points should be deleted that were obtained through conversion from lengths within 5% of $L_\infty$ (see Fig. 5.6 for an example of such points);
3) the points selected should fit along, or close to, a straight line, and one *single* outlier may be excluded, particularly when it is based on few fish only.

Concerning the first of these criteria, it might be added that point $P_1$ corresponds to the length class whose lower class limit represents an estimate of $L'$ as required for equation (5.9). The third of these criteria must not be misunderstood to provide an excuse for the wholesale deletion of points until one's preconceived notion of linearity is achieved; rather it allows deletion of *one* point. When

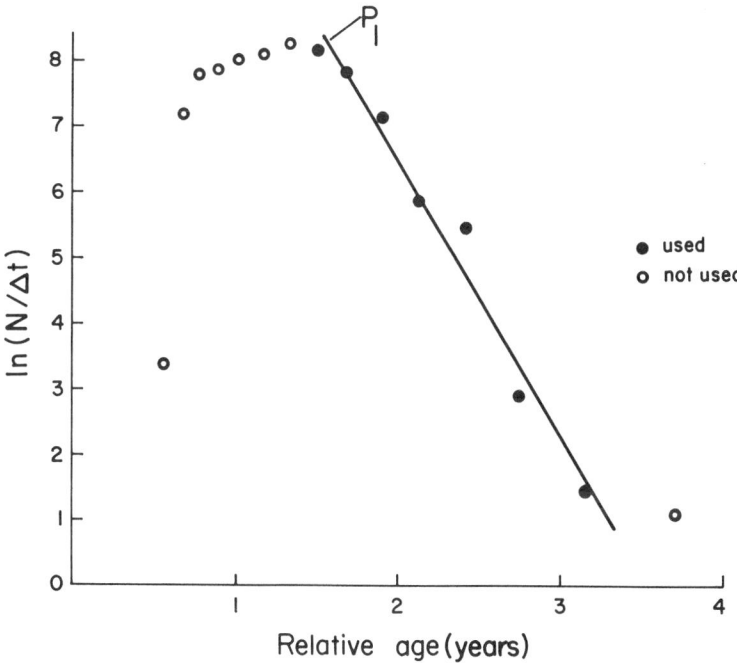

Fig. 5.6. Length-converted catch curve for yellow striped goatfish (*Upeneus vittatus*) from Manila Bay, Philippines, showing a point pertaining to a length close to $L_\infty$ which should not be used in the computation of Z (from Pauly 1982a).

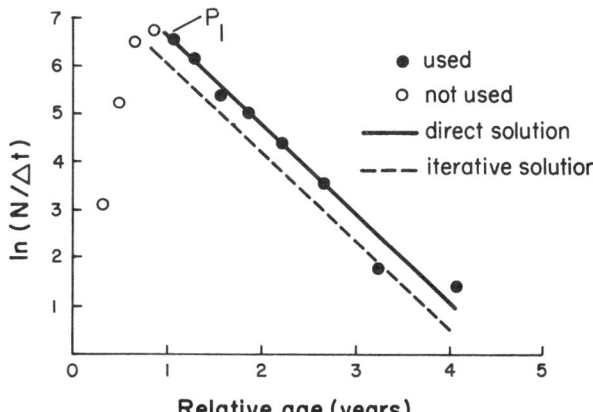

Fig. 5.7. Length-converted catch curve, based on equation (5.25) and the data of Table 5.4. The broken line, which parallels the catch curve, was obtained using equation (5.28). As shown in Example 5.9, the two lines provide virtually identical estimates of Z.

the curve as a whole seems to deviate from linearity, the appropriate approach should be to test whether this deviation is significant or not, using any of the statistical tests available for this purpose (e.g., Guilford and Fruchter 1978, p. 277-280).

Non-linearity of length-converted catch curves (see e.g., Fig. 5.4), that is their response to systematic changes in fishing effort or recruitment are akin to those of age-structured catch curves. The exhaustive discussions of the general properties of catch curves in Beverton and Holt (1956) and Ricker (1975) also apply to length-converted catch curves.

When reviewing the draft of this book, P. Sparre (pers. comm.) derived a form of a length-converted catch curve which involves none of the approximations in (5.16) and (5.25), by defining

- $N(t_1, t_2)$ = number of fish caught between ages $t_1$ and $t_2$, with $\Delta t = t_2 - t_1$
- $t_{L'}$ = the age corresponding to $L'$ (see above for definition of $L'$)
- $E = F/Z$ (see below for a more detailed definition)

from which

$$N(t_1, t_2) = N_{t'} e^{-Z(t_1 - t_{L'})} \cdot E(1 - e^{-Z\Delta t}) \qquad \ldots 5.26)$$

or

$$\ln N(t_1, t_2) = -Zt_1 + Zt_{L'} + \ln\{N_{t'} \cdot E(1 - e^{-Z\Delta t})\} \qquad \ldots 5.27)$$

which leads, with some rearrangement, to a new equation for a length-converted catch curve of the form

$$\ln \frac{N_i}{(1 - e^{-Z\Delta t_i})} = a - Zt'_i \qquad \ldots 5.28)$$

where $N_i$ is the number of fish in a given length class i; $\Delta t_i$ the time needed to growth through class i and $t'_i$ the relative age corresponding to the *lower* limit of class i.

Equation (5.28), although it can be solved only iteratively, has the definite advantage that no approximation is involved, as opposed to equation (5.25) where both the division of $N_i$ by $\Delta t_i$ and the use of relative ages corresponding to the midlengths of the length classes involve approximations.

Thus, equation (5.28) can be used to test the accuracy of the results obtained through equation (5.16) or (5.25). Example 5.8, which is typical of the many cases investigated so far, shows that equation (5.25) (and consequently 5.16 also) provide values of Z which differ only by a small fraction (less than 1%) from those obtained iteratively from equation (5.28). Therefore, the simpler model (5.25) generates results which are estimates of Z, and not only "proportional to Z", as suggested in Gulland (1983).

Further inferences from length-converted catch curves

Length-converted catch curves, in addition to allowing for the direct estimation of Z from length-frequency data, have the added advantage over "age-structured" catch curves of allowing a number of inferences to be drawn through detailed examination of the left, ascending arm of the curve, which is generally ignored in catch-curve analysis.

When the selection curve of the gear used to sample the data at hand is known, M can be estimated from the left side of a catch curve (Munro 1984). Conversely, when natural mortality is known, the selection curve of the gear can be inferred from the shape of the ascending arm of a length-converted catch curve. Only the latter of these two methods will be discussed here, as Munro's method, although quite elegant, has data requirements which limit its applicability.

Table 5.6 illustrates the derivation of selection data (probabilities of capture, by length) based on the left side of a selection curve and an estimate of M. The computational steps involved here are as follows:

(i) Set up a table which draws together all information needed for further analysis (these values are in square brackets in Table 5.6).

(ii) Compute times to grow from one class midpoint to the next and write $\Delta t$ values as in Table 5.6.

(iii) Interpolate mortalities (Mortality I in Table 5.6) between Z and M (whose values should pertain to the highest length class with zero catch; see Table 5.6). The step size for the interpolations is estimated from $(Z - M)/(n + 1)$ where n is the number of classes for which mortality must be interpolated (here, n = 4).

(iv) The mortalities estimated in (iii) are estimates of the mortality *within* a given length class. The mortality *between* adjacent length classes (Mortality II) are estimated by taking means between adjacent length classes (see Table 5.6).

(v) Compute numbers available from equation given in Table 5.6, starting with number of fish in the first class where the probability of capture is equal to unity (i.e., corresponding to point $P_1$).

(vi) Obtain probabilities of capture by dividing, for each length class, the number caught ($C_i$) by the number available ($N_i$).

The method as outlined here is extremely useful in that it derives quantities which are normally obtained from costly selection experiments from readily obtained length-frequency samples and a reasonable estimate of M, which is easy to obtain when growth parameters are available (see below).

In stocks that are unexploited, the estimate of Z obtained from the catch curve can serve as the estimate of M; otherwise, the computations remain the same except, obviously that the interpolations between Z and M are superfluous because the same value of Z = M is used throughout. The special case, Z = M, formed the basis of the approach of Pauly et al. (in press) to estimate approximate selection curves from the backward projection of the straight segment of a length-con-

Table 5.6. Derivation of a selection curve from the left side of a length-converted catch curve (all values in square brackets must be available before attempting to complete table).

| Class limits[a] | | | Numbers caught ($C_i$) | $\Delta t$ (class midpoint to midpoint)[b] | Mortality I (M → Z)[c] | Mortality II (means) | Numbers available ($N_i$)[d] | $P = C_i/N_i$ |
|---|---|---|---|---|---|---|---|---|
| Lower | Upper | Midpoint | | | | | | |
| 2 | 4 | 3 | [0] | — | [M = 1.14] | — | — | [0] |
| 4 | 6 | 5 | 5 | 0.158 | 1.28 | 1.35 | 448 | 0.0112 |
| 6 | 8 | 7 | 29 | 0.171 | 1.42 | 1.49 | 362 | 0.0801 |
| 8 | 10 | 9 | 114 | 0.188 | 1.56 | 1.63 | 281 | 0.4057 |
| 10 | 12 | 11 | 161 | 0.208 | 1.70 | 1.77 | 207 | 0.7778 |
| 12=L' | 14 | 13 | [143][e] | — | [Z = 1.84] | — | [143][e] | [1.00] |

[a] Actual upper class limits are 3.999, 5.999, etc., but are rounded for convenience.

[b] Computed from $\frac{1}{KD} \ln \left\{ \frac{L_\infty^D - L_2^D}{L_\infty^D - L_1^D} \right\}$ where $L_1$, $L_2$ are the lower and upper class limits, respectively.

[c] Values between Z and M interpolated linearly.

[d] Computed from $N_i = N_{i+1} e^{Z\Delta t}$, where $N_{i+1}$ is the number available in a given length class and $N_i$ the number available in the next lower length class.

[e] This number may be taken as the actual number caught in the first length class that is fully selected (i.e., corresponding to $P_1$). However, a better approach is to compute this number from the equation of the catch curve, for the midpoint in question. In this example, the two values of N are similar.

verted catch curve. This approach is now superseded by the more versatile and accurate method illustrated by Table 5.6.

The accuracy of the method outlined here depends critically on the following assumption being met:

(i) The gear in question is a trawl or has a selection curve similar to that of a trawl (where it is only the smaller fish that are selected against).
(ii) The smallest fish caught ($L_{min}$) are fully recruited.
(iii) The value of M used for the fish just below $L_{min}$ and the mortalities generated by interpolation between M and the Z value for the fully selected animals are accurate.

The first of these assumptions can be easily verified. The second, which will often be violated, implies that the resulting probabilities will not strictly refer to a *selection* curve, but to a *resultant* curve, i.e., to the product of a selection with a recruitment curve (Gulland 1969). Whether this assumption is met or not will thus affect the *interpretation* of the results, but not their computation.

The third of these assumptions can be assessed quite straightforwardly. The effects of changes in the value of M used on the probabilities of capture are easy to compute (see Appendix I for a brief introduction to sensitivity analysis). Anon. (1982) compared estimates of length at first capture obtained from selection experiments with length at first capture estimated through the approach proposed here (but using the special case where M is set equal to Z, see above) and obtained a good match for the cases investigated, Mediterranean sardines and hakes.

Chapter 2 should be consulted for the interpretation and use of selection curves, notably for the computation of mean lengths at first capture.

Estimating Z from a pseudo-catch curve

When the average size of the animals of a population under investigation displays a significant relationship to the water depth, or distance from the coast (or any other environmental gradient), it will generally be difficult to obtain size-frequency samples representative of the population as a whole. Various schemes of stratified sampling may be applied to deal with such a situation. However, as far as the estimation of Z is concerned, the best approach may be to actually *use*, in conjunction with a "pseudo-catch curve" as defined in Pauly (1980c), the gradient along which the population is distributed.

Here the method is applied to the case where the mean size of fish increases and their numbers decrease with water depth—the environmental gradient one is most likely to encounter.

To apply the pseudo-catch curve method, the following items are required:

1) data allowing quantification of the size-depth relationship (this might be a relationship involving mean length and depth, or mean weight and depth; in the case of the former a length-weight relationship is also needed). An example of such relationship is given as Fig. 5.8;

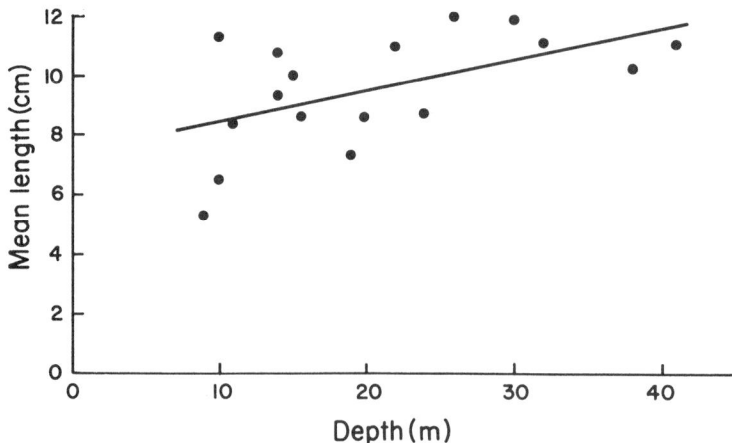

Fig. 5.8. Relationship between mean length and water depth in slipmouths *(Leiognathus splendens)* caught off Southeast Kalimantan, Indonesia (from Pauly 1980c).

2) catch-per-effort data stratified by depth and representative of the whole depth range inhabited by the investigated population. An example of such data is given as Fig. 5.9;
3) the growth parameters $L_\infty$, K (or $W_\infty$, K) and D of the VBGF.

The method consists of (1) using the size-depth relationship and the growth parameters to compute the mean (relative) age corresponding to the size at each depth for which a catch-per-effort value is available; (2) dividing the mean weight at depth into the corresponding c/f value to obtain the average "number at depth"; (3) plotting the natural logarithm of the numbers at depth against the corresponding relative age (see Fig. 5.10 for an example), and estimating $(-)Z$ from the slope.

The computations involved are outlined in Example 5.9.

This method, as emphasized in Pauly (1980c), was developed mainly to estimate Z from data which have been gathered and/or published for miscellaneous purposes and which could not be used directly for the construction of a real length-converted catch curve.

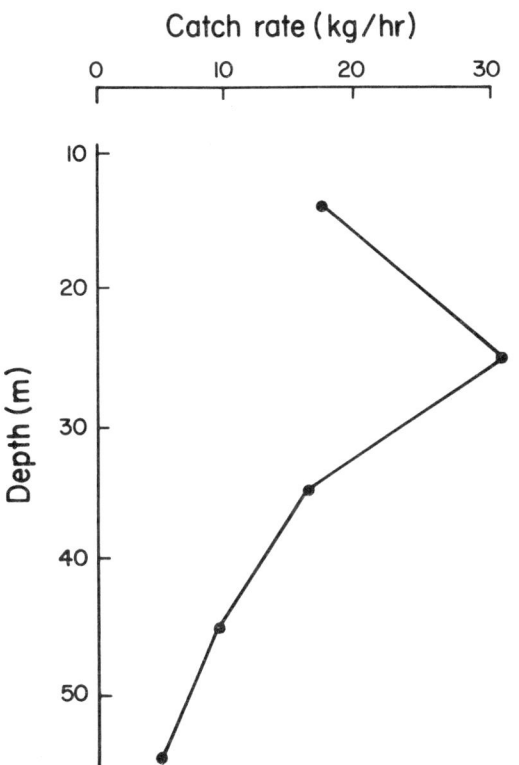

Fig. 5.9. Relationship between average catch per effort of *Leiognathus splendens* and water depth in western Indonesian waters (from Pauly 1977).

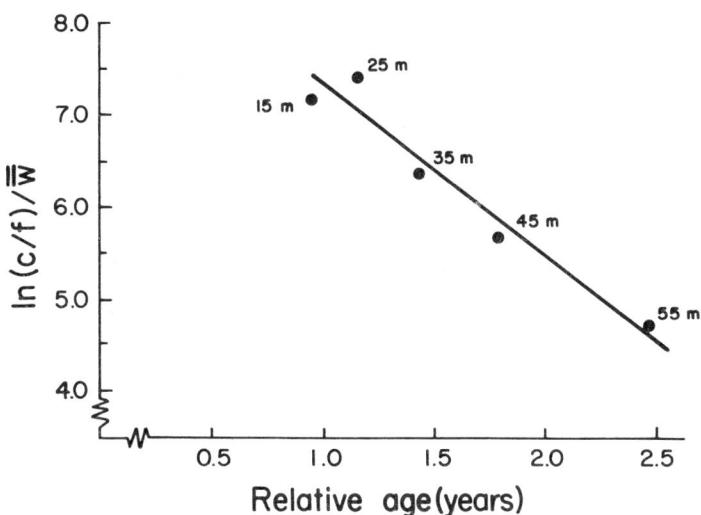

Fig. 5.10. Pseudo-catch curve for *Leiognathus splendens* in western Indonesian waters (see Example 5.9 for derivation and interpretation).

## SIMULTANEOUS ESTIMATION OF Z AND K

Saila and Lough (1981), based on a model developed by Ebert (1973), presented a method for the estimation of total mortality which has the advantage of also estimating the value of K of the VBGF given a set value for the asymptotic length $L_{(\infty)}$, an assumed value for the length at recruitment ($L_r$) and two successive mean lengths ($\overline{L}_1, \overline{L}_2$) obtained twice within a year ($t_1, t_2$) at times that are as far apart as possible.

Given these inputs (and a value of D when the generalized VBGF is used), K can be estimated from

$$K = \frac{\ln \frac{L_\infty^D - \overline{L}_2^D}{L_\infty^D - \overline{L}_1^D}}{(t_1 - t_2) \cdot D} \qquad \ldots 5.29)$$

while Z is estimated iteratively as the value which fulfills

$$\frac{\sum_{x=0}^{N} e^{-Zx} - b \cdot \sum_{x=0}^{N} e^{-(KD(t_1 + x) + Zx)}}{\sum_{x=0}^{N} e^{-Zx}} = \frac{\overline{L}_1^D}{L_{(\infty)}^D} \quad \ldots 5.30)$$

and

$$\frac{\sum_{x=0}^{N} e^{-Zx} - b \cdot \sum_{x=0}^{N} e^{-(KD(t_2 + x) + Zx)}}{\sum_{x=0}^{N} e^{-Zx}} = \frac{\overline{L}_2^D}{L_{(\infty)}^D} \quad \ldots 5.31)$$

where

$$N = \text{integer part of } \{ [-(\ln 0.0001)/Z] + 1 \} \quad \ldots 5.32)$$

and

$$b = (L_{(\infty)}^D - L_r^D)/L_{(\infty)}^D \quad \ldots 5.33)$$

A table (5.7) is provided here from which $t_1$, $t_2$ values can be read off, given the months of sampling and of recruitment (i.e., the months during which the length-frequency data were sampled from which $\overline{L}_1$, $\overline{L}_2$ and $L_r$ were estimated). Assumptions of this method are that (a) the VBGF and equation (5.1) describe the growth and mortality, respectively, of the investigated stock; (b) recruitment occurs during a brief period of time, and only once a year; (c) interannual variations of recruitment are negligible, i.e., the stock has a stable population with a stationary age distribution; and (d) $\overline{L}_1$, $\overline{L}_2$, $L_r$ and $L_{(\infty)}$ are good estimates of the actual values.

Of these assumptions, (c) may be the most crucial one, and the one whose validity may be the most difficult to assess. It must be understood, however, that this assumption is made not only here,

Table 5.7. Values of $t_1$ and $t_2$ for use with $L_1$ and $L_2$ values, given the month of recruitment.[a]

| Sampling months (for $L_1$ and $L_2$) | \multicolumn{12}{c}{Month of recruitment} |
|---|---|---|---|---|---|---|---|---|---|---|---|---|
| | J | F | M | A | M | J | J | A | S | O | N | D |
| J | 0 | 1 | 0.909 | 0.818 | 0.727 | 0.636 | 0.546 | 0.455 | 0.364 | 0.273 | 0.182 | 0.091 |
| F | 0.091 | 0 | 1 | 0.909 | 0.818 | 0.727 | 0.636 | 0.546 | 0.455 | 0.364 | 0.273 | 0.182 |
| M | 0.182 | 0.091 | 0 | 1 | 0.909 | 0.818 | 0.727 | 0.636 | 0.546 | 0.455 | 0.364 | 0.273 |
| A | 0.273 | 0.182 | 0.091 | 0 | 1 | 0.909 | 0.818 | 0.727 | 0.636 | 0.546 | 0.455 | 0.364 |
| M | 0.364 | 0.273 | 0.182 | 0.091 | 0 | 1 | 0.909 | 0.818 | 0.727 | 0.636 | 0.546 | 0.455 |
| J | 0.455 | 0.364 | 0.273 | 0.182 | 0.091 | 0 | 1 | 0.909 | 0.818 | 0.727 | 0.636 | 0.546 |
| J | 0.546 | 0.455 | 0.364 | 0.273 | 0.182 | 0.091 | 0 | 1 | 0.909 | 0.818 | 0.727 | 0.636 |
| A | 0.636 | 0.546 | 0.455 | 0.364 | 0.273 | 0.182 | 0.091 | 0 | 1 | 0.909 | 0.818 | 0.727 |
| S | 0.727 | 0.636 | 0.546 | 0.455 | 0.364 | 0.273 | 0.182 | 0.091 | 0 | 1 | 0.909 | 0.818 |
| O | 0.818 | 0.727 | 0.636 | 0.546 | 0.455 | 0.364 | 0.273 | 0.182 | 0.091 | 0 | 1 | 0.909 |
| N | 0.909 | 0.818 | 0.727 | 0.636 | 0.546 | 0.455 | 0.364 | 0.273 | 0.182 | 0.091 | 0 | 1 |
| D | 1 | 0.909 | 0.818 | 0.727 | 0.636 | 0.546 | 0.455 | 0.364 | 0.273 | 0.182 | 0.091 | 0 |

[a]To use this table, select appropriate column (= month of recruitment, and read from that column values of $t_1$ and $t_2$, given the month at which sampling for $L_1$ and $L_2$ took place ($t_1$ can be, but is not necessarily, the month of recruitment). Values may be interpolated linearly for dates of the month; in this case, recruitment and table values should be viewed as pertaining to the 15th of the corresponding month. Interpolation must not be done between 1 and 0.

but also in the various equations used to estimate Z from mean size data, as well as in all "catch curve" related methods (see above). The validity of assumption (b), on the other hand, can be assessed quite straightforwardly, e.g., by plotting the available length-frequency data and inspecting them visually for the pattern of recruitment (see Fig. 5.11). Assumption (a) is made throughout this manual and requires no further comment.

The method presented here for estimating Z and K simultaneously, as incorporated in Program FB 13, generates results that are very sensitive to small errors affecting the input parameters, particularly the values of $\overline{L}_1^D - L_r^D$ and $\overline{L}_2^D - L_r^D$. On the other hand, the values of $t_1$ and $t_2$ have a comparatively smaller effect on the results. Still, they will be improved by using exact values of $t_1$, $t_2$ for which reason a table (5.7) was included here which can be used to obtain directly the appropriate values of $t_1$, $t_2$, given the months of recruitment and sampling. The table also allows for interpolations when the exact dates in the months are known.

As this method—and a number of other methods discussed in this manual—involve the use of mean lengths, a routine has been included in Program FB 13 which can be used to compute rapidly the weighted mean lengths (or mean weights, or any weighted mean for that matter) from size-frequency data. The routine also computes the standard deviation of the variates and the standard error of the mean. This use of the routine is illustrated in Example 5.3 (see also Table 5.8).

Table 5.8. Length-frequency data for the goby *(Glossogobius giurus)* from Cardona, Laguna de Bay, Philippines.[a]

| Lower class limit (cm) | 1958 A | S | O | N | D | J | F | M | 1959 A | M | J | J |
|---|---|---|---|---|---|---|---|---|---|---|---|---|
| 4 | 1 | 3 | — | — | — | — | — | — | — | — | — | — |
| 6 | 138 | 113 | 1 | 9 | 2 | — | — | — | — | — | — | — |
| 8 | 153 | 62 | 40 | 65 | 126 | 12 | 5 | 6 | — | — | — | — |
| 10 | 49 | 36 | 111 | 49 | 127 | 55 | 52 | 56 | 21 | — | — | — |
| 12 | 9 | 25 | 43 | 20 | 65 | 50 | 84 | 77 | 50 | 6 | 3 | 8 |
| 14 | — | 7 | 3 | 1 | 14 | 25 | 36 | 38 | 53 | 37 | 6 | 36 |
| 16 | — | 1 | — | — | 3 | 9 | 4 | 8 | 26 | 43 | 17 | 18 |
| 18 | — | — | — | — | — | — | — | 3 | 12 | 15 | 13 | 4 |
| 20 | — | — | — | — | — | — | — | 1 | 4 | 6 | 5 | 3 |
| 22 | — | — | — | — | — | — | — | — | 1 | 4 | — | 2 |
| 24 | — | — | — | — | — | — | — | — | — | 1 | — | — |
| Σ | 350 | 247 | 198 | 144 | 337 | 151 | 181 | 189 | 167 | 112 | 44 | 71 |
| Mean length | 8.58 | 8.93 | 11.07 | 10.15 | 10.83 | 12.52 | 12.80 | 10.99 | 14.69 | 16.89 | 17.50 | 15.99 |
| Inputs | | $\overline{\overline{L}}_1 = 9.5$ (Sept) | | | | | | | | $\overline{\overline{L}}_2 = 16.8$ (June) | | |

[a] Adapted from data in Marquez (1960).

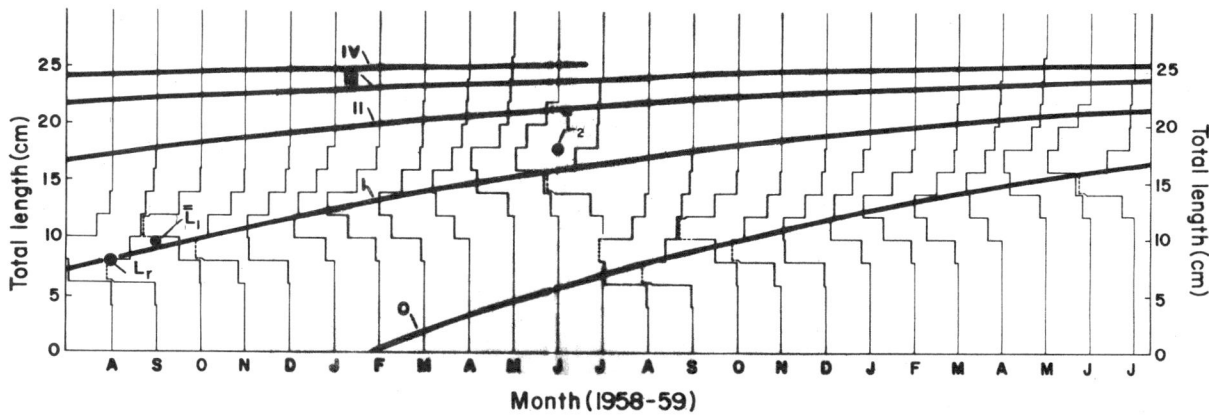

Fig. 5.11. Growth curve of the white goby *(Glossogobius giurus)* in Laguna de Bay, Philippines as estimated using Ebert's method (based on data in Table 5.8 and Example 5.10).

## ESTIMATION OF Z/K

While the estimation of Z requires either a knowledge of the growth parameters of a stock, or that the age of at least a few fish is known, a number of methods exist which allow for the estimation of a parameter—Z/K—which is closely related to Z, yet require no information on age or growth for its estimation.

A few of these methods have been presented above (cumulative plots, length-converted catch curves); in these, use of 1 (one) instead of the value of K leads to the estimation of Z/K instead of Z.

Powell (1979) derived a general model for the estimation of Z/K from which he derived four special cases, as follows:

### 1st case: the Beverton and Holt formula of 1956

Probably the simplest method for estimating Z/K is to rewrite equation (5.9) such that

$$Z/K = \frac{D(L_\infty^D - \overline{L}^D)}{\overline{L}^D - L'^D} \quad \ldots 5.34)$$

where all parameters are defined as in (5.9). This model is illustrated in Example 5.11. However, the reservations mentioned earlier with regards to (5.9) apply to this model also.

### 2nd case: using the variance of the mean length

Powell (1979) derived for the estimation of Z/K the equation

$$Z/K = \frac{2C^2}{1 - C^2} \quad \ldots 5.35)$$

where in terms of the special VBGF

$$C^2 = (s.d._{(L)})^2 / (\overline{L} - L')^2 \quad \ldots 5.36)$$

where $\overline{L}$ and $L'$ are defined as previously, and where $s.d._{(L)}$ is the standard deviation of the L values used in computing $\overline{L}$.

Several applications of equation (5.36) suggest that this model produces values of Z/K which are generally biased downward (see Example 5.11). On the other hand, the model does not require any estimate of asymptotic size, which might be viewed as an advantage over equation (5.34).

### 3rd case: using a nomogram and the mean weight of fish in the catch

Fig. 5.12 reproduces a nomogram presented by Powell (1979) to roughly estimate Z/K from the mean weight of fish in the catch and a few ancillary values.

### 4th case: estimating Z/K from the shape of the length-frequency distribution

Fig. 5.13 gives a redrawn version of Fig. 110 in Powell (1979), which may be used to obtain a crude, preliminary estimate of Z/K given a set of length-frequency data representative of a given population in which individual growth is described by the special VBGF.

The main reasons why Powell's graphs (Figs. 5.12 and 5.13) are given here is not their feature of allowing crude estimates of Z/K. Rather these graphs, particularly Fig. 5.13, have been included because they *show* how Z/K is related to major properties of fish stocks.

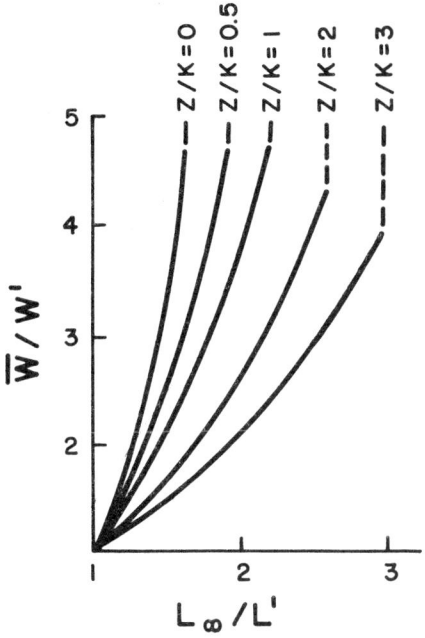

Fig. 5.12. Powell's nomogram for the estimation of Z/K (special VBGF) from the relationship between the mean weight ($\overline{W}$) in the catch, the asymptotic length and the lowest size at full retention (L' and W').

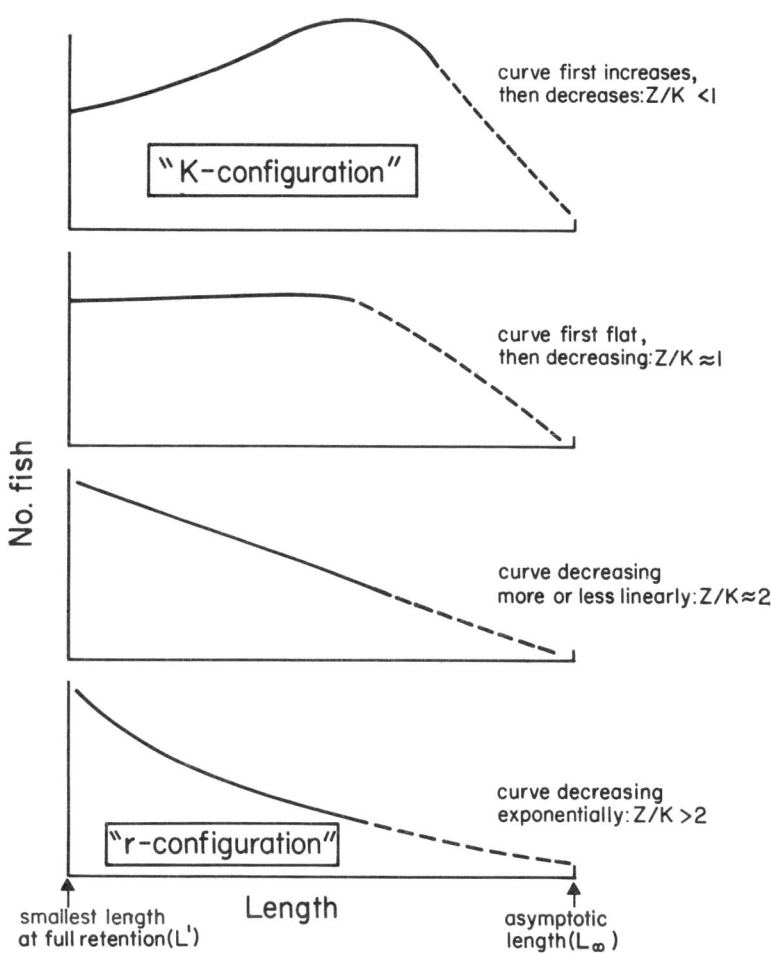

Fig. 5.13. Overall shapes of length-frequency plots, given different values of Z/K (special VBGF). Adapted from Powell (1979, Fig. 110) and Johnson (1981, Figs. 1 and 2). See text for definitions of r- and K-configurations.

For example, Fig. 5.13 shows that fish with very low mortalities and even slower growth, e.g., the whitefish of unexploited northern Canadian lakes (Johnson 1981), display such a considerable "pile-up effect" (see above for definition) that large fish are more numerous than fish of intermediate size, a phenomenon which Johnson calls "K-configuration", as opposed to the "r-configuration" occurring when fish numbers decrease exponentially with size (see Figs. 5.13 and 5.14).

Whether fishes with a clear "K-configuration" occur in the tropics is unclear; this would be surprising, however, given that the ratio M/K (and hence Z/K also) is generally higher in tropical fishes than in temperate fishes (see below). The ecology texts listed in Chapter 11 may be consulted, incidentally, for definitions of "r- and K-strategies", from which Johnson (1981) derived the concept of r- and K-configurations.

## METHODS FOR SPLITTING Z INTO M AND F

Two methods will be presented here which allow division of estimates of Z into their constituent parts, M and F, while a third (the method of Csirke and Caddy) is discussed in Chapter 10.

These methods are (1) plotting different values of Z on their corresponding effort and (2) analysis of tag return data.

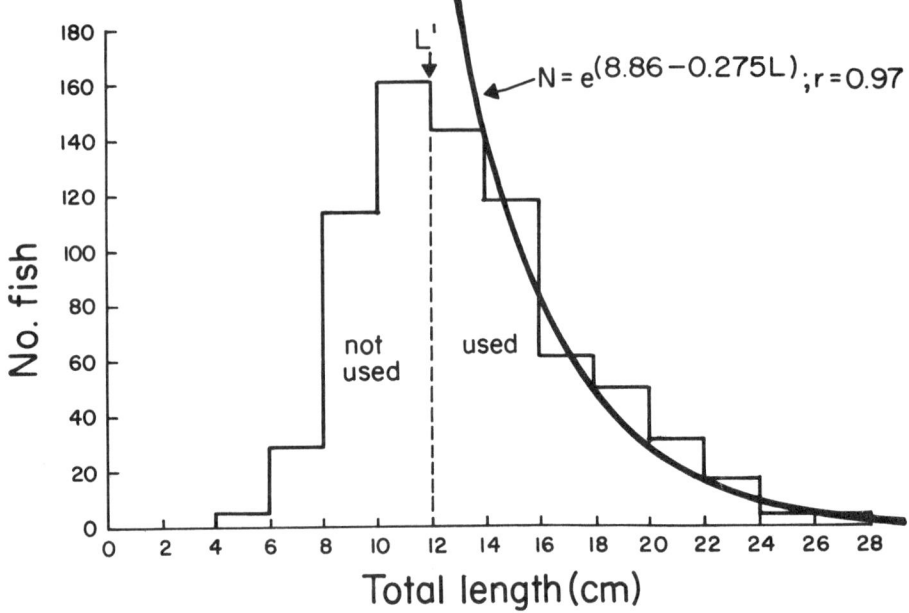

Fig. 5.14. Length-frequency data from Table 5.4, fitted with an exponential curve to demonstrate that Z/K for *Epinephelus sexfasciatus* is 2 or greater (see text, Fig. 5.13 and Example 5.11).

Plot of Z on effort

When two or more values of Z are available which pertain to different periods (years or groups of years) with different levels of fishing effort (f) (as for example in Table 5.9), a linear plot of Z on f will provide an estimate of M through the relationship

$$Z = M + qf \qquad \ldots 5.37)$$

Table 5.9. Data for estimating M and q for *Selaroides leptolepis* from the Gulf of Thailand.[a]

| Year | Effort[b] | $\overline{L}$ | $Z$[c] |
|---|---|---|---|
| 1966 | 2.08 | 13.25 | 2.41 |
| 1967 | 2.08 | 13.01 | 2.69 |
| 1968 | 3.50 | 19.99 | 2.72 |
| 1969 | 3.60 | 13.07 | 2.62 |
| 1970 | 3.80 | 12.37 | 3.73 |
| 1972 | 7.19 | 12.30 | 3.88 |
| 1973 | 9.94 | 12.01 | 4.61 |
| 1974 | 6.06 | 12.60 | 3.30 |
| $\overline{X}$ | 4.87 | 12.70 | 3.25 |

[a] Based on data in Boonyubol and Hongskul (1978).
[b] In millions of trawling hours.
[c] As estimated from $Z = K \cdot (L_\infty - \overline{L})/(\overline{L} - L')$, with $L_\infty = 20$ cm, $K = 1.16$ and $L' = 10$ cm.

where q is the "catchability coefficient", which relates effort to fishing mortality such that

$$F = q \cdot f \qquad \ldots 5.38)$$

Equation (5.38), it must be realized, applies only when f measures *effective* effort (as opposed to *nominal* effort, as expressed, e.g., by simple "number of boats") and provides a measure of effort which is indeed proportional to F (see Rothschild 1977, and contributions in Gulland 1964).

A program for estimating the values of M and q is superfluous here as equation (5.38) provides yet another linear regression with intercept equal to M and slope equal to q (see Example 5.13 and Fig. 5.15).

When only one value of Z is available, or when the available values of Z and f cover too small a range for reasonable values of M and q to be obtained, the catchability coefficient (q) may be estimated through

$$q = (\overline{Z} - M)/\overline{f} \qquad \ldots 5.39)$$

where $\overline{Z}$ is the mean of the available values of Z (or a single value of Z) and $\overline{f}$ is the mean of the values of f (or a single value of f), M being an independent estimate of natural mortality. (See **Ricker 1975**, p. 172-174, and Example 5.15.)

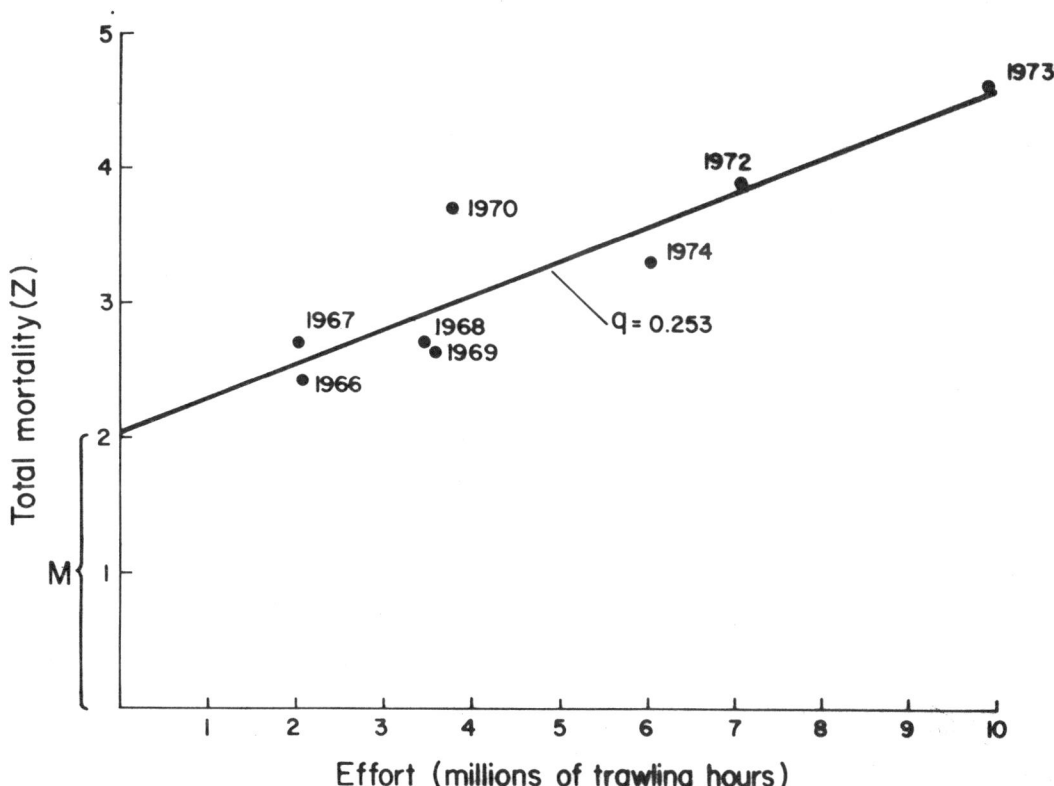

Fig. 5.15. Plot of total mortality (Z) on effort for the yellow striped trevally *(Selaroides leptolepis)* in the Gulf of Thailand trawl fishery, to obtain values of M and q (based on data in Table 5.9 and Example 5.13).

Analysis of tagging data

There is a very voluminous literature on methods to estimate mortalities by means of tagging studies. Reviews may be found in **Jones (1977), Ricker (1975)** and **White et al. (1982).** Only one case will be discussed here, namely that of tagging experiments in which all tagging is performed at one time (say over a period of a few days) and in which both fishing and natural mortality can be assumed constant during the period of the experiment.

In such cases, the analysis consists of simply plotting the natural logarithm of the number of recoveries, grouped by time intervals, on the number of the time intervals, or

$$\ln N_r = a + br' \qquad \ldots 5.40)$$

where $\ln N_r$ is the natural logarithm of the number of recoveries ($N_r$) per time interval and where $r'$ is the time interval number (starting with 0, see Table 5.10). The slope of such a plot provides, with sign changed, an estimate of Z, while the intercept a can be used to estimate F through the relationship

$$F = \frac{e^a \cdot Z}{N_o (1 - e^{-Z})} \qquad \ldots 5.41)$$

where $N_o$ is the total number of fish tagged and released (and provided there is no significant tag shedding, tag-induced mortality or non-recovery of tagged fish).

Table 5.10. Number of tagged and recovered chub mackerels *(Rastrelliger neglectus)*, grouped according to time spent at large after releasing.[a]

| No. of month (r')[b] | No. of recoveries |
|---|---|
| 0 | 1,052 |
| 1 | 748 |
| 2 | 165 |
| 3 | 46 |
| 4 | 8 |

[a]Area II, Gulf of Thailand, 1961 experiment. Total number released was $N_o = 5,230$. From Table XXI in Hongskul (1974).
[b]The first time period at large is coded 0, the following periods 1, 2, 3, etc.

Natural mortality is obtained by subtracting F from Z; then Z, F and M are converted to annual rates by multiplication by the number of times one of the time intervals is contained in a year (see Example 5.13).

Equations (5.40) and (5.41) are adapted from Gulland (1969, p. 76) whose chapter on tagging should be consulted for details on the method, particularly with regard to potential sources of errors.

It should be mentioned moreover, that tagging studies in other than well-monitored, single-species pelagic stocks (e.g., tuna and mackerels) are, in the tropics at least, generally very difficult to conduct successfully, particularly with regard to sufficient numbers of returns. Also, such studies are often too expensive to be cost-effective (Stephenson 1981; Pauly 1982a).

METHOD FOR OBTAINING INDEPENDENT ESTIMATES OF M

It has been demonstrated by various authors that the values of the parameter K of the VBGF are closely linked with longevity in fish (see e.g., Beverton and Holt 1959). This can be demonstrated on the basis of the observation that in nature the oldest fish of a stock generally grow to about 95% of their asymptotic length (Taylor 1958; Beverton 1963). This rule, which was derived from growth data used in conjunction with the special VBGF, does not strictly apply to large fish, such as tuna (see Pauly 1981). Still, in small fish at least, when

$$L_t = L_\infty (1 - e^{-K(t - t_o)}) \qquad \ldots 5.42)$$

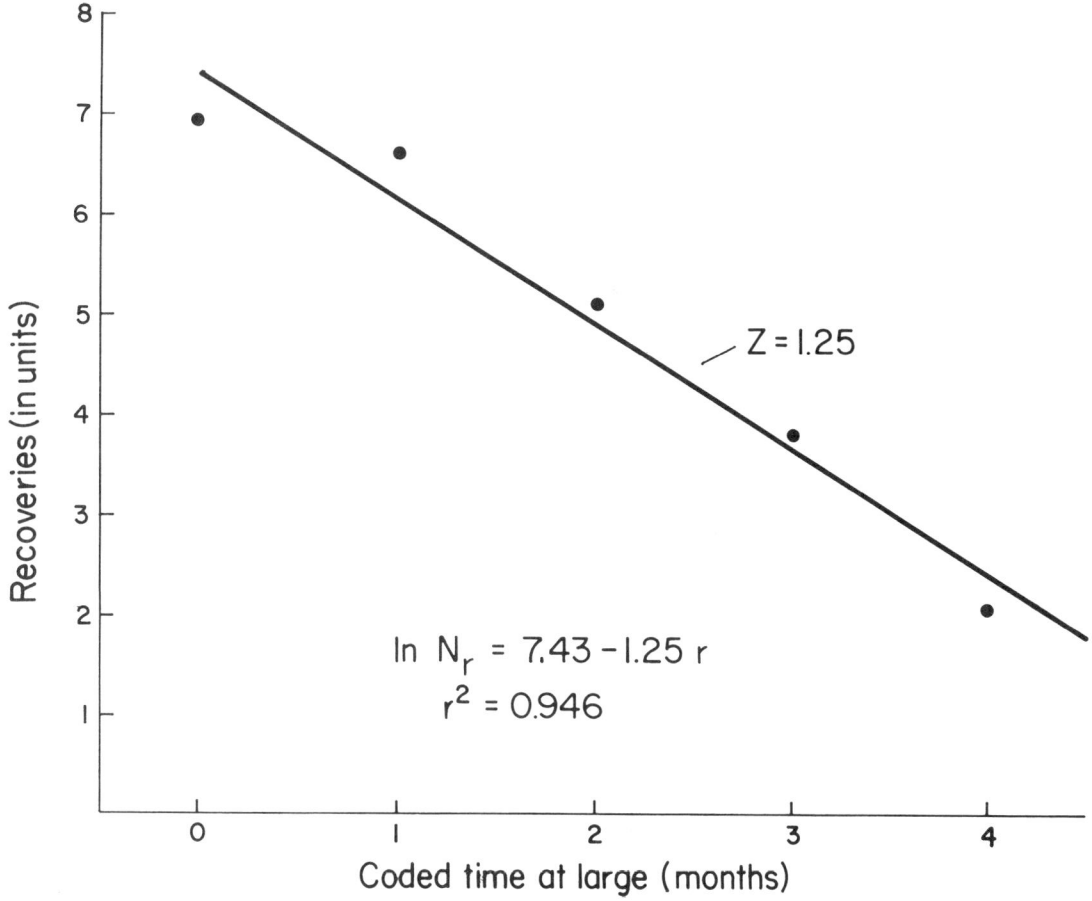

Fig. 5.16. Analysis of tag return data for chub mackerel *(Rastrelliger neglectus)* from the Gulf of Thailand (based on data in Table 5.10 and Example 5.13).

then

$$t - t_o = \frac{\ln(1 - (L_t/L_\infty))}{-K} \quad \ldots 5.43)$$

or, inserting 95% of $L_\infty$ for $L_{max}$

$$t_{max} - t_o = \frac{2.9957}{K} \quad \ldots 5.44)$$

or, ignoring $t_o$

$$t_{max} \approx \frac{3}{K} \quad \ldots 5.45)$$

where $t_{max}$ is the longevity of the fish in question.

That natural mortality should, in fishes, be inversely correlated with longevity and hence be correlated with K, seems obvious (see also equation 5.5). Natural mortality should also inversely correlate with size, since large fish should have, as a rule, fewer predators than small fish.

Natural mortality can also be demonstrated to be correlated to mean environmental temperature in fishes, although the interpretation of this phenomenon is still open (Pauly 1980b).

These various interrelationships can be expressed for length growth data by the multiple regression

$$\log M = -0.0066 - 0.279 \log L_\infty + 0.6543 \log K + 0.463 \log \overline{T} \quad \ldots 5.46)$$

and for weight growth data by

$$\log M = -0.2107 - 0.0824 \log W_\infty + 0.6757 \log K + 0.4687 \log \overline{T} \qquad \ldots 5.47)$$

where M is the natural mortality in a given stock, $L_\infty$ (total length, in cm) and $W_\infty$ (live weight, in g) being the asymptotic size of that stock; K (as well as $L_\infty$ and $W_\infty$) refers to the special VBGF and is expressed on an annual basis; the value of $\overline{T}$ is the annual mean temperature (°C) of the water in which the stock in question lives. These equations are incorporated in Program FB 15. [Negative temperature values for polar fishes, down to $-2°C$ may be used for input in Program FB 15, because an "effective physiological temperature" (Pauly 1980b), which happens to be always positive, is computed internally for all values of $T < 3.5°$ and $T \geqslant -2.0°C$.]

In general, the estimates of M provided by equations (5.46) and (5.47) are quite reasonable, especially because a very large number (175) of *independent* estimates of M have been used for their derivation. Also the fish considered covered an extremely wide range of sizes, taxa and habitats.

However, estimates of M obtained from these expressions may be biased upward in the case of strongly schooling fishes, such as the sardine-like fishes and downward in the case of polar fishes. Correction factors and a further discussion of equations (5.46) and (5.47) are given in Pauly (1980b), along with all data used in the derivation.

Equations (5.46) and (5.47) are incorporated into Program FB 15, which estimates M given the appropriate growth parameters of the special VBGF and an estimate of T, such as may be obtained from an oceanographic atlas (see Example 5.14).

# EXPLOITATION RATES AND POTENTIAL YIELDS

Certain stock assessment methods, such as Beverton and Holt's relative yield-per-recruit assessment (Beverton and Holt 1966) and Jones' (1974) length cohort analysis (see following chapters) make exhaustive use of exploitation rates, which define the fraction (in numbers) of an age class which will be caught during the fished life span (or: E = number caught/number dying of all causes).

In terms of mortality rates, the exploitation rate is defined by

$$E = \frac{F}{F + M} = \frac{F}{Z} \qquad \ldots 5.48)$$

Another definition of E is given by

$$E = 1 - \frac{M/K}{Z/K} \qquad \ldots 5.49)$$

which implies that the exploitation rate of a stock can be assessed without their age or growth parameters being known (see Example 5.15).

When, on the other hand, only M and E are known, F can be estimated from

$$F = M \cdot E/(1 - E) \qquad \ldots 5.50)$$

Gulland (1971) suggested that in a stock that is optimally exploited, fishing mortality should be about equal to natural mortality, or

$$F_{opt} \approx M \qquad \ldots 5.51)$$

which corresponds to

$$E_{opt} \approx 0.5 \qquad \ldots 5.52)$$

and which also leads to the well-known equation

$$P_y \approx 0.5 \, M \, B_o \qquad \ldots 5.53)$$

which states that the potential yield of a stock is about equal to half the virgin biomass ($B_o$) times the natural mortality prevailing in that stock (see Gulland 1971 p. x, xi for the two approaches that lead to this model).

Although widely used, equation (5.53) has been criticized by a number of authors, notably Francis (1974) and Caddy and Csirke (1983) who showed that the assumption $M \approx F_{opt}$ does not apply in a large number of stocks, notably in stocks of fish and shrimps low in the food chain.

Beddington and Cooke (1983) investigated equation (5.53) in great detail and concluded, on the basis of numerous simulations, that equation (5.53) generally overestimates potential yields by a factor which is itself a function of M. Thus, they showed that, for values of M ranging between 0.2 and 1, equation (5.53) overestimates potential yields by a factor of 2-3. For higher values of M—as often occurs in small tropical fish—equation (5.53) possibly overestimates potential yields by a factor of 3-4.

Thus, rather than $E_{opt} \approx 0.5$, it could well be that the optimum exploitation rate is—particularly in small fish with high recruitment variability—as low as 0.2 or, tentatively

$$P_y \approx 0.2 \, M \, B_o \qquad \ldots 5.54)$$

Clearly, these results are very important and warrant further research on this topic. Also, they make it imperative to use approximations such as discussed here only in the last resort, and then very conservatively, e.g., by relying on (5.54) rather than (5.53).

Recommended reading: Although less abundant than the literature on growth, the literature on mortality is quite large. Some useful reviews are: Beverton and Holt (1956, 1959), Robson and Chapman (1961), Gulland (1969, 1971) and Ricker (1975).

Suggested research topics: Compare estimates of Z obtained from catch curves of commercially important fish with estimates obtained from mean sizes in the catch (using different equations to compute the latter). Attempt to estimate M from Z and effort data, and compare the estimate(s) of M with independent estimates obtained from expressions (5.46 and 5.47). Attempt to partition F into different fishing gears, and M into different predators. Investigate changes in F and in M.

**Estimation of Z and its standard error from the maximum age of a fish sample.**   EXAMPLE 5.1

Rodrigues (1968) aged 115 male specimens of the croaker *(Micropogon furnieri)* caught off Caera State, Brazil. The maximum age was 7 years. What is the total mortality in the stock from which the 115 fish were taken, if $t_c$ is set at zero?

To obtain Z and its standard error, first read off the value of $c_1$ and $c_2$ corresponding to n = 115. These values, interpolated between the values for n = 110 and n = 120, are 0.198 and 0.049, respectively. Then perform

| Keystrokes | Results | |
|---|---|---|
| 197 ↑ .198 X ÷ | 0.72 | Z |
| $X^2$ .049 X √x | 0.16 | s.e.$_{(Z)}$ |

Other values of Z and s.e.$_{(Z)}$ in Brazilian fishes are given in Table 5.3.

---

EXAMPLE 5.2  **Estimation of Z from the mean weight of the catch (iterative solution).**

If the following set of growth parameters of the special VBGF (corresponding to a small tuna are available) $W_\infty$ = 10 kg, $t_o$ = —0.8, with $t_c$ = 0.95 and the mean weight in the catch is equal to $\overline{\overline{W}}$ = 5 kg; what is the total mortality? The tolerated error of Z will be 0.001.

Computations:

1) Read sides 1 and 2 of Program FB 10.

2) Initialize

| | Keystrokes | Results | |
|---|---|---|---|
| | 10 ↑ .5 ↑ .95 ↑ | | |
| | .8 CHS f a 5 f b | | |
| 1st guess for Z = 4 | .001 f e 4A | —2.47 | [f(a)] |
| 2nd guess for Z = 0.1 | 0.1B | 3.34 | [f(b)] |
| 3) Estimate total mortality: | E | 0.58 | (Z) |

Note: Depending on the values of f(a) and f(b), the iteration time can go beyond one minute.

**Estimation of Z from the mean length of the catch.**                                      **EXAMPLE 5.3**

Case I: Thompson and Munro (1978) give for the Jamaican grouper *(Epinephelus guttatus)* the parameter values $L_\infty$ = 52 cm, K = 0.28 (D = 1), $L'$ = 34 and L = 38.7. What is the total mortality?

| Keystrokes | Result | |
|---|---|---|
| .28 ↑ 52 ↑ 38.7— | | |
| X 38.7 ↑ 34 -- ÷ | 0.792 | (Z) |

Case II: Table 5.4 gives length-frequency data (averaged over one year to simulate equilibrium) for another grouper *(Epinephelus sexfasciatus)* from the Philippines. The data are used to illustrate the operation of the routine in Program FB 13 for the rapid computation of mean lengths and the effects of the omission of large fish on the estimated values of Z.

1) Load sides 1 and 2 of Program FB 13

2) Store $L'$, $\Delta L$ and initialize; keystrokes: 12 ↑ 2 f b

3) Enter frequencies needed for computation of the mean length and its standard error

   Keystrokes: 143 A 118 A 61 A 50 A 32 A 17 A 4 A

4) Compute the mean length and its standard error

| Keystroke | Results | |
|---|---|---|
| B | 425 | (n) |
| | 15.951 | ($\bar{L}$) |
| | 3.018 | (s.d.$_{(L)}$) |
| | 0.146 | (s.e.$_{(\bar{L})}$) |

5) Now recompute the mean length after adding the last frequency, which was omitted in step (3).

| Keystroke | Results | |
|---|---|---|
| 4 AB | 429 | (n) |
| | 16.054 | ($\bar{L}$) |
| | 3.186 | (s.d.$_{(L)}$) |
| | 0.154 | (s.e.$_{(\bar{L})}$) |

6) Finally, compute Z for the two values of $\bar{L}$ (15.951 and 16.054) using the same keystroke sequence as given in Case I of this Example.
   The results should be Z values equal to 1.868 when the last frequency is omitted, and 1.93 when it is included.

This Example illustrates that the values of Z obtained from mean lengths are quite sensitive to the inclusion of the few fish in the largest size classes (see text for a discussion of the problem that this represents). It will also be noted that an extraneous knowledge of $L'$ is required by this method, as opposed to what occurs when semi-graphical methods are used (cumulative plots, length-converted catch curves).

**EXAMPLE 5.4** | **Estimation of Z using Jones' method.**

Data from Table 5.4

Computations

1) Read side 1 of Program FB 11.

2) Enter $L_\infty$, D, $\Delta L$, $L_{max}$ and initialize

   Keystrokes: 30.9 ↑ 1 ↑ 2 ↑ 26

3) Enter all catches, starting with that corresponding to the largest fish

| Keystrokes | Results | |
|---|---|---|
| 4 A | 1.589 | ln $(L_\infty^D - L_i^D)$ |
|  | 1.386 | ln C $(L_i, \infty)$ |
| 4 A | 1.932 | .... |
|  | 2.079 | .... |
| 17 A | 2.186 | .... |
|  | 3.219 | .... |
| etc. | | |

4) Plot the ln $(L_\infty^D - L_i^D)$ and ln C $(L_i^D, \infty)$ data as in Fig. 5.2 and select points to be included in linear regression (see Fig. 5.2 for points selected).

5) Re-initialize, and re-enter data

   Keystrokes: 30.9 ↑ 1 ↑ 2 ↑ 26 f a 4 A 4 A R/S 17 A R/S 32 A R/S 50 A R/S 61 A R/S 118 A R/S 143 A R/S 161 A R/S

6) Compute parameters of linear regression and estimate Z/K.

| Keystroke | Results | |
|---|---|---|
| E | 0.998 | ($r^2$) |
|  | −5.235 | (a) |
|  | 3.846 | (b = Z/K) |

7) Calculate Z through multiplication of Z/K with K.

| Keystroke | Result | |
|---|---|---|
| .51 x | 1.961 | (Z) |

As will be shown further below, this result (Z = 1.961) is very similar to those obtained using a number of different methods (i.e., various forms of the length-converted catch curve) if the same data points are included in the analysis.

**Estimation of Z using Sparre's method.**  EXAMPLE 5.5

Data from Table 5.4

Computations

1) Read side 1 of Program FB 11.

2) Enter $L_\infty$, D, $\Delta L$, $L_{max}$ and initialize

   Keystrokes: 30.9 ↑ 1 D 26 f a

3) Enter K

   Keystrokes: 30.9 ↑ 1 ↑ 2 ↑ 26 fa

4) Enter all catches, starting with that corresponding to the largest fish

   | Keystrokes | Results | |
   |---|---|---|
   | 4 B | 3.611 | $t'_{L_i}$ |
   |     | 1.386 | ln C $(L_i, \infty)$ |
   | 4 B | 2.940 | .... |
   |     | 2.079 | .... |
   | 17 B | 2.441 | .... |
   |      | 3.219 | .... |
   | etc. | | |

5) Plot the $t'_{L_i}$ and ln C $(L_i, \infty)$ data as in Fig. 5.3 and select points to be included in the linear regression (see Fig. 5.3 for points selected).

6) Re-initialize and re-enter data

   Keystrokes: 30.9 ↑ 1 ↑ 2 ↑ 26 f a .51 STO 1 4 B 4 B R/S 17 B R/S 32 B R/S 50 B R/S 61 B R/S 118 B R/S 143 B R/S 161 B R/S

7) Compute parameters of linear regression and estimate Z

   | Keystroke | Results | |
   |---|---|---|
   | E | 0.998 | ($r^2$) |
   |   | 7.959 | (a) |
   |   | −1.961 | (b = −Z) |

It will be noted that the result (Z = 1.961) is exactly the same as that obtained using Jones' method.

**EXAMPLE 5.6**  Estimating Z from length-frequency data using a length-converted catch curve in which the "piling-up" effect is corrected for by the use of growth rates.

Data from Table 5.4.

1) Use Program FB 9 to compute the growth rate (dl/dt) and relative ages ($t'$) corresponding to the class midpoints in Table 5.4; also compute ln N(dl/dt) for each class midpoint, and record results as shown here.

| Class midpoint (cm) | N | dl/dt | ln N (dl/dt) | $t'$ | Remarks |
|---|---|---|---|---|---|
| 5 | 5 | 13.21 | 4.190 | 0.346 | not used, ascending part of curve |
| 7 | 29 | 12.19 | 5.868 | 0.504 | |
| 9 | 114 | 11.17 | 7.149 | 0.675 | |
| 11 | 161 | 10.15 | 7.399 | 0.863 | |
| 13 | 143 | 9.129 | 7.174 | 1.07 | used, descending straight part of catch curve |
| 15 | 118 | 8.109 | 6.864 | 1.30 | |
| 17 | 61 | 7.089 | 6.069 | 1.57 | |
| 19 | 50 | 6.069 | 5.715 | 1.87 | |
| 21 | 32 | 5.049 | 5.085 | 2.23 | |
| 23 | 17 | 4.029 | 4.227 | 2.67 | |
| 25 | 4 | 3.009 | 2.488 | 3.25 | |
| 27 | 4 | 1.989 | 2.074 | 4.06 | |

2) Plot these data as in Fig. 5.5 and select points to be included in regression.

3) Compute parameters of a length-converted catch curve using linear regression (standard Pac SDO 3A), using $t'$ for the x-axis and ln N·(dl/dt) for the y-axis. When x- and y-values (see above) have been entered, compute parameters of catch curve:

| Keystroke | Results | |
|---|---|---|
| C | 0.974 | ($r^2$) |
| | 9.087 | (a) |
| | −1.831 | (b) |

Thus Z is equal to 1.83, a value close to those estimated from the same data set using different methods (see Examples 5.3, 5.4 and 5.5).

It will also be noted that the plot in Fig. 5.4 gives no reason to delete the last point (that corresponding to $t' \approx 4$ years), which however, had to be deleted in Figs. 5.2 and 5.3.

**EXAMPLE 5.7** Showing that not correcting for the "piling-up" effect leads to negatively biased estimates of Z.

Data from Example 5.6

1) Use the linear regression program (standard Pac SDO 3A) to estimate the parameters of a plot of ln N on $t'$, using only the values of N and $t'$ in Example 5.6 corresponding to fishes with class midpoints ranging from 13 to 27 cm. Read sides 1 and 2 of SDO 3A, enter data, with x = $t'$ and y = ln N.

2) Estimate parameters of regression line

| Keystroke | Results | |
|---|---|---|
| C | 0.951 | ($r^2$) |
| | 6.331 | (a) |
| | −1.322 | (b) |

3) Since the value of K in Table 5.4 was equal to 0.51 and D = 1, Z is obtained by adding 0.51 to the absolute value of the slope or

| Keystrokes | Result | |
|---|---|---|
| CHS .51 + | 1.832 | (Z) |

As might be seen from Example 5.6 Z = 1.83 is a value that was obtained when directly accounting for the "piling-up" effect. Thus, not accounting for this effect indeed leads to slopes with absolute values equal to Z − KD.

**EXAMPLE 5.8** Estimation of Z from a length-converted catch curve (using $N/\Delta t$) with subsequent improvement using Sparre's method.

Data from Table 5.4

Computations

1) Read sides 1 and 2 of Program FB 12

2) Enter $L_\infty$, $\Delta L$, K, D and initialize

   Keystrokes: 30.9 ↑ 2 ↑ .51 ↑ 1 f a

3) Enter class midlengths and frequencies

| Keystrokes | Results | |
|---|---|---|
| 5 ↑ 5A | 3.497 | (ln ($N/\Delta t$)) |
| | 0.346 | ($t'$) |
| 7 ↑ 29A | 5.174 | (ln ($N/\Delta t$)) |
| | 0.504 | ($t'$) |
| etc. | . . . | |

Continued

**Example 5.8 (cont.)**

4) Plot values of ln (N/Δt) against $t'$ and identify points to be included in the catch curve; the points selected should range from class midpoints 13 to 27 cm (see Fig. 5.7).

5) Re-enter class midlengths and frequencies to be used in regression

|  | Keystrokes | Results |
|---|---|---|
|  | 13 ↑ 143 A | 6.480 |
|  |  | 1.071 |
| now press | Σ+ | 1 |
|  | 15 ↑ 118 A | 6.169 |
|  |  | 1.303 |
| again press | Σ+ | 2 |
|  | etc. | ... |

6) When all 8 pairs of values to be used in the regression have been entered, proceed with

| Keystroke | Results |
|---|---|
| E | 0.974 ($r^2$) |
|  | 8.406 (a) |
|  | 1.839 (Z) |

It will be noted that this result is virtually identical to that obtained in Examples 5.6 and 5.7. However, the methods in these two Examples and that used above are approximate. The value of Z obtained here will thus be used as an input to the iterative routine proposed by P. Sparre, which gives exact results, as follows:

7) Store 1.839 as first value of Z and initialize new routine

   Keystrokes: 1.839 f b

8) Then re-enter class midpoints and frequencies to be used in regression

|  | Keystrokes | Results |
|---|---|---|
|  | 13 ↑ 143 B | 6.066 (ln (N/(1 − $e^{-Z\Delta t}$))) |
|  |  | 0.964 ($t'_{L_i}$) |
| now press | Σ+ | 1 |
|  | 15 ↑ 118 B | 5.778 (ln (N/(1 − $e^{-Z\Delta t}$))) |
|  |  | 1.183 ($t'_{L_i}$) |
| again press | Σ+ | 2 |
|  | etc. | ... |

9) When all 8 pairs of values are entered, obtain the new estimate of Z through

| Keystroke | Results |
|---|---|
| E | 0.968 ($r^2$) |
|  | 7.814 (a) |
|  | 1.850 (Z) |

The new value of Z is so close to the initial value (% difference = 0.6) that there is no need for further iterations: Z will remain near 1.85 anyway.

**EXAMPLE 5.9**

**Construction of a pseudo-catch curve for *Leiognathus splendens* caught off Kalimantan, Indonesia (adapted from Pauly 1980c).**

1) The mean length/water-depth relationship in Fig. 5.8 can be expressed by the relationship

$$\overline{\overline{L}} = 7.36 + 0.106 \, m$$

where m is the depth in meters ($r = 0.544$, $P < 5\%$). The values of $L_\infty$, K and D used here are 14.3 cm, 1.04 and 1, respectively, while the length/weight relationship (cm, g) is given by

$$W = 0.011 \, L^{3.22}$$

2) The catch/effort data, as read off Fig. 5.9, are given below for each depth, along with the corresponding mean length, mean weights, numbers caught and relative ages, as computed using Program FB 1, FB 9 and simple divisions.

| Depth | c/f (kg) | $\overline{L}$ (cm) | $\overline{\overline{W}}$ (g) | $(c/f)/\overline{\overline{W}}$ | t' |
|---|---|---|---|---|---|
| 15 | 18.0 | 8.95 | 12.3 | 1,463 | 0.95 |
| 25 | 31.0 | 10.0 | 18.3 | 1,694 | 1.16 |
| 35 | 14.9 | 11.1 | 25.6 | 582 | 1.44 |
| 45 | 9.63 | 12.1 | 33.7 | 286 | 1.80 |
| 55 | 4.97 | 13.2 | 44.6 | 111 | 2.47 |

3) Program SD-03A ("curve fitting") is then used to estimate the parameters of the regression of $\ln (c/f)/\overline{\overline{W}}$ on $t'$. The results are

| Keystroke | Results | |
|---|---|---|
| C | 0.952 | ($r^2$) |
|   | 9.203 | (a) |
|   | −1.862 | (−Z) |

The main result, the value of Z of 1.86, is reasonable and might serve as input in models requiring estimates of total mortality.

**EXAMPLE 5.10** | **Estimation of K and Z in a stock of the white goby** *(Glossogobius giurus)* **using Ebert's method as improved by Saila and Lough (1981).**

Data from Table 5.8

Computations

1) By inspection of the data in Table 5.8, the month of recruitment is set as August (1958); and the length at recruitment set at 8 cm (as the mean length in the two most abundant length classes in August).

2) Two sampling months, September (1958) and June (1959) are selected which, together with August as month of recruitment, provide, using Table 5.7, values of $t_1$ and $t_2$ equal to 0.091 and 0.909, respectively.

3) The mean lengths $\bar{\bar{L}}_1$ and $\bar{\bar{L}}_2$ are computed by combining the monthly means for August, September and October, and the means for May, June and July, respectively (see Table 5.8). (Combining the samples has the effect of reducing the effects of sampling variability on the estimates of $\bar{\bar{L}}_1$ and $\bar{\bar{L}}_2$).

4) $L_{(\infty)}$ is estimated from the largest fish in Table 5.8 as 26.5 cm.

5) Read sides 1 and 2 of Program FB 13 and enter parameters estimated above.

   Keystrokes: 8 ↑ 9.5 ↑ 16.8 ↑ 1 f a .091 ↑ .909 ↑ 26.5 R/S

6) Enter initial guess of Z and iterate

| | Keystroke | Results | |
|---|---|---|---|
| | 1E | 1 | ($Z_1$) |
| | | 1.103 | ($Z_2$)* |
| | | ..... | etc. |
| | | 0.686 | (K) |
| value reached after 8 iterations | | 3.143 | (Z final) |

*When the second value of Z has a negative sign, this means that the initial guess of Z was much too high. In this case, press R/S, set STO 0 to 8 to zero, and start again with step 5.

**Estimating Z/K from length-frequency data.**  EXAMPLE 5.11

Case I

Thompson and Munro (1974) estimated $L_{(\infty)}$ from $L_{max}$ in *Epinephelus striatus* as approximately 90 cm, while K could not be estimated reliably. The mean length at unexploited oceanic banks off Jamaica is 69 cm, with $L' = 60$ cm. What is the value of M/K (special VBGF)?

Computation

|  | Keystrokes | Results |  |
|---|---|---|---|
|  | 90 ↑ |  |  |
|  | 69 — |  |  |
|  | 69 ↑ |  |  |
|  | 60 — ÷ | 2.33 | (M/K) |

Let's assume the mean length of *Epinephelus striatus* in a certain exploited area is 65 cm, with $L_{(\infty)} = 90$ cm and $L' = 60$. What is the value of Z/K?

Computation

|  | Keystrokes | Results |  |
|---|---|---|---|
|  | 90 ↑ |  |  |
|  | 65 — |  |  |
|  | 65 ↑ |  |  |
|  | 60 — ÷ | 5.00 | (Z/K) |

Case II

The data in Table 5.4 and a value of $L' = 12$ cm are used to compute Z/K using equations (5.35) and (5.36). First the value of $C^2$ is computed, using parameter values computed with Program FB 13 (see Example 5.3 for computation of mean length (16.054) and s.d.$_{(L)}$ (3.186) and equation (5.35):

|  | Keystrokes | Results |  |
|---|---|---|---|
|  | 3.186 x² |  |  |
|  | 16.054 ↑ 12 |  |  |
|  | — x² ÷ | 0.618 | ($C^2$) |

Then use value of $C^2$ to compute Z/K, using equation (5.31)

|  | Keystrokes | Results |  |
|---|---|---|---|
|  | .618 ↑ |  |  |
|  | 2 x 1 ↑ |  |  |
|  | .618 — ÷ | 3.236 | (Z/K) |

This value of Z/K, when multiplied with the value of K given in Table 5.4 (0.51) leads to an estimate of Z = 1.65 which is lower than that obtained using other methods (see Examples 5.3 to 5.9)(see text).

Case III

The length-frequency data in Table 5.4 have been drawn in Fig. 5.14. It might be seen that, beyond $L'$ the frequencies decline exponentially, a feature which is made more visible by the exponential curve superimposed on the data. Hence, using Fig. 5.14 as reference, we infer that Z/K is equal to or higher than 2, a fact substantiated by all previous analyses.

**EXAMPLE 5.12** — Estimating M and q from a plot of Z values against their corresponding values of effort.

Data from Table 5.9

Computation

1) Read sides 1 and 2 of SDO 3A (linear regression)

2) Initialize and enter data

   Keystrokes: f b 2.08 ↑ 2.41 A 2.08 ↑ 2.69 A 3.5 ↑ 2.72 A 3.6 ↑ 2.62 A 3.8 ↑ 3.73 A 7.19 ↑ 3.88 A 9.94 ↑ 4.61 A 6.06 ↑ 3.3 A

3) Obtain results

| Keystrokes | Results | |
|---|---|---|
| C | 0.81 | ($r^2$) |
|  | 2.03 | (a) |
|  | 0.25 | (b) |
| DSP 3 | 0.253 | (q) |
| x ≥ y | 2.034 | (M) |

Thus the results are q = 0.253 and M = 2.03.

---

**EXAMPLE 5.13** — Estimating F and M for chub mackerel *(Rastrelliger neglectus)* from tagging data.

Data from Table 5.10

Computation

1) Read side 1 of Program FB 14

2) Enter data from Table 5.10

   Keystrokes: f a 1052 A 748 A 165 A 46 A 8 A

3) Obtain $r^2$, a and b of regression line (see Fig. 5.16), and estimates of F and M

| Keystrokes | Results | |
|---|---|---|
| E | 0.96 | ($r^2$) |
|  | 7.43 | (a) |
|  | −1.25 | (b) |
| enter $N_o$ 5230 f e | 0.56 | (F) |
|  | 0.69 | (M) |

Gulland (1969) should be consulted for details on this method, as well as possible sources of bias and errors.

**EXAMPLE 5.14** | **Obtaining an independent estimate of M for a fish whose growth parameters are known.**

---

Estimate M in *Selaroides leptolepis* from the Gulf of Thailand. The growth parameters are: $L_\infty$ = 20 cm (total length), K = 1.16, CD = 1, while the mean water temperature in which the fish occur is about 27°C.

Computation

1) Read side 1 of Program FB 15.

2) Enter $L_\infty$, K and T

| Keystrokes | Results | |
|---|---|---|
| 20 ↑ 1.16 ↑ | | |
| 27 A | 2.17 | (M) |

It will be noted that this value is rather close to the value of M (= 2.03) obtained in Example 5.12. Thus it would have been possible, instead of plotting Z on f to obtain M, to simply use the mean value of Z and the mean effort in Table 5.9 to obtain q using equation (5.39) i.e.:

| Keystrokes | Results | |
|---|---|---|
| 3.25 ↑ 2.17 | | |
| —4.87 ÷ | | |
| DSP 3 | 0.222 | (q) |

This value of q compares rather well with the one estimated previously (0.253). This approach to estimating q should be used when the scatter of the Z and f value about the regression line makes the estimate of M look dubious, or, obviously when only one pair of f and Z values is available.

**Estimation of the exploitation rate from mean lengths.**  EXAMPLE 5.15

Thompson and Munro (1974) estimated $L_\infty$ from $L_{max}$ in *Epinephelus striatus* as approximately 90 cm, while K could not be reliably estimated. The mean length on unexploited oceanic banks off Jamaica is 69 cm, with $L' = 60$ cm and $D = 1$. What is M/K? (The answer is computed using equation (5.34).)

|   | Keystrokes | Results |   |
|---|---|---|---|
|   | 90 ↑ 69 – |   |   |
|   | 69 ↑ 60 – ÷ | 2.33 | (M/K) |

However, the mean length of *E. striatus* in exploited fishing grounds is 65 cm (again with $L_{(\infty)} = 90$ and $L' = 60$ cm). What is Z/K? (Using equation (5.34) again.)

|   | Keystrokes | Results |   |
|---|---|---|---|
|   | 90 ↑ 65 – |   |   |
|   | 65 ↑ 60 – ÷ | 5.00 | (Z/K) |

What is the exploitation rate in the exploited fishing grounds? (The answer is computed using equation (5.49).)

|   | Keystrokes | Results |   |
|---|---|---|---|
|   | 2.33 ↑ 5 ÷ |   |   |
|   | CHS 1 + | 0.53 | (E) |

The stock of *E. striatus* investigated here is thus under very intensive exploitation (see p. 77). It will be noted that this inference is made here without the growth parameters of *E. striatus* being known.

# 6. Estimation of Population Size

## INTRODUCTION

This chapter presents four methods by means of which the size of fish populations can be estimated. These are:
a) tagging
b) Leslie's method
c) swept-area method
d) using catch data and fishing mortality

Tagging and Leslie's methods are used to estimate the numbers of fish in a given population or stock, while the other methods are generally used to estimate the total weight of a fish stock (standing stock or biomass) at a given time. Other methods such as virtual population analysis and cohort analysis are discussed in the next chapter which is devoted to methods for estimating "past" populations.

There are still other methods which can be used to estimate stock sizes, i.e., acoustic methods and egg surveys. Specialized manuals should be consulted for these, such as Forbes and Nakken (1972) for acoustic surveys, and Saville (1977) for egg surveys.

## POPULATION SIZE THROUGH TAGGING (PETERSEN ESTIMATES)

Suppose a certain number of marked fishes (T) are released into a body of water, after which some time is allowed for the marked fish to mix thoroughly with the fish already present in the water body. Upon fishing, a certain number of fish (n) are captured of which a smaller number (m) consists of marked fish. The simplest equation for estimating the size of the population (N) is then

$$N = T \cdot n/m \qquad \ldots 6.1)$$

the standard error of N being given by

$$s.e._{(N)} = \left(T^2 n (n - m)/m^3\right)^{1/2} \qquad \ldots 6.2)$$

For these equations to provide reasonable estimates of N, the following assumptions among others, must be met:
1) The natural mortality and vulnerability to fishing gears of tagged and untagged animals are the same.
2) The tagged fish are randomly distributed in the population.
3) Tags are not lost.
4) There is no immigration nor emigration of fish into or out of the stock.
5) All tagged fish are reported.

See Jones (1977) and Ricker (1975) for more details on this and related methods, and for discussions on how to account for some of the bias inherent in the method.

Table 6.1 gives some variants of Petersen's method, which are illustrated in Example 6.1. Other models for the interpretation of tagging data exist, such as Jolly's method. An HP 67/97 program for population size estimates based on this method (Jolly 1965; Ricker 1975, p. 132-134) is included in the HP Users' Library Solutions booklet devoted to "Biology".

Table 6.1. Variants of equations (6.1) and (6.2) suggested by various authors. See also Program FB 16 and Example 6.1. Adapted from Jones (1977).

| Reference | Type of sampling[a] | Estimates of population size (N) | standard error of N |
|---|---|---|---|
| (A) Bailey (1951) | Direct | $N = \dfrac{T \cdot n}{m}$ | $s.e._{(N)} = \left(\dfrac{T^2 n(n-m)}{m^3}\right)^{1/2}$ |
| (B) Bailey (1952) | Direct | $N = \dfrac{T(n+1)}{m+1}$ | $s.e._{(N)} = \left(\dfrac{T^2(n+1)(n-m)}{(m+1)^2(m+2)}\right)^{1/2}$ |
| (C) Chapman (1951) Schaefer (1951) | Direct | $N = \dfrac{(T+1)(n+1)}{m+1} - 1$ | $s.e._{(N)} = \left(N^2\left[\dfrac{N}{nT} + 2\left(\dfrac{N}{nT}\right)^2 + 6\left(\dfrac{N}{nT}\right)^3\right]\right)^{1/2}$ |
| (D) Bailey (1951) | Inverse | $N = \dfrac{n(T+1)}{m} - 1$ | $s.e._{(N)} = \left(\dfrac{(T-m+1)(N+1)(N-T)}{m(T+2)}\right)^{1/2}$ |

[a]"Direct" sampling means that sampling is continued until a predetermined sample size (n) is obtained; "inverse" sampling means that sampling is carried out until a predetermined number of tagged animals (m) is obtained.

## STANDING STOCK ESTIMATION WITH THE SWEPT-AREA METHOD

In areas where the bottom is smooth enough for trawling, the standing stock sizes of demersal fishes (B) can be obtained from the relationship

$$B = \dfrac{\overline{c/f} \cdot A}{a \cdot X_1} \qquad \ldots 6.3)$$

where $\overline{c/f}$ is the mean catch/effort obtained during a survey (or in a given stratum), A the total survey (or stratum) area and a the area swept by the trawl in one unit of effort (e.g., one hour), $X_1$ being the proportion of the fish in the path of the net which are actually retained by it ($1/X_1$ may be termed "escapement factor").

For trawlers such as those used in Southeast Asia, a value of $X_1 = 0.5$ is commonly used in survey work (Isarankura 1971; Saeger et al. 1976; SCSP 1978), and for the Gulf of Thailand at least, there is some evidence that this value is appropriate (Pauly 1980d).

For the western Indian Ocean south of the equator, it has been suggested, on the other hand, that all fish in the path of the trawl might be caught, which corresponds to $X_1 = 1$ (Gulland 1979, p. 3), a figure also suggested by Dickson (1974). The difference between these two values of $X_1$ (0.5 & 1) is difficult to resolve and attempts should be made, wherever possible, to substantiate the values of $X_1$ used in an assessment by as much corroborative evidence as possible, because the value of $X_1$ used in equation (6.3) has a very strong effect on standing stock estimates. Using $X_1 = 0.5$, for example instead of $X_1 = 1$ doubles the estimated value of B.

The surface swept by the gear in one unit of effort is computed from the expression

$$a = t \cdot V \cdot h \cdot X_2 \qquad \ldots 6.4)$$

where V is the speed of the trawler, over ground, when trawling, h is the length of the trawl's head rope (see Fig. 6.1), t is the time spent trawling and $X_2$ is a fraction equal to the effective width of the net divided by the length of the head rope.

In the Caribbean, a value of $X_2$ = 0.6 was used by Klima (1976), while in Southeast Asian waters values of $X_2$ ranging from 0.66 (Shindo 1973) to 0.4 (SCSP 1978) have been proposed, with 0.5 possibly being (for Southeast Asian waters at least) the best compromise (Pauly 1980d).

Gulland (1969) showed that

$$F = \frac{a \cdot f X_1}{A} \qquad \ldots 6.5)$$

i.e., that the fishing mortality exerted on a given stock is equal to the product of the area swept in a year by the combined activity of a fleet of trawlers (a · f) times $X_1$, divided by the total area inhabited by the stock in question. The swept area method, thus, can be used both to estimate standing stocks and fishing mortality (Example 6.2). The method has been adapted, under certain assumptions pertaining to the behavior of fish, to line fishing over coral reefs (Wheeler and Ommaney 1953; Gulland 1979).

## POPULATION SIZE FROM CATCH AND FISHING MORTALITY

Sekharan (1974), based on Beverton and Holt (1957) showed that:

$$\frac{Y}{F} = \overline{N} \cdot \overline{\overline{W}} \qquad \ldots 6.6)$$

from which one obtains

$$\frac{Y}{F} = \overline{B} \qquad \ldots 6.7)$$

where Y is the annual catch, in weight, F the instantaneous fishing mortality rate (on an annual basis), $\overline{N}$ the mean number of fish in the stock, $\overline{\overline{W}}$ their mean weight, and $\overline{B}$ the mean biomass in the course of a year.

This relationship, simple as it is, can also be used with great advantage, e.g., to estimate the standing stock of exploited coral reef fish, as suggested by Marshall (1980) on the basis of difficulties with the standard methods for estimating the biomass of coral reef fish (reviewed in Russel et al. 1978).

Equation (6.7) obviously can be rewritten

$$F = Y/\overline{B} \qquad \ldots 6.8)$$

which can be used to estimate fishing mortality from the catch and an independent estimate of $\overline{B}$, as obtained from the swept area method (see above) or by an acoustic survey. (See Example 6.3).

## POPULATION SIZE AS ESTIMATED BY LESLIE'S METHOD

When the fish population of a body of water is fished down so rapidly that the effects of recruitment, immigration and natural mortality can be neglected, we have

$$c/f = qN_o - q\Sigma_t \qquad \ldots 6.9)$$

which expresses that catch per effort (c/f) in a given time period (t) plotted against the cumulative catch up to that period ($\Sigma_t$) gives a straight line, the slope of which is an estimate of the catchability coefficient (q) and whose intercept $qN_o$, divided by q provides an estimate of $N_o$, the population size prior to its reduction by fishing (Example 6.1, Case I, Table 6.2). When the special case applies that effort is constant for the period under consideration, the c/f values can be replaced by catch values, in which case F is estimated instead of q[a] (Example 6.4, Case II, Table 6.3).

Table 6.2. Successive sample sizes of reef eels *(Kaupichthys hyoproroides)* from an isolated Bahamian patch reef.[a]

| Samples | No. of fish collected | Effort[b] |
|---------|----------------------|-----------|
| A       | 5                    | 1         |
| B       | 4                    | 1         |
| C       | 3                    | 1         |
| D + E   | 1                    | 2         |

[a]Based on data in Smith (1973, Table 5, Station I).
[b]The unit of effort is "22 fluid ounces of emulsified rotenone applied from a plastic squeeze bottle".

Table 6.3. Successive sample sizes of bluehead wrasses *(Thalassoma bifasciatum)* from an isolated Bahamian patch reef.[a]

| Samples | No. of fish collected | Effort[b] |
|---------|----------------------|-----------|
| A       | 8                    | 1         |
| B       | 5                    | 1         |
| C       | 4                    | 1         |

[a]Based on data in Smith (1973, Table 6, Station X).
[b]The unit of effort is "22 fluid ounces of emulsified rotenone applied from a plastic squeeze bottle".

---

[a]This feature of the model was pointed out by E. Ursin (pers. comm.).

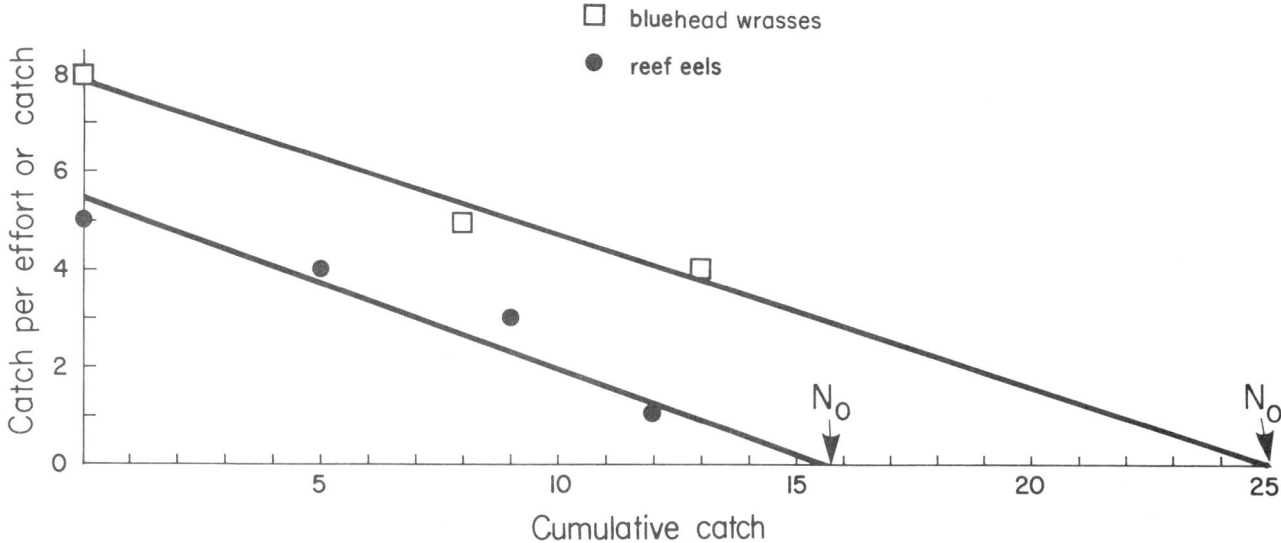

Fig. 6.1. Leslie plots for reef eels *(Kaupichthys hyoproroides)* and bluehead wrasses *(Thalassoma bifasciatum)* from an isolated Bahamian reef patch, with estimates of virgin population sizes (based on data in Tables 6.2, 6.3 and Example 6.4).

Recommended reading: For reviews of some of the voluminous literature on tagging see Ricker (1975) and Jones (1977). Kato and Yamada (1975) give application of a rather sophisticated method (Jolly-Seber) to a stock of seabreams in southern Japan, while Yap and Furtado (1980) give an application of various methods to a stock from a Malaysian river. The swept-area method is discussed in more detail in Gulland (1969). Ricker (1975) gives a discussion of Leslie's and related methods with several examples.

Suggested research topics: Use several methods to estimate population sizes on reefs, in enclosed or semi-enclosed water bodies, determine which methods give comparable results and why. Compare the population size of adjacent areas in relation to different fishing intensities.

**Petersen population estimate of tigerfish** *(Hydrocynus vittatus)* **in the Sanyati Gorge, Lake Kariba, Zimbabwe.**

EXAMPLE 6.1

Langerman (1980) conducted marking and tagging experiments on tigerfish *(Hydrocynus vittatus)* (Fam. Characinidae) in Sanyati Gorge, Lake Kariba, and concluded that under the conditions in and around that reservoir, tagging was superior to marketing with fluorescent dye. In an experiment conducted in 1979, $T = 984$ fish were tagged and released. Upon fishing one day later with a chartered vessel, 3,253 fish were caught, 68 of which bore tags. If the various assumptions involved in Petersen population estimates were met, what was the population size and its standard error?

Computation

1) Read sides 1 and 2 of Program FB 16

2) Enter data and initialize

   Keystrokes 984 ↑ 3253 ↑ 68 f a

3) Calculate population size using different formulae (see Table 6.1)

| | Keystrokes | Results | |
|---|---|---|---|
| | A | 47,073 | (N) |
| | | 5,648 | s.e.$_{(N)}$ |
| | B | 46,405 | (N) |
| | | 5,487 | s.e.$_{(N)}$ |
| | C | 46,451 | (N) |
| | | 5,680 | s.e.$_{(N)}$ |

Since sampling was direct, option D (inverse sampling) need not be considered. Note that the results using the three sets of equations give similar results; Langerman's paper also suggests that the assumptions involved in Petersen estimates were reasonably met. The population of tigerfish in the part of Sanyati Gorge for which the experiment was representative was about $46{,}600 \pm 560$.

EXAMPLE 6.2

**Use of the swept-area method to estimate demersal standing stock size and fishing mortality in San Miguel Bay, Philippines.**

A) Standing Stock

Vakily (1982) gives the following data for typical trawlers operating in San Miguel Bay, Philippines:
- Trawling speed 2 knots (conversion knots to km/h : kn · 1.83 = km/h)
- Length of headrope 17 m (headrope length/actual spread of net = 0.5 = $X_2$)
- Fraction of fish in the part of the net that are retained by the gear ($X_1$) = 0.50 (assumed)
- Mean catch per hour (in 1979-80): 33.5 kg
- Total area of San Miguel Bay = 840 km$^2$

The estimation of the surface swept during one hour (a) is thus (according to equation 6.4):

| Keystrokes | | Results |
|---|---|---|
| 2 ↑ (knots) | | |
| 1.83 X (convers. to km/h) | | |
| 0.017 X (headrope, in km) | | |
| .5 X ($X_2$) | 0.031 | (a, in km$^2$) |

The standing stock (B) is then obtained via equation (6.3) and

| Keystrokes | | Results |
|---|---|---|
| 0.0335 ↑ ($\overline{c/f}$, in tonnes) | | |
| 840 X (area of SM Bay) | | |
| X ⇌ Y (put a in display) | | |
| .5 X ÷ (use $X_1$ and finish) | 1,809.065 | (B, in tonnes) |

B) Fishing mortality

Vakily (1982) gives 5,966 km$^2$ for the surface area swept annually by all trawlers in San Miguel Bay. The fishing mortality induced by trawlers according to equation (6.5) is thus

| Keystrokes | | Results |
|---|---|---|
| 5,966 ↑ (area swept annually) | | |
| 0.5 X ($X_1$) | | |
| 840 ÷ (area of bay) | 3.551 | (F) |

EXAMPLE 6.3

**Applications of the relationships linking catch, fishing mortality and mean standing stock size.**

Case 1: Estimation of average standing stock

Sekharan (1974) gives for oil sardine *(Sardinella longiceps)* and for mackerel *(Rastrelliger kanagurta)* from southwestern Indian waters the following data (all on an annual basis):

|  | Z | M | F | Y (tonnes) |
|---|---|---|---|---|
| S. longiceps | 1.66 | 1.12 | 0.54 | 210,000 |
| R. kanagurta | 2.05 | 0.90 | 1.15 | 65,000 |

What are the mean standing stock sizes?

**Computation**

| Keystrokes | Results |
|---|---|
| 210,000 ↑ .54 ÷ | 388,889 ($\overline{B}$) (or ≈ 390,000 tonnes) |
| 65,000 ↑ 1.15 ÷ | 56,522 ($\overline{B}$) (or ≈ 57,000 tonnes) |

Case 2: Estimation of fishing mortality

Anon. (1979b, Table 12, p. 161) gives for carangid spp. *(Trachurus* spp., *Caranx rhonchus)* for 1970 to 1976 a mean annual catch of 465,000 t. Acoustic surveys conducted in the region under consideration (West African Coast from Mauritania to Liberia) provided an average carangid standing stock estimate of 4,200,000 t. What is the fishing mortality inflicted on carangids?

**Computation**

| Keystrokes | Results |
|---|---|
| 465,000 ↑ 4,200,000 ÷ | 0.11 ($\overline{F}$) |

As concluded in Anon. (1979b) "for fish of moderate longevity, this is a low but not insignificant value which suggests that stocks are lightly to moderately exploited."

**EXAMPLE 6.4** | Estimation of unfished population size ($N_o$) by means of Leslie's equation.

Case I: effort changing
Data from Table 6.2

Computation

1) Read side 1 of Program FB 17

2) Initialize and enter catch and effort data

    Keystrokes: f a 5 ↑ 1 A 4 ↑ 1 A 3 ↑ 1 A 1 ↑ 2 A

3) Calculate $r^2$, q and $N_o$

| | Keystrokes | Results | |
|---|---|---|---|
| | E | 0.88 | ($r^2$) |
| | | 5.39 | (a = q $N_o$) |
| | | −0.35 | (b = −q) |
| | | 15.46 | ($N_o$) |

Case II: effort constant
Data from Table 6.3

Computation

1) Read side 1 of Program FB 17

2) Initialize and enter catch data

    Keystrokes: f a 8 B 5 B 4 B

3) Calculate $r^2$, F and $N_o$

| | Keystrokes | Results | |
|---|---|---|---|
| | E | 0.98 | ($r^2$) |
| | | 7.86 | (a = F $N_o$) |
| | | −0.31 | (b = −F) |
| | | 25.05 | ($N_o$) |

Note the interesting result that the catchability (q) is similar with both fishes i.e., their susceptibility to rotenone is similar (see also Fig. 6.1).

# 7. Estimation of Past Population Sizes
## Using Virtual Population Analysis and Cohort Analysis

INTRODUCTION

The following four methods form an extremely powerful set of tools for the analysis of catch data from which reliable estimates of past population sizes (in numbers) and fishing mortality can be derived.

These four methods are:
— Virtual population analysis (VPA)
— Cohort analysis
— Length cohort analysis
— Length-structured VPA

Beverton and Holt (1957, p. 179) showed that the catch ($C_i$) from a population during a unit time period (i) is equal to the product of the population size at the beginning of the time period ($N_i$) times the fraction of the deaths caused by fishing, times the fraction of total deaths, or

$$C_i = \frac{F_i}{Z_i} (1 - e^{-Z_i}) \, N_i \qquad \ldots 7.1)$$

where  $F_i$ is the fishing mortality in the ith period
M is the natural mortality, generally assumed constant for all periods
and  $Z_i = F_i + M$

The version of Beverton and Holt's catch equation which has become most widely used for stock assessment purposes, however, is

$$\frac{N_{i+1}}{C_i} = \frac{Z_i \cdot e^{-Z_i}}{F_i (1 - e^{-Z_i})} \qquad \ldots 7.2)$$

also written

$$\frac{C_i}{N_{i+1}} = \frac{F_i}{Z_i} (e^{Z_i} - 1) \qquad \ldots 7.2a)$$

which is the equation in Gulland's (1965) virtual population analysis and which can be derived from (7.1) by substituting for $N_i$ the relationship

$$N_i = N_{i+1} \cdot e^{Z_i} \qquad \ldots 7.3)$$

Equation (7.2) is used with catch-at-age data from the whole of a fishery, and covering most of the life span of a given cohort* (thus VPA is used to estimate *retroactively* the size of *past* cohorts), an estimate of M and a (guessed) value of the fishing mortality that affected the oldest age group of a given cohort (terminal F, or $F_t$). The terminal fishing mortality ($F_t$) and the terminal catch ($C_t$) are used to estimate the size of the terminal population ($N_t$), either from

$$N_t = \frac{C_t \cdot Z_t}{F_t (1 - e^{-Z_t})} \qquad \ldots 7.4)$$

or from

$$N_t = C_t \cdot Z_t / F_t \qquad \ldots 7.5)$$

---

*A cohort is a group of fish born at the same time, and exposed throughout their lives to the same mortalities.

Generally, equation (7.4) is used when the cohort is not extinct past $N_t$ (and $C_t$), while equation (7.5) is used when $C_t$ includes the last remnants of a cohort (Mesnil 1980). Then, using $N_t$ as initial value of $N_{i+1}$, $F_i$ and $N_i$ values are estimated sequentially from older to younger age groups ("backward") by repeatedly solving equations (7.2) and (7.3), respectively.

Several authors have investigated the properties of equation (7.2) and its variants and their findings are summarized in Table 7.1.

Table 7.1. Review of work on the sensitivity of virtual population analysis and cohort analysis.

| Equation No. | Author of equation | Sensitivity analysis by | Property investigated | Main result(s) |
|---|---|---|---|---|
| (7.1) | Beverton and Holt (1957) based on Baranov (1918) | Jones (1961) | Convergence of F-values toward true solution | "Backward" computation ensures convergence; forward computation leads to divergence |
| (7.1) | Beverton and Holt (1957) based on Baranov (1918) | Murphy (1965), Tomlinson (1970) | Convergence of F-values toward true solution | Confirmed Jones' result |
| (7.2) | Gulland (1965) | Pope (1972) | Errors due to erroneous $F_t$ | Rapid convergence toward true F granted $F_i$'s are high |
|  |  |  | Sampling error of catches | Graph given to assess effects of sampling errors on $F_i$'s |
| (7.2) | Gulland (1965) | Agger et al. (1971) | Sampling error of catches | "Relative error of F is about half the relative error of that found in the catches" |
| (7.2) | Gulland (1965) | Agger et al. (1973) | Erroneous M value | If M is overestimated, F is generally underestimated, and conversely |
| (7.2) | Gulland (1965) | Ulltang (1977) | M varying between years, and other properties | Stock sizes will be under- or overestimated, but relative changes will be approximately correct; see original paper for other properties |
| (7.2) | Gulland (1965) | Sims (1982) | Effects of seasonal fishing | Effects not severe unless M and/or F are not very high |
| (7.11) | Pope (1972) | Pope (1972) | Choice of M | Value of M > 0.3 for one time increment (generally 1 year) should not be used |
| (7.9) | Jones (1974) | Jones (1979) | Choice of $L_\infty$ and M/K | Graphs given showing influence of $L_\infty$ and M/K on results and "critical" value of M/K determined |
| (7.9) | Jones (1974) | Sparre (1979) | Choice of M exponential body growth* emigration* difference with VPA version | The same results were obtained independently: No limitation as to value of M; differs herein from cohort analysis; results highly sensitive to length increments: with large increments, F is overestimated and stock size is underestimated |
| (7.9) | Jones (1974) | Pauly (this chapter) | Choice of M difference with VPA version (effect of length class increment) |  |

*See Sparre (1979) for this part of his results.

# DERIVATION OF A LENGTH-STRUCTURED VPA MODEL

Generalizing equation (7.2) for any time interval ($\Delta t$) gives

$$\frac{N_{i+\Delta t}}{C_i} = \frac{Z_i \cdot e^{-Z_i \cdot \Delta t}}{F_i (1-e^{-Z_i \cdot \Delta t})} \qquad \ldots 7.6)$$

or

$$C_i = N_{i + \Delta t} \frac{F_i}{Z_i} (e^{Z_i \Delta t} - 1) \qquad \ldots 7.6a)$$

with all other parameters defined as in (7.2); these equations allow for structuring catch data in terms of length, rather than time intervals.

Converting length to age requires the use of a mathematical expression of fish growth. Used here is the generalized VBGF (see Chapter 4). Thus, any age $t_1$ pertaining to a length $L_1$ can be obtained from

$$t_1 = \frac{-\ln(1 - \frac{L_1^D}{L_\infty^D})}{KD} + t_o \qquad \ldots 7.7)$$

and similarly for age $t_2$, pertaining to $L_2$. From the length-age relationships for $L_1$ and $L_2$, $\Delta t$ is obtained as the difference between $t_2$ and $t_1$, or after some rearrangement

$$\Delta t = \frac{\ln(\frac{L_\infty^D - L_1^D}{L_\infty^D - L_2^D})}{KD} \qquad \ldots 7.8)$$

which can be substituted for $\Delta t$ in equation (7.6).

Thus, given catch-at-length data from a stock with stable age distribution, equation (7.6) can be used in a fashion similar to equation (7.2) to estimate, starting from a (guessed) terminal fishing mortality (affecting the largest length group) the number of fish in the smaller size classes and the fishing mortalities affecting them.

When equation (7.6) is used in conjunction with values of $\Delta t$ that are not constant (i.e., when the $\Delta t$ values are computed from length-converted ages), the results obtained will not apply to a specific cohort of fish, but rather pertain (for a given value of M) to the population sizes (per length class) that must have existed, on the average, for the observed catch to have been produced by the estimated values of F. The method is thus analogous to Jones' length cohort analysis (Jones 1974, 1979, 1981) which, in terms of the generalized VBGF is expressed by

$$N_1 \approx (N_2 \cdot X_L + C_{1,2}) X_L \qquad \ldots 7.9)$$

where

$$X_L = \left(\frac{L_\infty^D - L_1^D}{L_\infty^D - L_2^D}\right)^{M/(2KD)} \qquad \ldots 7.10)$$

where $C_{1,2}$ is the number of fish caught in a given time period with stable age distribution with length between $L_1$ and $L_2$ and where $N_1$ and $N_2$ represent the population size (in number) with length $L_1$ and $L_2$, respectively.

Jones' length cohort analysis is particularly helpful in that it requires, in addition to the value of D (see Chapter 4), a knowledge of only 2 parameters, $L_\infty$ and the ratio M/K; the latter, as shown by Beverton and Holt (1959) tends to vary less between different groups of fish than either K or M alone (see also Chapter 5). However, a problem with Jones' method is that it is derived from the approximate "cohort analysis" of Pope (1972) i.e.,

$$N_i \approx N_{i+1} \cdot e^M + C_i \cdot e^{M/2} \qquad \ldots 7.11)$$

through generalizing for any time interval i.e.,

$$N_i \approx N_{i + \Delta t} e^{M \Delta t} + C_i e^{M \Delta t/2} \qquad \ldots 7.12)$$

Since equation (7.6), which gives precise results and the approximation in (7.9) can both be used to obtain estimates of population size and fishing mortality from the same set of catch-at-length data, equation (7.6) can be used to assess the closeness of the approximation involved in (7.9). This is done in the example in Table 7.2. As might be seen in this table, the combination of parameter values used generates a mean difference between the results obtained with Jones' method and those obtained using equation (7.6) of only 0.7% for the population estimates and 2.2% for the fishing mortality estimates.

However, regrouping the catch data in Table 7.2 into larger and larger length class intervals produces increasing differences between the fishing mortality estimates (and population estimates) obtained by the two methods (Table 7.3, Fig. 7.1), suggesting that Jones' length cohort analysis may indeed be quite sensitive to coarse groupings of the catch data.

Varying the value of natural mortality used for the analysis produces, on the other hand, virtually no additional differences between the results of the two methods, i.e., the difference remained close to 2% for M = 0.1 to M = 1.0.

## DISCUSSION OF THE LENGTH-STRUCTURED VPA MODEL

The main drawback of the length-structured VPA proposed here (equations 7.6 and 7.6a) and of length cohort analysis (equation 7.9) is the necessary assumption of a stable age distribution, which

Table 7.2. Comparison of results obtained using Jones' length cohort analysis and VPA using catch-at-length data on *Merluccius merluccius* off Senegal.

| Length (cm) | Catch[a] ('000) | Population ('000) | | | Fishing mortality (annual basis) | | |
|---|---|---|---|---|---|---|---|
| | | A | B | C (% diff.) | A | B | C (% diff.) |
| 6 | 1,823 | 98,919 | 98,238 | −0.7 | 0.040 | 0.040 | 0.0 |
| 12 | 14,463 | 84,393 | 83,801 | −0.7 | 0.386 | 0.392 | 1.3 |
| 18 | 25,227 | 59,476 | 59,010 | −0.8 | 1.066 | 1.111 | 4.2 |
| 24 | 8,134 | 27,623 | 27,428 | −0.7 | 0.647 | 0.661 | 2.2 |
| 30 | 3,889 | 15,968 | 15,849 | −0.7 | 0.491 | 0.500 | 1.8 |
| 36 | 2,959 | 9,861 | 9,782 | −0.8 | 0.592 | 0.605 | 2.4 |
| 42 | 1,871 | 5,501 | 5,455 | −0.8 | 0.647 | 0.666 | 3.1 |
| 48 | 653 | 2,819 | 2,797 | −0.8 | 0.385 | 0.392 | 1.8 |
| 54 | 322 | 1,691 | 1,678 | −0.8 | 0.288 | 0.293 | 1.7 |
| 60 | 228 | 1,057 | 1,048 | −0.9 | 0.307 | 0.313 | 1.6 |
| 66 | 181 | 621 | 616 | −0.8 | 0.401 | 0.412 | 2.7 |
| 72 | 96 | 314 | 312 | −0.6 | 0.389 | 0.399 | 2.6 |
| 78 | 16 | 149 | 148 | 0.0 | 0.110 | 0.111 | 0.9 |
| 84 ($L_{ter}$) | 46 ($C_t$) | 92 ($N_t$) | 92 ($N_t$) | — | 0.280 ($F_t$) | 0.280 ($F_t$) | — |

[a]From Table 6 in Anon. (1978b) who also provided (for D = 1): $L_\infty$ = 130 cm, K = 0.1 and M = 0.28.

A = Jones' length cohort analysis.
B = New method (VPA with length-at-age data).
C = (B/A − 1) · 100 = C (% diff.).

Table 7.3. Comparison of results using Jones' length cohort analysis (A) and length-structured VPA (B) (24-cm classes) (see also Table 7.2).

| Length (cm) | Catch ('000) | Population size A | B | % diff. | Fishing mortality A | B | % diff. |
|---|---|---|---|---|---|---|---|
| 12 | 51,713 | 93,010 | 84,379 | −9.3 | 0.487 | 0.646 | 32.6 |
| 36 | 5,805 | 11,592 | 10,265 | −11.4 | 0.357 | 0.482 | 35.0 |
| 60 | 521 | 1,236 | 1,087 | −12.1 | 0.234 | 0.308 | 31.6 |
| 84 | 46 ($L_{ter}$) | 92 ($N_t$) | 92 ($N_t$) | — | 0.280 ($F_t$) | 0.280 ($F_t$) | — |
| >84 | — | — | — | — | — | — | $\bar{x}$ = 33.1 |

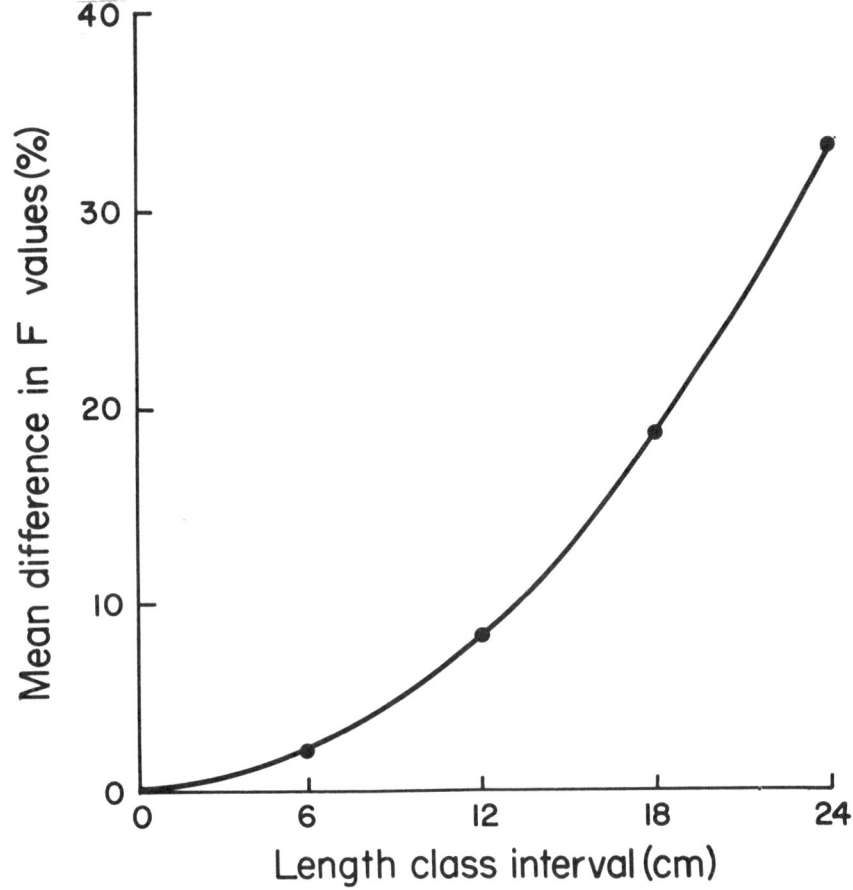

Fig. 7.1. Relationship between the length class interval in which catch data are grouped and the percentage difference between the results obtained using Jones' length cohort analysis and length-structured VPA. The calculation of the percentage difference is illustrated in Tables 7.2 and 7.3, which also document two of the four points plotted in this figure.

is not required in age-structured VPA. However, a number of methods have become widely accepted and used for stock assessment which rest on the same assumption of a stable age distribution, such as the estimation of total mortality from catch curves or from the mean length of fish in catch samples (see Chapter 5). As in the case of the procedure recommended for use with the above methods, a stable age distribution can be simulated in the case of length-structured VPA or length cohort analysis by averaging catch data for a length of time during which recruitment and fishing mortality can be assumed to have been constant.

Jones' length cohort analysis has the following advantages over the new method proposed here:
— it does not require separate estimates of K and M, but only of the ratio M/K, and
— it provides direct solutions, i.e., the solution does not need to be obtained iteratively, as in the case of solutions to (7.6)

On the other hand, Jones' method appears quite sensitive to coarse grouping of the catch data, a feature which may limit the applicability of the method where it may be most needed, e.g., when working with catch statistics of commercially graded penaeid shrimps (see Jones and Van Zalinge 1981).

## APPLICATIONS OF AGE-STRUCTURED VPA AND COHORT ANALYSIS

Following are applications of the four methods in Table 7.4. Example 7.1, based on the data in Table 7.5, presents an application of VPA to Moroccan sardines (see also Fig. 7.2). Example 7.2, based on the data in Table 7.6, presents an application of cohort analysis to the Peruvian anchoveta. As might be seen from Table 7.6, the estimates of fishing mortality in young fish obtained by cohort analysis (and hence, by VPA) are virtually independent of the first guess of terminal mortality. This property is most useful, and is one of the main reasons why these methods have become so popular, at least around the North Atlantic.

Table 7.4. Some properties of four methods for the analysis of sequential catch data.

| data requirement \ solution | iterative, but precise | direct, but approximate |
|---|---|---|
| catch-at-age data (single cohort) | VPA<br>Murphy (1965)<br>Gulland (1965) | Pope's cohort analysis (1972) |
| catch-at-length data (stable age distribution) | length-structured VPA | Jones' length cohort analysis (1974) |

## APPLICATION OF LENGTH COHORT ANALYSIS AND LENGTH-STRUCTURED VPA

Among the various methods presented in this manual, length cohort analysis and length-structured VPA may potentially be the most useful for tropical fisheries. However, to obtain population sizes and fishing mortalities based on these methods, it is necessary to have good catch-at-length data.

Converting catch in weight to catch-at-length data is rather straightforward, given length-frequency data representative of the catch, and the parameters of the length-weight relationship in the stock in question. A step-by-step approach to this conversion is given in Example 7.3. Once catch-at-length data are obtained, either length cohort analysis or length-structured VPA can be applied, as illustrated in Examples 7.4 and 7.5 and Table 7.7.

Table 7.5. Estimation by means of Gulland's virtual population analysis of the population (in numbers) and the fishing mortality (F) of a cohort of sardines *(Sardina pilchardus)* caught off Morocco.[a]

| Year of capture | Trimester | Catch | Population | F (per trimester) | Annual F |
|---|---|---|---|---|---|
| 1973 | 3 | 15,624 | 14,382,198 | 0.00 | |
| | 4 | 139,836 | 11,761,034 | 0.01 | |
| 1974 | 1 | 66,207 | 9,502,830 | 0.01 | |
| | 2 | 33,191 | 7,720,459 | 0.00 | ≈ 0.18 (1974) |
| | 3 | 514,256 | 6,290,998 | 0.09 | |
| | 4 | 319,612 | 4,686,819 | 0.08 | |
| 1975 | 1 | 106,583 | 3,548,903 | 0.03 | |
| | 2 | 383,842 | 2,809,370 | 0.16 | ≈ 0.75 (1975) |
| | 3 | 235,246 | 1,954,320 | 0.14 | |
| | 4 | 434,354 | 1,388,058 | 0.42 | |
| 1976 | 1 | 37,926 | 746,801 | 0.06 | |
| | 2 | 39,819 | 577,202 | 0.08 | ≈ 0.65 (1976) |
| | 3 | 118,049 | 436,651 | 0.35 | |
| | 4 | 34,226 | 251,483 | 0.16 | |
| 1977 | 1 | 5,225 | 175,063 | 0.03 | |
| | 2 | 7,859 | 138,612 | 0.06 | |
| | 3 | 17,538 ($C_t$) | 106,394 ($N_t$) | 0.20 ($F_t$) | |

[a] From Anon. (1978a, Table 1, p. 33) who also suggests values of M = 0.8 (per year, hence 0.2 per trimester) and of $F_t$ = 0.8 (per year, hence 0.2 per trimester).

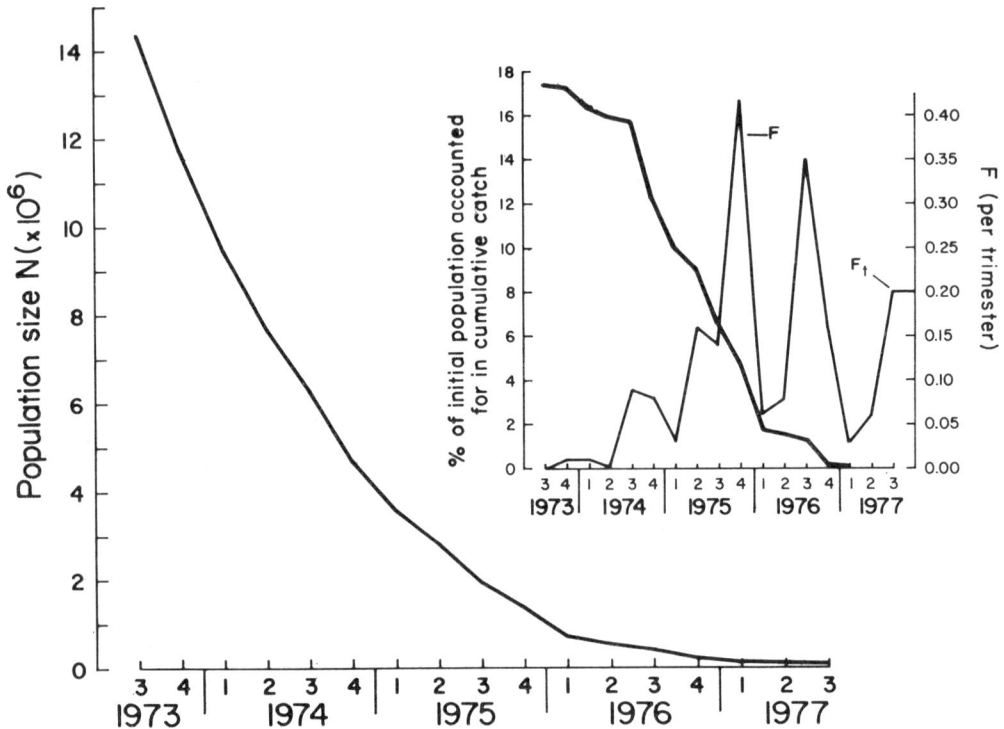

Fig. 7.2. Population sizes of a cohort of Moroccan sardines *(Sardina pilchardus)* as estimated by (age-structured) virtual population analysis (based on data in Table 7.5 and Example 7.1).

Table 7.6. Estimation of the population size in numbers (N) and fishing mortality (F) of a cohort of Peruvian anchovy *(Engraulis ringens)* by means of Pope's cohort analysis.

| Time of capture Year | Months | Catch[a] (in millions of individuals) | $N^b$ (in millions) | $F^c$ (per 2 months) | $F^d$ (per 2 months) | $F^e$ (per 2 months) |
|---|---|---|---|---|---|---|
| 1968 | Nov-Dec | 8,230 | 1,858,412 | 0.00 | 0.00 | 0.00 |
| 1969 | Jan-Feb | 120,060 | 1,514,092 | 0.09 | 0.09 | 0.09 |
|  | Mar-Apr | 168,580 | 1,130,999 | 0.18 | 0.18 | 0.18 |
|  | May-June | 21,380 | 773,446 | 0.03 | 0.03 | 0.03 |
|  | Jul-Aug | 0 | 613,899 | 0.00 | 0.00 | 0.00 |
|  | Sep-Oct | 21,860 | 502,618 | 0.05 | 0.05 | 0.05 |
|  | Nov-Dec | 7,410 | 391,729 | 0.02 | 0.02 | 0.02 |
| 1970 | Jan-Feb | 7,390 | 314,016 | 0.03 | 0.03 | 0.03 |
|  | Mar-Apr | 15,560 | 250,408 | 0.07 | 0.07 | 0.07 |
|  | May-June | 6,420 | 190,937 | 0.04 | 0.04 | 0.04 |
|  | Jul-Aug | 0 | 150,517 | 0.00 | 0.00 | 0.00 |
|  | Sep-Oct | 43,310 | 123,233 | 0.49 | 0.47 | 0.50 |
|  | Nov-Dec | 27,220 | 61,706 | 0.67 | 0.62 | 0.69 |
| 1971 | Jan-Feb | 0 | 25,891 | 0.00 | 0.00 | 0.00 |
|  | Mar-Apr | 11,160 | 21,198 | 0.87 | 0.75 | 0.94 |
|  | May-June | 1,290 | 7,257 | 0.22 | 0.17 | 0.25 |
|  | Jul-Aug | 0 | 4,775 | 0.00 | 0.00 | 0.00 |
|  | Sep-Oct | 1,020 | 3,909 | 0.34 | 0.25 | 0.41 |
|  | Nov-Dec | 1,160 | 2,278 | 0.83 | 0.51 | 1.21 |
| 1972 | Jan-Feb | 0 | 815 | 0.00 | 0.00 | 0.00 |
|  | Mar-Apr | 110 $C_t$ | $N_t$ = 667 | $F_t$ = 0.20 | $F_t$ = 0.10 | $F_t$ = 0.40 |

[a] Data adapted from Table 8.6 of Ricker (1975). Note that both F and M refer to a 2-month period and should be multiplied by 6 to obtain annual rates (e.g., M = 0.2 = 1.2/6).

[b] Rounded figures. Actual computation (based on $F_t$ = 0.20) used 10 significant digits.

[c] Assuming $F_t$ = 0.20 and M = 0.20, which provide, with equation (7.2) the estimate of $N_t$ = 667.

[d] Assuming $F_t$ = 0.10 and M = 0.20, population estimates omitted. Note convergence toward the F-values obtained by using $F_t$ = 0.20.

[e] Assuming $F_t$ = 0.40 and M = 0.20, population estimates omitted. Note convergence toward the F-values obtained by using $F_t$ = 0.20 or $F_t$ = 0.10.

Unfortunately, the catch and landing data-collection systems of most tropical countries are not geared toward collecting catch and landing data *and* length-frequency data representative of that catch, with the result that the methods outlined here generally cannot be applied to those fisheries. Yet these methods are extremely well-suited for use in tropical fisheries, where fishing is often conducted with a multitude of gears, the number and sampling properties of which are difficult to assess. Using such methods, it is thus possible to assess the impact on the fish themselves of all those gears in the form of values of F which can be used to state whether too many or not enough fish of certain sizes are being captured by the fishery as a whole or segments of it.

Finally, another important property of VPA and related methods is that the resulting population estimates of young (small) fish are estimates of absolute recruitment. Recruitment, as discussed in more detail in Chapter 9, is generally extremely difficult to estimate although it is an extremely important parameter.

It seems thus appropriate to stress here the need for fishery biologists working in tropical countries to help their fisheries department set up a catch reporting system which—at least for major fisheries—will allow for catch-at-length, and later catch-at-age data to emerge.

Table 7.7. Estimation of population size and exploitation rate for a West African stock of hake *(Merluccius merluccius)* based on Jones' length cohort analysis.[a]

| Length (in cm) | Catch (in thousands) | Population (in thousands) | Exploitation rate (F/Z) | Annual Z | Annual F |
|---|---|---|---|---|---|
| 6 | 1,823 | 98,919 | 0.13 | 0.32 | 0.04 |
| 12 | 14,463 | 84,393 | 0.58 | 0.67 | 0.39 |
| 18 | 25,227 | 59,476 | 0.79 | 1.35 | 1.07 |
| 24 | 8,134 | 27,623 | 0.70 | 0.93 | 0.65 |
| 30 | 3,889 | 15,968 | 0.64 | 0.77 | 0.49 |
| 36 | 2,959 | 9,861 | 0.68 | 0.87 | 0.59 |
| 42 | 1,871 | 5,501 | 0.70 | 0.93 | 0.65 |
| 48 | 653 | 2,819 | 0.58 | 0.67 | 0.39 |
| 54 | 322 | 1,691 | 0.51 | 0.57 | 0.29 |
| 60 | 228 | 1,057 | 0.52 | 0.59 | 0.31 |
| 66 | 181 | 621 | 0.59 | 0.68 | 0.40 |
| 72 | 96 | 314 | 0.58 | 0.67 | 0.39 |
| 78 | 16 | 149 | 0.28 | 0.39 | 0.11 |
| 84 ($L_{ter}$) | 46 ($C_t$) | 92 ($N_t$) | 0.50 ($E_t$) | (0.56) | (0.28) |

[a]The catch-at-length data are from Anon. (1978b, Table 6, p. 78) from which (p. 17) the parameter values $L_\infty$ = 130, K = 0.10, M = 0.28, M/KD = 2.8 and D = 1 also stem. The results (population estimates and E-values) presented here differ from those in Anon. (1978b) both because of the different $E_t$ used, and because of various inconsistencies in the original analysis.

Recommended reading: The literature on VPA and cohort analysis is growing rapidly as far as applications are concerned. However, both Gulland (1965)* and Jones (1974) are technically unpublished papers which are rather hard to get, while Ricker's (1975) discussion of VPA and cohort analysis is rather opaque. Best is to get Pope (1972)* for both VPA and cohort analysis, and the recent manual of Jones (1981) or Jones and van Zalinge (1981) for length cohort analysis. For those who understand French, the best introduction to (age-structured) VPA and cohort analysis will be that of Mesnil (1980).

Suggested research topics: Convert catch data in weight to catch-at-length data using the method outlined in Example 7.3, and apply these data to either length cohort analysis or length-structured VPA. Then using the method of Jones (1979), assess the impact of a change in fishing mortality, mesh size or both. Use the results to assess the relative impact of several fisheries exploiting the same stock (e.g., a small-scale inshore fishery and a large-scale offshore fishery).

---

*Gulland (1965) and Pope (1972) have been reprinted and included in the reader recently edited by Cushing (1983).

**EXAMPLE 7.1**

**Population sizes and fishing mortality of Moroccan sardines** *(Sardina pilchardus)* **as determined by Gulland's virtual population analysis.**

Data: catch-at-age data of Table 7.5

Computation

1) Read sides 1 and 2 of Program FB 18.

2) Initialize, enter M, terminal fishing mortality and terminal catch.

   Keystrokes: .0001 STO O .2 ↑ .2 ↑ 17538 f a. This results in $N_t$ = 106394.09

3) Enter the catch from the period immediately preceding that during which the terminal catch was made.

|  | Keystrokes | Results |  |
|---|---|---|---|
|  | 7859 A | 0.06 | $(F_i)$ |
|  |  | 138611.82 | $(N_i)$ |
| now enter the next earlier catch | 5225 A | 0.03 | $(F_i)$ |
|  |  | 175062.55 | $(N_i)$ |
| and so on | ..... | ....... |  |
| until you arrive at | 15624 A | 0.00 | $(F_i)$ |
|  |  | 14382197.51 | $(N_i)$ |

The results of virtual population analysis (VPA) should be recorded in a manner similar to that used for Table 7.5.

**EXAMPLE 7.2**  Population sizes and fishing mortality of Peruvian anchoveta *(Engraulis ringens)* as determined by Pope's cohort analysis.

---

Data: Catch-at-age data of Table 7.6

Computation

1) Read sides 1 and 2 of Program FB 18.

2) Initialize, enter M and estimate the terminal population, with a terminal catch of 110 million fish and a terminal F of 0.2.

   Keystrokes: .0001 STO O .2 ↑ .2 ↑ 110 f a  This results in $N_t$ = 667.31.

3) Enter the catch from the period immediately preceding that during which the terminal catch was made.

|  | Keystrokes | Results |  |
|---|---|---|---|
|  | 0 B | 0.000 | ($F_i$) |
|  |  | 815.51 | ($N_i$) |
| now enter the next earlier catch | 1160 B | 0.83 | ($F_i$) |
|  |  | 227.51 | ($N_i$) |
| and so on | ..... |  |  |
| until you arrive at | 8230 B | 0.00 | ($F_i$) |
|  |  | 1858412.26 | ($N_i$) |

The cohort analysis, which should be recorded in a manner similar to Table 7.6 is now essentially complete. Its results (the $F_i$ and $N_i$ values) can be used to assess the stock directly (e.g., was the fishing mortality too high?) or may be used as input in other models (e.g., those requiring estimates of absolute recruitment). (Alternatively, $F_i$ values considered more reasonable than the first $F_t$ can be used as new $F_t$ and the analysis run again.)

**EXAMPLE 7.3**

**Conversion of length-frequency data to catch-at-length data, given data on bulk catch and a length-weight relationship.**

Data from Table 5.8. We shall assume that the length-weight relationship of *Glossogobius giurus* is described by $W = 0.01 L^3$, where W is expressed in g and L in cm.

Computation

1) Read sides 1 and 2 of Program FB 20.

2) Enter the parameters a and b of L/W relationship.

   Keystrokes: .01 ↑ 3 f b

3) Then enter lower limit of smallest length class considered, and width of length class (see Table 5.8, August sample).

   Keystrokes: 4 ↑ 2 f c

4) Now enter frequencies, successively

   Keystrokes: 1 C 138 C 153 C 49 C 9 C

   (The numbers appearing after each entry are the mean weights of the fish in each length class)

5) Compute total weight of sample

   | Keystroke | Results | |
   |---|---|---|
   | E | 2530 | (weight of sample) |
   |   | 7.23 | (mean fish weight) |

6) Now assume 100 kg (= 100,000 g) of *Glossogobius giurus* had been caught in August. This would imply, given that the length-frequency sample is representative of the catch, that the equivalent of this sample has been caught 100,000/2,530 = *39.53 times*; thus each of the frequency in the length-frequency sample must be multiplied by the raising factor 39.53. The resulting numbers are catch-at-length data, as used in length-cohort analysis and length-structured VPA.

**EXAMPLE 7.4** | **Population sizes and exploitation rate of West African hake** *(Merluccius merluccius)* **as determined by Jones' length cohort analysis.**

Data: Catch-at-length data of Table 7.7

Computation

1) Read side 1 of Program FB 19.

2) Enter parameters needed, initialize and calculate $N_t$.

    Keystrokes: 130 STOA 2.8 ↑ 1 f b 84 ↑ 6 f c .5 ↑ 46 f d      Result: 92 ($N_t$)

3) Enter the catch for the length interval immediately preceding that to which $C_t$ refers.

|  | Keystrokes | Results |  |
|---|---|---|---|
|  | 16 A | 148.68 | ($N_i$) |
|  |  | 0.28 | ($E_i$) |
| now enter the catch pertaining to the next smaller length class | 96 A | 313.71 | ($N_i$) |
|  |  | 0.58 | ($E_i$) |
| and so on | .... | ...... |  |
| until you arrive at | 1823 A | 98919.30 | ($N_i$) |
|  |  | 0.13 | ($E_i$) |

Unless you have a value of M (rather than just a value of M/KD), the length cohort analysis is now completed.

4) If a value of M is available, values of Z and F (both on an annual basis) can be estimated by performing

|  | Keystrokes | Results |  |
|---|---|---|---|
| store M | .28 STO2 |  |  |
| estimate Z | .5 B | 0.56 | (Z) |
| and F |  | 0.28 | (F) |
| corresponding to | .28 B | 0.39 | (Z) |
| the values of E |  | 0.11 | (F) |
|  | etc. (see Table 7.3) |  |  |

It must be realized that as opposed to VPA and cohort analysis performed on catch-at-age data, length "cohort" analysis does not estimate population numbers pertaining to a specific cohort. Rather, the "population" estimates are the number needed to account for the catch at each size.

**Population sizes and fishing mortality of West African hake as determined by length-structured VPA.**   EXAMPLE 7.5

Data: catch-at-length data of Table 7.7 (the data are the same as those in Table 7.2, which also gives the source for $L_\infty$ = 130 cm, K = 0.10, D = 1 and M = 0.28).

Computation

1) Read sides 1 and 2 of Program FB 20.

2) Enter parameters needed:

   Keystrokes: 130 STO A .1 STO C 1 STO D .28 STO 2 84 STOI 6 STO E 10 ↑ 4 CHS $Y^X$ STO O

3) Estimate terminal population:

|  | Keystrokes | Results |  |
|---|---|---|---|
| enter $F_t$ | .28 ↑ |  |  |
| and $C_t$ | 46 f a | 92 | ($N_t$) |
| 4) Run VPA: | 16 A | 148.499 | (F) |
|  |  | 0.111 | (N) |
|  | 96 A | 311.813 | (F) |
|  |  | 0.399 | (N) |
|  | etc. |  |  |
| until | 1823 A | 98238... | (N) |
|  |  | 0.040 | (F) |

Note that the results are almost the same as those obtained with Jones' length cohort analysis. (See also Table 7.2.)

# 8. Yield-Per-Recruit Assessment

## INTRODUCTION

This chapter contains some of the most horrible-looking equations used in fish population dynamics, and an attempt to explain how these equations are derived would certainly deter all but the most enthusiastic readers. Thus, rather than derive any of the equations included in this chapter, I will simply present them, and hope that they will gradually become familiar, especially after frequent use and consulting the original literature.

A new concept needs to be introduced at this stage, that of the "recruit". Although the definition may vary between authors, we may here visualize recruits as 1) fully metamorphosed young fish, 2) fish whose growth is described adequately by some form of the VBGF, 3) fish whose instantaneous rate of natural mortality is similar to that of the adults, and 4) fish which occur at (or swim into) the fishing ground(s). Such recruits have an average age $t_r$, an average length $L_r$ and an average weight $W_r$. Upon reaching the age $t_r$, the recruits may be caught immediately, in which case the mean age at first capture ($t_c$) is equal to the age at recruitment ($t_c = t_r$). Alternatively, the recruits may be caught at a more advanced age (and a correspondingly larger size, $L_c$ and $W_c$). In such case, the number of recruits actually entering the fishery ($R_c$) will be less than the initial number of recruits ($R_r$), or

$$R_c = R_r \cdot e^{-M(t_c - t_r)} \qquad \ldots 8.1)$$

Now, there is, for each combination of $t_c$ and F values, a yield per recruit (Y/R = catch in weight, per recruit) the value of which can be estimated from various equations whose exact form depends on the model used to describe the growth of the fish. In the following paragraphs, equations for the estimation of Y/R will be given for various forms of the VBGF, i.e.,

Case I: 
$$W_t = W_\infty (1 - e^{-K(t - t_o)})^3 \qquad \ldots 8.2)$$

or special VBGF, as based on conversion from length using the isometric length-weight relationship

$$W = (c.f./100)L^3 \qquad \ldots 8.3)$$

Case II:
$$W_t = W_\infty (1 - e^{-K(t - t_o)})^b \qquad \ldots 8.4)$$

which is a form of the special VBGF where the exponent (b) of the length-weight relationship is allowed to take values other than 3, i.e.,

$$W = a \cdot L^b, b \neq 3 \qquad \ldots 8.5)$$

Case III:
$$W_t = W_\infty (1 - e^{-KD(3/b)(t - t_o)})^{b/D} \qquad \ldots 8.6)$$

the generalized VBGF for growth in weight.

# ESTIMATION OF YIELD PER RECRUIT

## Case I

Case I is that of Beverton and Holt (1957) for computing yield per recruit. The equation they proposed for this purpose is:

$$Y/R_r = F \cdot e^{-Mr_2} W_\infty \left\{ \frac{1-e^{-Zr_3}}{Z} - \frac{3e^{-Kr_1}(1-e^{-(Z+K)r_3})}{Z+K} \right.$$
$$\left. + \frac{3e^{-2Kr_1}(1-e^{-(Z+2K)r_3})}{Z+2K} - \frac{e^{-3Kr_1}(1-e^{-(Z+3K)r_3})}{Z+3K} \right\} \quad \ldots 8.7)$$

where  $Z = F + M$
$r_1 = t_c - t_o$
$r_2 = t_c - t_r$
$r_3 = t_{max} - t_c$

with $W_\infty$, K and $t_o$ being growth parameters, $t_c$ the mean age at first capture, $t_r$ the mean age at recruitment and $t_{max}$ "the maximum age of significant contribution to the fishery" or more simply, the longevity of the fish in question (see Ricker 1975).

The effect of the exact value of $t_{max}$ is generally very small, and equation (8.7) can be considerably simplified by setting $t_{max} = \infty$, in which case equation (8.7) becomes

$$Y/R_r = F \cdot e^{-Mr_2} W_\infty \left\{ \frac{1}{Z} - \frac{3e^{-Kr_1}}{Z+K} + \frac{3e^{-2Kr_1}}{Z+2K} - \frac{e^{-3Kr_1}}{Z+3K} \right\} \quad \ldots 8.8)$$

in which all other parameters are defined as in equation (8.7).

Both equations (8.7) and (8.8) can be used to assess the effect of different values of $t_c$ (corresponding, e.g., to a given mesh size) and values of F (corresponding to a certain amount of fishing effort) on the yield per recruit (Examples 8.1 and 8.2). The results of such computations are generally presented in the form of "yield curves", as in Fig. 8.1, from which the effect of increasing mesh size (e.g., from a size generating $t_c = 0.2$ yr to a size generating $t_c = 0.3$ yr) can be assessed.

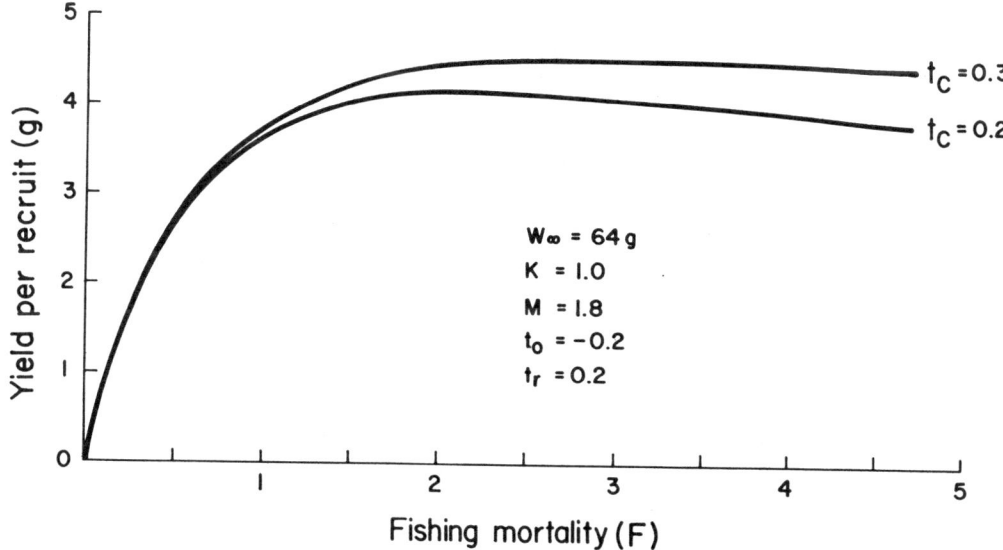

Fig. 8.1. Yield per recruit as a function of fishing mortality for the slipmouth *(Leiognathus splendens)* for two values of mean age at first capture (based on Example 8.1).

Another, more elaborate form of presenting the results of a yield-per-recruit analysis is the "yield-isopleth diagram", which shows the response of yield per recuit to both $t_c$ and F over a wide range of both parameters, to allow the best selection of mesh size for given F, or a best F for a given mesh size (see Fig. 8.2). Program FB 21 can be used for this purpose.

Equation (8.7) requires the estimation of six constants (in addition to $t_c$ and F which are used as variables) while equation (8.8) requires five constants.

In 1964, Beverton and Holt presented a modified version of their yield equation which requires only three input parameters, M/K, c (= $L_c/L_\infty$) and E (= F/Z) and which has the form

$$Y'/R_r = E(1-c)^{M/K} \cdot \left\{ 1 - \frac{3(1-c)}{1 + \frac{(1-E)}{(M/K)}} + \frac{3(1-c)^2}{1 + \frac{2(1-E)}{(M/K)}} - \frac{(1-c)^3}{1 + \frac{3(1-E)}{(M/K)}} \right\} \quad \ldots 8.9)$$

Here, however, it is not a yield per recruit in units of weight that is estimated, but something ($Y'/R_r$) proportional to it; this doesn't really matter because the absolute number of recruits ($R_r$) is not known anyway. Management advice is most often based on relative yield (see Example 8.3 and Fig. 8.3). Values of $Y'/R_r$ have been tabulated by Beverton and Holt (1964) for a wide range of M/K, c and E values. Given appropriate inputs, program FB 21 provides the same values as those in Beverton and Holt (1964), whose paper, however, should still be consulted for more details.

[The relationship between ordinary $Y/R_r$ (as given in Equation (8.8)) and $Y'/R_r$ is given by $Y/R_r = (Y'/R_r) \cdot (W_\infty \cdot \exp - M(t_r - t_o))$].

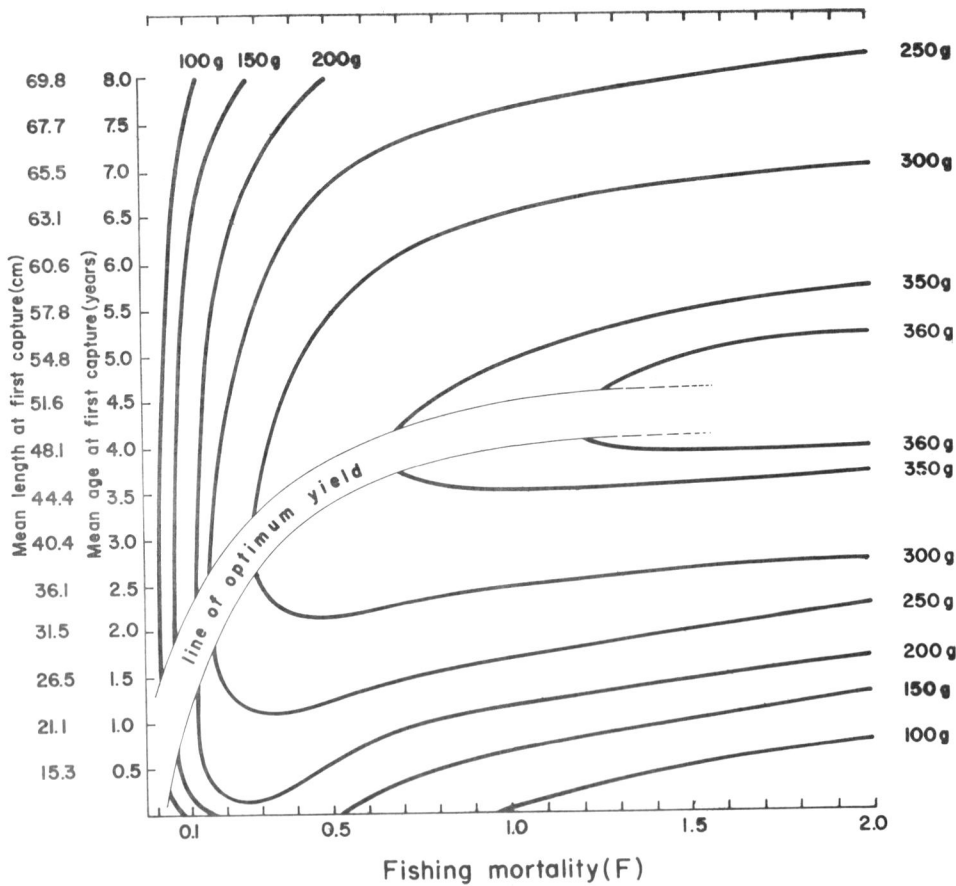

Fig. 8.2. Yield isopleth diagram for the snapper *(Lutjanus sanguineus)* of the South China Sea (from Pauly 1979b; see Example 8.2).

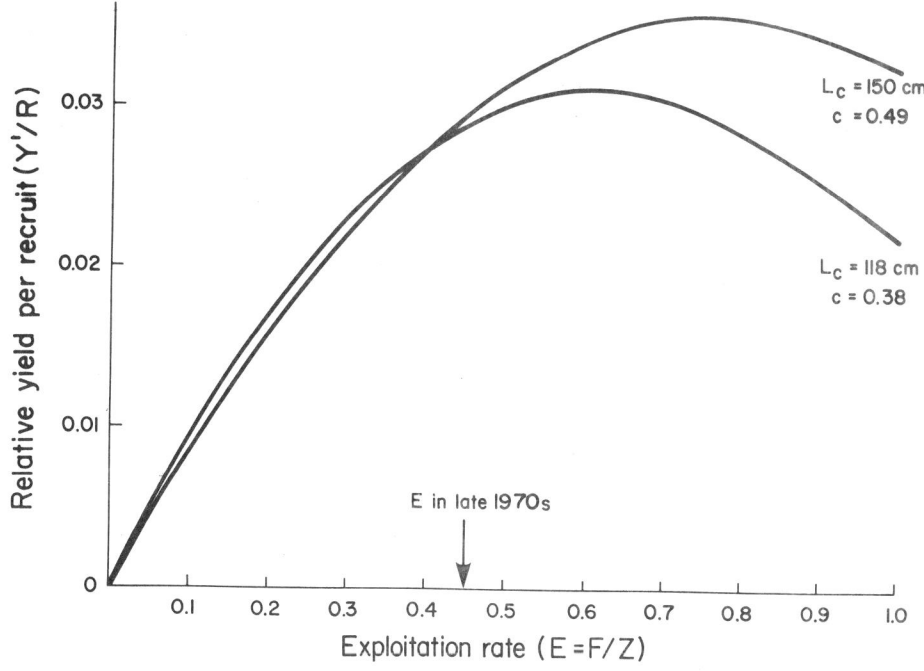

Fig. 8.3. Stock assessment of the swordfish *(Xiphias gladius)* off Florida, based on the **relative yield-per-recruit concept (based on Example 8.3).**

Case II

All three equations given above assume that growth in weight is isometric. This is often not the case and the value of b in the length-weight relationship generally ranges between 2.5 and 3.5 (see Chapter 2). The weight-at-age data of Table 8.1 were constructed to represent such a case, with b = 3.3.

Two methods are available to use the yield equations given above, even when growth is allometric.

The first of these methods simply consists of proceeding as if the length-weight relationship were isometric, i.e., of calculating a mean condition factor (which assumes b = 3) from the length-weight data at hand, then to use this mean condition factor to convert $L_\infty$ to $W_\infty$. This method stems from Beverton and Holt (1957).

[For the data of Table 8.1, a mean condition factor of 1.887 is obtained which can be used to convert the value of $L_\infty$ = 186.5 cm obtained from a Ford-Walford Plot to a value of $W_\infty$ = 122.6 kg

Table 8.1. Growth data of a hypothetical tuna reaching 146.5 cm ($L_{max}$) and 60 kg ($W_{max}$).[a]

| Age (years) | FL (cm) | Weight (g) |
|---|---|---|
| 1 | 35 | 648 |
| 2 | 55 | 2,879 |
| 3 | 75 | 8,011 |
| 4 | 90 | 14,622 |
| 5 | 105 | 24,318 |
| 6 | 115 | 32,833 |

[a]Adapted from the data in Table 4.4, using the length-weight relationship $W = 0.0052L^{3.3}$. Note that $W_{max}$ = 60,000 g corresponds to a value of D = 0.47. The mean c.f. obtained from the length-weight data is 1.887. M is set at 0.3 and $t_{max} = \infty$.

(Table 8.2). The value of K is that provided by the same Ford-Walford plot, while the value of $t_o$ is the mean of six estimates of $t_o$ obtained by solving the growth equation for that parameter (by means of Program FB 9). Then the growth parameters are used to estimate $t_c$ from $W_c$, $t_c$ is set equal to $t_r$, and equation (8.8) is used to estimate $Y/R_r$ (see Table 8.2 and Fig. 8.4).]

The second of these methods consists of calculating growth parameters directly from the weight data, and setting b = 3 (this can be done easily with the programs presented in Chapter 4). This results in values of K and $t_o$ different from those that would have been obtained by computing the growth parameters from length data (see Table 8.2). However, once these parameter values have been derived from b = 3, any of the three equations given above can be used to estimate yield per recruit (see Table 8.2 and Fig. 8.4). This method was suggested by Paulik and Gales (1964).

Table 8.2. Parameter values of different growth equations based on the data of Table 8.1 for use in yield-per-recruit analysis. ($W_\infty$ and K values stem from Ford-Walford plots.)

| Method | D | $W_\infty$ (kg) | K | $t_o$ [a] | b | $t_c$ [b] |
|---|---|---|---|---|---|---|
| Beverton and Holt (1957) | 1 | 122.60 | 0.150 | −0.535 | 3 | 2.28 |
| Paulik and Gales (1964) | 1 | 194.36 | 0.129 | −0.265 | 3 | 2.45 |
| Jones (1957) | 1 | 162.25 | 0.150 | −0.795 | 3.3 | 2.35 |
| Generalized VBGF | 0.47 | 85.95 | 0.582 | −2.035 | 3.3 | 2.39 |

[a] Obtained by solving the VBGF with the empirical size and age values in Table 8.1 and the corresponding set of asymptotic size, K, b and D values and Program FB 9, then by taking the mean of the resulting 6 estimates of $t_o$.

[b] Based on a mean weight at first capture $W_c$ = 5 kg.

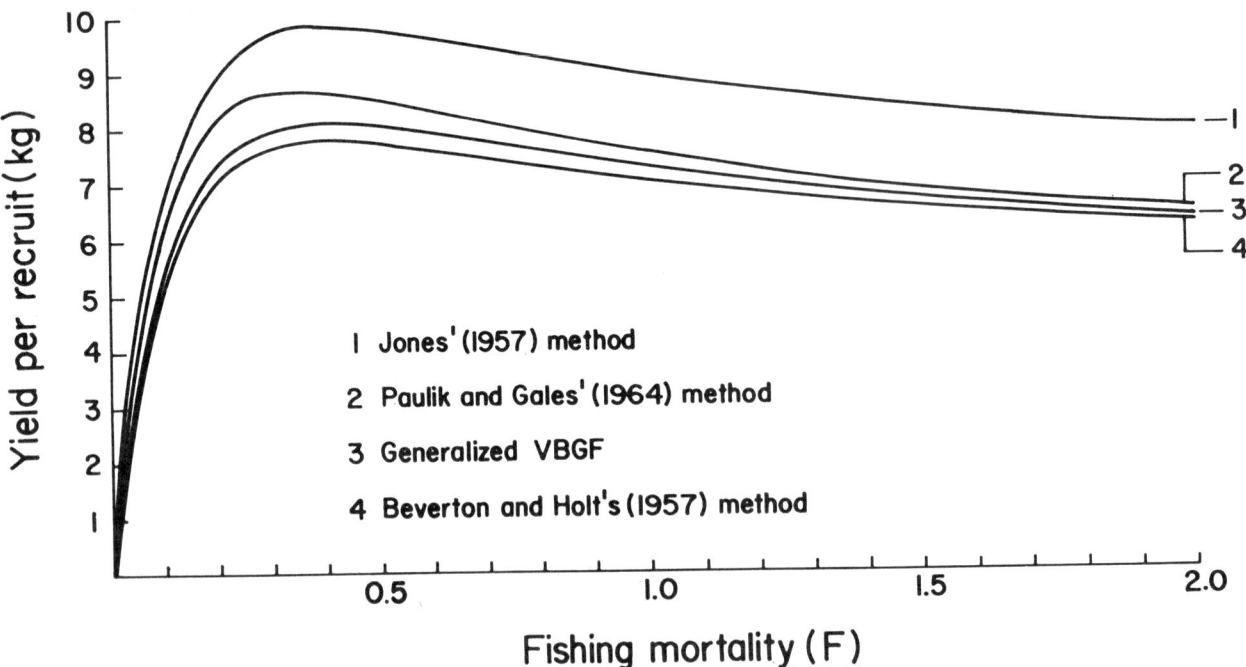

Fig. 8.4. Comparison of yield curves based on different methods to compensate for allometry when performing a yield-per-recruit analysis (see Table 8.2, Example 8.4 and text).

Another method for dealing with allometry in yield-per-recruit computations is the use of the incomplete $\beta$-function, as proposed by Jones (1957).

Here, the yield per recruit, when $t_{max} = \infty$, is given by

$$Y/R_r = F/K \cdot e^{Zr_1 - Mr_2} W_\infty \{\beta [X, P, Q]\} \qquad \ldots 8.10)$$

where  $X = e^{-Kr_1}$
       $P = Z/K$
       $Q = b + 1$ (b being the length/weight exponent),
and    $\beta$ = being the symbol of the incomplete beta function
with   $r_1 = t_c - t_o$
and    $r_2 = t_c - t_r$

Tables of the incomplete $\beta$-function have been presented by Wilimovsky and Wicklund (1963); these tables are not needed here because Program FB 22 estimates the appropriate values of the incomplete $\beta$-function (see Example 8.4, Fig. 8.4 and text below).

Case III

The incomplete $\beta$-function, besides allowing for the integration of the special VBGF with $b \neq 3$, also allows for the integration of the generalized VBGF and its use in yield-per-recruit analysis. When the generalized VBGF is used, and $t_{max} = \infty$, we have

$$Y/R_r = \frac{F \cdot b}{3\,KD} \cdot e^{Zr_1 - Mr_2} W_\infty \{\beta [X, P, Q]\} \qquad \ldots 8.11)$$

where  $X = e^{-3KDr_1/b}$
       $P = Zb/3KD$
and    $Q = (b/D) + 1$

with $r_1$ and $r_2$ being defined as above.

Thus, using the data of Table 8.1, first to estimate D (from $W_{max}$ and Program FB 9) then to estimate $W_\infty$ and K, with D = 0.47 and b = 3.3, it is possible to obtain growth parameters suitable for incorporation into equation (8.11) (see Table 8.2). Program FB 22 can then be used to estimate $Y/R_r$ values for these, or any other combination of growth parameters (see Example 8.5).

## COMPARISON OF VARIOUS EQUATIONS FOR YIELD-PER-RECRUIT ESTIMATION

Of the various equations available for the estimation of yield per recruit, the first [equation (8.7)] is the one which contains the most parameters. In fact, of the parameters used, one ($t_{max}$) is quite superfluous and may be set for most practical purposes equal to $\infty$, especially when Z is high (see Ricker 1975, p. 257).

Equation (8.8), on the other hand, is still widely used (when $b \approx 3$) and several examples are available of its application to tropical stocks (see recommended reading).

Equation (8.9) is particularly useful in situations where a detailed knowledge of the growth and mortality of the stock in question is not available. The results obtained from this equation are proportional to those obtained by means of equation (8.8) and allow a quick assessment of a fishery (Fig. 8.3).

Of the several methods available for compensating for allometry in yield-per-recruit analysis, that of Jones (1957) gave the results which differed most from those obtained using the generalized

VBGF, which serves as a benchmark (Fig. 8.4). The marked differences between the results obtained by Jones' method and the other methods are to a large extent due to growth beyond the ages considered in Table 8.1. This suggests that Jones' method is least robust with regard to violations of the assumption that $t_{max} = \infty$ in equation (8.10).

Paulik and Gales (1964) and Ricker (1975, p. 225) suggested that the "Chapman-Richards" curve (Richards 1959), which is essentially a form of the generalized VBGF, could be easily integrated by means of the incomplete $\beta$-function. Published examples have been wanting. This account (i.e., Case III) closes the gap.

## THE USE OF THE YIELD-PER-RECRUIT MODEL: A WARNING

The yield-per-recruit model, although very elegant and still suited to the management of certain stocks (such as the North Sea plaice *(Pleuronectes platessa)*) should be used with caution.

Fishermen are not interested in an imaginary "yield per recruit"; they are interested in a physical *yield* of fish, and this yield is the product of the yield per recruit *times* the absolute number of recruits produced in the stock. Yield is directly proportional to yield per recruit over a wide range of fishing mortalities only if it can be assumed that there is no relationship—over a wide range of F values—between the size of the parental stock of fish and its progeny (see chapter on stock-recruitment relationships).

Where this assumption does not apply—and it does not seem to apply to more than a few stocks—the values of F and $t_c$ needed to produce a maximum yield per recruit could well also generate an abysmally low yield, because the "best" value of F (the one maximizing yield per recruit) could also reduce the parental stock to a level at which virtually no recruits are produced.

Moreover, it must be realized that the finding of yield-per-recruit analyses apply to long-term or *equilibrium situations* only. In the short term, an increase of fishing mortality or a decrease in size at first capture always results in higher yields, even when the yield-per-recruit analysis predicts lower yields. Similarly, a decrease of fishing mortality or an increase in size at first capture always results in lower yields in the short term, although in the long run higher yields may be reached.

The duration of the transition period can be of several years in fish which have a high longevity and are subjected to exploitation over a number of years, as in a number of temperate stocks such as cod or halibut. In short-lived animals, the transition period will be much shorter; in the case of *very* short-lived animals, such as most penaeid shrimps, the distinction between "immediate" and "long-term" effect does not even apply, because the stocks are never in equilibrium. This and related problems are reviewed in Garcia and Le Reste (1981) who present a number of methods for the quantification of short- and long-term effects of changes in fishing mortality and mesh size (see also Jones 1981).

Another important feature of the yield-per-recruit model is that yield per recruit is maximized at low values of F only in the case of large, long-lived, low mortality fish, such as the swordfish *(Xiphias gladius)* (see Fig. 8.3). In small tropical fish, the values of F which maximize yield per recruit are generally extremely high (see Fig. 8.1). Thus, managing a tropical fishery based on a species of small fish (let alone a multispecies fishery based on such fish) using only yield-per-recruit analyses can be very misleading (see Pauly 1979b; Pauly and Martosubroto 1980).

It may be mentioned, finally, that in temperate waters, an (arbitrary) agreement has emerged to generally limit F (for assessment of stocks whose stock-recruitment relationships are unknown) to the value which corresponds to 1/10 of the rate of increase of yield per recruit that can be obtained by increasing F, at low levels of F (Gulland and Boerema 1973). This concept, called $F_{0.1}$ is illustrated in Fig. 8.5, Table 8.3 and Example 8.6. The $F_{0.1}$ concept may be viewed as a surrogate for MEY (Maximum Economic Yield, see Fig. 12.7), applicable in situations where economic data on the performance of a fishery are lacking. A concept analogous to $F_{0.1}$, but for use in conjunction with effort ($f_{0.1}$) is proposed in Chapter 12.

Table 8.3. Data for the computation of $F_{0.1}$ for *Nemipterus marginatus* from the South China Sea (see Example 8.6).

| F | $Y/R_r$ | Diff/10[a] | F | $Y/R_r$ | Diff/10[a] |
|---|---|---|---|---|---|
| 0.00 | 0.000 | | | | |
| 0.01 | 0.030 | 3.00 | 1.0 | 1.215 | |
| 0.1 | 0.270 | 2.40 | 1.1 | 1.247 | 0.32 |
| 0.2 | 0.485 | 2.15 | 1.2 | 1.272 | 0.25 |
| 0.3 | 0.656 | 1.71 | 1.3 | 1.293 | 0.21 |
| 0.4 | 0.794 | 1.38 | 1.4 | 1.310 | 0.17 |
| 0.5 | 0.905 | 1.11 | 1.5 | 1.323 | 0.13 |
| 0.6 | 0.995 | 0.90 | 1.6 | 1.334 | 0.11 |
| 0.7 | 1.068 | 0.73 | 1.7 | 1.342 | 0.08 |
| 0.8 | 1.127 | 0.59 | 1.8 | 1.348 | 0.06 |
| 0.9 | 1.175 | 0.48 | 1.9 | 1.352 | 0.04 |
| 1.0 | 1.215 | 0.40 | 2.0 | 1.355 | 0.03 |

[a]The difference between two succeeding $Y/R_r$ values, divided by ten is here used as approximation of the slope of the yield-per-recruit curve between the two values in question.

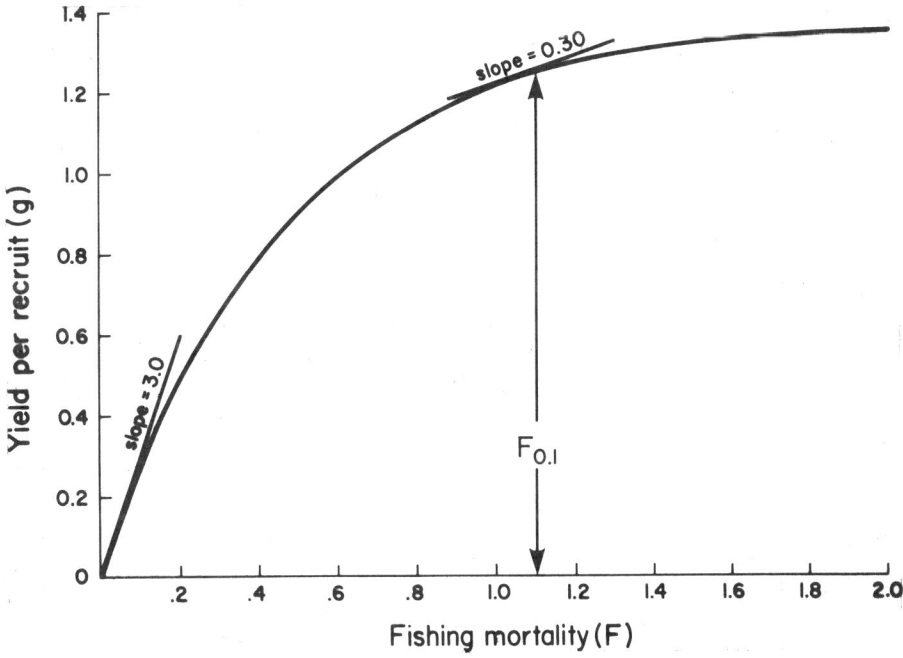

Fig. 8.5. Yield-per-recruit curve of the threadfin bream *(Nemipterus marginatus)* from the South China Sea, showing the position of $F_{0.1}$ (based on data in Table 8.3 and Example 8.6).

## AN ALTERNATIVE USE OF BEVERTON AND HOLT'S YIELD EQUATION

An interesting property of the yield equation of Beverton and Holt (1957) is that it can be used in a given stock to estimate the proportion of fish above or below a certain size. Thus, when the special VBGF is used, the total standing stock (biomass) of fish above the size at first capture ($t_c$) is given, assuming $t_{max} = \infty$, by

$$B_c = R_c \cdot F \cdot W_\infty \left( \frac{1}{Z} - \frac{3e^{-Kr_1}}{Z+K} + \frac{3e^{-2Kr_1}}{Z+2K} - \frac{e^{-3Kr_1}}{Z+3K} \right) \qquad \ldots 8.12)$$

where $R_c$ is the number of recruits of age $t_c$, and $r_1 = t_c - t_o$.

A factor (k) can be defined which relates the biomass of fish of and above a certain age ($t_k$) to the biomass of all fish of and above age $t_c$ such that

$$B_k/k = B_c \qquad \ldots 8.13)$$

The value of k will depend on the value of Z, but not on $W_\infty$, or $R_c$ which are the same in both parts of the stock ($B_c$ and $B_k$). Thus, the value of k, when $t_{max} = \infty$ can be estimated by the equation

$$k = \frac{\exp(-Zr_3) \cdot \{\frac{1}{Z} - \frac{3\exp(-Kr_2)}{Z+K} + \frac{3\exp(-2Kr_2)}{Z+2K} - \frac{\exp(-3K_2)}{Z+3K}\}}{\frac{1}{Z} - \frac{3\exp(-Kr_1)}{Z+K} + \frac{3\exp(-2Kr_1)}{Z+2K} - \frac{\exp(-3Kr_1)}{Z+3K}} \qquad \ldots 8.14)$$

with $r_1 = t_c - t_o$; $r_2 = t_k - t_o$; and $r_3 = t_k - t_c$.

This equation can be used to estimate, e.g., the proportion of the total stock which consists of fish at or above the age at first maturity ($t_m$), by setting $t_m = t_k$, that is:

$$r_1 = t_c - t_o;\ r_2 = t_m - t_o;\ \text{and}\ r_3 = t_m - t_c.$$

This technique has been recently used to estimate the standing stock size of potentially mature fish in the Gulf of Thailand (Pauly 1980d) and can also be used to convert catch data obtained by a given mesh size to those that would have been obtained had another mesh size been used. This expression is based on an analogous equation presented by Hempel and Sarhage (1959) to estimate the expected proportion of undersized and discarded fish in a trawl fishery. Program FB 23 can be used to estimate values of k for any value of F given a value of M, and values of $t_o$, $t_c$ and $t_k$ (see Example 8.7).

Recommended reading: The book in which Beverton and Holt (1957) originally presented their model has been reprinted and still is a mine of good ideas—although it is often quite hard to follow. Ricker (1975) gives a review of the whole yield-per-recruit approach, including the earlier work of Baranov (1918) who was the pioneer in this field. Tropical applications of the yield-per-recruit approach are to be found, e.g., in Bayliff (1967), Le Guen (1971), Jones (1976b) and Sinoda et al. (1979).

Suggested research topics: Whenever growth data are available, reasonable estimates of M can be obtained (see Chapter 5); yield-per-recruit computations can then be performed. Attempts should be made to perform such assessments routinely and to suggest appropriate mesh sizes. In fisheries that have stabilized at a given level of effort and/or those consisting of short-lived fish, yield may be divided by $Y/R_c$ to obtain estimates of recruitment, which may be compared with absolute recruitment estimates obtained from length cohort analysis.

**EXAMPLE 8.1**

**Estimating the yield per recruit obtainable from the slipmouth** *(Leiognathus splendens)* **in western Indonesian waters.**

Data: $W_\infty = 64$ g, $K = 1.0$, $t_o = -0.2$, $t_c = 0.2$, $t_r = 0.2$, $M = 2$, $b = 3$, $D = 1$ (adapted from Pauly 1980c).

Computation

1) Read sides 1 and 2 of Program FB 21

2) Enter parameters (except for b and D).

   Keystrokes: 64 STO B1 STO1 2STO2.2 CHS STO0 .2 STO D .2 STOI

3) Calculate $Y/R_c$ and $Y/R_r$ for $F = 0.5$ to $F = 5$ in steps of 0.5

| Keystrokes | Results | |
|---|---|---|
| .5 B | 2.247 | $(Y/R_c)$ |
|      | 2.247 | $(Y/R_r)$ |
| 1 B  | 3.199 | $(Y/R_c)$ |
|      | 3.199 | $(Y/R_r)$ |
| etc. | ..... | |
| 5 B  | 3.566 | $(Y/R_c)$ |
|      | 3.566 | $(Y/R_r)$ |

4) Plot the values of $Y/R_r$ onto a graph, and repeat with $t_c = 0.3$. A plot such as Fig. 8.1 will be obtained, which allows for the assessment that, for all values of fishing mortality considered, the mesh size which generates $t_c = 0.3$ will produce a greater yield than that which generates $t_c = 0.2$.

**EXAMPLE 8.2**  **Estimating the yield per recruit obtainable from the snapper** *(Lutjanus sanguineus)* **in the South China Sea.**

Data: $W_\infty$ = 12226 g, K = 0.154, $t_o$ = −0.67, D = 1, $t_{max}$ = 10 years (assumed), M = 0.33, with $t_r = t_o$, and $t_c$ = 2 years, b = 3 (adapted from Lai and Hsi 1974 and Pauly 1979b). Note that the age at recruitment is arbitrary.

Computation

1) Read sides 1 and 2 of Program FB 21

2) Enter parameters (b is assumed 3 and D is assumed 1 and need not be entered)

   Keystrokes: 12226 STO B .154 STO1 .33 STO2 10 STO A .67 CHS STO0 2 STO D .67 CHS STO I

3) Calculate $Y/R_c$ and $Y/R_r$ for F = 1

   | Keystrokes | Results | |
   |---|---|---|
   | 1 A | 660.924 | ($Y/R_c$) |
   | | 273.839 | ($Y/R_r$) |

4) Repeat with different value of F, e.g.

   | Keystrokes | Results | |
   |---|---|---|
   | .5 A | 708.999 | ($Y/R_c$) |
   | | 293.757 | ($Y/R_r$) |

5) Setting $t_{max} = \infty$ (i.e., using a very large number) and the same set of other parameters allows one to reproduce the yield isopleth diagram in Fig. 8.2.

**EXAMPLE 8.3**

**Yield-per-recruit assessment of Atlantic swordfish** *(Xiphias gladius)*.

Data: Berkeley and Houde (1980) give for swordfish caught off Florida: $L_\infty$ = 309 (fork length, in cm; ♂ and ♀), K = 0.0949, M = 0.18 (hence M/K = 1.9), $L_c$ = 118 (hence c = $L_c/L_\infty$ = 0.38).

Computation

1) Read sides 1 and 2 of Program FB 21

2) Enter parameters needed

   Keystrokes: 1.9 STO 8 .38 STOC

3) Compute the relative yield per recruit for different values of E (= F/Z)

   | Keystrokes | Results | |
   |---|---|---|
   | .1 C | 0.009 | $(Y'/R_r)$ |
   | .2 C | 0.017 | $(Y'/R_r)$ |
   | etc. | ..... | |
   | 1 C | 0.022 | $(Y'/R_r)$ |

4) Plot these values onto a graph, and repeat with a different value of c (e.g., 0.49). The result should look similar to Fig. 8.3 from which the assessment can be made that an increase of $L_c$ from 118 to 150 cm would not result in a marked increase of yield per recruit under the present (late 1970s) exploitation rate, but would lead to an increased yield per recruit under higher exploitation rates.

**EXAMPLE 8.4**

**Computation of yield per recruit in cases where weight growth is allometric (Jones' method).**

Data: Growth and other parameters from Tables 8.1 and 8.2

Computation

1) Read sides 1 and 2 of Program FB 22

2) Enter parameters needed

   Keystrokes: 162.25 STO B .15 STO A 1 STO D 3.3 STO E .3 STO 0 .795 CHS ↑ 2.35 f a 2.35 f c

3) Calculate yield per recruit for F = 0.1 to F = 2.0

| | Keystrokes | Results | |
|---|---|---|---|
| | .1 A (and wait . . .) | 0.018 | ($\beta$) |
| | | 6.773 | ($Y/R_c$) |
| | | 6.773 | ($Y/R_r$) |
| | etc. | | |
| | 2 A (and wait . . .) | 2.648...−06 | ($\beta$) |
| | | 7.936 | ($Y/R_c$) |
| | | 7.936 | ($Y/R_r$) |

4) Plot the $Y/R_r$ values against the F-values. The graph that emerges should look as line 1 in Fig. 8.4 (but see text).

---

**Computation of yield per recruit using the generalized VBGF.**

Data: Growth and other parameters from Table 8.2

Computation

1) Read sides 1 and 2 of Program FB 22

2) Enter parameters needed

   Keystrokes: 85.95 STO B .582 STO A .47 STO D .3 STO O 2.035 CHS ↑ 2.39 f a 2.39 f c

3) Calculate yield per recruit for F = 0.1 to F = 2

| | Keystrokes | Results | |
|---|---|---|---|
| | .1 B | 0.027 | ($\beta$) |
| | | 5.444 | ($Y/R_c$) |
| | | 5.444 | ($Y/R_r$) |
| | etc. | . . . . . | |
| | 2 B | 3.490...−07 | ($\beta$) |
| | | 6.347 | ($Y/R_c$) |
| | | 6.347 | ($Y/R_r$) |

4) Plot the $Y/R_r$ values against the F-values. The graph that emerges should look as line 3 in Fig. 8.4

**EXAMPLE 8.5**

**EXAMPLE 8.6**  Estimating $F_{0.1}$ for *Nemipterus marginatus* from the South China Sea.

Data: $W_\infty$ = 210 g, K = 0.42, $t_o$ = −0.41 (D = 1, b = 3), M = 1.73, $t_c$ = 0.26, $t_r$ = −0.41 (from Pauly and Martosubroto 1980).

Computation

1) Read sides 1 and 2 of Program FB 21

2) Enter parameters needed

   Keystrokes: 210 STO B .42 STO 1 1.73 STO2 .41 CHS STO0 .26STO D .41CHS STO I

3) Compute $Y/R_r$ at a very low value of F, e.g., F = 0.01

   | Keystrokes | Results | |
   |---|---|---|
   | .01 B | 0.096 | $(Y/R_c)$ |
   |  | 0.030 | $(Y/R_r)$ |

Near the origin, $Y/R_r$ increases from 0 to 0.03 when F increases from 0 to 0.01, thus the slope of the yield curve at the origin is close to 0.030/0.01 i.e.:

|  | Keystrokes | Results | |
|---|---|---|---|
|  | .01 ÷ | 2.999 | (slope near origin) |
| increase per unit of F near origin: | DSP 2 | 3.00 | (slope near origin) |

4) Then compute $Y/R_r$ for values of F ranging from 0.1 to 2, in steps of 0.1, record data and draw resulting graph (see Fig. 8.5 and Table 8.3).

5) Calculate increase in yield associated with each 0.1 increment of F, and divide this difference by 10 to obtain approximate slope (i.e., change in $Y/R_r$ per unit change in F).

6) Locate slope value closest to 1/10 of value of slope near the origin (corresponding to $F_{0.1}$). This value is 0.32, corresponding to $F_{0.1}$ = 1.1 (see Table 8.3). The next closest value is 0.25, corresponding to F = 1.1-1.2. Thus, the best value, corresponding to 0.30 will be close to F = 1.1, which we may take as our estimate of $F_{0.1}$ (see Fig. 8.5).

**EXAMPLE 8.7**

**Estimating the proportion (k) of adult slipmouth** *(Leiognathus splendens)* **in the total stock, under two different exploitation regimes.**

Data: $K = 1.0$, $t_o = -0.2$, $t_c = 0.2$, $M = 1.8$ (see Fig. 8.1); to be estimated are values of k for $F = 0$ and $F = 1$, with $t_k = 1$ year.

Computation

1) Read side 1 of Program FB 23

2) Enter needed parameter values

    Keystrokes: 1 STO1 .2 CHS STO0 1.8 STO2 .2 STOC 1 STOA

3) Calculate values of k for $F = 0$ and $F = 1$

    | Keystrokes | Results | |
    |---|---|---|
    | 0A | 0.55 | ($k_o$) |
    | 1A | 0.32 | ($k_1$) |

Thus, as expected, we find at $F = 1$ a smaller biomass of adults (32% of total stock) than at $F = 0$, where the adults contribute 55% of the total stock.

# 9. Stock-Recruitment Relationships

## INTRODUCTION

Clearly, there can be no production of young fish (recruits) if no adult fish are left (by a fishery) to mature, spawn, and produce eggs which hatch and grow to become recruits (see Fig. 9.1A).

The females of most fish species are extremely fecund, producing during their adult lives several thousand eggs, sometimes millions. This fecundity has led many fishery biologists to believe that even a very limited parental biomass should be sufficient to allow a complete "restocking" after each spawning season. It was assumed that features of the abiotic environment (e.g., oceanographic conditions) mainly determine how many of the spawned eggs survive to become recruits, the size of the spawning stock, except for stock sizes very close to zero, being virtually irrelevant in determining recruit numbers. The situation in which the number of recruits in a given stock is determined mainly by factors other than parental biomass is called "lack of a stock-recruitment relationship". Early proponents of this view include Beverton and Holt (1957) (see also Beverton 1963).

However, work conducted in the 1960s and 1970s suggests that many fish stocks do display stock-recruitment relationships, as demonstrated in Parrish (1978) and Saville (1980). Also, it was shown for most of the stocks which collapsed in the last three decades that "recruitment overfishing" was the cause (Murphy 1966, 1977, 1980; Saville 1980).

However, stock-recruitment relationships generally cannot be established directly by plotting an index of recruitment on parental biomass. Rather, it is necessary to account simultaneously for a stock-recruitment relationship and the biotic and/or abiotic factor(s) which may affect that relationship. In tropical stocks, this approach has allowed e.g., Csirke (1980) to demonstrate a strong effect of oceanographic conditions on the recruitment of the Peruvian anchovy. Ricker (1975, p. 275-280), Bakun and Parrish (1980) and Bakun et al. (1982) have discussed methods to identify various factors affecting recruitment using multiple regression analysis (for which Program FB 7, with slight modifications, can be used).

To date four types of stock-recruitment relationships are commonly recognized:
1) Recruitment increasing rather steeply toward an asymptote (this model, paradoxically is the model generally used for illustrating *a lack* of stock-recruitment relationships, see Figs. 9.1B and 9.2).
2) Recruitment increasing in proportion to a power of parental biomass or of the number of eggs shed (Fig. 9.1C).
3) Recruitment increasing more or less steeply toward a maximum at an intermediate size of parental stock (P), then decreasing with increasing values of P (Fig. 9.1D and 9.3).
4) None of the above, but stock-recruitment *sensu stricto* conforming to 1, 2 or 3 *after* the simultaneous effects of environmental factors (biotic or abiotic) are removed, as in Csirke (1980).

Examples of relationships of types 1 and 3, the most commonly used, are illustrated here (Examples 9.1 and 9.2). These two examples must be taken with a grain of salt, however, because the first displays considerable scatter (as is typical of most such plots), while the second is based on points derived by a method which gives only approximate results.

At present, research in fish recruitment is in a state of flux, with a lot of new ideas and insufficient data to test them. Reviews covering what little is known of stock-recruitment relationships in tropical fish are given in Sharp (1980) for pelagics, by Sale (1980) for coral reef fish, Murphy (1982) for miscellaneous fish and Garcia (1983) for penaeid shrimps.

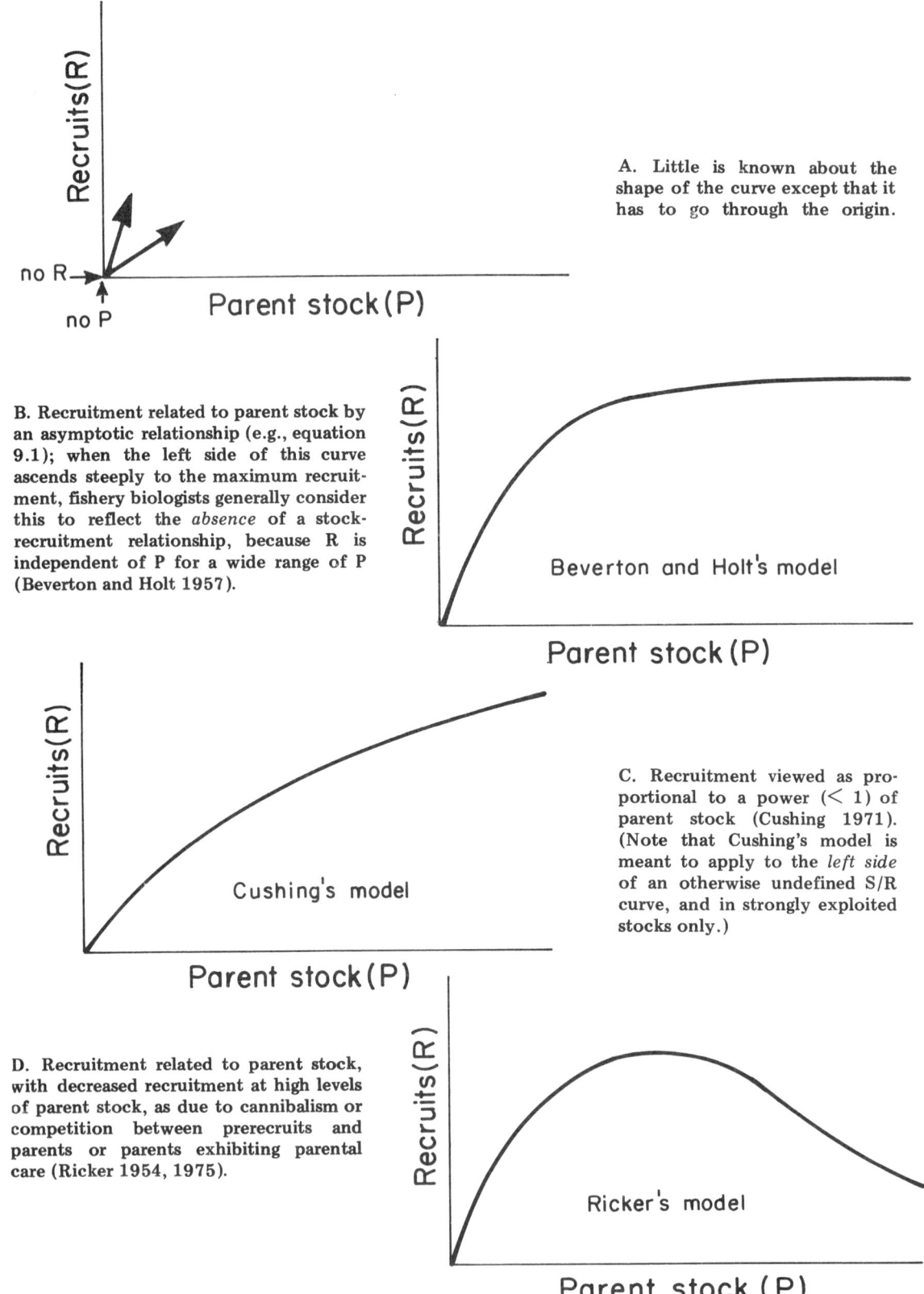

Fig. 9.1. Types of stock-recruitment relationships used in fishery research.

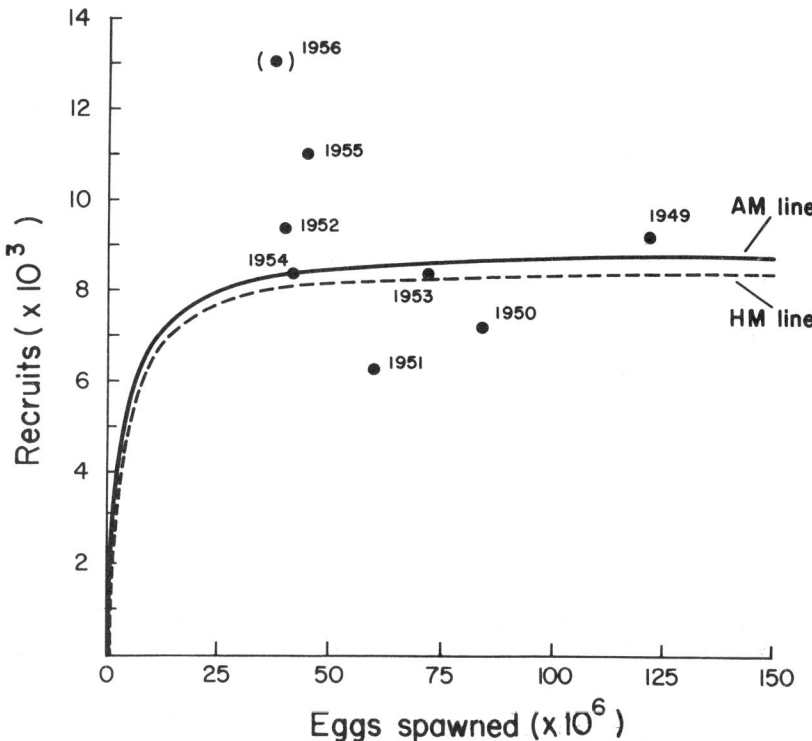

Fig. 9.2. Beverton and Holt type stock-recruitment relationship for the sea bream *(Taius tumifrons)* (East China Sea).

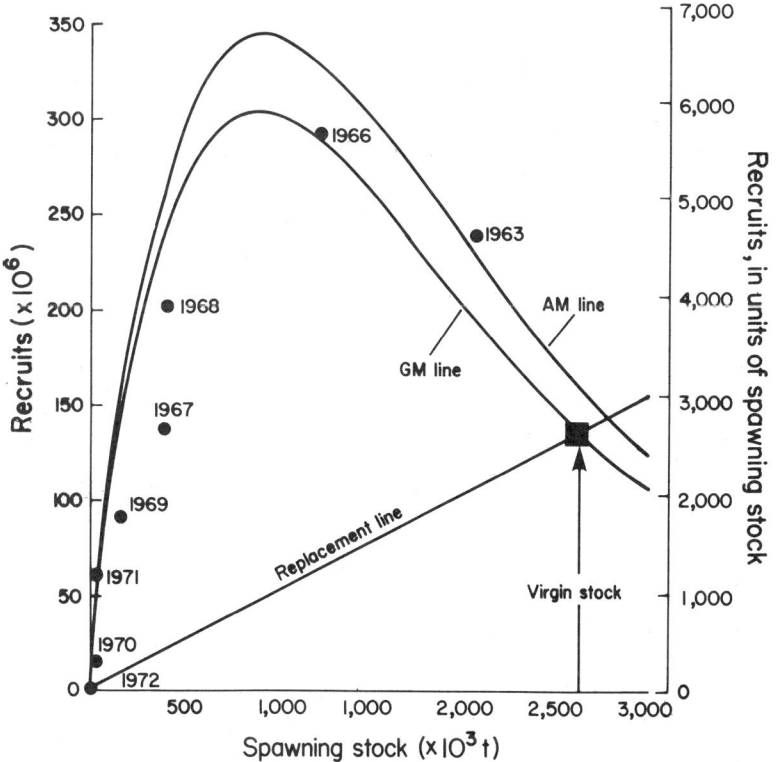

Fig. 9.3. Stock-recruitment data of false trevally *(Lactarius lactarius)* in the Gulf of Thailand, fitted with Ricker curves (GM and AM) (based on data in Table 9.2 and Example 9.3).

# THE STOCK-RECRUITMENT RELATIONSHIP OF BEVERTON AND HOLT*

In this model, the relationship between the number of recruits (R) and the spawning stock size (P) is given by

$$R = \frac{1}{\alpha' + \beta'} \quad \ldots 9.1)$$

Expression (9.1) can be expressed as a linear relationship of the form

$$\frac{P}{R} = \beta' + \alpha' P \quad \ldots 9.2)$$

As this plot involves the use of inverses (e.g., 1/R), the estimated values of $\alpha'$ and $\beta'$ provide, for each value of P, estimated values of recruitment ($\hat{R}$) whose sum ($\Sigma \hat{R}$) is actually lower than the sum of the empirical values of R ($\Sigma R$). This is due to the fact that the use of inverse values implies the use of a harmonic mean (HM) in fitting equation (9.1) and to the fact that the harmonic mean of a series of values is always less than the arithmetic mean (AM) of these values.

An approximate conversion of the estimated recruitment values $\hat{R}_{HM}$ to the corresponding $\hat{R}_{AM}$ values can be obtained, however, by performing

$$C = \frac{\Sigma R \text{ (empirical values)}}{\Sigma R \text{ (harmonic mean values)}} \quad \ldots 9.3)$$

and by multiplying the recruitment values of the HM line by the constant C (Ricker 1975).

An application of this model is given in Example 9.1, based on the data in Table 9.1.

Table 9.1. Data for the derivation of a Beverton and Holt type relationship for sea bream *(Taius tumifrons)* from the East China Sea. Figures derived from Murphy (1972, Fig. 3, based on Shindo 1960).

| No. | Year | Eggs spawned No. x $10^6$ | Recruits No. x $10^3$ | P/R |
|---|---|---|---|---|
| 1 | 1949 | 122 | 9.2 | 13.3 |
| 2 | 1950 | 84 | 7.2 | 11.7 |
| 3 | 1951 | 60 | 6.3 | 9.52 |
| 4 | 1952 | 40 | 9.4 | 4.26 |
| 5 | 1953 | 72 | 8.4 | 8.57 |
| 6 | 1954 | 42 | 8.3 | 5.06 |
| 7 | 1955 | 45 | 11.0 | 4.09 |
| not used[a] | 1956 | (38) | (13.0) | (2.92) |

[a]Use of the 1956 value generates a negative intercept in equation (9.2), and hence a negative value of $\beta'$ in equation (9.1). See Users' Instruction for FB 24.

---

*Beverton and Holt (1957) actually presented *two* stock-recruitment models. Their second model, however, is in its form—if not in its derivation—similar to Ricker's model discussed further below.

# RICKER'S STOCK-RECRUITMENT RELATIONSHIPS

First form of Ricker's curve

The stock-recruitment relationship proposed by Ricker (1954, 1975) can be written

$$R = \alpha P e^{-\beta P} \qquad \ldots 9.4)$$

where  R is the number of recruits
P is the size of parental stock (in weight, in numbers, or as egg production)
$\alpha$ is an index of stock-independent mortality

and  $\beta$ is an index of stock-dependent mortality

Equation (9.4) can be rewritten

$$\ln R - \ln P = \ln a - bP \qquad \ldots 9.5)$$

which has the form of a linear regression $y = a + bx$, where $y = \ln R - \ln P$, $x = P$, $a = \ln \alpha$ and $b = \beta$.
Once $\alpha$ and $\beta$ are estimated, maximum recruitment ($R_m$) is obtained by

$$R_m = \alpha/\beta e \qquad \ldots 9.6)$$

where e (= 2.1783) is the base of the natural logarithms. Also, the parental stock at maximum recruitment ($P_m$) can be estimated by the equation

$$P_m = 1/\beta \qquad \ldots 9.7)$$

The relationships between the parameters $\alpha$ and $\beta$ in the first form of Ricker's curve to $\alpha'$ and $\beta'$ in Beverton and Holt's curve are discussed in Chapter 11 (p. 156).
When P and R are expressed in the same units, a "level of replacement abundance" can be found where P = R. This replacement level ($P_r$) can be estimated through

$$P_r = \frac{\ln \alpha}{\beta} = R_r \qquad \ldots 9.8)$$

For most purposes, it is reasonable to assume that (the average size of) the virgin parental stock ($P_v$) should be equal to $P_r$, which allows, when an estimate of $P_v$ is available, for the original units of recruitment to be converted to units of P through multiplication with $P_v/P_r$ (see Table 9.2).
Program FB 25 can be used to estimate the parameters of the first type of Ricker curve (see Example 9.2).

Table 9.2. Data for the derivation of Ricker type stock-recruitment relationships for the false trevally *(Lactarius lactarius)* from the Gulf of Thailand.[a]

| Year | P (in thousand tonnes) | R (in millions) | R (in units of P)[b] |
|---|---|---|---|
| virgin stock | 2,660 | — | (2,660) |
| 1963 | 2,087 | 239 | 4,606.8 |
| 1966 | 1,277 | 292 | 5,628.4 |
| 1967 | 422 | 138 | 2,660.0 |
| 1968 | 444 | 202 | 3,893.6 |
| 1969 | 191 | 90.8 | 1,750.2 |
| 1970 | 29.8 | 15.5 | 298.77 |
| 1971 | 37.8 | 55.5 | 1,069.8 |
| 1972 | 4.0 | 8.9 | 171.55 |

[a] From Pauly (1980d); the values presented here should be considered tentative due to several approximations made for the estimation of the number of recruits.
[b] See Example 9.3.

## Second form of Ricker's curve

When recruitment and parental stock are expressed in the same units, equation (9.4) can be rewritten in the form

$$R = Pe^{a(1 - P/P_r)} \qquad \ldots 9.9)$$

where $P_r$ is the replacement abundance, and where a new parameter (a) is introduced, which is defined as

$$a = P_r \beta = \ln \alpha \qquad \ldots 9.10)$$

Thus, equation (9.9) can be rewritten

$$\ln R - \ln P = a - \frac{a}{P_r} P \qquad \ldots 9.11)$$

which has the form of a linear regression where $y = \ln R - \ln P$ and $x = P$, with the intercept of this regression providing an estimate of a and its slope an estimate of $a/P_r$.

Equation (9.9), as well as equation (9.4), incidentally, provide estimates of the geometric mean (GM) value of R at a given P; generally, GM values estimate the most probable values of recruitment for the observed P values, while the arithmetic mean (AM) curve estimates the long-term arithmetic average value of recruitment obtained at a given P (Ricker 1975, p. 283).

Thus, conversion of the GM curve to an AM curve is indicated especially when the R values are widely scattered about the stock-recruitment curve. Program FB 25 can be used for this conversion, which is performed according to the method given in Ricker (1975, p. 275 and 283-288) (see Example 9.2).

In temperate, single-species fisheries, the establishment of a stock-recruitment relationship of the type discussed here is sufficient for most purposes of fishery management, since the best strategy generally is to optimize the level of surplus recruitment (= the number of recruits produced in excess of replacement level, see Fig. 9.3).

This strategy also may be indicated in the case of tropical single-species fisheries, such as sardines, anchovies, chub mackerels or scads. In the case of multispecies fisheries, the establishment of a stock-recruitment relationship in one species is not sufficient—obviously—for deriving an optimum fishing strategy for the whole multispecies stock (see Chapter 12).

Recommended reading: The classic paper of Ricker (1954) is an excellent introduction to the field, which is also reviewed in Ricker (1975). Parrish (1978) edited a volume of papers on the subject of stock-recruitment relationships which contains many important contributions. Sharp (1980) presents an even more up-to-date review of the subject. Several contributions included in Pauly and Murphy (1982) are also of relevance to the topic, particularly as far as the tropics are concerned. Garcia (1983) discussed in detail the stock-recruitment relationships of tropical and subtropical shrimp and the numerous pitfalls (potential and realized) in the interpretation of such relationships. Shepherd (1982) recently proposed a versatile stock-recruitment model which has the Cushing, Beverton and Holt and Ricker models as special cases.

Suggested research topics: Every attempt should be made to estimate recruitment from stocks that are suitably well-documented, especially by using VPA and related methods. Attempts should be made to identify the factors which most strongly affect recruitment in a fishery and to derive from the properties of these factors the best strategy for the exploitation of the resource.

**EXAMPLE 9.1**

**Estimating the parameters of a Beverton and Holt type stock-recruitment relationship** (*Taius tumifrons*, East China Sea).

Data from Table 9.1

Computation

1) Read side 1 of Program FB 24

2) Enter P and R data

   Keystrokes: f a 122 ↑ 9.2 A 84 ↑ 7.2 A 60 ↑ 6.3 A 40 ↑ 9.4 A 72 ↑ 8.4 A 42 ↑ 8.3 A 45 ↑ 11 A

3) Estimate parameters of curve

   | Keystroke | Results | |
   |---|---|---|
   | E | 0.857 | ($r^2$) |
   |   | 0.116 | ($\alpha'$) |
   |   | 0.371 | ($\beta'$) |

4) To obtain estimate of $R_{HM}$ and $R_{AM}$, re-enter the P values

   Keystrokes 122 D 84 D 60 D 40 D 72 D 42 D 45 D

5) Then estimate $R_{HM}$ and $R_{AM}$ for any given value of P

   | Keystroke | Results | |
   |---|---|---|
   | 10C | 6.541 | $R_{HM}$ |
   |     | 6.827 | $R_{AM}$ |
   | etc. | ... | |

The data can thus be plotted in the form of curves as in Fig. 9.2

**EXAMPLE 9.2** | **Estimating the parameters of Ricker type recruitment curves (first and second forms).**

Data from Table 9.2

Computation

1) Read sides 1 and 2 of Program FB 25

2) Enter P and R data (first form of curve)

    Keystrokes: f a 2087 ↑ 239 A 1277 ↑ 292 A 422 ↑ 138 A 444 ↑ 202 A 191 ↑ 90.8 A 29.8 ↑ 15.5 A 37.8 ↑ 55.5 A 4 ↑ 8.9 A

3) Calculate parameters of stock recruitment curve (first form):

| | Keystrokes | Results | |
|---|---|---|---|
| | E | 0.694 | ($r^2$) |
| | | 0.886 | ($\alpha$) |
| | | 0.001 | ($\beta$) |
| | | 937.348 | ($P_m$) |
| | | 305.516 | ($R_m$) |

4) Since $\beta$ is not precise enough, do:    RCL B DSP 5    0.00107   ($\beta$)

5) Assuming that the value of P in the virgin stock ($P_v$) corresponds to $P_r$, estimate the ratio $R_r/P_r$

    2660 f d    0.05188   ($R_r/P_r$)

6) To convert the original values of R in units of P do:

| | Keystrokes | Results | |
|---|---|---|---|
| | DSP 1 | | |
| | 239 ↑ | | |
| | .05188 ÷ | 4606.8 | ($R_{(1963)}$) |
| | 292 ↑ | | |
| | .05188 ÷ | 5628.4 | ($R_{(1966)}$) |
| | etc. | ... | |
| | | (see Table 9.2) | |

7) To obtain parameters of stock-recruitment curve (second form), first enter P and new R data:

    Keystrokes: f a 2087 ↑ 4606.8 A 1277 ↑ 5628.4 A 422 ↑ 2660 A 444 ↑ 3893.6 A 191 ↑ 1750.2 A 29.8 ↑ 298.77 A 37.8 ↑ 1069.8 A 4 ↑ 171.55 A

(continued)

**Example 9.2 (cont.)**

(continued from p. 136)

8) To calculate parameters of new curve do:

| | Keystrokes | Results | |
|---|---|---|---|
| | f e | 0.694 | ($r^2$) |
| | | 2.838 | ($P_r/P_m$) |
| | | 2659.599 | ($P_r$) |

9) The parameter values obtained pertain to a GM curve; to obtain recruitment values corresponding to an AM curve, re-enter the P and R values:

Keystrokes: 2087 ↑ 4606.8 D 1277 ↑ 5628.4 D 422 ↑ 2660 D 444 ↑ 3893.6 D 191 ↑ 1750.2 D 29.8 ↑ 298.77 D 37.8 ↑ 1069.8 D 4 ↑ 171.55 D

10) When all P and new R values have been re-entered, the ratio between $R_{(AM)}$ and $R_{(GM)}$ values is obtained by:

| | Keystrokes | Results | |
|---|---|---|---|
| | f·c | 1.13 | ($R_{AM}/R_{GM}$) |

11) Which allows one to draw GM and RM curves by entering P values, and calculating the corresponding $R_{(GM)}$ and $R_{(AM)}$ values, i.e.,

| | | | |
|---|---|---|---|
| | 10 B | 168.96 | ($R_{(GM)}$) |
| | | 190.84 | ($R_{(AM)}$) |
| | 100 B | 1534.91 | ($R_{(GM)}$) |
| | | 1733.67 | ($R_{(AM)}$) |
| | etc. | ... | |
| | | (see Fig. 9.4) | |

# 10. Surplus-Yield Models

## INTRODUCTION

Based on earlier work by Baranov (1927), Graham (1935) and others, Schaefer (1954, 1957) presented a model which, in its recent formulation (e.g., Ricker 1975 or Schnute 1977) can be used for stock assessment when a minimum of data is available (only catch-and-effort data are required) and which has been applied, with varying success, to a number of fisheries throughout the world.

The assumptions made for the derivation of this model are as follows:

1) Any fish population newly colonizing a given, finite ecosystem grows in weight until it approaches the maximum carrying capacity (most often in terms of available food) of this ecosystem, after which its increase in total weight gradually ceases as the stock size comes closer (asymptotically) to the carrying capacity of the environment ($B_\infty$),
2) $B_\infty$ more or less corresponds to the virgin stock (= unfished biomass, $B_v$),
3) the growth, in time, of the fish biomass toward $B_\infty$ may be described by a logistic curve, the first derivative of which, $dB/dt$, has a maximum at $B_\infty/2$ and zero values at $B_\infty$ and $B = 0$ (Fig. 10.1),

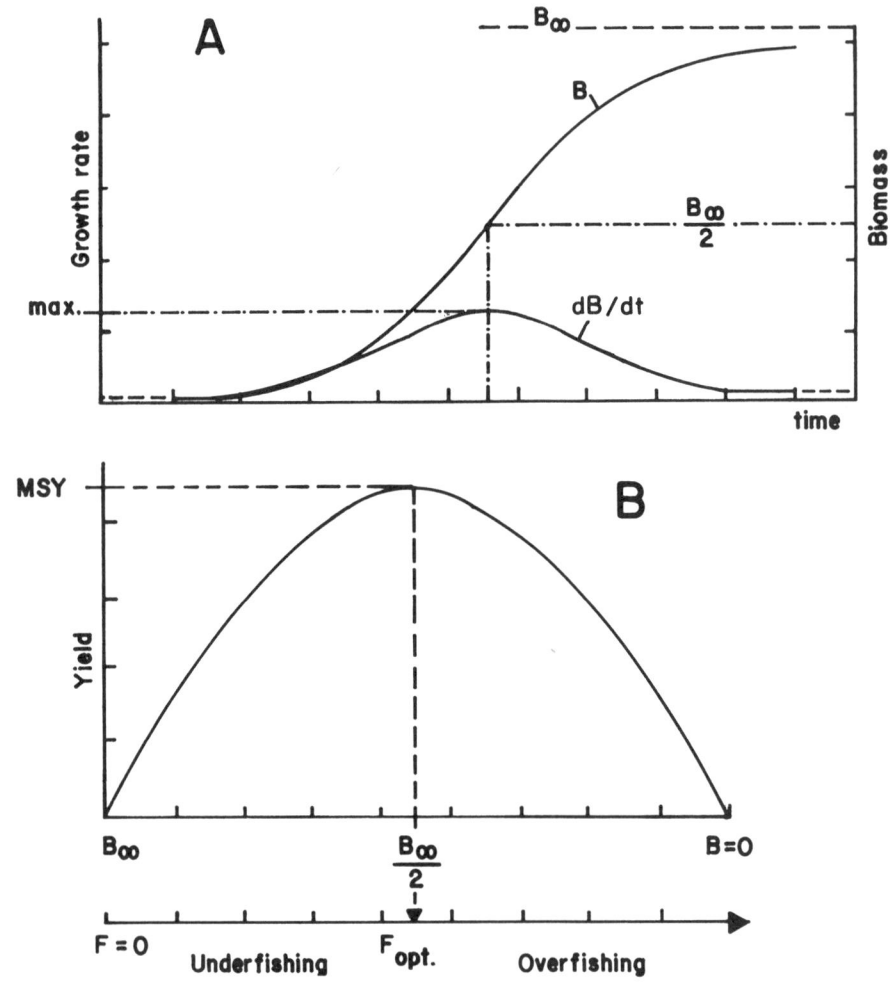

Fig. 10.1. The simple Schaefer model. A) the logistic curve and its first derivative. B) the yield-biomass and the yield-effort relationships.

4) the fishing effort which reduces $B_\infty$ to half its original value will produce the highest net growth of the stock, that is the maximum *surplus yield* available to a fishery (Fig. 10.1),

5) the maximum surplus yield in (4) can be sustained indefinitely (hence, the term maximum sustainable yield), as long as the biomass of the exploited stock is maintained at $B_\infty/2$.

There is biological evidence to make these assumptions appear reasonable (Odum 1971; Silliman and Gutsell 1958). Some reasons for the low surplus production at stock size $> B_\infty/2$ are given here (from Ricker 1975):

"1) Near maximum stock density, efficiency of reproduction, and often the actual number of recruits, is less than at smaller densities. In the latter event, reducing the stock will increase recruitment.

2) When food supply is limited, food is less efficiently converted to fish flesh by a large stock than by a smaller one. Each fish of the larger stock gets less food individually; hence, a larger fraction is used merely to maintain life, and a smaller fraction for growth.

3) An unfished stock tends to contain older individuals, relatively, than a fished stock. This makes for decreased production, in at least two ways. a) Larger fish tend to eat larger foods, so an extra step may be inserted in the food pyramid, with consequent loss of efficiency of utilization of the basic food production. b) Older fish convert a smaller fraction of the food they eat into new flesh—partly, at least because mature fish annually divert much substance to maturing eggs and milt."

The main reason larger fish convert a smaller fraction of their food into new flesh, however, is due to the fact that oxygen is needed for synthesis of body substance, and the relative gill size (= gill surface/body weight) decreases sharply as fish get larger, down to a point where the body is so badly supplied with $O_2$ that most of it is used for maintenance, with very little left for synthesis of new body substance or surplus production (Pauly 1981).

From the assumptions listed above, two very important features of the Schaefer and related models follow, namely that the growth of a stock is a function of its size and of its size only—and that, therefore, a stock should respond by changes in its growth rate (dB/dt) instantaneously to any change of its size (e.g., by fishing). Thus, we have

$$\frac{dB}{dt} = \frac{r_m B (B_\infty - B)}{B_\infty} \qquad \ldots 10.1)$$

where B is the stock size, $B_\infty$ is the carrying capacity of the environment, $r_m$ is the intrinsic rate of growth of the stock in question.

Quite clearly, the assumption that a stock reacts instantaneously to change of its size is not realistic. Therefore, the concept of "equilibrium" is used here, and this refers to the situation which exists when a given fishing mortality ($F_E$) has been exerted long enough for a stock to have adjusted its size and rate of net growth such that the relationship expressed in equation (10.1) is fulfilled. The following series of equations, adapted from Ricker (1975) assumes equilibrium conditions, as expressed by the subscript "E". We start from

$$Y_E = \frac{dB}{dt} = F_E \cdot B_E \qquad \ldots 10.2)$$

where $Y_E$, the equilibrium yield (per unit of time) is equal to the net growth rate of the stock maintained by a fishing mortality $F_E$ at the equilibrium level $B_E$.

Combining equations (10.2) and (10.1) and rearranging gives

$$Y_E = r_m B_E - \left(\frac{r_m}{B_\infty}\right) B_E^2 \qquad \ldots 10.3)$$

Expression (10.3) has the form of a parabola (Fig. 10.1B). The first derivative of (10.3) with respect to $B_E$ can be equated to zero and solved for $B_E$, which gives the value of $B_E$ (= $B_{opt}$) for which yield is maximum or

$$B_{opt} = \frac{B_\infty}{2} \qquad \ldots 10.4)$$

The maximum value of $Y_E$ is commonly named *maximum sustainable yield* (MSY). Thus, substituting (10.4) into (10.3) gives

$$\text{MSY} = \frac{r_m \cdot B_\infty}{4} \qquad \ldots 10.5)$$

Also, substituting $F_{opt} \cdot B_{opt}$ for MSY in (10.5) and dividing both sides by expression (10.4) gives the fishing mortality at MSY ($F_{opt}$):

$$F_{opt} = \frac{r_m}{2} \qquad \ldots 10.6)$$

and, since fishing mortality is proportional to effort, we also have

$$f_{opt} = \frac{r_m}{2q} \qquad \ldots 10.7)$$

where $f_{opt}$ is the fishing effort which brings about MSY and q is the catchability coefficient.

Since we have

$$B_E = B_\infty - \frac{F_E B_\infty}{r_m} \qquad \ldots 10.8)$$

equation (10.3) can be rewritten

$$Y_E = B_\infty F_E - \left(\frac{B_\infty}{r_m}\right) F_E^2 \qquad \ldots 10.9)$$

and, substituting $qf_E$ for $F_E$ gives

$$Y_E = af_E - bf_E^2 \qquad \ldots 10.10)$$

where
$$a = qB_\infty \qquad \ldots 10.11)$$

and
$$b = \frac{q^2 B_\infty}{r_m} \qquad \ldots 10.12)$$

Thus, when the stock is in equilibrium, surplus yield is a parabolic function of stock size (B), or of fishing mortality (F) or of effort (f). Therefore, catch and effort data can be fitted easily by the linear regression

$$\frac{Y_E}{f_E} = a - bf_E \qquad \ldots 10.13)$$

The definition of $f_{opt}$ in expression (10.7) and of a and b in (10.10) gives the following identities

$$f_{opt} = \frac{r_m}{2q} = \frac{q B_\infty \cdot r_m}{2 q^2 B_\infty} = \frac{a}{2b} \qquad \ldots 10.14)$$

[($f_{opt} = \frac{a}{2b}$), it will be noted, could also have been obtained by differentiating (10.10), equating to zero and solving for $f_E$.]

Thus, as Ricker (1975, p. 316) emphasizes "—maximum sustainable yield optimum rate of fishing [$f_{opt}$] can be estimated from the relation of equilibrium yield to equilibrium effort, without knowing the catchability (q) of the fish." This very important feature considerably simplifies the model originally proposed by Schaefer (1954, 1957), making it particularly well-suited to the investigation of tropical stocks.

## THE "EQUILIBRIUM" PROBLEM

This leaves only one problem which remains associated with the model, namely the determination of what an "equilibrium situation" actually is.

Many authors, implicitly assuming that the stock reacts instantaneously to changes of its size simply plot the yield per effort of a given year against the effort of the corresponding year. This procedure is illustrated in Example 10.1 which is based on Table 10.1.

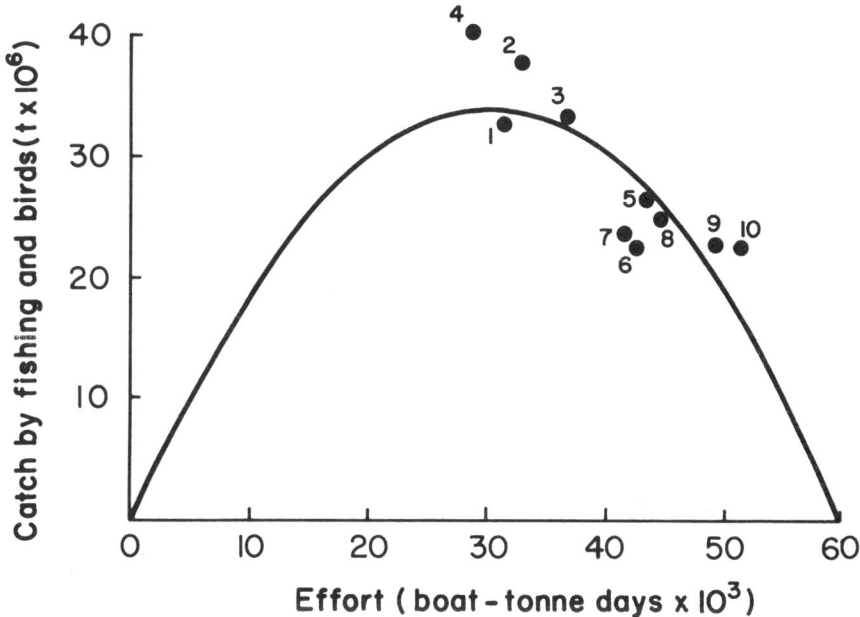

Fig. 10.2. Yield curve of Peruvian anchoveta *(Engraulis ringens)* off Peru, just prior to the collapse of the fishery (based on data in Table 10.1 and Example 10.1).

Table 10.1. Catch-and-effort data for anchoveta *(Engraulis ringens)* off Peru, prior to stock collapse (from Murphy 1972).

| No. | Season | Total catch[a] ($t \times 10^6$) | Total effort[b] |
|-----|--------|-----------------------|---------------|
| 1  | 1960-61 | 32.89 | 31.413 |
| 2  | 1961-62 | 37.78 | 32.999 |
| 3  | 1962-63 | 33.25 | 36.579 |
| 4  | 1963-64 | 28.86 | 40.367 |
| 5  | 1964-65 | 26.82 | 43.191 |
| 6  | 1965-66 | 22.26 | 42.716 |
| 7  | 1966-67 | 23.73 | 41.636 |
| 8  | 1967-68 | 25.04 | 44.634 |
| 9  | 1968-69 | 22.77 | 49.284 |
| 10 | 1969-70 | 22.64 | 52.048 |

[a]This "catch" accounts for the fish taken by the fishery, by guano birds and by fish predation.
[b]This "effort" accounts for both the fishery and the predatory animals (fish and birds) but is expressed in thousand of boat-tonnes per day.

Gulland (1969), on the other hand, suggested plotting the yield per effort of a given year against the mean effort $(\overline{f})$ of the present and preceding year(s), with the number of annual effort values to be included depending on the longevity and mortality of the fish under exploitation, i.e., on the number of year classes significantly contributing to the fishery. This technique, which is illustrated in Table 10.2 and Fig. 10.3, has been criticized by a number of authors (e.g., Roff and Fairbairn 1980; Walter 1975). The latter author also proposed an alternative, graphical method to simulate equilibrium condition.

Schnute (1977) presented a rigorous method for dealing with the problem caused by data drawn from a non-equilibrium situation. Only a simplified version of his model is presented here which has the form

$$\ln\left(\frac{U_i}{U_{i-1}}\right) = r_m - q \cdot \left(\frac{f_i + f_{i-1}}{2}\right) - \frac{r_m}{qB_\infty} \cdot \left(\frac{U_i + U_{i-1}}{2}\right) \qquad \ldots 10.15)$$

where $U_i$ is the mean c/f prevailing in a given year i. This model has the form of a multiple regression whose intercept ($a = r_m$) and slopes ($b_1 = -q$; $b_2 = -\frac{r_m}{qB_\infty}$) lead to estimates of $r_m$ and q and $B_\infty$, respectively. This makes the model superior to the original formulation of Schaefer (1954) which, rather than providing estimates of q, required a knowledge of this parameter. Mohn (1980), however, suggests that the model is quite unstable when "noisy" catch-and-effort data are used (see also Example 10.2) and it would seem best to compare the results obtained by it with estimates e.g., of MSY obtained using another model (see Fig. 10.3).

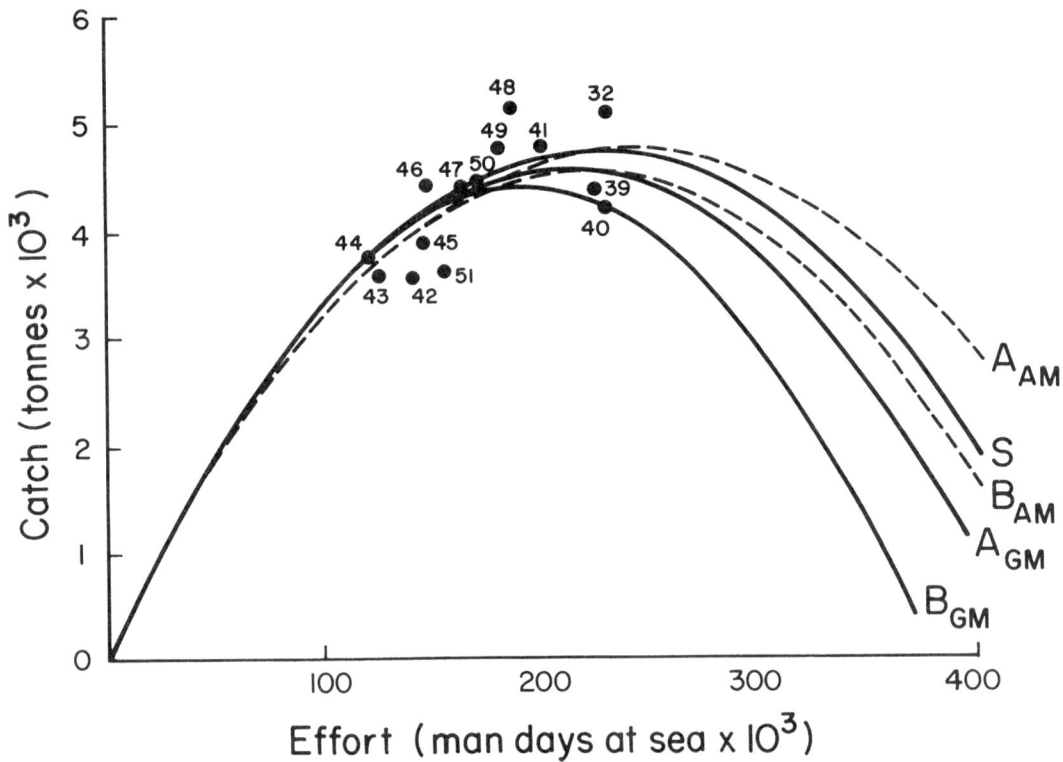

Fig. 10.3. Yield curves for the red snapper *(Lutjanus campecheanus)* fishery on the Bank of Campeche, Mexico. Note strong difference between curves obtained through arithmetic mean (AM) and those obtained through geometric mean regressions (GM); yield curve $A_{AM}$ corresponds to that in Klima (1976, Fig. 3); the corresponding GM curve ($A_{GM}$), because of the scatter of the data points, suggests a lower value of $f_{opt}$. Similarly, the yield curves obtained by using only contemporary effort ($A_{AM}$, $A_{GM}$) differ from those obtained by also using the preceding years' effort ($B_{AM}$, $B_{GM}$). Curve S results from an application of Schute's model (but see Example 10.2).

Table 10.2. Catch-and-effort data for the red snapper fishery on Campeche Bank, Gulf of Mexico, illustrating Gulland's method to simulate equilibrium conditions. From Klima (1976, Table 8, Figs. 2 and 3).

| No. | Year | Catch ($t \times 10^3$) | Contemporary effort (man-days at sea $\times 10^3$) | Average effort I (contemp. + previous year) | Average effort II (contemp. + 2 preceding years) |
|---|---|---|---|---|---|
| 1 | 1937 | 4.91 | 227 | — | — |
| 2 | 1938 | 5.02 | 224 | 225.5 | — |
| 3 | 1939 | 4.25 | 220 | 222.0 | 223.7 |
| 4 | 1940 | 4.14 | 227 | 223.5 | 223.7 |
| 5 | 1941 | 4.79 | 201 | 214.0 | 216.0 |
| 6 | 1942 | 3.46 | 141 | 171.0 | 189.7 |
| 7 | 1943 | 3.57 | 125 | 133.0 | 155.7 |
| 8 | 1944 | 3.77 | 123 | 124.0 | 129.7 |
| 9 | 1945 | 3.98 | 145 | 134.0 | 131.0 |
| 10 | 1946 | 4.37 | 149 | 147.0 | 135.0 |
| 11 | 1947 | 4.24 | 164 | 156.5 | 152.7 |
| 12 | 1948 | 5.06 | 182 | 173.0 | 165.0 |
| 13 | 1949 | 4.79 | 179 | 180.5 | 175.0 |
| 14 | 1950 | 4.38 | 166 | 172.5 | 175.7 |
| 15 | 1951 | 3.53 | 156 | 161.0 | 167.0 |

## SOME MODIFICATIONS OF THE PARABOLIC MODEL

There are various modifications of the basic model in which curves are fitted which differ from a parabola (e.g., Fox 1970; Pella and Tomlinson 1969). Of these variants, only the model of Fox (1970) is presented here.

Put simply, this model consists of plotting the natural logarithm of yield per effort on effort or

$$\ln \frac{Y_E}{f_E} = a - bf_E \qquad \ldots 10.16)$$

instead of plotting yield per effort on effort, as in the case of expression (10.10). This provides the following set of relationships

$$f_{opt} = 1/b \qquad \ldots 10.17)$$

$$MSY = (e^a - 1)/b \qquad \ldots 10.18)$$

and

$$Y_E = fe^a \cdot e^{-bf_E} \qquad \ldots 10.19)$$

Other useful relationships may be found in Fox (1970) or Ricker (1975, p. 330-331). In this model, the value of $B_{opt}$ is always 37% of $B_\infty$, as opposed to 50% in the parabolic model [see expression (10.4)].

Program FB 26 can be used, given a set of yield (= catch in weight) and effort data, to assess the state of a fishery by using the Schaefer (parabolic) and the Fox (exponential) model, by one single entry of data. Values of MSY and $f_{opt}$ are estimated; also values of $r^2$ for the regression equations (10.13) and (10.16) are given which allow comparison of the fit of each of the two models to a given set of data.

Here, the Schaefer and Fox models are fitted to data by means of a GM regression (see Chapter 4 for a definition), which has the effect of automatically accounting for uncertainty:
— when $r^2$ is low (that is when both catch and effort are estimated with large errors, and/or when the catch is strongly affected by environmental perturbations), the GM regression will provide lower (more conservative) estimates of optimum effort than an AM regression,
— when $r^2$ is high (that is when there is a tight relationship between the catch and effort data), the GM regression will have a slope and an intercept similar to those of an AM regression.

This feature, generally not considered when fitting surplus production models to data, seems particularly appropriate in light of the fact that costly investments are often based solely on the values of optimum effort generated by surplus production models.

An application of Fox's model is given in Example 10.3 (see also Fig. 10.4 and Table 10.3).

The models discussed above, although representing considerable simplifications or improvements of the model presented by Schaefer (1954, 1957), have a major drawback in that they require measures of effort, which are often unavailable and/or unreliable.

It is, however, not fishing effort itself which "generates" a surplus yield of an exploited stock, but fishing mortality. In an exploited fish stock, on the other hand, fishing mortality is often not directly measurable, because of the simultaneous effect of natural mortality.

To resolve this, Csirke and Caddy (1983) suggested to plot annual catch (Y) as a parabolic function of total mortality (Z), i.e.,

$$Y = a + b_1 Z + b_2 Z^2 \qquad \ldots 10.20)$$

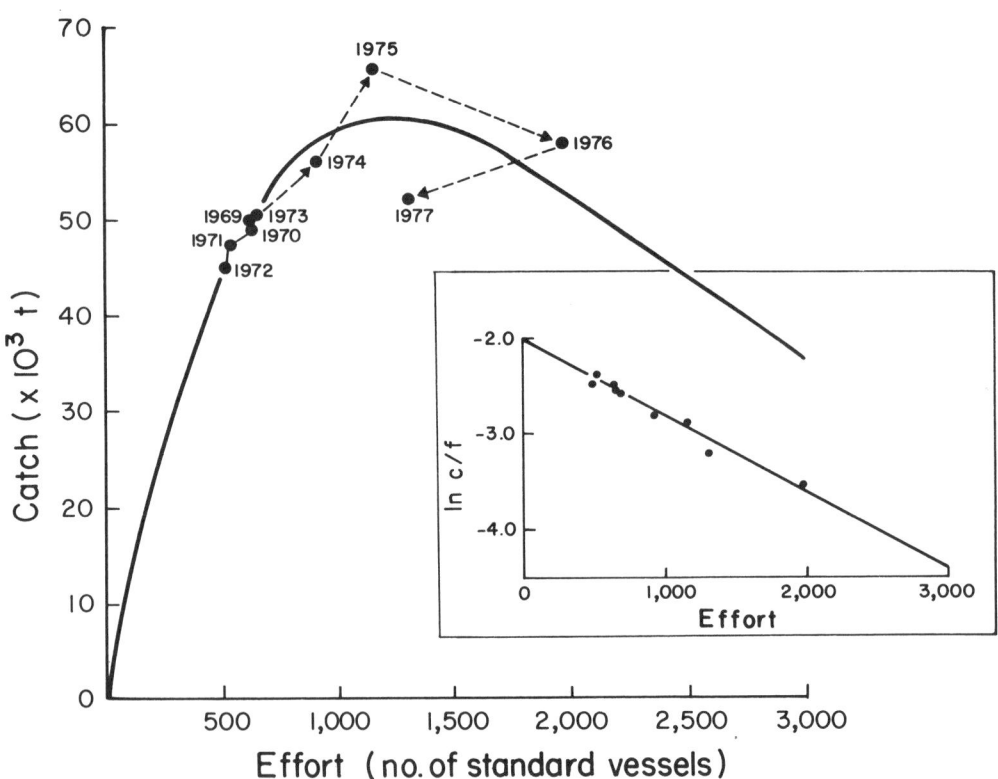

Fig. 10.4. Yield curve for the north Java coast trawl fishery (based on data in Table 10.3 and Example 10.3).

Table 10.3. Catch-and-effort data from the north Java demersal trawl fishery (all species aggregated) (from Dwiponggo 1979).

| No. | Year | Catch t x $10^3$ | Effort No. of standard vessels |
|---|---|---|---|
| 1 | 1969 | 50 | 623 |
| 2 | 1970 | 49 | 628 |
| 3 | 1971 | 47.5 | 520 |
| 4 | 1972 | 45 | 513 |
| 5 | 1973 | 51 | 661 |
| 6 | 1974 | 56 | 919 |
| 7 | 1975 | 66 | 1,158 |
| 8 | 1976 | 58 | 1,970 |
| 9 | 1977 | 52 | 1,317 |

where $Z = F + M$, from which the following parameters can be estimated.

$$M = \frac{-b_1 + \sqrt{b_1^2 - 4ab_2}}{2b_2} \quad \ldots 10.21)$$

$$Z_{opt} = -\frac{b_1}{2b_2} \quad \ldots 10.22)$$

$$F_{opt} = -\frac{b_1}{2b_2} - M \quad \ldots 10.23)$$

$$r_m = 2F_{opt} \quad \ldots 10.24)$$

$$MSY = a - (b_1^2/4b_2) \quad \ldots 10.25)$$

and

$$B_\infty = \frac{MSY \cdot 4}{r_m} \quad \ldots 10.26)$$

An application of this method is given in Example 10.4 (see also Fig. 10.5 and Table 10.4).

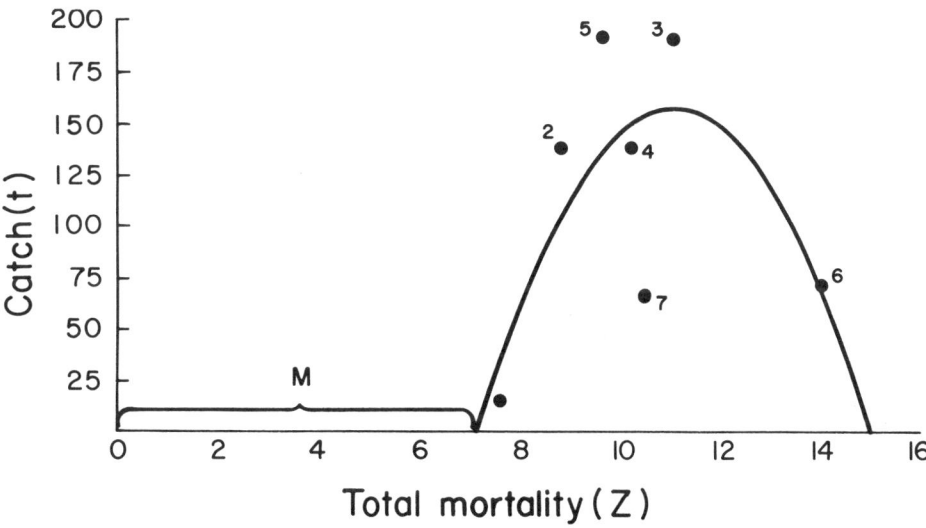

Fig. 10.5. Yield curve of shorthead anchovy (*Stolephorus heterolobus*) at Ysabel Passage, near New Hanover, Papua New Guinea. M = natural mortality. Numbers refer to those in Example 10.4.

A further property of the model of Csirke and Caddy is that Z in equation (10.20) above can be replaced by Z/K, the latter being a parameter which can be estimated from the average length composition of the fish catch and without an exact knowledge of the growth parameters of the fish in question (see Chapter 5). The modified model thus becomes

$$Y = a' + b_1' (Z/K) + b_2' (Z/K)^2 \qquad \ldots 10.27)$$

with
$$M/K = \frac{-b_1' + \sqrt{b_1'^2 - 4a'b_2'}}{2b_2'} \qquad \ldots 10.28)$$

and
$$Z_{opt}/K = -b_1'/2a' \qquad \ldots 10.29)$$

The parameter $Z_{opt}/K$ corresponds to an optimum mean length in the catch ($\overline{L}_{opt}$), the value of which may be estimated by trial and error, e.g., from

$$\frac{Z_{opt}}{K} = \frac{L_\infty - \overline{L}_{opt}}{\overline{L}_{opt} - L'} \qquad \ldots 10.30)$$

Finally, E = F/Z may be estimated for each value of Z/K from the equation

$$E = 1 - (M/K)/(Z/K) \qquad \ldots 10.31)$$

which can be used, along with the estimate of M/K, e.g., to estimate the relative yield per recruit obtained at each level of Z/K (see Chapter 8). See Chapter 5 for definitions of $\overline{L}$, $L'$ and E.

All of these parameters, it should be mentioned are either solutions of, or are implicit in the Schaefer model. The point here is that they can all be derived from quantities (catch, total mortality) that can be estimated rather straightforwardly, e.g., using one of the various methods presented in Chapter 5.

When catch data are not available, catch-per-effort data (c/f = U) can be used in a linear regression of the form

$$U = a - bZ \qquad \ldots 10.32)$$

where
$$M = (a - U_\infty)/b \qquad \ldots 10.33)$$

and where $U_\infty$ is the catch per effort corresponding to $B_\infty$, i.e., to the unexploited biomass or virgin stock (assuming that $B_v \approx B_\infty$). Generally, when catch-per-effort data are available, it will be possible to estimate $U_\infty$ by using the first two catch-per-effort values in a developing fishery ($U_1$, $U_2$) and defining

$$U_\infty \approx 2U_1 - U_2 \qquad \ldots 10.34)$$

(Obviously, data from biomass survey in an unexploited stock can be used to estimate both $U_\infty$ and $B_\infty$ directly). Using $U_\infty$ and equation (10.32), it is then possible to estimate $F_{opt}$ as

$$F_{opt} = U_\infty/(2b) \qquad \ldots 10.35)$$

while a knowledge of $B_\infty$ can be used to estimate MSY from $F_{opt}$

$$MSY = 0.5 B_\infty \cdot F_{opt} \qquad \ldots 10.36)$$

## APPLYING SURPLUS-YIELD MODELS TO MULTISPECIES STOCKS

In demersal fisheries, especially in the tropics, the catch tends to consist of a multitude of species for which individual assessments are often impossible or inappropriate.

Table 10.4. Catch and total mortality estimates of shorthead anchovy *(Stolephorus heterolobus)* in Ysabel Passage, near New Hanover, Papua New Guinea. Data from Dalzell (1984); Z estimates based on mean lengths.

| No. | Year | Catch (t) | Total mortality (Z) |
|---|---|---|---|
| 1 | 1972 | 14 | 7.6 |
| 2 | 1973 | 138 | 8.8 |
| 3 | 1976 | 191 | 11.0 |
| 4 | 1977 | 138 | 10.2 |
| not used | 1978 | (404) | (11.7) |
| 5 | 1979 | 192 | 9.6 |
| 6 | 1980 | 72 | 14.0 |
| 7 | 1981 | 66 | 10.5 |

It has been a common practice to treat the various fish of tropical and other multispecies stocks as one single entity, applying the Schaefer or Fox model to the total multispecies catch of these fisheries (see Example 10.3 and FAO 1978). Pope (1979) recently provided a theoretical basis for this approach, while some of the problems associated with it were discussed in Pauly (1979b). See also Chapter 12.

Recommended reading: Ricker (1975) gives a good account of the historical development of surplus yield models, but it is best to read also some of the original papers on the topic, notably those by Graham (1943), Schaefer (1954, 1957), Silliman and Gutsell (1958), Schaefer and Beverton (1963), Gulland (1969) and Schnute (1977).

Suggested research topics: Crucial with surplus yield models is the availability of long time-series of catch-and-effort data (or, in the case of Csirke and Caddy's model, of catch and total mortality data); it is worthwhile to estimate these parameters reliably in an ongoing fishery. Where possible, one should also attempt to reconstruct time-series of total mortality (e.g., from length-frequency data) for use with available time series of catch.

**EXAMPLE 10.1**

**Estimating MSY and optimum effort for a single-species pelagic fishery by means of the Schaefer model.**

Data from Table 10.1

Computation

1) Read sides 1 and 2 of Program FB 26

2) Enter catch and effort data

    Keystrokes: f a 32.89 ↑ 31.413 A 37.78 ↑ 32.999 A 33.25 ↑ 36.579 A 28.86 ↑ 40.367 A 26.82 ↑ 43.191 A 22.26 ↑ 42.716 A 23.73 ↑ 41.636 A 25.04 ↑ 44.634 A 22.77 ↑ 49.284 A 22.64 ↑ 52.048 A

3) Estimate parameters of plot of c/f on f, MSY and $f_{opt}$

| | Keystrokes | Results | |
|---|---|---|---|
| | E | 0.874 | ($r^2$) |
| | | 2.285 | (a) |
| | | −0.038 | (b) |
| | D | 29.879 | ($f_{opt}$) |
| | | 34.133 | (MSY) |

4) Use Program FB 26 to draw yield curve

| | Keystrokes | Results | |
|---|---|---|---|
| enter $f_1$ | 10 C | 19.024 | ($Y_1$) |
| enter $f_2$ | 20 C | 30.402 | ($Y_2$) |
| etc. | .... | .... | |

The result should look similar to Fig. 10.2 from which it appears that the fishery in the early 70s was in deep trouble. In fact, as Murphy (1972) pointed out "it shows that [ . . . ] a 20% increase in total effort [ . . . ] will drive the stock to extinction [and] it is not hard to imagine nature providing this increase or its equivalent, either through a negative perturbation of reproductive success, an increase in predation or some combination of these".

The negative perturbation came in the form of a strong "El Niño" and the stock collapsed.

**EXAMPLE 10.2**   Application of Schnute's model to the red snapper fishery on Campeche Bank, Mexico.

Data from Table 10.2

Computation

1) Read sides 1 and 2 of Program FB 27

2) Initialize and enter catch and effort data

   Keystrokes: 4.91 ↑ 227 f a 5.02 ↑ 224 A 4.25 ↑ 220 A 4.14 ↑ 227 A 4.79 ↑ 201 A
   3.46 ↑ 141 A 3.57 ↑ 125 A 3.77 ↑ 123 A 3.98 ↑ 145 A 4.37 ↑ 149 A
   4.24 ↑ 164 A 5.06 ↑ 182 A 4.79 ↑ 179 A 4.38 ↑ 166 A 3.53 ↑ 156 A

3) Calculate parameters of regression

   | | Keystrokes | Results | |
   |---|---|---|---|
   | | E | 0.006 | ($R^2$) |
   | | | 0.268 | (a) |
   | | | −0.001 | ($b_1$) |
   | | | −6.359 | ($b_2$) |

4) Estimate fishery-related parameters

   | | Keystrokes | Results | |
   |---|---|---|---|
   | | f e | 0.268 | ($r_m$) |
   | | | 0.001 | (q) |
   | | | 70.309 | ($B_\infty$) |
   | | | 223.558 | ($f_{opt}$) |
   | | | 4.712 | (MSY) |

As might be seen in Fig. 10.3, the yield curve based on Schnute's model (S) resembles quite closely the curve obtained by fitting the catch figures to the average of contemporary and the preceding year's effort (curve $B_{AM}$). Intuitively, this result makes sense since Schnute's model in fact uses the same averaged effort and is fitted with an AM multiple regression. The abysmally low value of $R^2$ (= 0.00635) sheds doubt on the reliability of the various parameter estimates, however.

EXAMPLE 10.3

**Estimating MSY and optimum effort for a multispecies demersal trawl fishery by means of Fox's model.**

Data from Table 10.3

Computation

1) Read sides 1 and 2 of Program FB 26

2) Enter catch and effort data

   Keystrokes: f a 50 ↑ 623 A 49 ↑ 628 A 47.5 ↑ 520 A 45 ↑ 513 A 51 ↑ 661 A 56 ↑ 919 A 66 ↑ 1158 ↑ 1970 A 52 ↑ 1317 A

3) Estimate parameters of plot of in c/f on f, $f_{opt}$ and MSY

   | Keystrokes | Results | |
   |---|---|---|
   | f e | 0.966 | ($r^2$) |
   | | −2.027 | (a) |
   | | −0.001 | (b) |
   | DSP 6 | −0.000799 | (b) |
   | DSP 2 f d | 1251.99 | ($f_{opt}$) |
   | | 60.66 | (MSY) |

4) Use Program FB 26 to plot draw yield curve

   | Keystrokes | Results | |
   |---|---|---|
   | 100 f c | 12.16 | ($Y_1$) |
   | 200 f c | 22.45 | ($Y_2$) |
   | etc. | ... | |

This example and Fig. 10.4 suggest that the level of effort applied in 1975 and 1977 was near optimum. Furthermore, the plot shows very nicely the effect on a rapid increase of effort, as in 1975 and 1976 the points of which are *above* the curve, while the point for 1977 is *below* the curve, as would be expected following a rapid decrease of effort. When effort remains unchanged for several years the yield should, on the average come to lie *on* the curve. However, demersal trawling has been banned in Indonesia, so we may never know.

**EXAMPLE 10.4**

**Estimation of MSY and $Z_{opt}$ using Csirke and Caddy's model.**

Data from Table 10.4

Computations

1) Read sides 1 and 2 of Program FB 28

2) Initialize and enter catch and mortality data

   Keystrokes: f a 14 ↑ 7.6 A 138 ↑ 8.8 A 191 ↑ 11 A 138 ↑ 10.2 A 192 ↑ 9.6 A 72 ↑ 14 A 66 ↑ 10.5 A

3) Calculate parameters of multiple regression

   | Keystroke | Results | |
   |---|---|---|
   | E | 0.495 | ($R^2$) |
   | | −1085.334 | (a) |
   | | 225.316 | ($b_1$) |
   | | −10.211 | ($b_2$) |

4) Calculate parameters of yield curves

   | Keystroke | Results | |
   |---|---|---|
   | f e | 7.104 | (M) |
   | | 11.033 | ($Z_{opt}$) |
   | | 3.928 | ($F_{opt}$) |
   | | 7.857 | ($r_m$) |
   | | 157.583 | (MSY) |
   | | 80.228 | ($B_\infty$) |

The results appear reasonable (particularly the value of M), but this was achieved by deleting one point (1978), which had a very high catch, such as might occur after an exceptionally good recruitment. Clearly, it would be appropriate here to assess the validity of the results, using another model.

# 11. The Intrinsic Rate of Population Increase

## INTRODUCTION

In the preceding chapters, various models (= equations) were presented, each of which illustrated a different aspect of the dynamics of fish populations.

It is the purpose of this chapter to demonstrate the interrelationships between some of these models, to show that several of the equations presented here actually reflect different aspects of the same processes.

The concept most helpful to show interrelationships between different models used in fish population dynamics is, paradoxically, rarely used in this field. It is the intrinsic rate of increase ($r_m$) of a population, which may be defined as "the innate capacity of (a) species to increase when population growth is not slowed down by competition" (Pielou 1978).

The $r_m$ concept is extremely important in quantitative ecology, and at least one chapter in every good ecology text is devoted to it (e.g., Odum 1971; Slobotkin 1980; Ricklefs 1979). In terms of Russel's Axiom (see Chapter 1), $r_m$ can be defined as

$$r_m = \frac{R^* + G^* - M^*}{B} \quad \ldots 11.1)$$

(when B is low) but this cannot be used for quantitative stock assessment purposes because Russel's axiom itself expresses things only qualitatively.

## MAXIMUM SUSTAINABLE YIELDS AND $r_m$

The intrinsic rate of increase ($r_m$) can be defined quantitatively in terms of the Schaefer model, where $r_m$, MSY and $B_\infty$, the carrying capacity of the environment are related such that:

$$MSY = \frac{r_m \cdot B_\infty}{4} \quad \ldots 11.2)$$

As discussed in Chapter 10, the Schaefer model is based on the assumption that the growth of a fish population released into a new environment can be described by a logistic growth curve. This curve has the form

$$B_t = \frac{B_\infty}{1 + e^{-r_m (t - t_i)}} \quad \ldots 11.3)$$

where $B_\infty$ is the carrying capacity of the environment in terms of weight, $r_m$ the intrinsic rate of population increase, and $t_i$ (=t at inflexion point) is a constant which adjusts the time scale to an origin such that $t - t_i = 0$ when $B_t = B_\infty/2$, $B_t$ being the biomass at time t. $B_\infty$ and $B_t$ may be replaced by $N_\infty$ and $N_t$ when equation (11.3) refers to numbers. When equation (11.3) is used to fit data from a selection experiment, $B_t$ is equivalent to the probability of capture, t to the length, and $t_i$ to $L_c$. (Refer to Chapter 3.)

Aquarium experiments demonstrate the growth of fish populations can often be approximated by a logistic curve (Silliman and Gutsell 1958, Fig. 3). In nature, cases of fish populations "exploding" into a new environment are obviously difficult to document. Some data, however, are available for Red Sea lizardfish *(Saurida undosquamis)* which penetrated into the Mediterranean via the Suez Canal, and after a lag phase (of genetic adjustment?) experienced a rapid increase of population size, as documented by catch-per-effort data off the Israel coast (Table 11.1).

As might be seen from Fig. 11.1 and Table 11.1, the course of the population increase reflected in the catch-per-effort data roughly corresponds to a logistic curve, the $r_m$ and $t_i$ values of which may

Table 11.1. Data on the growth of a newly established Mediterranean population of *Saurida undosquamis*, a Red Sea immigrant. Data from Ben-Yami and Glaser (1974, Fig. 5B).

| Code year | Catch/effort (kg/h) |
|---|---|
| 1 | 1 |
| 2 | 2 |
| 3 | 3 |
| 4 | 75 |
| 5 | 78 |

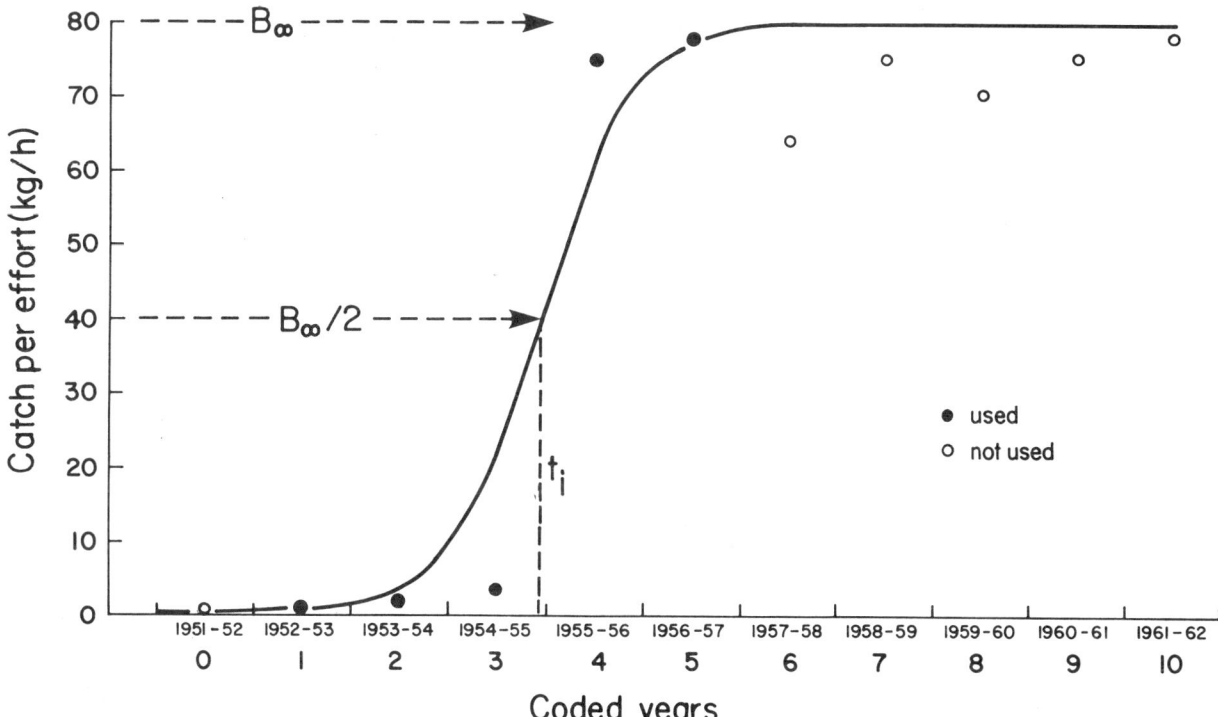

Fig. 11.1. Logistic growth curve fitted to catch-per-effort data on a newly established Mediterranean population of lizardfish *(Saurida undosquamis)* (based on data in Table 11.1, and see Example 11.1 for selection of points used in curve fitting).

be estimated by means of Program FB 28 (Example 11.1). MacCall (1980) presented data on a temperate fish *(Engraulis mordax)* suggesting a similar logistic increase of biomass.

Equation (11.2) suggests that when an estimate is available of the virgin biomass of a given population ($B_v$, or $B_o$ in Gulland 1971) and when it is legitimate to set $B_\infty \approx B_v$ (it is *not* always the case, see Pauly 1979b, or May et al. 1979), all that is needed to obtain a preliminary estimate of (future) MSY (also called Potential Yield, $P_y$) is an estimate of $r_m$.

Several, rather elaborate methods are used by ecologists to estimate $r_m$. One of them is the calculation of $r_m$ from so-called "life tables" (see Pielou 1978, Ricklefs 1979). This method has data requirements which fishery biologists will find quite hard to meet and only two studies have come to my attention which estimates $r_m$ using this approach in fish (Murphy 1967, Pitcher and Hart 1982). Two HP 67/97 programs are available to estimate $r_m$ from life tables. Demography I and Demography II, both in the HP Users' Library Solutions booklet devoted to "Biology".

Blueweiss et al. (1978) have shown that $r_m$ in animals and various small organisms is inversely related to body weight and presented a double logarithmic plot of $r_m$ on "mean adult body weight" ($\overline{W}$) spanning 22 orders of magnitude. I have added several values to the plot presented by Blueweiss et al. (1978) which pertain to fish and whales, the latter expanding the range covered by the plot to 24 orders of magnitude (Fig. 11.2).

Although the fit, particularly in organisms ranging from $10^{-6}$ to $10^0$ g is not particularly good, a clear relationship emerges which allows, when mean adult body weight is known, a rough estimate of $r_m$ through the relationship

$$r_m \approx 9.13 \cdot \overline{W}^{-0.26} \qquad \ldots 11.4)$$

where $r_m$ is expressed on a yearly basis and $\overline{W}$ is grams, and computed from $\overline{W} = (W_{max} + W_m)/2$; $W_{max}$ is the maximum weight reached by the adults of a stock and $W_m$ is their weight at first maturity (see Example 11.2).

Combining expression (11.4) with expression (11.2) gives

$$P_y \approx 2.3 \cdot \overline{W}^{-0.26} B_v \qquad \ldots 11.5)$$

which can be used to obtain first estimates of MSY, i.e., potential yield, when only virgin stock size and mean adult body weight are known.

The results obtained by means of this equation may thus be compared with those obtained using Gulland's (1971) well-known relationship

$$P_y \approx 1/2 \cdot M \cdot B_v \qquad \ldots 11.6)$$

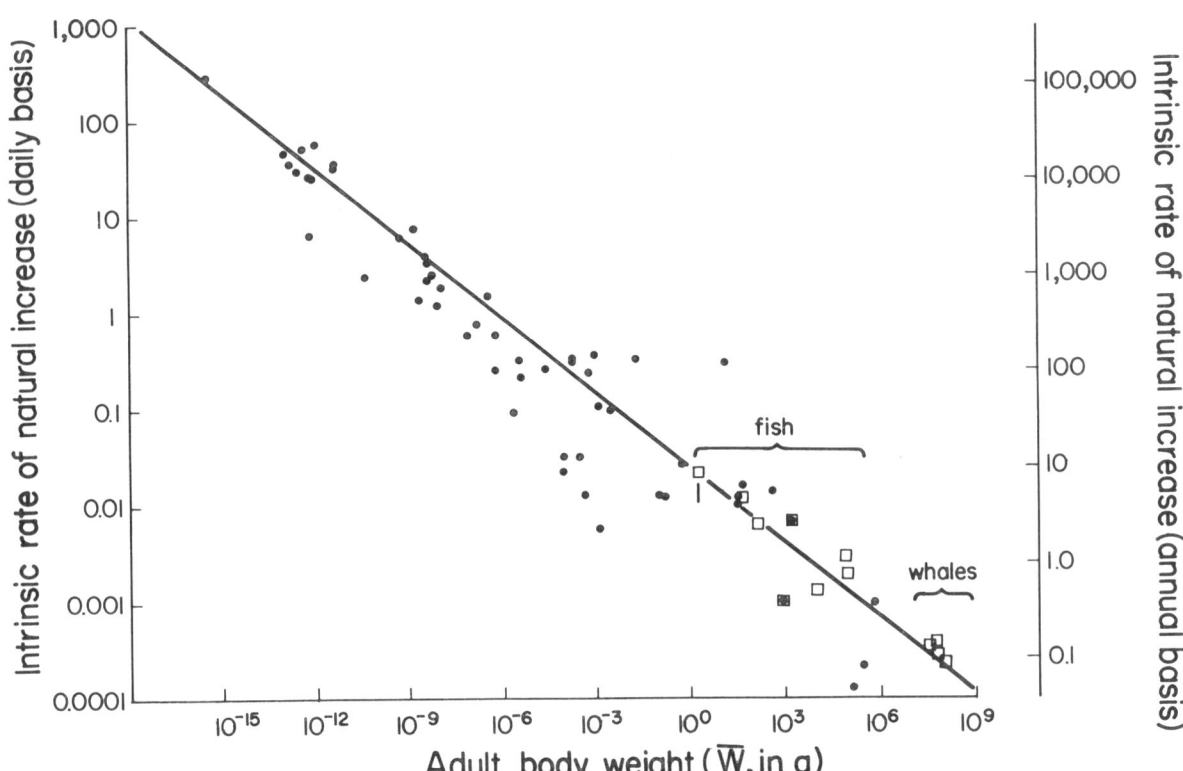

Fig. 11.2. Relationship between intrinsic rate of population increase ($r_m$) and adult body weight for various organisms. (The dots and the line are from Blueweiss et al. 1978; the open squares were added by Pauly 1982a.)

See also Example (11.3). Expressions (11.5) and (11.6) are rough approximations; with expression (11.5) the major problem is the fact that the built-in relationship between $\overline{W}$ and $r_m$ is based on a linear regression whose scatter of data is not negligible, while the major drawback of expression (11.6) is that the resulting $P_y$ estimates are directly proportional to and thus highly sensitive to, the value of M used. Also, the validity of (11.6) rests on the assumption that $F_{opt} = M$ which probably does not apply in most stocks (see p. 77).

## STOCK-RECRUITMENT RELATIONSHIPS AND $r_m$

Another integrative property of $r_m$ is that it can also be shown to be an implicit parameter of both Beverton and Holt and Ricker-type stock-recruitment curves. This property, which was discussed by Murphy (1967) and Eberhardt (1977) will be here touched upon only briefly because its various ramifications have not yet been fully investigated. Starting with the second form of Ricker's stock-recruitment curve (see Chapter 9), one can define

$$a = P_r/P_m \qquad \ldots 11.7)$$

where $P_r$ is the replacement abundance of parent stock and $P_m$ is the parent stock producing maximum recruitment (see Chapter 9 for details on these definitions). Subsitution into Ricker's second stock-recruitment curve gives:

$$R = P e^{P_r/P_m - P/P_m} \qquad \ldots 11.8)$$

Now, it is obvious that as P approaches zero, the second term of the exponent ($P/P_m$) will also tend to approach zero.* Division of both sides of (11.8) with P, when P is very small, yields:

$$R/P = e^{P_r/P_m} \qquad \ldots 11.9)$$

Since the ratio R/P expresses the ratio between total births in two successive generations at very low population sizes there is an identity between (11.9) and the equation used in the ecological literature

$$N_T/N_o = e^{r_m \cdot T} \qquad \ldots 11.10)$$

where, at very low population sizes

$N_o$ is the total number of animals in the population at the beginning of a generation
$N_T$ is the number of animals at the end of that generation
T is the generation time

and where

$r_m$ is the ubiquitous intrinsic rate of increase.

In view of this identity:

$$P_r/P_m = r_m \cdot T \qquad \ldots 11.11)$$

---

*In Murphy (1967) the word "zero" has been erroneously replaced by "unity."

which may be called "Murphy's identity". An application of this identity is given in the following paragraphs.

The generation time, T, of an animal is generally quite difficult to estimate (but see Slobotkin 1980, Fig. 5.2). However, it appears that a great number of the small fish caught in tropical waters have growth parameters suggesting a rather short life span (2-4 years) and an age at first maturity ($t_m$) of generally one year (Banerji and Krishnan 1973; Qasim 1973a, 1973b). High natural mortality and lack of substantial post-maturity growth will cause a mean generation time of about 1 year in such fish, or:

$$r_m \approx P_r/P_m \qquad \ldots 11.12)$$

Only one data set is readily available which can be used to test these conjectures. In Chapter 9, Example 9.4, a value of $P_r/P_m$ was estimated for *Lactarius lactarius*, a fish with the characteristics given in the above paragraph and this value was 2.84.

The value of $W_\infty$ used in Pauly (1980d) was 193 g, which may roughly correspond to $W_{max}$, while the value of $W_m$ is 57.3 g. Hence, $\overline{W}$, as defined above, is (193 + 57)/2 = 125 g, from which $r_m$ is estimated, via equation 11.4, to be 2.60. Conversely, T can be estimated from

$$T = 2.84/2.60 = 1.09 \qquad \ldots 11.13)$$

which is similar to the value assumed previously.

While Murphy (1967) investigated the second form of Ricker's curve, Eberhardt (1977) demonstrated a link between the first form of Ricker's curve and the logistic growth curve, which led to the identities

$$\alpha = e^{r_m} \qquad \ldots 11.14)$$

and

$$\beta = r_m/N_\infty \qquad \ldots 11.15)$$

while the link between Beverton and Holt's stock-recruitment curve and the logistic growth curve was established through the identities

$$\alpha' = (1 - e^{-r_m})/N_\infty \qquad \ldots 11.16)$$

and

$$\beta' = e^{-r_m} \qquad \ldots 11.17)$$

The parameters $\alpha'$ in Ricker's curve and $\beta'$ in Beverton and Holt's curve are often called "density-independent terms"; given equations (11.15) and (11.17), their relationship is given by

$$\alpha = 1/\beta' \qquad \ldots 11.18)$$

The "density-dependent terms" ($\beta$ in Ricker's curve, $\alpha'$ in Beverton and Holt's curve) are also closely related, and are approximately the same when $r_m$ is small, diverging up to 20% when $r_m$ is large; this is expressed by the approximations

$$\alpha' \approx \beta \approx (1 - e^{-r_m})/N_\infty \qquad \ldots 11.19)$$

which applies when $r_m$ is small (Eberhardt 1977; Pitcher and Hart 1982).

The presentation of these interrelationships between different models and the example for *Lactarius lactarius* given above are not meant to suggest that values of $r_m$ obtained say from equation (11.4) and from stock-recruitment relationships should necessarily coincide. Rather, the suggestion made earlier by Murphy (1967) is reiterated that there might be here a type of interrelationship worth pursuing further which might lead to a further integration of the various concepts used in fishery biology.

Indeed, as the following, last chapter should demonstrate, there is a great need for attempts to integrate concepts derived from fish population dynamics with some of those derived by theoretical ecologists, and thus to cross-pollinate the two disciplines.

Recommended reading: Since a good background in ecological theory should help the fishery biologist put her or his field into perspective, it may be appropriate to list here some ecological texts, all of which discuss, among other things, the intrinsic rate of increase of populations and related concepts, e.g., Slobotkin (1980), Odum (1971), Ricklefs (1979) and Pielou (1978). These books also contain most of the references needed to plunge into the ecological literature.

Suggested research topics: Since $r_m$ is so closely related to yields, it would seem that attempts to estimate this parameter from life tables of commercial fish populations should represent worthwhile research projects (see Pitcher and Hart 1982 for data requirements and method). Such a study also would allow one to identify factors (such as temperature or fecundity) other than body weight which may help to predict values of $r_m$, or to improve estimates obtained from plots such as Fig. 11.2.

EXAMPLE 11.1

**Estimating the intrinsic rate of increase for an "exploding" population of lizardfish** *(Saurida undosquamis)*.

Data from Table 11.1 and Fig. 11.1. (Only the data points for the years 1952-53 to 1956-57 are used for the computation. The earlier points were too low to be precisely read off the original figure in Ben-Yami and Glaser (1974). The later points, on the other hand, probably indicate a drop in biomass occurring after the initial build-up.)

Computation

1) Read side 1 of Program FB 29

2) Enter set value of $B_\infty$, and $B_t$ and t data

   Keystrokes: 80 f a 1 ↑ 1 A 2 ↑ 2 A 3 ↑ 75 ↑ 4 A 78 ↑ 5 A

3) Calculate $r^2$, $r_m$ and $t_i$

   | | Keystrokes | Results | |
   |---|---|---|---|
   | | E | 0.854 | ($r^2$) |
   | | | 2.244 | ($r_m$) |
   | | | 3.437 | ($t_i$) |

4) Confirm that $t_i$ corresponds to $B_\infty/2$

   | | C | 40.000 | ($B_\infty/2$) |
   |---|---|---|---|

By entering other t values and pressing the C-Key, data points for a curve such as in Fig. 11.1 can be obtained. It must be realized, however, that the values of $r_m$ and $t_i$ obtained here depend critically on the choice of points included in the computation and of 80 kg/hr as the c/f figure corresponding to $B_\infty$; the estimate of $r_m$ is thus tentative.

**EXAMPLE 11.2**

**Estimating $r_m$ from the mean weight ($\overline{W}$) of the adults in a given stock.**

1) Read side 1 of Program FB 29

Case I

2) Estimate $\overline{W}$: Thompson and Munro (1978) give data from which $W_{max}$ in Jamaican *Epinephelus guttatus* can be estimated at 2,324 g, while $W_m$, the mean weight at first maturity is about 243 g. Thus, to obtain $\overline{W}$, we perform

|  | Keystrokes | Results |
|---|---|---|
|  | 2,324 ↑ | — |
|  | 243 + 2 ÷ | 1,283.5 ($\overline{W}$) |
| 3) Estimate $r_m$ from $\overline{W}$ | f e | 1.42 ($r_m$) |

Case II

4) Estimate $\overline{W}$: Pauly (1980d) gives a value of 193 g for $W_\infty$ in *Lactarius lactarius* from the Gulf of Thailand. Using this as an estimate of $W_{max}$ and using $W_m = W_{max} \cdot 0.3 = 57.9$, we obtain $\overline{W}$ from:

|  | Keystrokes | Results |
|---|---|---|
|  | 193 ↑ |  |
|  | 57.9 + 2 ÷ | 125.45 ($\overline{W}$) |
| 5) Estimate $r_m$ from $\overline{W}$ | f e | 2.60 ($r_m$) |

It must be realized that these two estimates of $r_m$ are rather crude and should not preclude attempts to estimate this important parameter independently.

**Estimating potential yields when catch-and-effort data are not available.**  EXAMPLE 11.3

1) Thompson and Munro (1978) give for the Caribbean grouper *Epinephelus guttatus* the following data: natural mortality = 0.68, $TL_{max}$, in cm = 53.7 cm (corresponding to $W_{max}$ = 2,324), approximate weight at first maturity = 243. From these data, adult body weight ($\overline{W}$) is computed as 1,283.5 g (see Example 11.2).

2) Estimating potential yield ($P_y$) from Gulland's equation (11.6) assuming $B_v$ = 1:

    | Keystrokes | Results |
    |---|---|
    | .68 ↑ (M) | |
    | .5 x | 0.34    ($P_y$) |

3) Estimating potential yield ($P_y$) from equation (11.5), also assuming $B_v$ = 1:

    | Keystrokes | Results |
    |---|---|
    | 1,283.5 ↑ (w) | |
    | .26 CHS | |
    | $y^x$ 2.3x | 0.36    ($P_y$) |

The estimates (0.34 and 0.36) are close enough to each other to feel confident that $P_y$ is about 1/3 of the virgin biomass per year. Obviously, this is so because this example is in a manual; real-life data do not always behave so nicely. In fact, Beddington and Cooke (1983) argue, quite cogently, that Gulland's equation (and consequently any other equation which gives similar results) has an extremely strong upward bias (see p. 77).

## 12. Multispecies Fisheries

INTRODUCTION

With few exceptions, the models discussed in the previous chapters were developed for use in conjunction with single-species stocks and fisheries.

When using such models, an implicit assumption is that the stock under investigation has only negligible interaction with other species, except for those interactions accounted for by the catch-all interaction term "M", natural mortality (caused mainly by predation).

This approach may be justified in temperate waters, where some stocks (e.g., cod, pollock, herring, salmon) sustain "aimed" fisheries, in which the fish not belonging to the target species form only a minor part of the catch (the "bycatch").

In tropical fisheries, especially in demersal fisheries, no single species is aimed at, generally, and there is no "bycatch" when the definition above is used, except in shrimp fisheries where the fish caught (often 90% of the total catch by weight) are frequently thrown overboard. Table 12.1 reproduces the typical catch of a Southeast Asian trawler. The large number of species, none of which is dominant, will be noted.

Table 12.1. A typical trawler catch (45 min haul) from the Java Sea (06° 12'S, 108° 26'E, 34-35 m depth) made on 5 September 1976 by *R/V Mutiara IV* showing the diversity of tropical demersal multispecies stocks. (Asterisks refer to weight and number raised from a sorted sample of 1 out of 5 boxes. Invertebrates not included.)

| No. | Family | Species | W (kg) | N |
|---|---|---|---|---|
| 1 | Ariidae | *Osteogeniosus militaris* | 3.4 | 17 |
| 2 | Balistidae | *Abalistes stellaris* | 0.5 | 1 |
| 3 | Carangidae | *Seriolina nigrofasciata* | 0.32 | 1 |
| 4 | Carangidae | *Scomberoides* sp. | 0.15 | 5 |
| 5 | Carangidae | *Alepes kalla* | 5.0* | 90* |
| 6 | Carangidae | *Alepes djedaba* | 7.50* | 290* |
| 7 | Carangidae | *Megalaspis cordyla* | 8.5* | 170* |
| 8 | Carangidae | *Selaroides leptolepis* | 0.25* | 10* |
| 9 | Carangidae | *Carangoides* spp. | 6.10* | 145* |
| 10 | Carangidae | *Atropus atropus* | 1.75* | 30* |
| 11 | Chirocentridae | *Chirocentrus dorab* | 0.80* | 5* |
| 12 | Clupeidae | *Anadontostoma chacunda* | 0.15* | 5* |
| 13 | Clupeidae | *Opisthopterus valenciennensis* | 1.10* | 15* |
| 14 | Clupeidae | *Dussumieria acuta* | 1.70* | 50* |
| 15 | Clupeidae | *Ilisha* sp. | 5.60* | 65* |
| 16 | Clupeidae | *Sardinella gibbosa* | 0.30* | 10* |
| 17 | Dasyatidae | not identified | 2.65 | 1 |
| 18 | Drepanidae | *Drepane longimana* | 0.35* | 5* |
| 19 | Engraulidae | *Stolephorus* spp. | 21.0* | 4,175* |
| 20 | Gerridae | *Pentaprion longimanus* | 15.25* | 1,165* |
| 21 | Fistulariidae | not identified | 0.15* | 10* |
| 22 | Formionidae | *Formio niger* | 0.2 | 1 |
| 23 | Lagocephalidae | not identified | 4.0 | 95 |
| 24 | Leiognathidae | *Leiognathus splendens* | 10.0* | 720* |
| 25 | Leiognathidae | *Leiognathus leuciscus* | 4.20* | 780* |
| 26 | Leiognathidae | *Leiognathus bindus* | 1.20* | 340* |
| 27 | Leiognathidae | *Secutor ruconius* | 1.20* | 380* |

Continued

Table 12.1 continued

| | | | | |
|---|---|---|---|---|
| 28 | Leiognathidae | *Secutor insidiator* | 2.80* | 560* |
| 29 | Lutjanidae | *Lutjanus sanguineus* | 4.0 | 1 |
| 30 | Lutjanidae | *Lutjanus johni* | 5.0* | 10* |
| 31 | Lutjanidae | *Lutjanus lineolatus* | 0.20* | 10* |
| 32 | Lutjanidae | *Caesio erythrogaster* | 0.10* | 5* |
| 33 | Mullidae | *Upeneus sulphureus* | 75.0* | 6,075* |
| 34 | Nemipteridae | *Nemipterus japonicus* | 3.0* | 15* |
| 35 | Nemipteridae | *Nemipterus bathybius* | 0.40* | 15* |
| 36 | Pentapodidae | *Pentapodus setosus* (?) | 0.25* | 5* |
| 37 | Platycephalidae | not identified | 0.25* | 5* |
| 38 | Plectorhynchidae | *Plectorhynchus pictus* | 0.40* | 15* |
| 39 | Pomadasydae | *Pomadasys maculatus* | 0.25* | 5* |
| 40 | Pomadasydae | *Pomadasys* sp. | 0.50* | 35* |
| 41 | Priacanthidae | *Priacanthus macracanthus* | 3.10* | 80* |
| 42 | Scombridae | *Scomberomorus guttatus* | 7.20* | 65* |
| 43 | Scombridae | *Scomberomorus commerson* | 2.6 | 14 |
| 44 | Scombridae | *Rastrelliger brachysoma* | 3.0* | 50* |
| 45 | Stromateidae | *Pampus chinensis* | 0.75 | 1 |
| 46 | Stromateidae | *Pampus argenteus* | 6.3* | 30* |
| 47 | Synodontidae | *Saurida tumbil* | 0.35 | 1 |
| 48 | Synodontidae | *Saurida elongata* | 3.75* | 45* |
| 49 | Synodontidae | *Saurida longimana* | 0.90* | 105* |
| 50 | Sphyraenidae | *Sphyraena obtusata* | 0.60* | 10* |
| 51 | Scienidae | not identified | 0.25* | 5* |
| 52 | Theraponidae | *Therapon* sp. | 3.75 | 100 |
| 53 | Triacanthidae | not identified | 1.0* | 25* |
| 54 | Trichiuridae | *Trichiurus lepturus* | 1.0* | 55* |
| 55 | Trichiuridae | *Lepturacanthus savala* | 2.0* | 25* |
| Σ | 29 families | 43 genera and over 55 spp | 231.02 | 15,939 |

The goal of fishery biologists studying a fishery is generally to obtain information upon which management measures (e.g., catch allocation, effort control) can be based. Most often, these management measures aim at one of the following items:
— to provide as high a sustained catch as possible
— to provide a reasonable income for as many people as possible
— to generate profits as high as possible for those who have invested in the fishery.

These items, it will be noted, are not necessarily compatible with each other and more often than not, they are mutually exclusive (Clark 1976).

When the policy is to maximize yields, three forms of overfishing must be prevented:
— growth overfishing, i.e., taking fish that are too small. (The methods used to detect and quantify growth overfishing are outlined in Chapter 8)
— recruitment overfishing, i.e., taking so many adult fish that recruitment of young fish to the fishery is affected. (The methods to detect and quantify recruitment overfishing are outlined in Chapter 9)
— ecosystem overfishing, i.e., inducing changes in stock composition through excessive fishing such that abundant species decline *without* the subsequent compensatory increase of another (group of) species.

Obviously, when exploiting with an unselective gear a community of widely different fish, some large and long-lived, others small and short-lived, it is not possible to prevent growth and recruitment overfishing of the most sensitive stocks. With increasing effort, some species will then gradually disappear resulting at high levels of exploitation in a complete alteration of the original food chains and catch compositions and in ecosystem overfishing as well. This, and related problems are reviewed in FAO (1978), Pope (1979), Pauly (1979b), and in several papers included in Pauly and Murphy (1982).

In the following, a brief discussion is given of approaches to modelling and managing multispecies systems.

## MODELLING MULTISPECIES SYSTEMS

### Two-species systems

Attempts by biologists to model quantitatively interacting species started, logically enough, with studying the two-species case. The pioneers in this field were Lotka (1925) and Volterra (1926), who suggested independently what are now known as the Lotka-Volterra equations,

$$\frac{dN_1}{dt} = [r_{m1} - m_1(c_1N_1 + c_2N_2)]N_1 \qquad \ldots 12.1a)$$

$$\frac{dN_2}{dt} = [r_{m2} - m_2(c_1N_1 + c_2N_2)]N_2 \qquad \ldots 12.1b)$$

which describe the rate of change, in numbers, of two competing species, where $r_{m1}$ and $r_{m2}$ are the intrinsic rates of increase of species 1 and species 2 respectively, $m_1$ and $m_2$ are positive proportionality constants, and $C_1$ and $C_2$ are interaction terms.

It can be shown (Gause 1934; von Bertalanffy 1951) that the systems represented by equations (12.1a and 12.1b) are stable only in the unlikely case that $r_{m1}/m_1 = r_{m2}/m_2$. In all other cases, one species (that with the highest $r_m/m$) will survive while the other will become extinct. This behavior, the "competitive exclusion principle" of Gause (1934) was demonstrated to occur in micro-habitats such as culture bottles and aquaria in a wide variety of animals, including tropical fish (Silliman 1975). A pair of Lotka-Volterra equations can also be formulated for a predator-prey system:

$$\frac{dN_1}{dt} = (r_m - c_1N_2)N_1 \qquad \ldots 12.2a)$$

$$\frac{dN_2}{dt} = (-g + c_2N_1)N_2 \qquad \ldots 12.2b)$$

where g is a coefficient of negative growth (decline) of the predators ($N_2$) in the absence of prey ($N_1$), while $r_m$ is the intrinsic rate of increase of the prey population, $c_1$ and $c_2$ being interaction terms. An interesting property of these equations is that they generate oscillations over time, under certain circumstances, in the number of prey and predators that are independent of environmental fluctuations, and can be used to explain the oscillating behavior of at least some terrestrial predator-prey systems. Such oscillations have rarely been reported from tropical waters, one exception being possibly Munro (1967) who discussed the oscillatory behavior of a tilapia-tigerfish *(Hydrocyon)* system in Lake McIlwaine, Zimbabwe.

An HP 67/97 program incorporating the Lotka-Volterra equation ("fox and rabbit case") was submitted by J. van Thielen to the HP67/97 Users Library (# 02752D); the "fox and rabbit case" can also be simulated on the HP67/97 with the help of the keystroke sequences in Green and Lewis (1979).

The Lotka-Volterra equations, while providing insight into various aspects of the interactions between species, have been often criticized because of their extreme simplicity and lack of realism, e.g., by Beverton and Holt (1957) who proposed a much more elaborate two-species model.

However, bringing some realism into the Lotka-Volterra system of equations is relatively straightforward. Larkin (1966), who briefly reviewed some earlier variants, suggested the following set for predator-prey interactions:

$$\frac{dN_1}{dt} = (r_{m1} - a_1 N_1 - c_1 N_2) N_1 \qquad \ldots 12.3a)$$

$$\frac{dN_2}{dt} = (r_{m2} - a_2 N_2 - c_2 N_1) N_2 \qquad \ldots 12.3b)$$

where $r_{m1}$ and $r_{m2}$ are the intrinsic rates of increase of the preys ($N_1$) and the predators ($N_2$), $a_1$ and $a_2$ are coefficients of intraspecific competition, $c_1$ and $c_2$ are interaction terms, expressing decrease for the prey in the presence of predator and increase of the predator in the presence of prey. This system of equations, which is far more realistic than the original Lotka-Volterra formulation, has the following properties:
- the abundance of predator and prey are mutually dependent
- the abundance of prey has an upper limit in the absence of predators
- the abundance of predators has a lower limit in the absence of prey (i.e., they switch to another prey and don't become extinct)

Larkin (1966) presented a discussion of the behavior of the predator-prey system in expression (12.3) under exploitation by a fishery. As this behavior is similar to that of the model developed by Pope (1979), we shall now go directly to the latter model.

Pope (1979) presented an equation which is extremely helpful in making species interaction visible. The model has the form

$$Y_T = aF_P - bF_P^2 + c_1 F_P F_Q + dF_Q - eF_Q^2 + c_2 F_P F_Q \qquad \ldots 12.4)$$

or

$$Y_T = \qquad Y_P \qquad + \qquad Y_Q$$

where P and Q are interacting species, a, b, d and e are constants of parabolic yield curves, $c_1$ and $c_2$ interaction terms, $Y_P$ and $Y_Q$ yields from species P and Q, respectively, given the fishing mortalities $F_P$ and $F_Q$ and where $Y_t$ is the total yield from the two-species system.

For example we could have

$$Y_T = 200F_P - 100F_P^2 - 25 F_P F_Q + 100F_Q - 50F_Q^2 + 25 F_P F_Q \qquad \ldots 12.5)$$

where P is an abundant prey, Q a less abundant predator and —25 and +25 are the interaction terms, positive for the predator whose yield increases in the presence of prey. (This example is illustrated in Fig. 12.2). Table 12.2 presents some combinations of values of a, b, d, e and $c_1$ and $c_2$ and indicates the type of interaction that these values suggest. Based on the values in Table 12.2 a series of four figures have been drawn (Figs. 12.1 to 12.4) as in Pope (1979) which demonstrate the effects of biological interactions on the combined yields of two interacting species.

In addition to illustrating biological interactions, Pope's model equation (12.4) also allows for a precise definition of what he calls "technological interactions", i.e., the fact that in a multispecies fishery (and in fact in "single" species fisheries also) catching a certain quantity of a given species necessarily implies catch of a certain quantity of other species. When the ratio of the fishing mortalities ($F_P$, $F_Q$) applied on species P and Q, respectively, remains constant for any level of $F_P$, a straight line is generated which starts at the origin and cuts through the yield isopleths (see lines

Table 12.2. Constants used for drawing Figs. 12.1 to 12.4.

| Fig. no. | Constants of yield curve and interaction terms | | | | | | System optimum | | |
|---|---|---|---|---|---|---|---|---|---|
| | a | b | d | e | $c_1$ | $c_2$ | MSY | $F_Q$ | $F_P$ |
| 12.1 | 200 | 100 | 200 | 100 | −25 | 25 | 200 | 1.00 | 1.00 |
| 12.2 | 200 | 100 | 100 | 50 | −25 | 25 | 150 | 1.00 | 1.00 |
| 12.3 | 100 | 50 | 50 | 25 | 10 | 25 | 146 | 2.25 | 1.79 |
| 12.4 | 100 | 50 | 50 | 25 | 5 | 10 | 94 | 1.36 | 1.20 |

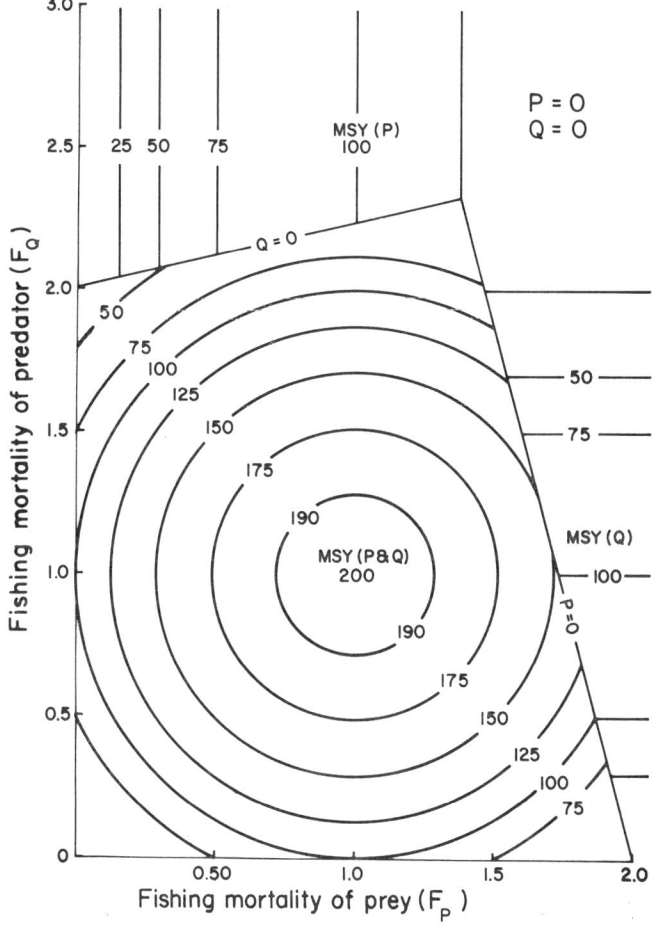

Fig. 12.1. Combined yield of two similar species, one preying to a small extent on the other (see constants of Table 12.2).

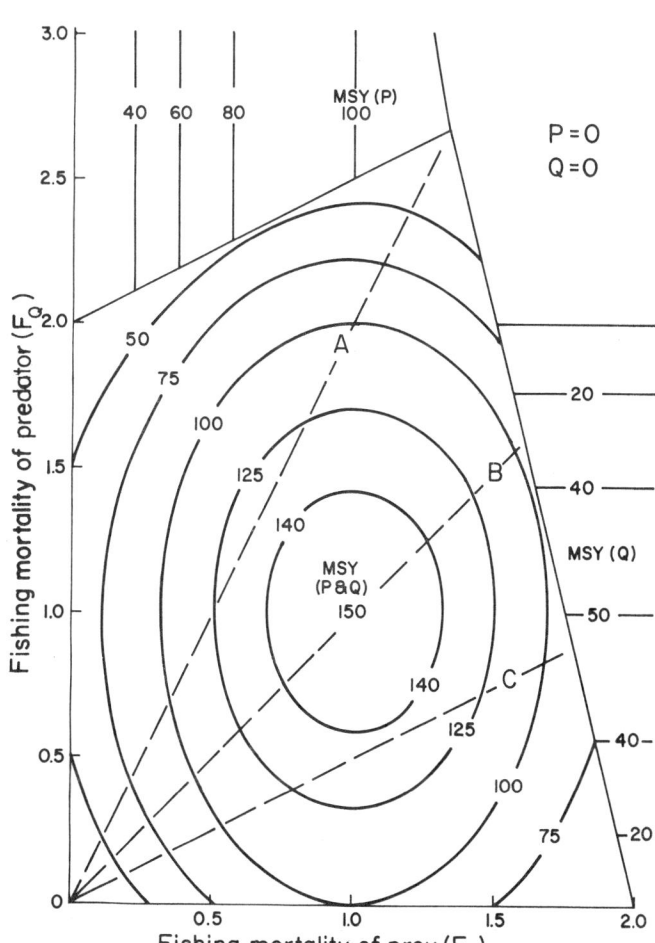

Fig. 12.2. Combined yield from a predator-prey system (see constants in Table 12.2). Lines A, B and C refer to three fixed F-ratios (see Fig. 12.5).

A, B, and C on Fig. 12.2). The interesting thing about such lines, however is that, while any F-ratio necessarily generates a parabolic yield curve (see Fig. 12.5 and Pope 1979 for a mathematical proof), this yield curve does not necessarily go through the maximum sustainable yield (MSY) of the whole system (see Figs. 12.1 and 12.5). As Pope (1979) demonstrated, the two-species system may be extended to any number of species with the overall conclusions remaining that

— For constant F-ratios, the total yield curve for any system composed of parabolic single species curves and linear interaction terms is itself a parabola.
— The F-ratio occurring in a given fishery does not necessarily generate the MSY, and the optimum F-ratios can be found only iteratively by changing F-ratios until MSY is reached.

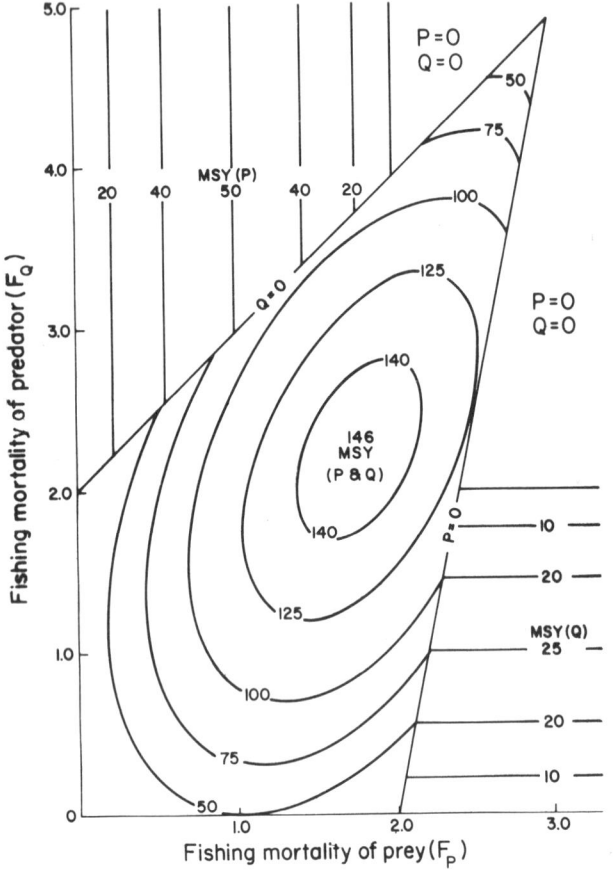

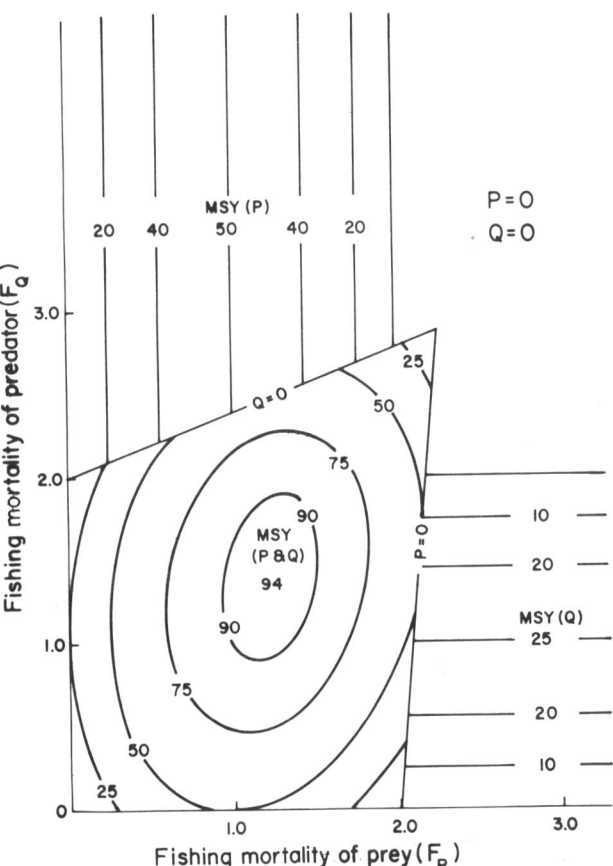

Fig. 12.3. Combined yield from a system in which each species strongly benefits from the presence of the other—mutualism (see constants in Table 12.2).

Fig. 12.4. Combined yield from a system in which each species, to a small extent, benefits from the presence of the other (see constants in Table 12.2).

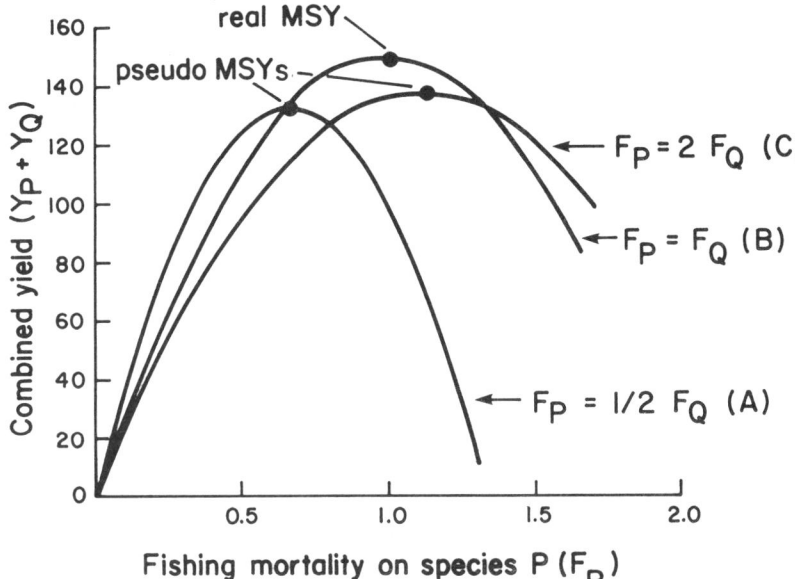

Fig. 12.5. Graph showing how the choice of a given constant ratio of fishing mortalities affects the shape and height of a yield curve; note that one optimum F-ratio leads to the real MSY of the two-species system (see also Fig. 12.2).

Pope's model is very useful in that it enables the user, at least in the two-species case—to literally *see* the interactions affecting the yields of the system. However, the constants (a, b, c, d, e) of the model cannot be estimated, for which reason it generally cannot be used directly for stock assessment purposes.

Concerning equation (12.4) it may finally be mentioned that the intrinsic rates of population increase ($r_m$) are implied in it, i.e.,

$$r_{mP} = 2F_{P \text{ (opt)}} \qquad \ldots 12.6a)$$

and

$$r_{mQ} = 2F_{Q \text{ (opt)}} \qquad \ldots 12.6b)$$

where $F_{P(opt)}$ and $F_{Q(opt)}$ are the fishing mortalities which generate MSY in species P and Q, respectively.

Program FB 30 is provided here to help the reader quickly calculate values of $Y_T$, $Y_P$ and $Y_Q$ for any set of constants as well as for finding the MSY and $F_{opt}$ values of the two-species system. It is hoped that exercises using this program and combinations of constants such as exemplified in Table 12.2 will help visualize the nature and effects of both technological and biological interactions (see Example 12.1).

N-species systems

It is only since the advent of electronic computers that it has become possible to model systems containing more than two species realistically. Particularly, the availability of computers made it possible to depart from simplifying approaches such as represented by equations (12.1) to (12.4) and to incorporate into the models, as suggested earlier by Beverton and Holt (1957), more realistic representations of growth, mortality, predation and other processes. This approach is taken in the large and complex "North Sea model" of Andersen and Ursin (1977), and in the various models of "multispecies VPA" presented by Pope (1979), Helgason and Gislason (1979) and Sparre (1980).

However, smaller simulation models, involving only a few trophic groups and the transfers between them can be used to test and validate hypotheses concerning the interactions within an exploited multispecies stock. This approach is best exemplified by Larkin and Gazey (1982) who designed a simulation model of the Gulf of Thailand stocks and fisheries and used it for testing mechanisms suggested by Pope (1979) and Pauly (1979b) to explain the observed changes in catch rates of different species groups. Such models, as well as the box model discussed below can also help in identifying gaps in our understanding of a system.

## METHOD FOR CONSTRUCTING QUANTITATIVE "BOX MODELS"

While the mathematical simulation of multispecies systems is generally so complex as to discourage all but very mathematically-oriented biologists, constructing "box" models of an ecosystem is rather straightforward. "Box" models are here defined as a class of models where emphasis is on the *graphical* representation of an ecosystem and where the taxa having similar ecological roles are grouped together in "boxes" (see Fig. 12.6).

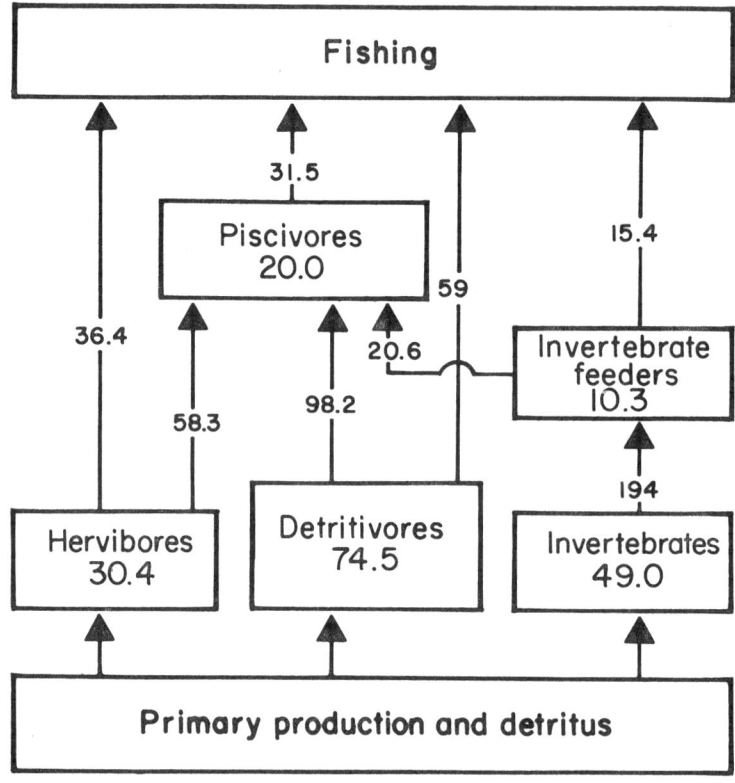

Fig. 12.6. Simplified trophic model of Bukit Merah Reservoir, Malaysia. The numbers in the boxes refer to annual mean standing stocks in tonnes, wet weight, while the numbers along the arrows express annual flows in tonnes (adapted from Yap 1983).

Box models can be either qualitative as in Pauly's (1975) model of a West-African lagoon, or quantitative as in Walsh's (1981) model of the Peruvian upwelling system.

Quantitative box models consist of four elements:
a) the taxa included in each box (see Table 12.3 for an example)
b) the biomass transfer between each box (i.e., the direction of the arrow linking the boxes with each other),

Table 12.3. Data for the construction of a quantitative box-model of Bukit Merah Reservoir, Malaysia. Adapted from Yap (1983).

| Trophic group of fish | Annual catch (tonnes) | Representative species[a] | F | M |
|---|---|---|---|---|
| Detritivores | 59.8 | *Labiobarbus festiva* | 0.58 | 2.22 |
| Herbivores | 36.4 | *Osteochilus hasselti* | 1.18 | 2.12 |
| Piscivores | 31.5 | *Oxyeleotris marmorata* | 2.61 | 1.68 |
| Invertebrate feeders | 15.4 | — | 1.5[b] | 2.0[b] |

[a]Species representative of their trophic group.
[b]Mean of 3 preceding values, taken in absence of other information.

c) the average biomass represented in each box, and
d) the average biomass transfer between boxes (i.e., the quantities represented by the **arrows**) (see Fig. 12.6).

Identifying the taxa to be included in the various boxes involves criteria relating to the size of the animals, to their distribution and to their feeding habits. Generally, it will be possible to **identify** groups separated by all three criteria, e.g.,

— large predators, e.g., sharks and groupers, which are large, tend to occur in deeper waters and feed on smaller fish,
— small, demersal, forage fish, e.g., slipmouths, which occur in relatively shallow waters and feed on zooplankton or zoobenthos, or
— small pelagics ... etc.

Since food and feeding habits cannot be determined for all species concerned, exhaustive use should be made of the available extensive literature on food and feeding habits of fish and of generalizations relating the morphology of fishes to their feeding habits.

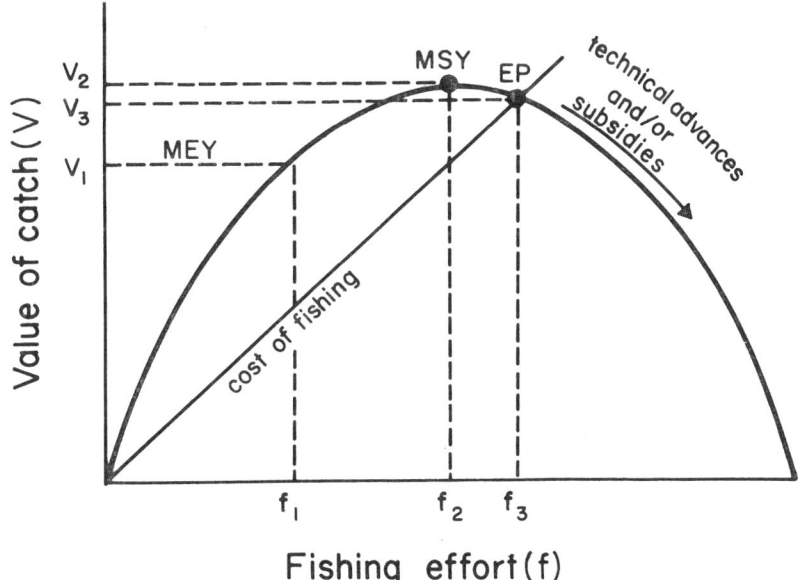

Fig. 12.7. A simple economic model of a fishery with fishing costs linearly proportional to effort. Note that MEY (maximum economic yield, i.e., the maximum difference between gross value of catch and cost of fishing) is achieved at a level of effort ($f_1$) lower than that needed ($f_2$) to obtain MSY (maximum sustainable yield). Under conditions of open access to fishing, fishing effort will increase until total costs equal the gross value of the catch (i.e., fishing reaches $f_3$, and the equilibrium point, EP) and at which profit for the average fishing unit is zero. Note also that lowering the cost line (e.g., by subsidizing the fishery) lowers the point at which equilibrium is reached, *and thus lowers the catch* (Smith 1981).

Examples of such generalizations are:
— large fish with strong, pointed teeth (sharks, conger eels, barracuda) are piscivorous (De Groot 1973)
— piscivorous fish tend to eat fish about one-quarter to one-fifth of their length (Ursin 1973; Cushing 1978)
— fish with long, coiled guts (longer than 3-4 times their body length) are generally detritivorous (Pauly 1975)
— fish with an extremely small mouth are generally zooplanktivorous
— generalist-type fish, such as snappers, are omnivorous
— the size of the spaces between the gill-rakers of pelagics gives a direct indication of the size of their favorite food, etc.

This list is not exhaustive but indicates some of the methods which can be used to group fish into feeding niches and hence into the various boxes of a model. Obviously, when detailed data are available on the food and feeding habits, ecological similarity ($\approx$ niche overlap) indices can be computed to quantify objectively the similarity in the diet of different fish to assist grouping. One such index is:

$$c_{ab} = 1 - \frac{1}{2} \Sigma \mid p_{aj} - p_{bj} \mid \qquad \ldots 12.7)$$

where $p_{aj}$ and $p_{bj}$ are the percentages of a certain food item j in the food of fish species a and b, respectively, the index having a value of zero when the two fish species have no food item in common, and of unity when both fish species have the same food items in the same percentage composition (see Colwell and Futuyama 1971, and Pianka 1973 for another index).

Obviously, grouping fish and invertebrates into boxes on the basis of their food and feeding habits makes the drawing of the arrows which link the various boxes quite easy, such that task (b) above becomes part of task (a). Putting numbers into the boxes is a little more complicated.

The first step is to obtain the mean standing stock in each box (or at least in most of them). The most straightforward method to obtain standing stock estimates is to conduct a trawl survey in the case of demersal stocks, or an acoustic survey in the case of pelagic stocks. In both cases, tagging-recapture experiments can also be conducted from which biomass and a number of other important parameters can be estimated.

These methods, however, are rather expensive, and in the following a method to bypass the problem is shown—at least as a first approach.

First, estimate the annual yield, by species group that is extracted from the system. Then, using methods selected from Chapter 5, first estimate fishing and natural mortality for species representative of each (or most) of the boxes of the model. Then estimate mean standing stock from Equation (6.7) or by means of any of the other methods available to estimate standing stock in Chapters 6 and 7.

It will generally not be possible to obtain estimates of mean biomasses ($\overline{B}$) for all fish included in each box. As a first approximation, however, all the fish in a given box may be assumed to have the same fishing mortality (they will have similar sizes and occur at similar places, so it is not a completely unreasonable assumption) (see Table 10.3). Putting numbers along the arrows linking boxes with each other is now relatively simple:
— for the arrow linking fish with the fishery, use the yield data themselves, i.e.,

$$Y = F \cdot \overline{B} \qquad \ldots 12.8)$$

— for the arrows linking predators and their prey use, assuming that all natural mortality is due to predation

$$Q = M \cdot \overline{B} \qquad \ldots 12.9)$$

where M is the natural mortality and Q is the wet weight of prey consumed by the predators. When a predation arrow goes to two or more predators, the value of Q is divided up in proportion of the biomass of each predator box (see Fig. 12.6).

From a box model such as in Fig. 12.6, the following quantities may be estimated:
a) food consumption per day and unit of weight of the animals in each box. Divide the amount ($\Sigma Q$) going into a box by $\overline{B}$, and then by 365, and
b) the food conversion rate within each box (or by trophic level if appropriate adjustments are made), calculated by dividing all matter leaving a box ($\Sigma[Y + Q]$) by all matter entering it.

The values of food consumption should generally fall between 3% and 6%/day, and those of food conversion rate, 5% to 25%. These ranges can also be used to complete empty boxes in the model, when values of Y and F are unobtainable, e.g., for zooplankton (see Fig. 12.6).

Quantitative box models, constructed along principles such as outlined here can serve the following purposes:
— summarizing the data available on a multispecies system
— allowing for an integration of a fishery with ecological data
— identifying those parts of the system where gaps in knowledge occur
— assessing the possible impact of exploiting one stock or the other.

Useful references that may be consulted when dealing with aquatic food chains and box models of exploited systems are Winberg (1971), Steele (1973), Boje and Tomczak (1978), Pauly (1979b), Jones (1982) and Polovina and Ow (1983).

## MANAGING MULTISPECIES FISHERIES

Fortunately, finding out what is necessary to manage a multispecies fishery rationally is most often less complicated than trying to understand how the system works in biological terms.

Throughout much of the world, as a rule, once exploitation of a stock has begun, the fishery rapidly moves toward overfishing because, in the absence of effective regulations, the point of equilibrium of a fishery occurs when the costs of fishing becomes as high as the gross returns from the fishery as shown in Fig. 12.7 and in Clark (1976).

Thus, managing a fishery (as opposed to developing one) is for most purposes synonymous with attempting to reduce or redirect fishing effort, in order either to increase the catch and/or to reduce losses due to overcapitalization, i.e., increase the income of those remaining in the fishery (see Fig. 12.7 and Smith 1981).

Pope (1979) suggested that fitting a parabolic yield curve to time series of catch-and-effort data from a multispecies fishery, although it may underestimate MSY, may be an appropriate method to identify an optimum level of aggregate effort, and this is, in fact, what is generally done in practice when time series of catch-and-effort data are available. However, Larkin (1982) pointed out that, contrary to expectations, "there is little evidence that total catches have fallen in tropical fisheries due to overfishing. Though catches of individual species have dropped, these often have been made up by increases of other species."

For example, the catch-and-effort data of the Gulf of Thailand demersal trawl fishery (Table 12.4) have been fitted with a total biomass Schaefer model (SCSP 1978) and a Fox model (FAO 1978) although the data do not really suggest a downward trend of total *catch* at high levels of effort (although the *catch-per-effort* rate decreased dramatically). For this reason, a more or less flat-topped model would fit the data (see Fig. 12.8).

Such a model is, for example

$$Y = Y_\infty (1 - e^{-\alpha f}) \qquad \ldots 12.10)$$

where $Y_\infty$ is the "asymptotic yield" while $\alpha$ is an empirical constant.

Obviously, when this model is used to reduce a set of catch-and-effort data, the need arises to somehow define an optimal level of effort (since infinite effort, giving $Y_\infty$, would clearly be an unreasonable proposition), especially when economic data are not available from which the equilibrium point and maximum economic yield can be defined.

In analogy to the $F_{0.1}$ concept discussed in Chapter 8, a level of catch and effort may be defined at which the slope of the yield curve is one-tenth of the slope at the origin ($Y_{0.1}$, $f_{0.1}$) by first defining the slope of equation (12.10)

$$\frac{dY}{df} = Y_\infty \cdot \alpha \cdot e^{-\alpha f} \qquad \ldots 12.11)$$

which, when $f = 0$, reduces to $Y_\infty \cdot \alpha$.

Thus, $f_{0.1}$ can be obtained from

$$Y_\infty \cdot \alpha/10 = Y_\infty \cdot \alpha \cdot e^{-\alpha f_{0.1}} \qquad \ldots 12.12)$$

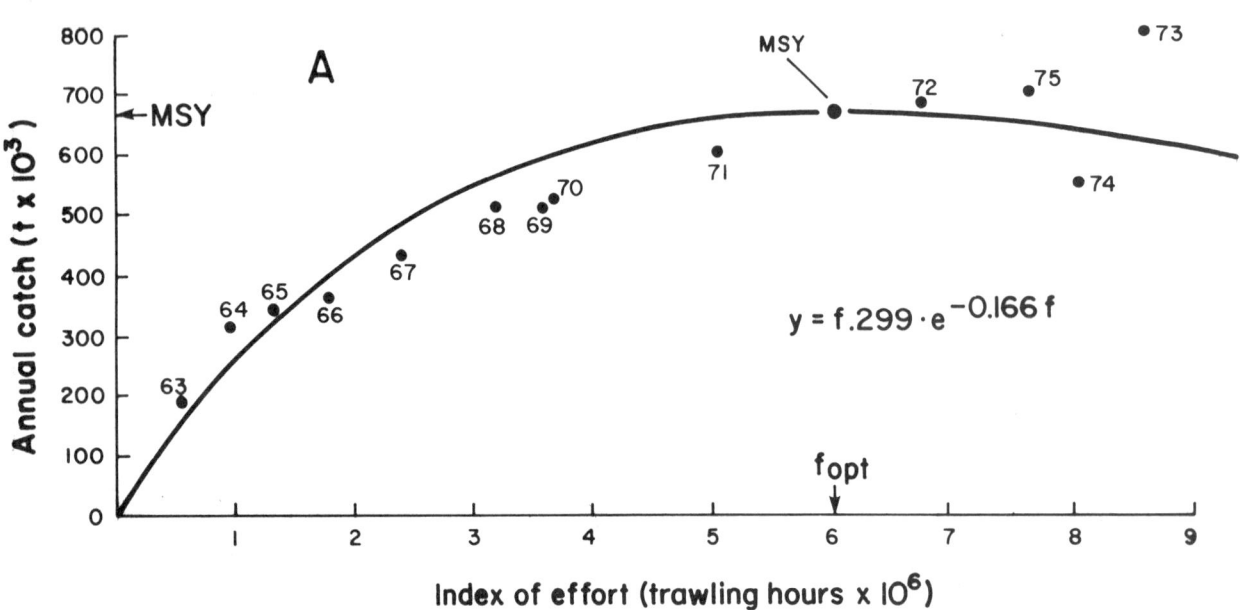

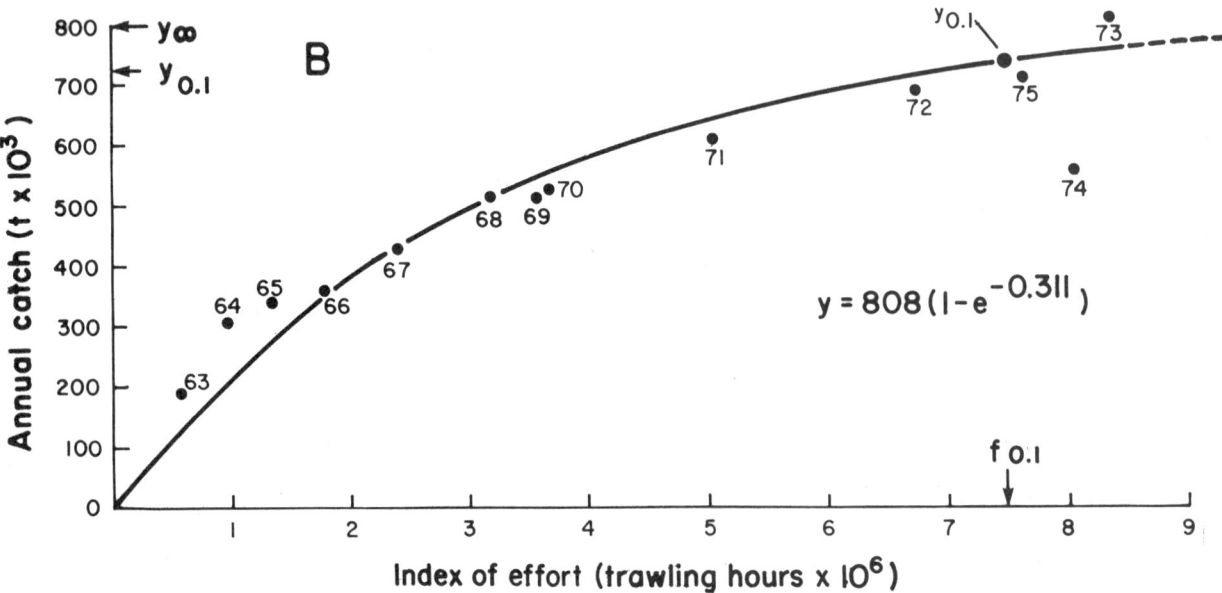

Fig. 12.8. Comparison of two yield models fitted to catch-and-effort data from a tropical multispecies fishery (the Gulf of Thailand trawl fishery). *Upper:* Fox model; *lower:* asymptotic yield model. Note that both models suggest that effort should be reduced, and yields stabilized in the neighborhood of 700,000 tonnes. (Based on Table 12.4 and Example 12.2).

or

$$\frac{\ln 10}{\alpha} = f_{0.1} \qquad \ldots 12.13)$$

while $Y_{0.1}$ is obtained from

$$Y_{0.1} = Y_{\infty} \cdot 0.9 \qquad \ldots 12.14)$$

Thus, paraphrasing Gulland and Boerema (1973) who introduced the $F_{0.1}$ concept, I wish to suggest that "the selection of 10% is arbitrary, but once the 10% figure is accepted, the corresponding catch can be calculated objectively. Thus it can be used to provide a commission or other management body objective guidance based on scientific grounds". An application of this model to a set of catch-and-effort data is given in Example 12.2 (see also Table 12.4) and Fig. 12.8.

To avoid misunderstandings, it is stressed here that equation (12.10) is not meant to describe the whole range of yield/effort relationships, which *must* exhibit a decline at very high levels of effort, but to help cope with a situation where the yield/effort relationship shows no maximum **and** where, therefore, a management goal different from MSY *must* be used.

Techniques on how to exploit a multispecies stock to obtain a desired species mix or avoid an undesired one are not available (Daan 1980). At least some of the following changes may be expected, however, given a steadily increasing level of effort on a demersal multispecies stock:
— a decline of the catch per effort (although not necessarily of the total catch as noted above)
— a rapid decrease and virtual extinction of very large fish (assuming that they are caught in the first place)
— a decrease in the average size of the fish caught
— an increase of the relative contributions of low-value, small-sized fish
— the unexpected increase of previously insignificant components of the system (e.g., squids or jellyfish).

I leave it to the reader to sort out these things in more detail.

Table 12.4. Nominal catch-and-effort data from the Gulf of Thailand Trawl Fishery. Data derived from Fig. 7 in Buzeta (1978).

| # | Year | Catch t x $10^3$ | Effort trawl-hours x $10^6$ |
|---|------|------------------|------------------------------|
| 1 | 1963 | 190 | 0.57 |
| 2 | 1964 | 310 | 0.98 |
| 3 | 1965 | 340 | 1.35 |
| 4 | 1966 | 360 | 1.8 |
| 5 | 1967 | 430 | 2.4 |
| 6 | 1968 | 510 | 3.2 |
| 7 | 1969 | 510 | 3.6 |
| 8 | 1970 | 520 | 3.7 |
| 9 | 1971 | 600 | 5.05 |
| 10 | 1972 | 680 | 6.75 |
| 11 | 1973 | 800 | 8.6 |
| 12 | 1974 | 550 | 8.05 |
| 13 | 1975 | 700 | 7.65 |

Recommended reading: The literature on tropical multispecies fisheries and on the modelling of such systems is rapidly growing. Useful contributions are FAO (1978), Pope (1979), Pauly (1979b), Saila and Roedel (1980), Munro (1983), Simpson (1982), Marten and Polovina (1982) and Larkin and Gazey (1982).

Suggested research topics: Evidently, it is difficult to define a research program that applies to all multispecies stocks. However, the following elements should be included in any basic fishery research program:
- monitoring total catch and catch per effort of the fishery
- monitoring catch per effort of various "indicator" species representing various groups of fish (e.g., large, medium- and small-sized)
- thorough study of the biology and population dynamics of the most abundant and of the most valuable species
- an attempt to construct a "box model" of the system in question
- an attempt to identify gear that would selectively remove certain groups of species (e.g., attempt to identify the best F-ratios in the system in question).

The various reviews included in Pauly and Murphy (1982) should be helpful in defining such a research program.

**EXAMPLE 12.1**

**Yields from a two-species (predator-prey) system.**

The yield-isopleths in Fig. 12.2 are meant to represent a predator-prey system and are based on the following set of assumed constants:

|  | Prey (P) |  | Predator (Q) |
|---|---|---|---|
| $a$ | = 200 | $d$ | = 100 |
| $b$ | = 100 | $e$ | = 50 |
| $c_1$ | = −25 | $c_2$ | = 25 |

Case I: Estimate $Y_P$ and $Y_Q$ for $F_P = 0.8$ and $F_Q = 0.8$ (i.e., using an F-ratio of 1:1):

1) Read sides 1 and 2 of Program FB 30

2) Enter constants:

   Keystrokes: 200 STO A 100 STO B 25 CHS STO 2 100 STO D 50 STO E 25 STO 3 .8 STO 0

3) Estimate $Y_P$, $Y_Q$ and $Y_T$ for $F_P = 1$

   | Keystrokes | Results | |
   |---|---|---|
   | .8 A | 80 | ($Y_P$) |
   | | 64 | ($Y_Q$) |
   | | 144 | ($Y_T$) |

Case II: Estimate "real" MSY, $F_{Q\,(opt)}$ and $F_{P\,(opt)}$ of the two-species system:

1) Read sides 1 and 2 of Program FB 30

2) Enter constants, including initial values $F'_P$ and $F'_Q$ (say, $F'_Q = 0.8$ and $F'_P = 1.2$).

   Keystrokes: 200 STO A 100 STO B 25 CHS STO 2 100 STO D 50 STO E 25 STO 3 .8 STO 0 1.2 STO 1

3) Enter $\Delta F$, TOL and estimate $F_{Q\,(opt)}$, $F_{P\,(opt)}$ and MSY:

   | Keystrokes | Results | |
   |---|---|---|
   | .05 ↑ | | |
   | 0.001 f a | 1.002 | ($F_{Q\,(opt)}$) |
   | | 0.998 | ($F_{P\,(opt)}$) |
   | | 150.000 | (MSY) |

Entering a smaller value of TOL (e.g., 0.0001) produces the exact values: $F_{Q\,(opt)} = 1.000$, $F_{P\,(opt)} = 1.000$ also with MSY = 150.000.

**EXAMPLE 12.2** — Fitting an asymptotic yield model to bulk catch-and-effort data from a multi-species fishery.

Data from Table 12.4

Computations

We take advantage of the fact that equation (12.10) has the same form as the special VBGF [see Chapter 4] (with $t_o = 0$) and use Program FB 3 (von Bertalanffy plot) to fit the data. Fitting the data is here viewed as finding the values of $\alpha$ and $Y_\infty$ for equation 12.10 which generate a curve that goes through the intercept (i.e., for which $t_o = 0$); $\alpha$ and $Y_\infty$ correspond to K and $L_\infty$ of the VBGF, respectively.

1) Read sides 1 and 2 of Program FB 3.

2) Select an initial value of $Y_\infty$ ($Y_\infty$ must always be higher than the highest reported catch). Upon visual inspection of Table 12.4, we select 850 (x $10^3$ tonnes) as an appropriate seed value. Thus

   Keystrokes: 850 ↑ 1 f a 190 ↑ .57 A 310 ↑ .98 A 340 ↑ 1.35 A 360 ↑ 1.8 A 430 ↑ 2.4 A 510 ↑ 3.2 A 510 ↑ 3.6 A 520 ↑ 3.7 A 600 ↑ 5.05 A 680 ↑ 5.75 A 800 ↑ 8.6 A 550 ↑ 8.05 A 700 ↑ 7.65 A

3) Obtain value of $r^2$, $\alpha$ and "$t_o$" corresponding to $Y_\infty = 850$

   | Keystrokes | Results | |
   |---|---|---|
   | E | 0.750 | ($r^2$) |
   | | 0.211 | ($\alpha$) |
   | | −0.854 | ("$t_o$") |

4) Since equation (12.10) implies that "$t_o$" = 0, the seed value of $Y_\infty = 850$ is too high, it is reduced to 825, which provides, upon repeating step 3 a value of "$t_o$" = −0.470. Thus, $Y_\infty$ must be lower, i.e., 810. This provides, upon repeating step 3 a value of "$t_o$" = −0.073. Clearly, we are on the right track. Further trials with 809 and 808 reveal that 808 gives a value of "$t_o$" very close to zero. Thus, for $Y_\infty = 808$ we have

   | Keystrokes | Results | |
   |---|---|---|
   | E | 0.607 | ($r^2$) |
   | | 0.311 | ($\alpha$) |
   | | 0.008 | ("$t_o$") |

5) Using Program FB 9, and replacing age by effort and length by yield, we obtain values for drawing the yield curve, by first entering the values of $\alpha$ in STO1 and $Y_\infty$ in store A (see Table 4.8) then entering the f values and pressing A.

6) Finally, $f_{0.1}$ and $Y_{0.1}$ are estimated from equations (12.13) and (12.14) by performing

   | | Keystrokes | Results | |
   |---|---|---|---|
   | | 10 LN | | |
   | | .311 ÷ | 7.404 | ($f_{0.1}$) |
   | and | 808 ↑ | | |
   | | .9 x | 727.200 | ($Y_{0.1}$) |

As might be seen in Fig. 12.8, $f_{0.1}$ and $Y_{0.1}$ are higher than $f_{opt}$ and MSY as obtained by using the Fox model (Fig. 12.8, upper). This example was meant to illustrate the asymptotic yield model, and not to perform an assessment of the Gulf of Thailand trawl fishery. For such an assessment, the data of Table 12.4 are inadequate, since they probably include fish caught outside the Gulf (Simpson 1982).

## Appendix I. Testing Models and Their Results: An Introduction to Sensitivity Analysis and the Jackknife

### INTRODUCTION

Throughout the twelve chapters of this book, various models have been presented through equations all of which provide, given appropriate inputs (e.g., data points), some useful output (a "statistic"). As the astute reader will have noted, neither the accuracy, nor the precision of the estimated statistics is discussed at length for any of the models presented in these twelve chapters and in fact, equations for estimating standard errors of estimates are given in a few cases only.

The reasons for this are two-fold:
- for a number of models, equations for the estimation of standard errors are either lacking, or inordinately complex, and
- a simple method exists, called the "jackknife", which can be used to estimate standard errors for the output of any model, thus making specific equations for each model superfluous.

While the jackknife method, presented in detail below, can be used to assess for any model the precision associated with estimates of a given statistic (i.e., the width of the confidence interval about that statistic), another method must be used to assess the "sensitivity" of a model to its input parameters.

Only "ordinary sensitivity analysis" will be discussed here; it has as its main objective "the identification of input parameters which, when changed by a fixed percentage, produce either a strong or a weak effect on the model output" (Majkowski 1982).

### SENSITIVITY ANALYSIS

In ordinary sensitivity analysis, only one parameter is changed at a time, usually by a fixed percentage (U %). The effect of the changes is expressed by a "D-measure"* which is used to express the changes in output caused by changes in the inputs. The D-measure relates the output values in the "perturbed" state (i.e., when the parameter values have been changed) to those in the "unperturbed" state (i.e., as occurs when the best available parameter estimates are used).

An example of a D-measure which can be used for a variety of purposes is

$$D = \frac{X - X^o}{X^o} \cdot 100 \qquad \ldots 1)$$

where $X$ and $X^o$ are perturbed and unperturbed outputs, respectively. Majkowski (1982), from whose paper this account is adapted, gave an application of ordinary sensitivity analysis to an equation commonly used in tropical fish stock assessment (equation 5.9). A summary of his analysis, based on the special VBGF and the parameter values $L_\infty$ = 28.9 cm, K = 0.46, $\overline{L}$ = 16.4 cm and L' = 12 cm, (for *Nemipterus peronii* from the Gulf of Thailand) is reproduced here (Appendix Table I.1).

The analysis led to the conclusion that equation (5.9) is extremely sensitive to changes in the value of $\overline{L}$ and that, therefore, every effort must be made, when using this equation, to ensure that $\overline{L}$ is estimated as reliably as possible.

Similarly, Moreau (1980), who applied ordinary sensitivity analysis to Beverton and Holt's yield-per-recruit model (see Chapter 8), found that the parameter which most influences the results is natural mortality. He concluded that, when using the yield-per-recruit model, attention must be devoted to increasing the accuracy and precision of estimates of M (rather than, e.g., spend resources on better estimates of growth parameters).

---

*Not to be mistaken for the parameter D in the generalized VBGF (see Chapter 4).

Appendix Table I.1. Values of the D-measure (formula 1) for various perturbations in the input parameters. The perturbed parameter is indicated in the first column of the table and magnitude of the perturbation (U%) in the first row of the table (from Majkowski 1982).

| U% | −40 | −20 | −10 | −5 | −1 | 1 | 5 | 10 | 20 | 40 |
|---|---|---|---|---|---|---|---|---|---|---|
| K | −40.00 | −20.00 | −10.00 | −5.00 | −1.00 | 1.00 | 5.00 | 10.00 | 20.00 | 40.00 |
| $L_\infty$ | −92.48 | −46.24 | −23.12 | −11.56 | −2.31 | 2.31 | 11.56 | 23.12 | 46.24 | 92.48 |
| $\overline{L}$ | −410.61 | 395.94 | 80.34 | 30.97 | 5.23 | −4.86 | −21.24 | −36.71 | −57.74 | −80.92 |
| $L'$ | −52.17 | −35.29 | −21.43 | −12.00 | −2.65 | 2.80 | 15.79 | 37.50 | 120.00 | −1,200.00 |

Two other forms of sensitivity analysis exist in addition to ordinary sensitivity analysis—extended deterministic sensitivity analysis and extended stochastic sensitivity analysis. They allow assessment of the impact of simultaneous changes of input parameters, for considering the effects of various types of error distributions in the input parameters, etc. (see Majkowski 1982). Ordinary sensitivity analysis as presented here, should suffice, however, for most models presented in this book.

## THE JACKKNIFE METHOD

The underlying principle of Tukey's "jackknife" method is (1) that a given statistic A, computed via a given model from a certain number (n) of data points will take different values ($A_{-i}$), depending upon which subset of the available data points are used for computation, and (2) that the distribution of the $A_{-i}$ values is related to the distribution of the statistic A itself (Miller 1974; Tukey 1977; Mosteller and Tukey 1977; Sokal and Rohlf 1981).

Computationally, the jackknife involves the following steps:

a) compute the value of the statistic A, using all available data points (n). This results in estimate $\hat{A}_1$ of the statistic in question,

b) then compute n new values of the statistic A, but omitting each time another of the n available data points. This results in n estimates of "$A_{i-1}$", each estimated by omitting a *single* data point (see Appendix Table I.2),

c) use the $A_{i-1}$ values to compute "pseudovalues" of A, ($\phi_i$), through the equation

$$\phi_i = (n \cdot \hat{A}_1) - [(n-1) \cdot A_i]$$

d) obtain a new estimate of A through

$$\hat{A}_2 = \frac{\Sigma \phi_i}{n} = \overline{\phi}$$

[In a perfect world, the two estimates of A ($\hat{A}_1$, $\hat{A}_2$) would be equal; in reality, they often are not. The standard error of A that is estimated by the jackknife (see below) pertains to $\hat{A}_2$, for which reason it may be more appropriate to stick to $\hat{A}_2$ as most useful estimator of A.]

e) the standard error of $\hat{A}_2$ is then computed from

$$s.e._{(A)} = \sqrt{(sd_\phi^2)/n}$$

where $sd_{(\phi)}$ is the standard deviation of the $\phi_i$ values.

The authors cited above give more detailed accounts of the jackknife, which is illustrated here—following a suggestion by S. Saila (pers. comm.)—by the computation of standard error for the output of a surplus production model (MSY and $f_{opt}$ as defined in Chapter 10).

Appendix Table I.2, which is an extension of Table 10.3, gives the catch-and-effort values used and/or omitted for the computation of the $A_{i-1}$ values (i.e., estimates of $MSY_{i-1}$ and $f_{opt\ i-1}$) computed by omitting the data points (i) pertaining to the years 1969 to 1977.

As might be seen, the results suggest rather small standard errors for the MSY and $f_{opt}$ values, which, multiplied with the appropriate $\hat{t}$ value (see Chapter 1), would yield a narrow confidence interval.

This application of the jackknife should have made the versatility of this method obvious. In principle, the method can be applied to all models presented in this book—except when the results are obtained through accumulation, where values cannot be omitted without distorting the final result entirely.

Table I.2. Application of the jackknife method to the surplus model (see also Chapter 10).

| # | Year | Catch[a] | Effort[b] | $A_{i-1}$ values | | Pseudovalues ($\phi_i$) | |
|---|------|----------|-----------|------------------|-----|------|------|
|   |      |          |           | $MSY_{i-1}$ | $f_{opt\ i-1}$ | $\phi_{msy}$ | $\phi_{f_{opt}}$ |
| 1 | 1969 | 50   | 623   | 60.6 | 1,253 | 63.3 | 1,442 |
| 2 | 1970 | 49   | 628   | 60.8 | 1,246 | 62.4 | 1,496 |
| 3 | 1971 | 47.5 | 520   | 60.5 | 1,275 | 64.1 | 1,264 |
| 4 | 1972 | 45   | 513   | 60.6 | 1,253 | 63.3 | 1,436 |
| 5 | 1973 | 51   | 661   | 60.7 | 1,250 | 62.9 | 1,461 |
| 6 | 1974 | 56   | 919   | 60.9 | 1,253 | 60.9 | 1,442 |
| 7 | 1975 | 66   | 1,158 | 59.8 | 1,237 | 70.1 | 1,567 |
| 8 | 1976 | 58   | 1,970 | 57.4 | 1,087 | 89.0 | 2,767 |
| 9 | 1977 | 52   | 1,317 | 63.2 | 1,337 | 43.2 | 767 |
| $\bar{X}$ | = | 52 | 923 | 60.5 | 1,244 | 64.2 | 1,509 |
| s.d. | = | 6.39 | 485 | 1.47 | 65.8 | 11.1 | 496 |
| s.e. | = | 2.13 | 162 | 0.491 | 21.9 | 3.70 | 165 |

[a] $10^3$ tonnes (see Table 10.3).
[b] No. of standard vessels (see Table 10.3).

## Appendix II. List of Programs and Program Listings

| | | | |
|---|---|---|---|
| FB 1 | Length-Weight Relationships | | 181 |
| FB 2 | Gear Selection | | 185 |
| FB 3 | Von-Bertalanffy Plot | | 189 |
| FB 4 | Ford-Walford Plot (GM) | | 193 |
| FB 5 | Gulland and Holt Plot | | 197 |
| FB 6 | Munro Plot | | 201 |
| FB 7a | Fitting Seasonally Oscillating Growth Data I | | 205 |
| FB 7b | Fitting Seasonally Oscillating Growth Data II | | 209 |
| FB 8 | Seasonal Growth from Tagging Data | | 213 |
| FB 9 | Generalized VBGF and Derivatives: Solutions | | 217 |
| FB 10 | Total Mortality from Mean Weight | | 221 |
| FB 11 | Z Using Jones' or Sparre's Method | | 225 |
| FB 12 | Length-Converted Catch Curves | | 229 |
| FB 13 | Z and K from Mean Lengths | | 233 |
| FB 14 | F and M from Tagging-Recapture Data | | 237 |
| FB 15 | Independent Estimates of M | | 241 |
| FB 16 | Population Size (Petersen's Method) | | 245 |
| FB 17 | Leslie's Equation | | 249 |
| FB 18 | VPA and Cohort Analysis | | 253 |
| FB 19 | Jones' Length Cohort Analysis | | 257 |
| FB 20 | Length-Structured VPA | | 261 |
| FB 21 | Yield Per Recruit (Special VBGF) | | 265 |
| FB 22 | Yield Per Recruit Via Incomplete $\beta$-Function | | 269 |
| FB 23 | Conversion Factor "k" | | 273 |
| FB 24 | Stock-Recruitment Curve of Beverton and Holt | | 277 |
| FB 25 | Ricker's Stock-Recruitment Curves | | 281 |
| FB 26 | Schaefer and Fox's Models | | 285 |
| FB 27 | Schnute's Yield Model | | 289 |
| FB 28 | Csirke and Caddy's Model | | 293 |
| FB 29 | Logistic Growth Curve | | 297 |
| FB 30 | Yields from Two Interacting Species | | 300 |

# User Instructions

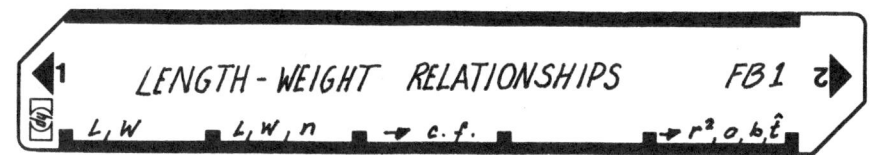

LENGTH-WEIGHT RELATIONSHIPS   FB 1

L,W    L,W,n  → c.f.    → $r^2, a, b, \hat{t}$

| STEP | INSTRUCTIONS | INPUT DATA/UNITS | KEYS | | OUTPUT DATA/UNITS |
|---|---|---|---|---|---|
| 1 | Initialize | | f | a | 0.000 |
| | DATA NOT WEIGHTED BY SAMPLE SIZE: | | | | |
| 2 | Enter L-W data pairs | L | ↑ | | L |
| | | W | A | | i |
| 3 | Remove erroneous data pairs | L | ↑ | | L |
| | | W | f | b | i-1 |
| | DATA WEIGHTED BY SAMPLE SIZE: | | | | |
| 4 | Enter L, W, n | L | ↑ | | L |
| | | W | ↑ | | W |
| | (No correction routine provided here. In case of an erroneous data entry, reinitialize and start again.) | n | B | | i |
| 5 | Calculate coefficients of L-W relationship | | E | | $r^2$ |
| | | | | | a |
| | (If L-W conversions are to be performed without a, b, or c.f. having been estimated internally, store "a" in A, "b" in B and "c.f." in C.) | | | | b |
| | | | | | $\hat{t}$ |
| 6 | Use "a" and "b" to estimate weight from length | L | D | | W |
| 7 | Use "a" and "b" to estimate length from weight | W | f | d | L |
| 8 | Calculate (mean) condition factor | | C | | c.f. |
| 9 | Use c.f. to estimate weight from length | L | f | C | W |
| 10 | Use c.f. to estimate length from weight | W | f | e | L |

181

## Program Listing (001 to 112)

| STEP | KEY ENTRY | KEY CODE | COMMENTS | STEP | KEY ENTRY | KEY CODE | COMMENTS |
|---|---|---|---|---|---|---|---|
| 001 | *LBLa | 21 16 11 | | 057 | × | -35 | |
| 002 | CLRG | 16-53 | | 058 | ST+5 | 35-55 05 | |
| 003 | P⇄S | 16-51 | | 059 | RCL1 | 36 01 | |
| 004 | CLRG | 16-53 | | 060 | RCLE | 36 15 | |
| 005 | CLX | -51 | | 061 | × | -35 | |
| 006 | RTN | 24 | | 062 | ST+4 | 35-55 04 | |
| 007 | *LBLA | 21 11 | | 063 | ISZI | 16 26 46 | |
| 008 | P⇄S | 16-51 | | 064 | RCLI | 36 46 | |
| 009 | ST+3 | 35-55 03 | | 065 | P⇄S | 16-51 | |
| 010 | LOG | 16 32 | | 066 | RTN | 24 | |
| 011 | X⇄Y | -41 | | 067 | *LBLE | 21 15 | |
| 012 | ST+0 | 35-55 00 | | 068 | P⇄S | 16-51 | |
| 013 | P⇄S | 16-51 | | 069 | SPC | 16-11 | |
| 014 | LOG | 16 32 | | 070 | RCL8 | 36 08 | |
| 015 | Σ+ | 56 | | 071 | RCL4 | 36 04 | |
| 016 | RTN | 24 | | 072 | RCL6 | 36 06 | |
| 017 | *LBLb | 21 16 12 | | 073 | × | -35 | |
| 018 | P⇄S | 16-51 | | 074 | RCL9 | 36 09 | |
| 019 | ST-3 | 35-45 03 | | 075 | ÷ | -24 | |
| 020 | LOG | 16 32 | | 076 | - | -45 | |
| 021 | X⇄Y | -41 | | 077 | ENT↑ | -21 | |
| 022 | ST-0 | 35-45 00 | | 078 | ENT↑ | -21 | |
| 023 | P⇄S | 16-51 | | 079 | RCL4 | 36 04 | |
| 024 | LOG | 16 32 | | 080 | X² | 53 | |
| 025 | Σ- | 16 56 | | 081 | RCL9 | 36 09 | |
| 026 | RTN | 24 | | 082 | ÷ | -24 | |
| 027 | *LBLB | 21 12 | | 083 | RCL5 | 36 05 | |
| 028 | P⇄S | 16-51 | | 084 | X⇄Y | -41 | |
| 029 | STOE | 35 15 | | 085 | - | -45 | |
| 030 | ST+9 | 35-55 09 | | 086 | ÷ | -24 | |
| 031 | R↓ | -31 | | 087 | STOB | 35 12 | |
| 032 | X⇄Y | -41 | | 088 | × | -35 | |
| 033 | ST+3 | 35-55 03 | | 089 | RCL6 | 36 06 | |
| 034 | LOG | 16 32 | | 090 | X² | 53 | |
| 035 | STO1 | 35 01 | | 091 | RCL9 | 36 09 | |
| 036 | R↓ | -31 | | 092 | ÷ | -24 | |
| 037 | ST+0 | 35-55 00 | | 093 | CHS | -22 | |
| 038 | LOG | 16 32 | | 094 | RCL7 | 36 07 | |
| 039 | STO2 | 35 02 | | 095 | + | -55 | |
| 040 | RCL1 | 36 01 | | 096 | ÷ | -24 | |
| 041 | × | -35 | | 097 | PRTX | -14 | |
| 042 | RCLE | 36 15 | | 098 | STOD | 35 14 | |
| 043 | × | -35 | | 099 | RCL6 | 36 06 | |
| 044 | ST+8 | 35-55 08 | | 100 | RCL4 | 36 04 | |
| 045 | RCL2 | 36 02 | | 101 | RCLB | 36 12 | |
| 046 | X² | 53 | | 102 | × | -35 | |
| 047 | RCLE | 36 15 | | 103 | - | -45 | |
| 048 | × | -35 | | 104 | RCL9 | 36 09 | |
| 049 | ST+7 | 35-55 07 | | 105 | ÷ | -24 | |
| 050 | RCL2 | 36 02 | | 106 | 10ˣ | 16 33 | |
| 051 | RCLE | 36 15 | | 107 | STOA | 35 11 | |
| 052 | × | -35 | | 108 | DSP9 | -63 09 | |
| 053 | ST+6 | 35-55 06 | | 109 | PRTX | -14 | |
| 054 | RCL1 | 36 01 | | 110 | RCLB | 36 12 | |
| 055 | X² | 53 | | 111 | DSP3 | -63 03 | |
| 056 | RCLE | 36 15 | | 112 | PRTX | -14 | |

### REGISTERS

| 0 | 1 | 2 | 3 | 4 | 5 | 6 | 7 | 8 | 9 |
|---|---|---|---|---|---|---|---|---|---|
| S0 used | S1 used | S2 used | S3 used | S4 $\Sigma x$ | S5 $\Sigma x^2$ | S6 $\Sigma y$ | S7 $\Sigma y^2$ | S8 $\Sigma xy$ | S9 $n$ |
| A $a$ | B $b$ | C $c.f.$ | D $r^2$ | E used | | | | I $i$ | |

# Program Listing (113 to end)

| STEP | KEY ENTRY | KEY CODE | | STEP | KEY ENTRY | KEY CODE |
|---|---|---|---|---|---|---|
| 113 | P⇄S | 16-51 | | 169 | *LBLc | 21 16 13 |
| 114 | S | 16 54 | | 170 | 3 | 03 |
| 115 | P⇄S | 16-51 | | 171 | Yˣ | 31 |
| 116 | X⇄Y | -41 | | 172 | RCLC | 36 13 |
| 117 | ÷ | -24 | | 173 | × | -35 |
| 118 | RCLB | 36 12 | | 174 | 1 | 01 |
| 119 | 3 | 03 | | 175 | 0 | 00 |
| 120 | - | -45 | | 176 | 0 | 00 |
| 121 | ABS | 16 31 | | 177 | ÷ | -24 |
| 122 | 1 | 01 | | 178 | RTN | 24 |
| 123 | RCLD | 36 14 | | 179 | *LBLe | 21 16 15 |
| 124 | - | -45 | | 180 | 1 | 01 |
| 125 | √x | 54 | | 181 | 0 | 00 |
| 126 | ÷ | -24 | | 182 | 0 | 00 |
| 127 | × | -35 | | 183 | × | -35 |
| 128 | RCL9 | 36 09 | | 184 | RCLC | 36 13 |
| 129 | 2 | 02 | | 185 | ÷ | -24 |
| 130 | - | -45 | | 186 | 3 | 03 |
| 131 | √x | 54 | | 187 | 1/X | 52 |
| 132 | × | -35 | | 188 | Yˣ | 31 |
| 133 | PRTX | -14 | | 189 | RTN | 24 |
| 134 | P⇄S | 16-51 | | | | |
| 135 | 0 | 00 | | | | |
| 136 | RTN | 24 | | | | |
| 137 | *LBLD | 21 14 | | | | |
| 138 | RCLB | 36 12 | | | | |
| 139 | Yˣ | 31 | | | | |
| 140 | RCLA | 36 11 | | | | |
| 141 | × | -35 | | | | |
| 142 | RTN | 24 | | | | |
| 143 | *LBLd | 21 16 14 | | | | |
| 144 | RCLA | 36 11 | | 200 | | |
| 145 | ÷ | -24 | | | | |
| 146 | RCLB | 36 12 | | | | |
| 147 | 1/X | 52 | | | | |
| 148 | Yˣ | 31 | | | | |
| 149 | RTN | 24 | | | | |
| 150 | *LBLC | 21 13 | | | | |
| 151 | P⇄S | 16-51 | | | | |
| 152 | RCL6 | 36 06 | | | | |
| 153 | RCL9 | 36 09 | | | | |
| 154 | ÷ | -24 | | 210 | | |
| 155 | 2 | 02 | | | | |
| 156 | + | -55 | | | | |
| 157 | RCL4 | 36 04 | | | | |
| 158 | RCL9 | 36 09 | | | | |
| 159 | ÷ | -24 | | | | |
| 160 | 3 | 03 | | | | |
| 161 | × | -35 | | | | |
| 162 | - | -45 | | | | |
| 163 | 10ˣ | 16 33 | | | | |
| 164 | STOC | 35 13 | | 220 | | |
| 165 | SPC | 16-11 | | | | |
| 166 | PRTX | -14 | | | | |
| 167 | P⇄S | 16-51 | | | | |
| 168 | RTN | 24 | | | | |

## LABELS

| A $L,W \rightarrow$ | B $L,W,n \rightarrow$ | C $\rightarrow c.f.$ | D $L \rightarrow W$ | E $\rightarrow r^2, a, b, \hat{t}$ | 0 |
| a initialize | b correct | c $L \rightarrow W$ | d $W \rightarrow L$ | e $W \rightarrow L$ | 1 |
| 0 | 1 | 2 | 3 | 4 | 2 |
| 5 | 6 | 7 | 8 | 9 | 3 |

## FLAGS / SET STATUS

| FLAGS | ON | OFF | TRIG | | DISP | |
|---|---|---|---|---|---|---|
| 0 | ☐ | ☒ | DEG | ☒ | FIX | ☒ |
| 1 | ☐ | ☒ | GRAD | ☐ | SCI | ☐ |
| 2 | ☐ | ☒ | RAD | ☐ | ENG | ☐ |
| 3 | ☐ | ☒ | | | n = 3,9 | |

# Program Description

**Program Title** Length – Weight Relationships
**Name** Daniel Pauly
**Date** January, 1982
**Address** ICLARM, MCC P.O. Box 1501
Makati, Metro Manila, Philippines

**Program Description, Equations, Variables, etc.** This program fits data to a length – weight relationship of the form

$$W = a \cdot L^b \qquad \ldots 1)$$

where $W$ is the weight and $L$ is the length of an animal. The fit is obtained by means of a linear regression of the form

$$\log_{10} W = \log_{10} a + b \log_{10} L \qquad \ldots 2)$$

whose goodness of fit is estimated by $r^2$.
Also, a condition factor (c.f.) is estimated by means of the expression

$$c.f. = W \cdot 100 / L^3 \qquad \ldots 3)$$

Both expression (1) and the condition factor can be used to perform length-to-weight and weight-to-length conversions.
When grams (live weight) and c.m. are used, the value of c.f. in most fishes will range between 0.5 and 1.5.

To test whether the values of $b$ estimated via expression (2) differ significantly from (3) (isometric growth), a value of $\hat{t}$ is computed with each value of $b$ which can be used in conjunction with a table of the t-distribution (d.f. = n-2).

$$\hat{t} = \frac{|b-3|}{\sqrt{1-r^2}} \cdot \frac{S_x}{S_y} \cdot \sqrt{n-2} \qquad \ldots 4)$$

as given in Sachs L. (1974, p. 339).

**Operating Limits and Warnings** Values of $b$ in equation (1) below 2.5 and 3.5 are questionable, and may reflect an error, or be based on too small a range of length and weight data.
An error message will appear after computation of $b$ if $r^2 = 1$, as may occur when $n$ is very low (2 or 3).

# User Instructions

**GEAR SELECTION** — FB2

Trawl Selection: N-cover ↑, N-codend ↓ correct → $L_c$

Gillnet Selection: Correct → % retained (B) → $a, b, r^2$; $C_A, C_B, L$ → % retained (A) → $L_A, L_B, S^2$

| STEP | INSTRUCTIONS | INPUT DATA/UNITS | KEYS | | OUTPUT DATA/UNITS |
|---|---|---|---|---|---|
| | **TRAWL SELECTION** | | | | |
| 1 | Enter lower class limit of smallest length class ($L_{min}$) | $L_{(min)}$ | f | a | 0.00 |
| 2 | Enter, for each length class, the number of fish in cover and in cod end | N cover | ↑ | | |
| | | N codend | A | | i |
| 3 | Remove erroneous data pair | N cover | ↑ | | |
| | | N codend | B | | i-1 |
| 4 | Calculate $L_c$ | | f | b | $L_c$ |
| | **GILLNET SELECTION** | | | | |
| 5 | Set flag 1 for asymmetric selection curves (or clear it for symmetrical curves) | | STF | 1 | |
| 6 | Enter smaller and larger mesh sizes and initialize | A | ↑ | | |
| | | B | f | e | 0.000 |
| 7 | Enter (for each length class represented in catch of both nets) the catches and class midlength, i.e. | $C_A$ | ↑ | | |
| | | $C_B$ | ↑ | | |
| | | $L_i$ | C | | counter |
| | Set FLAG 0 to view data | | | | |
| 8 | To remove erroneous entries, perform | $C_A$ | ↑ | | |
| | | $C_B$ | ↑ | | |
| | | $L_i$ | f | e | counter-1 |
| 9 | To estimate parameters of regression line and mesh selection parameters, press | | E | | $r^2$ |
| | | | | | a |
| | | | | | b |
| | | | | | $L_A$ |
| | | | | | $L_B$ |
| | | | | | s.d. |
| 10 | To obtain probabilities of capture, by length, do for mesh size A | Length | D | | frac. retained |
| | and similarly for B | Length | f | d | frac. retained |

## Program Listing (001 to 112)

| STEP | KEY ENTRY | KEY CODE | COMMENTS | STEP | KEY ENTRY | KEY CODE | COMMENTS |
|---|---|---|---|---|---|---|---|
| 001 | *LBLa | 21 16 11 | | | 057 | R↑ | 16-31 |
| | 002 | CLRG | 16-53 | | 058 | F0? | 16 23 00 |
| | 003 | 1 | 01 | | 059 | PRTX | -14 |
| | 004 | - | -45 | 060 | 060 | X⇄Y | -41 |
| | 005 | ST02 | 35 02 | | 061 | F0? | 16 23 00 |
| | 006 | CLX | -51 | | 062 | PRTX | -14 |
| | 007 | RTN | 24 | | 063 | X⇄Y | -41 |
| | 008 | *LBLA | 21 11 | | 064 | Σ+ | 56 |
| | 009 | ST00 | 35 00 | | 065 | RTN | 24 |
| 010 | 010 | + | -55 | | 066 | *LBLc | 21 16 13 |
| | 011 | RCL0 | 36 00 | | 067 | F1? | 16 23 01 |
| | 012 | X⇄Y | -41 | | 068 | LN | 32 |
| | 013 | ÷ | -24 | | 069 | R↓ | -31 |
| | 014 | ST+1 | 35-55 01 | 070 | 070 | X⇄Y | -41 |
| | 015 | 1 | 01 | | 071 | ÷ | -24 |
| | 016 | ST+2 | 35-55 02 | | 072 | LN | 32 |
| | 017 | RCL2 | 36 02 | | 073 | R↑ | 16-31 |
| | 018 | RTN | 24 | | 074 | F0? | 16 23 00 |
| | 019 | *LBLB | 21 12 | | 075 | PRTX | -14 |
| 020 | 020 | ST00 | 35 00 | | 076 | X⇄Y | -41 |
| | 021 | + | -55 | | 077 | F0? | 16 23 00 |
| | 022 | RCL0 | 36 00 | | 078 | PRTX | -14 |
| | 023 | X⇄Y | -41 | | 079 | X⇄Y | -41 |
| | 024 | ÷ | -24 | 080 | 080 | Σ- | 16 56 |
| | 025 | ST-1 | 35-45 01 | | 081 | RTN | 24 |
| | 026 | 1 | 01 | | 082 | *LBLE | 21 15 |
| | 027 | ST-2 | 35-45 02 | | 083 | P⇄S | 16-51 |
| | 028 | RCL2 | 36 02 | | 084 | SPC | 16-11 |
| | 029 | RTN | 24 | | 085 | RCL8 | 36 08 |
| 030 | 030 | *LBLb | 21 16 12 | | 086 | RCL4 | 36 04 |
| | 031 | RCL2 | 36 02 | | 087 | RCL6 | 36 06 |
| | 032 | 1 | 01 | | 088 | × | -35 |
| | 033 | + | -55 | | 089 | RCL9 | 36 09 |
| | 034 | RCL1 | 36 01 | 090 | 090 | ÷ | -24 |
| | 035 | - | -45 | | 091 | - | -45 |
| | 036 | RTN | 24 | | 092 | ENT↑ | -21 |
| | 037 | *LBLe | 21 16 15 | | 093 | ENT↑ | -21 |
| | 038 | CLRG | 16-53 | | 094 | RCL4 | 36 04 |
| | 039 | P⇄S | 16-51 | | 095 | X² | 53 |
| 040 | 040 | CLRG | 16-53 | | 096 | RCL9 | 36 09 |
| | 041 | F1? | 16 23 01 | | 097 | ÷ | -24 |
| | 042 | LN | 32 | | 098 | RCL5 | 36 05 |
| | 043 | ST01 | 35 01 | | 099 | X⇄Y | -41 |
| | 044 | R↓ | -31 | 100 | 100 | - | -45 |
| | 045 | F1? | 16 23 01 | | 101 | ÷ | -24 |
| | 046 | LN | 32 | | 102 | STOB | 35 12 |
| | 047 | ST00 | 35 00 | | 103 | × | -35 |
| | 048 | CLX | -51 | | 104 | RCL6 | 36 06 |
| | 049 | RTN | 24 | | 105 | X² | 53 |
| 050 | 050 | *LBLC | 21 13 | | 106 | RCL9 | 36 09 |
| | 051 | F1? | 16 23 01 | | 107 | ÷ | -24 |
| | 052 | LN | 32 | | 108 | CHS | -22 |
| | 053 | R↓ | -31 | | 109 | RCL7 | 36 07 |
| | 054 | X⇄Y | -41 | 110 | 110 | + | -55 |
| | 055 | ÷ | -24 | | 111 | ÷ | -24 |
| | 056 | LN | 32 | | 112 | PRTX | -14 |

### REGISTERS

| 0 Σ | 1 | 2 $L_A$ | 3 $L_B$ | 4 S | 5 | 6 | 7 | 8 | 9 |
|---|---|---|---|---|---|---|---|---|---|
| S0 A | S1 B | S2 | S3 | S4 used | S5 used | S6 used | S7 used | S8 used | S9 i |
| A a | B b | | C 2a/A+B | D | | E | | I | |

# Program Listing (113 to end)

| STEP | KEY ENTRY | KEY CODE | | STEP | KEY ENTRY | KEY CODE |
|---|---|---|---|---|---|---|
| 113 | RCL6 | 36 06 | | 169 | F1? | 16 23 01 |
| 114 | RCL4 | 36 04 | | 170 | LN | 32 |
| 115 | RCL8 | 36 12 | | 171 | RCL2 | 36 02 |
| 116 | x | -35 | | 172 | - | -45 |
| 117 | - | -45 | | 173 | $x^2$ | 53 |
| 118 | RCL9 | 36 09 | | 174 | RCL4 | 36 04 |
| 119 | ÷ | -24 | | 175 | $x^2$ | 53 |
| 120 | STOA | 35 11 | | 176 | 2 | 02 |
| 121 | PRTX | -14 | | 177 | x | -35 |
| 122 | RCLB | 36 12 | | 178 | ÷ | -24 |
| 123 | PRTX | -14 | | 179 | CHS | -22 |
| 124 | P≠S | 16-51 | | 180 | $e^x$ | 33 |
| 125 | RCLA | 36 11 | | 181 | RTN | 24 |
| 126 | 2 | 02 | | 182 | *LBLd | 21 16 14 |
| 127 | x | -35 | | 183 | F1? | 16 23 01 |
| 128 | RCL0 | 36 00 | | 184 | LN | 32 |
| 129 | RCL1 | 36 01 | | 185 | RCL3 | 36 03 |
| 130 | + | -55 | | 186 | - | -45 |
| 131 | ÷ | -24 | | 187 | $x^2$ | 53 |
| 132 | STOC | 35 13 | | 188 | RCL4 | 36 04 |
| 133 | RCL0 | 36 00 | | 189 | $x^2$ | 53 |
| 134 | x | -35 | | 190 | 2 | 02 |
| 135 | RCLB | 36 12 | | 191 | x | -35 |
| 136 | ÷ | -24 | | 192 | ÷ | -24 |
| 137 | CHS | -22 | | 193 | CHS | -22 |
| 138 | F1? | 16 23 01 | | 194 | $e^x$ | 33 |
| 139 | $e^x$ | 33 | | 195 | RTN | 24 |
| 140 | PRTX | -14 | | | | |
| 141 | F1? | 16 23 01 | | | | |
| 142 | LN | 32 | | | | |
| 143 | STO2 | 35 02 | | | | |
| 144 | RCLC | 36 13 | | | | |
| 145 | RCL1 | 36 01 | | 200 | | |
| 146 | x | -35 | | | | |
| 147 | CHS | -22 | | | | |
| 148 | RCLB | 36 12 | | | | |
| 149 | ÷ | -24 | | | | |
| 150 | F1? | 16 23 01 | | | | |
| 151 | $e^x$ | 33 | | | | |
| 152 | PRTX | -14 | | | | |
| 153 | F1? | 16 23 01 | | | | |
| 154 | LN | 32 | | 210 | | |
| 155 | STO3 | 35 03 | | | | |
| 156 | RCLC | 36 13 | | | | |
| 157 | RCL0 | 36 00 | | | | |
| 158 | RCL1 | 36 01 | | | | |
| 159 | - | -45 | | | | |
| 160 | x | -35 | | | | |
| 161 | RCLB | 36 12 | | | | |
| 162 | $x^2$ | 53 | | | | |
| 163 | ÷ | -24 | | | | |
| 164 | √x | 54 | | 220 | | |
| 165 | PRTX | -14 | | | | |
| 166 | STO4 | 35 04 | | | | |
| 167 | RTN | 24 | | | | |
| 168 | *LBLD | 21 14 | | | | |

## LABELS

| A Enter trawl data | B correct trawl data | C → $L_c$ | D Enter gillnet data | E → gillnet selection |
|---|---|---|---|---|
| a → $L_c$ | b → frac. retained | c store $L_{min}$ | d | e |
| 0 | 1 | 2 | 3 | 4 |
| 5 | 6 | 7 | 8 | 9 |

## FLAGS

0 display of $\ln c_R/c_B$
1
2
3

## SET STATUS

| FLAGS | TRIG | DISP |
|---|---|---|
| ON OFF | | |
| 0 ☒ ☒ | DEG ☒ | FIX ☒ |
| 1 ☒ ☒ | GRAD ☐ | SCI ☐ |
| 2 ☐ ☒ | RAD ☐ | ENG ☐ |
| 3 ☐ ☒ | | n = 3 |

# Program Description

**Program Title** Gear Selection
**Name** Daniel Pauly
**Date** Oct., 1981
**Address** ICLARM, MCC P.O. Box 1501
Makati, Metro Manila, Philippines

**Program Description, Equations, Variables, etc.** This program is (a) an implementation of the method of Baranov/Holt to estimate the selectivity of a pair of gillnet, each of which is assumed to have a symmetrical (normal) selection curve with equal variance.

A linear regression is used which has the form

$$y = a + bx$$

where $Y = \ln \frac{C_A}{C_B}$, where $C_A$ is the catch by length class of a gill net with mesh size A, while $C_B$ is the corresponding catch for B, and where x corresponds to the class midlength. The optimum lengths ($L_A$, $L_B$) are obtained from

$$L_A = (-2a \cdot A)/(b(A+B))$$

and correspondingly for $L_B$, while the standard deviation of the selection curves is given by

$$s.d. = \sqrt{(2a(A-B)/(b^2(A+B))}$$

once $L_A$, $L_B$ and $s$ have been estimated, the probability of capture at a given length $L$ is given by

$$P_A = \exp((L - L_A)^2 / (-2 s.d.^2))$$

and correspondingly for $L_B$. The possibility is offered by setting FLAG 1 to plot $\ln(C_A/C_B)$ on $\ln$ length, rather than on length itself. This results in asymmetrical selection curves.

This program (b) also estimates mean length at first capture ($L_c$) based on data from a trawl selection experiment, using the equation

$$L_c = L_n + 1 - \Sigma y_i$$

where $L_n$ is the lower class limit of the highest length class considered, while $\Sigma y_i$ is the sum of the fractions retained. Both parts of this program are based on Gulland (1969, p. 84-95).

**Operating Limits and Warnings** The assumptions used in the derivation of the equations above must be considered when applying the methods, and the original literature must be considered for possible sources of errors.

For the trawl selection, the length classes must be full centimeter; $L_c$ is expressed in cm.

In both methods, classes with zero catches for both mesh sizes must not be included.

# User Instructions

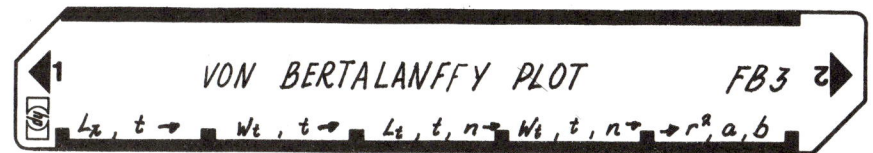

**VON BERTALANFFY PLOT**     FB3

$L_t, t \rightarrow \;\; W_t, t \rightarrow \;\; L_t, t, n \rightarrow \;\; W_t, t, n \rightarrow \;\; r^2, a, b$

| STEP | INSTRUCTIONS | INPUT DATA/UNITS | KEYS | | OUTPUT DATA/UNITS |
|---|---|---|---|---|---|
| I | LENGTH GROWTH: Enter $L(\infty)$ and D | $L(\infty)$ | ↑ | | $L(\infty)$ |
|   |   | D | f | a | 0.000 |
| a | Data not weighted by sample size: | | | | |
| 1 | Enter $L_t$, t values | $L_t$ | ↑ | | $L_t$ |
|   |   | t | A | | i |
| b | Data weighted by sample size: | | | | |
| 2 | Enter $L_t$, t, n values | $L_t$ | ↑ | | $L_t$ |
|   |   | t | ↑ | | t |
|   |   | n | C | | i |
| 3 | Calculate $r^2$, K and $t_0$ | | E | | $r^2$ |
|   |   | | | | K |
|   |   | | | | $t_0$ |
| II | WEIGHT GROWTH: Enter $W(\infty)$, D and b | $W(\infty)$ | ↑ | | $W(\infty)$ |
|   |   | D | ↑ | | D |
|   |   | b | f | b | 0.000 |
| a | Data not weighted by sample size: | | | | |
| 4 | Enter $W_t$, t values | $W_t$ | ↑ | | $W_t$ |
|   |   | t | B | | i |
| b | Data weighted by sample size: | | | | |
| 5 | Enter $W_t$, t, n values | $W_t$ | ↑ | | $W_t$ |
|   |   | t | ↑ | | t |
|   |   | n | D | | i |
| 6 | Calculate $r^2$, K, $t_0$ | | f | e | $r^2$ |
|   |   | | | | K |
|   |   | | | | $t_0$ |

## Program Listing (001 to 112)

| STEP | KEY ENTRY | KEY CODE | | STEP | KEY ENTRY | KEY CODE |
|---|---|---|---|---|---|---|
| 001 | *LBLa | 21 16 11 | | 057 | RCL3 | 36 03 |
| 002 | CLRG | 16-53 | | 058 | ÷ | -24 |
| 003 | STO0 | 35 14 | | 059 | PRTX | -14 |
| 004 | R↓ | -31 | | 060 | RTN | 24 |
| 005 | STOA | 35 11 | | 061 | *LBLc | 21 16 13 |
| 006 | CLX | -51 | | 062 | SPC | 16-11 |
| 007 | RTN | 24 | | 063 | RCL4 | 36 04 |
| 008 | *LBLC | 21 13 | | 064 | RCL6 | 36 06 |
| 009 | STOC | 35 13 | | 065 | × | -35 |
| 010 | ST+9 | 35-55 09 | | 066 | RCL9 | 36 09 |
| 011 | R↓ | -31 | | 067 | ÷ | -24 |
| 012 | STO1 | 35 01 | | 068 | CHS | -22 |
| 013 | R↓ | -31 | | 069 | RCL8 | 36 08 |
| 014 | RCL0 | 36 14 | | 070 | + | -55 |
| 015 | $y^x$ | 31 | | 071 | STO0 | 35 00 |
| 016 | RCLA | 36 11 | | 072 | RCL6 | 36 06 |
| 017 | RCL0 | 36 14 | | 073 | $x^2$ | 53 |
| 018 | $y^x$ | 31 | | 074 | RCL9 | 36 09 |
| 019 | − | -45 | | 075 | ÷ | -24 |
| 020 | CHS | -22 | | 076 | CHS | -22 |
| 021 | LN | 32 | | 077 | RCL7 | 36 07 |
| 022 | STO2 | 35 02 | | 078 | + | -55 |
| 023 | RCL1 | 36 01 | | 079 | P⇄S | 16-51 |
| 024 | × | -35 | | 080 | STO1 | 35 01 |
| 025 | RCLC | 36 13 | | 081 | P⇄S | 16-51 |
| 026 | × | -35 | | 082 | RCL4 | 36 04 |
| 027 | ST+8 | 35-55 08 | | 083 | $x^2$ | 53 |
| 028 | RCL2 | 36 02 | | 084 | RCL9 | 36 09 |
| 029 | $x^2$ | 53 | | 085 | ÷ | -24 |
| 030 | RCLC | 36 13 | | 086 | CHS | -22 |
| 031 | × | -35 | | 087 | RCL5 | 36 05 |
| 032 | ST+7 | 35-55 07 | | 088 | + | -55 |
| 033 | RCL2 | 36 02 | | 089 | P⇄S | 16-51 |
| 034 | RCLC | 36 13 | | 090 | STO0 | 35 00 |
| 035 | × | -35 | | 091 | RCL1 | 36 01 |
| 036 | ST+6 | 35-55 06 | | 092 | P⇄S | 16-51 |
| 037 | RCL1 | 36 01 | | 093 | × | -35 |
| 038 | $x^2$ | 53 | | 094 | STO3 | 35 03 |
| 039 | RCLC | 36 13 | | 095 | RCL0 | 36 00 |
| 040 | × | -35 | | 096 | $x^2$ | 53 |
| 041 | ST+5 | 35-55 05 | | 097 | RCL3 | 36 03 |
| 042 | RCL1 | 36 01 | | 098 | ÷ | -24 |
| 043 | RCLC | 36 13 | | 099 | PRTX | -14 |
| 044 | × | -35 | | 100 | RCL0 | 36 00 |
| 045 | ST+4 | 35-55 04 | | 101 | P⇄S | 16-51 |
| 046 | ISZI | 16 26 46 | | 102 | RCL0 | 36 00 |
| 047 | RCLI | 36 46 | | 103 | P⇄S | 16-51 |
| 048 | RTN | 24 | | 104 | ÷ | -24 |
| 049 | *LBLE | 21 15 | | 105 | STO3 | 35 03 |
| 050 | GSBc | 23 16 13 | | 106 | CHS | -22 |
| 051 | RCLA | 36 11 | | 107 | RCL0 | 36 14 |
| 052 | RCL0 | 36 14 | | 108 | ÷ | -24 |
| 053 | $y^x$ | 31 | | 109 | PRTX | -14 |
| 054 | LN | 32 | | 110 | RCL4 | 36 04 |
| 055 | X⇄Y | -41 | | 111 | RCL9 | 36 09 |
| 056 | − | -45 | | 112 | ÷ | -24 |

### REGISTERS

| 0 used | 1 used | 2 used | 3 used | 4 $\Sigma x$ | 5 $\Sigma x^2$ | 6 $\Sigma y$ | 7 $\Sigma y^2$ | 8 $\Sigma xy$ | 9 $\Sigma n$ |
|---|---|---|---|---|---|---|---|---|---|
| S0 used | S1 used | S2 | S3 | S4 | S5 | S6 | S7 | S8 | S9 |
| A $L_{(\infty)}$ | B $W_{(\infty)}$ | C used | D $D$ | E $b$ | | | | I $i$ | |

# Program Listing (113 to end)

| STEP | KEY ENTRY | KEY CODE | COMMENTS | STEP | KEY ENTRY | KEY CODE | COMMENTS |
|---|---|---|---|---|---|---|---|
| 113 | RCL3 | 36 03 | | 169 | ST+5 | 35-55 05 | |
| 114 | × | -35 | | 170 | RCL1 | 36 01 | |
| 115 | CHS | -22 | | 171 | RCLC | 36 13 | |
| 116 | RCL6 | 36 06 | | 172 | × | -35 | |
| 117 | RCL9 | 36 09 | | 173 | ST+4 | 35-55 04 | |
| 118 | ÷ | -24 | | 174 | ISZI | 16 26 46 | |
| 119 | + | -55 | | 175 | RCLI | 36 46 | |
| 120 | RTN | 24 | | 176 | RTN | 24 | |
| 121 | *LBLb | 21 16 12 | | 177 | *LBLe | 21 16 15 | |
| 122 | CLRG | 16-53 | | 178 | GSBc | 23 16 13 | |
| 123 | STOE | 35 15 | | 179 | RCLB | 36 12 | |
| 124 | R↓ | -31 | | 180 | RCLE | 36 15 | |
| 125 | STOD | 35 14 | | 181 | 1/X | 52 | |
| 126 | R↓ | -31 | | 182 | Yˣ | 31 | |
| 127 | STOB | 35 12 | | 183 | RCLD | 36 14 | |
| 128 | CLX | -51 | | 184 | Yˣ | 31 | |
| 129 | RTN | 24 | | 185 | LN | 32 | |
| 130 | *LBLD | 21 14 | | 186 | X≷Y | -41 | |
| 131 | STOC | 35 13 | | 187 | - | -45 | |
| 132 | ST+9 | 35-55 09 | | 188 | RCL3 | 36 03 | |
| 133 | R↓ | -31 | | 189 | ÷ | -24 | |
| 134 | STO1 | 35 01 | | 190 | PRTX | -14 | |
| 135 | R↓ | -31 | | 191 | RTN | 24 | |
| 136 | RCLE | 36 15 | | 192 | *LBLA | 21 11 | |
| 137 | 1/X | 52 | | 193 | 1 | 01 | |
| 138 | Yˣ | 31 | | 194 | GSBC | 23 13 | |
| 139 | RCLD | 36 14 | | 195 | RTN | 24 | |
| 140 | Yˣ | 31 | | 196 | *LBLB | 21 12 | |
| 141 | RCLB | 36 12 | | 197 | 1 | 01 | |
| 142 | RCLE | 36 15 | | 198 | GSBD | 23 14 | |
| 143 | 1/X | 52 | | 199 | RTN | 24 | |
| 144 | Yˣ | 31 | | | | | |
| 145 | RCLD | 36 14 | | | | | |
| 146 | Yˣ | 31 | | | | | |
| 147 | - | -45 | | | | | |
| 148 | CHS | -22 | | | | | |
| 149 | LN | 32 | | | | | |
| 150 | STO2 | 35 02 | | | | | |
| 151 | RCL1 | 36 01 | | | | | |
| 152 | × | -35 | | | | | |
| 153 | RCLC | 36 13 | | | | | |
| 154 | × | -35 | | | | | |
| 155 | ST+8 | 35-55 08 | | | | | |
| 156 | RCL2 | 36 02 | | | | | |
| 157 | X² | 53 | | | | | |
| 158 | RCLC | 36 13 | | | | | |
| 159 | × | -35 | | | | | |
| 160 | ST+7 | 35-55 07 | | | | | |
| 161 | RCL2 | 36 02 | | | | | |
| 162 | RCLC | 36 13 | | | | | |
| 163 | × | -35 | | | | | |
| 164 | ST+6 | 35-55 06 | | | | | |
| 165 | RCL1 | 36 01 | | | | | |
| 166 | X² | 53 | | | | | |
| 167 | RCLC | 36 13 | | | | | |
| 168 | × | -35 | | | | | |

## LABELS

| A $L_t, t \to$ | B $L_t, t, n \to$ | C $W_t, t \to$ | D $W_t, t, n \to$ | E $\to r^2, K, t_0, \omega$ | 0 |
|---|---|---|---|---|---|
| a initialize (L) | b initialize (W) | c used | d | e $\to r^2, K, t_0, (W)$ | 1 |
| 0 | 1 | 2 | 3 | 4 | 2 |
| 5 | 6 | 7 | 8 | 9 | 3 |

## FLAGS / SET STATUS

| FLAGS | ON | OFF | TRIG | | DISP | |
|---|---|---|---|---|---|---|
| 0 | ☐ | ☒ | DEG | ☒ | FIX | ☒ |
| 1 | ☐ | ☒ | GRAD | ☐ | SCI | ☐ |
| 2 | ☐ | ☒ | RAD | ☐ | ENG | ☐ |
| 3 | ☐ | ☒ | | | n = 3 | |

# Program Description

**Program Title:** Von Bertalanffy Plot
**Name:** Daniel Pauly
**Address:** ICLARM, MCC P.O. Box 1501, Makati, Metro Manila, Philippines
**Date:** August, 1980

**Program Description, Equations, Variables, etc.** The generalized Von Bertalanffy Growth Formula has for length the form

$$L_t = L_{(\infty)} \left(1 - e^{-KD(t-t_0)}\right)^{1/D} \quad \ldots 1)$$

and for weight the form

$$W_t = W_{(\infty)} \left(1 - e^{-KD\frac{3}{b}(t-t_0)}\right)^{b/D} \quad \ldots 2)$$

where $b$ is the exponent of the length-weight relationship. Equation (1) can be rewritten as

$$\ln\left(1 - \left(\frac{L_t}{L_\infty}\right)^D\right) = KDt_0 - KDt \quad \ldots 3)$$

which has the form of a linear regression, where $\ln\left(1 - \left(\frac{L_t}{L_\infty}\right)^D\right) = y$, $t = x$ and $KDt_0 = a$. Thus, given a preliminary estimate of $L_\infty$ (which is here coded $L(\infty)$) and a value of $D$, the values of $K$ and $t_0$ can be easily estimated and the preliminary value of $L(\infty)$ improved iteratively, until a maximum value of $r^2$ is reached. The method is similar for weight growth, except that values of $W^{1/b}$ are used instead of the weights themselves.

Weighting factors other than $n$ may be used; the inverse ($1/x$) of the standard error of the mean size in each age group is, for example, a very appropriate weighting factor.

**Operating Limits and Warnings** 1) The values of $L(\infty)$ and $W(\infty)$ must always be higher than the size-at-age data. 2) A value of $D$ must always be entered (e.g. $D=1$ in the case of the normal, or "special" von Bertalanffy Growth Formula). 3) The value of $t_0$ can be used only when the ages entered are <u>absolute</u> ages.

# User Instructions

| STEP | INSTRUCTIONS | INPUT DATA/UNITS | KEYS | | OUTPUT DATA/UNITS |
|---|---|---|---|---|---|
| | **LENGTH GROWTH** | | | | |
| 1 | Enter first length-at-age value and D | $L_t$ | ↑ | | $L_t$ |
| | | D | f | a | 0.000 |
| 2 | Enter remaining length-at-age values | $L_t$ | A | | $i$ |
| 3 | Calculate $r^2$, K and $L_\infty$ | | E | | $r^2$ |
| | | | | | K |
| | | | | | $L_\infty$ |
| | **WEIGHT GROWTH** | | | | |
| 1 | Enter first weight-at-age value, D and b | $W_t$ | ↑ | | $W_t$ |
| | | D | ↑ | | D |
| | | b | f | b | 0.000 |
| 2 | Enter remaining weight-at-age values | $W_t$ | B | | $i$ |
| 3 | Calculate $r^2$, K and $W_\infty$ | | E | | $r^2$ |
| | | | | | K |
| | | | | | $W_\infty$ |

## Program Listing (001 to 112)

| STEP | KEY ENTRY | KEY CODE | | STEP | KEY ENTRY | KEY CODE |
|---|---|---|---|---|---|---|
| 001 | *LBLa | 21 16 11 | | 057 | ÷ | -24 |
| 002 | CLRG | 16-53 | | 058 | STO3 | 35 03 |
| 003 | P⇄S | 16-51 | | 059 | × | -35 |
| 004 | CLRG | 16-53 | | 060 | RCL6 | 36 06 |
| 005 | STO0 | 35 14 | | 061 | $x^2$ | 53 |
| 006 | R↓ | -31 | | 062 | RCL9 | 36 09 |
| 007 | STOA | 35 11 | | 063 | ÷ | -24 |
| 008 | CLX | -51 | | 064 | CHS | -22 |
| 009 | RTN | 24 | | 065 | RCL7 | 36 07 |
| 010 | *LBLb | 21 16 12 | | 066 | + | -55 |
| 011 | CLRG | 16-53 | | 067 | ÷ | -24 |
| 012 | P⇄S | 16-51 | | 068 | PRTX | -14 |
| 013 | CLRG | 16-53 | | 069 | √x | 54 |
| 014 | STOE | 35 15 | | 070 | RCL3 | 36 03 |
| 015 | R↓ | -31 | | 071 | X⇄Y | -41 |
| 016 | STOD | 35 14 | | 072 | ÷ | -24 |
| 017 | R↓ | -31 | | 073 | STO3 | 35 03 |
| 018 | STOB | 35 12 | | 074 | LN | 32 |
| 019 | CLX | -51 | | 075 | RCLD | 36 14 |
| 020 | RTN | 24 | | 076 | ÷ | -24 |
| 021 | *LBLA | 21 11 | | 077 | PRTX | -14 |
| 022 | RCLD | 36 14 | | 078 | RCL6 | 36 06 |
| 023 | $y^x$ | 31 | | 079 | RCL4 | 36 04 |
| 024 | STOB | 35 12 | | 080 | RCL3 | 36 03 |
| 025 | RCLA | 36 11 | | 081 | × | -35 |
| 026 | RCLD | 36 14 | | 082 | - | -45 |
| 027 | $y^x$ | 31 | | 083 | RCL9 | 36 09 |
| 028 | STOC | 35 13 | | 084 | ÷ | -24 |
| 029 | RCLB | 36 12 | | 085 | RCL3 | 36 03 |
| 030 | RCLD | 36 14 | | 086 | CHS | -22 |
| 031 | 1/X | 52 | | 087 | 1 | 01 |
| 032 | $y^x$ | 31 | | 088 | + | -55 |
| 033 | STOA | 35 11 | | 089 | ÷ | -24 |
| 034 | RCLC | 36 13 | | 090 | P⇄S | 16-51 |
| 035 | RCLB | 36 12 | | 091 | RCLD | 36 14 |
| 036 | Σ+ | 56 | | 092 | 1/X | 52 |
| 037 | RTN | 24 | | 093 | $y^x$ | 31 |
| 038 | *LBLE | 21 15 | | 094 | F2? | 16 23 02 |
| 039 | P⇄S | 16-51 | | 095 | GTOC | 22 13 |
| 040 | SPC | 16-11 | | 096 | PRTX | -14 |
| 041 | RCL8 | 36 08 | | 097 | RTN | 24 |
| 042 | RCL4 | 36 04 | | 098 | *LBLB | 21 12 |
| 043 | RCL6 | 36 06 | | 099 | RCLE | 36 15 |
| 044 | × | -35 | | 100 | 1/X | 52 |
| 045 | RCL9 | 36 09 | | 101 | $y^x$ | 31 |
| 046 | ÷ | -24 | | 102 | RCLD | 36 14 |
| 047 | - | -45 | | 103 | $y^x$ | 31 |
| 048 | ENT↑ | -21 | | 104 | STOA | 35 11 |
| 049 | ENT↑ | -21 | | 105 | RCLB | 36 12 |
| 050 | RCL4 | 36 04 | | 106 | RCLE | 36 15 |
| 051 | $x^2$ | 53 | | 107 | 1/X | 52 |
| 052 | RCL9 | 36 09 | | 108 | $y^x$ | 31 |
| 053 | ÷ | -24 | | 109 | RCLD | 36 14 |
| 054 | RCL5 | 36 05 | | 110 | $y^x$ | 31 |
| 055 | X⇄Y | -41 | | 111 | STOC | 35 13 |
| 056 | - | -45 | | 112 | RCLA | 36 11 |

### REGISTERS

| 0 | 1 | 2 | 3 | 4 | 5 | 6 | 7 | 8 | 9 |
|---|---|---|---|---|---|---|---|---|---|
| S0 used | S1 used | S2 used | S3 used | S4 $\Sigma x$ | S5 $\Sigma x^2$ | S6 $\Sigma y$ | S7 $\Sigma y^2$ | S8 $\Sigma xy$ | S9 $i$ |
| A $L_1$/used | B $W_1$/used | C used | D $D$ | E $b$ | I | | | | |

# Program Listing (113 to end)

| STEP | KEY ENTRY | KEY CODE | COMMENTS |
|---|---|---|---|
| 113 | RCLD | 36 14 | |
| 114 | 1/X | 52 | |
| 115 | Y^x | 31 | |
| 116 | RCLE | 36 15 | |
| 117 | Y^x | 31 | |
| 118 | STOB | 35 12 | |
| 119 | RCLC | 36 13 | |
| 120 | RCLA | 36 11 | |
| 121 | Σ+ | 56 | |
| 122 | RTN | 24 | |
| 123 | *LBLe | 21 16 15 | |
| 124 | SF2 | 16 21 02 | |
| 125 | GTOΓ | 22 15 | |
| 126 | *LBLC | 21 13 | |
| 127 | RCLE | 36 15 | |
| 128 | Y^x | 31 | |
| 129 | PRTX | -14 | |
| 130 | RTN | 24 | |

## LABELS

| A $L \rightarrow$ | B $W \rightarrow$ | C | D | E $\rightarrow r^2, K, L_\infty$ | 0 |
| a $L_t, D \rightarrow$ | b $W_t, D, b \rightarrow$ | c | d | e $\rightarrow r^2, K, W_\infty$ | 1 |
| 0 | 1 | 2 | 3 | 4 | 2 Weight ? |
| 5 | 6 | 7 | 8 | 9 | 3 |

## FLAGS / SET STATUS

FLAGS: 0 ON☐ OFF☐ ; 1 ON☐ OFF☐ ; 2 ON☒ OFF☒ ; 3 ON☐ OFF☐

TRIG: DEG☒ GRAD☐ RAD☐

DISP: FIX☒ SCI☐ ENG☐ n = 3

# Program Description

**Program Title** Ford-Walford Plot (GM)
**Name** Daniel Pauly
**Date** August 1980
**Address** ICLARM, MCC P.O. Box 1501, Makati, Metro Manila, Philippines

**Program Description, Equations, Variables, etc.** When size-at-age data at equal time interval (year, month, week) are available, 2 parameters of the VBGF can be estimated from

$$L_{t+1}^D = a + bL_t^D \quad \ldots 1)$$

where

$$L_\infty = \left(\frac{a}{(1-b)}\right)^{1/D} \quad \ldots 2)$$

and

$$K = \ln b / D \quad \ldots 3)$$

However, since both $L_t$ and $L_{t+1}$ are measured with the same error, a geometric mean, or type II regression is used. For this purpose the parameters $a$ & $b$ of an arithmetic mean, or type I regression are first calculated, then used in conjunction with the correlation coefficient $(r)$ estimated along with $a$ & $b$ to obtain the slope and intercept of the GM regression through the relationships

$$b' = b/r \quad \ldots 4)$$

and

$$a' = \bar{Y} - (b'\bar{X}) \quad \ldots 5)$$

where $\bar{Y}$ and $\bar{X}$ are the means of the $L_{t+1}$ and $L_t$ values. $a'$, $b'$ are parameters of the GM regression, respectively (Ricker, 1975).

**Operating Limits and Warnings** Size-at-age data must be equidistant, and there must be at least 2 pairs of $L_{t+1}$, $L_t$ values. When weight-at-age data are used, the exponent $(b)$ of the length/weight relationship must be entered (e.g. $b=3$).
A value of D <u>must</u> be entered; when using the normal, or "special" VBGF, enter $D=1$.

## Program Listing (113 to end)

| STEP | KEY ENTRY | KEY CODE | COMMENTS |
|---|---|---|---|
| 113 | 1/X | 52 | |
| 114 | Yˣ | 31 | |
| 115 | RCLD | 36 14 | |
| 116 | Yˣ | 31 | |
| 117 | STO2 | 35 02 | |
| 118 | RCL1 | 36 01 | |
| 119 | − | −45 | |
| 120 | RCL0 | 36 00 | |
| 121 | ÷ | −24 | |
| 122 | RCL1 | 36 01 | |
| 123 | RCL2 | 36 02 | |
| 124 | + | −55 | |
| 125 | 2 | 02 | |
| 126 | ÷ | −24 | |
| 127 | F0? | 16 23 00 | |
| 128 | PRTX | −14 | |
| 129 | X⇄Y | −41 | |
| 130 | CHS | −22 | |
| 131 | F0? | 16 23 00 | |
| 132 | PRTX | −14 | |
| 133 | CHS | −22 | |
| 134 | Σ+ | 56 | |
| 135 | F0? | 16 23 00 | |
| 136 | PRTX | −14 | |
| 137 | RTN | 24 | |
| 138 | *LBLb | 21 16 12 | |
| 139 | RCLE | 36 15 | |
| 140 | 1/X | 52 | |
| 141 | Yˣ | 31 | |
| 142 | GTOc | 22 16 13 | |
| 143 | *LBLd | 21 16 14 | |
| 144 | RCLE | 36 15 | |
| 145 | Yˣ | 31 | |
| 146 | PRTX | −14 | |
| 147 | RTN | 24 | |
| 148 | *LBLc | 21 16 13 | |
| 149 | RCLD | 36 14 | |
| 150 | Yˣ | 31 | |
| 151 | STOB | 35 12 | |
| 152 | x̄ | 16 53 | |
| 153 | X⇄Y | −41 | |
| 154 | RCLB | 36 12 | |
| 155 | − | −45 | |
| 156 | STOB | 35 12 | |
| 157 | x̄ | 16 53 | |
| 158 | RCLB | 36 12 | |
| 159 | ÷ | −24 | |
| 160 | PRTX | −14 | |
| 161 | RTN | 24 | |
| 162 | *LBLe | 21 16 15 | |
| 163 | SF2 | 16 21 02 | |
| 164 | GTOE | 22 15 | |
| 165 | *LBLC | 21 13 | |
| 166 | SF0 | 16 21 00 | |
| 167 | RTN | 24 | |

### LABELS

| A enter L's | B enter W's | C Print | D →r², k, L∞ | E |
|---|---|---|---|---|
| a initialize | b W(∞)→K | c L(∞)→K | d →r², K, W∞ | e |
| 0 | 1 | 2 | 3 | 4 |
| 5 | 6 | 7 | 8 | 9 |

### FLAGS
0 Print?
1
2 Weight?
3

### SET STATUS

| FLAGS | | | TRIG | | DISP | |
|---|---|---|---|---|---|---|
| | ON | OFF | DEG | ☒ | FIX | ☒ |
| 0 | ☒ | ☒ | GRAD | ☐ | SCI | ☐ |
| 1 | ☐ | ☐ | RAD | ☐ | ENG | ☐ |
| 2 | ☒ | ☒ | | | n = 3 | |
| 3 | ☐ | ☐ | | | | |

# Program Description

**Program Title:** Gulland and Holt Plot
**Name:** Daniel Pauly
**Address:** ICLARM, MCC P.O. Box 1501, Makati, Metro Manila, Philippines
**Date:** Sept., 1980

**Program Description, Equations, Variables, etc.** Gulland and Holt (1959) demonstrated that estimates of $K$ and $L_\infty$ can be obtained by means of the relationship

$$\underbrace{\frac{L_2 - L_1}{t_2 - t_1}}_{Y} \approx a + b \underbrace{\frac{L_1 + L_2}{2}}_{X} \qquad \ldots 1)$$

where $L_1$ and $L_2$ are the length of fishes at time $t_1$ and $t_2$, respectively. When the period $\Delta t$ ($= t_2 - t_1$) is short relative to the total life span of the fish, the equation yields an estimate of $K$ through

$$K \approx -b \qquad \ldots 2)$$

while $L_\infty$ is estimated through

$$L_\infty \approx \frac{a}{b} \qquad \ldots 3)$$

These equations can be easily expanded to cases pertaining to growth in weight by using values of $W^{1/b}$ instead of the length values, and to the generalized VBGF by replacing the length values by $L^D$ values. A set of value for the asymptotic size ($L_{(\infty)}$) may be used in which case a "forced" Gulland and Holt Plot results, i.e.:

$$K \approx \frac{\bar{Y}}{L_{(\infty)} - \bar{X}} \qquad \ldots 4)$$

which can be easily expanded to weight growth and to the generalized VBGF.

**Operating Limits and Warnings** 1) A value of $D$ <u>must</u> be entered, i.e. $D = 1$, in the case of the special VBGF and $D < 1$ in the case of the generalized VBGF.
2) The original paper by Gulland and Holt (1959) should be consulted for a method (and table) to estimate the error involved in using the approximations in equations (2) and (3). When the print option is used with weights, the output are $\bar{W}^{1/b}$ and $\Delta W^{1/b}/\Delta t$ values.

# User Instructions

| STEP | INSTRUCTIONS | INPUT DATA/UNITS | KEYS | | OUTPUT DATA/UNITS |
|---|---|---|---|---|---|
| | **GROWTH IN LENGTH** | | | | |
| 1 | Enter $L_{(\infty)}$, D and initialize | $L_{(\infty)}$ | ↑ | | $L_{(\infty)}$ |
| | | D | f | a | 0.000 |
| 2 | Enter data triplets | $L_1$ | ↑ | | $L_1$ |
| | | $L_2$ | ↑ | | $L_2$ |
| | | $\Delta t$ | A | | i |
| 3 | Remove erroneous data triplet | $L_1$ | ↑ | | $L_1$ |
| | | $L_2$ | ↑ | | $L_2$ |
| | | $\Delta t$ | D | | i − 1 |
| 4 | Calculate mean value of K and its C.V. | | E | | $\bar{K}$ |
| | | | | | C.V. |
| | **GROWTH IN WEIGHT** | | | | |
| 5 | Enter $W_{(\infty)}$, D, b and initialize | $W_{(\infty)}$ | ↑ | | $W_{(\infty)}$ |
| | | D | ↑ | | D |
| | | b | f | b | 0.000 |
| 6 | Enter data triplets | $W_1$ | ↑ | | $W_1$ |
| | | $W_2$ | ↑ | | $W_2$ |
| | | $\Delta t$ | B | | i |
| 7 | Remove erroneous data triplet | $W_1$ | ↑ | | $W_1$ |
| | | $W_2$ | ↑ | | $W_2$ |
| | | $\Delta t$ | f | d | i − 1 |
| 8 | Calculate mean value of K and its C.V. | | E | | $\bar{K}$ |
| | | | | | C.V. |

NOTES: The $\Delta t$ should be expressed in days. The K values are annual values. For print option, press STF 0. To clear print option, perform CLF 0.

# Program Listing

| STEP | KEY ENTRY | KEY CODE |
|---|---|---|
| 001 | *LBLa | 21 16 11 |
| 002 | CLRG | 16-53 |
| 003 | P⇄S | 16-51 |
| 004 | CLRG | 16-53 |
| 005 | STOD | 35 14 |
| 006 | Y^x | 31 |
| 007 | STOA | 35 11 |
| 008 | CLX | -51 |
| 009 | RTN | 24 |
| 010 | *LBLA | 21 11 |
| 011 | STOC | 35 13 |
| 012 | R↓ | -31 |
| 013 | RCL0 | 36 14 |
| 014 | Y^x | 31 |
| 015 | CHS | -22 |
| 016 | RCLA | 36 11 |
| 017 | + | -55 |
| 018 | LN | 32 |
| 019 | X⇄Y | -41 |
| 020 | RCLD | 36 14 |
| 021 | Y^x | 31 |
| 022 | CHS | -22 |
| 023 | RCLA | 36 11 |
| 024 | + | -55 |
| 025 | LN | 32 |
| 026 | X⇄Y | -41 |
| 027 | − | -45 |
| 028 | RCLC | 36 13 |
| 029 | ÷ | -24 |
| 030 | 3 | 03 |
| 031 | 6 | 06 |
| 032 | 5 | 05 |
| 033 | × | -35 |
| 034 | F0? | 16 23 00 |
| 035 | PRTX | -14 |
| 036 | F2? | 16 23 02 |
| 037 | RTN | 24 |
| 038 | Σ+ | 56 |
| 039 | RTN | 24 |
| 040 | *LBLE | 21 15 |
| 041 | SPC | 16-11 |
| 042 | x̄ | 16 53 |
| 043 | PRTX | -14 |
| 044 | STO0 | 35 00 |
| 045 | S | 16 54 |
| 046 | RCL0 | 36 00 |
| 047 | ÷ | -24 |
| 048 | PRTX | -14 |
| 049 | RTN | 24 |
| 050 | R/S | 51 |
| 051 | *LBLb | 21 16 12 |
| 052 | CLRG | 16-53 |
| 053 | P⇄S | 16-51 |
| 054 | CLRG | 16-53 |
| 055 | STOE | 35 15 |
| 056 | X⇄Y | -41 |
| 057 | STOD | 35 14 |
| 058 | X⇄Y | -41 |
| 059 | ÷ | -24 |
| 060 | Y^x | 31 |
| 061 | STOB | 35 12 |
| 062 | CLX | -51 |
| 063 | RTN | 24 |
| 064 | *LBLB | 21 12 |
| 065 | STOC | 35 13 |
| 066 | R↓ | -31 |
| 067 | RCLD | 36 14 |
| 068 | RCLE | 36 15 |
| 069 | ÷ | -24 |
| 070 | Y^x | 31 |
| 071 | CHS | -22 |
| 072 | RCLB | 36 12 |
| 073 | + | -55 |
| 074 | LN | 32 |
| 075 | X⇄Y | -41 |
| 076 | RCLD | 36 14 |
| 077 | RCLE | 36 15 |
| 078 | ÷ | -24 |
| 079 | Y^x | 31 |
| 080 | CHS | -22 |
| 081 | RCLB | 36 12 |
| 082 | + | -55 |
| 083 | LN | 32 |
| 084 | X⇄Y | -41 |
| 085 | − | -45 |
| 086 | RCLC | 36 13 |
| 087 | ÷ | -24 |
| 088 | 3 | 03 |
| 089 | 6 | 06 |
| 090 | 5 | 05 |
| 091 | × | -35 |
| 092 | F0? | 16 23 00 |
| 093 | PRTX | -14 |
| 094 | F2? | 16 23 02 |
| 095 | RTN | 24 |
| 096 | Σ+ | 56 |
| 097 | RTN | 24 |
| 098 | R/S | 51 |
| 099 | *LBLD | 21 14 |
| 100 | SF2 | 16 21 02 |
| 101 | GSBA | 23 11 |
| 102 | Σ− | 16 56 |
| 103 | RTN | 24 |
| 104 | *LBLd | 21 16 14 |
| 105 | SF2 | 16 21 02 |
| 106 | GSBB | 23 12 |
| 107 | Σ− | 16 56 |
| 108 | RTN | 24 |

## LABELS

| | | | | | |
|---|---|---|---|---|---|
| A enter L | B enter W | C print | D corr. L | E →K̄, c.v. | 0 print option |
| a initialize L | b initialize W | c | d corr. W | e | 1 |
| 0 | 1 | 2 | 3 | 4 | 2 corrections |
| 5 | 6 | 7 | 8 | 9 | 3 |

## FLAGS / SET STATUS

FLAGS: 0 ON☒ OFF☒; 1 ☐ ☐; 2 ☒ ☒; 3 ☐ ☐
TRIG: DEG☒ GRAD☐ RAD☐
DISP: FIX☒ SCI☐ ENG☐ n=3

## REGISTERS

| 0 used | 1 | 2 | 3 | 4 | 5 | 6 | 7 | 8 | 9 |
|---|---|---|---|---|---|---|---|---|---|
| S0 | S1 | S2 | S3 | S4 Σx | S5 used | S6 used | S7 used | S8 used | S9 i |
| A L^D_(∞) | B W^%_(∞) | C used | D D | E b | I | | | | |

# Program Description

**Program Title:** Munro Plot
**Name:** Daniel Pauly
**Date:** Sept., 1980
**Address:** ICLARM, MCC P.O. Box 1501
Makati, Metro Manila, Philippines

**Program Description, Equations, Variables, etc.**

Munro (1982) suggested that

$$\log_e (L_\infty - L_a) - \log_e (L_\infty - L_b) = K(b - a) \quad \ldots 1)$$

which becomes, in terms of the generalized VBGF and using a different notation

$$\ln (L_{(\infty)}^D - L_1^D) - \ln (L_{(\infty)}^D - L_2^D) = KD(t_2 - t_1) \quad \ldots 2)$$

Given a value of $D$ and a first value of $L_{(\infty)}$, equation (2) can be used to obtain single values of $K$ (one for each triplet of $L_1$, $L_2$ and $\Delta t$ ($= t_2 - t_1$) values). The calculated values of $K$ have the property of being close to each other when an optimal value of $L_{(\infty)}$ has been selected, and to differ widely from others when the selected value of $L_{(\infty)}$ is too high or too low.

Thus, by calculating, for a given value of $L_{(\infty)}$ the coefficient of variation of the $K$-values (C.V. of $\bar{K}$ = s.d. of $K$-values / $\bar{K}$), one may select by trial and error the value of $L_{(\infty)}$ which produces the lowest C.V. in the $K$-values and which thus corresponds to $L_\infty$ (= best $L_{(\infty)}$).

The method resembles the "forced" Gulland and Holt Plot in that data at unequal time interval can be used. It has, however, the advantage of providing exact solutions (= $K$-values) irrespective of the value of $\Delta t$.

**Operating Limits and Warnings**
1) $L_{(\infty)}$ must be higher than any $L_2$ value.
2) $\Delta t$ must be expressed in days.
3) The $K$-values are put on an annual basis automatically.
4) A value of $D$ must be entered; set $D = 1$ when using the normal or "special" VBGF.

# User Instructions

FB 7a
FITTING SEASONALLY OSCILLATING GROWTH DATA I
initialize
input

| STEP | INSTRUCTIONS | INPUT DATA/UNITS | KEYS | | OUTPUT DATA/UNITS |
|---|---|---|---|---|---|
| 1 | Read sides 1 and 2 of card I and initialize | 10 | 10 | ↑ | 10.00 |
| | | 5 | 5 | $y^x$ | 100000.00 |
| | | | f | a | 100000.00 |
| | | | | | |
| 2 | Enter data | $t$ | ↑ | | $t$ |
| | | $L_i^D$ | ↑ | | $L_i^D$ |
| | | $L_{(\infty)}^D$ | A | | $i$ |
| | | | | | |
| 3 | Read sides 1 and 2 of card II, and go to Users Instructions, Part II. | | | | |

NOTES:
1) Input routine takes about 15 seconds per data triplet.
2) $L_{(\infty)}^D$ is entered with each set of length-at-age values.

## Program Listing (001 to 112)

| STEP | KEY ENTRY | KEY CODE | COMMENTS | STEP | KEY ENTRY | KEY CODE | COMMENTS |
|---|---|---|---|---|---|---|---|
| 001 | *LBLa | 21 16 11 | | | 057 | RCLC | 36 13 | |
| | 002 | CLRG | 16-53 | | | 058 | x | -35 | |
| | 003 | ST00 | 35 00 | | | 059 | RCL5 | 36 05 | |
| | 004 | ST04 | 35 04 | | 060 | 060 | RCLB | 36 12 | |
| | 005 | ST07 | 35 07 | | | 061 | x | -35 | |
| | 006 | ST09 | 35 09 | | | 062 | + | -55 | |
| | 007 | P⇄S | 16-51 | | | 063 | RCL4 | 36 04 | |
| | 008 | CLRG | 16-53 | | | 064 | RCLA | 36 11 | |
| | 009 | RAD | 16-22 | | | 065 | x | -35 | |
| 010 | 010 | RTN | 24 | | | 066 | + | -55 | |
| | 011 | *LBLA | 21 11 | | | 067 | RCL1 | 36 01 | |
| | 012 | STOD | 35 14 | | | 068 | + | -55 | |
| | 013 | ÷ | -24 | | | 069 | P⇄S | 16-51 | |
| | 014 | CHS | -22 | | 070 | 070 | ST05 | 35 05 | |
| | 015 | 1 | 01 | | | 071 | RCLA | 36 11 | |
| | 016 | + | -55 | | | 072 | x | -35 | |
| | 017 | LN | 32 | | | 073 | X⇄Y | -41 | |
| | 018 | ST0D | 35 14 | | | 074 | ST04 | 35 04 | |
| | 019 | X⇄Y | -41 | | | 075 | + | -55 | |
| 020 | 020 | STOC | 35 13 | | | 076 | ST0D | 35 14 | |
| | 021 | 2 | 02 | | | 077 | P⇄S | 16-51 | |
| | 022 | x | -35 | | | 078 | RCL8 | 36 08 | |
| | 023 | Pi | 16-24 | | | 079 | RCLC | 36 13 | |
| | 024 | x | -35 | | 080 | 080 | x | -35 | |
| | 025 | SIN | 41 | | | 081 | RCL7 | 36 07 | |
| | 026 | RCLC | 36 13 | | | 082 | RCLB | 36 12 | |
| | 027 | X⇄Y | -41 | | | 083 | x | -35 | |
| | 028 | RCLC | 36 13 | | | 084 | + | -55 | |
| | 029 | 2 | 02 | | | 085 | RCL5 | 36 05 | |
| 030 | 030 | x | -35 | | | 086 | RCLA | 36 11 | |
| | 031 | Pi | 16-24 | | | 087 | x | -35 | |
| | 032 | x | -35 | | | 088 | + | -55 | |
| | 033 | COS | 42 | | | 089 | RCL2 | 36 02 | |
| | 034 | RCLD | 36 14 | | 090 | 090 | + | -55 | |
| | 035 | ST+8 | 35-55 08 | | | 091 | RCL9 | 36 09 | |
| | 036 | x² | 53 | | | 092 | RCLC | 36 13 | |
| | 037 | ST+9 | 35-55 09 | | | 093 | x | -35 | |
| | 038 | R↓ | -31 | | | 094 | RCL8 | 36 08 | |
| | 039 | GSB0 | 23 14 | | | 095 | RCLB | 36 12 | |
| 040 | 040 | - | -45 | | | 096 | x | -35 | |
| | 041 | ST0E | 35 15 | | | 097 | + | -55 | |
| | 042 | P⇄S | 16-51 | | | 098 | RCL6 | 36 06 | |
| | 043 | RCL3 | 36 03 | | | 099 | RCLA | 36 11 | |
| | 044 | RCLC | 36 13 | | 100 | 100 | x | -35 | |
| | 045 | x | -35 | | | 101 | + | -55 | |
| | 046 | RCL2 | 36 02 | | | 102 | RCL3 | 36 03 | |
| | 047 | RCLB | 36 12 | | | 103 | + | -55 | |
| | 048 | x | -35 | | | 104 | P⇄S | 16-51 | |
| | 049 | + | -55 | | | 105 | ST07 | 35 07 | |
| 050 | 050 | RCL1 | 36 01 | | | 106 | RCLC | 36 13 | |
| | 051 | RCLA | 36 11 | | | 107 | x | -35 | |
| | 052 | x | -35 | | | 108 | X⇄Y | -41 | |
| | 053 | + | -55 | | | 109 | ST06 | 35 06 | |
| | 054 | RCL0 | 36 00 | | 110 | 110 | RCLB | 36 12 | |
| | 055 | + | -55 | | | 111 | x | -35 | |
| | 056 | RCL6 | 36 06 | | | 112 | + | -55 | |

Comment (spanning steps ~011–040): These steps (and also step 009) may be deleted and the program may then be used for multiple linear regression analysis. 24 steps are available for linearizing transformations (e.g. taking log).

### REGISTERS

| 0 | 1 | 2 | 3 | 4 | 5 | 6 | 7 | 8 | 9 |
|---|---|---|---|---|---|---|---|---|---|
| $a$ | $b_1$ | $b_2$ | $b_3$ | used | used | used | used | used | used |

| S0 | S1 | S2 | S3 | S4 | S5 | S6 | S7 | S8 | S9 |
|---|---|---|---|---|---|---|---|---|---|
| $c_0$ | $c_1$ | $c_2$ | $c_3$ | $c_4$ | $c_5$ | $c_6$ | $c_7$ | $c_8$ | $c_9$ |

| A | B | C | D | E | I |
|---|---|---|---|---|---|
| used | used | used | used | used | counter |

# Program Listing (113 to end)

| STEP | KEY ENTRY | KEY CODE | COMMENTS | STEP | KEY ENTRY | KEY CODE | COMMENTS |
|---|---|---|---|---|---|---|---|
| | 113 RCL0 | 36 14 | | | 169 RCL6 | 36 06 | |
| | 114 + | -55 | | 170 | 170 × | -35 | |
| | 115 1 | 01 | | | 171 RCLE | 36 15 | |
| | 116 + | -55 | | | 172 RCL7 | 36 07 | |
| | 117 1/x | 52 | | | 173 × | -35 | |
| | 118 STOD | 35 14 | | | 174 P⇄S | 16-51 | |
| | 119 RCLE | 36 15 | | | 175 ST-6 | 35-45 06 | |
| 120 | 120 × | -35 | | | 176 R↓ | -31 | |
| | 121 STOE | 35 15 | | | 177 ST-5 | 35-45 05 | |
| | 122 RCL7 | 36 07 | | | 178 R↓ | -31 | |
| | 123 × | -35 | | | 179 ST-4 | 35-45 04 | |
| | 124 ST+3 | 35-55 03 | | 180 | 180 P⇄S | 16-51 | |
| | 125 RCLE | 36 15 | | | 181 RCLD | 36 14 | |
| | 126 RCL6 | 36 06 | | | 182 RCL6 | 36 06 | |
| | 127 × | -35 | | | 183 × | -35 | |
| | 128 ST+2 | 35-55 02 | | | 184 STOE | 35 15 | |
| | 129 RCLE | 36 15 | | | 185 RCL6 | 36 06 | |
| 130 | 130 RCL5 | 36 05 | | | 186 × | -35 | |
| | 131 × | -35 | | | 187 RCLE | 36 15 | |
| | 132 ST+1 | 35-55 01 | | | 188 RCL7 | 36 07 | |
| | 133 RCLE | 36 15 | | | 189 × | -35 | |
| | 134 RCL4 | 36 04 | | 190 | 190 RCLD | 36 14 | |
| | 135 × | -35 | | | 191 RCL7 | 36 07 | |
| | 136 ST+0 | 35-55 00 | | | 192 x² | 53 | |
| | 137 RCLD | 36 14 | | | 193 × | -35 | |
| | 138 RCL4 | 36 04 | | | 194 P⇄S | 16-51 | |
| | 139 × | -35 | | | 195 ST-9 | 35-45 09 | |
| 140 | 140 STOE | 35 15 | | | 196 R↓ | -31 | |
| | 141 RCL4 | 36 04 | | | 197 ST-8 | 35-45 08 | |
| | 142 × | -35 | | | 198 R↓ | -31 | |
| | 143 RCLE | 36 15 | | | 199 ST-7 | 35-45 07 | |
| | 144 RCL5 | 36 05 | | 200 | 200 P⇄S | 16-51 | |
| | 145 × | -35 | | | 201 ISZI | 16 26 46 | |
| | 146 RCLE | 36 15 | | | 202 RCLI | 36 46 | |
| | 147 RCL6 | 36 06 | | | 203 RTN | 24 | |
| | 148 × | -35 | | | 204 *LBLD | 21 14 | |
| | 149 RCL7 | 36 07 | | | 205 STOC | 35 13 | |
| 150 | 150 P⇄S | 16-51 | | | 206 R↓ | -31 | |
| | 151 R↓ | -31 | | | 207 STOB | 35 12 | |
| | 152 ST-2 | 35-45 02 | | | 208 R↓ | -31 | |
| | 153 R↓ | -31 | | | 209 STOA | 35 11 | |
| | 154 ST-1 | 35-45 01 | | 210 | 210 RCLD | 36 14 | |
| | 155 R↓ | -31 | | | 211 RCL0 | 36 00 | |
| | 156 ST-0 | 35-45 00 | | | 212 RCL1 | 36 01 | |
| | 157 R↓ | -31 | | | 213 RCLA | 36 11 | |
| | 158 RCLE | 36 15 | | | 214 × | -35 | |
| | 159 × | -35 | | | 215 + | -55 | |
| 160 | 160 ST-3 | 35-45 03 | | | 216 RCL2 | 36 02 | |
| | 161 P⇄S | 16-51 | | | 217 RCLB | 36 12 | |
| | 162 RCLD | 36 14 | | | 218 × | -35 | |
| | 163 RCL5 | 36 05 | | | 219 + | -55 | |
| | 164 × | -35 | | 220 | 220 RCL3 | 36 03 | |
| | 165 STOE | 35 15 | | | 221 RCLC | 36 13 | |
| | 166 RCL5 | 36 05 | | | 222 × | -35 | |
| | 167 × | -35 | | | 223 + | -55 | |
| | 168 RCLE | 36 15 | | | 224 RTN | 24 | |

## LABELS

| A enter data | B | C | D used | E |
|---|---|---|---|---|
| a initialize | b | c | d | e |
| 0 | 1 | 2 | 3 | 4 |
| 5 | 6 | 7 | 8 | 9 |

## FLAGS

| 0 | 1 | 2 | 3 |
|---|---|---|---|

## SET STATUS

| FLAGS | TRIG | DISP |
|---|---|---|
| ON OFF | DEG ☐ | FIX ☒ |
| 0 ☐ ☒ | GRAD ☐ | SCI ☐ |
| 1 ☐ ☒ | RAD ☒ | ENG ☐ |
| 2 ☐ ☒ | | n = 2 |
| 3 ☐ ☒ | | |

# Program Description I

**Program Title** Fitting seasonally oscillating Growth data I
**Name** D. Pauly and G. Gaschütz   **Date** July, 1979
**Address** ICLARM, MCC P.O. Box 1501
Makati, Metro Manila, Philippines

**Program Description, Equations, Variables, etc.** 1) Given a preliminary value of $L_{(\infty)}$, a value of $D$ and length-at-age data, the program (Part I and II) estimates the values of the parameters $K$, $t_0$, $t_s$ and $C$ of the equation

$$L_t^D = L_\infty^D \left(1 - e^{-KD(t-t_0) + C \cdot \frac{KD}{2\pi} \cdot \sin 2\pi \cdot (t - t_s)}\right) \quad \ldots (1)$$

which is a version of the generalized VBGF suitable to describe seasonally oscillating length growth of animals, e.g. of fishes.

2) The parameter estimation is based on multiple regression analysis; the calculation of the regression coefficients is based on the program "Multiple Regression Analysis" No. 50584, HP 67/97 Users' Library (Europe) by Tapio Westerlund. By deleting step 009, and steps 012 to 034, the present program can also be used for solving multiple regression problems involving 3 independent variables (see Program Listing). In such cases, the second part of this program may be used for estimating $R^2$. (The regression coefficients ($a$, $b_1$, $b_2$, and $b_3$) are stored in STO 0 to STO 3).

3) The large number ($10^5$) used when initializing may be replaced by any large number of similar magnitude.

4) The program accepts only the year as time (age) unit. The appropriate conversions may be performed when entering the data.

**Operating Limits and Warnings** 1) $L_{(\infty)}^D - L_t^D$ must always be a positive number.

2) The values of time (age) must always be expressed in years or fractions thereof.

# User Instructions

**FB 7b**
◀ 1　FITTING SEASONALLY OSCILLATING GROWTH DATA II　2 ▶
→ $R^2$　　→ $L_t^D$　　→ $K, t_0, t_s, C$

| STEP | INSTRUCTIONS | INPUT DATA/UNITS | KEYS | | OUTPUT DATA/UNITS |
|---|---|---|---|---|---|
| 3 | You have already read in sides 1 and 2 of this program card, if not, do it now. | | | | 0.000 |
| 4 | Calculate $R^2$ | | A | | $R^2$ |
| 5 | Calculate KD, $t_0$, $t_s$ and C | | E | | KD |
| | | | | | $t_0$ |
| | | | | | $t_s$ |
| | | | | | C |
| 6 | To estimate the length corresponding to a given t value, perform | $L^D_{(\infty)}$ | STO | A | $L^D_{(\infty)}$ |
| 7a | Then calculate value of $L_t$ | t | C | | $L_t^D$ |
| 7b | Step 7 may be repeated at will, e.g. in order to draw a seasonally oscillating growth curve. | D | 1/x | $Y^x$ | $L_t$ |
| 8 | If $L_t$ values are to be calculated without the parameters having been estimated internally, perform [RAD], then | $L^D_{(\infty)}$ | STO | A | $L^D_{(\infty)}$ |
| | | KD | STO | 4 | KD |
| | | $t_0$ | STO | 5 | $t_0$ |
| | | $t_s$ | STO | 6 | $t_s$ |
| | | C | STO | 7 | C |
| | and go to step 7. | | | | |

NOTES:
1) When C output is negative, transform C and $t_s$ according to instructions in Program Description II.
2) Setting C = 0 in step 8 estimates values of $L_t$ for the unseasonalized VBGF.

## Program Listing (001 to 112)

| STEP | KEY ENTRY | KEY CODE | COMMENTS | STEP | KEY ENTRY | KEY CODE | COMMENTS |
|---|---|---|---|---|---|---|---|
| 001 | *LBLA | 21 11 | | 057 | RCLA | 36 11 | |
| 002 | 3 | 03 | | 058 | × | -35 | |
| 003 | ST04 | 35 04 | | 059 | RCLD | 36 14 | |
| 004 | P⇄S | 16-51 | | 060 | RCL5 | 36 05 | |
| 005 | RCL7 | 36 07 | | 061 | × | -35 | |
| 006 | RCL4 | 36 04 | | 062 | RCLE | 36 15 | |
| 007 | × | -35 | | 063 | - | -45 | |
| 008 | RCL5 | 36 05 | | 064 | RCLB | 36 12 | |
| 009 | RCL5 | 36 05 | | 065 | × | -35 | |
| 010 | × | -35 | | 066 | - | -45 | |
| 011 | - | -45 | | 067 | RCLC | 36 13 | |
| 012 | STOA | 35 11 | | 068 | RCLA | 36 11 | |
| 013 | RCL8 | 36 08 | | 069 | × | -35 | |
| 014 | RCL4 | 36 04 | | 070 | RCLB | 36 12 | |
| 015 | × | -35 | | 071 | RCLB | 36 12 | |
| 016 | RCL6 | 36 06 | | 072 | × | -35 | |
| 017 | RCL5 | 36 05 | | 073 | - | -45 | |
| 018 | × | -35 | | 074 | ÷ | -24 | |
| 019 | - | -45 | | 075 | P⇄S | 16-51 | |
| 020 | STOB | 35 12 | | 076 | ST05 | 35 05 | |
| 021 | RCL9 | 36 09 | | 077 | P⇄S | 16-51 | |
| 022 | RCL4 | 36 04 | | 078 | RCLD | 36 14 | |
| 023 | × | -35 | | 079 | RCL5 | 36 05 | |
| 024 | RCL6 | 36 06 | | 080 | × | -35 | |
| 025 | RCL6 | 36 06 | | 081 | RCLE | 36 15 | |
| 026 | × | -35 | | 082 | - | -45 | |
| 027 | - | -45 | | 083 | X⇄Y | -41 | |
| 028 | STOC | 35 13 | | 084 | RCLB | 36 12 | |
| 029 | RCL4 | 36 04 | | 085 | × | -35 | |
| 030 | RCL2 | 36 02 | | 086 | - | -45 | |
| 031 | RCL1 | 36 01 | | 087 | RCLA | 36 11 | |
| 032 | P⇄S | 16-51 | | 088 | ÷ | -24 | |
| 033 | RCL8 | 36 08 | | 089 | P⇄S | 16-51 | |
| 034 | × | -35 | | 090 | ST06 | 35 06 | |
| 035 | RCL1 | 36 01 | | 091 | RCL5 | 36 05 | |
| 036 | - | -45 | | 092 | P⇄S | 16-51 | |
| 037 | STOD | 35 14 | | 093 | RCL6 | 36 06 | |
| 038 | R↓ | -31 | | 094 | × | -35 | |
| 039 | RCL8 | 36 08 | | 095 | X⇄Y | -41 | |
| 040 | × | -35 | | 096 | RCL5 | 36 05 | |
| 041 | RCL2 | 36 02 | | 097 | × | -35 | |
| 042 | - | -45 | | 098 | + | -55 | |
| 043 | × | -35 | | 099 | RCLD | 36 14 | |
| 044 | STOE | 35 15 | | 100 | + | -55 | |
| 045 | RCL3 | 36 03 | | 101 | RCL4 | 36 04 | |
| 046 | RCL8 | 36 08 | | 102 | ÷ | -24 | |
| 047 | P⇄S | 16-51 | | 103 | CHS | -22 | |
| 048 | RCL3 | 36 03 | | 104 | P⇄S | 16-51 | |
| 049 | × | -35 | | 105 | ST07 | 35 07 | |
| 050 | - | -45 | | 106 | RCLI | 36 46 | |
| 051 | RCL4 | 36 04 | | 107 | RCL4 | 36 04 | |
| 052 | × | -35 | | 108 | - | -45 | |
| 053 | RCLD | 36 14 | | 109 | 1 | 01 | |
| 054 | RCL6 | 36 06 | | 110 | - | -45 | |
| 055 | × | -35 | | 111 | STOA | 35 11 | |
| 056 | + | -55 | | 112 | RCL0 | 36 00 | |

### REGISTERS

| 0 $a$ | 1 $b_1$ | 2 $b_2$ | 3 $b_3$ | 4 used/K | 5 used/$t_0$ | 6 used/$t_5$ | 7 used/c | 8 used | 9 used |
|---|---|---|---|---|---|---|---|---|---|
| S0 $c_0$ | S1 $c_1$ | S2 $c_2$ | S3 $c_3$ | S4 $c_4$ | S5 $c_5$ | S6 $c_6$ | S7 $c_7$ | S8 $c_8$ | S9 $c_9$ |
| A used | B used | C used | D used | E used | | | | I $n$ | |

# Program Listing (113 to end)

| STEP | KEY ENTRY | KEY CODE | COMMENTS | STEP | KEY ENTRY | KEY CODE | COMMENTS |
|---|---|---|---|---|---|---|---|
| 113 | RCL8 | 36 08 | | 169 | ÷ | -24 | |
| 114 | × | -35 | | 170 | CHS | -22 | |
| 115 | RCL7 | 36 07 | | 171 | TAN⁻¹ | 16 43 | |
| 116 | RCL1 | 36 01 | | 172 | Pi | 16-24 | |
| 117 | × | -35 | | 173 | ÷ | -24 | |
| 118 | + | -55 | | 174 | 2 | 02 | |
| 119 | RCL6 | 36 06 | | 175 | ÷ | -24 | |
| 120 | RCL2 | 36 02 | | 176 | PRTX | -14 | |
| 121 | × | -35 | | 177 | STO6 | 35 06 | |
| 122 | + | -55 | | 178 | GSBa | 23 16 11 | |
| 123 | RCL5 | 36 05 | | 179 | SIN | 41 | |
| 124 | RCL3 | 36 03 | | 180 | RCL4 | 36 04 | |
| 125 | × | -35 | | 181 | × | -35 | |
| 126 | + | -55 | | 182 | RCL3 | 36 03 | |
| 127 | RCL8 | 36 08 | | 183 | GSBa | 23 16 11 | |
| 128 | x² | 53 | | 184 | ÷ | -24 | |
| 129 | RCL1 | 36 46 | | 185 | 1/X | 52 | |
| 130 | ÷ | -24 | | 186 | PRTX | -14 | |
| 131 | STOE | 35 15 | | 187 | STO7 | 35 07 | |
| 132 | - | -45 | | 188 | RTN | 24 | |
| 133 | STOD | 35 14 | | 189 | *LBLC | 21 13 | |
| 134 | RCL9 | 36 09 | | 190 | STOB | 35 12 | |
| 135 | RCL0 | 36 10 | | 191 | RCL6 | 36 06 | |
| 136 | - | -45 | | 192 | - | -45 | |
| 137 | STOE | 35 15 | | 193 | GSBa | 23 16 11 | |
| 138 | ÷ | -24 | | 194 | SIN | 41 | |
| 139 | STOB | 35 12 | | 195 | RCL7 | 36 07 | |
| 140 | RCLE | 36 15 | | 196 | × | -35 | |
| 141 | RCLD | 36 14 | | 197 | Pi | 16-24 | |
| 142 | - | -45 | | 198 | ÷ | -24 | |
| 143 | RCLA | 36 11 | | 199 | 2 | 02 | |
| 144 | ÷ | -24 | | 200 | ÷ | -24 | |
| 145 | STOC | 35 13 | | 201 | RCL4 | 36 04 | |
| 146 | RCLD | 36 14 | | 202 | × | -35 | |
| 147 | RCL4 | 36 04 | | 203 | RCLB | 36 12 | |
| 148 | ÷ | -24 | | 204 | RCL5 | 36 05 | |
| 149 | RCLC | 36 13 | | 205 | - | -45 | |
| 150 | ÷ | -24 | | 206 | RCL4 | 36 04 | |
| 151 | STOD | 35 14 | | 207 | × | -35 | |
| 152 | RCLB | 36 12 | | 208 | + | -55 | |
| 153 | RTN | 24 | | 209 | CHS | -22 | |
| 154 | *LBLE | 21 15 | | 210 | eˣ | 33 | |
| 155 | RAD | 16-22 | | 211 | CHS | -22 | |
| 156 | RCL1 | 36 01 | | 212 | 1 | 01 | |
| 157 | CHS | -22 | | 213 | + | -55 | |
| 158 | PRTX | -14 | | 214 | RCLA | 36 11 | |
| 159 | STO4 | 35 04 | | 215 | × | -35 | |
| 160 | CHS | -22 | | 216 | RTN | 24 | |
| 161 | RCL0 | 36 00 | | 217 | *LBLa | 21 16 11 | |
| 162 | X⇄Y | -41 | | 218 | Pi | 16-24 | |
| 163 | ÷ | -24 | | 219 | × | -35 | |
| 164 | CHS | -22 | | 220 | 2 | 02 | |
| 165 | STO5 | 35 05 | | 221 | × | -35 | |
| 166 | PRTX | -14 | | 222 | RTN | 24 | |
| 167 | RCL3 | 36 03 | | | | | |
| 168 | RCL2 | 36 02 | | | | | |

## LABELS

| A → $R^2$ | B | C → $L_t$ | D | E → $K, t_0, t_s, C$ | 0 |
|---|---|---|---|---|---|
| a → $\pi \times 2z$ | b → $\pi \div 2 \div$ | c | d | e | 1 |
| 0 | 1 | 2 | 3 | 4 | 2 |
| 5 | 6 | 7 | 8 | 9 | 3 |

## FLAGS / SET STATUS

| FLAGS | ON | OFF | TRIG | | DISP | |
|---|---|---|---|---|---|---|
| 0 | ☐ | ☒ | DEG | ☐ | FIX | ☒ |
| 1 | ☐ | ☒ | GRAD | ☐ | SCI | ☐ |
| 2 | ☐ | ☒ | RAD | ☒ | ENG | ☐ |
| 3 | ☐ | ☒ | | | n = 3 | |

# Program Description II

**Program Title** Fitting Seasonally Oscillating Growth Data II
**Name** D. Pauly and G. Gaschütz
**Date** July, 1979
**Address** ICLARM, MCC P.O. Box 1501
Makati, Metro Manila, Philippines

**Program Description, Equations, Variables, etc.** (See also Program Description I)

5) The routine for the estimation of $R^2$ is taken from "Statistics for Multiple Regression Analysis" No. 50585, HP 67/97 Users' Library (Europe) by Tapio Westerlund.

6) Due to size limitation, the program may not always produce positive values of C. If a negative value of C is encountered, the following transformations should be applied

    a) change $-C$ to $+C$

and    b) add 0.5 to the value of $t_s$.

Although the two sets of C and $t_s$ values (original and transformed) are equivalent in their effects on a growth curve, the use of the transformed values agrees better with the definition of C given in the text.

7) Program No. 50585 (see 5) above) may be used subsequently to this program to obtain additional statistics for the multiple linear regression (e.g., to obtain standard errors and F-values for the regression coefficients).

**Operating Limits and Warnings**
1) The values of time (age) must always be expressed in years or fractions thereof.

2) Do not forget, when applicable, the transformations recommended in 6).

3) Steps 6, 7 and 8 must follow step 5.

# User Instructions

**FB 8 — SEASONAL GROWTH FROM TAGGING DATA**

| STEP | INSTRUCTIONS | INPUT DATA/UNITS | KEYS | | OUTPUT DATA/UNITS |
|---|---|---|---|---|---|
| 1 | Enter D and initialize | D | f | a | 0.000 |
| 2 | Enter data | $L_1$ | ↑ | | $L_1$ |
| | | $L_2$ | ↑ | | $L_2$ |
| | | $\Delta t$ | ↑ | | $\Delta t$ |
| | | $T\ (°C)$ | A | | $i$ |
| 3 | Estimate $a$, $b_1$, $b_2$ and $R^2$ | | E | | $R^2$ |
| | | | | | $a$ |
| | | | | | $b_1$ |
| | | | | | $b_2$ |
| 4 | To estimate value of $L_\infty$ and $K$, enter $\bar{T}$ * N.B. $K$ will be expressed in the units of time selected for $\Delta t$. | $\bar{T}$ | C | | $L_\infty$ |
| | | | | | $K$ |
| 5 | To estimate value of $C$, enter $T_S$, $T_W$ and $\bar{T}$ * | $T_S$ | ↑ | | |
| | | $T_W$ | ↑ | | |
| | | $\bar{T}$ | f | c | $C$ |
| 6 | To estimate value of $K$ based on a forcing value of $L_{(\infty)}$, do | $L_{(\infty)}$ | ↑ | | |
| | | $\bar{T}$ | f | e | $K$ |

NOTES:
* $T_S$ : highest mean monthly temperature in a year
* $T_W$ : lowest mean monthly temperature in a year
* $\bar{T}$ : mean annual temperature

## Program Listing (001 to 112)

| STEP | KEY ENTRY | KEY CODE | COMMENTS | STEP | KEY ENTRY | KEY CODE | COMMENTS |
|---|---|---|---|---|---|---|---|
| 001 | *LBLa | 21 16 11 | | | 057 | RCLB | 36 12 | |
| | 002 | CLRG | 16-53 | | 058 | RCLC | 36 13 | |
| | 003 | P⇄S | 16-51 | | 059 | × | -35 | |
| | 004 | ST00 | 35 00 | 060 | 060 | ST+3 | 35-55 03 | |
| | 005 | P⇄S | 16-51 | | 061 | 1 | 01 | |
| | 006 | CLX | -51 | | 062 | ST+0 | 35-55 00 | |
| | 007 | RTN | 24 | | 063 | RCL0 | 36 00 | |
| | 008 | *LBLA | 21 11 | | 064 | RTN | 24 | |
| | 009 | P⇄S | 16-51 | | 065 | *LBL1 | 21 01 | |
| 010 | 010 | ST04 | 35 04 | | 066 | ST+i | 35-55 45 | |
| | 011 | R↓ | -31 | | 067 | RCLI | 36 46 | |
| | 012 | ST03 | 35 03 | | 068 | 3 | 03 | |
| | 013 | R↓ | -31 | | 069 | − | -45 | |
| | 014 | RCL0 | 36 00 | 070 | 070 | STOI | 35 46 | |
| | 015 | Yˣ | 31 | | 071 | R↓ | -31 | |
| | 016 | ST02 | 35 02 | | 072 | x² | 53 | |
| | 017 | R↓ | -31 | | 073 | ST+i | 35-55 45 | |
| | 018 | RCL0 | 36 00 | | 074 | RTN | 24 | |
| | 019 | Yˣ | 31 | | 075 | *LBLE | 21 15 | |
| 020 | 020 | STOI | 35 01 | | 076 | RCL0 | 36 00 | |
| | 021 | RCL2 | 36 02 | | 077 | RCL4 | 36 04 | |
| | 022 | + | -55 | | 078 | × | -35 | |
| | 023 | 2 | 02 | | 079 | RCL7 | 36 07 | |
| | 024 | ÷ | -24 | 080 | 080 | x² | 53 | |
| | 025 | RCL4 | 36 04 | | 081 | − | -45 | |
| | 026 | RCL2 | 36 02 | | 082 | ST00 | 35 14 | |
| | 027 | RCL1 | 36 01 | | 083 | RCL0 | 36 00 | |
| | 028 | − | -45 | | 084 | RCL3 | 36 03 | |
| | 029 | RCL3 | 36 03 | | 085 | × | -35 | |
| 030 | 030 | ÷ | -24 | | 086 | RCL8 | 36 08 | |
| | 031 | P⇄S | 16-51 | | 087 | RCL9 | 36 09 | |
| | 032 | STOC | 35 13 | | 088 | × | -35 | |
| | 033 | R↓ | -31 | | 089 | − | -45 | |
| | 034 | STOB | 35 12 | 090 | 090 | × | -35 | |
| | 035 | R↓ | -31 | | 091 | STOC | 35 13 | |
| | 036 | STOA | 35 11 | | 092 | RCL0 | 36 00 | |
| | 037 | 7 | 07 | | 093 | RCL1 | 36 01 | |
| | 038 | STOI | 35 46 | | 094 | × | -35 | |
| | 039 | R↓ | -31 | | 095 | RCL7 | 36 07 | |
| 040 | 040 | GSB1 | 23 01 | | 096 | RCL8 | 36 08 | |
| | 041 | 8 | 08 | | 097 | × | -35 | |
| | 042 | STOI | 35 46 | | 098 | − | -45 | |
| | 043 | RCLB | 36 12 | | 099 | STOA | 35 11 | |
| | 044 | GSB1 | 23 01 | 100 | 100 | RCL0 | 36 00 | |
| | 045 | 9 | 09 | | 101 | RCL2 | 36 02 | |
| | 046 | STOI | 35 46 | | 102 | × | -35 | |
| | 047 | RCLC | 36 13 | | 103 | RCL7 | 36 07 | |
| | 048 | GSB1 | 23 01 | | 104 | RCL9 | 36 09 | |
| | 049 | RCLA | 36 11 | | 105 | × | -35 | |
| 050 | 050 | RCLB | 36 12 | | 106 | − | -45 | |
| | 051 | × | -35 | | 107 | STOB | 35 12 | |
| | 052 | ST+1 | 35-55 01 | | 108 | × | -35 | |
| | 053 | RCLA | 36 11 | | 109 | RCLC | 36 13 | |
| | 054 | RCLC | 36 13 | 110 | 110 | X⇄Y | -41 | |
| | 055 | × | -35 | | 111 | − | -45 | |
| | 056 | ST+2 | 35-55 02 | | 112 | RCL0 | 36 14 | |

### REGISTERS

| 0 | 1 | 2 | 3 | 4 | 5 | 6 | 7 | 8 | 9 |
|---|---|---|---|---|---|---|---|---|---|
| $n$ | $\Sigma xy$ | $\Sigma x_z$ | $\Sigma y_z$ | $\Sigma x^2$ | $\Sigma y^2$ | $\Sigma z^2$ | $\Sigma x$ | $\Sigma y$ | $\Sigma z$ |
| S0 | S1 | S2 | S3 | S4 | S5 | S6 | S7 | S8 | S9 |
| $D$ | $L_1^0$ | $L_2^0$ | $\Delta t$ | $T(°C)$ | | | | | |
| A | B | C | D | E | | | I | | |
| $a$ | $b$ | $c$ | used | used | | | used | | |

# Program Listing (113 to end)

| STEP | KEY ENTRY | KEY CODE | COMMENTS | STEP | KEY ENTRY | KEY CODE | COMMENTS |
|---|---|---|---|---|---|---|---|
| | 113 RCL0 | 36 00 | | | 169 PRTX | -14 | |
| | 114 RCL5 | 36 05 | | 170 | 170 RCLB | 36 12 | |
| | 115 x | -35 | | | 171 PRTX | -14 | |
| | 116 RCL8 | 36 08 | | | 172 RCLC | 36 13 | |
| | 117 X² | 53 | | | 173 PRTX | -14 | |
| | 118 - | -45 | | | 174 RTN | 24 | |
| | 119 x | -35 | | | 175 *LBLC | 21 13 | |
| 120 | 120 RCLA | 36 11 | | | 176 RCLC | 36 13 | |
| | 121 X² | 53 | | | 177 x | -35 | |
| | 122 - | -45 | | | 178 RCLA | 36 11 | |
| | 123 ÷ | -24 | | | 179 + | -55 | |
| | 124 STOC | 35 13 | | 180 | 180 RCLB | 36 12 | |
| | 125 RCLB | 36 12 | | | 181 ÷ | -24 | |
| | 126 RCLA | 36 11 | | | 182 P⇄S | 16-51 | |
| | 127 RCLC | 36 13 | | | 183 RCL0 | 36 00 | |
| | 128 x | -35 | | | 184 1/X | 52 | |
| | 129 - | -45 | | | 185 Yˣ | 31 | |
| 130 | 130 RCLD | 36 14 | | | 186 CHS | -22 | |
| | 131 ÷ | -24 | | | 187 PRTX | -14 | |
| | 132 STOB | 35 12 | | | 188 RCLB | 36 12 | |
| | 133 RCL9 | 36 09 | | | 189 RCL0 | 36 00 | |
| | 134 RCLC | 36 13 | | 190 | 190 ÷ | -24 | |
| | 135 RCL8 | 36 08 | | | 191 CHS | -22 | |
| | 136 x | -35 | | | 192 P⇄S | 16-51 | |
| | 137 - | -45 | | | 193 RTN | 24 | |
| | 138 RCLB | 36 12 | | | 194 *LBLc | 21 16 13 | |
| | 139 RCL7 | 36 07 | | | 195 STOI | 35 46 | |
| 140 | 140 x | -35 | | | 196 R↓ | -31 | |
| | 141 - | -45 | | | 197 - | -45 | |
| | 142 RCL0 | 36 00 | | | 198 RCLC | 36 13 | |
| | 143 ÷ | -24 | | | 199 x | -35 | |
| | 144 STOA | 35 11 | | 200 | 200 RCLI | 36 46 | |
| | 145 RCL9 | 36 09 | | | 201 RCLC | 36 13 | |
| | 146 x | -35 | | | 202 x | -35 | |
| | 147 RCL8 | 36 12 | | | 203 RCLA | 36 11 | |
| | 148 RCL2 | 36 02 | | | 204 + | -55 | |
| | 149 x | -35 | | | 205 2 | 02 | |
| 150 | 150 + | -55 | | | 206 x | -35 | |
| | 151 RCLC | 36 13 | | | 207 ÷ | -24 | |
| | 152 RCL3 | 36 03 | | | 208 PRTX | -14 | |
| | 153 x | -35 | | | 209 RTN | 24 | |
| | 154 + | -55 | | 210 | 210 *LBLe | 21 16 15 | |
| | 155 RCL9 | 36 09 | | | 211 RCLC | 36 13 | |
| | 156 X² | 53 | | | 212 x | -35 | |
| | 157 RCL0 | 36 00 | | | 213 RCLA | 36 11 | |
| | 158 ÷ | -24 | | | 214 + | -55 | |
| | 159 - | -45 | | | 215 X⇄Y | -41 | |
| 160 | 160 RCL6 | 36 06 | | | 216 ÷ | -24 | |
| | 161 RCL9 | 36 09 | | | 217 P⇄S | 16-51 | |
| | 162 X² | 53 | | | 218 RCL0 | 36 00 | |
| | 163 RCL0 | 36 00 | | | 219 P⇄S | 16-51 | |
| | 164 ÷ | -24 | | 220 | 220 1/X | 52 | |
| | 165 - | -45 | | | 221 Yˣ | 31 | |
| | 166 ÷ | -24 | | | 222 RTN | 24 | |
| | 167 PRTX | -14 | | | | | |
| | 168 RCLA | 36 11 | | | | | |

## LABELS

| A → enter data | B | C $\bar{T} → L_0, K$ | D | E → $R^2, o, b, c$ |
|---|---|---|---|---|
| a initialize | b | c $\bar{T}_s, \bar{T}, T_w → C$ | d | e $L_{(o)}, \bar{T} → K$ |
| 0 | 1 | 2 | 3 | 4 |
| 5 | 6 | 7 | 8 | 9 |

## FLAGS

| 0 | | | |
|---|---|---|---|
| 1 | | | |
| 2 | | | |
| 3 | | | |

## SET STATUS

| FLAGS | | TRIG | DISP |
|---|---|---|---|
| | ON OFF | | |
| 0 | ☐ ☒ | DEG ☒ | FIX ☒ |
| 1 | ☐ ☒ | GRAD ☐ | SCI ☐ |
| 2 | ☐ ☒ | RAD ☐ | ENG ☐ |
| 3 | ☐ ☒ | | n = 3 |

# Program Description

**Program Title** Seasonal Growth from Tagging Data
**Name** Daniel Pauly
**Date** January, 1982
**Address** ICLARM, MCC P.O. Box 1501
Makati, Metro Manila, Philippines

**Program Description, Equations, Variables, etc.** A multiple regression of the form

$$Y = a + b_1 X_1 + b_2 X_2 \qquad \ldots 1)$$

is used to estimate the parameters $L_\infty$ and $K$ of the VBGF. The following definitions apply

$$Y = L_2^D - L_1^D / t_2 - t_1 \quad \text{and} \quad X_1 = L_1^D + L_2^D / 2 \quad, \text{where } L_1 \text{ and}$$

$L_2$ are the length at tagging and at recapture, respectively, corresponding to the times $t_1$ and $t_2$, while $X_2$ is the mean water temperature when a given fish was at large ($\bar{T}$). Thus, given a series of $L_1$ and $L_2$ data, of the times at large and their corresponding temperatures, the growth parameters can be estimated from

$$L_\infty = \left( \frac{a + (b_2 \bar{T})}{-b_1} \right)^{1/D} \qquad \ldots 2)$$

and

$$K = -b/D \qquad \ldots 3)$$

and

$$C = (b_2 (T_S - T_W)) / 2 (a + (b_2 \bar{T})) \qquad \ldots 4)$$

where $T_S$ is the highest (summer) and $T_W$ the lowest (winter) mean monthly temperatures in the water body in question, while $\bar{T}$ is the mean annual temperature.

In analogy to the "forced Gulland and Holt Plot" (see Program FB 5), forcing value of $L_\infty$ can be used in conjunction with equation 2), which allows for $K$ to be estimated even when the fish used represented a narrow range of lengths only.

**Operating Limits and Warnings** 1) a value of $D$ must be entered, i.e., $D = 1$ when the special VBGF is used, and $D < 1$ when the generalized VBGF is used.
2) the values of $L_\infty$, $K$ and $C$ obtained by this method are approximate and should be confirmed whenever possible, using other methods.

# User Instructions

**GENERALIZED VBGF AND DERIVATIVES : SOLUTIONS    FB9**

$t \to L_t$ ; $\to L_i$ ; $t \to W_t$ ; $\to W_i$ ; $W_t \to t$ ; $L_t \to t$ ; $W_t \to dw/dt$ ; $L_t \to dl/dt$ ; $W_t, t \to t_0$ ; $L_t, t \to t_0$

| STEP | INSTRUCTIONS | INPUT DATA/UNITS | KEYS | | OUTPUT DATA/UNITS |
|---|---|---|---|---|---|
| 1 | Enter, in any order, the required constants | | | | |
| | | $L_\infty$ | STO | A | $L_\infty$ |
| | | $W_\infty$ | STO | B | $W_\infty$ |
| | | $K$ | STO | 1 | $K$ |
| | | $t_0$ | STO | 0 | $t_0$ |
| | | $D$ | STO | D | $D$ |
| | | $b^*$ | STO | E | $b$ |
| 2 | Find solutions: | | | | |
| 2.0 | length at a given age | $t$ | A | | $L_t$ |
| 2.1 | weight at a given age | $t$ | B | | $W_t$ |
| 2.2 | age at a given length | $L_t$ | C | | $t$ |
| 2.3 | age at a given weight | $W_t$ | f | c | $t$ |
| 2.4 | $t_0$ for a given length and age | $L_t$ | f | | $L_t$ |
| | | $t$ | E | | $t_0$ |
| 2.5 | $t_0$ for a given weight and age | $W_t$ | f | | $W_t$ |
| | | $t$ | f | e | $t_0$ |
| 2.6 | length at inflection point of curve ** | | f | a | $L_i$ |
| 2.7 | weight at inflection point of curve | | f | b | $W_i$ |
| 2.8 | growth rate at a given length | $L_t$ | D | | $dl/dt$ |
| 2.9 | growth rate at a given weight | $W_t$ | f | d | $dw/dt$ |
| 3 | Estimate d and D from $W_{max}$ (in grams). Enter $W_{max}$ | $W_{max}$ | GTO | 7 | |
| | | | R/S | | $d$ |
| | | | | | $D$ |

NOTES:
* Exponent of length-weight relationship.
** Step 2.6 can be performed only when $D < 1$.

## Program Listing (001 to 112)

| STEP | KEY ENTRY | KEY CODE | COMMENTS | STEP | KEY ENTRY | KEY CODE | COMMENTS |
|---|---|---|---|---|---|---|---|
| 001 | *LBL2 | 21 02 | | 057 | RTN | 24 | |
| 002 | RCLD | 36 14 | | 058 | *LBLC | 21 13 | |
| 003 | 1/X | 52 | | 059 | GSB1 | 23 01 | |
| 004 | Y^x | 31 | | 060 | RCL0 | 36 00 | |
| 005 | RTN | 24 | | 061 | + | -55 | |
| 006 | *LBL3 | 21 03 | | 062 | RTN | 24 | |
| 007 | RCLD | 36 14 | | 063 | *LBL1 | 21 01 | |
| 008 | RCLE | 36 15 | | 064 | RCLA | 36 11 | |
| 009 | ÷ | -24 | | 065 | ÷ | -24 | |
| 010 | Y^x | 31 | | 066 | RCLD | 36 14 | |
| 011 | RTN | 24 | | 067 | Y^x | 31 | |
| 012 | *LBL4 | 21 04 | | 068 | CHS | -22 | |
| 013 | RCL1 | 36 01 | | 069 | 1 | 01 | |
| 014 | RCLD | 36 14 | | 070 | + | -55 | |
| 015 | x | -35 | | 071 | LN | 32 | |
| 016 | x | -35 | | 072 | CHS | -22 | |
| 017 | RTN | 24 | | 073 | RCL1 | 36 01 | |
| 018 | *LBL5 | 21 05 | | 074 | RCLD | 36 14 | |
| 019 | 3 | 03 | | 075 | x | -35 | |
| 020 | RCLE | 36 15 | | 076 | ÷ | -24 | |
| 021 | ÷ | -24 | | 077 | RTN | 24 | |
| 022 | x | -35 | | 078 | *LBLc | 21 16 13 | |
| 023 | RTN | 24 | | 079 | GSB0 | 23 00 | |
| 024 | *LBL6 | 21 06 | | 080 | RCL0 | 36 00 | |
| 025 | RCL1 | 36 01 | | 081 | + | -55 | |
| 026 | RCLD | 36 14 | | 082 | RTN | 24 | |
| 027 | x | -35 | | 083 | *LBL0 | 21 00 | |
| 028 | x | -35 | | 084 | RCLB | 36 12 | |
| 029 | CHS | -22 | | 085 | ÷ | -24 | |
| 030 | e^x | 33 | | 086 | RCLD | 36 14 | |
| 031 | RTN | 24 | | 087 | RCLE | 36 15 | |
| 032 | *LBLA | 21 11 | | 088 | ÷ | -24 | |
| 033 | RCL0 | 36 00 | | 089 | Y^x | 31 | |
| 034 | - | -45 | | 090 | CHS | -22 | |
| 035 | GSB6 | 23 06 | | 091 | 1 | 01 | |
| 036 | CHS | -22 | | 092 | + | -55 | |
| 037 | 1 | 01 | | 093 | LN | 32 | |
| 038 | + | -55 | | 094 | CHS | -22 | |
| 039 | GSB2 | 23 02 | | 095 | RCL1 | 36 01 | |
| 040 | RCLA | 36 11 | | 096 | GSB5 | 23 05 | |
| 041 | x | -35 | | 097 | RCLD | 36 14 | |
| 042 | RTN | 24 | | 098 | x | -35 | |
| 043 | *LBLB | 21 12 | | 099 | ÷ | -24 | |
| 044 | RCL0 | 36 00 | | 100 | RTN | 24 | |
| 045 | - | -45 | | 101 | *LBLE | 21 15 | |
| 046 | GSB5 | 23 05 | | 102 | STO2 | 35 02 | |
| 047 | GSB6 | 23 06 | | 103 | X⇌Y | -41 | |
| 048 | CHS | -22 | | 104 | GSB1 | 23 01 | |
| 049 | 1 | 01 | | 105 | RCL2 | 36 02 | |
| 050 | + | -55 | | 106 | - | -45 | |
| 051 | RCLE | 36 15 | | 107 | CHS | -22 | |
| 052 | RCLD | 36 14 | | 108 | RTN | 24 | |
| 053 | ÷ | -24 | | 109 | *LBLe | 21 16 15 | |
| 054 | Y^x | 31 | | 110 | STO2 | 35 02 | |
| 055 | RCLB | 36 12 | | 111 | X⇌Y | -41 | |
| 056 | x | -35 | | 112 | GSB0 | 23 00 | |

### REGISTERS

| 0 $t_0$ | 1 $K$ | 2 used | 3 | 4 | 5 | 6 | 7 | 8 | 9 |
|---|---|---|---|---|---|---|---|---|---|
| S0 | S1 | S2 | S3 | S4 | S5 | S6 | S7 | S8 | S9 |
| A $L_\infty$ | B $W_\infty$ | C | D $D$ | E $b$ | I | | | | |

## Program Listing (113 to end)

| STEP | KEY ENTRY | KEY CODE | STEP | KEY ENTRY | KEY CODE |
|---|---|---|---|---|---|
| 113 | RCL2 | 36 02 | 169 | *LBLd | 21 16 14 |
| 114 | − | −45 | 170 | STO2 | 35 02 |
| 115 | CHS | −22 | 171 | RCLB | 36 12 |
| 116 | RTN | 24 | 172 | X≷Y | −41 |
| 117 | *LBLa | 21 16 11 | 173 | ÷ | −24 |
| 118 | RCLD | 36 14 | 174 | RCL0 | 36 14 |
| 119 | LN | 32 | 175 | RCLE | 36 15 |
| 120 | $e^x$ | 33 | 176 | ÷ | −24 |
| 121 | CHS | −22 | 177 | $Y^x$ | 31 |
| 122 | 1 | 01 | 178 | 1 | 01 |
| 123 | + | −55 | 179 | − | −45 |
| 124 | GSB2 | 23 02 | 180 | RCL2 | 36 02 |
| 125 | RCLA | 36 11 | 181 | × | −35 |
| 126 | × | −35 | 182 | RCL1 | 36 01 |
| 127 | RTN | 24 | 183 | × | −35 |
| 128 | *LBLb | 21 16 12 | 184 | 3 | 03 |
| 129 | RCLE | 36 15 | 185 | × | −35 |
| 130 | RCLD | 36 14 | 186 | RTN | 24 |
| 131 | − | −45 | 187 | *LBL7 | 21 07 |
| 132 | RCLE | 36 15 | 188 | SPC | 16-11 |
| 133 | ÷ | −24 | 189 | LOG | 16 32 |
| 134 | RCLE | 36 15 | 190 | . | −62 |
| 135 | RCLD | 36 14 | 191 | 0 | 00 |
| 136 | ÷ | −24 | 192 | 3 | 03 |
| 137 | $Y^x$ | 31 | 193 | 5 | 05 |
| 138 | RCLB | 36 12 | 194 | 7 | 07 |
| 139 | × | −35 | 195 | 4 | 04 |
| 140 | RTN | 24 | 196 | × | −35 |
| 141 | *LBLD | 21 14 | 197 | . | −62 |
| 142 | GSBC | 23 13 | 198 | 6 | 06 |
| 143 | STO2 | 35 02 | 199 | 7 | 07 |
| 144 | RCL0 | 36 00 | 200 | 4 | 04 |
| 145 | − | −45 | 201 | 2 | 02 |
| 146 | GSB6 | 23 06 | 202 | + | −55 |
| 147 | CHS | −22 | 203 | PRTX | −14 |
| 148 | 1 | 01 | 204 | 3 | 03 |
| 149 | + | −55 | 205 | × | −35 |
| 150 | RCLD | 36 14 | 206 | CHS | −22 |
| 151 | 1/X | 52 | 207 | 3 | 03 |
| 152 | 1 | 01 | 208 | ÷ | −55 |
| 153 | − | −45 | 209 | STOD | 35 14 |
| 154 | $Y^x$ | 31 | 210 | PRTX | −14 |
| 155 | RCLA | 36 11 | 211 | RTN | 24 |
| 156 | RCLD | 36 14 | | | |
| 157 | ÷ | −24 | | | |
| 158 | × | −35 | | | |
| 159 | RCL1 | 36 01 | | | |
| 160 | × | −35 | | | |
| 161 | RCLD | 36 14 | | | |
| 162 | × | −35 | | | |
| 163 | RCL2 | 36 02 | | | |
| 164 | RCL0 | 36 00 | | | |
| 165 | − | −45 | | | |
| 166 | GSB6 | 23 06 | | | |
| 167 | × | −35 | | | |
| 168 | RTN | 24 | | | |

### LABELS

| A $t \to L_t$ | B $t \to W_t$ | C $L_t \to t$ | D $L_t \to dL/dt$ | E $L_t, t \to t_o$ | 0 |
|---|---|---|---|---|---|
| a $\to L_i$ | b $\to W_i$ | c $W_t \to t$ | d $W_t \to dW/dt$ | e $W_t, t \to t_o$ | 1 |
| 0 used | 1 used | 2 used | 3 used | 4 used | 2 |
| 5 used | 6 used | 7 $\to d, D$ | 8 | 9 | 3 |

### FLAGS / SET STATUS

| FLAGS | ON | OFF | TRIG | | DISP | |
|---|---|---|---|---|---|---|
| 0 | ☐ | ☒ | DEG | ☒ | FIX | ☒ |
| 1 | ☐ | ☒ | GRAD | ☐ | SCI | ☐ |
| 2 | ☐ | ☒ | RAD | ☐ | ENG | ☐ |
| 3 | ☐ | ☒ | | | n = 3 | |

# Program Description

**Program Title** Generalized VBGF and Derivatives: Solutions
**Name** Daniel Pauly
**Address** ICLARM, MCC P.O. Box 1501
Makati, Metro Manila, Philippines
**Date** Dec., 1981

**Program Description, Equations, Variables, etc.** The generalized von Bertalanffy Growth Formula (VBGF) has for length the form

$$L_t = L_\infty (1 - e^{-KD(t-t_0)})^{1/D} \quad \ldots 1)$$

and its derivative is

$$dl/dt = \frac{L_\infty}{D}(1-e^{-KD(t-t_0)})^{1/D-1} \cdot KD \cdot e^{-KD(t-t_0)} \quad \ldots 2)$$

when $D < 1$, there is an inflexion point at time

$$t_i = t_0 - \frac{\ln D}{KD} \quad \ldots 3)$$

and at length

$$L_i = L_\infty (1 - e^{(\ln D)})^{1/D} \quad \ldots 4)$$

the generalized VBGF for weight is

$$W_t = W_\infty (1 - e^{-KD\frac{3}{b}(t-t_0)})^{3/D} \quad \ldots 5)$$

the first derivative of which is

$$dw/dt = W_\infty \, 3K (1 - e^{-KD\frac{3}{b}(t-t_0)})^{b/D-1} \cdot e^{-KD\frac{3}{b}(t-t_0)} \quad \ldots 6)$$

the weight at the inflexion point being given by

$$W_i = W_\infty \left(\frac{b-D}{b}\right)^{b/D} \quad \ldots 7)$$

Equations 1) and 5) correspond to the normal, or "special" VBGF when $D=1$ and $b=3$. D and d are estimated from equations 26) and 27) in Pauly (1981).

**Operating Limits and Warnings** 1) Equations 3) and 4) have no solutions when $D=1$.

2) $L_t$ and $W_t$ must always be lower than $L_\infty$ and $W_\infty$, respectively.

# User Instructions

| STEP | INSTRUCTIONS | INPUT DATA/UNITS | KEYS | | OUTPUT DATA/UNITS |
|---|---|---|---|---|---|
| 1 | Enter $W_\infty$, $K$, $t_c$ and $t_o$ | $W_\infty$ | ↑ | | |
| | | $K$ | ↑ | | |
| | | $t_c$ | ↑ | | |
| | | $t_o$ | f | a | 0.000 |
| 2 | Enter $\bar{W}$ | $\bar{W}$ | f | b | $\bar{W}$ |
| 3 | Enter TOL (tolerated error, e.g. 0.001) | TOL | f | e | TOL |
| 4 | Calculate $f(a)$ and $f(b)$ : | | | | |
| | enter a high Z-value | Z(a) | A | | $f(a)$ |
| | enter a low Z-value | Z(b) | B | | $f(b)$ |
| | Note: $f(a)$ must be negative, $f(b)$ positive; if this is not the case, enter new values of Z(a) and/or Z(b). | | | | |
| 5 | Iterate for Z | | E | | Z |

## Program Listing (001 to 112)

| STEP | KEY ENTRY | KEY CODE | COMMENTS | STEP | KEY ENTRY | KEY CODE | COMMENTS |
|---|---|---|---|---|---|---|---|
| 001 | *LBLa | 21 16 11 | | | 057 | ÷ | -24 | |
| | 002 | - | -45 | | 058 | RCLB | 36 12 | |
| | 003 | X⇄Y | -41 | | 059 | X⇄Y | -41 | |
| | 004 | STO1 | 35 01 | 060 | 060 | - | -45 | |
| | 005 | × | -35 | | 061 | STOD | 35 14 | |
| | 006 | STO5 | 35 05 | | 062 | RCLB | 36 12 | |
| | 007 | X⇄Y | -41 | | 063 | - | -45 | |
| | 008 | STO4 | 35 04 | | 064 | RCLC | 36 13 | |
| | 009 | CLX | -51 | | 065 | RCLB | 36 12 | |
| 010 | 010 | RTN | 24 | | 066 | - | -45 | |
| | 011 | *LBLe | 21 16 15 | | 067 | ÷ | -24 | |
| | 012 | STOE | 35 15 | | 068 | X<0? | 16-45 | |
| | 013 | RTN | 24 | | 069 | GTO1 | 22 01 | |
| | 014 | *LBLb | 21 16 12 | 070 | 070 | 1 | 01 | |
| | 015 | STO6 | 35 06 | | 071 | X≤Y? | 16-35 | |
| | 016 | RTN | 24 | | 072 | GTO1 | 22 01 | |
| | 017 | *LBLA | 21 11 | | 073 | RCLB | 36 12 | |
| | 018 | STOB | 35 12 | | 074 | RCLC | 36 13 | |
| | 019 | GSBD | 23 14 | | 075 | - | -45 | |
| 020 | 020 | STO8 | 35 08 | | 076 | ABS | 16 31 | |
| | 021 | RTN | 24 | | 077 | 4 | 04 | |
| | 022 | *LBLB | 21 12 | | 078 | ÷ | -24 | |
| | 023 | STOA | 35 11 | | 079 | RCLD | 36 14 | |
| | 024 | STOC | 35 13 | 080 | 080 | RCLC | 36 13 | |
| | 025 | GSBD | 23 14 | | 081 | - | -45 | |
| | 026 | STO7 | 35 07 | | 082 | ABS | 16 31 | |
| | 027 | STO9 | 35 09 | | 083 | X≤Y? | 16-35 | |
| | 028 | RTN | 24 | | 084 | GTO1 | 22 01 | |
| | 029 | *LBLE | 21 15 | | 085 | RCL1 | 36 46 | |
| 030 | 030 | RCL8 | 36 08 | | 086 | RCLD | 36 14 | |
| | 031 | X=0? | 16-43 | | 087 | RCLB | 36 12 | |
| | 032 | GTO5 | 22 05 | | 088 | - | -45 | |
| | 033 | RCLB | 36 12 | | 089 | ABS | 16 31 | |
| | 034 | RCLC | 36 13 | 090 | 090 | X>Y? | 16-34 | |
| | 035 | - | -45 | | 091 | GTO2 | 22 02 | |
| | 036 | ABS | 16 31 | | 092 | X⇄Y | -41 | |
| | 037 | RCLE | 36 15 | | 093 | RCLC | 36 13 | |
| | 038 | X>Y? | 16-34 | | 094 | RCLB | 36 12 | |
| | 039 | GTO5 | 22 05 | | 095 | - | -45 | |
| 040 | 040 | 2 | 02 | | 096 | ENT↑ | -21 | |
| | 041 | ÷ | -24 | | 097 | ABS | 16 31 | |
| | 042 | EEX | -23 | | 098 | ÷ | -24 | |
| | 043 | CHS | -22 | | 099 | × | -35 | |
| | 044 | 9 | 09 | 100 | 100 | RCLB | 36 12 | |
| | 045 | RCLB | 36 12 | | 101 | + | -55 | |
| | 046 | × | -35 | | 102 | STOD | 35 14 | |
| | 047 | + | -55 | | 103 | GTO2 | 22 02 | |
| | 048 | STO1 | 35 46 | | 104 | *LBL1 | 21 01 | |
| | 049 | RCLB | 36 08 | | 105 | RCLB | 36 12 | |
| 050 | 050 | RCL7 | 36 07 | | 106 | RCLC | 36 13 | |
| | 051 | RCL8 | 36 08 | | 107 | + | -55 | |
| | 052 | - | -45 | | 108 | 2 | 02 | |
| | 053 | RCLA | 36 11 | | 109 | ÷ | -24 | |
| | 054 | RCLB | 36 12 | 110 | 110 | STOD | 35 14 | |
| | 055 | - | -45 | | 111 | *LBL2 | 21 02 | |
| | 056 | ÷ | -24 | | 112 | RCLB | 36 12 | |

### REGISTERS

| 0 used | 1 $K$ | 2 $Z$ | 3 $W_\infty$ | 4 $K(t_c-t_0)$ | 5 | 6 $\bar{W}$ | 7 used | 8 used | 9 used |
|---|---|---|---|---|---|---|---|---|---|
| S0 | S1 | S2 | S3 | S4 | S5 | S6 | S7 | S8 | S9 |

| A used | B used | C used | D used | E TOL | I |
|---|---|---|---|---|---|

# Program Listing (113 to end)

| STEP | KEY ENTRY | KEY CODE | | STEP | KEY ENTRY | KEY CODE |
|---|---|---|---|---|---|---|
| 113 | STOA | 35 11 | | 169 | $e^x$ | 33 |
| 114 | RCL8 | 36 08 | 170 | 170 | RCL3 | 36 03 |
| 115 | ST07 | 35 07 | | 171 | × | -35 |
| 116 | RCLD | 36 14 | | 172 | 3 | 03 |
| 117 | STOB | 35 12 | | 173 | × | -35 |
| 118 | GSBD | 23 14 | | 174 | RCL1 | 36 01 |
| 119 | ST08 | 35 08 | | 175 | RCL3 | 36 03 |
| 120 | RCL9 | 36 09 | | 176 | + | -55 |
| 121 | × | -35 | | 177 | ÷ | -24 |
| 122 | X<0? | 16-45 | | 178 | − | -45 |
| 123 | GT03 | 22 03 | | 179 | RCL5 | 36 05 |
| 124 | RCLA | 36 11 | 180 | 180 | 3 | 03 |
| 125 | STOC | 35 13 | | 181 | × | -35 |
| 126 | RCL7 | 36 07 | | 182 | CHS | -22 |
| 127 | ST09 | 35 09 | | 183 | $e^x$ | 33 |
| 128 | *LBL3 | 21 03 | | 184 | RCL3 | 36 03 |
| 129 | RCL9 | 36 09 | | 185 | × | -35 |
| 130 | ABS | 16 31 | | 186 | RCL1 | 36 01 |
| 131 | RCL8 | 36 08 | | 187 | 3 | 03 |
| 132 | ABS | 16 31 | | 188 | × | -35 |
| 133 | X≤Y? | 16-35 | | 189 | RCL3 | 36 03 |
| 134 | GTOE | 22 15 | 190 | 190 | + | -55 |
| 135 | RCLB | 36 12 | | 191 | ÷ | -24 |
| 136 | RCLC | 36 13 | | 192 | − | -45 |
| 137 | STOB | 35 12 | | 193 | 1 | 01 |
| 138 | X≷Y | -41 | | 194 | + | -55 |
| 139 | STOC | 35 13 | | 195 | RCL4 | 36 04 |
| 140 | STOA | 35 11 | | 196 | × | -35 |
| 141 | RCL8 | 36 08 | | 197 | RCL6 | 36 06 |
| 142 | RCL9 | 36 09 | | 198 | − | -45 |
| 143 | ST08 | 35 08 | | 199 | RTN | 24 |
| 144 | X≷Y | -41 | 200 | | | |
| 145 | ST09 | 35 09 | | | | |
| 146 | ST07 | 35 07 | | | | |
| 147 | GTOE | 22 15 | | | | |
| 148 | *LBL5 | 21 05 | | | | |
| 149 | RCLB | 36 12 | | | | |
| 150 | RTN | 24 | | | | |
| 151 | *LBLD | 21 14 | | | | |
| 152 | ST03 | 35 03 | | | | |
| 153 | RCL5 | 36 05 | | | | |
| 154 | 2 | 02 | 210 | | | |
| 155 | × | -35 | | | | |
| 156 | CHS | -22 | | | | |
| 157 | $e^x$ | 33 | | | | |
| 158 | × | -35 | | | | |
| 159 | 3 | 03 | | | | |
| 160 | × | -35 | | | | |
| 161 | RCL1 | 36 01 | | | | |
| 162 | 2 | 02 | | | | |
| 163 | × | -35 | | | | |
| 164 | RCL3 | 36 03 | 220 | | | |
| 165 | + | -55 | | | | |
| 166 | ÷ | -24 | | | | |
| 167 | RCL5 | 36 05 | | | | |
| 168 | CHS | -22 | | | | |

## LABELS

| A → f(a) | B → f(b) | C | D | E → Z |
|---|---|---|---|---|
| a enter constants | b enter w̄ | c used | d | e enter TOL |
| 0 | 1 used | 2 used | 3 used | 4 |
| 5 used | 6 | 7 | 8 | 9 |

## FLAGS

| 0 | 1 | 2 | 3 |
|---|---|---|---|

## SET STATUS

| FLAGS ON OFF | TRIG | DISP |
|---|---|---|
| 0 ☐ ☒ | DEG ☒ | FIX ☒ |
| 1 ☐ ☒ | GRAD ☐ | SCI ☐ |
| 2 ☐ ☒ | RAD ☐ | ENG ☐ |
| 3 ☐ ☒ | | n = 3 |

# Program Description

**Program Title** Total Mortality from Mean Weight
**Name** Daniel Pauly
**Address** ICLARM, MCC P.O. Box 1501
Makati, Metro Manila, Philippines
**Date** Sept. 1980

**Program Description, Equations, Variables, etc.** Total mortality ($Z$) can be estimated iteratively from the equation

$$\bar{W} = W_\infty \left\{ 1 - \frac{3Z \exp(-a)}{Z+K} + \frac{3Z \exp(-2a)}{Z+2K} - \frac{Z \exp(-3a)}{Z+3K} \right\} \quad ..1)$$

where $a = K(t_c - t_0)$, $W_\infty$, $K$ and $t_0$ being parameters of the special von Bertalanffy Growth Formula. Where $t_c$ is the mean age at first capture obtained by a given gear and where $\bar{W}$ is the mean weight of the fishes in the catch (Gulland, 1969). "Knife-edge" selection (at $t_c$) is assumed.

The method of iteration used here is the "regula falsi" as incorporated in HP 67/97 program "solution to $f(x) = 0$" (HP 67/97 MA1 08A, Math Pac).

**Operating Limits and Warnings** The iteration time in (1) can be quite long ($\approx 1$ min.) and depends on the values $f(a)$ and $f(b)$, which should be both close to zero, and on TOL, with low TOL values increasing iteration time.

# User Instructions

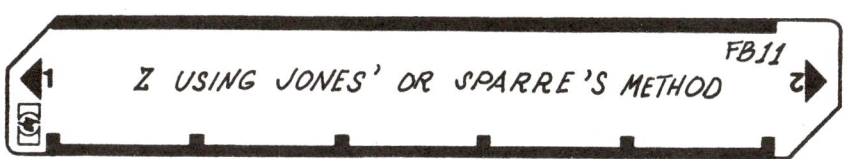

**Z USING JONES' OR SPARRE'S METHOD** — FB11

| STEP | INSTRUCTIONS | INPUT DATA/UNITS | KEYS | | OUTPUT DATA/UNITS |
|---|---|---|---|---|---|
| | _Jones' Method_ | | | | |
| 1 | Enter $L_\infty$, D, $\Delta L$ and $L_{max}$ * | $L_\infty$, D, $\Delta L$, $L_{max}$ | f | a | 0.000 |
| 2 | Enter successive catches, starting with the catch in highest length class with non-zero catch | C | A | | $\ln(L_\infty - L_1)$, $\ln C(L_1, \infty)$ |
| 3 | If the values obtained in step 2 are to be used for estimation of $Z/KD$, press R/S | | R/S | | i |
| 4 | When all catch values have been entered, do | | E | | $r^2$, a, $b = Z/KD$ |
| 5 | To obtain value of Z, multiply by K·D | K·D | × | | Z |
| | _Sparre's Method_ | | | | |
| 6 | same as step 1 above | | | | |
| 7 | Enter K·D ; if not available, enter 1 | K·D | STO | 1 | |
| 8 | Enter successive catches, starting with the catch in highest length class with non-zero catch | C | B | | (rel.) age, $\ln C(L_1, \infty)$ |
| 9 | If values obtained in step 8 are to be used for estimation of $Z/KD$, press R/S | | R/S | | i |
| 10 | When all catch values have been entered, do (and multiply $Z/KD$ with KD if K is available) | | E | | $r^2$, a, or $Z/KD$ |

* Note: Value of $L_{max} + \Delta L$ (class interval) must be $< L_\infty$; also: $L_{max}$ is the lower limit of its class.

# Program Listing

| STEP | KEY ENTRY | KEY CODE |
|---|---|---|
| 001 | *LBLa | 21 16 11 |
| 002 | CLRG | 16-53 |
| 003 | P⇌S | 16-51 |
| 004 | CLRG | 16-53 |
| 005 | STO2 | 35 02 |
| 006 | R↓ | -31 |
| 007 | STOI | 35 46 |
| 008 | R↓ | -31 |
| 009 | STOD | 35 14 |
| 010 | R↓ | -31 |
| 011 | STO0 | 35 00 |
| 012 | CLX | -51 |
| 013 | RTN | 24 |
| 014 | *LBLA | 21 11 |
| 015 | SPC | 16-11 |
| 016 | ST+3 | 35-55 03 |
| 017 | RCL0 | 36 00 |
| 018 | RCLD | 36 14 |
| 019 | Y^x | 31 |
| 020 | RCL2 | 36 02 |
| 021 | RCLD | 36 14 |
| 022 | Y^x | 31 |
| 023 | - | -45 |
| 024 | LN | 32 |
| 025 | PRTX | -14 |
| 026 | RCL3 | 36 03 |
| 027 | LN | 32 |
| 028 | PRTX | -14 |
| 029 | RCL2 | 36 02 |
| 030 | RCLI | 36 46 |
| 031 | - | -45 |
| 032 | STO2 | 35 02 |
| 033 | R↓ | -31 |
| 034 | R/S | 51 |
| 035 | X⇌Y | -41 |
| 036 | Σ+ | 56 |
| 037 | RTN | 24 |
| 038 | *LBLB | 21 12 |
| 039 | SPC | 16-11 |
| 040 | ST+3 | 35-55 03 |
| 041 | RCL0 | 36 00 |
| 042 | RCLD | 36 14 |
| 043 | Y^x | 31 |
| 044 | RCL2 | 36 02 |
| 045 | RCLD | 36 14 |
| 046 | Y^x | 31 |
| 047 | - | -45 |
| 048 | RCLD | 36 00 |
| 049 | RCLD | 36 14 |
| 050 | Y^x | 31 |
| 051 | ÷ | -24 |
| 052 | LN | 32 |
| 053 | CHS | -22 |
| 054 | RCL1 | 36 01 |
| 055 | ÷ | -24 |
| 056 | PRTX | -14 |
| 057 | RCL3 | 36 03 |
| 058 | LN | 32 |
| 059 | PRTX | -14 |
| 060 | RCL2 | 36 02 |
| 061 | RCLI | 36 46 |
| 062 | - | -45 |
| 063 | STO2 | 35 02 |
| 064 | R↓ | -31 |
| 065 | R/S | 51 |
| 066 | X⇌Y | -41 |
| 067 | Σ+ | 56 |
| 068 | RTN | 24 |
| 069 | *LBLE | 21 15 |
| 070 | P⇌S | 16-51 |
| 071 | RCL8 | 36 08 |
| 072 | RCL4 | 36 04 |
| 073 | RCL6 | 36 06 |
| 074 | x | -35 |
| 075 | RCL9 | 36 09 |
| 076 | ÷ | -24 |
| 077 | - | -45 |
| 078 | ENT↑ | -21 |
| 079 | ENT↑ | -21 |
| 080 | RCL4 | 36 04 |
| 081 | X² | 53 |
| 082 | RCL9 | 36 09 |
| 083 | ÷ | -24 |
| 084 | RCL5 | 36 05 |
| 085 | X⇌Y | -41 |
| 086 | - | -45 |
| 087 | ÷ | -24 |
| 088 | STOB | 35 12 |
| 089 | x | -35 |
| 090 | RCL6 | 36 06 |
| 091 | X² | 53 |
| 092 | RCL9 | 36 09 |
| 093 | ÷ | -24 |
| 094 | CHS | -22 |
| 095 | RCL7 | 36 07 |
| 096 | + | -55 |
| 097 | ÷ | -24 |
| 098 | SPC | 16-11 |
| 099 | PRTX | -14 |
| 100 | RCL6 | 36 06 |
| 101 | RCL4 | 36 04 |
| 102 | RCLB | 36 12 |
| 103 | x | -35 |
| 104 | - | -45 |
| 105 | RCL9 | 36 09 |
| 106 | ÷ | -24 |
| 107 | STOA | 35 11 |
| 108 | PRTX | -14 |
| 109 | RCLB | 36 12 |
| 110 | PRTX | -14 |
| 111 | P⇌S | 16-51 |
| 112 | RTN | 24 |

### LABELS

| A | B | C | D | E | 0 |
|---|---|---|---|---|---|
| a | b | c | d | e | 1 |
| 0 | 1 | 2 | 3 | 4 | 2 |
| 5 | 6 | 7 | 8 | 9 | 3 |

### FLAGS / SET STATUS

| FLAGS | TRIG | DISP |
|---|---|---|
| ON OFF | DEG ☐ | FIX ☐ |
| 0 ☐ ☐ | GRAD ☐ | SCI ☐ |
| 1 ☐ ☐ | RAD ☐ | ENG ☐ |
| 2 ☐ ☐ |  | n = |
| 3 ☐ ☐ |  |  |

### REGISTERS

| 0 $L_\infty$ | 1 $K$ | 2 $L'_{max}$ | 3 $\Sigma C$ | 4 | 5 | 6 | 7 | 8 | 9 |
|---|---|---|---|---|---|---|---|---|---|
| S0 | S1 | S2 | S3 | S4 $\Sigma x$ | S5 $\Sigma x^2$ | S6 $\Sigma y$ | S7 $\Sigma y^2$ | S8 $\Sigma xy$ | S9 $\Sigma n$ |
| A intercept | B slope | C | D $D$ | E | | | I $\Delta L$ | | |

# Program Description

**Program Title** $Z$ Using Jones' or Sparre's Method
**Name** Daniel Pauly
**Address** ICLARM, MCC P.O. Box 1501, Makati
Metro Manila, Philippines
**Date** Sept. 1983

**Program Description, Equations, Variables, etc.**

Jones (1981) showed that $Z/K$ is equal to the slope of the straight part of a plot $\ln C$ on $\ln(L_\infty - L_1)$, where $C$ is the cumulative catch (starting from the highest length class) corresponding to a given length class of which $L_1$ is the lower class limit.

The method has been modified by Sparre (MS) who showed that $K$ can be estimated from the slope of the straight part of a plot of $\ln C$ on the age corresponding to $L_1$, where both $\ln C$ and $L_1$ are defined as above. When $K$ is not known, using 1 instead of $K$ for the transformation of length to age makes the slope of the plot equal to $Z/K$.

Both methods were here modified for use with the generalized VBGF, by addition of the parameter $D$ where appropriate. Also, the ages in Sparre's method are replaced by relative ages.

**Operating Limits and Warnings** (1) Proper selection of the $x$ and $y$ values to be included in the computation of $Z$ or $Z/K$ requires that a graph be made from which the points belonging to the straight section are selected.

(2) Do not use the method with data obtained from a gear that selects for or against larger sizes.

# User Instructions

**LENGTH-CONVERTED CATCH CURVES**    FB12

initial Z: L, N →    improved Z: L, N →    → $r^2, a, Z$

| STEP | INSTRUCTIONS | INPUT DATA/UNITS | KEYS | | OUTPUT DATA/UNITS |
|---|---|---|---|---|---|
| | *Preliminary estimation of Z or Z/K* | | | | |
| 1 | Enter $L_\infty$, $\Delta L$, K, D and initialize (if K is unknown, enter 1 instead) | $L_\infty$ | ↑ | | |
| | | $\Delta L$ | ↑ | | |
| | | K | ↑ | | |
| | | D | f | a | 0.000 |
| 2 | Enter class midpoint and frequency | L | ↑ | | |
| | | N | A | | $\ln(N/\Delta t)$ |
| | | | | | $t'_i$ |
| 3 | If data pair is to be included in linear regression, do (do Σ− instead of Σ+ to remove erroneous entries) | | Σ+ | | i |
| 4 | When all values to be included have been entered, press | | E | | $r^2$ |
| | | | | | a |
| | *Iteration for improving estimate of Z or Z/K* | | | | Z or Z/K |
| 5 | Enter preliminary value of Z (or Z/K) and re-initialize | | f | b | Z or Z/K |
| 6 | Enter class midpoint and frequency | L | ↑ | | |
| | | N | B | | $\ln(N/1-e^{-Z\Delta t})$ |
| | | | | | $t'_i$ |
| 7 | If data pair is to be included in regression, do (do Σ− instead of Σ+ to remove erroneous entries) | | Σ+ | | i |
| 8 | When all values to be included have been entered, press | | E | | $r^2$ |
| | | | | | a |
| 9 | Stop if new value of Z or Z/K is close to initial value. If not repeat steps 6-9 using last value of Z or Z/K as input in step 6. Repeat until convergence is achieved. | | | | Z or Z/K |

## Program Listing (001 to 112)

| STEP | KEY ENTRY | KEY CODE | COMMENTS | STEP | KEY ENTRY | KEY CODE | COMMENTS |
|---|---|---|---|---|---|---|---|
| 001 | *LBLa | 21 16 11 | | 057 | + | -55 | |
| 002 | P⇄S | 16-51 | | 058 | 1/X | 52 | |
| 003 | CLRG | 16-53 | | 059 | RCL0 | 36 00 | |
| 004 | P⇄S | 16-51 | | 060 | × | -35 | |
| 005 | STOD | 35 14 | | 061 | LN | 32 | |
| 006 | R↓ | -31 | | 062 | SPC | 16-11 | |
| 007 | ST01 | 35 01 | | 063 | PRTX | -14 | |
| 008 | R↓ | -31 | | 064 | RCL8 | 36 08 | |
| 009 | 2 | 02 | | 065 | RCLC | 36 13 | |
| 010 | ÷ | -24 | | 066 | - | -45 | |
| 011 | STOC | 35 13 | | 067 | GSB1 | 23 01 | |
| 012 | X⇄Y | -41 | | 068 | PRTX | -14 | |
| 013 | ST05 | 35 05 | | 069 | RTN | 24 | |
| 014 | CLX | -51 | | 070 | *LBL0 | 21 00 | |
| 015 | RTN | 24 | | 071 | RCLC | 36 13 | |
| 016 | *LBLb | 21 16 12 | | 072 | + | -55 | |
| 017 | ST04 | 35 04 | | 073 | GSB1 | 23 01 | |
| 018 | P⇄S | 16-51 | | 074 | RCL8 | 36 08 | |
| 019 | 0 | 00 | | 075 | RCLC | 36 13 | |
| 020 | ST04 | 35 04 | | 076 | - | -45 | |
| 021 | ST05 | 35 05 | | 077 | GSB1 | 23 01 | |
| 022 | ST06 | 35 06 | | 078 | - | -45 | |
| 023 | ST07 | 35 07 | | 079 | RTN | 24 | |
| 024 | ST08 | 35 08 | | 080 | *LBL1 | 21 01 | |
| 025 | ST09 | 35 09 | | 081 | RCL5 | 36 05 | |
| 026 | P⇄S | 16-51 | | 082 | ÷ | -24 | |
| 027 | CLX | -51 | | 083 | RCLD | 36 14 | |
| 028 | RTN | 24 | | 084 | $Y^x$ | 31 | |
| 029 | *LBLA | 21 11 | | 085 | CHS | -22 | |
| 030 | ST00 | 35 00 | | 086 | 1 | 01 | |
| 031 | R↓ | -31 | | 087 | + | -55 | |
| 032 | ST08 | 35 08 | | 088 | LN | 32 | |
| 033 | GSB0 | 23 00 | | 089 | CHS | -22 | |
| 034 | ST07 | 35 07 | | 090 | RCL1 | 36 01 | |
| 035 | RCL8 | 36 08 | | 091 | ÷ | -24 | |
| 036 | GSB1 | 23 01 | | 092 | RCLD | 36 14 | |
| 037 | RCL0 | 36 00 | | 093 | ÷ | -24 | |
| 038 | RCL7 | 36 07 | | 094 | RTN | 24 | |
| 039 | ÷ | -24 | | 095 | *LBLE | 21 15 | |
| 040 | LN | 32 | | 096 | P⇄S | 16-51 | |
| 041 | SPC | 16-11 | | 097 | SPC | 16-11 | |
| 042 | PRTX | -14 | | 098 | RCL8 | 36 08 | |
| 043 | X⇄Y | -41 | | 099 | RCL4 | 36 04 | |
| 044 | PRTX | -14 | | 100 | RCL6 | 36 06 | |
| 045 | RTN | 24 | | 101 | × | -35 | |
| 046 | *LBLB | 21 12 | | 102 | RCL9 | 36 09 | |
| 047 | ST00 | 35 00 | | 103 | ÷ | -24 | |
| 048 | R↓ | -31 | | 104 | - | -45 | |
| 049 | ST08 | 35 08 | | 105 | ENT↑ | -21 | |
| 050 | GSB0 | 23 00 | | 106 | ENT↑ | -21 | |
| 051 | RCL4 | 36 04 | | 107 | RCL4 | 36 04 | |
| 052 | × | -35 | | 108 | $X^2$ | 53 | |
| 053 | CHS | -22 | | 109 | RCL9 | 36 09 | |
| 054 | $e^x$ | 33 | | 110 | ÷ | -24 | |
| 055 | CHS | -22 | | 111 | RCL5 | 36 05 | |
| 056 | 1 | 01 | | 112 | X⇄Y | -41 | |

### REGISTERS

| 0 used | 1 K | 2 used | 3 used | 4 $z_1$ | 5 $L_\infty$ | 6 used | 7 used | 8 used | 9 |
|---|---|---|---|---|---|---|---|---|---|
| S0 | S1 | S2 | S3 | S4 $\Sigma x$ | S5 $\Sigma x^2$ | S6 $\Sigma y$ | S7 $\Sigma y^2$ | S8 $\Sigma xy$ | S9 $\Sigma n$ |
| A $a$ | B $b$ | C $\Delta L/2$ | D $D$ | E | | | | I | |

# Program Listing (113 to end)

| STEP | KEY ENTRY | KEY CODE | COMMENTS |
|---|---|---|---|
| 113 | – | -45 | |
| 114 | ÷ | -24 | |
| 115 | STOB | 35 12 | |
| 116 | x | -35 | |
| 117 | RCL6 | 36 06 | |
| 118 | X² | 53 | |
| 119 | RCL9 | 36 09 | |
| 120 | ÷ | -24 | |
| 121 | CHS | -22 | |
| 122 | RCL7 | 36 07 | |
| 123 | + | -55 | |
| 124 | ÷ | -24 | |
| 125 | PRTX | -14 | |
| 126 | RCL6 | 36 06 | |
| 127 | RCL4 | 36 04 | |
| 128 | RCLB | 36 12 | |
| 129 | x | -35 | |
| 130 | – | -45 | |
| 131 | RCL9 | 36 09 | |
| 132 | ÷ | -24 | |
| 133 | STOA | 35 11 | |
| 134 | PRTX | -14 | |
| 135 | RCLB | 36 12 | |
| 136 | CHS | 22 | |
| 137 | PRTX | -14 | |
| 138 | P⇌S | 16-51 | |
| 139 | RTN | 24 | |

## LABELS

| A $L, N \rightarrow$ | B $L, N \rightarrow$ | C | D | E $\rightarrow r, a, z$ | 0 |
| a $L_0, K, D, \Delta L \rightarrow$ | b | c | d | e | 1 |
| 0 $L \rightarrow \Delta t$ | 1 $L \rightarrow t'$ | 2 enter Z & clear registers | 3 | 4 | 2 |
| 5 | 6 | 7 | 8 | 9 | 3 |

## FLAGS / SET STATUS

FLAGS ON/OFF: 0, 1, 2, 3 all off
TRIG: DEG ☒, GRAD ☐, RAD ☐
DISP: FIX ☒, SCI ☐, ENG ☐, n = 3

# Program Description

**Program Title** Length-converted catch curves
**Name** Daniel Pauly
**Date** Sept. 1983
**Address** ICLARM, MCC P.O. Box 1501
Makati, Metro Manila, Philippines

**Program Description, Equations, Variables, etc.** Given inputs of $L_\infty$, $K$, $D$ and $\Delta L$ (the class interval) and length-frequency data, this program computes values of $\ln N/\Delta t$ and $t'$ (relative age) as used for drawing length-converted catch curves of the type described by Pauly (1982a, 1983). Once the points have been graphed, the data pairs can be selected which are to be included in the estimation of $Z$, using linear regression (1). The points needed are then reentered and $Z$ is estimated from

$$\ln (N/\Delta t) = a - Zt' \qquad \ldots 1)$$

The value of $Z$ obtained from (1) can then be used as input ($Z_1$) in the equation of P. Sparre (pers. comm.), i.e.

$$\ln (N/1-e^{-Z_1 \Delta t}) = a - Z_2 t' \qquad \ldots 2)$$

where $Z_2$ is an improved estimate of $Z$. If the value of $Z_1$ and $Z_2$ differ markedly (which will rarely occur), $Z_2$ can be used as input for another iteration, which will then produce a value of $Z$ improved further ($Z_3$), etc.

**Operating Limits and Warnings** Selection of points to be included in the regression must be done carefully (see text); particularly, no points belonging to the ascending part of the curve must be included, nor points estimated from lengths within 5% of $L_\infty$.

# User Instructions

## Z and K FROM MEAN LENGTHS — FB 13

| STEP | INSTRUCTIONS | INPUT DATA/UNITS | KEYS | | OUTPUT DATA/UNITS |
|---|---|---|---|---|---|
| | *Estimation of Mean Size and its Standard Error* | | | | |
| 1 | Store lower class limit of lowest size considered, class interval and initialize ($S = L$ or $W$) | $S'$ $\Delta S$ | $f$ | $b$ | 0.000 |
| 2 | Enter frequency, starting from the lowest class (enter zero when appropriate) | $N_i$ | $A$ | | $i$ |
| 3 | When all frequencies have been entered, compute the mean size, the standard deviation of the size values and the standard error of the mean | | $B$ | | $\Sigma n$ $\bar{s}$ s.d.$_{(S)}$ s.e.$_{(\bar{s})}$ |
| | *Z and K from Mean Length* | | | | |
| 1 | Initialize and enter $L_r, L_1, L_2$ and $D$ | $L_r$ $L_1$ $L_2$ $D$ | ↑ ↑ ↑ $f$ | $a$ | 0.000 |
| 2 | Enter $t_1, t_2$ and $L_{(\infty)}$ | $t_1$ $t_2$ $L_{(\infty)}$ | ↑ ↑ R/S | | 0.000 |
| 3 | Enter initial value of Z and iterate | $Z$ | $E$ | | $Z_1$ $Z_2$ $Z_3$ etc. ⋮ $K$ $Z$ |

## Program Listing (001 to 112)

| STEP | KEY ENTRY | KEY CODE | COMMENTS | STEP | KEY ENTRY | KEY CODE | COMMENTS |
|---|---|---|---|---|---|---|---|
| 001 | *LBLa | 21 16 11 | | 057 | RCLE | 36 15 | |
| 002 | CLRG | 16-53 | | 058 | ÷ | -24 | |
| 003 | STOD | 35 14 | | 059 | 1 | 01 | |
| 004 | $y^x$ | 31 | | 060 | + | -55 | |
| 005 | STO0 | 35 00 | | 061 | INT | 16 34 | |
| 006 | R↓ | -31 | | 062 | STOI | 35 46 | |
| 007 | RCLD | 36 14 | | 063 | *LBL0 | 21 00 | |
| 008 | $y^x$ | 31 | | 064 | RCLE | 36 15 | |
| 009 | STO1 | 35 01 | | 065 | RCL8 | 36 08 | |
| 010 | R↓ | -31 | | 066 | × | -35 | |
| 011 | RCLD | 36 14 | | 067 | STO0 | 35 00 | |
| 012 | $y^x$ | 31 | | 068 | CHS | -22 | |
| 013 | STO2 | 35 02 | | 069 | $e^x$ | 33 | |
| 014 | CLX | -51 | | 070 | ST+1 | 35-55 01 | |
| 015 | R/S | 51 | | 071 | RCL8 | 36 08 | |
| 016 | RCLD | 36 14 | | 072 | × | -35 | |
| 017 | $y^x$ | 31 | | 073 | ST+2 | 35-55 02 | |
| 018 | STO3 | 35 03 | | 074 | RCL9 | 36 09 | |
| 019 | R↓ | -31 | | 075 | RCL8 | 36 08 | |
| 020 | STO9 | 35 09 | | 076 | + | -55 | |
| 021 | − | -45 | | 077 | RCLC | 36 13 | |
| 022 | STOC | 35 13 | | 078 | × | -35 | |
| 023 | RCL3 | 36 03 | | 079 | RCL0 | 36 00 | |
| 024 | RCL2 | 36 02 | | 080 | + | -55 | |
| 025 | − | -45 | | 081 | CHS | -22 | |
| 026 | RCL3 | 36 03 | | 082 | $e^x$ | 33 | |
| 027 | ÷ | -24 | | 083 | ST+4 | 35-55 04 | |
| 028 | STO8 | 35 12 | | 084 | RCL8 | 36 08 | |
| 029 | RCL0 | 36 00 | | 085 | × | -35 | |
| 030 | RCL3 | 36 03 | | 086 | ST+5 | 35-55 05 | |
| 031 | ÷ | -24 | | 087 | RCL8 | 36 08 | |
| 032 | STO6 | 35 06 | | 088 | RCLI | 36 46 | |
| 033 | RCL3 | 36 03 | | 089 | X=Y? | 16-33 | |
| 034 | RCL0 | 36 00 | | 090 | GTO1 | 22 01 | |
| 035 | − | -45 | | 091 | 1 | 01 | |
| 036 | RCL3 | 36 03 | | 092 | ST+8 | 35-55 08 | |
| 037 | RCL1 | 36 01 | | 093 | GTO0 | 22 00 | |
| 038 | − | -45 | | 094 | *LBL1 | 21 01 | |
| 039 | ÷ | -24 | | 095 | RCL1 | 36 01 | |
| 040 | LN | 32 | | 096 | RCL4 | 36 04 | |
| 041 | RCLC | 36 13 | | 097 | RCLB | 36 12 | |
| 042 | ÷ | -24 | | 098 | × | -35 | |
| 043 | STOC | 35 13 | | 099 | − | -45 | |
| 044 | EEX | -23 | | 100 | RCL1 | 36 01 | |
| 045 | 4 | 04 | | 101 | ÷ | -24 | |
| 046 | CHS | -22 | | 102 | RCL6 | 36 06 | |
| 047 | STO7 | 35 07 | | 103 | − | -45 | |
| 048 | CLX | -51 | | 104 | STO0 | 35 00 | |
| 049 | RTN | 24 | | 105 | RCL6 | 36 06 | |
| 050 | *LBLE | 21 15 | | 106 | 1 | 01 | |
| 051 | SPC | 16-11 | | 107 | − | -45 | |
| 052 | STOE | 35 15 | | 108 | RCL2 | 36 02 | |
| 053 | PRTX | -14 | | 109 | × | -35 | |
| 054 | RCL7 | 36 07 | | 110 | RCL5 | 36 05 | |
| 055 | LN | 32 | | 111 | RCLB | 36 12 | |
| 056 | CHS | -22 | | 112 | × | -35 | |

### REGISTERS

| 0 | 1 | 2 | 3 | 4 | 5 | 6 | 7 | 8 | 9 |
|---|---|---|---|---|---|---|---|---|---|
| used | used | used | | used | used | $L_P^D/L_{(\infty)}^D$/used | TOL/$S'$ | $X/\Delta S$ | $t_2$/used |
| S0 | S1 | S2 | S3 | S4 | S5 | S6 | S7 | S8 | S9 |

| A | B | C | D | E | I |
|---|---|---|---|---|---|
| | $L_\infty^D - L_P^D / L_{(\infty)}^D$ | KD | D | Z | N |

## Program Listing (113 to end)

| STEP | KEY ENTRY | KEY CODE | COMMENTS | STEP | KEY ENTRY | KEY CODE | COMMENTS |
|---|---|---|---|---|---|---|---|
|  | 113 | + | -55 |  | 169 | ST+4 | 35-55 04 |
|  | 114 | RCL0 | 36 00 | 170 | 170 | RCL7 | 36 07 |
|  | 115 | X⇄Y | -41 |  | 171 | RCL8 | 36 08 |
|  | 116 | ÷ | -24 |  | 172 | 2 | 02 |
|  | 117 | CHS | -22 |  | 173 | ÷ | -24 |
|  | 118 | RCLE | 36 15 |  | 174 | + | -55 |
|  | 119 | + | -55 |  | 175 | ST02 | 35 02 |
| 120 | 120 | ST00 | 35 00 |  | 176 | $x^2$ | 53 |
|  | 121 | X>0? | 16-44 |  | 177 | RCL3 | 36 03 |
|  | 122 | GTO2 | 22 02 |  | 178 | × | -35 |
|  | 123 | GTO3 | 22 03 |  | 179 | ST+5 | 35-55 05 |
|  | 124 | *LBL2 | 21 02 | 180 | 180 | RCL2 | 36 02 |
|  | 125 | RCL7 | 36 07 |  | 181 | RCL3 | 36 03 |
|  | 126 | 1 | 01 |  | 182 | × | -35 |
|  | 127 | 0 | 00 |  | 183 | ST+9 | 35-55 09 |
|  | 128 | × | -35 |  | 184 | RCL8 | 36 08 |
|  | 129 | RCLE | 36 15 |  | 185 | ST+7 | 35-55 07 |
| 130 | 130 | RCL0 | 36 00 |  | 186 | 1 | 01 |
|  | 131 | - | -45 |  | 187 | ST+6 | 35-55 06 |
|  | 132 | ABS | 16 31 |  | 188 | RCL6 | 36 06 |
|  | 133 | X>Y? | 16-34 |  | 189 | RTN | 24 |
|  | 134 | GTO4 | 22 04 | 190 | 190 | *LBLB | 21 12 |
|  | 135 | RCLC | 36 13 |  | 191 | SPC | 16-11 |
|  | 136 | RCLD | 36 14 |  | 192 | RCL4 | 36 04 |
|  | 137 | ÷ | -24 |  | 193 | PRTX | -14 |
|  | 138 | SPC | 16-11 |  | 194 | RCL9 | 36 09 |
|  | 139 | PRTX | -14 |  | 195 | X⇄Y | -41 |
| 140 | 140 | RCL0 | 36 00 |  | 196 | ÷ | -24 |
|  | 141 | PRTX | -14 |  | 197 | PRTX | -14 |
|  | 142 | RTN | 24 |  | 198 | RCL5 | 36 05 |
|  | 143 | *LBL3 | 21 03 |  | 199 | RCL4 | 36 04 |
|  | 144 | RCLE | 36 15 | 200 | 200 | ÷ | -24 |
|  | 145 | . | -62 |  | 201 | RCL9 | 36 09 |
|  | 146 | 9 | 09 |  | 202 | RCL4 | 36 04 |
|  | 147 | × | -35 |  | 203 | ÷ | -24 |
|  | 148 | ST00 | 35 00 |  | 204 | $x^2$ | 53 |
|  | 149 | GTO2 | 22 02 |  | 205 | - | -45 |
| 150 | 150 | *LBL4 | 21 04 |  | 206 | √x | 54 |
|  | 151 | 0 | 00 |  | 207 | PRTX | -14 |
|  | 152 | ST01 | 35 01 |  | 208 | RCL4 | 36 04 |
|  | 153 | ST02 | 35 02 |  | 209 | √x | 54 |
|  | 154 | ST04 | 35 04 | 210 | 210 | ÷ | -24 |
|  | 155 | ST05 | 35 05 |  | 211 | PRTX | -14 |
|  | 156 | ST08 | 35 08 |  | 212 | RTN | 24 |
|  | 157 | RCL0 | 36 00 |  |  |  |  |
|  | 158 | STOE | 35 15 |  |  |  |  |
|  | 159 | GTOE | 22 15 |  |  |  |  |
| 160 | 160 | *LBLb | 21 16 12 |  |  |  |  |
|  | 161 | CLRG | 16-53 |  |  |  |  |
|  | 162 | ST08 | 35 08 |  |  |  |  |
|  | 163 | R↓ | -31 |  |  |  |  |
|  | 164 | ST07 | 35 07 | 220 |  |  |  |
|  | 165 | CLX | -51 |  |  |  |  |
|  | 166 | RTN | 24 |  |  |  |  |
|  | 167 | *LBLA | 21 11 |  |  |  |  |
|  | 168 | ST03 | 35 03 |  |  |  |  |

### LABELS

| A $N_i \rightarrow$ | B $\rightarrow \bar{s}$, etc. | C | D | E iterate Z | 0 |
|---|---|---|---|---|---|
| a initialize(2) | b initialize(3) | c | d | e | 1 |
| 0 used | 1 used | 2 used | 3 used | 4 used | 2 |
| 5 | 6 | 7 | 8 | 9 | 3 |

### FLAGS / SET STATUS

| FLAGS | ON | OFF | TRIG |  | DISP |  |
|---|---|---|---|---|---|---|
| 0 | ☐ | ☒ | DEG | ☒ | FIX | ☒ |
| 1 | ☐ | ☒ | GRAD | ☐ | SCI | ☐ |
| 2 | ☐ | ☒ | RAD | ☐ | ENG | ☐ |
| 3 | ☐ | ☒ |  |  | n = 3 |  |

# Program Description

**Program Title** Z and K from Mean Lengths
**Name** Daniel Pauly   **Date** Sept., 1982
**Address** ICLARM, MCC P.O. Box 1501
Makati, Metro Manila, Philippines

**Program Description, Equations, Variables, etc.** As demonstrated by Ebert (1973), estimates of $K$ and $Z$ can be obtained from 2 mean lengths, a value of $L_{(\infty)}$, a length at recruitment ($L_r$) and times $t_1$ and $t_2$ (corresponding to the mean lengths) by solving two equations, which become, in terms of the generalized VBGF

$$\frac{\sum_{x=0}^{N} e^{-Zx} - b \sum_{x=0}^{N} e^{-(KD(t_1+x)+Zx)}}{\sum_{x=0}^{N} e^{-Zx}} = \frac{L_1^D}{L_{(\infty)}^D} \quad \ldots 1)$$

and

$$\frac{\sum_{x=0}^{N} e^{-Zx} - b \sum_{x=0}^{N} e^{-(KD(t_2+x)+Zx)}}{\sum_{x=0}^{N} e^{-Zx}} = \frac{L_2^D}{L_{(\infty)}^D} \quad \ldots 2)$$

where $b = L_{(\infty)}^D - L_r^D / L_{(\infty)}^D$, while $N$ is the integer portion of $Y$, when $Y = 1 + (-\log_e 0.0001/Z)$. As shown by Saila and Lough (1981), these equations have an explicit solution for $K$, i.e.

$$K = \ln \frac{L_{(\infty)}^D - L_2^D}{L_{(\infty)}^D - L_1^D} \Big/ (t_1 - t_2) \cdot D \quad \ldots 3)$$

Once $K$ has been calculated, the value of $Z$ is obtained using a very simplified version of the algorithm given in Ebert (1973, p. 286).

**Operating Limits and Warnings** Iterating time can be quite long when dealing with low values of $Z$; it saves time therefore, to enter initial guesses that are assumed higher than the true values (rather than the reverse).
$Z$ is estimated with an error of less than 0.001.

# User Instructions

F and M from TAGGING - RECAPTURE DATA FB14

| STEP | INSTRUCTIONS | INPUT DATA/UNITS | KEYS | | OUTPUT DATA/UNITS |
|---|---|---|---|---|---|
| 1 | Initialize | | f | a | 0.000 |
| 2 | Enter the $N_r$ values | $N_r$ | A | | coded time |
| 3 | Calculate $r^2$, a and b | | E | | $r^2$ |
| | | | | | a |
| | | | | | b |
| 4 | Enter $N_0$ and calculate F and M | $N_0$ | f | e | F |
| | | | | | M |

# Program Listing

| STEP | KEY ENTRY | KEY CODE | COMMENTS | STEP | KEY ENTRY | KEY CODE | COMMENTS |
|---|---|---|---|---|---|---|---|
| 001 | *LBLa | 21 16 11 | | 049 | RCL4 | 36 04 | |
| 002 | CLRG | 16-53 | | 050 | RCLB | 36 12 | |
| 003 | P⇄S | 16-51 | | 051 | × | -35 | |
| 004 | CLRG | 16-53 | | 052 | − | -45 | |
| 005 | CLX | -51 | | 053 | RCL9 | 36 09 | |
| 006 | RTN | 24 | | 054 | ÷ | -24 | |
| 007 | *LBLA | 21 11 | | 055 | STOA | 35 11 | |
| 008 | LN | 32 | | 056 | PRTX | -14 | |
| 009 | RCL0 | 36 00 | | 057 | RCLB | 36 12 | |
| 010 | Σ+ | 56 | | 058 | PRTX | -14 | |
| 011 | 1 | 01 | | 059 | P⇄S | 16-51 | |
| 012 | ST+0 | 35-55 00 | | 060 | RTN | 24 | |
| 013 | RCL0 | 36 00 | | 061 | *LBLe | 21 16 15 | |
| 014 | 1 | 01 | | 062 | RCLB | 36 12 | |
| 015 | − | -45 | | 063 | $e^x$ | 33 | |
| 016 | RTN | 24 | | 064 | CHS | -22 | |
| 017 | *LBLE | 21 15 | | 065 | 1 | 01 | |
| 018 | P⇄S | 16-51 | | 066 | + | -55 | |
| 019 | SPC | 16-11 | | 067 | × | -35 | |
| 020 | RCL8 | 36 08 | | 068 | RCLB | 36 12 | |
| 021 | RCL4 | 36 04 | | 069 | CHS | -22 | |
| 022 | RCL6 | 36 06 | | 070 | RCLA | 36 11 | |
| 023 | × | -35 | | 071 | $e^x$ | 33 | |
| 024 | RCL9 | 36 09 | | 072 | × | -35 | |
| 025 | ÷ | -24 | | 073 | X⇄Y | -41 | |
| 026 | − | -45 | | 074 | ÷ | -24 | |
| 027 | ENT↑ | -21 | | 075 | SPC | 16-11 | |
| 028 | ENT↑ | -21 | | 076 | PRTX | -14 | |
| 029 | RCL4 | 36 04 | | 077 | ST00 | 35 00 | |
| 030 | $x^2$ | 53 | | 078 | RCLB | 36 12 | |
| 031 | RCL9 | 36 09 | | 079 | CHS | -22 | |
| 032 | ÷ | -24 | | 080 | RCL0 | 36 00 | |
| 033 | RCL5 | 36 05 | | 081 | − | -45 | |
| 034 | X⇄Y | -41 | | 082 | PRTX | -14 | |
| 035 | − | -45 | | 083 | RTN | 24 | |
| 036 | ÷ | -24 | | | | | |
| 037 | STOB | 35 12 | | | | | |
| 038 | × | -35 | | | | | |
| 039 | RCL6 | 36 06 | | | | | |
| 040 | $x^2$ | 53 | | | | | |
| 041 | RCL9 | 36 09 | | | | | |
| 042 | ÷ | -24 | | 090 | | | |
| 043 | CHS | -22 | | | | | |
| 044 | RCL7 | 36 07 | | | | | |
| 045 | + | -55 | | | | | |
| 046 | ÷ | -24 | | | | | |
| 047 | PRTX | -14 | | | | | |
| 048 | RCL6 | 36 06 | | | | | |

## LABELS

| A $N_r \to$ | B | C | D | E $\to r^2, a, b$ | 0 |
|---|---|---|---|---|---|
| a initialize | b | c | d | e | 1 |
| 0 | 1 | 2 | 3 | 4 | 2 |
| 5 | 6 | 7 | 8 | 9 | 3 |

## FLAGS / SET STATUS

| FLAGS ON OFF | TRIG | DISP |
|---|---|---|
| 0 ☐ ☒ | DEG ☒ | FIX ☒ |
| 1 ☐ ☒ | GRAD ☐ | SCI ☐ |
| 2 ☐ ☒ | RAD ☐ | ENG ☐ |
| 3 ☐ ☒ | | n = 3 |

## REGISTERS

| 0 used | 1 | 2 | 3 | 4 | 5 | 6 | 7 | 8 | 9 |
|---|---|---|---|---|---|---|---|---|---|
| S0 | S1 | S2 | S3 | S4 $\Sigma x$ | S5 $\Sigma x^2$ | S6 $\Sigma y$ | S7 $\Sigma y^2$ | S8 $\Sigma xy$ | S9 $n$ |
| A $a$ | B $b$ | C | D | E | I | | | | |

# Program Description

**Program Title:** F and M from Tagging - Recapture Data
**Name:** Daniel Pauly
**Date:** Sept. 1980
**Address:** ICLARM, MCC P.O. Box 1501
Makati, Metro Manila, Philippines

**Program Description, Equations, Variables, etc.** Total mortality (Z) may be estimated from the equation

$$\ln N_r = a + b_{r'} \quad \ldots 1)$$

where $N_r$ is the number of recoveries per time interval, where $r'$ is the coded time interval (starting with $r'=0$, then $r'=1, 2, 3$ etc.), and where b, with sign changed is equal to Z.

Total mortality may then be split into F and M by means of the expression

$$F = \frac{e^a \cdot Z}{N_0 (1 - e^{-Z})} \quad \ldots 2)$$

where $N_0$ is the total number of fish tagged and released and $a$ is the intercept of equation (1) (Gulland, 1969).

**Operating Limits and Warnings**
1) Gulland, (1969, section 6) should be consulted for details and sources of bias and errors.
2) Do not forget to put the mortality values (M, F) on an annual basis.

# User Instructions

**INDEPENDENT ESTIMATES OF M** — FB15

$L_\infty, K, T \to M$    $W_\infty, K, T \to M$

| STEP | INSTRUCTIONS | INPUT DATA/UNITS | KEYS | | OUTPUT DATA/UNITS |
|---|---|---|---|---|---|
| 1 | Enter $L_\infty, K, \bar{T}$ and obtain M (special VBGF) | $L_\infty$ | ↑ | | |
| | | $K$ | ↑ | | |
| | | $\bar{T}$ | A | | M |
| 2 | Enter $W_\infty, K, \bar{T}$ and obtain M (special VBGF) | $W_\infty$ | ↑ | | |
| | | $K$ | ↑ | | |
| | | $\bar{T}$ | B | | M |
| 3 | IF the estimate of M pertain to Clupeidae, or polar fishes ($\bar{T} < 3.5°C$) see "operating limits and warnings." | | | | |

# Program Listing

| STEP | KEY ENTRY | KEY CODE |
|---|---|---|
| 001 | *LBLA | 21 11 |
| 002 | 3 | 03 |
| 003 | . | -62 |
| 004 | 5 | 05 |
| 005 | X>Y? | 16-34 |
| 006 | GSBC | 23 13 |
| 007 | R↓ | -31 |
| 008 | LOG | 16 32 |
| 009 | . | -62 |
| 010 | 4 | 04 |
| 011 | 6 | 06 |
| 012 | 3 | 03 |
| 013 | 4 | 04 |
| 014 | x | -35 |
| 015 | X≷Y | -41 |
| 016 | LOG | 16 32 |
| 017 | . | -62 |
| 018 | 6 | 06 |
| 019 | 5 | 05 |
| 020 | 4 | 04 |
| 021 | 3 | 03 |
| 022 | x | -35 |
| 023 | + | -55 |
| 024 | X≷Y | -41 |
| 025 | LOG | 16 32 |
| 026 | . | -62 |
| 027 | 2 | 02 |
| 028 | 7 | 07 |
| 029 | 9 | 09 |
| 030 | x | -35 |
| 031 | - | -45 |
| 032 | . | -62 |
| 033 | 0 | 00 |
| 034 | 0 | 00 |
| 035 | 6 | 06 |
| 036 | 6 | 06 |
| 037 | - | -45 |
| 038 | 10^x | 16 33 |
| 039 | RTN | 24 |
| 040 | *LBLC | 21 13 |
| 041 | R↓ | -31 |
| 042 | . | -62 |
| 043 | 1 | 01 |
| 044 | 3 | 03 |
| 045 | 8 | 08 |
| 046 | 2 | 02 |
| 047 | 7 | 07 |
| 048 | x | -35 |
| 049 | CHS | -22 |
| 050 | . | -62 |
| 051 | 8 | 08 |
| 052 | 7 | 07 |
| 053 | 6 | 06 |
| 054 | 6 | 06 |
| 055 | 1 | 01 |
| 056 | + | -55 |
| 057 | e^x | 33 |
| 058 | e^x | 33 |
| 059 | ENT↑ | -21 |
| 060 | RTN | 24 |
| 061 | *LBLB | 21 12 |
| 062 | 3 | 03 |
| 063 | . | -62 |
| 064 | 5 | 05 |
| 065 | X>Y? | 16-34 |
| 066 | GSBC | 23 13 |
| 067 | R↓ | -31 |
| 068 | LOG | 16 32 |
| 069 | . | -62 |
| 070 | 4 | 04 |
| 071 | 6 | 06 |
| 072 | 2 | 02 |
| 073 | 7 | 07 |
| 074 | x | -35 |
| 075 | X≷Y | -41 |
| 076 | LOG | 16 32 |
| 077 | . | -62 |
| 078 | 6 | 06 |
| 079 | 7 | 07 |
| 080 | 5 | 05 |
| 081 | 7 | 07 |
| 082 | x | -35 |
| 083 | + | -55 |
| 084 | X≷Y | -41 |
| 085 | LOG | 16 32 |
| 086 | . | -62 |
| 087 | 0 | 00 |
| 088 | 8 | 08 |
| 089 | 2 | 02 |
| 090 | 4 | 04 |
| 091 | x | -35 |
| 092 | - | -45 |
| 093 | . | -62 |
| 094 | 2 | 02 |
| 095 | 1 | 01 |
| 096 | 0 | 00 |
| 097 | 7 | 07 |
| 098 | - | -45 |
| 099 | 10^x | 16 33 |
| 100 | RTN | 24 |

| LABELS | | | | | | FLAGS | SET STATUS | | |
|---|---|---|---|---|---|---|---|---|---|
| A $L_e, K, \bar{T} \to M$ | B $W_e, K, \bar{T} \to M$ | C Temp. Correct | D | E | 0 | | FLAGS | TRIG | DISP |
| a | b | c | d | e | 1 | | ON OFF | DEG ☒ | FIX ☒ |
| 0 | 1 | 2 | 3 | 4 | 2 | | 0 ☐ ☒ | GRAD ☐ | SCI ☐ |
| 5 | 6 | 7 | 8 | 9 | 3 | | 1 ☐ ☒ | RAD ☐ | ENG ☐ |
| | | | | | | | 2 ☐ ☒ | | n = 2 |
| | | | | | | | 3 ☐ ☒ | | |

| REGISTERS | | | | | | | | | |
|---|---|---|---|---|---|---|---|---|---|
| 0 | 1 | 2 | 3 | 4 | 5 | 6 | 7 | 8 | 9 |
| S0 | S1 | S2 | S3 | S4 | S5 | S6 | S7 | S8 | S9 |
| A | | B | | C | | D | | E | I |

# Program Description

**Program Title** Independent Estimates of M
**Name** Daniel Pauly
**Address** ICLARM, MCC P.O. Box 1501
Makati, Metro Manila, Philippines
**Date** Sept., 1980

**Program Description, Equations, Variables, etc.** As demonstrated in Pauly (1980b), reasonable estimates of M can be obtained from the empirical relationships

$$\log_{10} M = -0.2107 - 0.0824 \log_{10} W_\infty + 0.6757 \log_{10} K + 0.4627 \log_{10} \bar{T} \qquad \ldots 1)$$

and

$$\log_{10} M = -0.0066 - 0.279 \log_{10} L_\infty + 0.6543 \log_{10} K + 0.4634 \log_{10} \bar{T} \qquad \ldots 2)$$

where $W_\infty$, $L_\infty$ and $K$ are parameters of the special v. Bertalanffy Growth Formula, and $\bar{T}$ the mean environmental temperature of the stock in question.

$W_\infty$ should be expressed in gram live weight, $L_\infty$ in cm total length, $K$ put on an annual basis and $\bar{T}$ expressed in °C.

An internal routine transforms, for temperatures lower than 3.5 °C (down to -2 °C), the $\bar{T}$ values to their corresponding "physiologically effective Temperature", $\bar{T}'$ (see Pauly 1980b, Fig. 1). The latter being always > 0 °C, negative temperature (down to -2 °C) can also be entered.

**Operating Limits and Warnings** 1) In the case of the Clupeidae (Herrings, Sardines etc.) the estimates of M provided by expressions (1) and (2) tend to be too high, and should be reduced by a factor of 0.8 to 0.6.
2) In the case of polar fishes (occurring at temp. < 3.5 °C) the estimates of M tend to be too low, and should be increased by a factor of 1.3.

# User Instructions

**POPULATION SIZE (PETERSEN'S METHOD) FB16**

| STEP | INSTRUCTIONS | INPUT DATA/UNITS | KEYS | | OUTPUT DATA/UNITS |
|---|---|---|---|---|---|
| 1 | Enter T, n and m  (fish tagged) | T | ↑ | | |
| | (all captures) | n | ↑ | | |
| | (recaptures of tagged fish) | m | f | a | 0. |
| 2 | Estimate population size (N) and its standard error. | | | | |
| | Case A | | A | | N |
| | | | | | s.e.(N) |
| | Case B | | B | | N |
| | | | | | s.e.(N) |
| | Case C | | C | | N |
| | | | | | s.e.(N) |
| | Case D | | D | | N |
| | | | | | s.e.(N) |

# Program Listing (001 to 112)

| STEP | KEY ENTRY | KEY CODE | | STEP | KEY ENTRY | KEY CODE |
|------|-----------|----------|---|------|-----------|----------|
| 001 | *LBLa | 21 16 11 | | | 057 | $x^2$ | 53 |
| 002 | STOC | 35 13 | | | 058 | RCLC | 36 13 |
| 003 | R↓ | -31 | | | 059 | 2 | 02 |
| 004 | STOB | 35 12 | | 060 | 060 | + | -55 |
| 005 | R↓ | -31 | | | 061 | × | -35 |
| 006 | STOA | 35 11 | | | 062 | ÷ | -24 |
| 007 | CLX | -51 | | | 063 | √X | 54 |
| 008 | RTN | 24 | | | 064 | PRTX | -14 |
| 009 | *LBLA | 21 11 | | | 065 | RTN | 24 |
| 010 | 010 | SPC | 16-11 | | 066 | *LBLC | 21 13 |
| 011 | RCLA | 36 11 | | | 067 | SPC | 16-11 |
| 012 | RCLB | 36 12 | | | 068 | RCLA | 36 11 |
| 013 | × | -35 | | | 069 | 1 | 01 |
| 014 | RCLC | 36 13 | | 070 | 070 | + | -55 |
| 015 | ÷ | -24 | | | 071 | RCLB | 36 12 |
| 016 | PRTX | -14 | | | 072 | 1 | 01 |
| 017 | RCLA | 36 11 | | | 073 | + | -55 |
| 018 | $x^2$ | 53 | | | 074 | × | -35 |
| 019 | RCLB | 36 12 | | | 075 | RCLC | 36 13 |
| 020 | 020 | × | -35 | | 076 | 1 | 01 |
| 021 | RCLB | 36 12 | | | 077 | + | -55 |
| 022 | RCLC | 36 13 | | | 078 | ÷ | -24 |
| 023 | - | -45 | | | 079 | 1 | 01 |
| 024 | × | -35 | | 080 | 080 | - | -45 |
| 025 | RCLC | 36 13 | | | 081 | PRTX | -14 |
| 026 | 3 | 03 | | | 082 | STOD | 35 00 |
| 027 | $Y^x$ | 31 | | | 083 | RCLA | 36 11 |
| 028 | ÷ | -24 | | | 084 | RCLB | 36 12 |
| 029 | √X | 54 | | | 085 | × | -35 |
| 030 | 030 | PRTX | -14 | | 086 | ÷ | -24 |
| 031 | RTN | 24 | | | 087 | RCL0 | 36 00 |
| 032 | *LBLB | 21 12 | | | 088 | RCLA | 36 11 |
| 033 | SPC | 16-11 | | | 089 | RCLB | 36 12 |
| 034 | RCLA | 36 11 | | 090 | 090 | × | -35 |
| 035 | RCLB | 36 12 | | | 091 | ÷ | -24 |
| 036 | 1 | 01 | | | 092 | $x^2$ | 53 |
| 037 | + | -55 | | | 093 | 2 | 02 |
| 038 | × | -35 | | | 094 | × | -35 |
| 039 | RCLC | 36 13 | | | 095 | + | -55 |
| 040 | 040 | 1 | 01 | | 096 | RCL0 | 36 00 |
| 041 | + | -55 | | | 097 | RCLA | 36 11 |
| 042 | ÷ | -24 | | | 098 | RCLB | 36 12 |
| 043 | PRTX | -14 | | | 099 | × | -35 |
| 044 | RCLA | 36 11 | | 100 | 100 | ÷ | -24 |
| 045 | $x^2$ | 53 | | | 101 | 3 | 03 |
| 046 | RCLB | 36 12 | | | 102 | $Y^x$ | 31 |
| 047 | 1 | 01 | | | 103 | 6 | 06 |
| 048 | + | -55 | | | 104 | × | -35 |
| 049 | × | -35 | | | 105 | + | -55 |
| 050 | 050 | RCLB | 36 12 | | 106 | RCL0 | 36 00 |
| 051 | RCLC | 36 13 | | | 107 | $x^2$ | 53 |
| 052 | - | -45 | | | 108 | × | -35 |
| 053 | × | -35 | | | 109 | √X | 54 |
| 054 | RCLC | 36 13 | | 110 | 110 | PRTX | -14 |
| 055 | 1 | 01 | | | 111 | RTN | 24 |
| 056 | + | -55 | | | 112 | *LBLD | 21 14 |

## REGISTERS

| 0 used | 1 | 2 | 3 | 4 | 5 | 6 | 7 | 8 | 9 |
|---|---|---|---|---|---|---|---|---|---|
| S0 | S1 | S2 | S3 | S4 | S5 | S6 | S7 | S8 | S9 |

| A  T | B  n | C  m | D | E | I |
|---|---|---|---|---|---|

# Program Listing (113 to end)

| STEP | KEY ENTRY | KEY CODE |
|---|---|---|
| 113 | SPC | 16-11 |
| 114 | RCLB | 36 12 |
| 115 | RCLA | 36 11 |
| 116 | 1 | 01 |
| 117 | + | -55 |
| 118 | × | -35 |
| 119 | RCLC | 36 13 |
| 120 | ÷ | -24 |
| 121 | 1 | 01 |
| 122 | - | -45 |
| 123 | PRTX | -14 |
| 124 | ST00 | 35 00 |
| 125 | RCLA | 36 11 |
| 126 | RCLC | 36 13 |
| 127 | - | -45 |
| 128 | 1 | 01 |
| 129 | + | -55 |
| 130 | RCL0 | 36 00 |
| 131 | 1 | 01 |
| 132 | + | -55 |
| 133 | × | -35 |
| 134 | RCL0 | 36 00 |
| 135 | RCLA | 36 11 |
| 136 | - | -45 |
| 137 | × | -35 |
| 138 | RCLC | 36 13 |
| 139 | RCLA | 36 11 |
| 140 | 2 | 02 |
| 141 | + | -55 |
| 142 | × | -35 |
| 143 | ÷ | -24 |
| 144 | √x | 54 |
| 145 | PRTX | -14 |
| 146 | RTN | 24 |

**LABELS**: A case A, B case B, C case C, D case D; a $T, n, m$ →

**FLAGS**: all OFF

**SET STATUS**: TRIG DEG, DISP FIX, n = 0

# Program Description

**Program Title:** Population Size (Petersen's Method)
**Name:** Daniel Pauly
**Address:** ICLARM, MCC P.O. Box 1501, Makati, Metro Manila, Philippines
**Date:** Jan. 1980

**Program Description, Equations, Variables, etc.** Jones (1977, Table 1) gives the following equations for estimating population size ($N$) and its variance (var $N$)

Formulae for estimating population size ($N$) by the Petersen method

| Reference | Type of sampling | Estimates of population size ($N$) | variance of ($N$) |
|---|---|---|---|
| (A) Bailey (1951) | Direct | $N = \dfrac{Tn}{m}$ | $\text{var } N = \dfrac{T^2 n(n-m)}{m^3}$ |
| (B) Bailey (1952) | Direct | $N = \dfrac{T(n+1)}{m+1}$ | $\text{var } N = \dfrac{T^2(n+1)(n-m)}{(m+1)^2(m+2)}$ |
| (C) Chapman (1951) Schaefer (1951) | Direct | $N = \dfrac{(T+1)(n+1)}{m+1} - 1$ | $\text{var } N = N^2\left[\dfrac{N}{nT} + 2\left(\dfrac{N}{nT}\right)^2 + 6\left(\dfrac{N}{nT}\right)^3\right]$ |
| (D) Bailey (1951) Chapman (1952) | Inverse | $N = \dfrac{n(T+1)}{m} - 1$ | $\text{var } N = \dfrac{(T-m+1)(N+1)(N-T)}{m(T+2)}$ |

where $T$ is the number of fish tagged (one tagging occasion), $n$ is the total number of individuals recaptured during the entire experiment, and $m$ is the number of tagged individuals recovered during the experiment.

Each of the methods (A-D) given here has its advantages and disadvantages and the original publications should be consulted for details, as well as Jones (1977) and Ricker (1975).

**Operating Limits and Warnings** "Direct" sampling means that sampling is continued until a predetermined sample size ($n$) is obtained; "inverse" sampling means that sampling is carried out until a predetermined number of tagged animals ($m$) is obtained. This distinction should be considered when computing $N$.

# User Instructions

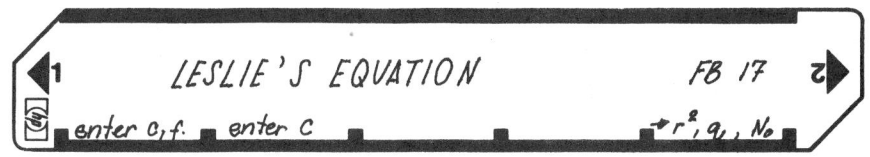

LESLIE'S EQUATION — FB 17
enter c, f.  enter c  → $r^2, q, N_0$

| STEP | INSTRUCTIONS | INPUT DATA/UNITS | KEYS | | OUTPUT DATA/UNITS |
|---|---|---|---|---|---|
| 1 | Initialize | | f | a | 0.00 |
| | **GENERAL CASE** | | | | |
| 2 | Enter catch-and-effort data | C | ↑ | | |
| | | f | A | | i |
| 3 | Compute $r^2$, a, b (= −q) and $N_0$ | | E | | $r^2$ |
| | | | | | a |
| | | | | | b |
| | | | | | $N_0$ |
| | **SPECIAL CASE (Effort Constant)** | | | | |
| 4 | Enter catch data | C | B | | i |
| 5 | Compute $r^2$, b (−F) and $N_0$ | | E | | $r^2$ |
| | | | | | a |
| | | | | | b |
| | | | | | $N_0$ |

# Program Listing

| STEP | KEY ENTRY | KEY CODE | COMMENTS | STEP | KEY ENTRY | KEY CODE | COMMENTS |
|---|---|---|---|---|---|---|---|
| 001 | 001 *LBLa | 21 16 11 | | | 049 ÷ | -24 | |
| | 002 CLRG | 16-53 | | 050 | 050 PRTX | -14 | |
| | 003 P⇄S | 16-51 | | | 051 RCL6 | 36 06 | |
| | 004 CLRG | 16-53 | | | 052 RCL4 | 36 04 | |
| | 005 CLX | -51 | | | 053 RCLB | 36 12 | |
| | 006 RTN | 24 | | | 054 × | -35 | |
| | 007 *LBLA | 21 11 | | | 055 - | -45 | |
| | 008 X⇄Y | -41 | | | 056 RCL9 | 36 09 | |
| | 009 ST00 | 35 00 | | | 057 ÷ | -24 | |
| 010 | 010 X⇄Y | -41 | | | 058 STOA | 35 11 | |
| | 011 ÷ | -24 | | | 059 PRTX | -14 | |
| | 012 RCL1 | 36 01 | | 060 | 060 RCLB | 36 12 | |
| | 013 Σ+ | 56 | | | 061 PRTX | -14 | |
| | 014 RCL0 | 36 00 | | | 062 P⇄S | 16-51 | |
| | 015 ST+1 | 35-55 01 | | | 063 RCLA | 36 11 | |
| | 016 1 | 01 | | | 064 RCLB | 36 12 | |
| | 017 ST+2 | 35-55 02 | | | 065 ÷ | -24 | |
| | 018 RCL2 | 36 02 | | | 066 CHS | -22 | |
| | 019 RTN | 24 | | | 067 PRTX | -14 | |
| 020 | 020 *LBLE | 21 15 | | | 068 RTN | 24 | |
| | 021 P⇄S | 16-51 | | | 069 *LBLB | 21 12 | |
| | 022 SPC | 16-11 | | 070 | 070 1 | 01 | |
| | 023 RCL8 | 36 08 | | | 071 GSBA | 23 11 | |
| | 024 RCL4 | 36 04 | | | 072 RTN | 24 | |
| | 025 RCL6 | 36 06 | | | | | |
| | 026 × | -35 | | | | | |
| | 027 RCL9 | 36 09 | | | | | |
| | 028 ÷ | -24 | | | | | |
| | 029 - | -45 | | | | | |
| 030 | 030 ENT↑ | -21 | | | | | |
| | 031 ENT↑ | -21 | | | | | |
| | 032 RCL4 | 36 04 | | 080 | | | |
| | 033 X² | 53 | | | | | |
| | 034 RCL9 | 36 09 | | | | | |
| | 035 ÷ | -24 | | | | | |
| | 036 RCL5 | 36 05 | | | | | |
| | 037 X⇄Y | -41 | | | | | |
| | 038 - | -45 | | | | | |
| | 039 ÷ | -24 | | | | | |
| 040 | 040 STOB | 35 12 | | | | | |
| | 041 × | -35 | | | | | |
| | 042 RCL6 | 36 06 | | 090 | | | |
| | 043 X² | 53 | | | | | |
| | 044 RCL9 | 36 09 | | | | | |
| | 045 ÷ | -24 | | | | | |
| | 046 CHS | -22 | | | | | |
| | 047 RCL7 | 36 07 | | | | | |
| | 048 + | -55 | | | | | |

## LABELS

| A enter $c,f$ | B enter $C$ | C | D | E →$r^2, a, b, N_0$ | 0 |
|---|---|---|---|---|---|
| a initialize | b | c | d | e | 1 |
| 0 | 1 | 2 | 3 | 4 | 2 |
| 5 | 6 | 7 | 8 | 9 | 3 |

## FLAGS / SET STATUS

| FLAGS | TRIG | DISP |
|---|---|---|
| ON OFF | DEG ☒ | FIX ☒ |
| 0 ☐ ☒ | GRAD ☐ | SCI ☐ |
| 1 ☐ ☒ | RAD ☐ | ENG ☐ |
| 2 ☐ ☒ | | n = 2 |
| 3 ☐ ☒ | | |

## REGISTERS

| 0 used | 1 used | 2 used | 3 | 4 | 5 | 6 | 7 | 8 | 9 |
|---|---|---|---|---|---|---|---|---|---|
| S0 | S1 | S2 | S3 | S4 $\Sigma x$ | S5 $\Sigma x^2$ | S6 $\Sigma y$ | S7 $\Sigma y^2$ | S8 $\Sigma xy$ | S9 $n$ |
| A $a = q \cdot N_0$ | B $b = -q$ | C | D | E | | | I | | |

# Program Description

**Program Title** Leslie's Equation
**Name** Daniel Pauly
**Address** ICLARM, MCC P.O. Box 1501, Makati, Metro Manila, Philippines
**Date** Sept. 1980

**Program Description, Equations, Variables, etc.** When a population is fished strongly enough to significantly reduce the catch/effort, and when the stock size reduction occurs fast enough for the effects of recruitment, mortality and immigration to be ignored, we have in Leslie's formulation

$$\frac{C_t}{f_t} = q N_0 - q \Sigma t \quad \ldots 1)$$

which states that catch/effort ($C_t/f_t$) in a given time period $t$, plotted against the cumulative catch up to that period ($\Sigma t$) gives a straight line, the slope of which, with sign changed is an estimate of the catchability coefficient ($q$) and the intercept of which ($q N_0$), divided by $q$ gives an estimate of the unfished stock size ($N_0$). When the special case applies that effort is, or can be assumed to be constant for all time periods, then the $C_t/f_t$ values are replaced by $C_t$, in which case a value of ($F$) is estimated instead of $q$.

Leslie's equation, as shown by Ricker (1975, p. 149-155) is simpler and often more appropriate than the related DeLury equation, also used to estimate $N_0$ and $q$ from cumulative catch data.

**Operating Limits and Warnings**

# User Instructions

**VPA and COHORT ANALYSIS** — FB 18

| STEP | INSTRUCTIONS | INPUT DATA/UNITS | KEYS | | OUTPUT DATA/UNITS |
|---|---|---|---|---|---|
| 1 | STO TOL* | TOL | STO | 0 | |
| 2 | Enter M, $F_t$, $C_t$ and calculate $N_t$ ($N_t$ = terminal population) | M | ↑ | | |
| | | $F_t$ | ↑ | | |
| | | $C_t$ | f' | a | $N_t$ |
| 3 | Calculate fishing mortality ($F_i$) in a given time interval, and population size at the beginning of that interval, going backward until all $C_i$ have been considered. | $C_i$ | A | | $F_i$ |
| | | | | | $N_i$ |
| 4 | Calculate $F_i$ and $N_i$ using cohort analysis | $C_i$ | B | | $F_i$ |
| | | | | | $N_i$ |

\* Tolerated error in VPA, e.g. 0.001

## Program Listing (001 to 112)

| STEP | KEY ENTRY | KEY CODE | COMMENTS | STEP | KEY ENTRY | KEY CODE | COMMENTS |
|---|---|---|---|---|---|---|---|
| 001 | *LBLa | 21 16 11 | | 057 | RCL9 | 36 09 | |
| 002 | ST07 | 35 07 | | 058 | RCL3 | 36 03 | |
| 003 | R↓ | -31 | | 059 | ÷ | -24 | |
| 004 | ST09 | 35 09 | | 060 | x | -35 | |
| 005 | R↓ | -31 | | 061 | RCL6 | 36 06 | |
| 006 | ST02 | 35 02 | | 062 | x | -35 | |
| 007 | 2 | 02 | | 063 | RCL4 | 36 04 | |
| 008 | ÷ | -24 | | 064 | $x^2$ | 53 | |
| 009 | CHS | -22 | | 065 | RCL5 | 36 05 | |
| 010 | $e^x$ | 33 | | 066 | x | -35 | |
| 011 | ST04 | 35 04 | | 067 | RCL7 | 36 07 | |
| 012 | RCL9 | 36 09 | | 068 | x | -35 | |
| 013 | RCL2 | 36 02 | | 069 | - | -45 | |
| 014 | + | -55 | | 070 | ST08 | 35 08 | |
| 015 | ST03 | 35 03 | | 071 | $x^2$ | 53 | |
| 016 | RCL7 | 36 07 | | 072 | RCL0 | 36 00 | |
| 017 | x | -35 | | 073 | X>Y? | 16-34 | |
| 018 | RCL3 | 36 03 | | 074 | GTO1 | 22 01 | |
| 019 | CHS | -22 | | 075 | RCL1 | 36 01 | |
| 020 | $e^x$ | 33 | | 076 | RCL5 | 36 05 | |
| 021 | CHS | -22 | | 077 | x | -35 | |
| 022 | 1 | 01 | | 078 | RCL8 | 36 08 | |
| 023 | + | -55 | | 079 | X⇄Y | -41 | |
| 024 | RCL9 | 36 09 | | 080 | ÷ | -24 | |
| 025 | x | -35 | | 081 | RCL9 | 36 09 | |
| 026 | ÷ | -24 | | 082 | X⇄Y | -41 | |
| 027 | RTN | 24 | | 083 | - | -45 | |
| 028 | *LBLA | 21 11 | | 084 | ST09 | 35 09 | |
| 029 | ST07 | 35 07 | | 085 | GTO0 | 22 00 | |
| 030 | R↓ | -31 | | 086 | *LBL1 | 21 01 | |
| 031 | ST06 | 35 06 | | 087 | RCL9 | 36 09 | |
| 032 | RCL4 | 36 04 | | 088 | SPC | 16-11 | |
| 033 | x | -35 | | 089 | PRTX | -14 | |
| 034 | RCL7 | 36 07 | | 090 | RCL2 | 36 02 | |
| 035 | RCL2 | 36 02 | | 091 | + | -55 | |
| 036 | CHS | -22 | | 092 | ST03 | 35 03 | |
| 037 | $e^x$ | 33 | | 093 | $e^x$ | 33 | |
| 038 | x | -35 | | 094 | RCL6 | 36 06 | |
| 039 | + | -55 | | 095 | x | -35 | |
| 040 | ST01 | 35 01 | | 096 | PRTX | -14 | |
| 041 | *LBL0 | 21 00 | | 097 | RTN | 24 | |
| 042 | RCL9 | 36 09 | | 098 | *LBLB | 21 12 | |
| 043 | CHS | -22 | | 099 | R↓ | -31 | |
| 044 | $e^x$ | 33 | | 100 | ST06 | 35 06 | |
| 045 | ST05 | 35 05 | | 101 | R↑ | 16-31 | |
| 046 | RCL2 | 36 02 | | 102 | RCL2 | 36 02 | |
| 047 | RCL9 | 36 09 | | 103 | 2 | 02 | |
| 048 | + | -55 | | 104 | ÷ | -24 | |
| 049 | ST03 | 35 03 | | 105 | $e^x$ | 33 | |
| 050 | RCL4 | 36 04 | | 106 | x | -35 | |
| 051 | $x^2$ | 53 | | 107 | X⇄Y | -41 | |
| 052 | RCL5 | 36 05 | | 108 | RCL2 | 36 02 | |
| 053 | x | -35 | | 109 | $e^x$ | 33 | |
| 054 | CHS | -22 | | 110 | x | -35 | |
| 055 | 1 | 01 | | 111 | + | -55 | |
| 056 | + | -55 | | 112 | ST05 | 35 05 | |

### REGISTERS

| 0 $TOL$ | 1 used | 2 $M$ | 3 $Z$ | 4 used | 5 used | 6 $N_{i+1}$ | 7 $C_i$ | 8 used | 9 $F$ |
|---|---|---|---|---|---|---|---|---|---|
| S0 | S1 | S2 | S3 | S4 | S5 | S6 | S7 | S8 | S9 |
| A | B | | C | | D | | E | | I |

# Program Listing (113 to end)

| STEP | KEY ENTRY | KEY CODE |
|---|---|---|
| 113 | RCL6 | 36 06 |
| 114 | X⇄Y | -41 |
| 115 | ÷ | -24 |
| 116 | LN | 32 |
| 117 | CHS | -22 |
| 118 | RCL2 | 36 02 |
| 119 | - | -45 |
| 120 | SPC | 16-11 |
| 121 | PRTX | -14 |
| 122 | RCL5 | 36 05 |
| 123 | PRTX | -14 |
| 124 | RTN | 24 |

**LABELS**

| A → Fi, Ni | B | C | D | E |
|---|---|---|---|---|
| a → initialize | b | c | d | e |
| 0 loop | 1 → Fi, Ni | 2 | 3 | 4 |
| 5 | 6 | 7 | 8 | 9 |

**FLAGS**: 0, 1, 2, 3

**SET STATUS**

FLAGS ON/OFF: 0 OFF, 1 OFF, 2 OFF, 3 OFF
TRIG: DEG
DISP: FIX, n = 2

# Program Description

**Program Title** VPA and Cohort Analysis
**Name** J. Pope* and D. Pauly
**Address** *MAFF Laboratory, Lowestoft, England
**Date** Oct. 1980

**Program Description, Equations, Variables, etc.** Program FB 18 calculates the value of $F$ which satisfies the equation

$$\frac{N_{i+1}}{C_i} = \frac{(F_i + M) \exp\{-(F_i + M)\}}{F_i (1 - \exp\{-(F_i + M)\})} \quad \ldots 1)$$

where $C_i$ is the catch at age $i$, $N_i$ and $N_{i+1}$ being the population sizes at the beginning and the end of the time period during which the catch $C_i$ was taken (Gulland 1965).

The computation proceeds backward, starting from a "terminal population" ($N_t$) which is estimated from

$$N_t = \frac{C_t \cdot (F_t + M)}{F_t (1 - \exp\{-(F_t + M)\})} \quad \ldots 2)$$

where $F_t$ is the (assumed) terminal fishing mortality and $C_t$ the terminal catch.

Equation (1) is solved iteratively, using the Newton method, and Pope's equation (1972) for cohort analysis to obtain approximations of the slope of 1).

An alternative to VPA is to estimate $N_i$ using Pope's approximation ("cohort analysis")

$$N_i \approx C_i \cdot e^{M/2} + N_{i+1} \cdot e^M \quad \ldots 3)$$

with $F_i$ being estimated from $N_i$, $N_{i+1}$ and $M$ (Pope 1972).

**Operating Limits and Warnings** Estimation of the $N_i$ and $F_i$-values must proceed backward, i.e. starting with $N_t$ as first estimate of $N_{i+1}$. The values of $N_i$ and $F_i$ will rapidly converge toward their true values, even when $F_t$ was a wild guess. The values of $N_i$ and $F_i$ immediately preceding $N_t$ and $F_t$ are to be treated with suspicion, however. They may be improved by using as $F_t$ one of the $F_i$-values obtained from a preliminary VPA.

When using cohort analysis, $M$-values should not be higher than 0.3 per time unit.

# User Instructions

JONES' LENGTH COHORT ANALYSIS FB19
→ N, E    → Z, F

| STEP | INSTRUCTIONS | INPUT DATA/UNITS | KEYS | | OUTPUT DATA/UNITS |
|---|---|---|---|---|---|
| 1 | Store parameters | $L_\infty$ | STO | A | |
| | | D | ↑ | | |
| | either | M | ↑ | | |
| | do | K | f | a | |
| | or | M/KD | ↑ | | |
| | | D | f | b | |
| | | | | | |
| 2 | Initialize | | | | |
| | a) enter upper limit of largest length | $L_{ter}$ | ↑ | | |
| | class and length class interval | $\Delta L$ | f | c | |
| | b) enter terminal exploitation rate (a | $E_t$ | ↑ | | |
| | guess)* and terminal catch | $C_t$ | f | d | $N_t$ |
| | | | | | |
| 3 | Run cohort analysis: enter $C_{1-2}$ | $C_{1-2}$ | A | | $N_1$ |
| | and compute $N_1$ and $E$ | | | | $E_{1-2}$ |
| | | | | | |
| 4 | To compute values of $Z$ and $F$, enter $M$ | M | STO | 2 | |
| | (if not done previously) and perform | $E_{1-2}$ | B | | $Z_{1-2}$ |
| | | | | | $F_{1-2}$ |
| 5 | Repeat step(s) 3 (and 4) until smallest | | | | |
| | length is reached | | | | |

NOTE:
*A value of $E = 0.5$, corresponding to $F_t = M$ will do for most purposes.

# Program Listing

| STEP | KEY ENTRY | KEY CODE | COMMENTS | STEP | KEY ENTRY | KEY CODE | COMMENTS |
|---|---|---|---|---|---|---|---|
| 001 | *LBLa | 21 16 11 | | 049 | PRTX | -14 | |
| 002 | ÷ | -24 | | 050 | RCL9 | 36 09 | |
| 003 | X⇄Y | -41 | | 051 | - | -45 | |
| 004 | STOD | 35 14 | | 052 | RCLC | 36 13 | |
| 005 | ÷ | -24 | | 053 | X⇄Y | -41 | |
| 006 | STO0 | 35 00 | | 054 | ÷ | -24 | |
| 007 | CLX | -51 | | 055 | PRTX | -14 | |
| 008 | RTN | 24 | | 056 | RTN | 24 | |
| 009 | *LBLe | 21 16 15 | | 057 | *LBLc | 21 16 13 | |
| 010 | RCLA | 36 11 | | 058 | STO8 | 35 12 | |
| 011 | RCLD | 36 14 | | 059 | X⇄Y | -41 | |
| 012 | Y^x | 31 | | 060 | STO8 | 35 08 | |
| 013 | RCL7 | 36 07 | | 061 | X⇄Y | -41 | |
| 014 | RCL0 | 36 14 | | 062 | - | -45 | |
| 015 | Y^x | 31 | | 063 | STO7 | 35 07 | |
| 016 | - | -45 | | 064 | CLX | -51 | |
| 017 | RCLA | 36 11 | | 065 | RTN | 24 | |
| 018 | RCLD | 36 14 | | 066 | *LBLB | 21 12 | |
| 019 | Y^x | 31 | | 067 | CHS | -22 | |
| 020 | RCL8 | 36 08 | | 068 | 1 | 01 | |
| 021 | RCLD | 36 14 | | 069 | + | -55 | |
| 022 | Y^x | 31 | | 070 | RCL2 | 36 02 | |
| 023 | - | -45 | | 071 | X⇄Y | -41 | |
| 024 | ÷ | -24 | | 072 | ÷ | -24 | |
| 025 | RCL0 | 36 00 | | 073 | SPC | 16-11 | |
| 026 | 2 | 02 | | 074 | PRTX | -14 | |
| 027 | ÷ | -24 | | 075 | RCL2 | 36 02 | |
| 028 | Y^x | 31 | | 076 | - | -45 | |
| 029 | STO6 | 35 06 | | 077 | PRTX | -14 | |
| 030 | RTN | 24 | | 078 | RTN | 24 | |
| 031 | *LBLA | 21 11 | | 079 | *LBLb | 21 16 12 | |
| 032 | STOC | 35 13 | | 080 | STOD | 35 14 | |
| 033 | GSBe | 23 16 15 | | 081 | R↓ | -31 | |
| 034 | RCL5 | 36 05 | | 082 | STO0 | 35 00 | |
| 035 | STO9 | 35 09 | | 083 | CLX | -51 | |
| 036 | x | -35 | | 084 | RTN | 24 | |
| 037 | RCLC | 36 13 | | 085 | *LBLd | 21 16 14 | |
| 038 | + | -55 | | 086 | X⇄Y | -41 | |
| 039 | RCL6 | 36 06 | | 087 | ÷ | -24 | |
| 040 | x | -35 | | 088 | STO5 | 35 05 | |
| 041 | STO5 | 35 05 | | 089 | RTN | 24 | |
| 042 | RCL7 | 36 07 | | 090 | | | |
| 043 | STO8 | 35 08 | | | | | |
| 044 | RCLB | 36 12 | | | | | |
| 045 | - | -45 | | | | | |
| 046 | STO7 | 35 07 | | | | | |
| 047 | RCL5 | 36 05 | | | | | |
| 048 | SPC | 16-11 | | | | | |

## LABELS

| A → $N_1, E$ | B $Z, F$ | C | D | E |
|---|---|---|---|---|
| a → $M/KD$ | b STD $M/KD$ | c → $L_1, L_2$ | d → $N_t$ | e → $XL$ |
| 0 | 1 | 2 | 3 | 4 |
| 5 | 6 | 7 | 8 | 9 |

## FLAGS

0, 1, 2, 3

## SET STATUS

| FLAGS | TRIG | DISP |
|---|---|---|
| ON OFF | DEG ☒ | FIX ☒ |
| 0 ☐ ☒ | GRAD ☐ | SCI ☐ |
| 1 ☐ ☒ | RAD ☐ | ENG ☐ |
| 2 ☐ ☒ | | n = 3 |
| 3 ☐ ☒ | | |

## REGISTERS

| 0 $M/KD$ | 1 $K$ | 2 $M$ | 3 $Z$ | 4 | 5 $N_2$ | 6 $X_L$ | 7 $L_1$ | 8 $L_2$ | 9 used |
|---|---|---|---|---|---|---|---|---|---|
| S0 | S1 | S2 | S3 | S4 | S5 | S6 | S7 | S8 | S9 |

| A $L_\infty$ | B $\Delta L$ | C $C_{1-2}$ | D $D$ | E | I |

# Program Description

**Program Title:** Jones' Length Cohort Analysis
**Name:** Daniel Pauly
**Date:** Feb., 1981
**Address:** ICLARM, MCC P.O. Box 1501, Makati, Metro Manila, Philippines

**Program Description, Equations, Variables, etc.** Pope's (1972) cohort analysis, generalized for any time interval $\Delta t$ is

$$N_1 = N_2 + \Delta t \cdot e^{M\Delta t} + C_{1-2}^{M\Delta t/2} \quad \ldots 1)$$

substituting length for age (using the generalized VBGF) and rearranging gives

$$N_1 = [(N_2 \cdot X_L) + C_{1-2}] \cdot X_L \quad \ldots 2)$$

where

$$X_L = \left\{ \frac{L_\infty^D - L_1^D}{L_\infty^D - L_2^D} \right\}^{M/2KD} \quad \ldots 3)$$

where $N_1$ is the number of fishes at length 1, while $C_{1-2}$ is the catch of fish of length $L_1$ to $L_2$. Having estimated a value of $N$ for the largest fish, successive applications of equation (1) lead to estimates of $N$ for the smaller fish. The rate of exploitation ($E = F/Z$) can be computed from

$$E = F/Z = \text{number caught} / \text{number dying}$$

$Z$ is then estimated from $E$ via

$$Z = M/(1-E) \quad \ldots 4)$$

and $F$ via $\quad F = Z - M \quad \ldots 5)$

The method is based on Jones (1974, 1981).

**Operating Limits and Warnings** The limitations of length cohort analysis are discussed in detail in papers by Jones (1974, 1981) and must be considered whenever this method is applied to a set of catch data. The results of length cohort analysis are sensitive to wide class intervals used for structuring the catch data; for this reason, it may be more appropriate to use length-structured VPA (program FB 20) whenever separate values of $M$ and $K$ are available.

# User Instructions

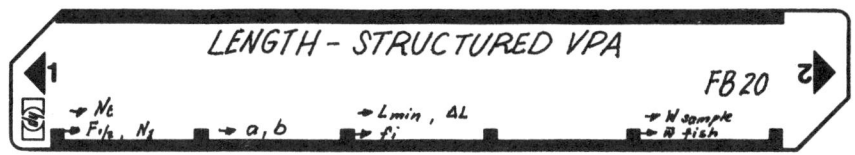

LENGTH - STRUCTURED VPA     FB 20

| STEP | INSTRUCTIONS | INPUT DATA/UNITS | KEYS | | OUTPUT DATA/UNITS |
|---|---|---|---|---|---|
| 1 | To initialize, enter constants | $L_\infty$ | STO | A | |
|   |   | K | STO | C | |
|   |   | D | STO | D | |
|   |   | M | STO | 2 | |
|   | (this value must be reentered for a new VPA) | $L_{ter.}$ | STO | I | |
|   |   | $\Delta L$ | STO | E | |
|   |   | TOL* | STO | O | |
| 2 | Calculate terminal population | $F_t$ | f | | |
|   |   | $C_t$ | f | 0 | $N_t$ |
| 3 | Run VPA, entering one $C_{i/2}$ after the other | $C_{i/2}$ | A | | $F_{i/2}$ |
|   |   |   |   |   | $N_i$ |
|   | * Tolerated error, e.g. 0.001 | | | | |
| 4 | To calculate the total weight of a sample, and its weight by length class, enter the parameters a and b of a length-weight relationship | a | f | | |
|   |   | b | f | b | |
| 5 | Then enter lower limit of smallest length class considered, and width of length class | $L_{min}$ | f | | |
|   |   | $\Delta L$ | f | c | |
| 6 | Then enter frequencies successively ** | $N_i$ | C | | $\bar{w}$ |
| 7 | To compute total weight of sample, and mean weight of fish in sample, press | | E | | W of sample |
|   |   |   |   |   | $\bar{W}$ of fish |

NOTE:
** Entering of frequencies should proceed from small to large sizes, and include zero frequencies.

## Program Listing (001 to 112)

| STEP | KEY ENTRY | KEY CODE | COMMENTS | STEP | KEY ENTRY | KEY CODE | COMMENTS |
|---|---|---|---|---|---|---|---|
| 001 | *LBLA | 21 11 | | | 057 | + | -55 |
| 002 | ST07 | 35 07 | | | 058 | ST03 | 35 03 |
| 003 | R↓ | -31 | | | 059 | RCL4 | 36 04 |
| 004 | ST06 | 35 06 | | 060 | 060 | $x^2$ | 53 |
| 005 | RCLA | 36 11 | | | 061 | RCL5 | 36 05 |
| 006 | RCLD | 36 14 | | | 062 | × | -35 |
| 007 | $y^x$ | 31 | | | 063 | CHS | -22 |
| 008 | RCLI | 36 46 | | | 064 | 1 | 01 |
| 009 | RCLD | 36 14 | | | 065 | + | -55 |
| 010 | $y^x$ | 31 | | | 066 | RCL9 | 36 09 |
| | 011 | - | -45 | | 067 | RCL3 | 36 03 |
| | 012 | RCLA | 36 11 | | 068 | ÷ | -24 |
| | 013 | RCLD | 36 14 | | 069 | × | -35 |
| | 014 | $y^x$ | 31 | 070 | 070 | RCL6 | 36 06 |
| | 015 | RCLI | 36 46 | | 071 | × | -35 |
| | 016 | RCLE | 36 15 | | 072 | RCL4 | 36 04 |
| | 017 | - | -45 | | 073 | $x^2$ | 53 |
| | 018 | STOI | 35 46 | | 074 | RCL5 | 36 05 |
| | 019 | RCLD | 36 14 | | 075 | × | -35 |
| 020 | 020 | $y^x$ | 31 | | 076 | RCL7 | 36 07 |
| | 021 | - | -45 | | 077 | × | -35 |
| | 022 | X⇄Y | -41 | | 078 | - | -45 |
| | 023 | ÷ | -24 | | 079 | ST08 | 35 08 |
| | 024 | LN | 32 | 080 | 080 | $x^2$ | 53 |
| | 025 | RCLC | 36 13 | | 081 | RCL0 | 36 00 |
| | 026 | ÷ | -24 | | 082 | X>Y? | 16-34 |
| | 027 | RCLD | 36 14 | | 083 | GTO1 | 22 01 |
| | 028 | ÷ | -24 | | 084 | RCL1 | 36 01 |
| | 029 | STOB | 35 12 | | 085 | RCL5 | 36 05 |
| 030 | 030 | RCL9 | 36 09 | | 086 | × | -35 |
| | 031 | GSBB | 23 12 | | 087 | RCL8 | 36 08 |
| | 032 | ST09 | 35 09 | | 088 | X⇄Y | -41 |
| | 033 | RCL2 | 36 02 | | 089 | ÷ | -24 |
| | 034 | GSBB | 23 12 | 090 | 090 | RCL9 | 36 09 |
| | 035 | ST02 | 35 02 | | 091 | X⇄Y | -41 |
| | 036 | 2 | 02 | | 092 | - | -45 |
| | 037 | ÷ | -24 | | 093 | ST09 | 35 09 |
| | 038 | CHS | -22 | | 094 | GTO0 | 22 00 |
| | 039 | $e^x$ | 33 | | 095 | *LBL1 | 21 01 |
| 040 | 040 | ST04 | 35 04 | | 096 | RCL9 | 36 09 |
| | 041 | RCL6 | 36 06 | | 097 | RCLB | 36 12 |
| | 042 | × | -35 | | 098 | ÷ | -24 |
| | 043 | RCL7 | 36 07 | | 099 | ST09 | 35 09 |
| | 044 | RCL2 | 36 02 | 100 | 100 | SPC | 16-11 |
| | 045 | CHS | -22 | | 101 | PRTX | -14 |
| | 046 | $e^x$ | 33 | | 102 | RCL2 | 36 02 |
| | 047 | × | -35 | | 103 | RCLB | 36 12 |
| | 048 | + | -55 | | 104 | ÷ | -24 |
| | 049 | ST01 | 35 01 | | 105 | ST02 | 35 02 |
| 050 | 050 | *LBL0 | 21 00 | | 106 | + | -55 |
| | 051 | RCL9 | 36 09 | | 107 | GSBB | 23 12 |
| | 052 | CHS | -22 | | 108 | $e^x$ | 33 |
| | 053 | $e^x$ | 33 | | 109 | RCL6 | 36 06 |
| | 054 | ST05 | 35 05 | 110 | 110 | × | -35 |
| | 055 | RCL2 | 36 02 | | 111 | PRTX | -14 |
| | 056 | RCL9 | 36 09 | | 112 | RTN | 24 |

### REGISTERS

| 0 $TOL/W_1$ | 1 used/$W_2$ | 2 $M/\Sigma f \cdot \bar{W}$ | 3 $Z/\Sigma f$ | 4 used/a | 5 used/b | 6 $N_q/L_{min}$ | 7 $C_{f_b}/\bar{W}$ | 8 used | 9 F |
|---|---|---|---|---|---|---|---|---|---|
| S0 | S1 | S2 | S3 | S4 | S5 | S6 | S7 | S8 | S9 |
| A $L_\infty$ | B $\Delta t$ | C $K$ | D $D$ | E $\Delta L$ | | | | I $L_s'$ | |

## Program Listing (113 to end)

| STEP | KEY ENTRY | KEY CODE | COMMENTS | STEP | KEY ENTRY | KEY CODE | COMMENTS |
|---|---|---|---|---|---|---|---|
| 113 | *LBLB | 21 12 | | 169 | PRTX | -14 | |
| 114 | RCLB | 36 12 | | 170 | RCL3 | 36 03 | |
| 115 | × | -35 | | 171 | ÷ | -24 | |
| 116 | RTN | 24 | | 172 | PRTX | -14 | |
| 117 | *LBLa | 21 16 11 | | 173 | RTN | 24 | |
| 118 | X≷Y | -41 | | | | | |
| 119 | STO9 | 35 09 | | | | | |
| 120 | RCL2 | 36 02 | | | | | |
| 121 | + | -55 | | | | | |
| 122 | RCL9 | 36 09 | | | | | |
| 123 | X≷Y | -41 | | | | | |
| 124 | ÷ | -24 | | 180 | | | |
| 125 | ÷ | -24 | | | | | |
| 126 | RTN | 24 | | | | | |
| 127 | *LBLb | 21 16 12 | | | | | |
| 128 | CLRG | 16-53 | | | | | |
| 129 | STO5 | 35 05 | | | | | |
| 130 | R↓ | -31 | | | | | |
| 131 | STO4 | 35 04 | | | | | |
| 132 | CLX | -51 | | | | | |
| 133 | RTN | 24 | | | | | |
| 134 | *LBLc | 21 16 13 | | 190 | | | |
| 135 | STOE | 35 15 | | | | | |
| 136 | R↓ | -31 | | | | | |
| 137 | STO6 | 35 06 | | | | | |
| 138 | RCL5 | 36 05 | | | | | |
| 139 | Yˣ | 31 | | | | | |
| 140 | RCL4 | 36 04 | | | | | |
| 141 | × | -35 | | | | | |
| 142 | STO0 | 35 00 | | | | | |
| 143 | CLX | -51 | | | | | |
| 144 | RTN | 24 | | 200 | | | |
| 145 | *LBLC | 21 13 | | | | | |
| 146 | ST+3 | 35-55 03 | | | | | |
| 147 | RCL6 | 36 06 | | | | | |
| 148 | RCLE | 36 15 | | | | | |
| 149 | + | -55 | | | | | |
| 150 | STO6 | 35 06 | | | | | |
| 151 | RCL5 | 36 05 | | | | | |
| 152 | Yˣ | 31 | | | | | |
| 153 | RCL4 | 36 04 | | | | | |
| 154 | × | -35 | | 210 | | | |
| 155 | STO1 | 35 01 | | | | | |
| 156 | RCL0 | 36 00 | | | | | |
| 157 | + | -55 | | | | | |
| 158 | 2 | 02 | | | | | |
| 159 | ÷ | -24 | | | | | |
| 160 | STO7 | 35 07 | | | | | |
| 161 | × | -35 | | | | | |
| 162 | ST+2 | 35-55 02 | | | | | |
| 163 | RCL1 | 36 01 | | | | | |
| 164 | STO0 | 35 00 | | 220 | | | |
| 165 | RCL7 | 36 07 | | | | | |
| 166 | RTN | 24 | | | | | |
| 167 | *LBLE | 21 15 | | | | | |
| 168 | RCL2 | 36 02 | | | | | |

### LABELS

| A → $F_{1/2}, N_t$ | B used | C $N_i$ → | D | E |
|---|---|---|---|---|
| a → $N_t$ | b $a, b$ → | c $L_{min}, \Delta L$ → | d | e |
| 0 used | 1 used | 2 | 3 | 4 |
| 5 | 6 | 7 | 8 | 9 |

### FLAGS

| 0 | 1 | 2 | 3 |
|---|---|---|---|

### SET STATUS

| FLAGS | | TRIG | DISP |
|---|---|---|---|
| | ON OFF | DEG ☒ | FIX ☒ |
| 0 | ☐ ☒ | GRAD ☐ | SCI ☐ |
| 1 | ☐ ☒ | RAD ☐ | ENG ☐ |
| 2 | ☐ ☒ | | n = 3 |
| 3 | ☐ ☒ | | |

# Program Description

**Program Title** Length-structured VPA
**Name** Daniel Pauly
**Address** ICLARM, MCC P.O. Box 1501
Makati, Metro Manila, Philippines

**Date** April, 1981

**Program Description, Equations, Variables, etc.** In analogy to Jones' (1974) conversion of Pope's (1972) cohort analysis to a method suitable for the analysis of catch-at-length data, Gulland's (1965) Virtual Population Analysis (VPA) can be used to estimate fishing mortality and population sizes from catch-at-length data. Gulland's VPA has the form

$$\frac{N_{i+1}}{C_i} = \frac{(F_i + M) \exp\{-(F_i + M)\}}{F_i \{1 - \exp -(F_i + M)\}} \quad \ldots 1)$$

Generalized for any time interval $\Delta t$, this becomes

$$\frac{N_{1+\Delta t}}{C_{1-2}} = \frac{(F_{1-2} + M) \Delta t \cdot \exp\{-(F_{1-2} + M) \Delta t\}}{(F_{1-2} \cdot \Delta t) \cdot \{1 - \exp(-(F_{1-2} + M) \Delta t)\}} \quad \ldots 2)$$

where $N_1$ is the number of fish of age 1 and $C_{1-2}$ and $F_{1-2}$ are the catch and fishing mortality, respectively, pertaining to fishes ranging from age 1 to age 2.

Converting length to age, in terms of the generalized VBGF gives for $\Delta t$

$$\Delta t = \frac{\ln\left\{\frac{L_\infty^D - L_1^D}{L_\infty^D - L_2^D}\right\}}{KD} \quad \ldots 3)$$

where $L_1$ and $L_2$ are the lengths pertaining to ages 1 and 2, respectively.

**Operating Limits and Warnings** The properties of the method are essentially the same as for VPA as far as convergence towards true fishing mortality is concerned, and the same as for Jones' length cohort analysis as far as sensitivity to $L_\infty$ and $K$ is concerned. The method, however, is insensitive to the effects of length class intervals that are very large, something which is not the case with Jones' length cohort analysis.

# User Instructions

**YIELD PER RECRUIT (Special VBGF) FB21**

| STEP | INSTRUCTIONS | INPUT DATA/UNITS | KEYS | | OUTPUT DATA/UNITS |
|---|---|---|---|---|---|
| | ORIGINAL VERSION (1957) | | | | |
| 1 | Enter parameter values | $W_\infty$ | STO | B | |
| | | $K$ | STO | 1 | |
| | | $M$ | STO | 2 | |
| | | $t_{max}$ | STO | A | |
| | | $t_o$ | STO | 0 | |
| | | $t_c$ | STO | D | |
| | | $t_r$ | STO | I | |
| 2 | Compute $Y/R$ | $F$ | A | | $Y/R_c$ |
| | | | | | $Y/R_r$ |
| | JONES' VERSION (1957) | | | | |
| 3 | Enter parameter values as above, omitting $t_{max}$ | | | | |
| 4 | Compute $Y/R$ | $F$ | B | | $Y/R_c$ |
| | | | | | $Y/R_r$ |
| | SIMPLIFIED VERSION (1966) | | | | |
| 5 | Enter parameter values | $M/K$ | STO | 8 | |
| | $(L_c/L_\infty =)$ | $C$ | STO | C | |
| 6 | Calculate relative $Y'/R$ | $E$ | C | | $Y'/R$ |

$Y/R_c$ = yield per recruit of age $t_c$

$Y/R_r$ = yield per recruit of age $t_r$. When $t_r$ is not available, set $t_r = t_o$

## Program Listing (001 to 112)

| STEP | KEY ENTRY | KEY CODE | | STEP | KEY ENTRY | KEY CODE |
|---|---|---|---|---|---|---|
| 001 | *LBLa | 21 16 11 | | 057 | RCL3 | 36 03 |
| 002 | RCL2 | 36 02 | | 058 | + | -55 |
| 003 | + | -55 | | 059 | ÷ | -24 |
| 004 | ST03 | 35 03 | | 060 | − | -45 |
| 005 | RCLD | 36 14 | | 061 | RCLB | 36 12 |
| 006 | RCL0 | 36 00 | | 062 | × | -35 |
| 007 | − | -45 | | 063 | RCL4 | 36 04 |
| 008 | ST05 | 35 05 | | 064 | × | -35 |
| 009 | RCLA | 36 11 | | 065 | *LBLb | 21 16 12 |
| 010 | RCLD | 36 14 | | 066 | SPC | 16-11 |
| 011 | − | -45 | | 067 | PRTX | -14 |
| 012 | ST06 | 35 06 | | 068 | RCLD | 36 14 |
| 013 | RTN | 24 | | 069 | RCLI | 36 46 |
| 014 | *LBLB | 21 12 | | 070 | − | -45 |
| 015 | ST04 | 35 04 | | 071 | RCL2 | 36 02 |
| 016 | GSBa | 23 16 11 | | 072 | × | -35 |
| 017 | RCL3 | 36 03 | | 073 | CHS | -22 |
| 018 | 1/X | 52 | | 074 | $e^x$ | 33 |
| 019 | RCL5 | 36 05 | | 075 | × | -35 |
| 020 | RCL1 | 36 01 | | 076 | PRTX | -14 |
| 021 | × | -35 | | 077 | RTN | 24 |
| 022 | CHS | -22 | | 078 | *LBLA | 21 11 |
| 023 | $e^x$ | 33 | | 079 | ST04 | 35 04 |
| 024 | 3 | 03 | | 080 | GSBa | 23 16 11 |
| 025 | × | -35 | | 081 | RCL6 | 36 06 |
| 026 | RCL1 | 36 01 | | 082 | RCL3 | 36 03 |
| 027 | RCL3 | 36 03 | | 083 | × | -35 |
| 028 | + | -55 | | 084 | CHS | -22 |
| 029 | ÷ | -24 | | 085 | $e^x$ | 33 |
| 030 | − | -45 | | 086 | CHS | -22 |
| 031 | RCL5 | 36 05 | | 087 | 1 | 01 |
| 032 | RCL1 | 36 01 | | 088 | + | -55 |
| 033 | × | -35 | | 089 | RCL3 | 36 03 |
| 034 | 2 | 02 | | 090 | ÷ | -24 |
| 035 | × | -35 | | 091 | RCL1 | 36 01 |
| 036 | CHS | -22 | | 092 | RCL3 | 36 03 |
| 037 | $e^x$ | 33 | | 093 | + | -55 |
| 038 | 3 | 03 | | 094 | ST07 | 35 07 |
| 039 | × | -35 | | 095 | RCL6 | 36 06 |
| 040 | RCL1 | 36 01 | | 096 | × | -35 |
| 041 | 2 | 02 | | 097 | CHS | -22 |
| 042 | × | -35 | | 098 | $e^x$ | 33 |
| 043 | RCL3 | 36 03 | | 099 | CHS | -22 |
| 044 | + | -55 | | 100 | 1 | 01 |
| 045 | ÷ | -24 | | 101 | + | -55 |
| 046 | + | -55 | | 102 | RCL5 | 36 05 |
| 047 | RCL5 | 36 05 | | 103 | RCL1 | 36 01 |
| 048 | RCL1 | 36 01 | | 104 | × | -35 |
| 049 | × | -35 | | 105 | CHS | -22 |
| 050 | 3 | 03 | | 106 | $e^x$ | 33 |
| 051 | × | -35 | | 107 | 3 | 03 |
| 052 | CHS | -22 | | 108 | × | -35 |
| 053 | $e^x$ | 33 | | 109 | × | -35 |
| 054 | RCL1 | 36 01 | | 110 | RCL7 | 36 07 |
| 055 | 3 | 03 | | 111 | ÷ | -24 |
| 056 | × | -35 | | 112 | − | -45 |

### REGISTERS

| 0 $t_0$ | 1 $K$ | 2 $M$ | 3 $Z$ | 4 $F$ | 5 $t_c - t_0$ | 6 $t_{max} - t_c$ | 7 used | 8 $M/K$ | 9 $1-c$ |
|---|---|---|---|---|---|---|---|---|---|
| S0 | S1 | S2 | S3 | S4 | S5 | S6 | S7 | S8 | S9 |

| A $t_{max}$ | B $W_\infty$ | C $c$ | D $t_c$ | E $E$ | I $t_r$ |
|---|---|---|---|---|---|

# Program Listing (113 to end)

| STEP | KEY ENTRY | KEY CODE | COMMENTS | STEP | KEY ENTRY | KEY CODE | COMMENTS |
|---|---|---|---|---|---|---|---|
| | 113 ST08 | 35 08 | | | 169 GTO6 | 22 16 12 | |
| | 114 RCL1 | 36 01 | | 170 | 170 *LBLC | 21 13 | |
| | 115 2 | 02 | | | 171 STOE | 35 15 | |
| | 116 x | -35 | | | 172 RCLC | 36 13 | |
| | 117 RCL3 | 36 03 | | | 173 CHS | -22 | |
| | 118 + | -55 | | | 174 1 | 01 | |
| | 119 ST07 | 35 07 | | | 175 + | -55 | |
| 120 | 120 RCL6 | 36 06 | | | 176 ST09 | 35 09 | |
| | 121 x | -35 | | | 177 3 | 03 | |
| | 122 CHS | -22 | | | 178 x | -35 | |
| | 123 e^x | 33 | | | 179 RCL8 | 36 08 | |
| | 124 CHS | -22 | | 180 | 180 1/X | 52 | |
| | 125 1 | 01 | | | 181 RCLE | 36 15 | |
| | 126 + | -55 | | | 182 CHS | -22 | |
| | 127 RCL5 | 36 05 | | | 183 1 | 01 | |
| | 128 RCL1 | 36 01 | | | 184 + | -55 | |
| | 129 x | -35 | | | 185 x | -35 | |
| 130 | 130 2 | 02 | | | 186 ST07 | 35 07 | |
| | 131 x | -35 | | | 187 1 | 01 | |
| | 132 CHS | -22 | | | 188 + | -55 | |
| | 133 e^x | 33 | | | 189 ÷ | -24 | |
| | 134 3 | 03 | | 190 | 190 CHS | -22 | |
| | 135 x | -35 | | | 191 1 | 01 | |
| | 136 RCL7 | 36 07 | | | 192 + | -55 | |
| | 137 ÷ | -24 | | | 193 RCL9 | 36 09 | |
| | 138 ST+8 | 35-55 08 | | | 194 X^2 | 53 | |
| | 139 RCL1 | 36 01 | | | 195 3 | 03 | |
| 140 | 140 3 | 03 | | | 196 x | -35 | |
| | 141 x | -35 | | | 197 RCL7 | 36 07 | |
| | 142 RCL3 | 36 03 | | | 198 2 | 02 | |
| | 143 + | -55 | | | 199 x | -35 | |
| | 144 ST07 | 35 07 | | 200 | 200 1 | 01 | |
| | 145 RCL6 | 36 06 | | | 201 + | -55 | |
| | 146 x | -35 | | | 202 ÷ | -24 | |
| | 147 CHS | -22 | | | 203 + | -55 | |
| | 148 e^x | 33 | | | 204 RCL9 | 36 09 | |
| | 149 CHS | -22 | | | 205 3 | 03 | |
| 150 | 150 1 | 01 | | | 206 Y^x | 31 | |
| | 151 + | -55 | | | 207 RCL7 | 36 07 | |
| | 152 RCL5 | 36 05 | | | 208 3 | 03 | |
| | 153 RCL1 | 36 01 | | | 209 x | -35 | |
| | 154 x | -35 | | 210 | 210 1 | 01 | |
| | 155 3 | 03 | | | 211 + | -55 | |
| | 156 x | -35 | | | 212 ÷ | -24 | |
| | 157 CHS | -22 | | | 213 - | -45 | |
| | 158 e^x | 33 | | | 214 RCL9 | 36 09 | |
| | 159 x | -35 | | | 215 RCL8 | 36 08 | |
| 160 | 160 RCL7 | 36 07 | | | 216 Y^x | 31 | |
| | 161 ÷ | -24 | | | 217 x | -35 | |
| | 162 RCL8 | 36 08 | | | 218 RCLE | 36 15 | |
| | 163 X⇄Y | -41 | | | 219 x | -35 | |
| | 164 - | -45 | | 220 | 220 RTN | 24 | |
| | 165 RCL8 | 36 12 | | | | | |
| | 166 x | -35 | | | | | |
| | 167 RCL4 | 36 04 | | | | | |
| | 168 x | -35 | | | | | |

## LABELS

| A B&H '57 | B Jones '57 | C B&H '66 | D | E |
|---|---|---|---|---|
| a used | b used | c | d | e |
| 0 | 1 | 2 | 3 | 4 |
| 5 | 6 | 7 | 8 | 9 |

## FLAGS

| 0 | 1 | 2 | 3 |
|---|---|---|---|

## SET STATUS

FLAGS ON/OFF: 0 ☐ ☒, 1 ☐ ☒, 2 ☐ ☒, 3 ☐ ☒

TRIG: DEG ☒, GRAD ☐, RAD ☐

DISP: FIX ☒, SCI ☐, ENG ☐, n = 3

# Program Description

**Program Title** _Yield per Recruit_
**Name** _Daniel Pauly_  **Date** _March, 1981_
**Address** _ICLARM, MCC P.O. Box 1501_
_Makati, Metro Manila, Philippines_

**Program Description, Equations, Variables, etc.** Program FB 20 estimates the yield per recruit, given growth and related parameters from any of the three equations

$$Y/R_r = F \cdot e^{-Mr_2} W_\infty \left\{ \frac{1-e^{-Zr_3}}{Z} - \frac{3e^{-Kr_1}(1-e^{-(Z+K)r_3})}{Z+K} \right.$$

$$\left. + \frac{3e^{-2Kr_1}(1-e^{-(Z+2K)r_3})}{Z+2K} - \frac{e^{-3Kr_1}(1-e^{-(Z+3K)r_3})}{Z+3K} \right\} \quad \ldots 1)$$

or

$$Y/R_r = F \cdot e^{-Mr_2} W_\infty \left\{ \frac{1}{Z} - \frac{3e^{-Kr_1}}{Z+K} + \frac{3e^{-2Kr_1}}{Z+2K} - \frac{e^{-3Kr_1}}{Z+3K} \right\} \quad \ldots 2)$$

where $Z = F+M$, $r_1 = t_c - t_0$, $r_2 = t_c - t_r$ and $r_3 = t_{max} - t_c$

or

$$Y'/R_r = E(1-C)^{M/K} \cdot \left\{ 1 - \frac{3(1-C)}{1 + \frac{K(1-E)}{M}} + \frac{3(1-C)^2}{1 + \frac{2K(1-E)}{M}} \right.$$

$$\left. - \frac{(1-C)^3}{1 + \frac{3K(1-E)}{M}} \right\} \quad \ldots 3)$$

proposed by Beverton and Holt (1957), Jones (1957), Beverton and Holt (1964).

**Operating Limits and Warnings** These equations must be used only in conjunction with the special VBGF (when D=1) and when weight growth is isometric.

# User Instructions

FB 22
YIELD PER RECRUIT VIA INCOMPLETE β-FUNCTION

| STEP | INSTRUCTIONS | INPUT DATA/UNITS | KEYS | | OUTPUT DATA/UNITS |
|---|---|---|---|---|---|
| 1 | Enter parameters | $W_\infty$ | STO | B | |
| | | $K$ | STO | A | |
| | | $D$ | STO | D | |
| | | $b$ | STO | E | |
| | | $M$ | STO | O | |
| | | $t_0$ | ↑ | | |
| | | $t_r$ | f | a | |
| | | $t_c$ | f | c | |
| | _SPECIAL VBGF (D = 1)_: | | | | |
| 2 | Calculate yield per recruit | $F$ | A | | $\beta$ |
| | | | | | $Y/R_c$ |
| | | | | | $Y/R_r$ |
| | _GENERALIZED VBGF (D ≠ 1)_: | | | | |
| 3 | Calculate yield per recruit | $F$ | B | | $\beta$ |
| | | | | | $Y/R_c$ |
| | | | | | $Y/R_r$ |

NOTES:
$Y/R_c$ = yield per recruit of age $t_c$
$Y/R_r$ = yield per recruit of age $t_r$
When $t_r$ is not available, set $t_r = t_0$

## Program Listing (001 to 112)

| STEP | KEY ENTRY | KEY CODE | COMMENTS | STEP | KEY ENTRY | KEY CODE | COMMENTS |
|---|---|---|---|---|---|---|---|
| 001 | *LBLA | 21 11 | | | 057 | RCL5 | 36 05 | |
| | 002 | STOI | 35 46 | | 058 | x | -35 | |
| | 003 | P⇄S | 16-51 | | 059 | RCL4 | 36 04 | |
| | 004 | RCL1 | 36 01 | 060 | 060 | + | -55 | |
| | 005 | RCL0 | 36 00 | | 061 | STO5 | 35 05 | |
| | 006 | − | -45 | | 062 | CLX | -51 | |
| | 007 | P⇄S | 16-51 | | 063 | RCL7 | 36 07 | |
| | 008 | RCLA | 36 11 | | 064 | x | -35 | |
| | 009 | x | -35 | | 065 | RCL6 | 36 06 | |
| 010 | 010 | CHS | -22 | | 066 | + | -55 | |
| | 011 | $e^x$ | 33 | | 067 | STO7 | 35 07 | |
| | 012 | STO3 | 35 03 | | 068 | RCL8 | 36 08 | |
| | 013 | RCLE | 36 15 | | 069 | 1 | 01 | |
| | 014 | RCLD | 36 14 | 070 | 070 | + | -55 | |
| | 015 | ÷ | -24 | | 071 | STO8 | 35 08 | |
| | 016 | 1 | 01 | | 072 | RCL2 | 36 02 | |
| | 017 | + | -55 | | 073 | RCL8 | 36 08 | |
| | 018 | STO2 | 35 02 | | 074 | − | -45 | |
| | 019 | RCLI | 36 46 | | 075 | x | -35 | |
| 020 | 020 | RCL0 | 36 00 | | 076 | RCL1 | 36 01 | |
| | 021 | + | -55 | | 077 | RCL8 | 36 08 | |
| | 022 | RCLA | 36 11 | | 078 | + | -55 | |
| | 023 | ÷ | -24 | | 079 | RCL8 | 36 08 | |
| | 024 | STOI | 35 01 | 080 | 080 | + | -55 | |
| | 025 | 1 | 01 | | 081 | ÷ | -24 | |
| | 026 | STO7 | 35 07 | | 082 | LSTX | 16-63 | |
| | 027 | STO6 | 35 06 | | 083 | 1 | 01 | |
| | 028 | STO4 | 35 04 | | 084 | − | -45 | |
| | 029 | 0 | 00 | | 085 | ÷ | -24 | |
| 030 | 030 | STO8 | 35 08 | | 086 | RCL3 | 36 03 | |
| | 031 | STO5 | 35 05 | | 087 | x | -35 | |
| | 032 | *LBL0 | 21 00 | | 088 | ENT↑ | -21 | |
| | 033 | STO9 | 35 09 | | 089 | ENT↑ | -21 | |
| | 034 | RCL1 | 36 01 | 090 | 090 | RCL4 | 36 04 | |
| | 035 | RCL8 | 36 08 | | 091 | x | -35 | |
| | 036 | + | -55 | | 092 | RCL5 | 36 05 | |
| | 037 | ENT↑ | -21 | | 093 | ÷ | -55 | |
| | 038 | ENT↑ | -21 | | 094 | STO4 | 35 04 | |
| | 039 | RCL2 | 36 02 | | 095 | X⇄Y | -41 | |
| 040 | 040 | + | -55 | | 096 | RCL6 | 36 06 | |
| | 041 | x | -35 | | 097 | x | -35 | |
| | 042 | RCL1 | 36 01 | | 098 | RCL7 | 36 07 | |
| | 043 | RCL8 | 36 08 | | 099 | + | -55 | |
| | 044 | + | -55 | 100 | 100 | STO6 | 35 06 | |
| | 045 | RCL8 | 36 08 | | 101 | X≠0? | 16-42 | |
| | 046 | + | -55 | | 102 | ÷ | -24 | |
| | 047 | ÷ | -24 | | 103 | RCL9 | 36 09 | |
| | 048 | LSTX | 16-63 | | 104 | X⇄Y | -41 | |
| | 049 | 1 | 01 | | 105 | X≠Y? | 16-32 | |
| 050 | 050 | + | -55 | | 106 | GTO0 | 22 00 | |
| | 051 | ÷ | -24 | | 107 | RCL3 | 36 03 | |
| | 052 | RCL3 | 36 03 | | 108 | RCL1 | 36 01 | |
| | 053 | x | -35 | | 109 | $Y^x$ | 31 | |
| | 054 | CHS | -22 | 110 | 110 | x | -35 | |
| | 055 | ENT↑ | -21 | | 111 | 1 | 01 | |
| | 056 | ENT↑ | -21 | | 112 | RCL3 | 36 03 | |

### REGISTERS

| 0 M | 1 P | 2 Q | 3 X | 4 used | 5 used | 6 used | 7 used | 8 used | 9 used |
|---|---|---|---|---|---|---|---|---|---|
| S0 $t_0$ | S1 $t_c$ | S2 $t_n$ | S3 | S4 | S5 | S6 | S7 | S8 | S9 |
| A K | B $W_\infty$ | C | D D | E b | I F | | | | |

## Program Listing (113 to end)

| STEP | KEY ENTRY | KEY CODE | COMMENTS | STEP | KEY ENTRY | KEY CODE | COMMENTS |
|---|---|---|---|---|---|---|---|
| | 113 | - | -45 | | 169 | STOA | 35 11 |
| | 114 | RCL2 | 36 02 | 170 | 170 | CLX | -51 |
| | 115 | $y^x$ | 31 | | 171 | RTN | 24 |
| | 116 | x | -35 | | 172 | *LBLa | 21 16 11 |
| | 117 | RCL1 | 36 01 | | 173 | P⇄S | 16-51 |
| | 118 | ÷ | -24 | | 174 | STO2 | 35 02 |
| | 119 | SPC | 16-11 | | 175 | R↓ | -31 |
| 120 | 120 | PRTX | -14 | | 176 | STO0 | 35 00 |
| | 121 | RCLB | 36 12 | | 177 | P⇄S | 16-51 |
| | 122 | x | -35 | | 178 | CLX | -51 |
| | 123 | RCLi | 36 46 | | 179 | RTN | 24 |
| | 124 | x | -35 | 180 | 180 | *LBLc | 21 16 13 |
| | 125 | RCLA | 36 11 | | 181 | P⇄S | 16-51 |
| | 126 | ÷ | -24 | | 182 | STO1 | 35 01 |
| | 127 | P⇄S | 16-51 | | 183 | P⇄S | 16-51 |
| | 128 | RCL1 | 36 01 | | 184 | CLX | -51 |
| | 129 | RCL0 | 36 00 | | 185 | RTN | 24 |
| 130 | 130 | - | -45 | | | | |
| | 131 | P⇄S | 16-51 | | | | |
| | 132 | RCLi | 36 46 | | | | |
| | 133 | RCL0 | 36 00 | | | | |
| | 134 | + | -55 | 190 | | | |
| | 135 | x | -35 | | | | |
| | 136 | $e^x$ | 33 | | | | |
| | 137 | x | -35 | | | | |
| | 138 | PRTX | -14 | | | | |
| | 139 | P⇄S | 16-51 | | | | |
| 140 | 140 | RCL1 | 36 01 | | | | |
| | 141 | RCL2 | 36 02 | | | | |
| | 142 | - | -45 | | | | |
| | 143 | P⇄S | 16-51 | | | | |
| | 144 | RCL0 | 36 00 | 200 | | | |
| | 145 | x | -35 | | | | |
| | 146 | CHS | -22 | | | | |
| | 147 | $e^x$ | 33 | | | | |
| | 148 | x | -35 | | | | |
| | 149 | PRTX | -14 | | | | |
| 150 | 150 | RTN | 24 | | | | |
| | 151 | *LBLB | 21 12 | | | | |
| | 152 | STOi | 35 46 | | | | |
| | 153 | RCLA | 36 11 | | | | |
| | 154 | P⇄S | 16-51 | 210 | | | |
| | 155 | STO5 | 35 05 | | | | |
| | 156 | P⇄S | 16-51 | | | | |
| | 157 | RCLD | 36 14 | | | | |
| | 158 | x | -35 | | | | |
| | 159 | 3 | 03 | | | | |
| 160 | 160 | x | -35 | | | | |
| | 161 | RCLE | 36 15 | | | | |
| | 162 | ÷ | -24 | | | | |
| | 163 | STOA | 35 11 | | | | |
| | 164 | RCLi | 36 46 | 220 | | | |
| | 165 | GSBA | 23 11 | | | | |
| | 166 | P⇄S | 16-51 | | | | |
| | 167 | RCL5 | 36 05 | | | | |
| | 168 | P⇄S | 16-51 | | | | |

### LABELS

| A $Y/R, D=1$ | B $Y/R, D\neq 1$ | C | D | E |
|---|---|---|---|---|
| a $t_0, t_r \rightarrow$ | b | c $t_c \rightarrow$ | d | e |
| 0 Loop for β | 1 | 2 | 3 | 4 |
| 5 | 6 | 7 | 8 | 9 |

### FLAGS

| 0 | 1 | 2 | 3 |

### SET STATUS

| FLAGS | TRIG | DISP |
|---|---|---|
| ON OFF | DEG ☒ | FIX ☒ |
| 0 ☐ ☒ | GRAD ☐ | SCI ☐ |
| 1 ☐ ☒ | RAD ☐ | ENG ☐ |
| 2 ☐ ☒ | | n = 3 |
| 3 ☐ ☒ | | |

# Program Description

**Program Title** Yield per Recruit via Incomplete β-Function
**Name** Daniel Pauly
**Address** ICLARM, MCC P.O. Box 1501
Makati, Metro Manila, Philippines
**Date** March 1981

**Program Description, Equations, Variables, etc.** Yield per recruit, as shown by Jones (1957) can be computed, when growth conforms to the special VBGF, by using

$$Y/R_r = F/K \cdot e^{-Zr_1} \cdot e^{-Mr_2} \cdot W_\infty \{B(X, P, Q)\} \quad \ldots 1)$$

where $X = e^{-Kr_1}$, $P = Z/K$, $Q = b+1$ (b being the exponent of the length-weight relationship) and $B$ being the symbol of the incomplete beta function, and where $r_1 = t_c - t_0$ and $r_2 = t_c - t_r$. Note here that $b$ may be $\neq 3$ (Jones (1957), Wilimovsky and Wicklund (1963), Ricker (1975)).

When the generalized VBGF is used to describe growth, yield per recruit can be computed from

$$Y/R_r = \frac{F \cdot b}{3KD} \cdot e^{Zr_1} \cdot e^{-Mr_2} W_\infty \{B(X, P, Q)\} \quad \ldots 2)$$

where $X = e^{-3KDr_1/b}$, $P = Zb/3KD$, $Q = (b/D)+1$ and $r_1$ and $r_2$ are defined as above.

The routine which estimates the values of the incomplete beta function is taken from program 00425D, submitted by R.H. Shudde to the U.S. User's Library.

**Operating Limits and Warnings** Execution time is about 40 seconds.

# User Instructions

CONVERSION FACTOR "k"　　FB 23

F → k

| STEP | INSTRUCTIONS | INPUT DATA/UNITS | KEYS | | OUTPUT DATA/UNITS |
|---|---|---|---|---|---|
| 1 | Enter parameters needed | K* | STO | 1 | |
| | | M* | STO | 2 | |
| | | $t_o$ | STO | 0 | |
| | | $t_c$ | STO | C | |
| | | $t_k$ | STO | A | |
| 2 | Calculate value of factor "k" | F* | A | | "k" |

NOTES:
* If no separate estimates of M and F are available, enter Z instead of M, and compute k for F = 0.

# Program Listing

| STEP | KEY ENTRY | KEY CODE |
|---|---|---|
| 001 | *LBLA | 21 11 |
| 002 | RCL2 | 36 02 |
| 003 | + | -55 |
| 004 | ST03 | 35 03 |
| 005 | 1/x | 52 |
| 006 | ST09 | 35 09 |
| 007 | ST05 | 35 05 |
| 008 | RCLC | 36 13 |
| 009 | RCL0 | 36 00 |
| 010 | - | -45 |
| 011 | ST07 | 35 07 |
| 012 | RCL1 | 36 01 |
| 013 | x | -35 |
| 014 | CHS | -22 |
| 015 | $e^x$ | 33 |
| 016 | 3 | 03 |
| 017 | x | -35 |
| 018 | RCL3 | 36 03 |
| 019 | RCL1 | 36 01 |
| 020 | + | -55 |
| 021 | ÷ | -24 |
| 022 | ST-9 | 35-45 09 |
| 023 | RCL7 | 36 07 |
| 024 | RCL1 | 36 01 |
| 025 | x | -35 |
| 026 | 2 | 02 |
| 027 | x | -35 |
| 028 | CHS | -22 |
| 029 | $e^x$ | 33 |
| 030 | 3 | 03 |
| 031 | x | -35 |
| 032 | RCL1 | 36 01 |
| 033 | 2 | 02 |
| 034 | x | -35 |
| 035 | RCL3 | 36 03 |
| 036 | + | -55 |
| 037 | ÷ | -24 |
| 038 | ST+9 | 35-55 09 |
| 039 | RCL7 | 36 07 |
| 040 | RCL1 | 36 01 |
| 041 | x | -35 |
| 042 | 3 | 03 |
| 043 | x | -35 |
| 044 | CHS | -22 |
| 045 | $e^x$ | 33 |
| 046 | RCL1 | 36 01 |
| 047 | 3 | 03 |
| 048 | x | -35 |
| 049 | RCL3 | 36 03 |
| 050 | + | -55 |
| 051 | ÷ | -24 |
| 052 | ST-9 | 35-45 09 |
| 053 | RCL5 | 36 05 |
| 054 | ST04 | 35 04 |
| 055 | RCLA | 36 11 |
| 056 | RCL0 | 36 00 |
| 057 | - | -45 |
| 058 | ST08 | 35 08 |
| 059 | RCL1 | 36 01 |
| 060 | x | -35 |
| 061 | CHS | -22 |
| 062 | $e^x$ | 33 |
| 063 | 3 | 03 |
| 064 | x | -35 |
| 065 | RCL1 | 36 01 |
| 066 | RCL3 | 36 03 |
| 067 | + | -55 |
| 068 | ÷ | -24 |
| 069 | ST-4 | 35-45 04 |
| 070 | RCL8 | 36 08 |
| 071 | RCL1 | 36 01 |
| 072 | x | -35 |
| 073 | 2 | 02 |
| 074 | x | -35 |
| 075 | CHS | -22 |
| 076 | $e^x$ | 33 |
| 077 | 3 | 03 |
| 078 | x | -35 |
| 079 | RCL1 | 36 01 |
| 080 | 2 | 02 |
| 081 | x | -35 |
| 082 | RCL3 | 36 03 |
| 083 | + | -55 |
| 084 | ÷ | -24 |
| 085 | ST+4 | 35-55 04 |
| 086 | RCL8 | 36 08 |
| 087 | RCL1 | 36 01 |
| 088 | x | -35 |
| 089 | 3 | 03 |
| 090 | x | -35 |
| 091 | CHS | -22 |
| 092 | $e^x$ | 33 |
| 093 | RCL1 | 36 01 |
| 094 | 3 | 03 |
| 095 | x | -35 |
| 096 | RCL3 | 36 03 |
| 097 | + | -55 |
| 098 | ÷ | -24 |
| 099 | ST-4 | 35-45 04 |
| 100 | RCL4 | 36 04 |
| 101 | RCLA | 36 11 |
| 102 | RCLC | 36 13 |
| 103 | - | -45 |
| 104 | RCL3 | 36 03 |
| 105 | x | -35 |
| 106 | CHS | -22 |
| 107 | $e^x$ | 33 |
| 108 | x | -35 |
| 109 | RCL9 | 36 09 |
| 110 | ÷ | -24 |
| 111 | RTN | 24 |

| LABELS | | | | | FLAGS |
|---|---|---|---|---|---|
| A →K | B | C | D | E | 0 |
| a | b | c | d | e | 1 |
| 0 | 1 | 2 | 3 | 4 | 2 |
| 5 | 6 | 7 | 8 | 9 | 3 |

SET STATUS

| FLAGS | | TRIG | DISP |
|---|---|---|---|
| | ON OFF | DEG ☒ | FIX ☒ |
| 0 | ☐ ☒ | GRAD ☐ | SCI ☐ |
| 1 | ☐ ☒ | RAD ☐ | ENG ☐ |
| 2 | ☐ ☒ | | n = 3 |
| 3 | ☐ ☒ | | |

### REGISTERS

| 0 $t_0$ | 1 $K$ | 2 $M$ | 3 $Z$ | 4 used | 5 $1/Z$ | 6 | 7 $r_1$ | 8 $r_2$ | 9 used |
|---|---|---|---|---|---|---|---|---|---|
| S0 | S1 | S2 | S3 | S4 | S5 | S6 | S7 | S8 | S9 |
| A $k$ | B | C $t_c$ | D | E | I | | | | |

# Program Description

**Program Title** Conversion Factor "k"
**Name** Daniel Pauly
**Date** March 1981
**Address** ICLARM, MCC P.O. Box 1501
Makati, Metro Manila, Philippines

**Program Description, Equations, Variables, etc.** Under equilibrium conditions, the proportion in the total stock (i.e. of the fish of age $t_c$ and above) of the fish of age $t_k$ and above is given by

$$k = \frac{\exp(-Zr_3) \cdot \left\{ \frac{1}{Z} - \frac{3\exp(-Kr_2)}{Z+K} + \frac{3\exp(-2Kr_2)}{Z+2K} - \frac{\exp(-3Kr_2)}{Z+3K} \right\}}{\frac{1}{Z} - \frac{3\exp(-Kr_1)}{Z+K} + \frac{3\exp(-2Kr_1)}{Z+2K} - \frac{\exp(-3Kr_1)}{Z+3K}} \quad \ldots 1)$$

where $r_1 = t_c - t_o$

$r_2 = t_k - t_o$

and $r_3 = t_k - t_c$

with the parameters $K$ and $t_o$ pertaining to the special VBGF (Hempel and Sarhage (1959), Pauly (1980d)).

**Operating Limits and Warnings** Use only in conjunction with the special VBGF (i.e. with $D = 1$).

# User Instructions

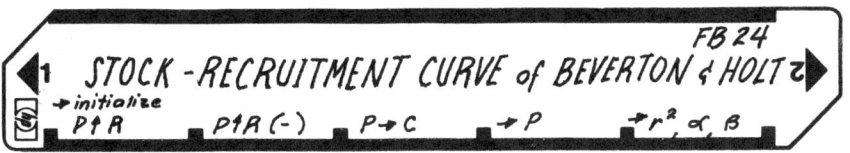

| STEP | INSTRUCTIONS | INPUT DATA/UNITS | KEYS | | OUTPUT DATA/UNITS |
|---|---|---|---|---|---|
| 1 | Initialize | | f | a | 0.000 |
| 2 | Enter P and R values | P | ↑ | | |
| | | R | A | | $i$ |
| 3 | Remove erroneous data pair | P | ↑ | | |
| | | R | B | | $i-1$ |
| 4 | Calculate $r^2$, $\alpha'$, $\beta'$ | | E | | $r^2$ |
| | | | | | $\alpha'$ |
| | | | | | $\beta'$ |
| 5 | Enter P-values* | P | D | | $i$ |
| 6 | Estimate R (HM & AM) for a given P-value | P | C | | $\hat{R}$ (HM) |
| | | | | | $\hat{R}$ (AM) |
| 7 | If P and R are expressed in the same units, calculate parameters of 2nd form of curve | | f | e | A |
| | | | | | $P_r$ (HM) |

NOTES:
* If an erroneous value of P is entered, perform: 0 STO 1, 0 STO 3, and start entering the P-values all over again.

# Program Listing

| STEP | KEY ENTRY | KEY CODE |
|---|---|---|
| 001 | *LBLa | 21 16 11 |
| 002 | CLRG | 16-53 |
| 003 | P⇌S | 16-51 |
| 004 | CLRG | 16-53 |
| 005 | CLX | -51 |
| 006 | RTN | 24 |
| 007 | *LBLA | 21 11 |
| 008 | ST+1 | 35-55 01 |
| 009 | R↓ | -31 |
| 010 | STO0 | 35 00 |
| 011 | R↑ | 16-31 |
| 012 | ÷ | -24 |
| 013 | RCL0 | 36 00 |
| 014 | F2? | 16 23 02 |
| 015 | GTO0 | 22 00 |
| 016 | Σ+ | 56 |
| 017 | RTN | 24 |
| 018 | *LBL0 | 21 00 |
| 019 | Σ- | 16 56 |
| 020 | RTN | 24 |
| 021 | *LBLB | 21 12 |
| 022 | SF2 | 16 21 02 |
| 023 | GTOA | 22 11 |
| 024 | *LBLE | 21 15 |
| 025 | P⇌S | 16-51 |
| 026 | SPC | 16-11 |
| 027 | RCL8 | 36 08 |
| 028 | RCL4 | 36 04 |
| 029 | RCL6 | 36 06 |
| 030 | x | -35 |
| 031 | RCL9 | 36 09 |
| 032 | ÷ | -24 |
| 033 | - | -45 |
| 034 | ENT↑ | -21 |
| 035 | ENT↑ | -21 |
| 036 | RCL4 | 36 04 |
| 037 | x² | 53 |

| STEP | KEY ENTRY | KEY CODE |
|---|---|---|
| 038 | RCL9 | 36 09 |
| 039 | ÷ | -24 |
| 040 | RCL5 | 36 05 |
| 041 | X⇌Y | -41 |
| 042 | - | -45 |
| 043 | ÷ | -24 |
| 044 | STOB | 35 12 |
| 045 | x | -35 |
| 046 | RCL6 | 36 06 |
| 047 | x² | 53 |
| 048 | RCL9 | 36 09 |
| 049 | ÷ | -24 |
| 050 | CHS | -22 |
| 051 | RCL7 | 36 07 |
| 052 | + | -55 |
| 053 | ÷ | -24 |
| 054 | PRTX | -14 |
| 055 | RCL6 | 36 06 |
| 056 | RCL4 | 36 04 |
| 057 | RCLB | 36 12 |
| 058 | x | -35 |
| 059 | - | -45 |
| 060 | RCL9 | 36 09 |
| 061 | ÷ | -24 |
| 062 | STOA | 35 11 |
| 063 | RCLB | 36 12 |
| 064 | PRTX | -14 |
| 065 | X⇌Y | -41 |
| 066 | PRTX | -14 |
| 067 | P⇌S | 16-51 |
| 068 | RTN | 24 |
| 069 | *LBLD | 21 14 |
| 070 | RCLA | 36 11 |
| 071 | X⇌Y | -41 |
| 072 | ÷ | -24 |
| 073 | RCLB | 36 12 |
| 074 | + | -55 |

| STEP | KEY ENTRY | KEY CODE |
|---|---|---|
| 075 | 1/X | 52 |
| 076 | ST+2 | 35-55 02 |
| 077 | 1 | 01 |
| 078 | ST+3 | 35-55 03 |
| 079 | RCL3 | 36 03 |
| 080 | RTN | 24 |
| 081 | *LBLC | 21 13 |
| 082 | SPC | 16-11 |
| 083 | RCLA | 36 11 |
| 084 | X⇌Y | -41 |
| 085 | ÷ | -24 |
| 086 | RCLB | 36 12 |
| 087 | + | -55 |
| 088 | 1/X | 52 |
| 089 | PRTX | -14 |
| 090 | RCL1 | 36 01 |
| 091 | RCL2 | 36 02 |
| 092 | ÷ | -24 |
| 093 | x | -35 |
| 094 | PRTX | -14 |
| 095 | RTN | 24 |
| 096 | *LBLe | 21 16 15 |
| 097 | RCLA | 36 11 |
| 098 | CHS | -22 |
| 099 | 1 | 01 |
| 100 | + | -55 |
| 101 | PRTX | -14 |
| 102 | RCLB | 36 12 |
| 103 | X⇌Y | -41 |
| 104 | ÷ | -24 |
| 105 | 1/X | 52 |
| 106 | PRTX | -14 |
| 107 | RTN | 24 |

## LABELS

| A data input | B correction | C est. R | D add R est. | E →r², α, β | 0 |
|---|---|---|---|---|---|
| a initialize | b | c | d | e A, Pr | 1 |
| 0 | 1 | 2 | 3 | 4 | 2 correction |
| 5 | 6 | 7 | 8 | 9 | 3 |

## FLAGS

0, 1, 2 correction, 3

## SET STATUS

**FLAGS**: 0 OFF, 1 OFF, 2 ON/OFF, 3 OFF
**TRIG**: DEG ☒, GRAD ☐, RAD ☐
**DISP**: FIX ☒, SCI ☐, ENG ☐, n = 3

## REGISTERS

| 0 used | 1 ΣR | 2 ΣR est. | 3 | 4 | 5 | 6 | 7 | 8 | 9 |
|---|---|---|---|---|---|---|---|---|---|
| S0 | S1 | S2 | S3 | S4 Σx | S5 Σx² | S6 Σy | S7 Σy² | S8 Σxy | S9 i |
| A β' | B α' | C | D | E | | | | I | |

# Program Description

**Program Title** Stock-recruitment curve of Beverton & Holt
**Name** Daniel Pauly
**Date** March 1979
**Address** Institut für Meereskunde
Kiel, FRG

**Program Description, Equations, Variables, etc.** The stock-recruitment relationship proposed by Beverton and Holt (1957) has the form

$$R = \frac{1}{\alpha' + \beta'/P}$$

, where $P$ is the size of the parental stock and $R$ is the number of recruits. When $P$ and $R$ are expressed in the same units, the formula can be rewritten as

$$R = \frac{1}{1 - A(1 - P/P_r)}$$

, where $A = 1 - \beta'$ and $\alpha' = A/P_r$, $P_r$ being the replacement abundance. The curve is fitted by means of:

$$\frac{P}{R} = \beta' + \alpha' P$$

that is by regressing $P/R$ on $P$. The R-line, obtained by inverting the values of $R$ represents the harmonic means (HM) of the expected recruitment for the various $P$-values. The conversion of HM-values to the corresponding arithmetic mean values (AM) follows the procedure outlined by Ricker (1975).

**Operating Limits and Warnings** The AM-values obtained through conversion from the HM-values are approximative (see Ricker 1975, p. 292). When a negative value of $\beta'$ is obtained, delete the values of $R$ and $P$ associated with the highest $P/R$ ratio and recalculate $\alpha'$ and $\beta'$.

# User Instructions

**RICKER'S STOCK-RECRUITMENT CURVES FB 25**

P♦R (2) → $R_{GM \& AM}$ → $R_{(GM)}$ → $R_{(AM)}/R_{(GM)}$ → $P_r/R_r$ → 2nd form
P♦R (10) → 1st form

| STEP | INSTRUCTIONS | INPUT DATA/UNITS | KEYS | | OUTPUT DATA/UNITS |
|---|---|---|---|---|---|
| 1 | Initialize | | f | a | 0.000 |
| | **1st FORM (R and P in different units)** | | | | |
| 2 | Enter P and R values | P | ↑ | | |
| | | R | A | | i |
| 3 | Remove erroneous data pair | P | ↑ | | |
| | | R | f | b | i-1 |
| 4 | Calculate parameters of stock-recruitment curve | | E | | $r^2$ |
| | | | | | $\alpha$ |
| | | | | | $\beta$ |
| | | | | | $P_m$ |
| | | | | | $R_m$ |
| 5 | Estimate $R_{(GM)}$ for a given P-value | P | C | | $\hat{R}_{(GM)}$ |
| 6 | If an estimate of $P_r$ is available, do: | $P_r$ | f | d | $P_r/R_r$ |
| | **2nd FORM (R and P in the Same Units)** | | | | |
| 7-8 | As 2 and 3 in 1st form | | | | |
| 9 | Calculate parameters of stock-recruitment curve | | f | e | $r^2$ |
| | | | | | $a (= P_r/P_m)$ |
| | | | | | $P_r$ |
| 10 | Reenter P and R values * | P | ↑ | | |
| | | R | D | | i |
| | When all values have been entered, do: | | f | c | $R_{(AM)}/R_{(GM)}$ |
| 11 | Estimate $R_{(GM)}$ & $R_{(AM)}$ from a given P-value | P | B | | $R_{(GM)}$ |
| | | | | | $R_{(AM)}$ |
| | *If an erroneous value of P and/or R was entered, perform: 0 STO 6 & 0 STO 7 and start entering P & R values all over again. | | | | |

## Program Listing (001 to 112)

| STEP | KEY ENTRY | KEY CODE | STEP | KEY ENTRY | KEY CODE |
|---|---|---|---|---|---|
| 001 | *LBLa | 21 16 11 | 057 | RCLB | 36 12 |
| 002 | CLRG | 16-53 | 058 | × | -35 |
| 003 | P⇄S | 16-51 | 059 | - | -45 |
| 004 | CLRG | 16-53 | 060 | RCL9 | 36 09 |
| 005 | CLX | -51 | 061 | P⇄S | 16-51 |
| 006 | RTN | 24 | 062 | ÷ | -24 |
| 007 | *LBLA | 21 11 | 063 | $e^x$ | 33 |
| 008 | LN | 32 | 064 | STOA | 35 11 |
| 009 | X⇄Y | -41 | 065 | F2? | 16 23 02 |
| 010 | STO0 | 35 00 | 066 | RTN | 24 |
| 011 | LN | 32 | 067 | PRTX | -14 |
| 012 | - | -45 | 068 | RCLB | 36 12 |
| 013 | RCL0 | 36 00 | 069 | CHS | -22 |
| 014 | F2? | 16 23 02 | 070 | STOB | 35 12 |
| 015 | GTO0 | 22 00 | 071 | PRTX | -14 |
| 016 | Σ+ | 56 | 072 | 1/X | 52 |
| 017 | RTN | 24 | 073 | PRTX | -14 |
| 018 | *LBL0 | 21 00 | 074 | RCLA | 36 11 |
| 019 | Σ- | 16 56 | 075 | RCLB | 36 12 |
| 020 | RTN | 24 | 076 | ÷ | -24 |
| 021 | *LBLb | 21 16 12 | 077 | 1 | 01 |
| 022 | SF2 | 16 21 02 | 078 | $e^x$ | 33 |
| 023 | GTOA | 22 11 | 079 | ÷ | -24 |
| 024 | *LBLE | 21 15 | 080 | PRTX | -14 |
| 025 | P⇄S | 16-51 | 081 | RTN | 24 |
| 026 | SPC | 16-11 | 082 | *LBLC | 21 13 |
| 027 | RCL8 | 36 08 | 083 | STO0 | 35 00 |
| 028 | RCL4 | 36 04 | 084 | RCLB | 36 12 |
| 029 | RCL6 | 36 06 | 085 | CHS | -22 |
| 030 | × | -35 | 086 | × | -35 |
| 031 | RCL9 | 36 09 | 087 | $e^x$ | 33 |
| 032 | ÷ | -24 | 088 | RCL0 | 36 00 |
| 033 | - | -45 | 089 | × | -35 |
| 034 | ENT↑ | -21 | 090 | RCLA | 36 11 |
| 035 | ENT↑ | -21 | 091 | × | -35 |
| 036 | RCL4 | 36 04 | 092 | RTN | 24 |
| 037 | $x^2$ | 53 | 093 | *LBLd | 21 16 14 |
| 038 | RCL9 | 36 09 | 094 | GSBC | 23 13 |
| 039 | ÷ | -24 | 095 | RCL0 | 36 00 |
| 040 | RCL5 | 36 05 | 096 | ÷ | -24 |
| 041 | X⇄Y | -41 | 097 | RTN | 24 |
| 042 | - | -45 | 098 | *LBLe | 21 16 15 |
| 043 | ÷ | -24 | 099 | SF2 | 16 21 02 |
| 044 | STOB | 35 12 | 100 | GSBE | 23 15 |
| 045 | × | -35 | 101 | LN | 32 |
| 046 | RCL6 | 36 06 | 102 | PRTX | -14 |
| 047 | $x^2$ | 53 | 103 | STO3 | 35 03 |
| 048 | RCL9 | 36 09 | 104 | RCLB | 36 12 |
| 049 | ÷ | -24 | 105 | ÷ | -24 |
| 050 | CHS | -22 | 106 | CHS | -22 |
| 051 | RCL7 | 36 07 | 107 | STO4 | 35 04 |
| 052 | + | -55 | 108 | PRTX | -14 |
| 053 | ÷ | -24 | 109 | RTN | 24 |
| 054 | PRTX | -14 | 110 | *LBL0 | 21 14 |
| 055 | RCL6 | 36 06 | 111 | STO5 | 35 05 |
| 056 | RCL4 | 36 04 | 112 | R↓ | -31 |

### REGISTERS

| 0 used | 1 | 2 | 3 a | 4 $P_r$ | 5 $R^1$ | 6 used | 7 $i$ | 8 | 9 |
|---|---|---|---|---|---|---|---|---|---|
| S0 | S1 | S2 | S3 | S4 $\Sigma x$ | S5 $\Sigma x^2$ | S6 $\Sigma y$ | S7 $\Sigma y^2$ | S8 $\Sigma xy$ | S9 $i$ |
| A a, α | B b | C | D | E | | I | | | |

# Program Listing (113 to end)

| STEP | KEY ENTRY | KEY CODE | COMMENTS | STEP | KEY ENTRY | KEY CODE | COMMENTS |
|---|---|---|---|---|---|---|---|
| 113 | STO0 | 35 00 | | 169 | x | -35 | |
| 114 | RCL4 | 36 04 | | 170 | PRTX | -14 | |
| 115 | ÷ | -24 | | 171 | RTN | 24 | |
| 116 | CHS | -22 | | | | | |
| 117 | 1 | 01 | | | | | |
| 118 | + | -55 | | | | | |
| 119 | RCL3 | 36 03 | | | | | |
| 120 | x | -35 | | | | | |
| 121 | $e^x$ | 33 | | | | | |
| 122 | RCL0 | 36 00 | | | | | |
| 123 | x | -35 | | | | | |
| 124 | LOG | 16 32 | | 180 | | | |
| 125 | RCL5 | 36 05 | | | | | |
| 126 | LOG | 16 32 | | | | | |
| 127 | - | -45 | | | | | |
| 128 | $x^2$ | 53 | | | | | |
| 129 | ST+6 | 35-55 06 | | | | | |
| 130 | 1 | 01 | | | | | |
| 131 | ST+7 | 35-55 07 | | | | | |
| 132 | RCL7 | 36 07 | | | | | |
| 133 | RTN | 24 | | | | | |
| 134 | *LBLc | 21 16 13 | | 190 | | | |
| 135 | RCL6 | 36 06 | | | | | |
| 136 | RCL7 | 36 07 | | | | | |
| 137 | 1 | 01 | | | | | |
| 138 | - | -45 | | | | | |
| 139 | STO0 | 35 00 | | | | | |
| 140 | ÷ | -24 | | | | | |
| 141 | RCL0 | 36 00 | | | | | |
| 142 | x | -35 | | | | | |
| 143 | RCL7 | 36 07 | | | | | |
| 144 | ÷ | -24 | | 200 | | | |
| 145 | 1 | 01 | | | | | |
| 146 | . | -62 | | | | | |
| 147 | 1 | 01 | | | | | |
| 148 | 5 | 05 | | | | | |
| 149 | 1 | 01 | | | | | |
| 150 | 8 | 08 | | | | | |
| 151 | x | -35 | | | | | |
| 152 | $10^x$ | 16 33 | | | | | |
| 153 | STO8 | 35 08 | | | | | |
| 154 | RTN | 24 | | 210 | | | |
| 155 | *LBLB | 21 12 | | | | | |
| 156 | STO0 | 35 00 | | | | | |
| 157 | RCL4 | 36 04 | | | | | |
| 158 | ÷ | -24 | | | | | |
| 159 | CHS | -22 | | | | | |
| 160 | 1 | 01 | | | | | |
| 161 | + | -55 | | | | | |
| 162 | RCL3 | 36 03 | | | | | |
| 163 | x | -35 | | | | | |
| 164 | $e^x$ | 33 | | 220 | | | |
| 165 | RCL0 | 36 00 | | | | | |
| 166 | x | -35 | | | | | |
| 167 | PRTX | -14 | | | | | |
| 168 | RCL8 | 36 08 | | | | | |

## LABELS

| A $P, R \rightarrow$ | B est. $R_{(GM)(AM)}$ | C est. $R_{(GM)}$ | D reenter P & R | E $\rightarrow$ 1st form |
|---|---|---|---|---|
| a Initialize | b correct. | c $\rightarrow R_{(AM)}/R_{(GM)}$ | d $\rightarrow P_r/R_r$ | e $\rightarrow$ 2nd form |
| 0 | 1 | 2 | 3 | 4 |
| 5 | 6 | 7 | 8 | 9 |

## FLAGS

| 0 | |
|---|---|
| 1 | |
| 2 | used |
| 3 | |

## SET STATUS

| FLAGS | TRIG | DISP |
|---|---|---|
| ON OFF | DEG ☒ | FIX ☒ |
| 0 ☐ ☐ | GRAD ☐ | SCI ☐ |
| 1 ☐ ☐ | RAD ☐ | ENG ☐ |
| 2 ☒ ☒ | | n = 3 |
| 3 ☐ ☐ | | |

# Program Description

**Program Title** Ricker's Stock Recruitment Curves
**Name** Daniel Pauly
**Date** March 1981
**Address** ICLARM, MCC P.O. Box 1501
Makati, Metro Manila, Philippines

**Program Description, Equations, Variables, etc.** The first of the stock-recruitment curves discussed in Ricker (1975) has the form

$$R = \alpha P e^{-\beta P} \qquad \ldots 1)$$

where $P$ is the parental stock size, $R$ the corresponding number of recruits, $\alpha$ is an index of density-independent mortality and $\beta$ an index of density dependent mortality.

The second form of the curve is

$$R = P e^{a(1 - P/P_r)} \qquad \ldots 2)$$

where $P_r$ is the replacement abundance (i.e. the point at which the replacement line cuts the stock-recruitment curve) and $a = P_r/P_m$, $P_m$ being the parent stock size at maximum recruitment.

The fitting of the curves and the estimation of the ratio $R_{(AM)}/R_{(GM)}$ follows the method outlined in Ricker (1975, p. 282-289) which should be consulted for details and further considerations.

**Operating Limits and Warnings** The geometric mean values ($R_{(GM)}$) are the most probable $R$ for the observed $P$-values, not the long-term (arithmetic mean) average $R$ obtained at a given $P$.

# User Instructions

**SCHAEFER AND FOX'S MODELS**    FB 26

Catch, Effort, correct.    Fox curve    Fox: fopt, MSY    Fox c/f line
Schaefer curve    Sch: fopt, MSY    Sch. c/f line

| STEP | INSTRUCTIONS | INPUT DATA/UNITS | KEYS | | OUTPUT DATA/UNITS |
|---|---|---|---|---|---|
| 1 | Initialize | | f | a | 0.000 |
| 2 | Enter catch-and-effort data | catch | ↑ | | |
|   |   | effort | A | | $i$ |
| 3 | Remove erroneous data pair | catch | ↑ | | |
|   |   | effort | B | | $i-1$ |
|   | **SCHAEFER MODEL** | | | | |
| 4 | Plot of c/f on f | | E | | $r^2$ |
|   |   | | | | $a$ |
|   |   | | | | $b$ |
| 5 | f opt and MSY | | D | | f opt |
|   |   | | | | MSY |
| 6 | Calculate catch for any level of effort | effort | C | | catch |
|   | **FOX MODEL** | | | | |
| 7 | Plot of ln c/f on f | | f | e | $r^2$ |
|   |   | | | | $a$ |
|   |   | | | | $b$ |
| 8 | f opt and MSY | | f | d | f opt |
|   |   | | | | MSY |
| 9 | Calculate catch for any level of effort | effort | f | c | catch |

## Program Listing (001 to 112)

| STEP | KEY ENTRY | KEY CODE | COMMENTS | STEP | KEY ENTRY | KEY CODE | COMMENTS |
|---|---|---|---|---|---|---|---|
| 001 | *LBLa | 21 16 11 | | | 057 | SPC | 16-11 | |
| | 002 | CLRG | 16-53 | | 058 | RCL8 | 36 08 | |
| | 003 | P⇌S | 16-51 | | 059 | RCL4 | 36 04 | |
| | 004 | CLRG | 16-53 | 060 | 060 | RCL6 | 36 06 | |
| | 005 | CLX | -51 | | 061 | × | -35 | |
| | 006 | RTN | 24 | | 062 | RCL9 | 36 09 | |
| | 007 | *LBLA | 21 11 | | 063 | ÷ | -24 | |
| | 008 | ST00 | 35 00 | | 064 | − | -45 | |
| | 009 | ÷ | -24 | | 065 | ENT↑ | -21 | |
| 010 | 010 | ST01 | 35 01 | | 066 | ENT↑ | -21 | |
| | 011 | LN | 32 | | 067 | RCL4 | 36 04 | |
| | 012 | ST02 | 35 02 | | 068 | $x^2$ | 53 | |
| | 013 | RCL0 | 36 00 | | 069 | RCL9 | 36 09 | |
| | 014 | ST+4 | 35-55 04 | 070 | 070 | ÷ | -24 | |
| | 015 | $x^2$ | 53 | | 071 | RCL5 | 36 05 | |
| | 016 | ST+5 | 35-55 05 | | 072 | X⇌Y | -41 | |
| | 017 | RCL2 | 36 02 | | 073 | − | -45 | |
| | 018 | ST+6 | 35-55 06 | | 074 | ÷ | -24 | |
| | 019 | $x^2$ | 53 | | 075 | STOB | 35 12 | |
| 020 | 020 | ST+7 | 35-55 07 | | 076 | × | -35 | |
| | 021 | RCL2 | 36 02 | | 077 | RCL6 | 36 06 | |
| | 022 | RCL0 | 36 00 | | 078 | $x^2$ | 53 | |
| | 023 | × | -35 | | 079 | RCL9 | 36 09 | |
| | 024 | ST+8 | 35-55 08 | 080 | 080 | ÷ | -24 | |
| | 025 | 1 | 01 | | 081 | CHS | -22 | |
| | 026 | ST+9 | 35-55 09 | | 082 | RCL7 | 36 07 | |
| | 027 | RCL1 | 36 01 | | 083 | + | -55 | |
| | 028 | RCL0 | 36 00 | | 084 | ÷ | -24 | |
| | 029 | Σ+ | 56 | | 085 | PRTX | -14 | |
| 030 | 030 | RTN | 24 | | 086 | √X | 54 | delete to obtain AM regression |
| | 031 | *LBLB | 21 12 | | 087 | RCLB | 36 12 | |
| | 032 | ST00 | 35 00 | | 088 | X⇌Y | -41 | |
| | 033 | ÷ | -24 | | 089 | ÷ | -24 | |
| | 034 | ST01 | 35 01 | 090 | 090 | STOB | 35 12 | |
| | 035 | LN | 32 | | 091 | RCL6 | 36 06 | |
| | 036 | ST02 | 35 02 | | 092 | RCL4 | 36 04 | |
| | 037 | RCL0 | 36 00 | | 093 | RCLB | 36 12 | |
| | 038 | ST-4 | 35-45 04 | | 094 | × | -35 | |
| | 039 | $x^2$ | 53 | | 095 | − | -45 | |
| 040 | 040 | ST-5 | 35-45 05 | | 096 | RCL9 | 36 09 | |
| | 041 | RCL2 | 36 02 | | 097 | ÷ | -24 | |
| | 042 | ST-6 | 35-45 06 | | 098 | STOA | 35 11 | |
| | 043 | $x^2$ | 53 | | 099 | PRTX | -14 | |
| | 044 | ST-7 | 35-45 07 | 100 | 100 | RCLB | 36 12 | |
| | 045 | RCL2 | 36 02 | | 101 | PRTX | -14 | |
| | 046 | RCL0 | 36 00 | | 102 | P⇌S | 16-51 | |
| | 047 | × | -35 | | 103 | RTN | 24 | |
| | 048 | ST-8 | 35-45 08 | | 104 | *LBLe | 21 16 15 | |
| | 049 | 1 | 01 | | 105 | SPC | 16-11 | |
| 050 | 050 | ST-9 | 35-45 09 | | 106 | RCL8 | 36 08 | |
| | 051 | RCL0 | 36 00 | | 107 | RCL4 | 36 04 | |
| | 052 | RCL1 | 36 01 | | 108 | RCL6 | 36 06 | |
| | 053 | Σ- | 16 56 | | 109 | × | -35 | |
| | 054 | RTN | 24 | 110 | 110 | RCL9 | 36 09 | |
| | 055 | *LBLE | 21 15 | | 111 | ÷ | -24 | |
| | 056 | P⇌S | 16-51 | | 112 | − | -45 | |

### REGISTERS

| 0 used | 1 used | 2 used | 3 FOX → | 4 Σx | 5 Σx² | 6 Σy | 7 Σy² | 8 Σxy | 9 n |
|---|---|---|---|---|---|---|---|---|---|
| S0 | S1 | S2 | S3 SCHAEFER → | S4 Σx | S5 Σx² | S6 Σy | S7 Σy² | S8 Σxy | S9 n |
| A intercept (a) | B slope (b) | C | D | | E | | | I | |

## Program Listing (113 to end)

| STEP | KEY ENTRY | KEY CODE | COMMENTS | STEP | KEY ENTRY | KEY CODE | COMMENTS |
|---|---|---|---|---|---|---|---|
| 113 | ENT↑ | -21 | | 169 | RTN | 24 | |
| 114 | ENT↑ | -21 | | 170 | *LBLD | 21 14 | |
| 115 | RCL4 | 36 04 | | 171 | SPC | 16-11 | |
| 116 | $x^2$ | 53 | | 172 | RCLA | 36 11 | |
| 117 | RCL9 | 36 09 | | 173 | RCLB | 36 12 | |
| 118 | ÷ | -24 | | 174 | CHS | -22 | |
| 119 | RCL5 | 36 05 | | 175 | 2 | 02 | |
| 120 | X≠Y | -41 | | 176 | × | -35 | |
| 121 | − | -45 | | 177 | ÷ | -24 | |
| 122 | ÷ | -24 | | 178 | PRTX | -14 | |
| 123 | STOB | 35 12 | | 179 | RCLA | 36 11 | |
| 124 | × | -35 | | 180 | $x^2$ | 53 | |
| 125 | RCL6 | 36 06 | | 181 | RCLB | 36 12 | |
| 126 | $x^2$ | 53 | | 182 | 4 | 04 | |
| 127 | RCL9 | 36 09 | | 183 | × | -35 | |
| 128 | ÷ | -24 | | 184 | CHS | -22 | |
| 129 | CHS | -22 | | 185 | ÷ | -24 | |
| 130 | RCL7 | 36 07 | | 186 | PRTX | -14 | |
| 131 | + | -55 | | 187 | RTN | 24 | |
| 132 | ÷ | -24 | | 188 | *LBLd | 21 16 14 | |
| 133 | PRTX | -14 | | 189 | RCLB | 36 12 | |
| 134 | √x | 54 | delete to obtain AM regression | 190 | 1/X | 52 | |
| 135 | RCLB | 36 12 | | 191 | CHS | -22 | |
| 136 | X≠Y | -41 | | 192 | SPC | 16-11 | |
| 137 | ÷ | -24 | | 193 | PRTX | -14 | |
| 138 | STOB | 35 12 | | 194 | RCLA | 36 11 | |
| 139 | RCL6 | 36 06 | | 195 | 1 | 01 | |
| 140 | RCL4 | 36 04 | | 196 | − | -45 | |
| 141 | RCLB | 36 12 | | 197 | $e^x$ | 33 | |
| 142 | × | -35 | | 198 | RCLB | 36 12 | |
| 143 | − | -45 | | 199 | ÷ | -24 | |
| 144 | RCL9 | 36 09 | | 200 | CHS | -22 | |
| 145 | ÷ | -24 | | 201 | PRTX | -14 | |
| 146 | STOA | 35 11 | | 202 | RTN | 24 | |
| 147 | PRTX | -14 | | | | | |
| 148 | RCLB | 36 12 | | | | | |
| 149 | PRTX | -14 | | | | | |
| 150 | RTN | 24 | | | | | |
| 151 | *LBLC | 21 13 | | | | | |
| 152 | STO0 | 35 00 | | | | | |
| 153 | RCLB | 36 12 | | | | | |
| 154 | × | -35 | | 210 | | | |
| 155 | RCLA | 36 11 | | | | | |
| 156 | + | -55 | | | | | |
| 157 | RCL0 | 36 00 | | | | | |
| 158 | × | -35 | | | | | |
| 159 | RTN | 24 | | | | | |
| 160 | *LBLc | 21 16 13 | | | | | |
| 161 | STO0 | 35 00 | | | | | |
| 162 | RCLB | 36 12 | | | | | |
| 163 | × | -35 | | | | | |
| 164 | RCLA | 36 11 | | 220 | | | |
| 165 | + | -55 | | | | | |
| 166 | $e^x$ | 33 | | | | | |
| 167 | RCL0 | 36 00 | | | | | |
| 168 | × | -35 | | | | | |

### LABELS

| A enter data | B correction | C catch | D MSY, fopt | E Schaefer Plot |
|---|---|---|---|---|
| a initialize | b | c catch | d MSY, fopt | e Fox Plot |
| 0 | 1 | 2 | 3 | 4 |
| 5 | 6 | 7 | 8 | 9 |

### FLAGS

| 0 |
|---|
| 1 |
| 2 |
| 3 |

### SET STATUS

| FLAGS | TRIG | DISP |
|---|---|---|
| ON OFF | | |
| 0 ☐ ☒ | DEG ☒ | FIX ☒ |
| 1 ☐ ☒ | GRAD ☐ | SCI ☐ |
| 2 ☐ ☒ | RAD ☐ | ENG ☐ |
| 3 ☐ ☒ | | n = 2 |

# Program Description

**Program Title:** Schaefer and Fox's Models
**Name:** Daniel Pauly
**Date:** Sept., 1980
**Address:** ICLARM, MCC P.O. Box 1501
Makati, Metro Manila, Philippines

**Program Description, Equations, Variables, etc.** When a fishery is in equilibrium, surplus yield can be described by a parabolic function of effort, i.e.

$$Y = af - bf^2 \qquad \ldots 1)$$

where $a$ and $b$ are constants and $f$ is fishing effort; Maximum Sustainable Yield (MSY) and optimum effort ($f$ opt.) can be estimated from the relationships

$$MSY = a^2/4b \qquad \ldots 2)$$

and

$$f\,opt. = a/2b \qquad \ldots 3)$$

The values of the constants $a$ & $b$ are generally obtained by plotting $c/f$ on effort, $a$ & $b$ being the intercept and the slope, respectively of the resulting linear regression (the model used here is a GM regression; see Ricker 1975).

When $\ln c/f$ is plotted on $f$, a yield curve is obtained which has the form

$$Y = fe^{a} \cdot e^{-bf} \qquad \ldots 4)$$

with $MSY = e^{a-1}/b$ and $f\,opt = 1/b$ $\qquad \ldots 5), 6)$

and where $a$ and $b$ are the intercept and slope, respectively of a GM regression of $\ln c/f$ on $f$ (Schaefer 1957, Fox 1970, Ricker 1975).

**Operating Limits and Warnings** The models are based on the assumptions that equilibrium effort and yield figures are used. When this is not the case, a bias will occur, whose magnitude is a function of both the life-span of the fish in question, and of the extent of the changes in effort (see Gulland (1969), for a method to simulate equilibrium conditions).
The results obtained here will differ slightly from those obtained using the more common AM regression.

# User Instructions

SCHNUTE'S YIELD MODEL FB27

| STEP | INSTRUCTIONS | INPUT DATA/UNITS | KEYS | | OUTPUT DATA/UNITS |
|---|---|---|---|---|---|
| 1 | Enter first pair of catch-and-effort data and initialize | $c$ | A | | |
| | | $f$ | $f$ | $b$ | 0.000 |
| 2 | Enter second and following data pairs | $c$ | A | | |
| | | $f$ | A | | $i$ |
| 3 | Calculate $R^2$ and coefficients of regression | | E | | $R^2$ |
| | | | | | $a$ |
| | | | | | $b_1$ |
| | | | | | $b_2$ |
| 4 | Estimate model parameters | | $f$ | $e$ | $r_m$ |
| | | | | | $q$ |
| | | | | | $B_\infty$ |
| | | | | | $f_{opt.}$ |
| | | | | | MSY |
| 5 | Estimate catch for any level of effort | $f$ | C | | catch |

## Program Listing (001 to 112)

| STEP | KEY ENTRY | KEY CODE | COMMENTS | STEP | KEY ENTRY | KEY CODE | COMMENTS |
|---|---|---|---|---|---|---|---|
| 001 | *LBLa | 21 16 11 | | 057 | $x^2$ | 53 | |
| 002 | CLRG | 16-53 | | 058 | ST+6 | 35-55 06 | |
| 003 | STOA | 35 11 | | 059 | RCLE | 36 15 | |
| 004 | R↓ | -31 | | 060 | RCLD | 36 14 | |
| 005 | STOC | 35 13 | | 061 | × | -35 | |
| 006 | RCLA | 36 11 | | 062 | ST+1 | 35-55 01 | |
| 007 | ÷ | -24 | | 063 | RCLD | 36 14 | |
| 008 | STOB | 35 12 | | 064 | RCLI | 36 46 | |
| 009 | CLX | -51 | | 065 | × | -35 | |
| 010 | RTN | 24 | | 066 | ST+2 | 35-55 02 | |
| 011 | *LBLA | 21 11 | | 067 | RCLE | 36 15 | |
| 012 | STOE | 35 15 | | 068 | RCLI | 36 46 | |
| 013 | R↓ | -31 | | 069 | × | -35 | |
| 014 | STOD | 35 14 | | 070 | ST+3 | 35-55 03 | |
| 015 | RCLE | 36 15 | | 071 | 1 | 01 | |
| 016 | ÷ | -24 | | 072 | ST+0 | 35-55 00 | |
| 017 | STOI | 35 46 | | 073 | RCL0 | 36 00 | |
| 018 | RCLB | 36 12 | | 074 | RTN | 24 | |
| 019 | + | -55 | | 075 | *LBLE | 21 15 | |
| 020 | 2 | 02 | | 076 | SPC | 16-11 | |
| 021 | ÷ | -24 | | 077 | RCL0 | 36 00 | |
| 022 | P⇄S | 16-51 | | 078 | RCL4 | 36 04 | |
| 023 | ST00 | 35 00 | | 079 | × | -35 | |
| 024 | RCLE | 36 15 | | 080 | RCL7 | 36 07 | |
| 025 | RCLA | 36 11 | | 081 | $x^2$ | 53 | |
| 026 | + | -55 | | 082 | - | -45 | |
| 027 | 2 | 02 | | 083 | STOD | 35 14 | |
| 028 | ÷ | -24 | | 084 | RCL0 | 36 00 | |
| 029 | ST01 | 35 01 | | 085 | RCL3 | 36 03 | |
| 030 | RCLI | 36 46 | | 086 | × | -35 | |
| 031 | RCLB | 36 12 | | 087 | RCL8 | 36 08 | |
| 032 | ÷ | -24 | | 088 | RCL9 | 36 09 | |
| 033 | LN | 32 | | 089 | × | -35 | |
| 034 | ST02 | 35 02 | | 090 | - | -45 | |
| 035 | RCLE | 36 15 | | 091 | × | -35 | |
| 036 | STOA | 35 11 | | 092 | STOC | 35 13 | |
| 037 | RCLD | 36 14 | | 093 | RCL0 | 36 00 | |
| 038 | STOC | 35 13 | | 094 | RCL1 | 36 01 | |
| 039 | RCLI | 36 46 | | 095 | × | -35 | |
| 040 | STOB | 35 12 | | 096 | RCL7 | 36 07 | |
| 041 | RCL2 | 36 02 | | 097 | RCL8 | 36 08 | |
| 042 | STOI | 35 46 | | 098 | × | -35 | |
| 043 | RCL1 | 36 01 | | 099 | - | -45 | |
| 044 | STOD | 35 14 | | 100 | STOA | 35 11 | |
| 045 | RCL0 | 36 00 | | 101 | RCL0 | 36 00 | |
| 046 | STOE | 35 15 | | 102 | RCL2 | 36 02 | |
| 047 | P⇄S | 16-51 | | 103 | × | -35 | |
| 048 | ST+8 | 35-55 08 | | 104 | RCL7 | 36 07 | |
| 049 | $x^2$ | 53 | | 105 | RCL9 | 36 09 | |
| 050 | ST+5 | 35-55 05 | | 106 | × | -35 | |
| 051 | RCLD | 36 14 | | 107 | - | -45 | |
| 052 | ST+7 | 35-55 07 | | 108 | STOB | 35 12 | |
| 053 | $x^2$ | 53 | | 109 | × | -35 | |
| 054 | ST+4 | 35-55 04 | | 110 | RCLC | 36 13 | |
| 055 | RCLI | 36 46 | | 111 | X⇄Y | -41 | |
| 056 | ST+9 | 35-55 09 | | 112 | - | -45 | |

### REGISTERS

| 0 $n$ | 1 $\Sigma XY$ | 2 $\Sigma XZ$ | 3 $\Sigma YZ$ | 4 $\Sigma X^2$ | 5 $\Sigma Y^2$ | 6 $\Sigma Z^2$ | 7 $\Sigma X$ | 8 $\Sigma Y$ | 9 $\Sigma Z$ |
|---|---|---|---|---|---|---|---|---|---|
| S0 used | S1 used | S2 used | S3 | S4 | S5 | S6 | S7 | S8 | S9 |
| A $a$ | B $b_1$ | C $b_2$ | D used | E used | I used | | | | |

## Program Listing (113 to end)

| STEP | KEY ENTRY | KEY CODE | COMMENTS | STEP | KEY ENTRY | KEY CODE | COMMENTS |
|---|---|---|---|---|---|---|---|
| | 113 RCLD | 36 14 | | | 169 RCLA | 36 11 | |
| | 114 RCL0 | 36 00 | | 170 | 170 PRTX | -14 | |
| | 115 RCL5 | 36 05 | | | 171 RCLB | 36 12 | |
| | 116 × | -35 | | | 172 PRTX | -14 | |
| | 117 RCL8 | 36 08 | | | 173 RCLC | 36 13 | |
| | 118 X² | 53 | | | 174 PRTX | -14 | |
| | 119 − | -45 | | | 175 RTN | 24 | |
| 120 | 120 × | -35 | | | 176 *LBLe | 21 16 15 | |
| | 121 RCLA | 36 11 | | | 177 SPC | 16-11 | |
| | 122 X² | 53 | | | 178 RCLA | 36 11 | |
| | 123 − | -45 | | | 179 PRTX | -14 | |
| | 124 ÷ | -24 | | 180 | 180 RCLB | 36 12 | |
| | 125 STOC | 35 13 | | | 181 CHS | -22 | |
| | 126 RCLB | 36 12 | | | 182 PRTX | -14 | |
| | 127 RCLA | 36 11 | | | 183 RCLC | 36 13 | |
| | 128 RCLC | 36 13 | | | 184 RCLB | 36 12 | |
| | 129 × | -35 | | | 185 × | -35 | |
| 130 | 130 − | -45 | | | 186 RCLA | 36 11 | |
| | 131 RCLD | 36 14 | | | 187 ÷ | -24 | |
| | 132 ÷ | -24 | | | 188 1/X | 52 | |
| | 133 STOB | 35 12 | | | 189 PRTX | -14 | |
| | 134 RCL9 | 36 09 | | 190 | 190 STOD | 35 14 | |
| | 135 RCLC | 36 13 | | | 191 RCLA | 36 11 | |
| | 136 RCL8 | 36 08 | | | 192 RCLB | 36 12 | |
| | 137 × | -35 | | | 193 CHS | -22 | |
| | 138 − | -45 | | | 194 ÷ | -24 | |
| | 139 RCLB | 36 12 | | | 195 2 | 02 | |
| 140 | 140 RCL7 | 36 07 | | | 196 ÷ | -24 | |
| | 141 × | -35 | | | 197 PRTX | -14 | |
| | 142 − | -45 | | | 198 GSBC | 23 13 | |
| | 143 RCL0 | 36 00 | | | 199 PRTX | -14 | |
| | 144 ÷ | -24 | | 200 | 200 RTN | 24 | |
| | 145 STOA | 35 11 | | | 201 *LBLC | 21 13 | |
| | 146 RCL9 | 36 09 | | | 202 STOI | 35 46 | |
| | 147 × | -35 | | | 203 RCLB | 36 12 | |
| | 148 RCLB | 36 12 | | | 204 × | -35 | |
| | 149 RCL2 | 36 02 | | | 205 RCLA | 36 11 | |
| 150 | 150 × | -35 | | | 206 ÷ | -24 | |
| | 151 + | -55 | | | 207 1 | 01 | |
| | 152 RCLC | 36 13 | | | 208 + | -55 | |
| | 153 RCL3 | 36 03 | | | 209 RCL0 | 36 14 | |
| | 154 × | -35 | | 210 | 210 × | -35 | |
| | 155 + | -55 | | | 211 RCLB | 36 12 | |
| | 156 RCL9 | 36 09 | | | 212 × | -35 | |
| | 157 X² | 53 | | | 213 CHS | -22 | |
| | 158 RCL0 | 36 00 | | | 214 RCLI | 36 46 | |
| | 159 ÷ | -24 | | | 215 × | -35 | |
| 160 | 160 − | -45 | | | 216 RTN | 24 | |
| | 161 RCL6 | 36 06 | | | | | |
| | 162 RCL9 | 36 09 | | | | | |
| | 163 X² | 53 | | | | | |
| | 164 RCL0 | 36 00 | | 220 | | | |
| | 165 ÷ | -24 | | | | | |
| | 166 − | -45 | | | | | |
| | 167 ÷ | -24 | | | | | |
| | 168 PRTX | -14 | | | | | |

LABELS: A data entry; C f → catch; E → R², σ, b₁, b₂; a initialize; e r_m, q, etc.

FLAGS: 0 OFF, 1 OFF, 2 OFF, 3 OFF

SET STATUS: TRIG DEG; DISP FIX, n = 3

# Program Description

**Program Title:** Schnute's Yield Model
**Name:** Daniel Pauly
**Date:** August 1982
**Address:** ICLARM, MCC P.O. Box 1501, Makati, Metro Manila, Philippines

**Program Description, Equations, Variables, etc.** Schnute (1977) demonstrated that given a time series of catch (C)-and-effort (f) data, several fisheries related parameters can be estimated from the multiple regression

$$\ln\left(\frac{U_i}{U_{i-1}}\right) = r_m - q \cdot \left(\frac{f_i + f_{i-1}}{2}\right) - \frac{r_m}{q \cdot B_\infty} \cdot \left(\frac{U_i + U_{i-1}}{2}\right) \quad \ldots 1)$$

where $U$ is the mean catch per effort ($C/f$) in a given year ($i$). Once $r_m$, $q$ and the term $r_m/q \cdot B_\infty$ have been estimated (as intercept and slopes of the regression, respectively), the catch can be estimated for any level of effort (including $f_{opt}$) from

$$Y_i = q \cdot B_\infty f_i \left(1 - (q/r_m) f_i\right) \quad \ldots 2)$$

while $f_{opt}$ can be estimated from

$$f_{opt} = r_m / 2q \quad \ldots 3)$$

Schnute (1977) gives a number of other equations pertaining to this model; the original paper should be consulted for these.

**Operating Limits and Warnings** See Schnute (1977) for limitations of the model.

# User Instructions

CSIRKE AND CADDY'S MODEL    FB 28

| STEP | INSTRUCTIONS | INPUT DATA/UNITS | KEYS | | OUTPUT DATA/UNITS |
|---|---|---|---|---|---|
| 1 | Initialize | | f | a | 0.000 |
| 2 | Enter catch and Z data | C | f | | |
|   | (or catch and Z/K data) | Z | A | | $i$ |
| 3 | Estimate parameters of parabola | | E | | $R^2$ |
|   | | | | | $a$ |
|   | | | | | $b_1$ |
|   | | | | | $b_2$ |
| 4 | To estimate fishery-related parameters, do | | f | e | $M$ |
|   | | | | | $Z_{opt}$ |
|   | | | | | $F_{opt}$ |
|   | | | | | $r_m$ |
|   | | | | | MSY |
|   | | | | | $B_\infty$ |
| 5 | Obtain data for drawing parabola | $Z_i$ | B | | $Y_i$ |

NOTE:
When Z/K values were used instead of the Z values, the first three outputs ($M$, $Z_{opt}$, $F_{opt}$) are replaced by estimate of $M/K$, $Z_{opt}/K$ and $F_{opt}/K$ respectively; the three other parameters are not estimated.

## Program Listing (001 to 112)

| STEP | KEY ENTRY | KEY CODE | COMMENTS | STEP | KEY ENTRY | KEY CODE | COMMENTS |
|---|---|---|---|---|---|---|---|
| 001 | *LBLa | 21 16 11 | | 057 | x | -35 | |
| 002 | CLRG | 16-53 | | 058 | RCL7 | 36 07 | |
| 003 | CLX | -51 | | 059 | $x^2$ | 53 | |
| 004 | RTN | 24 | | 060 | - | -45 | |
| 005 | *LBLA | 21 11 | | 061 | STOD | 35 14 | |
| 006 | ENT↑ | -21 | | 062 | RCL0 | 36 00 | |
| 007 | $x^2$ | 53 | | 063 | RCL3 | 36 03 | |
| 008 | X≷Y | -41 | | 064 | x | -35 | |
| 009 | R↑ | 16-31 | | 065 | RCL8 | 36 08 | |
| 010 | R↑ | 16-31 | | 066 | RCL9 | 36 09 | |
| 011 | STOC | 35 13 | | 067 | x | -35 | |
| 012 | R↑ | 16-31 | | 068 | - | -45 | |
| 013 | STOB | 35 12 | | 069 | x | -35 | |
| 014 | R↑ | 16-31 | | 070 | STOC | 35 13 | |
| 015 | STOA | 35 11 | | 071 | RCL0 | 36 00 | |
| 016 | 7 | 07 | | 072 | RCL1 | 36 01 | |
| 017 | STOI | 35 46 | | 073 | x | -35 | |
| 018 | R↓ | -31 | | 074 | RCL7 | 36 07 | |
| 019 | GSB1 | 23 01 | | 075 | RCL8 | 36 08 | |
| 020 | 8 | 08 | | 076 | x | -35 | |
| 021 | STOI | 35 46 | | 077 | - | -45 | |
| 022 | RCLB | 36 12 | | 078 | STOA | 35 11 | |
| 023 | GSB1 | 23 01 | | 079 | RCL0 | 36 00 | |
| 024 | 9 | 09 | | 080 | RCL2 | 36 02 | |
| 025 | STOI | 35 46 | | 081 | x | -35 | |
| 026 | RCLC | 36 13 | | 082 | RCL7 | 36 07 | |
| 027 | GSB1 | 23 01 | | 083 | RCL9 | 36 09 | |
| 028 | RCLA | 36 11 | | 084 | x | -35 | |
| 029 | RCLB | 36 12 | | 085 | - | -45 | |
| 030 | x | -35 | | 086 | STOB | 35 12 | |
| 031 | ST+1 | 35-55 01 | | 087 | x | -35 | |
| 032 | RCLA | 36 11 | | 088 | RCLC | 36 13 | |
| 033 | RCLC | 36 13 | | 089 | X≷Y | -41 | |
| 034 | x | -35 | | 090 | - | -45 | |
| 035 | ST+2 | 35-55 02 | | 091 | RCLD | 36 14 | |
| 036 | RCLB | 36 12 | | 092 | RCL0 | 36 00 | |
| 037 | RCLC | 36 13 | | 093 | RCL5 | 36 05 | |
| 038 | x | -35 | | 094 | x | -35 | |
| 039 | ST+3 | 35-55 03 | | 095 | RCL8 | 36 08 | |
| 040 | 1 | 01 | | 096 | $x^2$ | 53 | |
| 041 | ST+0 | 35-55 00 | | 097 | - | -45 | |
| 042 | RCL0 | 36 00 | | 098 | x | -35 | |
| 043 | RTN | 24 | | 099 | RCLA | 36 11 | |
| 044 | *LBL1 | 21 01 | | 100 | $x^2$ | 53 | |
| 045 | ST+i | 35-55 45 | | 101 | - | -45 | |
| 046 | RCLI | 36 46 | | 102 | ÷ | -24 | |
| 047 | 3 | 03 | | 103 | STOC | 35 13 | |
| 048 | - | -45 | | 104 | RCL8 | 36 12 | |
| 049 | STOI | 35 46 | | 105 | RCLA | 36 11 | |
| 050 | R↓ | -31 | | 106 | RCLC | 36 13 | |
| 051 | $x^2$ | 53 | | 107 | x | -35 | |
| 052 | ST+i | 35-55 45 | | 108 | - | -45 | |
| 053 | RTN | 24 | | 109 | RCLD | 36 14 | |
| 054 | *LBLE | 21 15 | | 110 | ÷ | -24 | |
| 055 | RCL0 | 36 00 | | 111 | STOB | 35 12 | |
| 056 | RCL4 | 36 04 | | 112 | RCL9 | 36 09 | |

### REGISTERS

| 0 $n$ | 1 $\Sigma xy$ | 2 $\Sigma xz$ | 3 $\Sigma yz$ | 4 $\Sigma x^2$ | 5 $\Sigma y^2$ | 6 $\Sigma z^2$ | 7 $\Sigma x$ | 8 $\Sigma y$ | 9 $\Sigma z$ |
|---|---|---|---|---|---|---|---|---|---|
| S0 | S1 | S2 | S3 | S4 | S5 | S6 | S7 | S8 | S9 |

| A $a$ | B $b_1$ | C $b_2$ | D used | E used | I |
|---|---|---|---|---|---|

# Program Listing (113 to end)

| STEP | KEY ENTRY | KEY CODE | COMMENTS | STEP | KEY ENTRY | KEY CODE | COMMENTS |
|---|---|---|---|---|---|---|---|
| | 113 RCLC | 36 13 | | | 169 x | -35 | |
| | 114 RCL8 | 36 08 | | 170 | 170 ÷ | -24 | |
| | 115 x | -35 | | | 171 PRTX | -14 | |
| | 116 - | -45 | | | 172 RCLB | 36 12 | |
| | 117 RCLB | 36 12 | | | 173 CHS | -22 | |
| | 118 RCL7 | 36 07 | | | 174 RCLC | 36 13 | |
| | 119 x | -35 | | | 175 2 | 02 | |
| 120 | 120 - | -45 | | | 176 x | -35 | |
| | 121 RCL0 | 36 00 | | | 177 ÷ | -24 | |
| | 122 ÷ | -24 | | | 178 PRTX | -14 | |
| | 123 STOA | 35 11 | | | 179 X⇌Y | -41 | |
| | 124 RCL9 | 36 09 | | 180 | 180 - | -45 | |
| | 125 x | -35 | | | 181 PRTX | -14 | |
| | 126 RCLB | 36 12 | | | 182 2 | 02 | |
| | 127 RCL2 | 36 02 | | | 183 x | -35 | |
| | 128 x | -35 | | | 184 PRTX | -14 | |
| | 129 + | -55 | | | 185 RCLB | 36 12 | |
| 130 | 130 RCLC | 36 13 | | | 186 $x^2$ | 53 | |
| | 131 RCL3 | 36 03 | | | 187 RCLC | 36 13 | |
| | 132 x | -35 | | | 188 4 | 04 | |
| | 133 + | -55 | | | 189 x | -35 | |
| | 134 RCL9 | 36 09 | | 190 | 190 ÷ | -24 | |
| | 135 $x^2$ | 53 | | | 191 CHS | -22 | |
| | 136 RCL0 | 36 00 | | | 192 RCLA | 36 11 | |
| | 137 ÷ | -24 | | | 193 + | -55 | |
| | 138 - | -45 | | | 194 PRTX | -14 | |
| | 139 RCL6 | 36 06 | | | 195 4 | 04 | |
| 140 | 140 RCL9 | 36 09 | | | 196 x | -35 | |
| | 141 $x^2$ | 53 | | | 197 X⇌Y | -41 | |
| | 142 RCL0 | 36 00 | | | 198 ÷ | -24 | |
| | 143 ÷ | -24 | | | 199 PRTX | -14 | |
| | 144 - | -45 | | 200 | 200 RTN | 24 | |
| | 145 ÷ | -24 | | | 201 *LBLB | 21 12 | |
| | 146 PRTX | -14 | | | 202 ENT↑ | -21 | |
| | 147 RCLA | 36 11 | | | 203 $x^2$ | 53 | |
| | 148 PRTX | -14 | | | 204 RCLC | 36 13 | |
| | 149 RCLB | 36 12 | | | 205 x | -35 | |
| 150 | 150 PRTX | -14 | | | 206 X⇌Y | -41 | |
| | 151 RCLC | 36 13 | | | 207 RCLB | 36 12 | |
| | 152 PRTX | -14 | | | 208 x | -35 | |
| | 153 RTN | 24 | | | 209 + | -55 | |
| | 154 *LBLe | 21 16 15 | | 210 | 210 RCLA | 36 11 | |
| | 155 RCLB | 36 12 | | | 211 + | -55 | |
| | 156 $x^2$ | 53 | | | 212 RTN | 24 | |
| | 157 RCLA | 36 11 | | | | | |
| | 158 RCLC | 36 13 | | | | | |
| | 159 x | -35 | | | | | |
| 160 | 160 4 | 04 | | | | | |
| | 161 x | -35 | | | | | |
| | 162 - | -45 | | | | | |
| | 163 √X | 54 | | | | | |
| | 164 RCLB | 36 12 | | 220 | | | |
| | 165 CHS | -22 | | | | | |
| | 166 + | -55 | | | | | |
| | 167 RCLC | 36 13 | | | | | |
| | 168 2 | 02 | | | | | |

## LABELS

| A $c, z \rightarrow$ | B $z \rightarrow c$ | C | D | E $(a, b_1, b_2), R^2$ |
|---|---|---|---|---|
| a initialise | b | c | d | e $\rightarrow M, Z_{opt}, etc.$ |
| 0 | 1 | 2 | 3 | 4 |
| 5 | 6 | 7 | 8 | 9 |

## FLAGS

| 0 | 1 | 2 | 3 |

## SET STATUS

| FLAGS | | TRIG | DISP |
|---|---|---|---|
| | ON OFF | DEG ☒ | FIX ☒ |
| 0 | ☐ ☒ | GRAD ☐ | SCI ☐ |
| 1 | ☐ ☒ | RAD ☐ | ENG ☐ |
| 2 | ☐ ☒ | | n = 3 |
| 3 | ☐ ☒ | | |

# Program Description

**Program Title:** Csirke and Coddy's Model
**Name:** Daniel Pauly
**Address:** ICLARM, MCC P.O. Box 1501, Makati, Metro Manila, Philippines
**Date:** August 1981

**Program Description, Equations, Variables, etc.** This program fits catch data as a parabolic function of contemporary total mortality, or

$$Y = a + b_1 Z + b_2 Z^2 \quad \ldots 1)$$

where $Y$ is the annual catch from a given fishery and $Z$ the total mortality of the fish in that fishery.

Once $a$, $b$ and $c$ have been estimated, various parameters for the fish stock in question can be estimated, i.e.

$$M = \frac{-b_1 + \sqrt{b_1^2 - 4ab_2}}{2} \quad \ldots 2)$$

$$F_{opt} = -b_1 / 2b_2 \quad \ldots 3)$$

$$MSY = a - (b_1^2 / 4b_2) \quad \ldots 4)$$

$$B_\infty = \sqrt{-4b_2 \cdot MSY}$$

$$r_m = -B_\infty / b_2 \quad \ldots 5)$$

This model, which was proposed by Csirke and Caddy (1983) may at times generate completely erroneous parameter values (e.g. negative values of $M$). It should therefore be used in conjunction with other models, whenever possible.

The routine used to fit equation 1) is adapted from the HP 67/97 Stat. Pac (ST1-13A)

**Operating Limits and Warnings** The results given by this model should be used with caution in cases where the estimate of $M$ differ widely from expected values; also, the multiple correlation coefficient ($R$) should be significant. Consult original description of this model for further details.

# User Instructions

**LOGISTIC GROWTH CURVE** — FB 29

| STEP | INSTRUCTIONS | INPUT DATA/UNITS | KEYS | | OUTPUT DATA/UNITS |
|---|---|---|---|---|---|
| | LOGISTIC GROWTH CURVE | | | | |
| 1 | Initialize and enter $B_\infty$ | $B_\infty$ | f | a | 0.000 |
| 2 | Enter $B_t$, $t$ values | $B_t$ | ↑ | | |
| | | $t$ | A | | $i$ |
| 3 | Remove erroneous values by performing | $B_t$ | ↑ | | |
| | | $t$ | D | | $i-1$ |
| 4 | Calculate values of $r^2$, $r_m$ and $t_i$ | | E | | $r^2$ |
| | | | | | $r_m$ |
| | | | | | $t_i$ |
| 5 | Estimate value of $B_t$ given a value of $t$ | $t$ | C | | $\hat{B_t}$ |
| | EMPIRICAL EQUATION OF BLUEWEISS et al (1978) | | | | |
| 6 | Enter mean weight of adults, in grams | $\bar{W}$ | f | e | $\hat{r_m}$ |

NOTE:
When using this program to fit data from a trawl selection experiment, $B_\infty = 1$, $B_t$ = fraction retained, $t$ = class midpoint, and $t_1 = L_c$. See also operating limits and warnings.

# Program Listing

| STEP | KEY ENTRY | KEY CODE |
|---|---|---|
| 001 | *LBLa | 21 16 11 |
| 002 | CLRG | 16-53 |
| 003 | P⇄S | 16-51 |
| 004 | CLRG | 16-53 |
| 005 | STOB | 35 12 |
| 006 | CLX | -51 |
| 007 | RTN | 24 |
| 008 | *LBLA | 21 11 |
| 009 | STO0 | 35 00 |
| 010 | X⇄Y | -41 |
| 011 | RCLB | 36 12 |
| 012 | X⇄Y | -41 |
| 013 | ÷ | -24 |
| 014 | 1 | 01 |
| 015 | - | -45 |
| 016 | LN | 32 |
| 017 | RCLD | 36 00 |
| 018 | F2? | 16 23 02 |
| 019 | GTOb | 22 16 12 |
| 020 | Σ+ | 56 |
| 021 | RTN | 24 |
| 022 | *LBLb | 21 16 12 |
| 023 | Σ- | 16 56 |
| 024 | RTN | 24 |
| 025 | *LBLE | 21 15 |
| 026 | P⇄S | 16-51 |
| 027 | SPC | 16-11 |
| 028 | RCL8 | 36 08 |
| 029 | RCL4 | 36 04 |
| 030 | RCL6 | 36 06 |
| 031 | × | -35 |
| 032 | RCL9 | 36 09 |
| 033 | ÷ | -24 |
| 034 | - | -45 |
| 035 | ENT↑ | -21 |
| 036 | ENT↑ | -21 |
| 037 | RCL4 | 36 04 |
| 038 | X² | 53 |
| 039 | RCL9 | 36 09 |
| 040 | ÷ | -24 |
| 041 | RCL5 | 36 05 |
| 042 | X⇄Y | -41 |
| 043 | - | -45 |
| 044 | ÷ | -24 |
| 045 | STO3 | 35 03 |
| 046 | × | -35 |
| 047 | RCL6 | 36 06 |
| 048 | X² | 53 |
| 049 | RCL9 | 36 09 |
| 050 | ÷ | -24 |
| 051 | CHS | -22 |
| 052 | RCL7 | 36 07 |
| 053 | + | -55 |
| 054 | ÷ | -24 |
| 055 | PRTX | -14 |
| 056 | RCL6 | 36 06 |
| 057 | RCL4 | 36 04 |
| 058 | RCL3 | 36 03 |
| 059 | × | -35 |
| 060 | - | -45 |
| 061 | RCL9 | 36 09 |
| 062 | ÷ | -24 |
| 063 | STOA | 35 11 |
| 064 | RCL3 | 36 03 |
| 065 | CHS | -22 |
| 066 | PRTX | -14 |
| 067 | STOC | 35 13 |
| 068 | P⇄S | 16-51 |
| 069 | RCLA | 36 11 |
| 070 | X⇄Y | -41 |
| 071 | ÷ | -24 |
| 072 | PRTX | -14 |
| 073 | RTN | 24 |
| 074 | *LBLC | 21 13 |
| 075 | RCLC | 36 13 |
| 076 | × | -35 |
| 077 | CHS | -22 |
| 078 | RCLA | 36 11 |
| 079 | + | -55 |
| 080 | $e^x$ | 33 |
| 081 | 1 | 01 |
| 082 | + | -55 |
| 083 | RCLB | 36 12 |
| 084 | X⇄Y | -41 |
| 085 | ÷ | -24 |
| 086 | RTN | 24 |
| 087 | *LBLD | 21 14 |
| 088 | SF2 | 16 21 02 |
| 089 | GTOA | 22 11 |
| 090 | RTN | 24 |
| 091 | *LBLe | 21 16 15 |
| 092 | . | -62 |
| 093 | 2 | 02 |
| 094 | 6 | 06 |
| 095 | CHS | -22 |
| 096 | $y^x$ | 31 |
| 097 | 9 | 09 |
| 098 | . | -62 |
| 099 | 1 | 01 |
| 100 | 3 | 03 |
| 101 | × | -35 |
| 102 | RTN | 24 |

## LABELS

| A $B_t, t \to$ | B | C $\to \hat{B}_t$ | D correct. | E $\to r^2, r_m, t_i$ |
|---|---|---|---|---|
| a initialize | b used | c | d | e $\to \hat{r}_m$ |
| 0 | 1 | 2 | 3 | 4 |
| 5 | 6 | 7 | 8 | 9 |

## FLAGS

| 0 | 1 | 2 used | 3 |
|---|---|---|---|

## SET STATUS

| FLAGS | | TRIG | DISP |
|---|---|---|---|
| | ON OFF | DEG ☒ | FIX ☐ |
| 0 | ☐ ☐ | GRAD ☐ | SCI ☐ |
| 1 | ☐ ☐ | RAD ☐ | ENG ☐ |
| 2 | ☒ ☒ | | n= |
| 3 | ☐ ☐ | | |

## REGISTERS

| 0 | 1 | 2 | 3 | 4 | 5 | 6 | 7 | 8 | 9 |
|---|---|---|---|---|---|---|---|---|---|
| S0 | S1 | S2 | S3 used | S4 $\Sigma x$ | S5 $\Sigma x^2$ | S6 $\Sigma y$ | S7 $\Sigma y^2$ | S8 $\Sigma xy$ | S9 $i$ |
| A $a$ | B $B_\infty$ | C $r_m$ | D | E | I | | | | |

# Program Description

**Program Title** Logistic Growth Curve
**Name** Daniel Pauly
**Date** April 1981
**Address** ICLARM, MCC P.O. Box 1501
Makati, Metro Manila, Philippines

**Program Description, Equations, Variables, etc.** The logistic growth curve has the form

$$B_t = \frac{B_\infty}{1 + e^{-r_m(t-t_i)}} \quad \ldots 1)$$

when $B_\infty$ is the carrying capacity, $r_m$ is the intrinsic rate of increase, $t_i$ is a constant which adjusts the time scale to an origin such that $t - t_i = 0$ when $B_t = B_\infty / 2$, and $B_t$ is the biomass at time $t$ ($B_\infty$ and $B_t$ may be replaced by $N_\infty$ and $N_t$, respectively when equation (1) pertains to numbers).

When an estimate of $B_\infty$ can be obtained independently (such as by averaging $B_{max}$ values over a certain period of time), $r_m$ and $t_i$ can be estimated by rewriting expression 1) to

$$\ln\left(\frac{B_\infty}{B_t} - 1\right) = r_m t_i - r_m t \quad \ldots 2)$$

which has the form of a linear regression whose slope and intercept allow for the estimation of $r_m$ and $t_i$, respectively.

Blueweiss et al (1978) demonstrated that, over an extremely wide range of weights, $r_m$ in various organisms can be estimated from the empirical equation

$$r_m = 9.13 \bar{w}^{-0.26}$$

, where $\bar{w}$ is the mean body weight of the adults of the species in question, in gram.

**Operating Limits and Warnings** All values of $B_t$ must be < than the values of $B_\infty$ and > than 0. When using the logistic to fit trawl mesh selection data, care must be taken to use fractions retained that are always < 1, but > 0. Also, these fractions must be plotted against the class midpoints, not against the lower class limit.

# User Instructions

YIELDS FROM TWO INTERACTING SPECIES   FB 30

| STEP | INSTRUCTIONS | INPUT DATA/UNITS | KEYS | | OUTPUT DATA/UNITS |
|---|---|---|---|---|---|
| 1 | Enter constants | $a$ | STO | A | |
| | | $b$ | STO | B | |
| | | $d$ | STO | D | |
| | | $e$ | STO | E | |
| | | $c_1$ | STO | 2 | |
| | | $c_2$ | STO | 3 | |
| | | $F_Q$ | STO | 0 | |
| 2 | Calculate field from two interacting species | $F_Q$ | STO | 0 | |
| | | $F_P$ | A | | $Y_P$ |
| | | | | | $Y_Q$ |
| | | | | | $Y_T$ |
| 3 | Calculate $F_P$(opt), and $F_Q$(opt) and MSY: | | | | |
| | Enter starting value of $F_P$ | $F_P'$ | STO | 1 | |
| | Enter starting value of $F_Q$ | $F_Q'$ | STO | 0 | |
| | Enter $\Delta F$ and TOL* | $\Delta F$ | ↑ | | |
| | | TOL | f | 0 | $F_Q$(opt) |
| | | | | | $F_P$(opt) |
| | | | | | MSY |

NOTE:
* $\Delta F$ = initial step size
  TOL = tolerated error of estimates
  (e.g. 0.01)

## Program Listing (001 to 112)

| STEP | KEY ENTRY | KEY CODE | STEP | KEY ENTRY | KEY CODE |
|---|---|---|---|---|---|
| 001 | *LBLa | 21 16 11 | 057 | GSBE | 23 15 |
| 002 | ST09 | 35 09 | 058 | CHS | -22 |
| 003 | R↓ | -31 | 059 | PRTX | -14 |
| 004 | ST07 | 35 07 | 060 | R/S | 51 |
| 005 | *LBLc | 21 16 13 | 061 | *LBLE | 21 15 |
| 006 | 0 | 00 | 062 | RCLA | 36 11 |
| 007 | STOI | 35 46 | 063 | RCL1 | 36 01 |
| 008 | RCL7 | 36 07 | 064 | × | -35 |
| 009 | 2 | 02 | 065 | RCL1 | 36 01 |
| 010 | ÷ | -24 | 066 | $x^2$ | 53 |
| 011 | ST07 | 35 07 | 067 | RCLB | 36 12 |
| 012 | ABS | 16 31 | 068 | × | -35 |
| 013 | RCL9 | 36 09 | 069 | - | -45 |
| 014 | X>Y? | 16-34 | 070 | RCL2 | 36 02 |
| 015 | GTOb | 22 16 12 | 071 | RCL0 | 36 00 |
| 016 | *LBLD | 21 14 | 072 | × | -35 |
| 017 | 0 | 00 | 073 | RCL1 | 36 01 |
| 018 | ST05 | 35 05 | 074 | × | -35 |
| 019 | *LBLC | 21 13 | 075 | STOC | 35 13 |
| 020 | 1 | 01 | 076 | + | -55 |
| 021 | RCL5 | 36 05 | 077 | X<0? | 16-45 |
| 022 | + | -55 | 078 | SF2 | 16 21 02 |
| 023 | ST05 | 35 05 | 079 | ST04 | 35 04 |
| 024 | GSBE | 23 15 | 080 | RCLD | 36 14 |
| 025 | RCL6 | 36 06 | 081 | RCL0 | 36 00 |
| 026 | X≠Y | -41 | 082 | × | -35 |
| 027 | ST06 | 35 06 | 083 | RCL0 | 36 00 |
| 028 | X>Y? | 16-34 | 084 | $x^2$ | 53 |
| 029 | GTO0 | 22 00 | 085 | RCLE | 36 15 |
| 030 | RCL7 | 36 07 | 086 | × | -35 |
| 031 | ST+i | 35-55 45 | 087 | - | -45 |
| 032 | GTOC | 22 13 | 088 | RCL3 | 36 03 |
| 033 | *LBL0 | 21 00 | 089 | RCL0 | 36 00 |
| 034 | RCL5 | 36 05 | 090 | × | -35 |
| 035 | 3 | 03 | 091 | RCL1 | 36 01 |
| 036 | X≤Y? | 16-35 | 092 | × | -35 |
| 037 | GTOB | 22 12 | 093 | ST08 | 35 08 |
| 038 | RCL7 | 36 07 | 094 | + | -55 |
| 039 | CHS | -22 | 095 | X<0? | 16-45 |
| 040 | ST07 | 35 07 | 096 | SF1 | 16 21 01 |
| 041 | GTO0 | 22 14 | 097 | P≠S | 16-51 |
| 042 | *LBLB | 21 12 | 098 | STO0 | 35 00 |
| 043 | ISZI | 16 26 46 | 099 | P≠S | 16-51 |
| 044 | RCLI | 36 46 | 100 | F0? | 16 23 00 |
| 045 | 2 | 02 | 101 | RTN | 24 |
| 046 | X=Y? | 16-33 | 102 | RCL4 | 36 04 |
| 047 | GTOc | 22 16 13 | 103 | + | -55 |
| 048 | GTOD | 22 14 | 104 | CHS | -22 |
| 049 | *LBLb | 21 16 12 | 105 | RTN | 24 |
| 050 | RCLi | 36 45 | 106 | *LBLA | 21 11 |
| 051 | PRTX | -14 | 107 | SPC | 16-11 |
| 052 | ISZI | 16 26 46 | 108 | ST01 | 35 01 |
| 053 | 1 | 01 | 109 | CF1 | 16 22 01 |
| 054 | RCLI | 36 46 | 110 | SF0 | 16 21 00 |
| 055 | X≤Y? | 16-35 | 111 | GSBE | 23 15 |
| 056 | GTOb | 22 16 12 | 112 | CF0 | 16 22 00 |

### REGISTERS

| 0 $F_Q$ | 1 $F_P$ | 2 $c_1$ | 3 $c_2$ | 4 used | 5 used | 6 used | 7 used | 8 used | 9 TOL |
|---|---|---|---|---|---|---|---|---|---|
| S0 used | S1 | S2 | S3 | S4 | S5 | S6 | S7 | S8 | S9 |
| A a | B b | C used | D d | E e | I used | | | | |

## Program Listing (113 to end)

| STEP | KEY ENTRY | KEY CODE | COMMENTS |
|---|---|---|---|
| 113 | F2? | 16 23 02 | |
| 114 | GTO1 | 22 01 | |
| 115 | F1? | 16 23 01 | |
| 116 | GTO3 | 22 03 | |
| 117 | RCL4 | 36 04 | |
| 118 | X<0? | 16-45 | |
| 119 | CLX | -51 | |
| 120 | PRTX | -14 | |
| 121 | P⇄S | 16-51 | |
| 122 | RCL0 | 36 00 | |
| 123 | P⇄S | 16-51 | |
| 124 | X<0? | 16-45 | |
| 125 | CLX | -51 | |
| 126 | PRTX | -14 | |
| 127 | + | -55 | |
| 128 | PRTX | -14 | |
| 129 | RTN | 24 | |
| 130 | *LBL3 | 21 03 | |
| 131 | RCL4 | 36 04 | |
| 132 | RCLC | 36 13 | |
| 133 | - | -45 | |
| 134 | X<0? | 16-45 | |
| 135 | CLX | -51 | |
| 136 | PRTX | -14 | |
| 137 | 0 | 00 | |
| 138 | PRTX | -14 | |
| 139 | X⇄Y | -41 | |
| 140 | PRTX | -14 | |
| 141 | RTN | 24 | |
| 142 | *LBL1 | 21 01 | |
| 143 | F1? | 16 23 01 | |
| 144 | GTO2 | 22 02 | |
| 145 | CLX | -51 | |
| 146 | PRTX | -14 | |
| 147 | P⇄S | 16-51 | |
| 148 | RCL0 | 36 00 | |
| 149 | P⇄S | 16-51 | |
| 150 | RCL8 | 36 08 | |
| 151 | - | -45 | |
| 152 | X<0? | 16-45 | |
| 153 | CLX | -51 | |
| 154 | PRTX | -14 | |
| 155 | PRTX | -14 | |
| 156 | RTN | 24 | |
| 157 | *LBL2 | 21 02 | |
| 158 | CLX | -51 | |
| 159 | PRTX | -14 | |
| 160 | PRTX | -14 | |
| 161 | PRTX | -14 | |
| 162 | RTN | 24 | |

### LABELS

| A → Y'S | B used | C used | D used | E used |
|---|---|---|---|---|
| a → MSY | b used | c used | d | e |
| 0 used | 1 used | 2 used | 3 used | 4 |
| 5 | 6 | 7 | 8 | 9 |

### FLAGS
0
1
2
3

### SET STATUS

FLAGS ON/OFF: 0 ON/OFF, 1 ON/OFF, 2 ON/OFF, 3 □ □

TRIG: DEG ☒, GRAD □, RAD □

DISP: FIX ☒, SCI □, ENG □, n = 2

# Program Description

**Program Title:** Yields from Two Interacting Species
**Name:** Daniel Pauly
**Address:** ICLARM, MCC P.O. Box 1501, Makati, Metro Manila, Philippines
**Date:** April, 1981

**Program Description, Equations, Variables, etc.** Pope (1979) showed that, if single-species yield curves can be described by parabolas, the total yield ($Y_T$) of a system of two interacting species $P$ and $Q$ should, as long as the ratio $F_P : F_Q$ remains constant, also correspond to a parabola, i.e.

$$Y_T = \underbrace{aF_P - bF_P^2 + c_1 F_P F_Q} + \underbrace{dF_Q - eF_Q^2 + c_2 F_P F_Q} \quad \ldots 1)$$

$$Y_T = \quad Y_P \quad + \quad Y_Q \quad \ldots 2)$$

where $a$ & $b$, and $d$ & $e$ are constants of the yield curves of the two different species (e.g. predator and prey) and where $c_1$ and $c_2$ express the intensity of the interactions occurring between these species ($c_1$ and $c_2$ have opposite signs in cases of predator-prey interactions). Pope (1979) also generalized equation (1) to an n-species system and showed that the overall yield curve of such systems are parabolic, as long as the F-ratios remain constant and no species drops out of the system.

This program estimates values of $Y_P$, $Y_Q$ and $Y_T$ for any combination of $a$, $b$, $c_1$, $c_2$, $d$, $e$, $F_Q$ and $F_P$ values as well as the MSY and optimal values of $F_P$ and $F_Q$ of the 2 species system.

The iterative subroutines included in this program are adapted from program # 02851 D submitted by B.W. Clare to the HP 67/97 (U.S.) User's Library.

**Operating Limits and Warnings** There might be combinations of constants and of $F_P'$ and $F_Q'$ for which the MSY cannot be located by the algorithm provided here. Iteration time is quite long; don't be impatient.

When computing $Y_P$, $Y_Q$ and $Y_T$, the combination of the interaction terms is omitted if one of the species drop out of the system; "dropping out" occurs when a partial yield (including the interaction term is smaller than zero).

# Appendix III. Use of Calculators Other Than HP 67/97

In this Appendix, a brief discussion is presented of the suitability of the models included in Chapters 1 to 12, and of the Programs FB 1 to FB 30 for implementation with calculators other than the HP 67/97, specifically the HP 65, HP 41C and HP 41CV of the Hewlett-Packard Company, TI-58 and TI-59 of Texas Instruments, Inc. and miscellaneous other scientific calculators.

## HP 65

Wholesale conversion of the programs in Appendix II for use on a HP 65 is possible only in the case of rather short programs (e.g., FB 14), using about half or less of the memory available on the HP 67/97. In some other cases, the sequential approach discussed under "miscellaneous calculators" may be applied (see below).

## HP 41C AND HP 41CV

Programs FB 1 to FB 30 have been found to run on an HP 41C without modifications in most cases; all tests were performed using pre-programmed HP 67/97 program cards and an HP 82104A Card Reader. When such a card reader and/or pre-programmed cards are not available, conversion of the programs in Appendix II can be performed using the selection of translated keystrokes in Appendix Table III.1.

Experienced users of HP 41C/41CV may also wish to use the large amount of memory available in these calculators to improve on the programs presented here, some of which had to be condensed (and thus rendered less user friendly) to fit into the limited memory space of the HP 67/97.

## TI-58

This model uses an "Algebraic Operating System" (AOS) as does the more advanced TI-59, which is radically different from the "Reverse Polish Notation" (RPN) implemented on HP calculators. The difference between AOS and RPN renders direct translation of HP programs into TI "language" particularly difficult. For this reason, a short program is presented in Appendix Fig. III.1, which, according to its author (Hoyer 1983) allows the running of programs written in RPN on TI-58 (and TI-59). The following paragraphs are a translation (from German) of the comments published along with this program.

"This program simulates on TI-58/59 the RPN as used on HP calculators. The necessary functions which operate the stack are defined by the keys A to E, as follows:

- A = Enter
- B = Clear stack
- C = Roll up (↑)
- D = Roll down (↓)
- E = Last X

Addition, subtraction, multiplication and division are performed via SBR+, SBR−, SBRX and SBR÷, respectively. The use of the TI's T-register to simulate the HP's Y-register makes it possible to use tests such as X=Y?, X > Y?, etc. This allows for even large RPN programs to be used with TI calculators after only small modifications".

## TI-59

Users of the more sophisticated TI-59 have, in addition to the possibility of using the program in Appendix Fig. III.1 the option of using a "RPN-simulator", available as a "Solid State Module" from Texas Instruments, Inc., which, when plugged in a TI-59, translates RPN programs (from HP 65 and HP 67/97) into AOS-compatible keystroke sequences. The very comprehensive manual which comes with the "RPN Simulator", gives all necessary details on the conversion. The memory avail-

Appendix Table III.1. Guide for the conversion of HP 97 keystrokes to HP 41C/41CV functions (shortened from Anon. 1979a).[a]

| HP 97 | HP 41 | HP 97 | HP 41 | HP 97 | HP 41 |
|---|---|---|---|---|---|
| f CLF 0 | CF 00 | GTO fa | GTO 15 | f SF 0 | SF 00 |
| f CLF 1 | CF 01 | ... | ... | f SF 1 | SF 01 |
| f CLF 2 | CF 02 | GTO fe | GTO 19 | f SF 2 | SF 02 |
| f CLF 3 | CF 22 | LBL 0 | LBL 00 | f SF 3 | SF 22 |
| f CL REG | 7CLREG | ... | ... | $\Sigma +$ | $\Sigma$ REG 14, $\Sigma +$ |
| DSP 0 | 7DSP0 | LBL 9 | LBL 09 | f $\Sigma -$ | $\Sigma$ REG 14, $\Sigma -$ |
| DSP 1 | 7DSP1 | LBL A | LBL 10, LBL A | f $\sin^{-1}$ | $\sin^{-1}$ or ASIN |
| ... | ... | ... | ... | f SPACE | ADV |
| DSP 9 | 7DSP9 | LBL E | LBL 14, LBL E | $\sqrt{x}$ | $\sqrt{x}$ or SQRT |
| f F? 0 | FS? 00 | LBL fa | LBL 15, LBL a | STO + 0 | STO ÷ 00 or ST ÷ 00 |
| f F? 1 | FS? 01 | ... | ... | etc. for other stores and subtraction, multiplication |  |
| f F? 2 | FS?C 02 | LBL fe | LBL 19, LBL e | and division |  |
| f F? 3 | FS?C 22 | f LOG | LOG |  |  |
| F1X | 7FIX | f LAST X | LASTX | STO 0 | STO 00 |
| GSB 0 | XEQ 00 | f $\pi$ | $\pi$ or PI | ... | ... |
| ... | ... | f STACK | 7PRSTK | STO 9 | STO 09 |
| GSB 9 | XEQ 00 | PRINT X | 7PRTX | STO A | STO 20 |
| GSB A | XEQ 10 | f P≶S | 7 P≶S | STO E | STO 24 |
| ... | ... | R↓ | R↓ or RDN | STO 1 | STO 25 |
| GSB E | XEQ 14 | f R↑ | R↑ | f x ≠ 0? | X ≠ 0? |
| GSB fa | XEQ 15 | f RAD | RAD | ... | ... |
| ... | ... | RCL 0 | RCL 00 | f x ≤ y? | X ≤ Y? |
| GSB fe | XEQ 19 | ... | ... | f $\bar{x}$ | $\Sigma$ REG 14, MEAN |
| GTO 0 | GTO 00 | RCL 9 | RCL 09 | $x^2$ | $X \uparrow 2$ or $X^2$ |
| ... | ... | RCL A | RCL 20 | $y^x$ | $Y \uparrow X$ or $Y^X$ |
| GTO 9 | GTO 09 | ... | ... |  |  |
| GTO A | GTO 10 | RCL E | RCL 24 |  |  |
| ... | ... | RCL I | RCL 25 |  |  |
| GTO E | GTO 14 | f S | $\Sigma$ REG 14, SDEV |  |  |

[a] This guide omits functions and keystroke sequences that are identical between both types of calculators, function and keystroke sequences which differ only trivially among themselves (e.g., GTO 0, GTO 1, GTO 3, etc.) and functions and keystroke sequences not used in FB 1 to 30.

Appendix Fig. III.1. Program for implementing RPN on TI-58/59 calculators (from Hoyer 1983).

| | | | | | | | | |
|---|---|---|---|---|---|---|---|---|
| 000 | 76 | LBL | 029 | 76 | LBL | 058 | 76 | LBL |
| 001 | 11 | A | 030 | 14 | D | 059 | 55 | ÷ |
| 002 | 42 | STO | 031 | 48 | EXC | 060 | 55 | ÷ |
| 003 | 00 | 00 | 032 | 02 | 02 | 061 | 32 | X:T |
| 004 | 32 | X⇄T | 033 | 48 | EXC | 062 | 95 | = |
| 005 | 48 | EXC | 034 | 01 | 01 | 063 | 35 | 1/X |
| 006 | 01 | 01 | 035 | 32 | X⇄T | 064 | 32 | X≤T |
| 007 | 48 | EXC | 036 | 91 | R/S | 065 | 71 | SBR |
| 008 | 02 | 02 | 037 | 76 | LBL | 066 | 95 | = |
| 009 | 43 | RCL | 038 | 15 | E | 067 | 76 | LBL |
| 010 | 00 | 00 | 039 | 82 | HIR | 068 | 75 | — |
| 011 | 91 | R/S | 040 | 11 | 11 | 069 | 85 | + |
| 012 | 76 | LBL | 041 | 91 | R/S | 070 | 32 | X:T |
| 013 | 12 | B | 042 | 76 | LBL | 071 | 94 | +/− |
| 014 | 25 | CLR | 043 | 85 | + | 072 | 95 | = |
| 015 | 29 | CP | 044 | 85 | + | 073 | 94 | +/− |
| 016 | 42 | STO | 045 | 32 | X≤T | 074 | 32 | X≤T |
| 017 | 01 | 01 | 046 | 95 | = | 075 | 71 | SBR |
| 018 | 42 | STO | 047 | 32 | X⇄T | 076 | 95 | = |
| 019 | 02 | 02 | 048 | 71 | SBR | 077 | 76 | LBL |
| 020 | 91 | R/S | 049 | 95 | = | 078 | 95 | = |
| 021 | 76 | LBL | 050 | 76 | LBL | 079 | 43 | RCL |
| 022 | 13 | C | 051 | 65 | × | 080 | 02 | 02 |
| 023 | 32 | X⇄T | 052 | 65 | × | 081 | 48 | EXC |
| 024 | 48 | EXC | 053 | 32 | X≤T | 082 | 01 | 01 |
| 025 | 01 | 01 | 054 | 95 | = | 083 | 32 | X≤T |
| 026 | 48 | EXC | 055 | 32 | X≤T | 084 | 91 | R/S |
| 027 | 02 | 02 | 056 | 71 | SBR | | | |
| 028 | 91 | R/S | 057 | 95 | = | | | |

able on a TI-59 should, moreover, be sufficient for implementing translated versions of most of the programs in Appendix II.

## MISCELLANEOUS CALCULATORS

Various "scientific" calculators, notably by Sharp and Casio, are nowadays available on which the reader might consider implementing modified versions of (at least some of) the programs in Appendix II. Direct conversion of these programs will generally be impossible, however, both because of the limited memory which most of these calculators have, and because of the lack of branching and looping functions (GOTO, GOSUB, FLAGS, etc.).

However, a number of the programs in Appendix II have a structure as in Fig. III.2, which allows their sequential implementation even with simple calculators. Programs (FB 1 to 5, 11, 12, 14, 17, 24, 25, 26 and 29) are in principle amenable to sequential implementation, along with a number of other programs (FB 6, 9, 13, 15, 16, 19, 21 and 23) which have an even simpler structure in which no linear regression is involved. These programs solve what are often lengthy equations by straightforward sequential computations, which also could be performed using a very simple scientific calculator and by tabulating intermediate results.

The following books, a small selection from a large population and written for calculators of various types to supplement manufacturer's user's instructions should help in the conversion of the programs in Appendix II and more generally, in the efficient use of calculators: McCarthy (1976), Smith (1977), Ball (1978) Green and Lewis (1978), Alt (1979) and Jarett (1982).

Appendix Fig. III.2. Basic structure of several programs in Appendix II, showing how the computation involved can be also performed step by step using programmable calculators with limited memory space (see text).

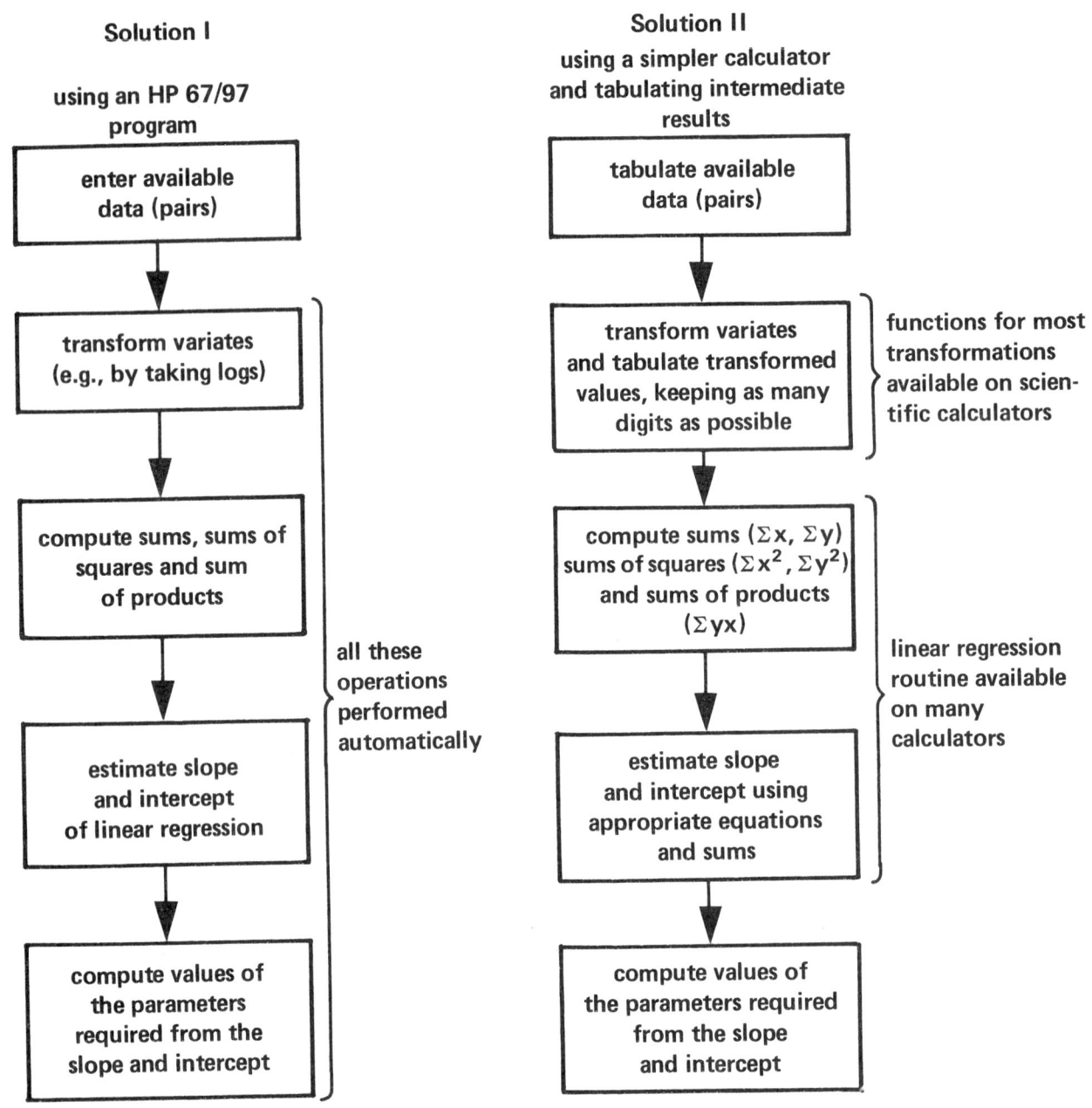

# List of Symbols and Their Definitions

The list of symbols given below corresponds as far as possible to the notation proposed by Holt et al. (1959), Holt (1960) and Ricker (1975). However, the need to accommodate numerous authors presenting different versions of the same basic models prevented the establishment of a rigorous, one-to-one correspondence between parameters, their symbols and their definitions.

The symbols are arranged alphabetically. Given are first the small, then the capital letters, then the corresponding Greek letters. Only the most common combination of symbol + subscript are given, because the possibility for permutation are too numerous.

The page number(s) in brackets refers to first usage, or most comprehensive definition (in some cases, equation, table or figure numbers are given instead of, or in addition to a text reference).

$a$
— intercept in an ordinary (AM) linear regression (p. 5)
— intercept in a multiple linear regression (p. 38)
— multiplicative term in a length/weight relationship (p. 5)
— exponent in equations (4.2a) and (4.3)
— area "swept" by a trawl per unit of effort (p. 92)
— parameter of a Ricker S/R curve ($a = \ln\alpha$) (p. 134)

$a'$
— intercept of a GM linear regression (p. 31)

$a_1, a_2$
— coefficient of intraspecific competition (Chapter 12)

$A$
— a statistic; see equations (1.2) and (1.3) (p. 178)
— fraction of fish dead after time t (equation 5.4)
— area inhabited by a stock; with the swept-area method, A is usually the total area included in the survey, or a given stratum thereof (p. 92)
— smaller mesh size in a gill net selection experiment (p. 13)

AM
— arithmetic mean; used to characterize "type I" or "predictive" regressions (p. 31)

AOS
— Algebraic Operating System, used in TI calculators (p. 305)

$\alpha$
— parameter of the "asymptotic yield" model (p. 171)
— density *independent* term in Ricker's S/R curve (p. 132, 156)

$\alpha'$
— density *dependent* term in Beverton and Holt's S/R curve (p. 132, 156)

$b$
— exponent of a length-weight relationship (p. 5)
— slope of an ordinary (AM) linear regression (p. 5)
— a constant (p. 68)

$b'$
— slope of a GM regression (p. 31)

$b_i$
— partial regression coefficient, i.e., one of several slopes in a multiple linear regression (p. 38)

$B$
— biomass, or stock size in weight (p. 1)
— larger mesh size in a gillnet selection experiment (p. 13)

$B_{opt}$
— optimum biomass, i.e., biomass generating MSY (p. 77, 139, 143)

$B_v$
— virgin stock size (= Gulland's $B_o$) (p. 77, 138, 153)

$B_\infty$
— environmental carrying capacity for a given stock, in weight (p. 138)

$\beta$
— symbol of the incomplete beta function (p. 119)
— density *dependent* term in Ricker's S/R curve (p. 132, 156)

$\beta'$
— density *independent* term in Beverton and Holt's S/R curve (p. 132, 156)

$c$
— the fraction $L_c/L_\infty$ (p. 116)

$c_{a\,b}$
— index of ecological similarity (p. 170)

$c/f$
— catch per unit of effort (p. 92)

c.f.
— condition factor, i.e., a single number expressing a length-weight relationship when isometry is assumed (p. 5)

cm — centimeter
$c_1, c_2$ — multiplyers for estimating Z and its standard error (p. 53, Table 5.2)
— interaction terms in Lotka-Volterra's equations and variants thereof (Chapter 12)
C — catch, in numbers (p. 13)
— parameter of the seasonally oscillating version of the VBGF (p. 37, Fig. 4.12)
— multiplicative factor for debiasing recruitment estimates in Beverton and Holt's S/R relationship (p. 132)
$C_t$ — terminal catch, as used in VPA and cohort analysis (p. 100)
$C^2$ — parameter in Powell's equation for estimation of Z/K (p. 70)
$C(L_1, \infty)$ — catch in number, from the lower limit ($L_1$) of a given length class upward (equation 5.12)
C.V. — coefficient of variation, i.e., C.V. = $\overline{X}/s.d._{(x_i)}$ (p. 33, 36)

d — power of weight to which anabolism is proportional (p. 23, 24)
d.f. — degree of freedom, i.e., "real" number of cases available for testing a statistical hypothesis (p. 3)
$dl/dt$ — growth rate, in length, of an average fish in a stock (p. 37)
$dw/dt$ — growth rate, in weight, of an average fish in a stock (p. 23)
$dB/dt$ — growth rate of a fish population, in weight (p. 138)
$dN/dt$ — growth rate of a fish population, in numbers (p. 163)
$dY/df$ — increase of catch per unit of effort (p. 122)
D — gill "surface factor", a parameter of the generalized VBGF (p. 23, 24)
— a measure of the "sensitivity" of the output to changes in the inputs of a given model (p. 23, 24)
$\Delta$ — any difference; examples are:
$\Delta L$ — length increment, width of length class in grouped data (p. 79)
$\Delta t$ — time difference, e.g., the time needed by an average fish to grow from the lower to the upper limit of a length class (p. 62)
$\Delta L/\Delta t$ — a growth rate expressed as difference equation (p. 45)
$\Delta T$ — a temperature difference, e.g., the difference between warmest ($T_s$) and coldest ($T_w$) mean monthly temperature (p. 40)
$\Delta S$ — size increment, when referring either to length or weight (p. 233)

e — base of the natural (or Naperian) logarithms; e = 2.71828 (p. 12)
E — exploitation rate; E = F/Z (p. 76)
— subscript to express equilibrium, steady state conditions, or stable age population. Used explicitly in Chapter 10 only, however, equilibrium assumption implicit in many models presented in this book (see p. 69-70)
$E_{opt}$ — exploitation rate producing MSY (p. 76)
$E_t$ — terminal exploitation rate, as used in Jones' length cohort analysis (Table 7.7)

f — fishing effort
$f_{opt}$ — level of effort generating MSY (p. 140)
$f_{0.1}$ — level of effort at which dY/df is 1/10 of its value when f is close to zero (p. 172-173)
F — instantaneous rate of fishing mortality (p. 52)
— symbol of the F-distribution (p. 212)
FL — Fork length; length of a fish when measured up to the central rays of the caudal fin (p. 31)
$F_{opt}$ — fishing mortality generating MSY (p. 76)
$F_t$ — terminal fishing mortality, as used in VPA and cohort analysis (p. 100)
$F_{0.1}$ — level of fishing mortality at which the marginal increase in yield per recruit reaches 1/10 of the marginal increase computed at a very low value of F (p. 120, 121)

$\phi$ — "pseudovalue" of an statistic; used with the jackknife (p. 178)

g — gram (p. 6)
— a coefficient of population decline; the opposite of $r_m$ (p. 163)
G* — biomass increase resulting from the growth of individual fishes; used in Russel's axiom (p. 1)
GM — geometric mean; used to characterize "type II", or "functional" regression (p. 31)

H — coefficient of anabolism, used in the derivation of the VBGF (p. 23)
HM — harmonic mean (p. 132)

| | |
|---|---|
| i | — symbol or subscript used for counting items; used here only in a few equations (particularly in Chapter 7) where the need for unambiguous definitions made its use necessary |
| I | — Roman numeral, equal to 1; used to express age (year) groups (Table 4.3) |
| k | — coefficient of catabolism (equation 4.1) |
| | — proportion of fish above age $t_k$ in a stock of fish (p. 121, 122) |
| kn | — knots = 1.852 km/h (p. 97) |
| K | — "stress factor", a parameter of the VBGF (p. 23) |
| ln | — $\log_e$, logarithm of base e (p. 13) |
| log | — $\log_{10}$, logarithm of base 10 (p. 5) |
| L | — "length" of a fish, shrimp, etc. (length itself is defined differently, depending on what is measured, see TL, SL, FL, etc.) (p. 5) |
| L′ | — a length not smaller than the smallest length of fish fully represented in catch samples; used to compute $\overline{L}$ (p. 55) |
| $\overline{L}$ | — mean length of fish, computed from L′ upward (p. 55) |
| | — mean of two lengths, e.g., mean of length at tagging ($L_1$) and at recapture ($L_2$) (p. 33, Table 4.6) |
| $\overline{\overline{L}}$ | — overall mean length of fish in catch samples (equation 5.10) |
| $L_c$ | — mean length of fish at first capture; equivalent to $L_{50}$ of other authors (Fig. 3.1) |
| $L_i$ | — length at the inflexion point of the generalized VBGF, when $D \neq 1$ (Table 4.8) |
| $L_{max}$ | — maximum length reached by the fish of a given stock (p. 29) |
| $L_{max.\ ever}$ | — largest size ever recorded from a given fish species (p. 29) |
| $L_{min}$ | — smallest length represented in one, or several samples (p. 10) |
| $L_n$ | — lower limit of highest length class considered in computing $L_c$ from trawl selection experiment data (equation 3.1) |
| $L_{opt}$ | — mean length above L′ in a stock maintained at MSY (p. 146) |
| $L_r$ | — mean length at first recruitment (p. 68, 114) |
| $L_t$ | — mean length at age t (p. 23) |
| $L_\infty$ | — asymptotic length, i.e., the mean length the fish of a given stock would reach if they were to grow forever (p. 23) |
| $L_{(\infty)}$ | — preliminary estimate of $L_\infty$, obtained, e.g., through equation (4.16) (see p. 29) |
| m | — number of fish marked (or tagged) for a Petersen population estimate (p. 91) |
| $m_1, m_2$ | — proportionality constants in the Lotka-Volterra equation (p. 163) |
| M | — instantaneous rate of natural mortality, i.e., of mortality due to all causes except fishing (p. 52) |
| M* | — biomass of fish dying of all causes other than fishing in Russel's axiom (p. 1) |
| MSY | — Maximum Sustainable Yield (p. 139) |
| n | — number of items in a sample, number of cases investigated, etc. (p. 6) |
| | — counter for items; similar in use to "i" (equation 3.1) |
| | — number of marked fish recovered in a Petersen population estimate (p. 91) |
| N | — size, in numbers, of a population (p. 91) |
| | — number of fish in a given size class of a catch sample (p. 60) |
| No | — abbreviation for number (p. 10) |
| $N_o$ | — initial number of fish in a cohort (p. 52) or a population (p. 94) |
| | — total number of fish tagged and released in an experiment (p. 74) |
| $N_r$ | — number of recoveries per time interval in a tagging experiment (p. 74) |
| $N_T$ | — number of fish at the end of a generation started with an initial number $N_o$ (p. 155) |
| $N_\infty$ | — environmental carrying capacity for a given stock, in numbers; corresponds to $B_\infty$ (see under this symbol) and to the parameter "K" in the ecological literature (p. 152) |
| p | — multiplicative factor in equation (4.2a) |
| $p_{ij}$ | — percentage in gut of species i of food item j (p. 170) |
| P | — constant in equations (8.10) and (8.11) |
| | — probability of capture (p. 12) |
| | — production (p. 53) |
| | — parents, or parental egg production in S/R relationships (p. 129) |
| $P_m$ | — parental stock producing maximum recruitment in a Ricker curve (p. 133) |
| $P_r$ | — replacement abundance of parental stock in a Ricker curve (p. 133) |

311

| | |
|---|---|
| $P_v$ | — parental abundance in the virgin (= unexploited) stock (p. 133) |
| $\bar{P}_y$ | — a predicted value of MSY, obtained for a developing fishery before catch-and-effort data become available (p. 77, 153) |
| $P_1$ | — first point, in a length-converted catch curve, that is included in the computation of Z; this point is by definition the first where, by definition, the probability of capture is 1 (Fig. 5.5) |
| P/B ratio | — production/biomass ratio, or "turnover rate" (total mortality) (p. 53) |
| $\pi$ | — pi = 3.1415 (p. 38) |
| q | — multiplicative factor in equation (4.2b) |
| | — catchability coefficient; q = F/f (equation 5.38) |
| Q | — constant used in equations (8.10) and (8.11) |
| | — weight of prey consumed by predators; (approximately equivalent to M* in p. 1) (p. 170) |
| r | — correlation coefficient (p. 6, 31) |
| $r^2$ | — coefficient of determination (p. 6) |
| r' | — coded number of a time interval in a tagging experiment (p. 74) |
| $r_m$ | — a constant of the logistic curve, interpreted as the intrinsic rate of natural increase when the curve describes the growth of a population (Chapters 10 and 11) |
| $r_1, r_2, r_3$ | — multiplyers used in yield per recruit equations (p. 115) |
| R | — number of recruits, as used in S/R curves (Chapter 9) |
| $R_c$ | — number of fish actually "recruiting" into the size groups available for capture (p. 114) |
| $R_m$ | — maximum recruitment predicted by a Ricker curve (p. 133) |
| $R_r$ | — number of fish recruiting to the fishing ground (p. 114) |
| R* | — weight added by recruitment in Russel's axiom (p. 1) |
| $R^2$ | — multiple coefficient of determination (Table 4.1, p. 38) |
| RPN | — Reverse Polish Notation, used in HP calculators (p. 305) |
| s.d. | — standard deviation of variates (p. 3) |
| s.e. | — standard error of a statistic (p. 3) |
| S | — fraction of fish surviving after time t (equation 5.3) |
| | — size, when referring to length or weight (p. 233) |
| $\Sigma$ | — summation sign (equation 3.1) |
| $\Sigma_t$ | — cumulative catch up to time t (p. 94) |
| t | — a given time (p. 33) |
| | — short for "t-statistic" (p. 3) |
| | — absolute age of a fish, e.g., as estimated from daily otolith rings (p. 26-28) |
| t' | — relative age of a fish (p. 26-28) often defined as $t' = t - t_o$ (p. 60-61) or $t' = (t - t_o) \cdot K$ (equation 5.14) |
| $t_c$ | — mean age at first capture (p. 114) |
| $t_i$ | — inflexion point of logistic curve (p. 152) |
| $t_m$ | — mean length at first maturity (p. 122, 156) |
| $t_{max}$ | — longevity (in the wild) (p. 42, 75) |
| $t_o$ | — the "age" fish would have had at length zero if they had always grown according to the VBGF; $t_o$ generally has a negative value, but does not express "prenatal growth" (p. 24) |
| $t_r$ | — mean age at recruitment (p. 114) |
| $t_s$ | — parameter of the seasonally oscillating version of the VBGF (p. 37, equation 4.49) |
| T | — total number of fish captured (marked and unmarked) in a Petersen population estimate (p. 91) |
| $\bar{T}$ | — mean annual water temperature, in °C (p. 75, 76) |
| TL | — "total" length; the length of a fish, measured with the lobes of the caudal fin bent until they are parallel to the body (p. 6) |
| TOL | — tolerated error, used in programs that approach a solution iteratively (p. 221) |
| $T_s$ | — highest mean monthly temperature (p. 40) |
| $T_w$ | — lowest mean monthly temperature (p. 40) |
| U | — mean catch per effort in a given year; more or less equivalent to $\bar{c}/f$ (p. 142) |
| $U_\infty$ | — mean catch per effort in a stock that has reached the carrying capacity of its environment (p. 146) |
| U% | — percent change of an input in sensitivity analysis (p. 177, Table I.1) |

| | |
|---|---|
| V | — Roman numeral (equal to 5) and used to express age (year) group (Table 4.3) |
| | — speed (i.e., velocity) over ground of a trawler—when trawling (p. 93) |
| VBGF | — abbreviation for Von Bertalanffy Growth Formula (p. 23) |
| W | — weight of a fish (live weight if not explicitly stated otherwise) (p. 5) |
| W' | — a weight not smaller than the smallest weight fully represented in catch samples (Fig. 5.12) |
| $\overline{W}$ | — mean weight of fish in catch samples, computed from W' upward (Fig. 5.12) |
| | — mean weight of fish within a given length class (p. 111) |
| | — mean adult weight of fish and other organisms, as used in equations (11.4), (11.5) and Fig. 11.2 (p. 154) |
| $\overline{\overline{W}}$ | — overall mean weight of fish in catch samples (equations 5.8 and 5.11) |
| $W_i$ | — weight at inflexion point of VBGF (Table 4.8) |
| $W_{max}$ | — maximum weight reached by the fish of a given stock (p. 29) |
| $W_{max.\ ever}$ | — largest size ever recorded from a given fish species (p. 29) |
| $W_t$ | — mean weight of fish at age t (p. 25) |
| $W_\infty$ | — asymptotic weight, i.e., the mean weight the fish of a given stock would reach if they were to grow forever (p. 25) |
| $W_{(\infty)}$ | — preliminary estimate of $W_\infty$, obtained e.g., through equation (4.17) (see p. 29) |
| x | — any variable (often used for the abscissa in 2-dimensional plots) (p. 6) |
| $\overline{x}$ | — the mean of a series of variates (Table 3.2, p. 31) |
| X | — Roman numeral, equal to 10, used to express age (year) group of fish (Fig. 5.4) |
| | — a constant in equations (8.10) and (8.11) |
| | — "perturbed" output in sensitivity analysis (p. 177) |
| $X^o$ | — "unperturbed" output in sensitivity analysis (p. 177) |
| $X_1$ | — proportion of fish in the path of a trawl net that is actually retained by it (p. 92) |
| $X_2$ | — width of a trawl net when operating, expressed as a fraction of its headrope length (p. 93) |
| y | — any variable (often used for the ordinate in 2-dimensional plots (p. 6) |
| $\overline{y}$ | — the mean of a series of variates (p. 31) |
| Y | — catch in weight (equation 1.1, p. 93) |
| $Y_{0.1}$ | — yield corresponding to $f_{0.1}$ (p. 173) |
| $Y_\infty$ | — "asymptotic" yield, i.e., maximum catch in a flat topped yield model (p. 171) |
| Y/R | — yield per recruit (p. 114) |
| Y'/R | — relative yield per recruit (p. 116) |
| Z | — instantaneous rate of total mortality (p. 52) |
| $Z_{opt}$ | — total mortality generating MSY (p. 145) |

# References

Agger, P., I. Boëtius and H. Lassen. 1971. On errors in the Virtual Population Analysis. I.C.E.S. C.M. 1971/H:16. 10 p. (Mimeo).*

Agger, P., I. Boëtius and H. Lassen. 1973. Error in the virtual population analysis: the effects of uncertainties in the natural mortality coefficient. J. Cons., Cons. Int. Explor. Mer 35(1): 93.

Allen, K.R. 1966. Determination of age distribution from age-length keys and length distributions, IBM 7090, 7094, FORTRAN IV. Trans. Am. Fish. Soc. 95: 230-231.

Allen, K.R. 1971. Relation between production and biomass. J. Fish. Res. Board Can. 28: 1573-1581.

Alt, H. 1979. Angewandte Mathematik, Finanzmathematik, Statistik, Informatik fuer UPN Rechner. Vieweg & Sohn. Braunschweig/Wiesbaden, Fed. Rep. of Germany.

Andersen, K.P. and E. Ursin. 1977. A multispecies extension to the Beverton and Holt theory of fishing, with accounts of phosphorus circulation and primary production. Medd. Danm. Fisk. Havunders. (N.S.) 7: 319-435.

Anon. 1978a. Report of the *ad hoc* working group on sardine (*Sardina pilchardus* Waldb.). CECAF/ECAF Ser./78/7. 35 p. FAO, Rome.

Anon. 1978b. Report of the *ad hoc* working group on hake (*Merluccius merluccius*, *M. senegalensis*, *M. cadenati*) in the Northern zone of CECAF. CECAF/ECAF Ser./78/9. 93 p. FAO, Rome.

Anon. 1979a. HP 82104A card reader owner's handbook. Hewlett-Packard Company, Corvallis, Oregon.

Anon. 1979b. Report of the *ad hoc* working group on West African coastal pelagic fish from Mauritania to Liberia (26°N to 5°N). CECAF/ECAF Ser./78/10. 161 p. FAO, Rome.

Anon. 1982. Comparative study of three methods for total mortality estimation, p. 91-125. *In* Report of the second technical consultation on stock assessment in the Balearic and Gulf of Lions statistical divisions, Casablanca, Morocco, 7-11 December 1981. FAO Fish. Tech. Rep. 263. 165 p.

Bagenal, T.B., editor. 1974. Ageing of fish. Unwin Bros. Ltd., Old Woking, Surrey, England.

Bailey, N.T.J. 1951. On estimating the size of mobile populations from recapture data. Biometrika 38: 293-306.

Bailey, N.T.J. 1952. Improvements in the interpretation of recapture data. J. Anim. Ecol. 21(1): 120-127.

Bakun, A. and R.H. Parrish. 1980. Environmental inputs to fishery population models for eastern boundary current regions, p. 67-104. *In* G. Sharp (Rapporteur) Workshop on the effects of environmental variation on the survival of larval pelagic fishes. Intergovernmental Oceanographic Commission Workshop Report No. 28, 323 p.

Bakun, A., J. Beyer, D. Pauly, J.G. Pope and G.D. Sharp. 1982. Ocean science in relation to living resources. Can. J. Fish. Aquat. Sci. 39: 1059-1070.

Ball, J.A. 1978. Algorithms for RPN calculators. John Wiley and Sons, New York.

Balon, E.K. 1974. Fishes of Lake Kariba, Africa. TFH Publications, Neptune City, New Jersey.

Banerji, S.K. and T.S. Krishnan. 1973. Acceleration of assessment of fish populations and comparative studies of similar taxonomic groups, p. 158-175. *In* Proceedings of the Symposium on Living Resources of the Seas Around India, Spec. Publ., Cent. Mar. Fish. Res. Inst., Cochin, India.

Baranov, F.I. 1914. The capture of fish by gillnets. Mater. Poznaniyu Russ. Rybolovsta. 3(6): 56-99. (In Russian).

Baranov, F.I. 1918. On the question of the biological basis of fisheries. Nauchn. Issled. Ikhtiologicheskii Inst. Izv. 1: 81-128. (In Russian).

Baranov, F.I. 1927. More about the poor catch of vobla. Byull. Rybn. Khoz. 7(7). (In Russian).

Baranov, F.I. 1976. Selected works on fishing gear. Vol. I: Commercial fishing techniques. Israel Program for Scientific Translations, Jerusalem.

Bayliff, W.H. 1967. Growth, mortality, and exploitation of the Engraulidae, with special reference to the anchoveta, *Cetengraulis mysticetus*, and the colorado, *Anchoa naso*, in the eastern Pacific Ocean. Inter-Am. Trop. Tuna Comm., Bull. 12(5): 365-432.

Beamish, R.J. and McFarlane. 1983. The forgotten requirement for age validation in fisheries biology. Trans. Am. Fish. Soc. 112: 735-743.

Beddington, J.R. and J.G. Cooke. 1983. The potential yield of fish stocks. FAO Fish. Tech. Pap. (242), 47 p.

Ben-Yami, M. and T. Glaser. 1974. The invasion of *Saurida undosquamis* (Richardson) into the Levant Basin—an example of biological effects of inter-oceanic canals. Fish. Bull. (U.S.) 72(2): 359-373.

Berkeley, S.A. and E.D. Houde. 1978. Biology of two exploited species of halfbeaks, *Hemirhamphus brasiliensis* and *H. balao* from Southeast Florida. Bull. Mar. Sci. 28: 624-644.

Berkeley, S.A. and E.D. Houde. 1980. Swordfish, *Xiphias gladius*, dynamics in the straits of Florida. I.C.E.S. C.M. 1980/H:59. 11 p. (Mimeo).

Berry, R.J. 1970. Shrimp mortality rates derived from fishery statistics. Proc. Gulf Caribb. Fish. Inst. 22: 66-78.

---

*Photocopies of this and of the other I.C.E.S. Council Meetings papers cited here can be obtained by writing to the I.C.E.S. Secretariat, Palaegade 2, DK-1261 Copenhagen, Denmark.

Bertalanffy, L. von. 1934. Untersuchungen über die Gesetzlichkeiten des Wachstums I. Roux'. Arch. Entwicklungsmech. 131: 613-652.

Bertalanffy, L. von. 1938. A quantitative theory of organic growth (Inquiries on growth laws. II) Hum. Biol. 10(2): 181-213.

Bertalanffy, L. von. 1951. Theoretische Biologie. Zweiter Band: Stoffwechsel, Wachstum. A. Franke A.G. Verlag, Bern.

Beverton, R.J.H. 1962. Long-term dynamics of certain North Sea fish populations, p. 242-259. In E.D. Le Cren and M.W. Holdgate (eds.) The exploitation of natural animal populations. Blackwell Scientific Publications, Oxford.

Beverton, R.J.H. 1963. Maturation, growth and mortality of clupeid and engraulid stocks in relation to fishing. Rapp. P.-V. Réun. Cons. Int. Explor. Mer 154: 44-67.

Beverton, R.J.H. and S.J. Holt. 1956. A review of methods for estimating mortality rates in fish populations, with special references to sources of bias in catch sampling. Rapp. P.-V. Réun. Cons. Int. Explor. Mer 140: 67-83.

Beverton, R.J.H. and S.J. Holt. 1957. On the dynamics of exploited fish populations. Fish. Invest. Ser. II Vol. 19, 533 p.

Beverton, R.J.H. and S.J. Holt. 1959. A review of the life-spans and mortality rates of fish in nature and their relation to growth and other physiological characteristics. Ciba Found. Colloq. on Ageing 5: 142-180.

Beverton, R.J.H. and S.J. Holt. 1964. Table of yield functions for fishery management. FAO Fish. Tech. Pap. 38. 49 p.

Beverton, R.J.H. and S.J. Holt. 1966. Manual of methods for fish stock assessment. Part 2. Tables of yield functions. FAO Fish. Tech. Pap. 38. Rev. 1: 67.

Blueweiss, L., H. Fox, V. Kudzma, D. Nakashima, R. Peters and S. Sams. 1978. Relationships between body size and some life-history parameters. Oecologia (Berlin) 37: 257-272.

Boje, R. and M. Tomczak, editors. 1978. Upwelling ecosystems. Springer Verlag, Berlin.

Boonyubol, M. and V. Hongskul. 1978. Demersal resources and exploitation in the Gulf of Thailand, 1960-1975, p. 56-70. In Report of the Workshop on the Demersal Resources of the Sunda Shelf, 31 October-6 November 1977, Penang, Malaysia. Part II. SCS/GEN/77/13. 120 p. South China Sea Fisheries Development and Coordinating Programme, Manila.

Brandt, A. von. 1972. Fish catching methods of the world. Fishing News Books, Ltd., Surrey, England.

Brothers, E.B. 1980. Age and growth studies on tropical fishes, p. 119-136. In S.B. Saila and P. Roedel (eds.) Stock assessment for tropical small-scale fisheries. Proceedings of an international workshop held 19-21 September 1979 at the University of Rhode Island. Int. Cent. Mar. Resource Dev., University of Rhode Island, Kingston.

Buzeta, R.B., editor. 1978. Report of the Workshop on the Demersal Resources of the Sunda Shelf, 31 October-6 November 1977, Penang, Malaysia. Part I. SCS/GEN/77/12. 51 p. South China Sea Fisheries Development and Coordinating Programme, Manila.

Caddy, J.F. and J. Csirke. 1983. Approximations to sustainable yields for exploited and unexploited stocks. Océanogr. Trop. 18(1): 3-15.

Carlander, K. 1969. Handbook of freshwater fishery biology. Vol. I. Iowa State University Press, Ames.

Carlander, K. 1977. Handbook of freshwater fishery biology. Vol. II. Iowa State University Press, Ames.

Chapman, D.G. 1951. Some properties of the hypergeometric distribution with applications to zoological sample census. Univ. Calif. Publ. Stat. 1: 131-160.

Chapman, D.W. 1968. Production, p. 182-196. In W.E. Ricker (ed.) Methods for assessment of fish production in fresh water. IBP Handbook No. 3. Blackwell Scientific Publications, Oxford.

Chatterjee, S. and B. Price. 1977. Regression analysis by example. John Wiley and Sons, New York.

Clark, C.W. 1976. Mathematical bioeconomics: the optimal management of renewable resources. Wiley Interscience, New York.

Colwell, R.K. and D.G. Futuyama. 1971. On the measurement of niche breadth and overlap. Ecology 52: 567-576.

Csirke, J. 1980. Recruitment in the Peruvian anchovy and its dependence on the adult population, p. 307-313. In A. Saville (ed.) The assessment and management of pelagic fish stocks. Rapp. P.-V. Réun. Cons. Int. Explor. Mer 177.

Csirke, J. and J.F. Caddy. 1983. Production modelling using mortality estimates. Can. J. Fish. Aquat. Sci. 40: 43-51. (With errata in Can. J. Fish. Aquat. Sci. 40: 255-256).

Cushing, D.H. 1971. The dependence of recruitment on parent stock in different groups of fishes. J. Cons., Cons. Int. Explor. Mer 33: 340-362.

Cushing, D.H. 1978. Upper trophic levels in upwelling areas, p. 101-110. In R. Boje and M. Tomczak (eds.) Upwelling ecosystems. Springer Verlag, Berlin.

Cushing, D.H. 1981. Fisheries biology: a study in population dynamics. 2nd ed. University of Wisconsin Press, Madison, Wisconsin.

Cushing, D.H., editor. 1983. Key papers on fish populations. IRL Press, Oxford, England.

Daan, N. 1980. A review of replacement of depleted stocks by other species and the mechanisms underlying such replacements, p. 405-421. In A. Saville (ed.) The assessment and management of pelagic fish stocks. Rapp. P.-V. Réun. Cons. Int. Explor. Mer 177.

Dalzell, P. 1984. The population biology and management of bait-fish in Papua New Guinea waters. Dept. Primary Industry, Fish. Res. Surv. Branch Report 84-05, Port Moresby, Papua New Guinea. 59 p.

De Groot, S.J. 1973. Gaps in the studies on behaviour of Indian Ocean flatfishes belonging to the Psettodidae and Cynoglossidae. J. Mar. Biol. Assoc., India 15(1): 251-261.

Dickson, W. 1974. A review of the efficiency of bottom trawls. Institute of Fishery Technology Research, Bergen. 30 p. (Mimeo).

Draper, N. and H. Smith. 1966. Applied regression analysis. John Wiley and Sons, New York.

Dwiponggo, A. 1979. Review of the demersal resources and fisheries in the Java Sea. Marine Fisheries Research Institute, Agency for Agricultural Research and Development, Ministry of Agriculture, Jakarta, Indonesia. 36 p. (Mimeo).

Ebert, T.A. 1973. Estimating growth and mortality rates from size data. Oecologia (Berlin) 11: 281-298.

Eggers, D.M., N.A. Rickard, D.G. Chapman and R.R. Whitney. 1982. A methodology for estimating area fished for baited hooks and traps along a ground line. Can. J. Fish. Aquat. Sci. 39: 448-453.

Eberhardt, L.L. 1977. Relationship between two stock-recruitment curves. J. Fish. Res. Board Can. 34: 425-428.

FAO. 1978. Some scientific problems of multi-species fisheries. Report of the Expert Consultation on Management of Multi-species Fisheries. FAO Fish Tech. Pap. 181. 42 p.

Forbes, S.T. and O. Nakken. 1972. Manual of methods for fisheries resource survey and appraisal. Part 2. The use of acoustic instruments for fish detection and abundance estimation. FAO Man. Fish. Sci. 5. 138 p.

Ford, E. 1933. An account of the herring investigations conducted at Plymouth during the years from 1924-1933. J. Mar. Biol. Assoc. U.K. 19: 305-384.

Fox, W.W. 1970. An exponential yield model for optimizing exploited fish populations. Trans. Am. Fish. Soc. 99: 80-88.

Francis, C.R. 1974. Relationship of fishing mortality to natural mortality at the level of maximum sustainable yield under the logistic stock production model. J. Fish. Res. Board Can. 31: 1539-1542.

Fridrikson, A. 1934. On the calculation of age-distribution within a stock of cod by means of relatively few age determinations as a key to measurements on a large scale. Rapp. P.-V. Réun. Cons. Int. Explor. Mer 86: 1-14.

Fryer, G. and T.D. Iles. 1972. The cichlid fishes of Africa. Their biology and evolution. TFH Publications, Neptune City, New Jersey.

Garcia, S. 1983. The stock-recruitment relationships in shrimps: reality or artifacts and misinterpretations? Océanogr. Trop. 18(1): 25-48.

Garcia, S. and L. Le Reste. 1981. Life cycles, dynamics, exploitation and management of coastal penaeid shrimp stocks. FAO Fish. Tech. Pap. 203. 215 p.

Garrod, D.J. 1961. The selection characteristics of nylon gillnets for *Tilapia esculenta* Graham. J. Cons., Cons. Int. Explor. Mer 26(2): 191-203.

Gaschütz, G., D. Pauly and N. David. 1980. A versatile BASIC program for fitting weight and seasonally oscillating length growth data. I.C.E.S. C.M. 1980/D:6 Statistics Cttee. 23 p. (Mimeo)

Gause, G.F. 1934. The struggle for existence. Williams and Wilkins, Baltimore.

Godoy, M.P. 1959. Age, growth, sexual maturity, behavior, migration, tagging and transplantation of the curimbat (*Prochilodus scrofa* Steindachner, 1881) of the Magi Guassu River, Sao Paulo State, Brazil. An. Acad. Bras. Cienc. 31(3): 447-477.

Gomez, K.A. and A.A. Gomez. 1976. Statistical procedures for agricultural research. The International Rice Research Institute, Los Baños, Laguna, Philippines.

Graham, M. 1929. Studies of age determination in fish. Part II. A survey of the literature. U.K. Min. Agric. Fish. Invest. (Ser. 2) 11(3): 50 p.

Graham, M. 1935. Modern theory of exploiting a fishery and application to North Sea trawling. J. Cons., Cons. Int. Explor. Mer 10: 264-274.

Graham, M. 1943. The fish gate. Faber and Faber Ltd., London.

Green, D.R. and J. Lewis. 1979. Science with pocket calculators. Wykeram Publications Ltd., London.

Guilford, J.P. and B. Fruchter. 1978. Fundamental statistics in psychology and education. McGraw Hill, New York.

Gulland, J.A., editor. 1964. On the measurement of abundance of fish stocks. Rapp. P.-V. Réun. Cons. Int. Explor. Mer 155.

Gulland, J.A. 1965. Estimation of mortality rates. Annex to Rep. Arctic. Fish. Working Group, I.C.E.S. C.M. 1965 (3). 9 p.

Gulland, J.A. 1966. Manual of sampling and statistical methods for fisheries biology. Part I. Sampling methods. FAO Man. Fish. Sci. 3. pag. var.

Gulland, J.A. 1969. Manual of methods for fish stock assessment. Part I. Fish population analysis. FAO Man. Fish. Sci. 4. 154 p.

Gulland, J.A. 1971. The fish resources of the oceans. FAO/Fishing News Books, Ltd., Surrey, England.

Gulland, J.A. 1979. Report of the FAO/IOP workshop on the fishery resources of the Western Indian Ocean south of the equator, p. 1-37. In IOFC/DEV/79/45. FAO, Rome.

Gulland, J.A. 1983. Fish stock assessment. A manual of basic methods. John Wiley and Sons, New York.

Gulland, J.A. and L.K. Boerema. 1973. Scientific advice on catch levels. Fish. Bull. (U.S.) 71: 325-335.

Gulland, J.A. and D. Harding. 1961. The selection of *Clarias mossambicus* (Peters) by nylon gillnets. J. Cons., Cons. Int. Explor. Mer 26(2): 215-222.

Gulland, J.A. and S.J. Holt. 1959. Estimation of growth parameters for data at unequal time intervals. J. Cons. Cons. Int. Explor. Mer 25(1): 47-49.

Hamley, J.M. 1975. Review of gillnet selectivity. J. Fish. Res. Board Can. 32(11): 1943-1969.

Hashem, M.T. 1972. The age, growth and maturity of *Labeo niloticus* Forsk. from the Nozha Hydrodome in 1968-1970. Bull. Inst. Oceanogr. Fish. (Egypt) 2: 84-102.

Helgason, T. and H. Gislason. 1979. VPA-analysis with species interactions due to predation. I.C.E.S. C.M. 1979/ G: 52. (Mimeo).

Hempel, G. and D. Sarhage. 1959. Zur Berechnung des Anteils nicht angelandeter und untermassigen Fische im Gesamtfang. Arch. Fischereiwiss. 10: 58-67.

Henderson, F. 1982. The dynamics of mean-size statistic in a changing fishery. FAO Fish. Tech. Pap. 116. 16 p.

Hoenig, J.M. 1984. Empirical use of longevity data to estimate mortality rates. Fish. Bull. (US) 81(4). (In press).

Hoenig, J.M. and W.D. Lawing. 1982. Estimating the total mortality rate using the maximum-order statistic for age. I.C.E.S. C.M. 1982/D: 7. Statistics Cttee. 13 p. (Mimeo).

Hoenig, N.A. and R.H. Choudary. 1983. Statistical considerations in fitting seasonal growth model for fishes. I.C.E.S. C.M. 1983/D: 25. Statistics Cttee. 22 p. (Mimeo)

Hohendorf, K. 1966. Eine Diskussion der Bertalanffy Funktionen und ihre Anwendung zur Charakterisierung des Wachstums von Fischen. Kiel. Meeresforsch. 22: 70-97.

Holt, S.J. 1960. Multilingual vocabulary and notation for fishery dynamics. FAO, Rome.

Holt, S.J. 1963. A method for determining gear selectivity and its application. Spec. Publ. Int. Comm. Northwest Atl. Fish. Spec. Publ. 5: 106-115.

Holt, S.J., J.A. Gulland and C. Taylor. 1959. A standard teminology and notation for fishery dynamics. J. Cons., Cons. Int. Explor. Mer 24: 239-242.

Hongskul, V. 1974. Population dynamics of Pla-tu, *Rastrelliger neglectus* (van Kampen) in the Gulf of Thailand. Proc. Indo-Pac. Fish. Counc. 15(111): 297-342.

Hoyer, H.J. 1983. UPN fuer TI-58/59. Chip (Wuerzburg, Fed. Rep. of Germany) No. 3. p. 128.

International Game Fish Association. 1978. World record marine fishes. Fort Lauderdale, Florida.

Isarankura, A.P. 1971. Assessment of stocks of demersal fish off the west coast of Thailand and Malaysia. IOC/DEV/ 71/20. Indian Ocean Fish. Comm. FAO, Rome, 20 p.

Ita, E.O. 1980. Contribution to the dynamics of mean-size statistics in a changing fishery. I. Family Citharinidae in Kainji Lake, Nigeria. Hydrobiologia 68: 269-277.

Jarett, K. 1982. HP41 : Synthetic programming made easy. Synthetix, Manhattan Beach, California.

Johnson, L. 1981. The thermodynamic origin of ecosystems. Can. J. Fish. Aquat. Sci. 38: 571-590.

Jolly, G.M. 1965. Explicit estimates from capture-recapture data with both death and immigration—stochastic model. Biometrika 52: 225-247.

Jones, R. 1957. A much simplified version of the fish yield equation. Doc. No. P. 21. Paper presented at the Lisbon joint meeting of International Commission Northwest Atlantic Fisheries, International Council for the Exploration of the Sea, and Food and Agriculture Organization of the United Nations. 8 p. (Mimeo).

Jones, R. 1961. The assessment of long-term effects of changes in gear selectivity and fishing effort. Mar. Res. (Scot.) 2: 1-19.

Jones, R. 1974. Assessing the long-term effects of changes in fishing effort and mesh size from length composition data. I.C.E.S. C.M. 1974/F: 33. 13 p. (Mimeo).

Jones, R. 1976a. Growth of fishes, p. 251-279. *In* D.H. Cushing and J.J. Walsh (eds.) The ecology of the seas. Blackwell Scientific Publications, Oxford.

Jones, R. 1976b. Mesh regulation in the demersal fisheries of the South China Sea area. SCS/76/WP/35. 75 p. South China Sea Fisheries and Development Coordinating Programme, Manila.

Jones, R. 1977. Tagging: theoretical methods and practical difficulties, p. 46-66. *In* J.A. Gulland (ed.) Fish population dynamics. Wiley Interscience, New York.

Jones, R. 1979. An analysis of a *Nephrops* stock using length composition data. Rapp. P.-V. Réun. Cons. Int. Explor. Mer 175: 259-269.

Jones, R. 1981. The use of length composition data in fish stock assessment (with notes on VPA and Cohort Analysis) FAO Fish. Circ. 734. 55 p.

Jones, R. 1982. Ecosystems, food chains and fish yields, p. 195-239. *In* D. Pauly and G.I. Murphy (eds.) Theory and management of tropical fisheries. ICLARM Conference Proceedings 9, 360 p. International Center for Living Aquatic Resources Management, Manila, Philippines and Division of Fisheries Research, Commonwealth Scientific and Industrial Research Organisation, Cronulla, Australia.

Jones, R. and N.P. van Zalinge. 1981. Estimates of mortality rate and population size for shrimps in Kuwait waters. Kuwait Bull. Mar. Sci. 2: 273-288.

Kato, F. and Y. Yamada. 1975. Estimation of abundance and related parameters of the age I red sea bream, *Pagrus major*, in Iida Bay, by the multiple tag-recapture census. Bull. Jap. Reg. Fish. Res. Lab. 26: 1-16.

Kesteven, G.L. 1947. On the ponderal index, or condition factor, as employed in fishery biology. Ecology 28(1): 78-80.

Kimura, D.L. 1977. Statistical assessment of the age-length key. J. Fish. Res. Board Can. 34(3): 317-324.

Klima, E.F. 1976. An assessment of the fish stocks and fisheries of the Campeche Bank. WECAF Studies No. 5. 24 p. FAO, Rome.

Lai, H-L. and C-L. Hsi. 1974. Age determination and growth of *Lutjanus sanguineus* (C & V) in the South China Sea. J. Fish. Soc. Taiwan 3(1): 39-57.

Langerman, J.D. 1980. An evaluation of mark and recapture techniques for estimating tigerfish biomass in Lake Kariba. Lake Kariba Fish. Res. Inst. Proj. Rep. 38. Department of National Parks and Wildlife Management, Zimbabwe. 12 p. (Mimeo).

Lara, F.J.S. 1951. A study of the life history of *Macrodon ancylodon* (Bloch & Schneider), a sciaenid fish occurring on the coast of Southern Brazil. An. Acad. Bras. Cienc. 23(3): 291-322.

Larkin, P.A. 1966. Exploitation in a type of predator-prey relationship. J. Fish. Res. Board Can. 23(3): 349-356.

Larkin, P.A. 1982. Directions for future research in tropical multispecies fisheries, p. 309-328. *In* D. Pauly and G.I. Murphy (eds.) Theory and management of tropical fisheries. ICLARM Conference Proceedings 9, 360 p. International Center for Living Resources Management, Manila, Philippines and Division of Fisheries Research, Commonwealth Scientific and Industrial Research Organisation, Cronulla, Australia.

Larkin, P.A. and W. Gazey. 1982. Application of ecological simulation models to management of tropical multispecies fisheries, p. 123-140. *In* D. Pauly and G.I. Murphy (eds.) Theory and management of tropical fisheries. ICLARM Conference Proceedings 9, 360 p. International Center for Living Aquatic Resources Management, Manila, Philippines and Division of Fisheries Research, Commonwealth Scientific and Industrial Research Organisation, Cronulla, Australia.

Laws, E.A. and J.W. Archie. 1981. Appropriate use of regression analysis in marine biology. Mar. Biol. 65(16): 13-16.

Le Cren, E.D. 1951. The length-weight relationship and seasonal cycle in gonad weight and condition in the perch *(Perca fluviatilis)*. J. Anim. Ecol. 20: 201-219.

Le Guen, J.C. 1971. Dynamique des populations de *Pseudotolithus (Fonticulus) elongatus* (Bowd. 1825) Poissons, Sciaenidae. Cah. O.R.S.T.O.M. Sr. Océanogr. 9(1): 3-84.

Lelek, A. and A.A. Wuddah. 1969. A note on the occurrence and length frequency distribution of *Tilapia* species caught in gillnets in Volta Lake, p. 186-189. *In* L.E. Obeng (ed.) Man-made lakes. The symposium. Ghana Universities Press.

Lotka, A.J. 1925. Elements of mathematical biology. Dover Publications, New York.

Loubens, G. 1980. Biologie de quelques espèces de poisson du lagon Néo-Calédonien III croissance. Cah. Ind. Pac. 2(2): 101-153.

Lowe-McConnell, R.H. 1975. Fish communities in tropical freshwaters. Longman, New York.

MacCall, A.D. 1980. Population models for the northern anchovy *(Engraulis mordax)*, p. 292-306. *In* A. Saville (ed.) The assessment and management of pelagic fish stocks. Rapp. P.-V. Réun. Cons. Int. Explor. Mer 177.

Majkowski, J. 1982. Usefulness and applicability of sensitivity analysis in a multispecies approach to fisheries management, p. 149-165. *In* D. Pauly and G.I. Murphy (eds.) Theory and management of tropical fisheries. ICLARM Conference Proceedings 9, 360 p. International Center for Living Aquatic Resources Management, Manila, Philippines and Division of Fisheries Research, Commonwealth Scientific and Industrial Research Organisation, Cronulla, Australia.

Manooch, C.S. and G.R. Huntsman. 1977. Age, growth and mortality of the red porgy *Pagrus pagrus*. Trans. Am. Fish. Soc. 106(1): 26-33.

Marquez, J.R.S. 1960. Age and size at sexual maturity of white goby *(Glosogobius giurus)*, a common species of fish in Laguna de Bay, with notes on its food habits. Philipp. J. Fish. 8(1): 71-99.

Marr, J.C. 1978. Book review: Fish population dynamics. J.A. Gulland (ed.) John Wiley and Sons. Aquaculture 15: 179.

Marshall, N. 1980. Fishery yields of coral reefs and adjacent shallow-water environments, p. 103-109. *In* S.B. Saila and P. Roedel (eds.) Stock assessment for tropical small-scale fisheries. Proceedings of an international workshop held 19-21 September 1979 at the University of Rhode Island. Int. Cent. Mar. Res. Dev., University of Rhode Island, Kingston.

Marten, G.G. and J.J. Polovina. 1982. A comparative study of fish yields from various tropical ecosystems, p. 255-289. *In* D. Pauly and G.I. Murphy (eds.) Theory and management of tropical fisheries. ICLARM Conference Proceedings 9, 360 p. International Center for Living Aquatic Resources Management, Manila, Philippines and Division of Fisheries Research, Commonwealth Scientific and Industrial Research Organisation, Cronulla, Australia.

May, R.M., J.R. Beddington, C.W. Clark, S.J. Holt and R.M. Laws. 1979. Management of multispecies fisheries. Science 205 (4403): 267-277.

McCarthy, G. 1976. Calculator calculus. Rev. ed. Educalc Publications, Laguna Beach, California.

McCombie, A.M. and F.E.J. Fry. 1960. Selectivity of gillnets for lake whitefish *Coregonus clupeaformis*. Trans. Am. Fish. Soc. 89(2): 176-184.

Menon, M.D. 1950. The use of bones, other than otoliths, in determining the age and growth-rate of fishes. J. Cons., Cons. Int. Explor. Mer 16: 311-335.

Mesnil, B. 1980. Théorie et pratique de l'analyse des cohortes. Rev. Trav. Inst. Pêches Marit. 44(2): 119-155.

Miller, R.G. 1974. The jackknife—a review. Biometrika 61: 1-15.

Mohn, R.K. 1980. Bias and error propagation in logistic production models. Can. J. Fish. Aquat. Sci. 37(8): 1276-1283.

Mohr, E. 1927. Bibliographie der Alters-und Wachstums-Bestimmung bei Fischen. J. Cons., Cons. Int. Explor. Mer 2(2): 236-258.

Mohr, E. 1930. Bibliographie der Alters-und Wachstums-Bestimmung bei Fischen. II Nachträge und Fortsetzung. J. Cons., Cons. Int. Explor. Mer 5(1): 88-100.

Mohr, E. 1934. Bibliographie der Alters-und Wachstums-Bestimmung bei Fischen. III Nachträge und Fortsetzung. J. Cons., Cons. Int. Explor. Mer 9(2): 377-391.

Moreau, J. 1980. Influence des divers parametres sur l'estimation du rendement par recrue: application aux pêches continentales. Cybium, 3e série 8: 67-75.

Mosteller, F. and J.W. Tukey. 1977. Data analysis and regression: a second course in statistics. Addison-Wesley, Massachusetts.

Muir, B.S. 1969. Gill size as a function of fish size. J. Fish. Res. Board Can. 26: 165-170.

Munro, J.L. 1967. The food of a community of East African freshwater fishes. J. Zool. 151: 389-415.

Munro, J.L. 1974. The mode of operation of Antillean fish traps and the relationships between ingress, escapement and catch. J. Cons., Cons. Int. Explor. Mer 35: 337-350.

Munro, J.L. 1982. Estimation of the parameters of the von Bertalanffy growth equation from recapture data at variable time intervals. J. Cons., Cons. Int. Explor. Mer 40(2): 199-200.

Munro, J.L., editor. 1983. Caribbean coral reef fishery resources. ICLARM Studies and Reviews 7, 276 p. International Center for Living Aquatic Resources Management, Manila, Philippines.

Munro, J.L. 1984. Estimation of natural mortality rates from selectivity and catch length-frequency data. Fishbyte 2(1): 11-14.

Munro, J.L. and R. Thompson. 1973. The biology, ecology, exploitation and management of Caribbean reef fishes. Part II. The Jamaican fishing industry, the area investigated and the objectives and methodology of the ODA/UWI Fisheries Ecology Research Project. Res. Rep. Zool. Dept., Univ. West Indies 3(II): 44 p.

Murphy, G.I. 1965. A solution of the catch equation. J. Fish. Res. Board Can. 22(1): 191-202.

Murphy, G.I. 1966. Population biology of the Pacific sardine *(Sardinops caerulea)*. Proc. Calif. Acad. Sci. 34: 1-84.

Murphy, G.I. 1967. Vital statistics of the Pacific sardine *(Sardinops caerulea)* and the population consequences. Ecology 48: 731-736.

Murphy, G.I. 1972. Fisheries in upwelling regions, with special reference to Peruvian waters. Geoforum 11: 63-71.

Murphy, G.I. 1977. Clupeoids, p. 282-308. In J.A. Gulland (ed.) Fish population dynamics. Wiley Interscience, New York.

Murphy, G.I. 1982. Recruitment of tropical fishes, p. 141-148. In D. Pauly and G.I. Murphy (eds.) Theory and management of tropical fisheries. ICLARM Conference Proceedings 9, 360 p. International Center for Living Aquatic Resources Management, Manila, Philippines and Division of Fisheries Research, Commonwealth Scientific and Industrial Research Organisation, Cronulla, Australia.

Nomura, H. and J. de Oliveira Chacon. 1976. Idade e crescimento da pescada-do-piani, *Plagoscion squamosissimus* (Heckel) (Osteichthyes, Sciaenidae), do agude Amanari (Maranguape, Caera). Rev. Ceres 23(127): 191-197.

Nomura, H., J. de Oliveira Chacon, L. Nemoto and I.M. de Mattos. 1976. Idade e crescimento do cangati, *Trachycorystes galeatus* (Linnaeus, 1776) (Osteichthyes, Nematognathi, Auchenipteridae) do agude Banabuiu (Quixada, Caera, Brasil). Rev. Bras. Biol. 36(2):521-525.

Nzioka, R.M. 1983. Biology of the small-spotted grunt *Pomadasys opercularis* (Playfair 1866) (Pisces: Pomadasydae) around Malindi in Kenya. Kenya J. Sci. Techn. 15(3): 69-81.

Odum, E.P. 1971. Fundamentals of ecology. 3rd ed. Saunder's International Student Edition, Philadelphia, Pennsylvania.

Pannella, G. 1971. Fish otoliths: daily growth layers and periodical patterns. Science 137 (4002): 1124-1127.

Parrish, B.B., editor. 1978. Fish stocks and recruitment. Rapp. P.-V. Réun. Cons. Int. Explor. Mer 164.

Paulik, G.J. and L.E. Gales. 1964. Allometric growth and Beverton and Holt yield equation. Trans. Am. Fish. Soc. 93: 369-381.

Pauly, D. 1975. On the ecology of a small West African lagoon. Ber. dt. Komm. Meeresforsch. 24(1): 46-62.

Pauly, D. 1976. The biology, fishery and potential for aquaculture of *Tilapia melanotheron* in a small West African lagoon. Aquaculture 7(1): 33-49.

Pauly, D. 1977. The Leiognathidae (Teleostei): their species, stocks and fisheries in Indonesia, with notes on the biology of *Leiognathus splendens* (Cuvier) Mar. Res. Indonesia 19: 73-93.

Pauly, D. 1978. A preliminary compilation of fish length growth parameters. Ber. Inst. f. Meereskunde Univ. Kiel No. 55, 200 p.

Pauly, D. 1979a. Gill size and temperature as governing factors in fish growth: a generalization of Von Bertalanffy's growth formula. Ber. Inst. f. Meereskunde Univ. Kiel. No. 63, xv + 156 p.

Pauly, D. 1979b. Theory and management of tropical multispecies stocks: a review with emphasis on the Southeast Asian demersal fisheries. ICLARM Studies and Reviews 1, 35 p. International Center for Living Aquatic Resources Management, Manila, Philippines.

Pauly, D. 1980a. A selection of simple methods for the assessment of tropical fish stocks. FAO Fish. Circ. No. 729 (FIRM/C729), 54 p.

Pauly, D. 1980b. On the interrelationships between natural mortality, growth parameters and mean environmental temperature in 175 fish stocks. J. Cons., Cons. Int. Explor. Mer 39(3): 175-192.

Pauly, D. 1980c. The use of a pseudo catch curve for the estimation of mortality rates in *Leiognathus splendens* (Pisces: Leiognathidae) in Western Indonesian Waters. Meeresforsch. 28(1): 56-60.

Pauly, D. 1980d. A new methodology for rapidly acquiring basic information on tropical fish stocks: growth, mortality and stock-recruitment relationships, p. 154-172. In S. Saila and P. Roedel (eds.) Stock assessment for tropical small-scale fisheries. Proceedings of an international workshop held 19-21 September 1979 at the University of Rhode Island. Int. Cent. Mar. Res. Dev., University of Rhode Island, Kingston.

Pauly, D. 1981. The relationships between gill surface area and growth performance in fish: a generalization of von Bertalanffy's theory of growth. Meeresforsch. 28(4): 251-282.

Pauly, D. 1982a. Studying single-species dynamics in a multispecies context, p. 33-70. *In* D. Pauly and G.I. Murphy (eds.) Theory and management of tropical fisheries. ICLARM Conference Proceedings 9, 360 p. International Center for Living Resources Management, Manila, Philippines and Division of Fisheries Research, Commonwealth Scientific and Industrial Research Organisation, Cronulla, Australia.

Pauly, D. 1982b. Notes on tropical multispecies fisheries, with a short bibliography on the food and feeding habits of tropical fish, p. 30-35 and 92-98. *In* Report of the Regional Training Course on Fisheries Stock Assessment, Samutprakarn, Thailand, 1 September-9 October 1981, Part II, Vol. 1. SCS/GEN/82/41, 238 p. South China Sea Fisheries Development and Coordinating Programme, Manila.

Pauly, D. 1982c. Further evidence for a limiting effect of gill size on the growth of fish: the case of the Philippine goby *(Mistichthys luzonensis)*. Kalikasan, Philipp. J. Biol. 11(2-3): 379-383.

Pauly, D. 1983. Some simple methods for the assessment of tropical fish stocks. FAO Fish Tech. Pap. 234. 52 p.

Pauly, D. and N. David. 1981. ELEFAN I, a BASIC program for the objective extraction of growth parameters from length-frequency data. Meeresforsch. 28(4): 205-211.

Pauly, D. and G. Gaschütz. 1979. A simple method for fitting oscillating length growth data, with a program for pocket calculators. I.C.E.S. C.M. 1979/G: 24. Demersal Fish Cttee. 26 p.

Pauly, D. and J. Ingles. 1981. Aspects of the growth and natural mortality of exploited coral reef fishes, p. 89-98. *In* E.D. Gomez, C.E. Burkeland, R.W. Buddemeier, R.E. Johannes, J.A. Marsh, Jr. and R.T. Tsuda (eds.) The reef and man. Proceedings of the Fourth International Coral Reef Symposium, Vol. 1. Marine Sciences Center, University of the Philippines, Quezon City, Philippines.

Pauly, D., J. Ingles and R.A. Neal. Application to shrimp stocks of objective methods for the estimation of vital statistics from length data. Proceedings of the NOAA/FAO Workshop on the Scientific Basis for the Management of Penaeid Shrimps, Florida, November 1981. (In press).

Pauly, D. and P. Martosubroto. 1980. The population dynamics of *Nemipterus marginatus* off Western Kalimantan, South China Sea. J. Fish Biol. 17: 263-273.

Pauly, D. and G.I. Murphy, editors. 1982. Theory and management of tropical fisheries. ICLARM Conference Proceedings 9, 360 p. International Center for Living Aquatic Resources Management, Manila, Philippines and Division of Fisheries Research, Commonwealth Scientific and Industrial Research Organisation, Cronulla, Australia.

Pauly, D. and N.A. Navaluna. 1983. Monsoon-induced seasonality in the recruitment of Philippine fishes, p. 823-833. *In* G. Sharp and J. Csirke (eds.) Proceedings of the Expert Consultation to Examine Changes in Abundance and Composition of Neritic Fish Stocks, San José, Costa Rica, 18-29 April 1983. FAO Fish. Tech. Rep. 231. Vol. 3.

Pella, J.J. and P.K. Tomlinson. 1969. A generalized stock production model. Inter-Am. Trop. Tuna Comm., Bull. 13: 419-496.

Pianka, E.R. 1973. The structure of lizard communities. Annu. Rev. Ecol. Syst. 4: 53-74.

Pielou, E.C. 1978. Population and community ecology. Gordon and Breach, New York.

Pitcher, T.J. and P.J.B. Hart. 1982. Fisheries ecology. AVI Publ. Co., Westport, Connecticut.

Polovina, J.J. and M.D. Ow. 1983. ECOPATH: a user's manual and program listings. Southwest Fish. Cent. Admin. Rep. H-82-23 NMFS, Honolulu. 46 p.

Pope, J.A., A.R. Margetts, J.M. Hamley and E.F. Akyüz. 1975. Manual of methods for fish stock assessment, Part III. Selectivity of fishing gear. FAO Fish. Tech. Pap. 41. Rev. 1. 65 p.

Pope, J.G. 1972. An investigation of the accuracy of Virtual Population Analysis. Int. Comm. Northwest Atl. Fish. Res. Bull. 9: 65-74.

Pope, J.G. 1979. Stock assessment in multispecies fisheries, with special reference to the trawl fisheries in the Gulf of Thailand. SCS/DEV/79/19. 106 p. South China Sea Fisheries Development and Coordinating Programme, Manila.

Postel, E. 1955. Contribution à l'étude de la biologie de quelques Scombridés de l'Atlantique tropico-oriental. Ann. Stn. océanogr. Salammbô (10). 168 p.

Powell, D.G. 1979. Estimation of mortality and growth parameters from the length-frequency in the catch. Rapp. P.-V. Réun. Cons. Int. Explor. Mer 175: 167-169.

Prabhu, M.S. 1952. Preliminary observations on the biology of *Chirocentrus dorab* Forsk. Cur. Sci. (India) 22(10): 309-310.

Qasim, S.Z. 1973a. An appraisal of the studies on maturation and spawning in marine teleosts from the Indian waters. Indian J. Fish. 20(1): 166-181.

Qasim, S.Z. 1973b. Some implications of the problems of age and growth in marine fishes from the Indian waters. Indian J. Fish. 20(2): 351-371.

Ralston, S. 1976. Age determination of a tropical reef butterfly fish utilizing daily growth rings in otoliths. Fish. Bull. (U.S.) 74(4): 990-994.

Randall, J.E. 1962. Tagging reef fishes in the Virgin Islands. Proc. Gulf Caribb. Fish. Inst. 14: 201-241.

Randall, J.E. 1968. Caribbean reef fishes. TFH Publications, Neptune City, New Jersey.

Richards, F.J. 1959. A flexible growth function for empirical use. J. Exp. Bot. 10: 290-300.

Ricker, W.E. 1954. Stock and recruitment. J. Fish. Res. Board Can. 11: 559-623.

Ricker, W.E. 1973. Linear regression in fishery research. J. Fish. Res. Board Can. 30: 409-434.

Ricker, W.E. 1975. Computation and interpretation of biological statistics of fish populations. Bull. Fish. Res. Board Can. (191). 382 p.

Ricker, W.E. 1979. Growth rates and models, p. 677-433. In W.S. Hoar, D.J. Randall and J.R. Brett (eds.) Fish physiology. Vol. III: Bioenergetics and growth. Academic Press, New York.

Ricklefs, R.E. 1979. Ecology. 2nd ed. Thomas Nelson, Sunbury-on-Thames, U.K.

Robson, D.S. and D.G. Chapman. 1961. Catch curves and mortality rates. Trans. Am. Fish. Soc. 90(2): 181-189.

Rodrigues, M.S. de Sousa. 1968. Idade e crescimento de cururuca, *Micropogon furnieri* (Demarest, 1822), na aguas caerenses. Arq. Est. Biol. Mar. Univ. Fed. Caer 8(1): 7-14.

Roff, D.A. and D.J. Fairbairn. 1980. An evaluation of Gulland's method for fitting the Schaefer model. Can. J. Fish. Aquat. Sci. 37(8): 1229-1235.

Rohlf, F.J. and R.R. Sokal. 1969. Statistical tables. Freeman and Co., San Francisco, California.

Rothschild, B.J. 1977. Fishing effort, p. 96-115. In J.A. Gulland (ed.) Fish population dynamics. John Wiley and Sons, New York.

Russel, E.S. 1931. Some theoretical considerations on the overfishing problem. J. Cons., Cons. Int. Explor. Mer 6(1): 3-20.

Russel, B.C., F.H. Talbot, G.R.V. Anderson and B. Goldman. 1978. Collection and sampling of reef fishes, p. 329-345. In D.R. Stoddart and R.E. Johannes (eds.) Coral reefs: research methods. UNESCO, Paris.

Sachs, L. 1974. Angewandte Statistik. Springer Verlag, Berlin.

Saeger, J., P. Martosubroto and D. Pauly. 1976. First report of the Indonesian-German demersal fisheries project (Result of a trawl survey in the Sunda Shelf area). Marine Fisheries Research Reports/Contributions of the Demersal Fisheries Project No. 1, Jakarta, p. 1-46.

Saila, S. and R.G. Lough. 1981. Mortality and growth estimation from size data—an application to some Atlantic herring larvae. Rapp. P.-V. Réun. Cons. Int. Explor. Mer 178: 7-14.

Saila, S.B. and P. Roedel, editors. 1980. Stock assessment for tropical small-scale fisheries. Proceedings of an international workshop held 19-21 September 1979 at the University of Rhode Island. Int. Cent. Mar. Res. Dev., University of Rhode Island, Kingston.

Sale, P.F. 1980. The ecology of fishes on coral reefs. Oceanogr. Mar. Biol. Annu. Rev. 18: 367-421.

Saville, A., editor. 1980. The assessment and management of pelagic fish stocks. Rapp. P.-V. Réun. Cons. Int. Explor. Mer 177. 517 p.

Schaefer, M.B. 1951. Estimation of size of animal populations by marking experiments. U.S. Fish Wildl. Serv., Fish. Bull. 52(69): 191-203.

Schaefer, M.B. 1954. Some aspects of the dynamics of populations important to the management of the commercial marine fisheries. Inter-Am. Trop. Tuna Comm., Bull. 1(2): 27-56.

Schaefer, M.B. 1957. A study of the dynamics of the fishery for yellowfin tuna in the eastern tropical Pacific Ocean. Inter-Am. Trop. Tuna Comm., Bull. 2: 247-268.

Schaefer, M. and R. Beverton. 1963. Fishery dynamics, their analysis and interpretation. In M.N. Hill (ed.) The sea Vol. 2. Wiley Interscience, New York.

Schnute, J. 1977. Improved estimates from Schaefer production model: theoretical considerations. J. Fish. Res. Board Can. 34(5): 583-603.

Sekharan, K.V. 1974. Estimates of the stocks of oil sardine and mackerel in the present fishing grounds off the west coast of India. Indian J. Fish. 21(1): 177-182.

SCSP. 1978. Report of the workshop on the demersal resources of the Sunda Shelf, 31 October-6 November 1977, Penang, Malaysia. Part II. SCS/GEN/77/13. 120 p. South China Sea Fisheries Development and Coordinating Programme, Manila.

Sharp, G. 1980. Report of the workshop on the effects of environmental variation on survival of larval pelagic fishes, p. 15-59. In G. Sharp (Rapporteur). Workshop on the effects of environmental variation on the survival of larval pelagic fishes. Intergovernmental Oceanographic Commission Workshop Report No. 28. 323 p.

Shepherd, J.G. 1982. A versatile new stock-recruitment relationship for fisheries and the construction of sustainable yield curves. J. Cons., Cons. Int. Explor. Mer 40(1): 67-75.

Shindo, S. 1960. Studies on the stock of yellow sea bream in the East China Sea. Bull. Sekai Reg. Fish. Res. Lab. 20: 1-198.

Shindo, S. 1973. General review of the trawl fishery and the demersal fish stocks of the South China Sea. FAO Fish. Tech. Pap. 120. 49 p.

Shul'man, G.E. 1974. Life cycles of fish; physiology and biochemistry. Isr. Progr. Sci. Transl. John Wiley and Sons, New York.

Silliman, R.P. 1975. Experimental exploitation of competing population. Fish. Bull. (U.S.) 73: 872-888.

Silliman, R.P. and J.S. Gutsell. 1958. Experimental exploitation of fish population. Fish. Bull. (U.S.) 58(133): 215-252.

Simpson, A.C. 1982. A review of the database on tropical multispecies stocks in the Southeast Asian region, p. 5-32. In D. Pauly and G.I. Murphy (eds.) Theory and management of tropical fisheries. ICLARM Conference Proceedings 9, 360 p. International Center for Living Aquatic Resources Management, Manila, Philippines and Division of Fisheries Research, Commonwealth Scientific and Industrial Research Organisation, Cronulla, Australia.

Sims, S.E. 1982. The effects of unevenly distributed catches on stock-size estimates using Virtual Population Analysis (Cohort Analysis) J. Cons., Cons. Int. Explor. Mer 40(1): 47-52.

Sinoda, M., S.M. Tan, Y. Watanabe and Y. Meemeskul. 1979. A method for estimating the best cod-end mesh size in the South China Sea area. Bull. Choshi Marine Lab., Chiba University 11: 65-80.

Slobotkin, L.B. 1980. Growth and regulation of animal populations. 2nd ed. Dover Publications, New York.

Smith, C.L. 1973. Small rotenone stations: a tool for studying coral reef communities. Amer. Mus. Novit. (2512). 21 p.

Smith, I.R. 1981. Improving fishing incomes when resources are overfished. Mar. Pol. 5: 17-22.

Smith, J.M. 1977. Scientific analysis on the pocket calculator. 2nd ed. John Wiley and Sons, New York.

Snedecor, G.W. and W.C. Cochran. 1967. Statistical methods. Iowa State University Press, Ames, Iowa.

Sokal, R.R. and F.J. Rohlf. 1981. Biometry. 2nd ed. Freeman and Company, San Francisco, California.

Sparre, P. 1979. Some necessary adjustments for using the common methods in eel assessments. Rapp. P.-V. Réun. Cons. Int. Explor. Mer 174: 41-44.

Sparre, P. 1980. A goal function of fisheries (Legion analysis) I.C.E.S. C.M. 1980/G: 40. (Mimeo).

Sparre, P. Methods for estimating natural mortality. FAO/DANIDA project: training in fish stock assessment. Mombasa, June 1983. Lecture notes. (MS).

Sprugel, D.G. 1983. Correcting for bias in log-transformed allometric equations. Ecology 64(1): 209-210.

Steele, J.H., editor. 1973. Marine food chains. Oliver and Boyd, Edinburgh.

Stephenson, D. 1981. Assessment of fishery resources—Gulf of Nicoya, Costa Rica, p. 187-203. In Small-scale fisheries in Central America: acquiring information for decision-making. Int. Cent. Mar. Res. Dev., University of Rhode Island, Kingston.

Suvorov, J.K. 1959. General ichthyology. VEB Deutscher Verlag der Wissenschaften, Berlin. (In German).

Taylor, C.C. 1958. Cod growth and temperature. J. Cons., Cons. Int. Explor. Mer 23: 366-370.

Taylor, C.C. 1962. Growth equations with metabolic parameters. J. Cons., Cons. Int. Explor. Mer 27(3): 270-286.

Thompson, R. and J.L. Munro. 1974. The biology, ecology and bionomics of Caribbean reef fishes: Serranidae (hinds and groupers). Res. Rep. Zool. Dept. Univ. West Indies 3 (Part Vb) Kingston, 82 p.

Thompson, R. and J.L. Munro. 1978. Aspects of the biology and ecology of Caribbean reef fishes: Serranidae (hinds and groupers). J. Fish Biol. 12: 115-146.

Tinker, S.W. 1978. Fishes of Hawaii. Hawaiian Services Inc., Honolulu.

Tomlinson, P.K. 1970. A generalization of the Murphy catch equation. J. Fish. Res. Board Can. 27: 821-825.

Tukey, J.W. 1977. Exploratory data analysis. Addison-Wesley, Reading, Massachusetts.

Ulltang, Ø. 1977. Sources of errors in and limitations of Virtual Population Analysis (Cohort Analysis). J. Cons., Cons. Int. Explor. Mer 37(3): 249-260.

Ursin, E. 1973. On the prey size preference of cod and dab. Medd. Dan. Fisk. Havunders. N.S. 7: 85-98.

van Sickle, J. 1977. Mortality rates from size distributions: the application of a conservation law. Oecologia (Berlin) 27: 311-318.

Vakily, J.M. 1982. Catch and effort in the trawl fishery, p. 65-94. In D. Pauly and A.N. Mines (eds.) Small-scale fisheries of San Miguel Bay, Philippines: biology and stock assessment. ICLARM Technical Reports 7, 143 p. Institute of Fisheries Development and Research, College of Fisheries, University of the Philippines in the Visayas, Quezon City, Philippines; International Center for Living Aquatic Resources Management, Manila, Philippines; and the United Nations University, Tokyo, Japan.

Volterra, V. 1926. Variations and fluctuations of individuals of animals living together, p. 409-448. In R.N. Chapman (ed.) Animal ecology. MacGraw-Hill, New York.

Walford, L.A. 1946. A new graphic method of describing the growth of animals. Biol. Bull. 90: 141-147.

Walsh, J.J. 1981. A carbon budget for overfishing off Peru. Nature (London) 290(5304): 300-304.

Walter, G.G. 1975. Graphical methods for estimating parameters in simple models of fisheries. J. Fish. Res. Board Can. 32: 2163-2168.

Weatherley, A.H. 1972. Growth and ecology of fish populations. Academic Press, London and New York.

Weber, E. 1980. Grundriss der biologischen Statistik. Gustav Fischer Verlag, Stuttgart and New York.

Wheeler, J. and F.D. Ommanney. 1953. Report on the Mauritius-Seychelles Fisheries Survey, 1948-1949. Col. Off. Fish. Publ. (London) 1(3). 148 p.

White, G.C., D.R. Anderson, K.P. Burnham and D.L. Otis. 1982. Capture-recapture and removal methods for sampling closed populations. LA-8787 NERP. Los Alamos National Laboratory, Los Alamos, New Mexico. 235 p.

Willimovsky, N.J. and E.C. Wicklund. 1963. Tables of the incomplete beta functions for the calculation of fish population yield. University of British Columbia, Vancouver, Canada.

Winberg, G.G. 1960. Rate of metabolism and food requirements of fishes. Minsk, USSR. Fish. Res. Board Can. Transl. Ser. No. 194. 239 p.

Winberg, G.G. 1961. New information on metabolic rate in fishes. Vopr. Ikhtiol. 1(1): 157-165. Fish. Res. Board Can. Transl. Ser. No. 362. 11 p.

Winberg, G.G., editor. 1971. Methods for the estimation of production of aquatic animals. Academic Press, London and New York.

Yap, S-Y. 1983. A holistic, ecosystem approach to investigating tropical multispecies reservoir fisheries. ICLARM Newsletter 6(2): 10-11.

Yap, S-Y. and J.I. Furtado. 1980. Evaluation of two tagging/marking techniques and their practical application in Osteochilus hasselti C. & V. (Cyprinidae) population estimates and movement at Subang Reservoir. Malaysia. Hydrobiologia 68(1): 35-48.

## Author Index

Included here exclusively are the names *of persons*, i.e., of authors, or other persons mentioned in **acknowledgements**. The names of persons that are parts of eponyms (e.g., *Schaefer* model, *Lotka-Volterra* equations) are not included. Self-references are omitted.

Agger, P. 101
Akyüz, E.F. 18
Allen, K.R. 53, 59
Alt, H. 307
Andersen, K.P. 168
Anderson, D.R. 73
Anderson, G.R.V. 93
Archie, J.W. 3, 31
Aye Pyo xvi

Bagenal, T. 28, 41
Bailey, N.T.J. 92, 248
Bakun, A. 129
Ball, J.A. 2, 307
Balon, E.K. 7
Banerji, S.K. 156
Baranov, F.I. 14, 18, 60, 101, 122, 138
Bayliff, W.H. 122
Beamish, R.J. 28
Beddington, J.R. 77, 153
Ben-Yami, M. 153, 158
Berkeley, S.A. 39, 125
Berry, R.J. 62
Bertalanffy, L. von 23, 24, 29, 41, 163
Beverton, R.J.H. 18, 28, 41, 53, 55, 58, 74, 76, 77, 93, 100, 101, 102, 115, 116, 117, 121, 122, 129, 130, 147, 164, 167, 268, 279
Beyer, J. 129
Blueweiss, L. 154, 299
Boerema, L.K. 120, 173
Boëtius, I. 101
Boje, R. 171
Boonyubol, M. 72
Brandt, A. von 18
Brothers, E.B. 28, 41
Burnham, K.P. 73
Buzeta, R.B. 173

Caddy, J.F. 77, 144, 296
Carlander, K. 5, 7
Chapman, D.G. 18, 58, 92, 248
Chapman, D.W. 53
Chatterjee, S. 3
Choudary, R.H. 38
Clare, B.W. 303

Clark, C.W. 153, 162, 171
Cochran, W.C. 2
Colwell, R.K. 170
Cooke, J.G. 77
Csirke, J. 77, 129, 144, 296, xvi
Cushing, D.H. 41, 108, 130, 170

Daan, N. 173
Dalzell, P. 147
David, N. 26, 37, 41
De Groot, S.J. 170
Dickson, W. 92
Draper, N. 2
Dwiponggo, A. 145

Eberhardt, L.L. 155
Ebert, T.A. 67, 236
Eggers, D.M. 18

Fairbairn, D.J. 142
Forbes, S.T. 91
Ford, E. 31
Fox, H. 154, 299
Fox, W.W. 143, 288
Francis, R.C. 77
Fridrikson, A. 59
Fruchter, B. 64
Fry, F.E.J. 18
Fryer, G. 41
Furtado, J.L. 95
Futuyama, D.G. 170

Gales, L.E. 118, 120
Garcia, S. 29, 120, 129, 134
Gaschütz, G. 26, 37, 208, 212
Gause, G.F. 163
Gazey, W. 168, 173
Gislason, H. 168
Glaser, T. 153, 158
Godoy, M.P. 55
Goldman, B. 93
Gomez, A.A. 2
Gomez, K.A. 2
Graham, M. 28, 138, 147

Green, D.R. 2, 163, 307
Guilford, J.P. 64
Gulland, J.A. 14, 18, 33, 34, 55, 59, 62, 64, 66, 73, 74,
    76, 77, 88, 92, 93, 95, 100, 101, 108, 120, 142,
    154, 155, 173, 188, 200, 224, 239, 264, 288, xiii,
    xiv
Gutsell, J.S. 139, 147, 152

Hamley, J.M. 14, 18
Harding, D. 14, 18
Hart, P.J.B. 153, 156, 157
Hashem, M.T. 28
Helgason, T. 168
Hempel, G. 122, 275
Henderson, F. 56
Hoenig, J.M. 53, 54, xiv
Hoenig, N.A. 38
Hohendorf, K. 33
Holt, S.J. 14, 33, 34, 41, 53, 55, 58, 74, 76, 77, 93, 100
    101, 102, 115, 116, 117, 121, 122, 129, 130, 153,
    164, 167, 200, 268, 279, 309
Hongskul, V. 72, 74
Houde, E.D. 39, 125
Hoyer, H.J. 305, 307
Hsi, C.-L. 124
Huntsman, G.R. 59

Iles, T.D. 41
Ingles, J. 39, 40, 60, 62, 65
Isarankura, A.P. 92
Ita, E.O. 56

Jarett, K. 307
Johnson, L. 71
Jolly, G.M. 91
Jones, R. 41, 56, 73, 76, 77, 95, 101, 102, 105, 108,
    118, 119, 122, 171, 227, 248, 259, 264, 268, 272

Kato, F. 95
Kesteven, G.L. 7
Kimura, D.L. 59
Klima, E.F. 93, 142, 143
Krishnan, T.S. 156
Kudzma, V. 154, 299

Lai, H.-L. 124
Langerman, J.D. 96
Lara, F.J.S. 55
Larkin, P.A. 164, 168, 171, 173
Lassen, H. 101
Lawing, W.D. 53, 54
Laws, E.A. 3, 31
Laws, R.M. 153
Le Cren, E.D. 7
Le Guen, J.C. 122
Lelek, A. 17
Le Reste, L. 120
Lewis, J. 2, 163, 307
Lotka, A.J. 163

Louben, G. 54
Lough, R.G. 67, 86, 236
Lowe-McConnell, R.H. 41

MacCall, A.D. 153
Majkowski, J. 177, 178
Manooch, C.S. 59
Margetts, J.M. 18
Marquez, J.R.S. 69
Marr, J.C. 1
Marshall, N. 93
Marten, G.G. 173
Martosubroto, P. 92, 120, 127
Mattos, L.M. de 55
May, R.M. 153
McCarthy, G. 307
McCombie, A.M. 18
McFarlane, G.A. 28
Meemeskul, Y. 18, 122
Menon, M.D. 28
Mesnil, B. 101, 108
Miller, R.G. 178
Mohn, R.K. 142
Mohr, E. 28
Mosteller, F. 178
Moreau, J. 177
Muir, B.S. 24
Munro, J.L. 18, 35, 60, 64, 79, 87, 90, 159, 160, 163,
    173, 203, xiii, xiv
Murphy, G.I. 101, 129, 132, 134, 141, 147, 148, 153,
    155, 156, 157, 163, 174

Nakashima, D. 154, 299
Nakken, O. 91
Navaluna, N.A. 59
Neal, R. 40, 65
Nemoto, L. 55
Nomura, H. 55
Nzioka, R.M. 62

Odum, E.P. 139, 152, 157
Oliviera-Chacon, J. de 55
Ommanney, F.D. 93
Otis, D.L. 73
Ow, M.D. 171

Palomares, L. xvi
Pannella, G. 28, 41
Parrish, B.B. 129, 134
Parrish, R.H. 129
Paulik, G.J. 118, 120
Pella, J.J. 143
Peters, R. 154, 299
Pianka, E.R. 170
Pielou, E.C. 152, 153, 157
Pitcher, T.J. 153, 156, 157
Polovina, J.J. 171, 173
Pope, J.A. 18
Pope, J.G. 101, 102, 108, 129, 147, 163, 164, 166,
    168, 171, 256, 259, 264, 304

Postel, E. 31, 44
Powell, D.G. 70, 71
Prabhu, M.S. 9
Price, B. 3

Qasim, S.Z. 156

Ralston, S. 27
Randall, 33, 34, 46
Richards, F.J. 120
Rickard, N.A. 18
Ricker, W.E. 2, 3, 7, 31, 41, 58, 73, 77, 95, 107, 115,
    119, 120, 122, 129, 130, 132, 134, 138, 139, 140,
    143, 147, 196, 248, 251, 272, 279, 284, 288, 309,
    xv
Ricklefs, R.E. 152, 153, 157
Robson, D.S. 58
Rodrigues, M.S. de Sousa 55, 78
Roedel, P. 173
Roff, D.A. 142
Rohlf, F.J. 2, 3, 8, 178
Rothschild, B.J. 73
Russel, B.C. 93
Russel, E.S. 1

Sachs, L. 184
Saeger, J. 92
Saila, S. 67, 86, 173, 178, 236, xvi
Sale, P.F. 129
Sams, S. 154, 299
Sarhage, D. 122, 275
Saville, A. 91, 129
Schaefer, M.B. 92, 138, 140, 142, 144, 147, 248, 288
Schnute, J. 138, 142, 147, 292
Sekharan, K.V. 93, 98
Sharp, G.D. 129, 134
Shepherd, J.G. 134
Shindo, S. 93, 132
Shudde, R.H. 272
Shul'man, G.E. 39, 41
Silliman, R.P. 139, 147, 152, 163
Simpson, A.C. 173, 176
Sims, S.E. 101
Sinoda, M. 18, 122
Slobotkin, L.B. 152, 156, 157

Smith, C.L. 94
Smith, H. 2
Smith, I.R. 169, 171
Smith, J.M. 2, 307
Snedecor, G.W. 2
Sokal, R.R. 2, 3, 8, 178
Sparre, P. 56, 64, 101, 227, 232, xvi
Sprugel, D.G. 3
Steele, J.H. 171
Stevenson, D. 74
Suvorov, J.K. 28

Talbot, F.H. 93
Tan, S.M. 18, 122
Taylor, C.C. 23, 28, 41, 74
Thompson, R. 60, 79, 87, 90, 159, 160
Tinker, S.W. 42
Tomczak, M. 171
Tomlinson, P.K. 101, 143
Tukey, J.W. 3, 178

Ulltang, Ø. 101
Ursin, E. 94, 168, 170, xiv

Vakily, J.M. 97
van Sickle, J. 60
van Zalinge, N.P. 105, 108
Volterra, V. 163

Walford, L.A. 31
Walsh, J.J. 168
Walters, G.G. 142
Watanabe, Y. 122
Weatherley, A.H. 7, 41
Weber, E. 2
Westerlund, T. 208, 212
Wheeler, J. 93
White, G.C. 73
Whitney, R.R. 18
Wicklund, E.C. 119, 272
Wilimovsky, N.J. 119, 272
Winberg, G.G. 24, 53, 171
Wuddah, A.A. 17

Yamada, Y. 95
Yap S.-Y. 95, 168, 169